CREATING MODERN CAPITALISM

CREATING
MODERN CAPITALISM

HOW ENTREPRENEURS, COMPANIES, AND
COUNTRIES TRIUMPHED IN THREE
INDUSTRIAL REVOLUTIONS

EDITED BY
Thomas K. McCraw

HARVARD UNIVERSITY PRESS
Cambridge, Massachusetts, and London, England

Printed in the United States of America

Third printing, 2000

Library of Congress Cataloging-in-Publication Data
Creating modern capitalism : how entrepreneurs, companies, and countries
triumphed in three industrial revolutions / edited by Thomas K. McCraw.
    p. cm.
  Includes bibliographical references and index.
  ISBN 0-674-17555-7 (cl : alk. paper).
  ISBN 0-674-17556-5 (p : alk. paper)
  1. Capitalism. 2. Industrial revolution. 3. Economic history.
I. McCraw, Thomas K.
HB501.C785 1997
338.09--dc21   97-15334

PREFACE

What is capitalism? How has it evolved over time? Why have some entrepreneurs, companies, and countries been able to make it work for them while others haven't?

This book gives a unique perspective on these questions. On one level, the answer to "What is capitalism?" is obvious, because capitalism's main benefits are so clear: a steady increase in incomes and a broadening of opportunity. The negative side is equally obvious: capitalism exalts material values over spiritual ones, and its market forces can have harsh consequences.

Beneath these manifest traits lie questions that are more subtle. Is capitalism the "natural" way to organize an economy? If it is, then why did it become ascendant so late in human history? Why did it develop in some cultures and countries but not others? Does capitalism require a certain mind-set—a preoccupation with the future rather than the past? Is there a national example of capitalism in its purest form, which might serve as a model for other countries? Is that example the United States? Japan? Germany? Britain? Some other country? Does capitalism go hand in hand with democratic government? Must it be preceded by democracy, or can authoritarian regimes better push developing countries down the capitalist path?

These questions are as challenging today as they were three centuries ago, when capitalism began to dominate a few national economies and then to spread gradually throughout the world. More recently, in the late twentieth century, the sudden collapse of socialism and communism has given new urgency to the questions. In the "emerging" national economies of Asia, Latin America, Africa, and Eastern Europe, policymakers and business leaders have begun to look more closely for models of successful capitalist development. For thoughtful people everywhere, understanding the anatomy of capitalism has become a crucial part of coming to terms with the modern world. No educated person can afford to neglect it, regardless of his or her attitude toward capitalism.

How should one pursue this understanding? The subject has many aspects: economic, cultural, political, aesthetic, and so on. Capitalism can be approached through academic disciplines that specialize in each of these areas. It can be usefully studied through biographies of great entrepreneurs, histories of successful companies, and analyses of important industries. It can be explored with theoretical models developed by economists, sociologists, political scientists, and others.

The most penetrating students of capitalism—Adam Smith, Karl Marx, Max Weber, R. H. Tawney, Joseph Schumpeter, John Maynard Keynes, Joan Robinson, R. H. Coase, Robert Heilbroner, Alfred D. Chandler Jr.—have all taken mixed approaches. All have written about several aspects of capitalism. Schumpeter once said that any worthwhile analysis of economic phenomena must contain elements of history, theory, and statistics.

This book, *Creating Modern Capitalism,* contains each of Schumpeter's three elements; but above all, it is a book of history. It has four sweeping chapters that examine the economic development of Britain, Germany, the United States, and Japan. Its other chapters are full of biographical sketches of remarkable people, such as Josiah Wedgwood, August Thyssen, Henry Ford, and Sakichi Toyoda. The book contains compelling histories of notable companies, among them Rolls-Royce, the Deutsche Bank, IBM, and Seven-Eleven Japan. All of these stories—whether of countries, companies, or people—have strong elements of drama. All are memorable. And all help us to understand the nature of economic success in the midst of constant change.

During the three years that the authors spent conceiving, researching, and writing this book, we came to certain conclusions about capitalism. We now think—in fact, we *know*—that there is no one best way to organize a capitalist system. Certainly there are a few essentials, such as private property and the rule of law. But as a general economic system, capitalism is flexible and adaptable in the extreme. It can operate effectively within diverse national contexts. Countries with profoundly different resource endowments, histories, religions, and cultures can accommodate a capitalist economy.

But constructive human agency cannot be taken for granted. Nor does economic progress come easily or automatically—to countries, companies, or people. It has to be pursued with energy and will. It requires purposeful acts and strenuous toil. It has to be constantly promoted or it will not be sustained.

At the most basic level, capitalism is best understood as an expression of human creativity. It is propelled by the dreams, aspirations, and efforts of individuals. So the authors of this book have taken care to show exactly who did what. Most of the book is about the entrepreneurs, companies, and governments that made four national economies prosperous. Fundamentally, the book is about *ideas and systems that worked* in the creation of modern capitalism.

CONTENTS

ILLUSTRATIONS

Following page 50

Map 1. The United Kingdom and Ireland

Josiah Wedgwood, portrait by Sir Joshua Reynolds
The Wedgwood factory called Etruria
Wedgwood showrooms, Portland House, Soho, London
The Portland vase, Wedgwood's most celebrated masterpiece of Jasper-ware
A cauliflower ware teapot, made in Staffordshire in the 1760s

Charles Stewart Rolls in 1906
Rolls at the wheel of the first Rolls-Royce
Henry Royce in late middle age
The Royal Air Force's Defiant fighter planes of World War II, powered with Rolls-Royce Merlin engines

Following page 134

Map 2. Germany in 1871
Map 3. Germany in 1919
Map 4. Germany in 1949

August Thyssen Sr., founder of major German steel, coal, and machinery companies
Thyssen, 1895
August's brother Josef Thyssen
Hedwig Thyssen and her children
Henrich Thyssen-Bornemisza and his family

Georg von Siemens, spokesman of the Deutsche Bank's Managing Board from 1870 to 1900
Headquarters of the Deutsche Bank in Berlin, 1929
Georg Solmssen, spokesman of the Deutsche Bank's Managing Board in 1933

CREATING MODERN CAPITALISM

INTRODUCTION

Thomas K. McCraw

For most of human history until about the seventeenth century, economic stagnation seemed to be the natural order of things all over the world.[1] People at every social level took it for granted and arranged their lives accordingly. They gave little thought to what later generations called "economic and social mobility." The idea of an "industrial revolution" or a "consumer economy" would have seemed incomprehensible to them. In Europe during the thousand years before 1700, per capita income grew at the minuscule rate of about 0.11 percent per year, or just over a tenth of a percent. There is no substantial reason to think that the rate was much more or less than that in most other parts of the world.[2]

In many countries, the coming of industrialization and the creation of modern capitalism ended this long economic stagnation and transformed the mind-set that went with it. As Karl Marx and Friedrich Engels wrote in 1848, a scant hundred years of capitalism had already "created more massive and more colossal productive forces than have all preceding generations together." And even as they wrote, the forces of capitalism were just beginning to gather steam. At the old annual growth rate of 0.11 percent, per capita income had doubled about every 630 years. But between 1820 and 1990, a period of only 170 years, it multiplied by a factor of about 10 in Great Britain, 15 in Germany, 18 in the United States, and 25 in Japan. The capitalist era, especially the period since 1820, has been unique in human history, a time of spectacular economic growth.[3]

This book explores some aspects of how that growth occurred, and particularly what entrepreneurs and business firms had to do with it.

The book's structure is a little unusual, with four chapters focusing on countries and eight others on companies. The chapters entitled "British

Capitalism," "German Capitalism," and so on, survey the evolution of each nation's business system. Here our vantage point is long-range, as from an orbiting satellite taking continuous time-lapse photographs. These country chapters provide an overview of the innovation and constant change that are the defining characteristics of capitalist systems.

The economist Joseph Schumpeter (1883–1950), one of the most astute of all analysts of capitalism, called it a process of "creative destruction"—an incessant sweeping out of old products, old processes, and old organizational forms by new ones. Schumpeter wrote that "The atmosphere of industrial revolutions—of 'progress'—is the only one in which capitalism can survive." He went on to say that "stabilized capitalism is a contradiction in terms." The contents of this book support his conclusions.[4]

The tumultuous process of creative destruction was carried out mostly by entrepreneurs operating through business firms. So, between the country chapters, we drop from the satellite view to helicopter height and examine the histories of at least two companies in each country: Wedgwood and Rolls-Royce in Great Britain; Thyssen Steel and Deutsche Bank in Germany; Ford, General Motors, and IBM in the United States; Toyota Motor and Seven-Eleven in Japan.

Each of these companies has been a champion performer in its particular industry. In choosing the firms to include in this book, we looked not only for top performers but also for examples that capture some of the essence of each country's economy. No company is necessarily "typical" of its national business system, because the systems themselves are too varied. But these firms are not atypical. It's hard to imagine the story of Rolls-Royce occurring anywhere other than Britain, or that of Ford anywhere but the United States.

A third component of the book is its comparative reference tools. These include a statistical appendix that also contains some time lines setting forth the chronology of each country's and company's development. Both the statistics and the time lines are indispensable to understanding the four countries' experience with capitalism, and they're worth your close attention.

Why do we focus on Britain, Germany, the United States, and Japan? Because all four countries have achieved outstanding economic growth, and are champions in their own right. Equally important, each has also exemplified a distinctive variety of capitalism. Britain, having started to industrialize in the late eighteenth century, represents the earliest instance of modern capitalist development.[5] Germany and the United States came next, exploding to world prominence late in the nineteenth century. Japan, which began to industrialize just before the twentieth century, became a significant force in certain industries by the 1930s. Then, in the generation after 1950, it achieved sensational growth.

All four of these countries are "capitalist," but their versions of capitalism are not identical. Nor do the four together exhaust the list of possible models. The historical record shows that there are many paths to capitalist success.

"Capital" and "Capitalism"

The term "capital" first appeared in its modern sense in about 1630. The *Oxford English Dictionary* gives a succinct definition: "accumulated wealth reproductively employed." Throughout history, human beings had quickly consumed almost all of what they produced. Sometimes they accumulated a little wealth, but they customarily spent it on displays that weren't very useful in improving common people's living standards. The pyramids of Egypt represented an enormous amount of accumulated wealth, but it was devoted to the afterlife of pharaohs. It produced a good deal of employment, but not with the continuing developmental effect that would have come if the same money had been spent on roads and canals. The pyramids are only one example of the practice of traditional societies all over the world.

Often the use of accumulated wealth did have the worthy result of producing spiritual inspiration through priceless art and architecture: the pyramids, the Forbidden City of China, the Parthenon of Greece, the cathedrals of medieval Europe. But accumulated wealth put to these uses wasn't "reproductively employed." So it didn't represent "capital" in the modern sense. Ironically, it did so later, when these monumental structures started attracting hordes of tourists.

"Capitalism" is a newer term than "capital," and it's harder to define. The word didn't come into existence until the 1850s, when it appeared as an antonym of "socialism." What exactly does "capitalism" mean?

At a minimum, a capitalist system is organized around a market economy that emphasizes private property, entrepreneurial opportunity, technological innovation, the sanctity of contracts, payment of wages in money, and the ready availability of credit. Under capitalism, property must be "alienable," that is, freely bought and sold. The "value" of a good or service means whatever price someone will pay for it. Previously, there had been widespread quasi-religious notions of a "just price" above which one charged at the peril of one's soul.[6] And buying anything on credit, even for purposes of investment, was often regarded as questionable. The transition from the old mind-set to the new was a long, gradual process that even today is not complete. We ourselves feel vestiges of the old virtues in our guilt (often appropriate) about the unrestrained use of consumer credit.

Capitalism relies heavily on investment credit as a means of financing innovation. In this respect the term "capitalism" goes beyond the dictionary definition of "capital," which is an economic concept and a factor of production common to all economies. Capitalism characteristically employs not only accumulated wealth but also financial resources that don't yet exist in tangible form. It employs "money of the mind," as credit has aptly been called. Banks, the primary sources of credit, lend out money far beyond their cash reserves, on the expectation that borrowers will employ the money, pay interest on it, and repay the principal in the *future*. In so doing, banks create money out of nothing but faith and informed expectation, subject of course to reserve requirements imposed by banking authorities. Entrepreneurs and companies borrow this money. To get still more of the capital they need, they may also issue stocks and bonds, often backed by nothing except the anticipation of a future return on the companies' products.

"Capitalists," then, are people who make bets on the future. The essence of capitalism is a psychological orientation toward the pursuit of future wealth and property. It's all about aspiration and striving, measured by gains and losses in wealth and income. It rests on a belief that economic growth, even substantial growth, is possible and desirable— for an individual, a family, a business firm, an industry, even an entire country.

Today most of us take this belief for granted. It is an unstated assumption behind much of what we do. But for many centuries, such a belief did not enter the minds of most people. Economic growth did not necessarily seem desirable, let alone possible. Nor was it commonly seen as related to individual effort. There was little expectation of change in any circumstance of life, economic or otherwise. Most people looked on the changes that did occur as the consequences of some outside force. They explained catastrophes such as the Black Death, which wiped out about a third of Europe's population during the fourteenth century, as God's punishment.[7]

Many ethical systems contained stern warnings about how the pursuit of riches imperiled the soul. "Many evil men are rich, and good men poor," the Athenian statesman Solon observed in the sixth century B.C. "It is easier for a camel to go through the eye of a needle, than for a rich man to enter into the Kingdom of God," cautioned the Gospel of Matthew. In some religions, including Christianity and Islam, lending money at interest was forbidden as sinful. In Japan as late as the mid-nineteenth century, merchants had the most money but the lowest status. They ranked not only below the samurai (warrior class), but also below craftsmen and the mass of agricultural peasantry. They stood at the bottom of Japanese society because their lives centered around buying low and selling high.

For much of human history, and in most societies across the world, the prevailing mind-set was antimaterialistic and antigrowth. Even people with strong acquisitive tendencies, ranging from the conqueror Genghis Khan to the Medici bankers of Florence, bent their efforts toward gaining a larger share of what was thought to be a pie of fixed size. Their gain was regarded as another's loss, by definition. Life was viewed as a seesaw. If someone went up, someone else had to go down. That's one reason why acquisitive people were often relegated to low social status, unless their success came from military conquest or was truly spectacular. Even in eighteenth-century England, a relatively modern capitalist society, most people thought it unseemly that merchants should try to become "gentlemen." Gentlemen devoted themselves to their lands and surrounding communities, or to the church, the army or navy, or the civil service. They didn't pursue money as an end in itself.

Partly because of this kind of mind-set, there was minimal economic growth in most of the world for several thousand years. Although life was "solitary, poor, nasty, brutish, and short," as the English philosopher Thomas Hobbes put it, life was not necessarily filled with hard labor. Most people tended to work in "lumps"—assiduously at planting and harvest periods, lackadaisically during the winter. Their sense of time came not from clocks but from the sun and the seasons.[8] Circumstances didn't encourage or even permit them to work in a way we would regard as efficient. As a result, individual incomes didn't rise.

Social mobility was extremely low. Few people were "free" in the sense that we now use that term. In 1772, the English economic writer Arthur Young estimated that the world contained about 775 million people, only 33.5 million of whom were "free."[9] The rest—96 percent of the total—were serfs, slaves, or vassals of some kind. They owed their loyalty and part of their labor to those above them in the social order, and ultimately to authoritarian kings, chieftains, or warlords.

Most agricultural lands in Europe were "entailed." They were parts of unitary feudal estates. They couldn't be sold or subdivided for ownership by individual farmers. Occupational and geographical mobility remained low. One usually did what one's parents had done. One lived where they had lived. A large proportion of the earth's people never in their lifetimes traveled more than thirty miles from their birthplaces. Incentives for change were very small. Institutional structures weren't geared toward economic growth. And so not much growth occurred.

One essential condition of a dynamic economy, and of capitalism itself, is a relatively free labor market. Individuals must have some control over the disposition of their work. They must have a choice about whom they wish to "sell" it to. They should also be able to keep most of their wages for themselves and their families. Yet for thousands of years, almost no free labor markets existed. Few jobs paid cash wages, and a portion of the returns of everyone's work went to the landlord, the chieftain, the king, the warlord.

Capitalism, by contrast, opened up labor markets and fostered cash wages systems. More broadly, capitalism promoted a dynamic, flexible, and future-oriented way of thinking. It injected a pattern of ceaseless and merciless competition into nearly every aspect of life. Politics, the military, even religion became more competitive, following the lead of the economic system and occasionally moving in advance of it. Martin Luther and John Calvin openly challenged the Church of Rome, which had dominated Europe's religious life for centuries. Their doctrines competed not only against Catholicism and Judaism, but against each other. And all of this religious competition tended to widen the opportunities for market forces to operate, and thereby to strengthen the spirit of capitalism even more.[10]

Capitalism as an economic system did not necessarily go hand in hand with democracy. It did not, by itself, "free" anyone from anything, except from some of the old social and familial bonds of mutual obligation. Capitalism did promote the dissolution of feudal restrictions, and helped to promote freer labor markets. But in so doing, it tended to facilitate a new form of exploitation, which its opponents came to call "wage slavery." A number of writers, following Karl Marx's original definition of capitalism, have emphasized that a capitalist system is not merely a market economy, but that it also implies a political system ruled by, or in the interests of, capitalists.[11]

There's a good deal of truth in this definition. In precapitalist systems, political power was determined mostly by noneconomic yardsticks. Military strength, inherited lands, and intricate systems of reciprocal obligations were the organizing principles of society. But once the market began to replace these older customs, political power began to gravitate toward those with new fortunes, and a series of wrenching social adjustments followed in train. That process is still going on, and the adaptations continue down to the present day.

Historically, some of these adaptations have been profound, and have gone in the wrong direction. Each of the four countries analyzed in this book has an embarrassing historical underside of which it is ashamed, or ought to be: Britain of its cruel treatment of subjugated peoples in parts of its empire; Japan of atrocities against East and South Asian peoples before and during World War II; the United States of whites' enslavement of African-Americans; Germany of the Holocaust, which in its organized mass murder was among the ghastliest episodes in all of human experience. But this book is a business history. It can't adequately cover those topics except to note that they proceeded right alongside capitalist development in each country. Capitalism didn't produce these tragedies in a direct sense. But it facilitated some of them, and it certainly didn't prevent them.

Over the very long term, one of the central problems of capitalist societies has been the vexing question of how to distribute equitably the bountiful fruits of economic growth. Where, exactly, does justice lie? Should early industrialists have been allowed to squeeze extravagant profits from the sweat of their workforce, which included large numbers of children? Should workers have had to labor endless hours in the squalor of "dark Satanic mills," as the poet William Blake called them?[12] In the nineteenth century, should the Rothschilds of Europe and the Rockefellers of America have been allowed to become so colossally wealthy? In our own lifetimes, could it possibly have been proper for the American investment banker Michael Milken to have "earned" $550 million in the single year 1987?

These are old kinds of questions, in part because the roots of capitalism go back a long way, to about the eleventh century. At that time, a few merchant families in southern Europe started to become wealthy enough to challenge the feudal nobility. But it was not until the sixteenth and seventeenth centuries that a more widespread capitalist class emerged. And not until the eighteenth did most of the other conditions of modern capitalism (credit systems, cash wages, incessant innovation) begin to flower. When Adam Smith published The Wealth of Nations in 1776, he showed how materialism and the pursuit of individual gain could be the central motivating principles of a new kind of society. In such a society, the economic pie need not be of fixed size. It could constantly grow. Commercial exchange could benefit the buyer, the seller, and the community as a whole. The more production and exchange, the better.

Best of all, such a trend was already under way. By the time his book appeared, Adam Smith's "invisible hand"—that powerful symbol of a market process in which millions of individual producers and consumers continually make economic decisions in their own self-interest, and thereby benefit society as a whole—was already guiding the economies of Britain and a few other parts of Europe. Of course, this was still capitalism in its infancy. Smith could hardly have predicted all of the potent forces it eventually would unleash. Nor could he have imagined that capitalism would take hold in so many different places and in so many different forms. Surely he would have been astonished at the phenomenal growth it produced in some nations' economies in the 200 years after his death in 1790.

Capitalism and Economic Performance

In the world's community of nations, each of the four countries covered in this book has been a star performer. Three brief tables will put their achievements in perspective.

In Table 1.1 we see the gulf between the economic performances of

Table 1.1   Gross Domestic Product per Capita on the Basis of Purchasing Power
Parity: A Sample of 12 Countries (U.S. = 100; absolute amount in
current dollars = $25,880)

High-Income Economies		Middle-Income Economies		Lower-Income Economies	
U.S.	100.0	South Korea	39.9	China	9.7
Japan	81.7	Thailand	26.9	India	4.9
Germany	75.3	Poland	21.2	Nigeria	4.6
U.K.	69.4	Brazil	20.9	Rwanda	1.3

Note: Purchasing Power Parity is a measure that converts incomes into dollars not on the
basis of current exchange rates but according to their ability to purchase a standardized
bundle of goods. On the basis of current exchange rates, the United States ranks as the fifth-
richest country, behind Switzerland, Japan, Denmark, and Norway.
Source: World Development Report 1996 (New York: Oxford University Press for The
World Bank, 1996), pp. 188–189, 223–225. The year reported is 1994.

the richest and poorest countries as of the mid-1990s, with the United
States at the top, Rwanda at the bottom, and a huge variation in between.
Of the 133 countries in the world with populations of over a million
each, only 25 are "high-income" nations. All 25 are capitalist economies.
No country with a communist economy has ever made it into the top
tier, and only by a severe definitional stretch would there be any socialist
economies in the high-income group. A capitalist economy is not a sufficient condition for sustained national affluence, and plenty of capitalist
countries have never made it into the top tier. But it does seem to be a
necessary condition.

The poorest group of countries includes the vast majority of the human population—the great masses of people in China, India, Indonesia,
Pakistan, Bangladesh, most of Africa, and much of Latin America. Of a
world population of about 5.6 billion, about 4.8 billion live outside the
high-income countries. This is 85 percent of the world's people. About
1.6 billion live in "middle-income" countries, and well over 3 billion, or
about 60 percent of the world's total, live in poor countries. So the rich
countries comprise only 15 percent of the earth's population. Most of
the other 85 percent are now trying to harness the forces of capitalism
for their own economic development.

Table 1.2 shows the growth performance over 170 years of the four
countries covered in this book. The big story here is in the far right-hand
column, the 1989 number as a multiple of the 1820 number. As men-

Table 1.2   Gross Domestic Product per Capita, 1820–1989 (in thousands of
             dollars at constant 1985 U.S. Prices)

	1820	1913	1950	1989	1989's figure as a multiple of 1820's
U.K.	$1.4	$4.0	$5.7	$13.5	10
Germany	0.9	2.6	3.3	14.0	15
U.S.	1.0	4.9	8.6	18.3	18
Japan	0.6	1.1	1.6	15.1	25

Note: The 1820 number for Japan is a rough estimate.
Source: Adapted from Angus Maddison, *Dynamic Forces in Capitalist Development* (New York: Oxford University Press, 1991), pp. 6–7.

tioned at the start of this chapter, per capita income in the U.K. increased by almost 10 times during that 170-year period, in Germany 15 times, in the U.S. 18 times, and in Japan 25 times. During the 8,000 years of recorded history, nothing like that had happened before. What we're looking at here is properly regarded as a miracle of capitalist economic growth.

In 1820 no responsible commentator would have predicted such phenomenal growth rates persisting over so long a time. With the single exception of Karl Marx, nobody of much importance in the eighteenth or nineteenth century fully grasped the revolutionary economic potential of capitalism. Many writers instead predicted a "steady state" economy. As Joseph Schumpeter once described the leading analysts from the Victorian period, "They were all stagnationists." They "had no idea of what the capitalist engine of production was going to achieve."[13] What it did in fact achieve is indicated by the high multiples appearing in the far right-hand column of Table 1.2.

As against the 0.11 annual percentage growth of per capita GDP in precapitalist times, consider the numbers in Table 1.3, which break down the aggregate figures in Table 1.2 into annual rates.

Here we see two different phenomena. First, we observe the miracle growth rates peculiar to industrial capitalism. Recall that in Japan, traditional society persisted until the Meiji Restoration of 1868. Up until that time Japan showed the usual precapitalist growth figure of 0.1 percent. After capitalist industrialization, Japan's long-run rate multiplied by a factor of 27, to 2.7 percent per year.[14]

Table 1.3   Long-Term Average Annual Compound Growth Rates of Gross Domestic Product per Capita

	1820–1870	1870–1989
U.K.	1.2%	1.4%
Germany	0.7	2.0
U.S.	1.5	1.8
Japan	0.1	2.7

Source: Adapted from Maddison, *Dynamic Forces in Capitalist Development,* p. 49.

The second phenomenon we see in Table 1.3, especially when we combine it with the aggregate numbers in Table 1.2, is the remarkable long-term effect of compound growth rates. With reference again to the numbers for Japan, at a compound rate of increase of 0.1 percent per year, an economy will double in size every 693 years. But at 2.7 percent growth per year, compounded, it will double every 26 years. At 6 percent, it will double about every 12 years, and at 12 percent about every 6 years. This remarkable consequence of compounded growth percentages is why small differences in interest rates are so important in business transactions. And it's one reason why in our own time a compound per capita growth rate of one percent per year in an industrialized country is poor, but 2 percent not bad and 3 percent very good.

Varieties of Capitalism

As you'll discover in the chapters on British, German, American, and Japanese capitalism, each country's business system has an idiosyncratic history. This history is related to each nation's culture, its political system, and external events such as war. Yet each system is a capitalist economy based on the market mechanism. So the countries have a lot in common. One of the challenges of this book, and of the general subject we're calling "varieties of capitalism," is to discover which elements are essential to any capitalist system and which are not. There are many routes to capitalist success, and to failure as well. Specific analyses of the British, German, American, and Japanese economies can be more informative than generic commentaries on "capitalism" abstractly conceived.

At a broad level, the superstructure of each country's business system encompasses its national culture, its prevailing value system and ideology, its political system, and its macroeconomic policies. In this book we concentrate on some of those elements but not others. We take note of differences in political systems and macroeconomic policies, but we don't emphasize them. We pay more attention to variations in regulatory systems and microeconomic policies, which affect business more directly.

Each type of business system contains its own distinctive strengths and weaknesses. These differences are reflected in the industrial structures of each nation, as well as in changes among those structures over time. By "varieties" of capitalism, we mean differences from country to country not only in the ways economic systems work, but in the ways individual companies are organized: What are their management systems? How do they select their technologies? Where do they get their financing? How do they govern their workforces?

We also mean the ways in which firms make connections with one another: Do they operate at only one stage of the production or marketing process? Do they make "horizontal" cartel agreements with other firms to divide markets and control prices? Do they develop formal or informal strategic alliances such as *keiretsu* (Japan), *Interessengemein-schaften* (Germany), loosely connected holding companies (Britain), or more tightly organized conglomerates (United States)? In what industries do they decide to integrate "vertically" and do both manufacturing and marketing within the same company?

The Three Industrial Revolutions

Just as the details of capitalism differ by location, we can distinguish different phases of development across time. One way of thinking about these cumulative processes of growth is the notion of three industrial revolutions. Professors debate over the wisdom of using the term "industrial revolution" at all, since there are no single years in which big spurts of economic activity suddenly occur. Instead the record shows a gradual rise in growth rates.[15]

Nor is it precisely correct to equate industrial revolutions with capitalism itself. Noncapitalist economies can produce technological wonders, as the Soviet Union did when it put the first person into space. But the congruence of technological advance with capitalist economic progress has been so very close historically that it is entirely proper to speak of industrial revolutions in tandem with capitalist development.

In this book we'll use the term "industrial revolution" mostly as an organizing device to separate one era from another. We won't argue that one period abruptly gave way to the next on a certain date, or that all countries went through each phase at the same time. But you'll be able to see how very different each of the industrial revolutions became from what went before it, and how the structures of modern capitalism were successively transformed.

Each of our three revolutions is exemplified by a characteristic set of industrial processes and products:

1. The First Industrial Revolution, 1760s–1840s
   a. Led by Great Britain, with the U.S., France, and the states that later made up Germany following after a lag of several decades.
   b. Agricultural productivity increased. Manufacturing, which for thousands of years had been based on human and animal energy, was powered more and more by water and by steam generated from coal. New canals facilitated water transport. Machine tools came into wider use. The factory system spread rapidly, and an industrial proletariat began to gather in cities. People started to work by the clock. The corporate form of business organization began to spread. Some companies employed several hundred persons each, and a few employed more than one thousand.
   c. Typical new products were steam engines and factory-produced items such as cotton textiles, ironware, and pottery.
2. The Second Industrial Revolution, 1840s–1950s
   a. Led by the United States, Great Britain, and a few European nations, especially Germany, France, and the Low Countries.
   b. Communication and transportation were revolutionized, first by the telegraph and railroad, then by the telephone, automobile, truck, and airplane. Production was increasingly powered by electric motors and the internal combustion engine. Corporations proliferated, becoming commonplace in all capitalist countries. Mass marketing arose. The international economy began to become much more integrated. "Big business" as we know it first appeared, and some companies built complex organizations with semi-autonomous divisions and many layers of management. A few very large firms, clustered in a small

number of industries, employed several hundred thousand persons each. In most industries, traditional small shops and medium-sized factories persisted alongside the new industrial giants, and that pattern endures to the present day. Starting in the mid-nineteenth century with the railroads, management became professionalized. By the close of the nineteenth century and the start of the twentieth, the first business schools began to appear.

   c. Typical products included "producers' goods" such as steel, turbines, and chemicals, plus a profuse array of new consumer goods, which were now mass-produced, branded, and individually packaged. Consumer durables such as automobiles, radios, home appliances, and ultimately television sets became focal points of daily life. Toward the end of the period, antibiotics were developed. The continuous introduction of new products of all kinds became the hallmark of modern capitalism.

3. The Third Industrial Revolution, 1950s to the Present
   a. Led by the United States, Japan, and Europe.
   b. The central trend of this era has been called the "rise of the information economy," or, somewhat misleadingly, the "coming of post-industrial society." More people began to work in services than in all other sectors put together. There was an immense increase in the volume of international trade, investment, and finance. Computer technology became pervasive, and "knowledge work" came to have surpassing importance. Together, these changes required a huge growth in the number of managers and other professionals serving business, such as accountants, engineers, lawyers, and consultants.

   Science-based products became the primary growth sectors in the developed world. The integrated circuit had a profound impact, rivalling that of the steam engine in the first industrial revolution and electricity in the second. Computers and other electronic items, plus synthetic chemicals and pharmaceuticals, dominated the outpouring of new products. Organized research and development intensified. Instantaneous global communication became possible on a large scale, and then almost indispensable for certain kinds of business. Firms in some industries grew gigantic. Then, in the 1980s, companies began

to "downsize" in response to domestic and international competition. Spans of control grew wider, layers of management
thinner. "Virtual corporations" became conceivable, though
unlikely to materialize in significant numbers.

c. Typical products included the VCR, the facsimile machine, the
cellular telephone, the personal computer with its vast range of
software, and a huge assortment of new pharmaceuticals, notably birth control pills.

Thinking Historically

That completes the basic outline of the business and economic history of
four industrialized countries over the last 200 years. Their role in creating
modern capitalism is set forth in the pages that follow. As you study this
material, it will be useful to distinguish not only among the three industrial revolutions, but also among different units of analysis. The major
units to focus on are the country, the industry, the company, and the
individual manager. As you read, try to determine how these four units
are interacting with each other. Ask yourself what is causing what. That's
a pivotal question in the study of history, of course. There is seldom a
clear answer to the question, but most things don't happen randomly.
You'll discern definite patterns of causation and historical development
within each country and across all four.

The American literary critic Bernard de Voto once wrote that "History
abhors determinism, but it cannot tolerate chance." He meant that history is actually about both determinism and chance, but that thinking
historically means being able to tell the difference. In our own lives, we're
all constantly bouncing between the extremes of individual volition on
the one hand and the sweep of impersonal forces on the other. We try to
make judgments about what we can change and what we must accept as
inevitable. We wonder how we might make a virtue of necessity and turn
circumstance into opportunity. We can't stop the rain, but we need not
get wet if we remember to carry an umbrella. And we might even be able
to collect and sell the water.[16]

So it was with our ancestors, who were just as intelligent and re-
sourceful as we like to think we ourselves are. And so it should be as we
come to terms with the countries, industries, companies, and individuals
in this book. Thinking historically has nothing to do with memorizing

dates and winning trivia contests. Instead it means charting changes and sequences over time and making judgments about them. It means discerning the boundaries between volition and inevitability. Ultimately it means being able to distinguish what's really important from what's not.

History offers a vast, incomparably rich storehouse of vicarious experience. But as you partake of this experience, perspective becomes vital. It's essential not only to see events and trends in hindsight, but also to imagine how they unfolded for contemporaries, who had no assurance of how things might turn out. The English historian F. W. Maitland urged us never to forget that what's now in the past was once in the future. The American poet Emily Dickinson put the same kind of thought in a slightly different way: "Forever is composed of Nows."

The next chapter, "Josiah Wedgwood and the First Industrial Revolution," is the first of several in this book concerned with the role of the individual entrepreneur. In later chapters we'll meet equally colorful characters such as August Thyssen (Germany), Henry Ford (United States), and Sakichi Toyoda (Japan). Josiah Wedgwood himself was a key figure in the industrial quickening that began in about the 1760s and wound up changing the world.

When most people think of industrial revolutions, they think of technological breakthroughs: the steam engine, the power loom, and machines with interchangeable parts. Such innovations were indeed the keys to what economists like to call the "supply side" of the First Industrial Revolution, by which they mean the revolution in production brought by technology.*

But there was a powerful demand side as well. Economic and social transitions were accompanied by substantial changes in consumer behavior, and innovations in marketing sometimes proved to be as important as those in technology. As Joseph Schumpeter once observed, "It was not enough to produce satisfactory soap, it was also necessary to induce people to wash."** In the eighteenth century, as today, consumers had to be persuaded that they "needed" the new products. So it was with the remarkable success of Josiah Wedgwood's pottery works, and with his broader role in the First Industrial Revolution. Using a variety of ingenious marketing devices, Wedgwood induced more and more people

---

*Technology is a theme of many important books on industrial revolutions, such as Phyllis Deane, *The First Industrial Revolution,* 2d ed. (Cambridge: Cambridge University Press, 1984), David S. Landes, *The Unbound Prometheus: Technological Change and Industrial Development in Western Europe from 1750 to the Present* (Cambridge: Cambridge University Press, 1969); and Joel Mokyr, *The Lever of Riches: Technological Creativity and Economic Progress* (New York: Oxford University Press, 1990).

**Joseph A. Schumpeter, *Business Cycles: A Theoretical, Historical, and Statistical Analysis of the Capitalist Process,* 2 vols. (New York: McGraw-Hill, 1939), p. 243.

to buy his products. The result was that the name Wedgwood became one of the first brands to be recognizable throughout the world.

This chapter's theme is the complex interaction between manufacturing and marketing. It also takes note of entrepreneurs' roles in promoting canals and other public works, and of the new industrial workforce's very mixed reaction to factory discipline, especially the tyranny of the time clock. Most of all, the chapter is about how Josiah Wedgwood and his partner Thomas Bentley built up the "brand equity" that the Wedgwood name came to represent.

That brand equity became an almost priceless asset, and it has endured for more than 230 years. Such a history of success raises the question of how significant the "first-mover advantage" is in the creation of a brand. It also invites us to speculate about how long other great brands of more recent vintage—Coca-Cola, Shell, Disney, Chanel, Seiko, Sony, Microsoft—may be expected to flourish.

❋ 2 ❋

JOSIAH WEDGWOOD AND THE FIRST
INDUSTRIAL REVOLUTION

Nancy F. Koehn

I saw the [industrial] field was spacious, and the soil so good, as to promise an ample recompense to any who should labour diligently in its cultivation.

—*Josiah Wedgwood*[1]

In June 1774, members of London's social elite made their way through the bustling streets of the West End to a stately Georgian building called Portland House. Here in five commercial showrooms, earls, dukes, and Queen Charlotte, the wife of George III, mingled with prosperous merchants and traders. They had all come to see the most famous set of china in England.

Commissioned by Catherine the Great of Russia at a price of £3,000 (about $330,000 today),[2] the 50-person dinner and dessert services consisted of 952 pieces, each hand-painted with a distinctive British scene.[3] It was an impressive sight. One of Queen Charlotte's attendants commented that "three rooms below and two above" were filled with china, "laid out on tables, everything that can be wanted to serve a dinner." The china was in pale creamware, the drawings in purple, the borders a wreath of leaves, and "the middle of each piece a particular view of all the remarkable places in the King's dominions."[4] Drawn from engravings and first-hand sketches, most of the scenes were detailed renderings of provincial mansions and elaborate gardens. The men and women crowding into Portland House were anxious to see whose properties had been reproduced for the Russian empress.

In contrast to the rest of the set, a few pieces pictured canal locks, a colliery, a papermill, and a dockyard. These few plates, teapots, and cups offered glimpses of an emerging England, inventive, industrial, and busy, a new world mixing with the traditional order.[5] Overall, this new china service that London elites clamored to see in mid-1774 was both a symbol and a product of the nation's evolving economy. Novel manufacturing methods and organizational arrangements of the First Industrial Revolution had been used for the expeditious production of the unadorned pieces. But the unique decoration on each piece, applied by skilled artisans using long-established practices, had taken 15 months to complete. So the whole project symbolized a fusion of old and new industrial processes.

The men responsible for the project were Josiah Wedgwood and his partner, Thomas Bentley. They owned and managed Wedgwood & Bentley, one of the most innovative and successful firms in Britain's expanding pottery industry. Both men had worked hard to obtain the Russian royal commission. They had earned smaller profits on the sale than projected, but their company and its wares had captured significant aristocratic attention and, therefore, prestige.[6] From Josiah Wedgwood's vantage point, elite sanction was a critical component in selling both luxury goods and more essential pottery to an expanding range of customers. As he wrote to his partner:

> It is really amazing how rapidly . . . [our china] has spread allmost over the whole Globe, & how universally it is liked. How much of this general use, & estimation, is owing to the mode of its introduction & how much to its real utility & beauty? are questions in which we may be a good deal interested for the government of our future Conduct . . . For instance, if a Royal, or Noble Introduction be as necessary to the sale of an Article *of Luxury,* as real Elegance & beauty, then the Manufacturer, if he consults his own interest will bestow as much pains, & expence too if necessary, in gaining the former of these advantages, as he would in bestowing the latter.[7]

Wedgwood and Bentley understood that in the emerging consumer society, marketing was as important as manufacturing.

What else did it mean to do business in an age when widespread economic change was altering the range of possibilities available to consumers and suppliers? How were individual entrepreneurs going to manage the challenges presented by new goods, markets, mechanical contrivances, and labor relations? The story of Josiah Wedgwood is that of a man living at an inflection point in the history of capitalism. Over the course of his career, organized manufacturing and marketing became much more significant in Britain's economic structure. Industrial productivity increased. At the same time, agricultural and commercial productivity grew. The nation's international trading patterns shifted.[8]

Most of these changes were gradual. A few were dramatic. Taken together, they altered irrevocably the pace, tenor, and scope of British life. As Henry Fielding, the author of *Tom Jones* and other novels, commented in 1751, "Nothing has wrought such an Alteration in this Order of People, as the Introduction of Trade. This hath indeed given a Face to the whole Nation, hath in great measure subverted the former State of Affairs, and hath almost totally changed the Manners, Customs and Habits of the People."[9] Josiah Wedgwood wanted to understand and profit from this transformation.

Wedgwood was born on or about July 12, 1730 (the date of his baptism) in Burslem, a Staffordshire village 150 miles northwest of London (see Map 1). He was the thirteenth and last child of Mary and Thomas Wedgwood. The father, Thomas, was a man of moderate means from a long line of potters. He himself owned a pot-works near the Burslem churchyard. Like those of most babies born in Britain and Europe at that time, Josiah's chances of dying in the first year of life were about one in six.[10] If he survived his first 12 months, he could be expected to live another 39 years. Actually he lived to be 65.

The young Josiah, from his earliest years as a potter's apprentice, used his own substantial gifts of intellectual curiosity, aesthetic sensitivity, and commercial imagination to make sense of his world. He wanted to exploit the opportunities offered by scientific progress and economic expansion. But he was motivated by more than money.[11] Throughout his life, he was also drawn to scientific experiment, politics, literature, philosophy, and even botany.

Josiah's dedication and creativity eventually paid handsome rewards. He became the most successful and respected potter in Europe. He played a major role in transforming social attitudes toward earthenware, expanding its markets, and implementing a host of organizational and production innovations. The British statesman William Gladstone said in 1863, looking back over the early years of the First Industrial Revolution, "Wedgwood was the greatest man who ever, in any age, or in any country . . . applied himself to the important work of uniting art with industry."[12]

Such accolades might have embarrassed Josiah, but would not have surprised him. Throughout most of his life, he remained sure of his purpose and confident of his abilities to elevate himself and his world. He wrote Bentley in 1766, before their partnership was formalized, that if Bentley himself "could really fall in love with, and make a Mistress of" this new pottery business, "I should have little or no doubt of our success." He went on to declare that "we have certainly the fairest prospect of inlarging this branch of Manufacture to our wishes, and as Genius will not be wanting, I am firmly perswaded that our *proffits* will be in proportion to our *application*."[13] As Josiah understood, inspiration was a necessary, though not sufficient, condition of success. It was going to take a lot of work to make the most of the opportunities afforded by the First Industrial Revolution.

The Pottery Industry and the Eighteenth-Century Economy

In 1730, when Josiah Wedgwood was born, pottery manufacture and commerce were the principal occupations in his home village. Burslem had a population of a thousand and was well on its way to becoming a town.[14] More than two-thirds of the residents earned their livelihood in nonagricultural occupations, up from 50 percent three decades earlier.[15] Burslem's inhabitants lived and worked in 150 thatched cottages, many of which were surrounded by hollows from which potters dug their clay and into which they carted ash piles and other waste from their kilns. The tradesmen of Burslem included two blacksmiths, a baker, a cobbler, a butcher, and a barber. Two general shops sold tobacco, soap, candles, sugar, buttons, and thread. One of them also sold cloth, books, knitting needles, and groceries such as rice, prunes, and spices.[16] At least eight alehouses, with names such as the Jolly Potters, provided libations to quench the community's thirst.[17]

Several primitive roads connected Burslem with London, Liverpool, and other markets. The roads were pretty rough, and in the winter often impassable even by packhorse.[18] In 1730, the nearest canal was 20 miles away and still under construction.

Burslem was an important community in the Staffordshire region, which was (and still is) the center of earthenware production in England. Earthenware, another name for pottery, is china made of clay. Earthenware differs from porcelain, which is made from a compound of refined clay, fusible rock, and flux, an oxide added to ceramic bodies to promote fusion during firing. Porcelain is usually fired to the point where it becomes translucent. Consequently, it is usually more fragile than earthenware.[19]

In 60 small Burslem workshops, most of them employing fewer than a dozen men and children, master earthenware craftsmen and their assistants made butter-pots, pitchers, and mugs from the red, brown, and orange-colored clays available locally. Known as coarseware, these simple, durable products were usually coated in colored salt-based glazes. As consumer products, they were fast replacing the wood and pewter dishes that most Britons had used for centuries. Coarseware was sold to wholesalers and retailers in local and London markets. British demand for finer wares was met by European and Far Eastern imports or by the delftware potteries in London and Bristol. Delftware was an elaborately decorated form of earthenware, vulnerable to scratches and breakage.[20]

By modern standards, a potter's tools were very simple. Most workshops had one or two wheels and at least one lathe to scrape the surface of the ware after the potter had "thrown," molded, and dried the clay. In the 1730s, both wheels and lathes were powered by human energy, as they had been for centuries. Earthenware manufacture at this time was a labor-intensive process, more dependent on individual craft and energy than on capital equipment or organizational capabilities. Even so, the necessary tools and inputs represented a substantial financial investment for most households.

The majority of pot-works had at least one oven, fueled by coal and usually measuring eight feet long by ten feet wide, standing fifteen feet high. Some potters also had special molds. A potter's oven cost £15, a wheel approximately £1, and a high-quality lathe £2 10s.[21] Counting raw materials and existing stock, a mid-sized workshop such as that inherited by Josiah's father was valued at about £40 (approximately $6,400 in today's dollars), exclusive of rent for the shop.[22] This was almost three times the annual income of a farm laborer and almost twice the yearly earnings of a collier.[23] Financial barriers to entry, plus the long training required, prevented much of the Staffordshire labor force from obtaining any kind of ownership stake in the pottery business.[24]

The industry was broadly representative of the national economy. Manufacturing in early eighteenth-century Britain was diverse, small in scale, and regionally concentrated by industry. Manufacturing output was spread across a broad range of industries: baking, milling, brewing, distilling, pottery, leather processing, building materials, and woolen textiles.[25] The last three sectors probably accounted for close to two-thirds of industrial output before 1750. The famous technological leaders of the First Industrial Revolution—cotton textiles, ironware, and engineering (manufacture of machinery)—made up less than 10 percent.[26]

Still, as early as 1740, almost 40 percent of men over the age of 20 labored in commercial or manufacturing enterprises, a higher fraction than was true for the rest of Europe. About 30 percent of British families farmed, and most of the remaining 30 percent were servants and other laborers.[27] During the middle decades of the eighteenth century, the British economy became even more industrialized, but agriculture and commerce steadily expanded along with manufacturing. Through a series of cost-reducing innovations, including the introduction of fodder crops into the rotations, agricultural output grew an average of 0.6 percent each year in the first half of the century.[28] Industrial output climbed an average 0.7 percent annually before 1760.[29] Though not high by twentieth-century criteria, they were significant gains at the time.

The starting date for the First Industrial Revolution is a hotly debated subject.[30] Historians and economists argue about the relative importance of labor, capital, and technological change in industrialization as well as about the contribution of agriculture and international trade in accounting for Britain's rising national product.[31] Most scholars agree, however, that in the middle decades of the century England's traditional and newer sectors experienced steady growth (see Table 2.1). The expansion of agricultural output slowed after 1760.[32] But output in commerce and manufacturing sectors—wool, iron, silk, cotton, beer, leather, soap—increased by more than 1 percent each year in the two decades after 1760, accelerating to 1.8 percent annually in the last 20 years of the century.[33] By eighteenth-century standards, this was very rapid growth.

Table 2.1   Growth of British Gross Domestic Product and of Industrial and Agricultural Output, 1700–1801 (% per annum)

Years	1700–60	1760–80	1780–1801
GDP	0.7	0.6	1.4
Industry	0.7	1.3	2.0
Agriculture	0.6	0.1	0.8

Source: Adapted from Nick Crafts, "The Industrial Revolution," in Roderick Floud and Donald McCloskey, eds., *The Economic History of Britain since 1700,* 2d ed. (Cambridge: Cambridge University Press, 1994), vol. 1, p. 47.

After 1780, cotton and iron manufacture became more significant components of industrial output, which itself was becoming an ever-larger part of national product. During the second half of the eighteenth century, the number of weavers more than doubled, and the number of men in the textile trades as a whole more than tripled.[34] By 1800, industry, commerce, and services made up more than half of Britain's national product.[35] Britain was one of the first countries in the world to pass the benchmark of having less than half its workforce deployed in agriculture.[36]

Businessmen and politicians working during Josiah Wedgwood's lifetime had no access to national income and productivity figures such as the ones quoted above. Such measurements are twentieth-century innovations, and the numbers cited here have been carefully calculated retrospectively, on the basis of incomplete data. By modern criteria, the growth figures mentioned are not very impressive, but they did represent quite a large increase at the time, and they underscore the far-reaching inventiveness and improvement that characterized the British economy.

As noted earlier, eighteenth-century manufacturing was usually centered in specific regions. Pig and bar iron were smelted in Shropshire and Worcestershire. Metalware was produced in factories and workshops around cities such as Birmingham, Wolverhampton, and Sheffield.[37] Woolens, linens, fustians (mixes of cotton and linen), and other cotton goods were made in northwest England.

As for mining, copper was centered in Cornwall, slate in North Wales, lead in Cumberland and Derbyshire. But the most important of all mining sectors was coal. Britain was richly endowed with coal reserves, and these played a critical role in the nation's industrialization. Coal was used in smelting iron and in many other manufactures. It was mined in Shropshire, Worcestershire, Yorkshire, South Wales, and Staffordshire. Coal mining, like the production of textiles, earthenware, and ships, engendered subsidiary trades, which grew up to serve the principal occupations in a particular area. Grindstone production drew artisans to Sheffield to make equipment for the ironware industry. The making of spindles, needles, combs, and cards developed in the textile regions. Crate manufacturing proliferated in Staffordshire as the earthenware sector expanded.

Many industries and regional economies became much more efficient during the eighteenth century. Few sectors, however, underwent the range of operational advances that earthenware manufacture did. In the decades surrounding Josiah Wedgwood's birth, a series of important developments in raw materials, casting processes, and firing methods increased the potential quality, quantity, and range of output. Before 1730, Staffordshire potters had begun working with white clays imported from southwest England, eventually combining them with local clays to produce a cream-colored ware, often called creamware, that was smoother to work with and more appealing to the eye.[38] These innovations marked the first stages in the production of earthenware that could compete with high-priced porcelain and delftware.[39]

In Burslem and other pottery centers, manufacturers experimented further with molds and casting processes to shape "useful" earthenware, those products used for domestic functional purposes, such as plates, cups, basins, and pitchers. Techniques for shaping the earthenware expanded to include not only "press molding"—the pushing of flat pieces of damp clay into brass or alabaster molds—but also a larger number of shapes made from plaster of Paris.[40] This development proved crucial to the evolution of "slip-casting," which offered potters a much wider range of shapes than those possible on the wheel or through press molding.[41] Slip-casting entailed pouring "slip," a creamy clay solution, into plaster molds, allowing the solution to dry, and then removing the unfired clay.

In the 1740s, Staffordshire potters also experimented with new firing and glazing methods for cream-colored earthenware. They combined fluid glaze mixtures with novel firing techniques. Instead of firing the clay once after a powdered glaze had been applied, a few master craftsmen began firing their clay unglazed. Then, while the ware was still in a porous or "biscuit" condition, they dipped it in the glaze, then fired it again to fuse the glaze.[42] As Josiah Wedgwood and other potters quickly realized, the two firings produced pottery more evenly finished and with less resultant waste.

By the mid-eighteenth century, the Staffordshire pottery industry blended traditional skills and practices with novel processes, products, and organizational forms—the fusion of old and new that was to be so neatly symbolized by Wedgwood & Bentley's exhibition at Portland House some years later. Many of these early innovations produced quick, visible results: whiter, more smoothly polished plates and cups. Others took longer to bear fruit. Whether they occurred gradually or swiftly, the improvements were cumulative, with each feeding on and often encompassing other recent discoveries. Taken together, these innovations played a critical role in transforming the industry to which Josiah was to devote his life.

Josiah's Early Years

Josiah Wedgwood's childhood seems to have been a happy one. His mother, Mary, was a small, organized woman of uncommon sensitivity and kindness.[43] When Josiah was born, she already had 12 children, including 6 under age 10. Mary was relatively well educated, and she passed to her children her faith in the ethical and practical power of human industry. Josiah's father, Thomas Wedgwood, came from a long line of potters, many of whom had accumulated sizable resources. But he himself was not particularly ambitious or prosperous. The family was neither rich nor poor by eighteenth-century standards.[44] Like other contemporary manufacturers, the Wedgwoods were of the "middling" sort, part of Britain's heterogeneous and growing commercial classes.[45]

Before he was old enough to begin learning the family craft, Josiah did washing, dairywork, and other chores. When he was not working, he had time to ride the cratemen's packhorses as they waited for their loads and to explore the countryside surrounding Burslem, collecting fossils and pottery shards. In his father's workshop, Josiah put his hands in clay, forming imitations of all kinds of objects that interested him.[46] He was a lively, joyful child.

At age 7, he was sent to school in Newcastle-under-Lyme, west of Burslem, where he studied reading, writing, figures, and chemistry. According to his teacher, Josiah was "a fair arithmetician and master of a capital hand."[47] In 1739, when he was 9, his father died, and the pottery works passed to Josiah's eldest brother, Thomas. Cash became short, and Josiah left school. He probably began work in the pottery at this time.[48]

In 1742, smallpox broke out in Staffordshire, infecting the 12-year-old Josiah and other Burslem children.[49] He spent many weeks in bed, his body covered with sores. In this illness, some biographers have seen the origins of his adult passion for books.[50]

The disease left Josiah's face pockmarked and his right knee weak and unreliable. Often he could not walk without crutches or a cane. Pain dogged him, limiting his ability to operate the foot pedal on the potter's wheel. So he took up modeling, glazing, and other parts of earthenware production in his brother's workshop.[51] In 1744, the 14-year-old Josiah was formally apprenticed to his eldest brother. In exchange for room, board, and training in the "art, Mistery, Occupation or Imployment of Throwing and Handleing," Josiah bound himself for five years to a standard series of conditions: "At Cards Dice or any other unlawful Games he shall not Play, Taverns or Ale Houses he shall not haunt or frequent, Fornication he shall not Commit—Matrimony he shall not Contract—from the Service of his said Master he shall not at any time depart or absent himself without his said Masters Leave."[52]

Josiah completed his apprenticeship and worked for his brother an additional three years as a journeyman.[53] Constantly tinkering with various stages of pottery making, he tested different oxides that imitated a more vibrant marbled finish on the ware. He also developed his own variations on tortoiseshell ware, named for its mottled glaze, which faintly resembled a turtle's shell. His brother's workshop manufactured primarily useful goods. But Josiah also tried his hand at making ornamental goods—vases, snuffboxes, and decorative knife handles.

In 1752, Josiah left the workshop. He may have been frustrated by his brother's lack of ambition or the limitations of the family business. Most likely he sought a wider realm in which to nurture and develop his gifts. He worked for two years in a pottery in nearby Stoke. Then, when he was 24, he entered into a partnership with Thomas Whieldon, an experienced potter of the nearby town of Fenton, who had a large workshop and was on his way to amassing a considerable fortune.[54] Aged 35 when Josiah came to work with him, Whieldon employed more than 20 assistants, who made stoneware, tortoiseshell, and creamware in a wide range of pieces.[55] He oversaw a larger and more diversified operation than any Josiah had previously known. In the mid-1750s, Whieldon's annual sales rose to £900 (about $145,000 in today's dollars).[56] Josiah spent five years in Whieldon's pottery, working extensively with colors and glazes. He also traveled regularly to sell snuffboxes and knife handles to the metalware and cutlery industries in Birmingham and Sheffield.[57]

In the 1750s, both of those cities were booming. A center for the growing metalware and iron industries, Birmingham had almost tripled its population since 1700. With almost 30,000 people it was now the fifth-largest city in Britain, behind London, Bristol, Norwich, and Newcastle.[58] Sheffield in 1754 had 12,000 inhabitants (by 1801 it would have 46,000).[59] In both Birmingham and Sheffield, Josiah could see the power of industrial capitalism unleashed: crowded, busy streets, sprawling growth, and an expanding number of consumer goods—brooches, tankards, toys, French pottery, books, and much more.[60] Table 2.2 shows the pattern of urban growth in Britain before and during the First Industrial Revolution.

Josiah observed the social changes that accompanied urban expansion. He and other contemporary observers were particularly struck by how quickly fortunes could be made (and lost) in this environment. The British statesman Lord Shelburne, after visiting Birmingham in the 1760s, noted that "It is not fifty years since the hardware began to make a figure [in the city], from thence begun by people not worth above three or four hundred pounds a-piece, some of whom are now worth three or four hundred thousand."[61] There is no evidence that Josiah exulted in the changes he witnessed. But apparently the symptoms of industrialization neither frightened nor dismayed him. For Josiah, economic transformation was to be understood and exploited.

By his middle twenties, he realized that success in earthenware manufacture demanded precise, systematic knowledge of production techniques and attention to changing customer wants. So in Whieldon's workshop he spent most of his time on the development of handling and glazing processes. At the age of 28, still working for Whieldon, he began

Table 2.2 Urban Growth in Early Modern England

	Population Totals (thousands)			
	c. 1600	c. 1700	c. 1750	1801
England	4,110	5,060	5,770	8,660
London	200	575	675	960
10 historic regional centers[a]	73	107	126	153
8 established ports[b]	53	81	128	190
4 "new" manufacturing towns[c]	11	27	70	262

a. Norwich, York, Salisbury, Chester, Worcester, Exeter, Cambridge, Coventry, Shrewsbury, Gloucester.

b. Bristol, Hull, Colchester, Newcastle, Ipswich, Great Yarmouth, King's Lynn, Southampton.

c. Birmingham, Manchester, Leeds, Sheffield.

Source: E. Anthony Wrigley, "Urban Growth and Agricultural Change: England and the Continent in the Early Modern Period," in Robert I. Rotberg and Theodore K. Rabb, eds., *Population and History: From the Traditional to the Modern World* (Cambridge: Cambridge University Press, 1986), p. 133.

keeping the first of many notebooks, which he called Experiment Books, to record the state of his own innovations. The firm's manufacture of earthenware at that time stood in great need of improvement, as he noted. With "the demand for our goods decreasing daily, and the trade universally complained of as being bad and in a declining condition," something new was wanted, he wrote, "to give a little spirit to the business."[62]

Using his own secret code to log specific formulas, Josiah kept these detailed notebooks for the rest of his career.[63] In them, he meticulously laid out the results of his experiments, always attempting to organize his thoughts on a systematic basis and to apply science to the manufacture of pottery.

On His Own

In May 1759, Wedgwood left Whieldon's workshop and established himself as an independent potter. He was 28, ambitious, and eager to test his talents. His new establishment at Burslem consisted of a cottage, two kilns, sheds, and workrooms, all of which he rented from his cousin John Wedgwood for £15 a year (about $2,100 in today's dollars).[64] For additional rent of £2.6, he acquired a potter's wheel. He hired as a journeyman another cousin, Thomas, at an annual salary of £22. Thomas was 24, and his experience centered around porcelain manufacture, enameling, and transfer printing, areas that complemented Josiah's own expertise.

It is not clear how Josiah financed this first venture. Perhaps he borrowed funds from wealthier relatives. He seems to have been short of money. He was six months late paying rent for the pottery works, and almost a quarter of the total rent was paid in goods.

For the next three years, Josiah, his cousin, and several hired hands manufactured tortoiseshell and other ware. Josiah began coating creamware in the new green and yellow glazes he had perfected while working with Whieldon. He applied these brilliant glazes to teapots and plates molded or pressed in many shapes, such as pineapples, cauliflowers, cabbages, and pears. He bought the ornate molds needed to produce these elaborate pieces from one of Whieldon's potters.

Pineapple and cauliflower were eye-catching, functional, and, most important, *novel*. These ornate pieces were immediately popular, and are still manufactured today. Of course, not all Britons in the mid-eighteenth century could afford to care about the fashionability of new products.[65] But as per capita and family incomes climbed, increasing numbers of consumers from the upper and middling ranks acquired new possessions.[66]

The rich built magnificent houses, sometimes demolishing Elizabethan and Jacobean mansions to make room for them. To fill their new homes, they commissioned furniture from Chippendale, Hepplewhite, Sheraton, and other designers. They created orangeries, greenhouses, and sumptuous gardens. Many great households had private menageries stocked with exotic animals.[67]

Within their means, Britons from the middling orders were no less zealous consumers. They bought clocks, linens, window curtains, books, cutlery, pottery, tobacco, chocolate, and tea. Some types of goods, such as table linens and books, had been used by the rich in the seventeenth century, but by 1750 were much more common. Tea, coffee, and chocolate were new products introduced from the Far East and the New World. Like espresso drinks in modern America, these new hot beverages took Great Britain by storm. In 1730, Britons had consumed 1.4 million pounds of tea each year, or about one-fourth of a pound per person. By 1800, annual tea consumption had risen to over 12 million pounds, or about 1.5 pounds per person.[68] Increased spending on new and established goods begat still more spending. Preparation of coffee, tea, and chocolate called for specialized equipment: cups, pitchers, pots, sugar bowls. Tobacco required pipes and snuffboxes. As households acquired books, they needed bookshelves. Table linens and pottery required new sideboards and china closets with glass doors. Throughout all this consumption ran a strong thirst for novelty. In furniture, pottery, fabrics, and millinery, consumers insisted on new fashions. The desire for novelty was so pervasive that the great wit Dr. Samuel Johnson grumbled that nowadays men were "to be hanged in a new way."[69]

Josiah Wedgwood understood all of this quite well. By the early 1760s, he was hard at work developing an improved creamware, the attractive white pottery made possible by earlier innovations. While working with Whieldon, he had experimented extensively with creamware. He was aware of the problems in its dipping and firing, but he also recognized its potential as both useful and ornamental ware. In color, it could compete with porcelain and delftware. But its durability and lower cost might appeal to a much broader market. Consumers who could not afford the expense of porcelain or the replacement cost of fragile delftware might scoop it up.

His chief technical problem seems to have been consistency of quality and color. His early creamware, like that of other potters, had varied from straw color to deep saffron. Josiah was certain that the market would be more efficiently served with a single pale color, a shade that did not vary across firings and that closely resembled porcelain.[70]

By 1762, he had made great progress using a body composed of ground flint and pipe clay and covered with a lead glaze. He had developed what he described as a "species of earthenware for the table quite new in its appearance, covered with a rich and brilliant glaze bearing sudden alterations of heat and cold, manufactured with ease and expedition, and consequently cheap."[71]

Josiah sent some of his creamware to Liverpool, where it was decorated by a new process now becoming fashionable for porcelain. This technique, called transfer-printing, allowed a wide array of intricate scenes or characters to be applied smoothly to any kind of china.[72] After printing, the ware was shipped back to Burslem for firing and often enameling.[73]

The demand for Josiah Wedgwood's goods outstripped his pot-works' capacity even before he made these improvements to creamware.[74] In late 1762, he moved production to the larger Brick House Works in Burslem. These rented premises consisted of five or six workshops, five ovens, and a brick dwelling for him as master potter.[75] He employed sixteen paid hands.[76] Three years later, now 35 years of age, he acquired even more workshop space from his cousin John.

The Partnership of Wedgwood & Bentley

In the early 1760s, Wedgwood rode frequently to Liverpool to do business with Sadler & Green, sales agents and merchants. He did not relish the 40-mile journey. Since his childhood bout with smallpox and the deterioration of his knee, riding had been difficult. Although as an adult he was hypochondriacal about other aspects of his physical condition, he was remarkably stoic about this handicap.[77] Like the twentieth-century American president Franklin D. Roosevelt, who was stricken with polio, Josiah Wedgwood sought to conquer his infirmity through sheer will. Throughout his life, he routinely subjected himself to grueling physical exercise.[78] These regimes also helped him control his appetite and weight, both of which he often worried about. He took care with the rest of his appearance, favoring unostentatious dress and a simple wig. His grey-blue eyes were resolute and full of humor. He carried his 5 foot, 6 inch frame and 12 stones (168 pounds) gracefully.

One day in early 1762, the 31-year-old Wedgwood set out on one of his arduous journeys to Liverpool. By the time he reached the port city, he had damaged his bad knee even more and had to lie in bed for many weeks.[79] While he was recuperating, his physician introduced him to Thomas Bentley. This meeting was a fortuitous one for both men. It inaugurated a long friendship of great depth and intimacy, as well as one of the most important business partnerships of the eighteenth century.[80] In 1769, Bentley formally became Wedgwood's partner in manufacturing and selling ornamental china. But from the time they met in 1762, the two men collaborated closely on a range of managerial issues. Until his death in 1780, Bentley brought his commercial experience, his social grace, and his entrepreneurial skills to bear on the business.[81] He oversaw the firm's London operations, developed new markets, and channeled Josiah's boundless enthusiasms in productive directions.[82]

At the time they met, Bentley was 32, about the same age as Wedgwood. The son of a Derbyshire gentleman, Bentley was classically educated. He was also well traveled and solidly established as a leading local merchant. A member of the Liverpool Philosophical Club, he had helped found the Public Library and the Nonconformist Academy.[83] Bentley was active in the movement to abolish slavery in England and its colonies. His mercantile and intellectual contacts spanned the Atlantic world. He was friends with the chemist Joseph Priestley, and when Benjamin Franklin was in Britain in the 1760s, he spent time with Bentley.[84]

Wedgwood and Bentley liked each other immediately. They sat up late night after night, smoking their pipes, discussing religion, commerce, art, chemistry, and poetry. As soon as Josiah was well enough, Bentley introduced him to some of his own circle of friends: the scientist Priestley, the portrait painters Chubbard and Caddick, the well-known watchmaker John Wyke, and other artistic and commercial men. After eight weeks' convalescence for his bad knee, Wedgwood was finally ready to go home. Back in Burslem, he wrote Bentley a lengthy letter, the first installment in what became a rich correspondence that spanned 18 years and covered a variety of subjects. National politics, romance, pottery prices, the latest London plays, Wedgwood's weight, all were fair game.

Like Wedgwood, Bentley was an active supporter of additional turnpikes and canals for the economic development of Britain. In the second half of the eighteenth century, Parliament approved hundreds of miles of turnpike construction, much of it initiated and funded regionally by local businessmen.[85] During the 1760s, Wedgwood lobbied aristocrats and politicians for road construction between Burslem and the ports of Chester and Liverpool. He himself invested heavily in several turnpike trusts, and he urged his brother John to do so as well: "We have another Turnpike broke out amongst us here betwixt Leek and Newcastle," he wrote. (Leek is seven miles northeast of Burslem.) Wedgwood said that "£2000 is wanting for this road" and that he had subscribed £500, intending that John would put up two or three hundred of it.[86]

At the same time, Wedgwood and Bentley began recruiting political and financial support for a canal that would link the port cities of Liverpool and Hull with the Staffordshire potteries. The Trent-Mersey canal, as the proposed waterway was to become known, was part of a large set of canals that would connect the four major rivers of England: the Trent, the Mersey, the Thames, and the Severn. To increase public support for the project, Bentley published a pamphlet that set out the case for the new canal, *A View of the Advantages of Inland Navigation with a Plan of a Navigable Canal*. Here he argued that the waterway would decrease travel time and carriage costs, encourage new and existing manufactures, and raise property values along the proposed route.[87] Wedgwood traveled across the Midlands drumming up commercial support for the canal.[88] On July 26, 1766, after more than six months of lobbying and negotiation among business interests and politicians, he cut the first sod of earth on the Trent-Mersey canal. From this time on, politics became yet another of Wedgwood's passions, and somehow in the midst of 12-hour workdays he made room for it.

Marriage had broadened his world still further. In 1764, he wed his distant cousin Sarah Wedgwood, the daughter of a wealthy cheesemaker of Cheshire.[89] Four years younger than Josiah, she was a kind, practical, and spirited woman, devoted to her husband and the eight children they had. (In 1796, the Wedgwoods' eldest child, Susannah, married the scientist Erasmus Darwin's son, Robert. Their own child and Wedgwood's grandson, Charles Darwin, was born in 1809. When Charles Darwin was 30, he married his first cousin, Emma Wedgwood, the daughter of Josiah II and granddaughter of Josiah Wedgwood. The Wedgwood family fortune then helped underwrite Darwin's famous voyage aboard the *Beagle,* which was a critical part of his research for *The Origin of Species.*)[90]

The marriage between Josiah and Sarah seems to have been a harmonious, satisfying partnership.[91] She helped with his experimental work, discussed commercial finances, and advised him on pottery design. She suggested, for example, that he decorate the lids of transfer-printed teapots and sugar bowls, which had previously been plain.[92] "I speak from experience in Female taste," Josiah told Bentley, "without which I should have made but a poor figure amongst my Potts, not one of which, of any consequence, is finished without the approbation of my Sally."[93]

The Business Expands

Sally Wedgwood and Thomas Bentley were both involved in Josiah's most significant expansion plans. By early 1765, sales of useful ware were booming, and it was clear that the business was outgrowing the Brick House facilities in Burslem. In 1769, Wedgwood sold about £7,000 of tableware and other useful goods (approximately $1 million today).[94] The market for vases, cameos, and other ornamental ware seemed prom-

Table 2.3 Profit and Turnover, Wedgwood Ornamental Ware, 1769–1775 (£)

Fiscal Year	Goods Sold	Expenses of Manufacturing and Selling	Goods on Hand at End of Year	Profit
August 1769–August 1770	2,404	1,921	3,164	[a]2,561
August 1770–August 1771	3,955	2,372	4,411	2,830
August 1771–August 1772	4,838	2,924	8,187	5,691
August 1772–August 1773	4,244	2,303	9,069	2,823
August 1773–August 1774	6,168	2,937	10,144	4,307
August 1774–December 1774	2,065	946	10,261	1,235
January 1775–December 1775	6,481	3,804	11,190	3,545

a. Profit figures also reflect receivables collected—often after a long lag—in a particular year, but do not capture carrying costs on inventory.

Source: Financial Accounts, 1775, W/M 1713, Moseley Collection, Wedgwood Manuscripts, Keele University Library.

ising. Creamware exports were climbing, helped significantly by Bentley's work as a wholesale agent. Table 2.3 gives the statistics for the ornamental ware part of the business as it developed in the late 1760s and early 1770s.

In 1766, Josiah paid £3,000 ($385,000 in today's dollars) for 350 acres located close to Burslem and in the path of the projected Trent & Mersey Canal. Construction began immediately on the factory and a nearby mansion for Josiah and Sally.[95] Wedgwood named the factory and estate Etruria after the region in central Italy where beautiful ancient pottery was then being excavated.[96] At the same time, he took his cousin Thomas Wedgwood into partnership to oversee production of all useful ware manufacture. This partnership allowed Josiah to concentrate on market expansion and his experiments, including the search for a new clay body for ornamental ware.[97]

In 1765, Wedgwood had opened an office in a small wholesale warehouse in London. Three years later, he began looking for showroom space there. He wanted facilities for retailing as well as premises large enough to show various table and dessert services completely set out. As he wrote to Bentley:

> Six or eight at least such services are absolutely necessary to be shewn in order to *do the needful* with the Ladys in the neatest, genteelest & best method. The same, or indeed a much greater variety of setts of Vases should decorate the Walls, & both these articles may, every few days, be so alter'd, revers'd, & transform'd as to render the whole a new scene, even to the same Company, every time they shall bring their friends to visit us. I need not tell you the many good effects this must produce, when business & amusement can be made to go hand in hand. Every new show, Exhibition, or rarity soon grows stale in London, & is no longer regarded after the first sight, unless utility, or some such variety . . . continue to recommend it to their notice.[98]

In March 1768, Wedgwood found the space he wanted. Over the next few years, he moved his showrooms to premises in nearby Portland House, and opened additional selling space in Bath and Dublin. He proposed to pay his salespeople in the showrooms on commission. As he pointed out to Bentley, this compensation scheme would help ensure that stock was not wasted, that business was conducted at "a moderate expence," and that "as great a quantity of goods as possible" was sold.[99]

Expansion plans were interrupted in May 1768 when Wedgwood's right knee collapsed, a serious recurrence of the old ailment. Erasmus Darwin and others recommended amputation, which was a fairly common procedure at that time. The operation was performed in Wedgwood's home without anesthetic, while Josiah remained conscious. Although he had frequently been depressed at the onset of one of his psychosomatic illnesses, he was stoic and resilient during this operation and recovery. Within three weeks, he was directing his business from bed and reporting to Bentley on his recuperation: "I am well even beyond my most sanguine expectations, my leg is allmost healed, the wound is not quite 2 inches by one & ½, I measur'd it with the compasses this morning when I dress'd it."[100] Soon he was fitted with a wooden leg, joking that next year he planned to throw a party to celebrate St. Amputation Day.[101]

The Etruria factory was completed in mid-1769, the same year that Bentley officially became Wedgwood's partner in the production of ornamental ware.[102] At the heart of the factory's organization was Wedgwood's insistence on specialized manufacture based on a carefully planned division of labor.[103] He separated the production of useful ware from that of vases and other ornamental ware, allocating workshops and kilns to each.[104] The shops were arranged in sequence in order to provide an efficient production line and to avoid unnecessary movement of workers or goods.[105]

The shops for both useful and ornamental ware incorporated the latest technology, including the engine-turning lathe, which used eccentric or elliptical motion to produce uniform, vertical fluting and other patterns on the pottery. Wedgwood's first engine-turning lathes were modeled on those he had seen in a Birmingham foundry and were built to his specifications for use in earthenware manufacture.[106] In 1782, Josiah installed a steam engine, manufactured by the nationally famous foundry Boulton & Watt, to grind flint and colors. When a French industrial spy visited Etruria in the mid-1780s, he described the factory and village of workmen's cottages as a small town unto itself, "a marvel of organization."[107]

Marketing

By the early 1760s, when the popularity of Wedgwood china was surging, the market for Staffordshire pottery was rapidly becoming a national one. Finished goods traveled by horse, ship, and canal barge to dealers in Newcastle, Yarmouth, Liverpool, Bath, and Bristol. Useful ware and small quantities of ornamental goods were sold in Leeds, which was a hub for cotton textile production, and in Birmingham and other industrial areas. But the overwhelming bulk of all pottery was sent directly to London, where large wholesale dealers bought earthenware in growing quantities, primarily for distribution to small retailers.[108] From Liverpool and Bristol, merchants shipped Staffordshire pottery to continental Europe and increasingly to America and the West Indies.[109]

Pottery exports reflected the broad outlines of British commerce. Throughout the eighteenth century, and especially after 1750, international trade became ever more important. Total imports into Britain climbed by 500 percent between 1700 and 1800, reexports (commodities imported into Britain and then exported) by 250 percent, and exports by more than 560 percent.[110] The composition of this trade reflected the economic transformation under way. Agricultural goods fell markedly as a fraction of exports, and by 1750, Britain had become a net importer of grains.[111] By contrast, manufactured exports, including woolens, metalwares, glass, cottons, and pottery, grew sixfold over the course of the century.[112] In 1700, over 80 percent of Britain's exports had gone to Europe. Seventy years later, European customers purchased only 30 percent of Britain's exports, while colonists on the North American mainland and in the West Indies took almost half. The remainder of exportable goods went to India, Ireland, and the Far East.[113]

Wedgwood was keen to sell his creamware internationally. By 1769, he could hardly contain his excitement about France's market potential: "Do you really think that we may make a *complete conquest* of France? Conquer France in Burslem? My blood moves quicker, I feel my strength increase for the contest."[114] Two years later, as domestic sales became sluggish and as stock piled up, Wedgwood concluded that "nothing but a *foreign market*" would ever keep the stock "within any tolerable bound."[115] His production had now grown so efficient that he needed new oulets. "Every *Gentle* & *Decent* push," he wrote, "should be made to have our things *seen* & *sold* at Foreign Markets."[116]

Toward this end, in 1771 Josiah sent unsolicited parcels of his pottery to 1,000 members of the German aristocracy and nobility. Each package cost about £20 and was accompanied by a circular letter advertising his products, and an invoice. This strategy was one of the earliest recorded examples of "inertia selling," that is, marketing to selected customers by shipping them unsolicited goods and offering them the opportunity either to purchase the items at set prices or return them to the manufacturer at no cost to themselves. It was a precursor of the practice of modern book and music clubs. Wedgwood's plan cost £20,000 ($2.7 million today) and involved very significant financial risk.[117] But, as he remarked, "We know that nothing great can be done without some risque, nor is there any *absolute certainty* in trade."[118] It was a successful gamble, as a majority of the selected customers purchased Wedgwood's goods.[119]

In the mid-1760s, however, Wedgwood's primary focus was still the domestic market. He sought a buoyant, growing demand for his useful pieces. Many of these products were new. Others had been available for years. How was one to create and sustain customer interest in the wares of a particular workshop or firm? What kind of competitive advantage could a company construct with customers when other suppliers were producing similar goods?

He had few precedents to follow in creating and sustaining customer loyalty. One of his responses to the challenge was to build his brand systematically. Brand marketing was virtually unheard of in the mid-eighteenth century. Only a handful of luxury goods, such as Chippendale furniture or Meissen porcelain, were known by their manufacturer's names. Until about 1770, most potters did not mark their products. The few earthenware and porcelain manufacturers that did, such as the Chelsea porcelain factory, generally used signs, symbols, or the location of the factory as identifying marks. Wedgwood changed this practice in the later 1760s by impressing his own name in the unfired clay. His works were thus much less vulnerable to forgery than those of other makers, and as Josiah understood, every piece advertised the Wedgwood name.[120] By 1772, everything made by Wedgwood, useful or ornamental, carried his name.[121]

Josiah realized that many Britons now had more money to spend on nonessential or luxury goods than had their counterparts in previous generations.[122] He also understood that much of this spending was directed toward social emulation. Eighteenth-century Britons, like modern consumers all over the world, tended to put their money where their aspirations were. They spent as the rich did, or at least as the income class right above them did. In 1767, the English political economist Nathaniel Forster bemoaned "the perpetual restless ambition in each of the inferior ranks to raise themselves to the level of those immediately above them," causing "fashionable luxury" to spread "like a contagion."[123]

Even so, there was not much movement toward economic parity. Although average per capita income increased almost 30 percent during the eighteenth century, the First Industrial Revolution did not distribute this income equally.[124] In 1688, the wealthiest 10 percent of Britons had received 44 percent of total income. By 1801, this group received 53 percent. At the same time, the fraction of income that went to the bottom 40 percent of the population held steady at between 10 and 11 percent.[125] But, as the U.S. experience in the 1980s and 1990s demonstrated, rising equality is not a necessary condition of the habit of emulative spending. The two may even be inversely correlated.

Josiah Wedgwood could not measure income distribution with any precision in the 1760s. He did not need to. He knew that the middling ranks wanted to ape their social betters, and he planned his sales strategy accordingly. In 1763, he presented George III's wife, Queen Charlotte, with a breakfast set of his finest creamware. Two years later, he produced a tea set for her, a sale that resulted in his appointment as "Potter to Her Majesty." His creamware quickly became known as Queensware. A young entrepreneur (he was 35 at the time) could hardly have hoped for more. In Josiah's eyes, nobility, aristocrats, and to a lesser extent the gentry were the principal conductors of fashion diffusion. By the late 1760s, Josiah had opened an office and showrooms in London to serve his growing clientele. In 1770, he instructed Bentley to scan the English Peerage for additional "lines, channels and connections."[126] These groups, he noted, were the "legislators in taste."[127]

Josiah actively sought aristocratic and noble commissions, and the explicit and implicit endorsements that accompanied these sales.[128] Like sportswear and cosmetics manufacturers today, he understood the value of celebrity sanction. He worked very hard to obtain it, absorbing significant costs in time and money in order to produce highly specialized individual commissions. While other potters avoided such orders, Wedgwood actively sought them.[129]

Once he had completed an aristocratic sale, Josiah lost no time in advertising it to a much larger, more profitable market. As he wrote his partner about the growing market for Wedgwood vases, "The Great People have had their Vases in their Palaces long enough for them to be seen and admired by the *Middling Class* of People, which Class we know are vastly, I had almost said, infinitely superior in number to the Great."[130] Wedgwood took out ads in London newspapers to celebrate his royal patronage. His company catalogues emphasized upscale potential at reasonable prices. His traveling salesmen carried samples of goods endorsed by aristocrats along with a sales manual of sorts, with marketing and collection guidelines.[131]

Specific Wedgwood pieces were named for members of the nobility. In 1779, Josiah suggested calling a set of flowerpots after the Duchess of Devonshire. These and other techniques, he said, "complete our notoriety to the whole Island" and help greatly in the sale of goods both useful and ornamental, by showing that "we are employ'd in a much higher scale than other Manufacturers."[132] Competitors, such as Duesbury of Derby, Turner & Abbott, Worcester porcelain, and others, followed Wedgwood's marketing lead. These manufacturers used newspaper advertising and London showrooms to sell their wares. Some sought aristocratic endorsements. But none deployed a marketing strategy that rivaled the scope, effectiveness, and sustainability of Wedgwood's.

The middling-class customers were to be won with quality and fashionability, rather than low prices.[133] From the mid-1760s on, Wedgwood priced his most successful useful line, Queensware, as much as 75 or 100 percent higher than competing products from other potteries.[134] His entire line of useful ware was more expensive than those of rivals. In 1770, for example, the wholesale price for a top-quality Wedgwood dinner plate was 8 pence (about $5 in today's dollars).[135] By contrast, other Staffordshire potters priced their best table plates at 2 pence each.[136]

Josiah was willing to reduce prices when the spread between his and competitors' prices became too great or when he wanted to expand sales of a product already popularized at a high price.[137] But he generally kept his prices noticeably above the industry average. "*Low prices,*" he wrote Bentley in 1772, "must beget a *low quality* in the manufacture, which will beget *contempt,* which will beget *neglect, & disuse,* and there is an end of the trade." But if any one manufacturer will keep up or improve the quality of its product, "that House may perhaps keep up its prices." In such a case, an economic downturn "will work a *particular good* to that house," for it "may continue to sell *Queensware at the usual prices* when the rest of the trade can scarcely give it away."[138] When Josiah thought that demand for one of his products was becoming saturated, he discontinued it, and reintroduced it only when he thought the market was once more ripe.

In exchange for the premium they paid, Wedgwood's customers received free shipping anywhere in England, and compensation for damage that occurred in transport. They also received a satisfaction-or-money-back guarantee, the first recorded example of such product support.[139]

Josiah's marketing strategy toward international outlets was similar to his domestic strategy. He paid special attention to British ambassadors and their wives, who were likely to be moved from one European capital city to another. He courted aristocrats, nobility, and gentry in France, Germany, Turkey, Portugal, Italy, even China.[140] Wedgwood's expanded showrooms displayed wares ordered by the crowned heads of Europe. The order from Catherine the Great for a 952-piece set of Wedgwood china, so impressively displayed to Londoners in 1774, was a conspicuous example. He charged premium prices for what was fast becoming some of the most fashionable china in the world. When the political economist Arthur Young visited the Wedgwood factory and other Staffordshire potteries in 1771, he noted that "some of the finest sort went to France," and that large quantities of creamware were sent to Ireland, Germany, Holland, Russia, Spain, the British colonies in the East Indies, and "much to America."[141] By 1783, Wedgwood was exporting almost 80 percent of his total production of ornamental and useful ware.[142]

Organizing the Workforce

The organization of work at Etruria and other late-eighteenth-century factories imposed new standards on craftsmen and laborers.[143] They were required to be punctual. They had to appear every day, six days a week, at the same time. They had to labor until the clock or the bell tolled. These rhythms contrasted sharply with those imposed by the sun and seasons or the requirements of a specific task, all of which determined the nature and pace of agricultural labor. Factory work was also much more routinized than that of preindustrial enterprise, which alternated between bouts of intense effort and idleness, like modern student life.[144]

Wedgwood devised several schemes to increase his craftsmen and laborers' punctuality and attendance. From his days at the Brick House, he had used a bell to summon workmen. According to his instructions, the bell was to be rung at 5:45 in the morning or a quarter of an hour before the men could see to take up their jobs; then at 8:30 for breakfast, at 9:00 to recall workers from the meal, at noon for dinner, at 12:30 to return to their tasks, and on until "the last bell when they can no longer see."[145] Josiah also hired a Clerk of the Manufactory, who was to arrive at Etruria before anyone else. The clerk's job was to:

> settle the people to their business as they come in—to encourage those who come regularly to their time, letting them know that their regularity is properly noticed . . . Those who come later than the hour appointed should be noticed, and if after repeated marks of disapprobation they do not come in due time, an account of the time they are deficient in should be taken, & so much of their wages stopt as the time comes to.[146]

To keep track of his workers' time, Wedgwood devised a primitive clocking-in system, the first in the history of business. He described it in precise terms. To save the trouble of the porters going round, tickets were printed with the names of all the workers. Each person took two of these tickets with him when he left work every evening. He delivered one of them into a box when he went through the lodge the next morning, and the other when he returned from dinner. The porter then, "looks over these tickets only; & if he finds any deficiency, goes to such places only where the defiance appears. If the persons have neglected or refused to deliver their tickets on going through, they are to be admonished the first time, the second time to pay a small fine to the poors box."[147] By the end of the eighteenth century, this innovative system had given way to the kind of punch-clock that is still in wide use today throughout the world.[148]

The overarching authority of the clock was not the only novel aspect of industrialization. Factory work also demanded precision, avoidance of waste, and obedience to an evolving managerial hierarchy. The challenge, according to Josiah, was to "make such *Machines* of the *Men* as cannot Err."[149] Early-eighteenth-century potters had worked by rule of thumb under dirty, inefficient, and arbitrary conditions. The mess and waste were natural companions to the craft.[150]

To encourage cleanliness and careful working habits, Wedgwood issued a detailed set of "Potters' Instructions" and "Rules and Regulations." The clerk or overseer in each workshop, plus the five to ten gen-

eral managers, such as the Clerk of the Manufactory and the Clerk of
Weights and Measures, received guidelines encompassing almost every
aspect of the manufacturing process and of factory discipline. The regulations prohibited workers from carrying ale or liquor into the manufactory, scaling the gates, writing obscene or other language on the walls,
playing games, and "striking or otherwise abusing an overlooker."[151]
Most of these offenses carried stiff financial penalties.[152] Striking a manager resulted in instant dismissal.

In addition to disciplining all his workers to function effectively under
the new regime, Josiah had to find the skilled artists and craftsmen essential to the production of useful and especially ornamental ware. To
do this, he decided to train his artists rather than rely on workers from
outside. The task, he wrote Bentley, was to make artists of "mere men."[153]
It made no sense to rely on the local labor market because "few hands
can be got to paint flowers in the style we want them. I may add, nor
any other work we do. *We must make them.* There is no other way. We
have stepped forward beyond the other Manufacturers & we must be
content to train up hands to suit our purpose."[154]

Although Wedgwood instituted policies to retrain existing hands, he
was much more successful working with new hires. In the early 1770s,
he established a drawing and modeling school for his apprentices. Eventually more than a quarter of the firm's total of 290 workers in the early
1790s were apprentices. Ten percent of these young artists and potters
were women.[155]

Product Management and Finance

By the time Etruria was in full operation, Wedgwood & Bentley had
become as renowned for its ornamental ware as for Queensware. In
1772, Josiah reported that the firm was producing "upwards of 100
Good Forms of Vases," many of which were manufactured with interchangeable handles and ornaments.[156]

He and Bentley always monitored their product lines carefully, at times
restricting output of various styles to keep them relatively scarce and
thus more desirable. The designs were mostly derivative, drawn from a
range of contemporary sources on classical and ancient pottery. Wedgwood modeled his Etruscan vases, in which red wax-based paint was

applied to black basalt, on the extensive collection of ancient Egyptian, Roman, and Greek vases owned by Britain's ambassador to the Court of Naples, Sir William Hamilton.[157]

Although Wedgwood & Bentley produced library busts, decorative candlesticks, portrait medallions, and cameos, the firm's most popular ornamental products were vases. In 1769, these vases were suddenly in great demand. Wedgwood noted that at the London showrooms there was "no getting to the door for Coaches, nor into the rooms for Ladies & Gentlemen . . . Vases was all the cry. We must endeavor to gratify this *universal passion*."[158] A visitor to Etruria described a similar "violent *Vase madness*" breaking out in Ireland.[159]

The surge in demand took the firm by surprise. Writing from London in late spring 1769, Wedgwood told Bentley to assign all "hands that can be spared" to vase production, and ordered a large number in two different styles. He said he could sell £1,000 worth of such vases ($133,000 today).[160] That order was filled within two months, but the firm still could not keep pace with the demand from London. To speed production, Wedgwood simplified decoration processes and ordered some vases to be finished by the firm's engine-powered lathes rather than by hand. But unmet orders continued to pile up. "Strange as it may sound," Wedgwood wrote Bentley, "I should be glad never to receive another order for *any particular kind* of Vases, & I should wish you to avoid taking such orders as much as you *decently* can, at least till we are got into a more methodical way of making *the same sorts over again,* & there is no other way of doing this but by having models & moulds of every shape & size we make."[161]

By late 1769, Wedgwood & Bentley had significant cash flow problems. The firm was spending larger than anticipated sums on raw materials, wages, and other costs, without collecting its bills fast enough to finance expanded production.[162] Wedgwood urged Bentley, "Collect. Collect," and "set all your hands & heads to work."[163] At the end of the year, despite having manufactured more than £12,000 worth of pottery in 1769 ($1.6 million today), the firm had debts totaling £4000 ($533,000) in addition to weekly wage costs of £100 ($13,300). Wedgwood complained of being "poor as a Church mouse."[164]

His response to this crisis was to initiate a thorough analysis of the firm's cost structure for vase production. This effort resulted in the preparation of Wedgwood's Price Book of Workmanship, which included "every expence of Vase making," from the crude materials to the retail counter in London, for each sort of vase.[165]

For Wedgwood, the most important discovery of his analysis was the distinction between fixed and variable costs. He advised Bentley to notice how large a share of the cost of manufacturing was borne by modeling and molds, rent, fuel, bookkeepers, and boys' wages. "Consider," the potter said, "that these expences move like clockwork, & are much the same whether the quantity of goods made be large or small." Thus, said Josiah, "you will see the vast consequence in most manufactures of *making the greatest quantity possible in a given time.*"[166]

In this context, he revised his earlier policy of actively soliciting special commissions. Such orders often involved high labor and materials costs for a small one-time increase in output. He cautioned Bentley to avoid made-to-order sales unless they had significant marketing value, such as the huge sale to Catherine the Great in 1774.[167] Wedgwood also lengthened production runs for certain ornamental wares, reduced stocks in market downturns, and kept careful tabs on sales and marketing costs.

Wedgwood and Capitalism

By the mid-1770s, Josiah Wedgwood and his partners, Thomas Bentley and Thomas Wedgwood, were the preeminent British pottery manufacturers. They were market leaders at home and important players in outlets abroad. His mounting commercial success reinforced his ardent belief in the logic and integrity of industrial capitalism. In 1783, he published his views on this subject in a short pamphlet, *An Address to the Young Inhabitants of the Pottery,* excerpts of which follow:

> I would request you to ask your parents for a description of the country we inhabit when they first knew it; and they will tell you, that the inhabitants bore all signs of poverty to a much greater degree than they do now. Their houses were miserable huts; the lands [were] poorly cultivated and . . . yielded little of value for the food of man or beast . . .
>
> Compare this picture, which I know to be a true one, with the present state of the same country. The workingmen earning nearly double their former wages—their houses mostly new and comfortable, and the lands, roads and every other circumstance bearing evident marks

of the most pleasing and rapid improvements. From whence, and from what cause has this happy change taken place? You will be beforehand with me in acknowledging a truth too evident to be denied by any one. Industry has been the parent of this happy change—A well directed and long continued series of industrious exertions, both in masters and servants, has so changed for the better the face of our country, its buildings, lands, roads, and not withstanding the present unfavourable appearances, I must say the manners and deportment of its inhabitants too, as to attract the notice and admiration of countries which had scarcely heard of us before; and how far these improvements may still be carried by the same laudable means which have brought us thus far, has been one of the most pleasing contemplations of my life.[168]

Josiah's workforce did not always share his unabashed faith in industrial capitalism. Many workers resented the enforced specialization of the factory system. Others found the training tedious and the rules of behavior overly restrictive. Some refused to take orders from factory foremen. Almost all workers resented their own dependence on the ebb and flow of market forces. These and other grievances led workers into confrontations with Wedgwood on several occasions between 1769 and 1790, when Josiah withdrew from active management of the business. In 1782 and 1789, Etruria workers staged demonstrations.[169]

These uprisings always surprised Josiah. He considered himself a benevolent employer. He supplied housing for his workers and subsidized a sick club, a kind of a primitive health insurance. The factory he had developed was the first standardized production system to be applied to pottery. He wanted to use his organizational, production, and marketing innovations not only to increase profits, but to achieve what he called "constant employment" for his workforce and capital equipment.[170] In return for these efforts on the workers' behalf, Josiah expected loyalty, punctuality, and consistently high performance. To the end of his life, Josiah could not understand why many of his workers were less than content with the social contract he had established at Etruria.

Epilogue

Josiah died in 1795, leaving a fortune estimated at £500,000 ($44 million today).[171] The business, which had been incorporated in 1790 as Josiah Wedgwood & Sons, passed to his second son, Josiah II, and his nephew,

Thomas Byerly. Neither proved equal to the task of running the firm efficiently. Production standards declined. The company's financial condition deteriorated. Market conditions worsened as the Napoleonic Wars dragged on and Continental markets were frequently unavailable. But sales remained relatively robust, climbing to over £43,000 in 1810 ($2.5 million today). Under often reluctant family management, the firm survived the nineteenth century, although revenues rarely exceeded their 1810 level.

In 1903, U.S. President Theodore Roosevelt commissioned a 1,300-piece dinner service for the White House, which was made in the Etruria factory. In 1940, production was moved to new, larger premises in nearby Barlaston, where it is still located today. In 1986, Waterford Crystal acquired Josiah Wedgwood & Sons, which continued to produce china in the Barlaston factory under the Wedgwood name.

Modern china manufacture is a blend of state-of-the-art technology, including robotics, and craft skills, some of which are virtually unchanged since the eighteenth century. Today about 5,500 people work in the Wedgwood Group factories in Stoke-on-Trent. In 1995, the Wedgwood Group of Waterford Wedgwood earned profits of 18.3 million Irish pounds ($28.3 million) on sales of 208 million Irish pounds ($322.4 million). In the same year, the bicentennial of Josiah I's death, Waterford Wedgwood paid its first year-end dividend in seven years.[172]

PROLOGUE TO CHAPTER 3

The Wedgwood chapter outlined the contours of British business in the early years of the First Industrial Revolution. The next chapter, "British Capitalism and the Three Industrial Revolutions," presents a broader and longer-range perspective. Here we return to our observation post in the orbiting satellite, and examine the equivalent of a long series of time-lapse photographs.

Throughout the history of modern capitalism, the orientation of British business has been distinctly individualistic and international. In this chapter we explore some of the reasons for that interesting combination. The kinds of questions raised here about Britain are posed later for Germany, the United States, and Japan: How and why did each country succeed in pulling off a capitalist revolution, while so many other countries failed? What was distinctive about its national style of doing business? How did its workforce respond to the pressures and the boredom inherent in factory employment? Because Britain was the first major nation to industrialize, these questions have some of the fascination common to "firsts" of any kind.

In issues involving national economic development, the most obvious things often turn out to be the most important. When the industrial era began, Britain was (and, of course, still is) an island nation located near a continent full of strong and ambitious rivals. So its leaders, in both government and business, paid a lot of attention to sea power. The English Channel was both a barrier against invasion and a cheap commercial route to continental ports. The world's oceans served like long-distance highways. In part because of the gains from water-borne commerce, Britain developed the first big domestic market for consumer goods, the first sizable middle class, and the largest overseas empire.

The British Empire, which had originated in modest commercial enterprises, grew rapidly during the First Industrial Revolution and reached its apogee at about the midpoint of the Second, in the latter part of the nineteenth century. Then, in the early years of the Third Industrial Revolution (the 1940s and 1950s), it collapsed altogether, along with the empires of other European countries.

This chapter raises some big questions. Many of them can be answered only partially, even with the most rigorous thinking and the best historical judgment. For example, what bearing did Britain's geopolitical stature during these very different eras have on its economic development? How did its citizens cope with the country's rapid rise in power and influence, and then its slow decline relative to some other countries? How difficult was the transition from the First to the Second Industrial Revolution, and how well might the country perform in the Third?

In reading the chapter, keep in mind that it is only an introduction to the subject. In only 43 pages, it covers more than 300 years of a many-layered story. So what you're about to encounter is very much a selective and sharply focused analysis. One of the premises of this book is that such an analysis is not only appropriate to the comparative study of capitalist systems, it's essential.

The United Kingdom and Ireland.

(Harvard Business School/Peter Amirault, Type A Co., 1997)

Josiah Wedgwood, portrait by Sir Joshua Reynolds, 1782. Wedgwood was 52 at the time, and a well-known national figure.

(Courtesy of The Trustees of The Wedgwood Museum, Barlaston, Stoke-on-Trent, Staffordshire, England)

The factory called Etruria. To facilitate transportation, the building was deliberately built adjacent to the new Trent-Mersey canal. Bells in the tower at top center summoned laborers to work. From 1772 to 1940, almost all Wedgwood production took place here (the building was demolished in the 1960s).

(Courtesy of The Trustees of The Wedgwood Museum, Barlaston, Stoke-on-Trent, Staffordshire, England)

Wedgwood showrooms, Portland House, Soho, London, where the set of china for Catherine the Great was exhibited in 1774. Note the display of cabinets, tables, and wide aisles, all retailing innovations of the late eighteenth century.

(Courtesy The Hulton Getty Picture Collection Limited, London, England)

The Portland vase, Wedgwood's most celebrated masterpiece of jasperware. One of the greatest technical achievements of eighteenth-century European pottery, it was copied from a famous Roman vase believed to date from the first century B.C. Wedgwood produced only a few dozen of these, mostly by commission.

(Courtesy of The Trustees of The Wedgwood Museum, Barlaston, Stoke-on-Trent, Staffordshire, England)

A cauliflower ware teapot, made in Staffordshire in the 1760s. For today's tastes the design may not be esthetically pleasing, but for the emerging middle-class market of the eighteenth century the novelty of this item had great appeal.

(Courtesy of The Trustees of The Wedgwood Museum, Barlaston, Stoke-on-Trent, Staffordshire, England)

The dashing Charles Stewart Rolls in 1906, the year of Rolls-Royce's founding.

(UPI/Corbis-Bettmann)

Charles Stewart Rolls at the wheel of the first Rolls-Royce. The Prince of Wales (later King George V) is in the front seat, Sir Charles Gust and Lord Langattock in the rear.
(UPI/Corbis-Bettmann)

Henry Royce in late middle age. Royce was a very difficult personality, but he was the design genius of the company, and the creative force behind its transition from making luxury cars to making aero engines.

(UPI/Corbis-Bettmann)

The Royal Air Force's Defiant fighter planes of World War II, powered with Rolls-Royce Merlin engines. The Merlin was the most important single product in the company's history, and a key to the victory over the Luftwaffe. More than 80,000 were produced by Rolls-Royce, and a similar number by other firms in association with Rolls-Royce. The Merlin powered other fighter planes as well as the Defiant: the Spitfire, Hurricane, and American P-51 Mustang.

(UPI/Corbis-Bettmann)

❧ 3 ❧

BRITISH CAPITALISM AND THE THREE
INDUSTRIAL REVOLUTIONS

Peter Botticelli

In 1851, at London's Hyde Park, Great Britain staged the first world's fair, to celebrate the nation's recent technical and material progress. Known as the "Great Exhibition," the fair was open for 141 days and attracted over 6 million visitors from many countries. The center of the exhibition was a giant glass and iron building called the Crystal Palace, crammed with the industrial products of 14,000 firms from all over the globe. Half of the palace was filled with foreign products, half with British goods, assembled and displayed to highlight Britain's superiority as the self-proclaimed "Workshop of the World."[1]

The novelist Charlotte Brontë visited the exhibition five times during 1851. She was profoundly impressed. "Its grandeur does not consist in one thing," she wrote to her father, "but in the unique assemblage of all things. Whatever human industry has created, you find there." She compared the array of manufactured goods to an Arabian bazaar, one such as "eastern Genii might have created. It seems as if magic only could have gathered this mass of wealth from all the ends of the Earth." Brontë wrote that the forces of industrial capitalism were like "supernatural hands" that had arranged the fair's displays with "a blaze of colours and marvellous power of effect."[2]

The Great Exhibition was a celebration of Britain's success as the first industrial nation. It was the ceremonial culmination of more than half a century of economic and political development, and its planners were implicitly holding up British capitalism as a model for other countries to follow.

At the time of the Great Exhibition of 1851, no precise statistics were available to measure national economic performance. Recent estimates, however, suggest that the faith many nineteenth-century Britons had in their country's economic dynamism was thoroughly justified (see Table 3.1).

As the introductory chapter of this book makes clear, these were remarkably high growth rates relative to preindustrial economic development. But by the standards of twentieth-century capitalist expansion, Britain's growth during the First Industrial Revolution was not especially impressive. The same is true for later years. Between 1856, when the Second Industrial Revolution was poised to begin, and 1973, when growth slowed throughout the world, Britain's overall rate of economic expansion averaged 1.9 percent annually. Unlike modern Germany and Japan, leading nations in the Second and Third Industrial Revolutions, Great Britain has never been able to include high-speed economic expansion in its social contract. In both the economic and political realms, the tradeoff between individual and societal interests has more often been resolved in favor of individual ones.

This is not to say that Britain has never actively managed its national economy. For much of the seventeenth century and most of the eighteenth, British statesmen tried to divert the economy toward geopolitical ends: to build national economic and military strength, and to increase government revenues. Since the early nineteenth century, however, Britain has taken a more laissez faire approach to economic development than has Germany or Japan.

The key questions of this chapter are how Great Britain came to dominate world markets during the First Industrial Revolution, and how it has remained an important capitalist nation ever since, even while experiencing some economic decline relative to the other countries analyzed in this book.

Table 3.1   British Economic Growth (% per year, in real terms)

1700–1780	1780–1801	1801–1831
0.7%	1.8%	2.7%

Note: Per capita GNP grew by .31 percent annually for the period 1700–60; .01 percent each year between 1760 and 1780; .35 percent from 1780–1801; and .52 percent from 1801–31. See N. F. R. Crafts, *British Economic Growth during the Industrial Revolution* (Oxford: Clarendon Press, 1985), p. 45.

Source: Adapted from Nick Crafts, "The Industrial Revolution," in Roderick Floud and Donald McCloskey, eds., *The Economic History of Britain since 1700*, 2d ed. (Cambridge: Cambridge University Press, 1994), vol. 1, p. 47.

State, Society, and the First Industrial Revolution*

In the late seventeenth century, Britain was not very rich by modern standards, but it was one of the two or three most prosperous countries in Europe. Its wealth flowed from a relatively productive agricultural sector, a vigorous commercial sector, and an emerging manufacturing sector of the kind we saw in the preceding chapter.[3] A majority of the nation's resources was controlled by a hierarchy of landed elites, some of whom were involved in industry (especially mining) as well as agriculture.[4] For centuries, at court and in Parliament, the great landed families had played a dominant role in English government.** They had clung tenaciously to their power, assets, and social status.

As industry expanded during the eighteenth and nineteenth centuries, newly prosperous merchants, manufacturers, and other business leaders posed challenges to this established system. But in Britain the struggle for political and social influence was resolved through compromise, unlike in Germany and France, where the battle between middle (business and professional) and noble (mainly landed) classes often ended in violence. In little more than a century, Britain successfully assimilated substantial economic, social, and political change, becoming by about 1850 the world's first modern society. It accomplished all of this without provoking mass violence, an achievement that owed much to the innovation and flexibility of British capitalism.

The political foundations of Britain's business system date back to the seventeenth century and the origins of the modern state. The "Glorious Revolution" of 1688 marked a turning point in the evolution of British constitutional government. The previous four hundred years had been marred by a long succession of civil and foreign wars. Since the Norman Conquest in 1066, factions of feudal lords had intermittently battled for

---

*Pp. 53–59 were written in part by Nancy F. Koehn and Thomas K. McCraw.

**In this chapter, "England" and "English" are differentiated from "Great Britain," "Britain," and "British," which also include Scotland, Wales, and, until the twentieth century, all of Ireland. William the Conqueror's great achievement after 1066 was in tying together the different regions of England into one of Europe's first unified systems of government. Wales was formally annexed in 1536. Scotland was formally joined to Great Britain in 1707. Ireland was formally annexed in 1800, though the country had been subject to British rule since 1171, often through brutal military action. The official name of the country is the United Kingdom of Great Britain and Northern Ireland.

the English throne. The seventeenth century was especially bloody. In 1649, the Stuart king, Charles I, was beheaded after losing a protracted civil war against an army raised by Parliament. The monarchy was restored in 1660, but the conflict between the Crown and Parliament continued until 1688, when the legislature finally won out. King James II, Charles I's grandson, was then forced to leave Britain. He was replaced by William of Orange, a Dutchman related to the Stuarts by birth and marriage. This political changeover of 1688 became known as the Glorious Revolution because it was accomplished without bloodshed.

Once King William had assumed control of the government, he was willing to make important concessions to legislative authority. One of his first acts was to summon Parliament, which had not been called by James II since 1685. Parliament, working with the new king and his wife, Mary Stuart (daughter of James II), now passed a series of important constitutional acts. The Bill of Rights, enacted in 1689, prohibited standing armies in peacetime and taxes not levied by Parliament. The bill also extended individuals' civil rights and outlawed cruel and unusual punishment. It called for frequent Parliaments, free elections to this body, and free speech by its members.

The Bill of Rights, together with several other important acts, ensured that Britain would be governed by a limited monarchy—by the king or queen acting with the regular consent of the legislature. Although the Glorious Revolution left the Crown in full command as head of the executive branch, the settlement made annual meetings of Parliament essential. The monarch would henceforth have to choose policies and chief ministers approved by a legislative majority. At a broad level, Britain would thus be ruled by a constitution which, in theory at least, granted to all British subjects a broad array of rights, including the right to own private property. Technically, Britain's constitution was and still is unwritten; it is not codified in a single document, but is the product of a system of laws that have evolved over many centuries.

Until the nineteenth century, any such constitutional system was unusual by European standards. In France, Russia, and other countries, the monarch *was* the law. Legally and practically, monarchs often used the apparatus of the state to exploit their countries' human and material resources. In eighteenth-century Russia, for example, Peter the Great ordered an entire city, St. Petersburg, to be built for no other reason than to serve as his capital.

THE BRITISH STATE, EARLY MODERN WARFARE, AND FINANCIAL INNOVATIONS

Of all Beings that have Existence only in the Minds of Men, nothing is more fantastical and nice than Credit; 'tis never to be forc'd; it hangs upon Opinion; it depends upon our passions of hope and fear; it comes many times unsought for, and often goes away without Reason; and when once lost, is hardly to be quite recover'd.

—the British political economist Charles Davenant[5]

One result of the Glorious Revolution was the new control that Parliament, and particularly the House of Commons, gained over public finances and military spending. In an era of frequent warfare, such parliamentary oversight translated into significant fiscal power. During the Nine Years War against France, for example (1688–97), military expenditures represented almost 75 percent of total government spending.[6]

Between 1689 and 1815, Britain fought no fewer than six major wars with France. A little more than 55 of these 126 years, therefore, were taken up in expensive combat.[7] Britain and France, together with their shifting coalitions of allies, spent huge sums. The Seven Years War of 1756–63 alone cost Britain about £160 million. This was more than twice its gross national product of 1760, and in that sense would be comparable to the United States fighting a war at the close of the twentieth century with a price tag of more than $13 trillion.[8] In the Seven Years War and other conflicts, Britain and France battled not only for military advantage, but also for colonies and economic dominance: for the authority to rule international trade, for access to raw materials, and for markets in which to sell domestic manufactures.[9]

To finance Britain's struggles with France, Parliament levied a variety of taxes, which a growing civil administration collected with some efficiency and without significant corruption.[10] During the eighteenth century, a growing percentage of military expenditures was funded through state borrowing. By the time of the American Revolution (1775–83), public borrowing financed 40 percent of military expenses.[11] The Treasury raised money by issuing government securities, usually in the form of long-term bonds with a guaranteed annual premium. The service costs of the resulting indebtedness were financed by the nation's increasingly effective tax system.

The critical role of credit in financing Britain's wars with France gave rise to institutional and financial innovations. One of the most important of these was the founding in 1694 of the Bank of England. The Bank was established as a *private* bank by a group of leading London financiers, who lent money to the government during the Nine Years War in return for a monopoly on joint-stock banking in England.[12] Working with the British Treasury, the Bank helped to coordinate the purchase and sale of government securities, and made the annual interest payments to debt holders.[13]

From the 1690s on, individuals and businesses could buy and sell public stocks and bonds on the London stock exchange. Beginning in 1698, prices of all the major government securities traded were printed twice weekly and circulated throughout Europe.[14] The availability of these securities, and their ease of transfer, provided businessmen with ideal short-term assets into which they could channel idle balances and from which they could quickly withdraw needed funds. For eighteenth-century firms, short-term borrowing and lending were extremely important. Because the distribution system was so slow and primitive, carrying costs remained high.[15] Business assets requiring short-term credit were often four to five times greater than a given company's fixed investments in plant and equipment. Government debt provided a low-risk asset that could be liquidated rapidly and was thus attractive to businesses and individuals.[16]

Other financial innovations, many of which had been pioneered by the Dutch, included the mortgage, the promissory note, and—most important of all—the bill of exchange, the forerunner of modern paper currency and bank checks.[17] Bills of exchange facilitated the quick transfer of funds between banks without the burden of physically shipping gold and silver coins, which were the only legal tender in early eighteenth-century Europe.

The use of bills of exchange, bank notes, and government securities opened new possibilities for domestic and international commerce. These novel instruments of credit helped to spread the risks associated with slow and intermittent communication between markets. Doing business on credit also served to keep capital markets functioning when the business cycle took one of its periodic dips.[18] The rapidity and flexibility with which Britain developed a vital, effective system of public and private credit in the early eighteenth century made it one of the leading countries in Europe in the realm of finance.

TRADE AND EMPIRE

By the early decades of the eighteenth century, London was challenging Amsterdam as the world's premier banking and trading center.[19] In 1700, London's population had reached about 575,000, a very large total for that time.[20] Bustling commerce in and around the city stimulated demand for goods and services within the British Isles as a whole and enabled the country to trade on a global scale.[21]

London's dynamism was a result of government policy as well as social developments. During much of the eighteenth century, most of the great powers of Europe considered trade, both domestic and international, to be a vital national asset that had to be protected by tariffs and other regulations, and defended by military force.[22] In a period of frequent, expensive warfare, a nation's commerce provided needed materials, domestic employment, and tax revenues. In 1718, the political economist Josiah Child commented on another advantage of international trade. The British ships that carried such commerce "bring with them a great access of Power (Hands as well as Money); many ships and Seamen bring justly the reputed Strength and Safety of England."[23] Commerce was, in itself, a vehicle for spreading British influence throughout the world.

During the seventeenth and eighteenth centuries, Britain, France, and other European states tended to manage their international commerce toward geopolitical ends. They used a range of policies such as tariffs, subsidies, and regulations, which together became known as "mercantilism."[24] One of the central aims of British mercantilism was to increase both exports and "re-exports," which was the name given to goods imported into Britain and then shipped on to foreign markets. These policies seem to have been highly successful, as Table 3.2 indicates.

Britain's exports to its North American and West Indian colonies grew faster than any other branch of its international commerce, rising from

Table 3.2   Growth of British Trade (% change in value from to 1699 to 1774)

	Asia	Americas	Ireland	Europe	All Colonies
Exports	590	775	560	90	700
Re-exports	450	310	570	250	410

Source: Adapted from Ralph Davis, "English Foreign Trade, 1700–1774," *Economic History Review,* 15 (1962), pp. 302–303.

about one-tenth of the nation's exports in 1700 to more than half by 1800.[25] Even independence did not stem the North Americans' demand for British manufactures. In the 1790s, the United States continued to purchase almost 90 percent of its manufactured imports from Britain.[26] This expansion of trade probably served as an important engine propelling Britain into the First Industrial Revolution.[27]

At the center of British trade policy toward its American colonies, at least until 1740, were the Navigation Acts, the first of which had been passed in 1651. These laws required that most commerce between America and the rest of the world pass through British ports on British ships. Britain's mercantilist policies also included prohibitions on American manufactures that competed with those of the mother country. There were also severe restrictions on direct trade between North America and the West Indies.

The eighteenth-century economy that grew up between lands bordering on the North Atlantic was a complex, dynamic set of trading relations. Although there were countless variations, trade often followed triangular or quadrangular patterns.[28] In one such pattern, British manufactures were shipped to Africa. There they were exchanged for black Africans, who were then sent as slaves to such destinations as South and Central America, the West Indian islands, and the southern colonies of North America. West Indian sugar (in the form of molasses) then traveled to refineries and distilleries in Europe or North America to be manufactured into rum. North American goods such as tobacco, rice, lumber, furs, and fish were then shipped to Britain for domestic distribution or re-export to Europe.

Until relations between the mother country and thirteen of the continental colonies became severely strained in the early 1770s, most Britons agreed that the nation's dominions in North America and the West Indies had three major economic functions: to serve as growing markets for British manufactures, to produce raw materials for use in the mother country, and to help defray the costs of managing and defending the empire as a whole. Many colonists, on the other hand, were less than enthusiastic about what they perceived as their own subservient role in Britain's mercantile system. Commercial exploitation by the mother country became an important colonial grievance in the years leading up to the American war for independence.

It is worth noting that the overseas British Empire had originated not as a coordinated government policy but rather as a series of independent commercial enterprises. In an effort to raise money and exploit foreign markets, the government had sold monopoly rights to a number of trading companies. The most famous of these, the East India Company, had been chartered by Queen Elizabeth I in 1599. In addition to monopolies on trade, the chartered companies were given quasi-official powers to govern the territories in which they operated. Thus, the British *raj,* or rule, of parts of India began with the directors of the East India Company.[29]

In strictly commercial terms, the great chartered companies were remarkably successful, so much so that they paved the way for their own demise.[30] By the middle of the eighteenth century, Britain's trade had grown sufficiently attractive that smaller firms and individual merchants began to challenge the chartered companies' dominance. Many more capitalists now had sufficient funds to finance long-distance voyages than had been the case a century earlier. And the rise of a strong Royal Navy, plus the development of maritime insurance, had reduced the risks of foreign trade.[31] The exclusivity of commerce enjoyed by the East India Company and similar concerns therefore declined steadily over the late eighteenth and early nineteenth centuries. British trade during those years evolved into a decentralized web of small, specialized firms. At the same time, many of the wealthiest merchants came to act as bankers, in turn financing a group of middle-level merchants who acted as wholesalers.[32]

Meanwhile, the geopolitical potential of specific territories had provided an important rationale for creating and sustaining the British Empire on an official governmental basis as well as an informal commercial one. The size of the Empire expanded and contracted with Britain's military fortunes. In 1763, for example, the nation's victory in the Seven Years War earned it control over all of Canada, much of India, all of East Florida, and numerous islands in the Atlantic Ocean and Caribbean Sea. Twenty years later, at the close of the American Revolution, Britain lost dominion over thirteen of its North American colonies. On balance, however, the British Empire grew very significantly over the eighteenth and early nineteenth centuries. By 1850, it had become one of the largest empires in history and arguably the most powerful since that of ancient Rome. By that time, the First Industrial Revolution was in full swing, and the Great Exhibition at the Crystal Palace was about to open its doors.

Building an Industrial Society

The First Industrial Revolution was a great age of civil engineering, in which Britain pioneered the building of a modern economic infrastructure. Beginning in the 1760s, a sophisticated network of canals was constructed to connect northern and western industrial cities such as Birmingham, Sheffield, and Manchester with the nation's major ports, especially London and Liverpool.[33] At the same time, many cities and towns were linked by improved toll roads. These were major advances over the rudimentary and poorly kept roads that had crisscrossed the British Isles for centuries.[34] Britain's upgraded infrastructure, together with the abolition in 1707 of customs duties between England and Scotland, laid the groundwork for a truly national market. All of this happened well before 1800, at a time when internal tariffs and primitive roads made such a concept as a national market almost unthinkable in much of continental Europe.

For the most part, Britain's infrastructure was privately financed and operated. Capital was provided by merchants, by landed aristocrats and gentry, and by industrial investors such as Josiah Wedgwood.[35] A fortuitous cycle evolved, in which investments in transportation coincided with technological innovations to spark industrial growth, and hence more investment.

One of the most important examples of this kind of integrated expansion was the pattern of growth in Britain's coal industry. Over the last half of the eighteenth century, infrastructural improvements helped lower the transport cost of coal by 50 percent.[36] Coal production both fueled and depended on steam engines, which after 1711 were used to pump water out of mines and later to lift coal to the surface.[37] Such savings in transportation and production technology greatly stimulated coal mining[38] (see Table 3.3).

In Britain, coal supplied the critical energy for both the First and Second Industrial Revolutions. With coal and the steam engine, Britain now had the necessary ingredients for one of the most important technological advances in the history of transportation: the railroad locomotive. In 1830, when the nation's first major railway was opened between Liverpool and Manchester, Britain entered the modern transportation age. The first locomotive, called the "Rocket," traveled as fast as 25 miles an hour. At a time when a loaded horse-drawn wagon needed not an hour but at

Table 3.3   British Coal Output (millions of tons per year)

1700	1750	1800	1830	1870	1994
3	5	15	30	110	31

Sources: For 1700 to 1830: Michael Flinn, *History of the British Coal Industry* (Oxford: Oxford University Press, 1984), vol. 2, p. 26. For 1870: B. R. Mitchell and Phyllis Deane, *Abstract of British Historical Statistics* (Cambridge: Cambridge University Press, 1962), p. 115. For 1994: Central Statistical Office, *Annual Abstract of Statistics, 1996* (London: HMSO, 1996), p. 174.

least a whole day to travel 25 miles, the railway represented almost blinding speed. Many people wondered if the human body could endure the strain.[39]

Most of the major technological innovations of the First Industrial Revolution involved the substitution of water- and steam-driven mechanical power for human and animal muscle. Historians and other social commentators have always made much of the machine's entrance onto the economic stage, and justifiably so. For the novelist Mary Shelley, the machine was an awesome and even terrifying new creature. It had to be treated with extreme care, lest it get out of hand. In her novel *Frankenstein* (1818), she depicted the machine as an unnatural kind of monster. She labeled it "the modern Prometheus," after the figure in Greek mythology who stole fire from the gods and delivered it to humanity.

COTTON TEXTILES

No industry better exemplified the First Industrial Revolution in Britain than did cotton textiles. It was by far the premier growth sector.[40] Through a combination of technology and modern factory organization, average throughput per cotton textile firm rose by a factor of thirteen between 1792 and 1850.[41] During the first three decades of the nineteenth century, real output in the industry grew by more than 5.5 percent annually.[42] By 1830, cotton cloth accounted for as much as half of Britain's total exports.[43] In less than a century, Manchester rose from obscurity to become one of Europe's foremost commercial centers: "Cottonopolis," it was called.

Within Great Britain, the cotton textile industry was shaped by ruthless competition. Rapid growth in demand, low barriers to entry, frequent technological innovations, and a high rate of firm bankruptcy all combined to form an environment in which monopolistic or oligopolistic competition became almost impossible. Although nineteenth-century politicians and other Britons often expressed concern that cartels and monopolies were taking over the industry, these worries were completely unfounded. From 1790 onward, hordes of entrepreneurs entered the market. The industry began to center around the region of Lancashire, and between 1835 and 1850, the number of cotton textile factories in Lancashire doubled, climbing from 676 to 1,235.[44]

By the 1830s and 1840s, world demand for inexpensive textiles was growing rapidly, and atomistic competition produced extraordinary interfirm volatility. That, in turn, spawned additional economic activity. The high rate of firm bankruptcies, for example, created a thriving second-hand market for textile machinery, which encouraged fresh waves of entrepreneurs to try their luck. A similar situation obtained in many other nineteenth-century British industries.[45] In brewing, chemicals, and the metal trades, swiftly rising demand made it almost impossible to limit supply through cartels and monopolies.[46]

Britain's nineteenth-century competitive dominance in cotton textiles was at least partly the result of its prowess in science and engineering. But Britain would learn the hard way that technology does not respect the boundaries of an individual firm or even a nation. The machines that revolutionized textile manufacturing could easily be transplanted to other countries, along with the expertise of British engineers and craftsmen. Toward the end of the eighteenth century, Parliament had banned the emigration of skilled mechanics and the export of machinery. But these laws were notoriously unsuccessful in stopping technology transfers. It took the emigration of only a handful of skilled mechanics to spread Britain's most advanced technology to other countries.[47] By the 1840s, the laws prohibiting emigration and machinery export were repealed.[48]

During most of the nineteenth century, British cotton firms tended to be relatively small, employing an average of about 150 workers.[49] Almost all such firms were family owned and had only a handful of partners.[50] Significantly, the legal principle of limited liability was not fully adopted in Britain until 1861. Before this time equity investors were usually responsible for paying 100 percent of a firm's debts, even if it required all of their personal assets to do so. Given the extreme risks in owning a business during the First Industrial Revolution, there was much to be said for fiscal conservatism and for close, hands-on supervision by company owners.[51]

BANKING AND INDUSTRY

It is natural to assume that the City of London, as the financial district was and still is called, supplied much of the capital for the First Industrial Revolution. In fact, the City provided only indirect support. By the mid-eighteenth century, Britain's banking system was engaged in two types of business. Within the City of London itself, a number of large "clearing" banks offered short-term finance, mainly for long-distance trade.[52] The clearing banks also acted as agents for small provincial banks, which provided short-term loans, called "overdrafts," while also "discounting" (buying at a discount) the domestic bills of exchange that circulated between London and the provinces. This two-tiered system aided industrial development by maintaining a smooth flow of domestic trade, but not by providing funds for long-term capital investment.

During boom periods, British manufacturing firms would sometimes look to the capital markets, but in most cases the pressures of competition seem to have discouraged this practice.[53] Given the heavy personal risks involved in manufacturing, a great many British entrepreneurs were determined to maintain their independence from creditors. Hence, most of the early industrial enterprises were self-financed, from the personal fortunes of owners and through reinvested profits.

Nevertheless, the "country" bankers outside London often had close personal ties to families who owned industrial firms. In many instances, country banks had been founded by industrialists and merchants themselves, so that one way to chart the progress of British industry over time is simply by measuring the proliferation of these institutions. In 1750, there were probably no more than a dozen country banks in all of Britain. By the 1780s, there were over 100, by 1810 over 600, and by the 1830s more than 1,000.[54]

Because the country bankers' business depended on trade generated by industrial output, they were often forced to abandon their strategy of extending only short-term credit. The economic historian Peter Mathias has noted that "a banker lent short for three months or six months, and then found that he could not get his money back at the due date. Provided the business was essentially sound and suffering only a liquidity crisis, the banker's interests were usually best served by not foreclosing."[55] So country bankers often supported manufacturing over the long run, despite their own preference not to do so.

INDUSTRIALISTS CONFRONT THE OLD ORDER

As Britain moved through the First Industrial Revolution, institutional rearrangements under capitalism came to represent a unique blending of the old with the new. Until the early twentieth century, the landed establishment continued to exert very significant, through declining, influence on British government.[56] From most outward appearances, landed elites remained the political, social, and fashion leaders of the country. Together, the great families continued to control enormous wealth. As late as 1873, these families along with the gentry owned 79 percent of the nation's land.[57]

But beginning in the late eighteenth century, individuals who owed their opportunities to the First Industrial Revolution had begun to challenge the landed aristocracy's dominance. Some of these individuals were of foreign descent, having fled religious persecution in their own countries. European Jews, French Huguenots, and other immigrants came to Britain as merchants and bankers, bringing with them their commercial contacts.[58]

In all countries at this time, foreign trade depended heavily on personal and family ties among merchants, manufacturers, and bankers. The Rothschilds, for example, started their banking empire in Frankfurt. After the Napoleonic Wars, they branched out to London, Paris, Vienna, and Naples. As a Jew, Nathan Rothschild, who arrived in England in 1798, found London a much safer place to borrow and lend capital than central Europe, where anti-Jewish violence was commonplace. During the eighteenth and early nineteenth centuries, Britain profited greatly by extending property rights to foreigners such as the Rothschilds, thereby enabling them to do business without risk of persecution.

In addition to foreign bankers and merchants, many entrepreneurs of the First Industrial Revolution came from "nonconformist" religious groups such as Quakers and Unitarians.[59] Even so, nonconformists, who were Protestants not belonging to the Church of England, were denied many rights in Britain. Among other things, they could not sit in Parliament unless they took communion in the established Church of England.[60]

For much of the eighteenth century, British manufacturers tended to be geographically isolated. Most industries developed in the north and west of England, seemingly far from the elite London world of politics, culture, and high finance. That isolation limited their influence in national affairs, including economic policy.

In spite of these social, religious, and geographical distances, other interests did begin to exercise influence in British life, thereby threatening the centuries-old dominion of landed elites. These interests included merchants, manufacturers, financiers, and eventually even working people. But the change did not happen overnight, of course. Economic, political, and social equality for all Britons did not arrive in a blaze with the First Industrial Revolution. The inroads against landed rule occurred gradually and at an uneven pace, over a very long period. The social decline of the British aristocracy continues even into our own time—in the popular debates about the vicissitudes of the royal family, for example.

Early stirrings of this profound long-term social transformation became evident during the last four decades of the eighteenth century, when British manufacturers began to organize themselves as a political force.[61] In 1766, for example, a coalition of manufacturers successfully lobbied Parliament to repeal the Stamp Act, which had laid a new colonial tax that was hurting their export business. Almost two decades later, the potter Josiah Wedgwood, the Birmingham chemical manufacturer Samuel Garbett, and other industrialists established the General Chamber of Manufacturers to oppose the government's commercial treaty with Ireland, which many feared would raise duties on English goods shipped there.[62] Wedgwood saw lasting benefits to an organization "of Delegates from all the main factories and places in England and Scotland."[63] The Chamber of Manufacturers, he noted to the manufacturer Matthew Boulton, "may be of great use" on issues other than Britain's trade with Ireland.[64] Wedgwood envisioned this industrial alliance working to solve common problems of excise taxes, tariff policy, transport costs, and regulation of prices.[65] During the last decades of the eighteenth century, industrial interests had uneven influence on policymaking. But by the end of that century, they were being heard in parlors, town meetings, trade fairs, and the halls of national government.

In this context, even representatives of landed interests, such as the statesman Edmund Burke, began to acknowledge the increasing significance of business interests. For Burke and other representatives of the traditional order, the forces of economic and social change were potentially explosive, as the French Revolution had demonstrated. In 1789, discontent at all levels of French society had suddenly spilled over, and the powerful but corrupt Bourbon dynasty had given way to a series of oppressive revolutionary regimes, ending with Napoleon's dictatorship. The upheavals of the French Revolution, stretching over a period of 26 years, damaged France's nascent industries and helped open the way for Britain to take the lead in important sectors of the emerging industrial economy.

Watching the chaos in France, Burke noted in 1790 that "Good order is the foundation of all good things."[66] Like many other Britons, he believed that the nation's constitutional government was more just and humane than that prevailing in France. The broad-based legitimacy of the British state and the relative openness of British social structures allowed the country to absorb and profit from industrialization without massive unrest. The absence of agrarian crises also helped the nation accommodate widespread change. Britain was occasionally threatened by domestic unrest, but never to the degree characteristic of many parts of Europe between 1789 and 1848, or on the scale of the American Civil War in the 1860s.

Through the 1820s, 1830s, and 1840s, a capitalist ideology bent on reforming the political system steadily gained influence in Britain. Members of Parliament had always been chosen by election, but until the 1800s the voting system was heavily weighted toward the landed aristocracy. Some MPs represented ancient boroughs that by the 1800s had become uninhabited sheep fields or were under water. By the late 1820s, Britain's voting system was under broad attack for being corrupt and unrepresentative. In 1832, Parliament passed the first of a series of laws to widen the franchise. In 1833, Parliament abolished slavery in all British colonies. In 1867 and 1884, Parliament passed reform bills that eventually gave the vote to most men. (After 1918 all adult men, plus women 30 and over, were allowed to vote. Universal adult suffrage was finally achieved in 1928.) This very gradual move toward democracy was calculated to help preserve Britain's social, political, and economic stability, and it succeeded.

But British business rarely spoke with one political voice. On a given issue, such as tariff duties, the income tax, state aid to schools, or factory regulation, the practical interests of one industrial group almost always conflicted with those of another. Therefore, even though the influence of

British industrialists in national policymaking increased during the nineteenth century, the landed gentry remained the dominant political force throughout the years of the First Industrial Revolution.[67]

The Second Industrial Revolution, 1840s to 1940s

At the beginning of the Second Industrial Revolution, no one doubted that the First Industrial Revolution had made Great Britain the most economically competitive nation in the world. The prevailing belief among British capitalists was that national prosperity depended on the zeal of individual entrepreneurs, and not on national development policy. In 1859, a best-selling author named Samuel Smiles confidently declared that "the strength, the industry, and the civilization of nations all depend upon individual character . . . In the just balance of nature, individuals, nations, and races will obtain just so much as they deserve, and no more."[68] Unfortunately for British capitalists, the Second Industrial Revolution proved to be a severe test of Smiles's faith in individual enterprise over some form of industrial planning.

THE EXPERIMENT WITH FREE TRADE, 1846–1931

Britain occupied a singular place in the global economy, and it became the first nation in Europe to reject the economic orthodoxy of mercantilism. In the 1840s, Parliament adopted a policy of almost unrestricted free trade. The rationale for this move was complex, but it owed much to the nation's steady rise in population during the decades after 1750, which made it politically important to keep food prices at a minimum through freer imports of grain.

Overcoming the mercantilist impulse took some time, however. After the Napoleonic wars ended in 1815, Parliament tried to limit food imports through tariffs. These were the so-called Corn Laws, which applied to wheat and other grains as well. But the demand in Britain for foreign grain was so high that Parliament began gradually to reduce the tariffs. In 1846, they were dropped altogether, and grain imports began to rise dramatically.[69] By the early twentieth century, the country was importing over half of its food and as much as seven-eighths of its raw materials.[70] Britain thus became unusually dependent on imported goods; between the 1870s and the 1920s, the value of imports equaled roughly one-quarter of the Gross National Product.[71]

Britain's commitment to free trade lasted from 1846 until 1931, when the Great Depression was at its worst.[72] A cynic might argue that the nation had lowered its tariffs in the first place only because, being the largest and most efficient producer in the world during the 1840s, it faced scant competition. There is some truth to this argument. Even as late as 1900, Britain was still so strong that it was second only to the United States in manufacturing output, though its population was much smaller. In 1899, the United States had 41 percent of the world's manufacturing output, Britain had 21 percent, Germany 15 percent, and Japan 1.2 percent.[73] And not until after World War II did America export more manufactured goods than did Britain.[74]

In nineteenth-century British politics, a majority of legislators could agree that trade was a vital national asset, and that free trade worked well for British merchants and consumers. There was much less agreement about the role of manufacturing. Britain's industrial and social fragmentation, which made national planning exceedingly difficult, undoubtedly contributed to the delay in setting industrial growth as a national priority. Finance took a higher status, since industrialists, traders, and bankers could easily agree on the need to maintain the gold standard and a positive balance of payments. Beyond this, there was little agreement on national economic policy. Only after the Second World War (1939–45) did any consensus develop behind the need for government to promote Britain's international competitiveness in industry.

For much of the nineteenth century and the first third of the twentieth, Britain stood almost alone in its commitment to free trade. During these years, the spirit of rapid industrial growth informed the trade protectionism of other countries. As later chapters of this book will show, the United States and Germany used high tariffs to restrict imports and to boost their domestic manufacturing. This protection of their home markets helped to enable the Americans and Germans to increase their industrial output very rapidly. Their rejection of free trade was especially troubling to Britain because it effectively shut out many British exports from the world's two fastest-growing consumer markets.

In the closing years of the nineteenth century, some British politicians and industrialists argued for retaliatory tariffs. But the majority were reluctant to do anything that might spark an international trade war. The City of London had much to lose in such a conflict, because British finance was so heavily concentrated in foreign investments. London was unquestionably the world's dominant financial center in the era leading up to 1914.[75] But its orientation was international, and not centered on the domestic economy. From 1911 to 1913, domestic share issues on the London stock exchange accounted for only about 18 percent of its business. During the same period, the total capital raised for domestic manufacturing firms was equal to only 3 percent of the capital exported to other countries. Other vested interests in free trade included the export industries (especially textiles), and the consumer-oriented "cheap food" lobby.[76]

BRITAIN'S FORMAL EMPIRE IN THE NINETEENTH CENTURY

Within Britain's numerous colonies, the smaller scale of merchant companies in the nineteenth century meant that private businesses could no longer exercise the quasi-governmental functions once fulfilled by the great chartered companies. (The East India Company lost its trade monopoly in 1813 and was legally disbanded in 1858.) Instead, the job of safeguarding colonies for British trade was gradually taken over by the government. By the middle of the nineteenth century, the era of informal commercial governance had given way to a formal, government-administered empire, with serious consequences for the mother country.

The empire brought oppression for indigenous colonial peoples around the world. It also imposed high administrative and military costs on Britain itself. Even so, by the late nineteenth century, several other European countries, notably France and Germany, had begun to compete openly with Britain for control of new territories in Asia and Africa. The majority of colonies cost more to maintain than they paid in revenues, and keeping up the appearances of a great empire took ever greater sums of money. Many Britons back home considered this money ill spent. What had begun in the 1600s as a series of commercial ventures sponsored by British merchants ended up as a public responsibility the nation could hardly afford.[77]

By the late nineteenth century, if not earlier, Britain's noncolonial markets were probably much more profitable than its colonial ones.[78] Overall, the Western Hemisphere was the most popular site for investors. British investment there grew at least three times as fast as in any other part of the world in the fifty years before World War I. The Americas attracted more British capital than did the United Kingdom itself, as Table 3.4 indicates.

Table 3.4   Distribution of Britain's Private Capital, 1865–1914

Americas	Europe	Rest of World	U.K.
37%	9%	24%	30%

Source: Adapted from Lance Davis and Robert Huttenback, *Mammon and the Pursuit of Empire* (Cambridge: Cambridge University Press, 1986), p. 46.

Colonies were often quite profitable for individual investors and entrepreneurs, though not in proportion to the overall cost of administering the Empire.[79] In South Africa, for instance, the diamond and gold-mining interests controlled by Cecil Rhodes in the late 1800s represented a vast potential source of wealth. But then, southern Africa was a volatile place, requiring large military forces to enforce British rule. As governor of the Cape colony, Rhodes fought against several African tribes for territories rich in gold and diamonds. Even worse, in 1899 the Boers of South Africa (white settlers of Dutch, German, and French Huguenot descent) started a war for independence that cost Britain a very high price in both money and lives to win.[80]

CAPITAL EXPORTS

By the late nineteenth century, Britain's accumulated pool of savings had grown so vast that the City of London was able to export prodigious amounts of capital. In 1914, on the eve of the First World War, the UK was still by far the leading source of foreign direct investment, accounting for almost half of the world's total. The United States was in a distant second place with about 19 percent.[81] Britain's dominance of overseas finance may actually have created a disincentive to invest in domestic manufacturing during the Second Industrial Revolution.

Many people in Britain complained that this investment pattern seemed to signal that the nation had implicitly decided to sacrifice its long-term potential for the sake of short-term profits. The consequence, it was argued, would be a weak Britain, unable to compete against countries that placed national interests over individual desires. Henry Dyer, a British engineer with much experience in Japan, wrote in 1904 that "the chief lesson to be learned from Japan is the need for a truly national spirit for the accomplishment of great ends." But in Britain's case, he asked, "is it not true that we have no real national policy, and that our statesmen drift according to their own whims or to what may be called accidental circumstances?"[82]

Britain's dependence on international trade and finance was very often criticized in the years before World War I. One popular commentator, E. E. Williams, warned in 1901 that "we live as a nation under an enormous danger, for we are at the mercy of foreign nations, not only for our food and for our clothes, but for our huge invested capital."[83] But given the profits available to investors in international markets, there was little incentive to change a system that had earlier made Britain the world's foremost economic power. Moreover, the geographical distribution of British investments on the eve of World War I would suggest that the nation had little to fear in the way of financial threats from its potential European enemies (see Table 3.5).

In the late nineteenth century and through much of the twentieth, "invisible" exports (investment capital, along with services such as insurance, and shipping) were indispensable sources of foreign exchange for Britain. This income was sorely needed in a country whose large urban population had a huge demand for imported food and raw materials. For "visible" merchandise Britain ran a trade deficit every single year between 1823 and 1913. Yet its overall current-account balance was positive in all but two of those years. From 1910 through 1913, for example, Britain bought £539,300 million more in overseas merchandise than it exported, but in those same years its invisible earnings totaled £1.3 billion.[84] As Table 3.6 shows, Britain would remain the world's most effective exporter of capital through most of the twentieth century.

If there was a long-term danger to Britain's economic competitiveness, it was in investing so little at home and having a relatively large percentage of the nation's savings invested in areas that would become the slowest-growing markets of the twentieth century, namely Latin America and the colonies. This is not to suggest that British investors were some-

Table 3.5   Distribution of British Overseas Investment, 1914

U.S.	Latin America	Colonies	Europe	Asia
21%	19%	46%	5%	9%

Note: The colonies' total includes India, South Africa, Canada, and Australia.
Source: Adapted from François Crouzet, *The Victorian Economy* (London: Methuen, 1982), p. 366.

how misguided. The City's natural desire to minimize risk was usually better served by investing in businesses located in areas removed from the conflicts of continental Europe.[85]

THE PROBLEM OF NATIONAL COMPETITIVENESS

As the Second Industrial Revolution progressed in the late nineteenth century, its apparent direction caused much anxiety in Britain. Actually, trade statistics gave little concern, as British manufacturing exports continued to dominate global markets—rather thoroughly, in fact (see Table 3.7). Still, a pessimist could argue that other countries were catching up fast (see Table 3.8).

British industrialists were justifiably alarmed by the speed with which competing firms in other countries were growing. American industrial output grew at an average of 4.7 percent per year between 1870 and 1913, and the figure for Germany was 4.1 percent. But for Britain it was only 2.1 percent.[86]

Britain was at an institutional disadvantage early in the Second Industrial Revolution because it did not have any giant companies in those

Table 3.6   Index of Foreign Investment (100 = country average, relative to population)

	U.S.	Germany	Japan	U.K.
1913	53	—	59	410
1937	76	19	9	417
1973	51	36	44	144

Note: The average performance includes France along with the four countries shown here.
Sources: Adapted, with permission, from a manuscript by Leslie Hannah, 1995. Numbers from John Dunning, *Explaining International Production* (London: Unwin Hyman, 1988); population data from Angus Maddison, *Dynamic Forces in Capitalist Development* (Oxford: Oxford University Press, 1991).

Table 3.7   Shares of World Manufacturing Exports before World War I (%)

	U.S.	Germany	Japan	Britain
1899	12	17	2	35
1913	14	20	3	32

Source: Adapted from R. C. O. Matthews, C. H. Feinstein, and J. C. Odling-Smee, *British Economic Growth, 1856–1973* (Stanford: Stanford University Press, 1982), p. 435.

industries most advantaged by economies of scale and scope. True, in steel, chemicals, and machinery, Britain would eventually develop large, vertically integrated firms. But that did not happen until long after such huge corporations had become the norm in these industries in the United States and Germany.[87] As Table 3.9 indicates, Britain's largest companies before World War I were in mature industries highly dependent on exports.

To the extent that size equaled competitive potential in the Second Industrial Revolution, Britain fell far behind the Americans after the turn of the century. United States Steel employed over five times as many workers as did Britain's largest firm, Fine Cotton Spinners and Doublers.[88] (And even this company, like the number five firm in the table, Calico Printers, was a loose federation, unlike the integrated firms normally implied by the term "big business.") But in a few industries, notably shipbuilding, Britain before 1914 still remained the workshop of the world (see Table 3.10).

Britain also had great strength in the arms business. One British firm, Vickers, was a particularly competent exporter of weapons, in addition

Table 3.8 Increase in Value of Manufacturing Exports, 1899–1913 (%)

U.S.	Germany	Japan	Britain
100	121	151	48

Note: Based on constant prices for 1913.
Source: Adapted from Alfred Maizels, *Industrial Growth and World Trade* (Cambridge: Cambridge University Press, 1963), pp. 432–433.

Table 3.9 Britain's Five Largest Manufacturing Employers, c. 1907

Employer	Industry	Employees (est.)
1. Fine Cotton Spinners & Doublers Assoc.	Textiles	30,000
2. Royal Dockyards	Shipbuilding	25,600
3. Armstrong, Whitworth	Armaments, Ships	25,000
4. Vickers Sons & Maxim	Armaments, Ships	22,500
5. Calico Printers Assoc.	Textiles	20,500

Source: Christine Shaw, "The Large Manufacturing Employers of 1907," in R. P. T. Davenport-Hines, ed., *Business in the Age of Depression and War* (London: Frank Cass, 1990), p. 11.

Table 3.10   Shipbuilding, 1913 (thousands of gross tons produced)

U.S.	Germany	Japan	Britain
276	465	65	1,932

Source: Adapted from Sidney Pollard and Paul Robertson, *The British Shipbuilding Industry, 1870–1914* (Cambridge, MA: Harvard University Press, 1979), p. 249.

to supplying the British government with the ships and guns it needed to rule a global empire.[89] For all the great European powers at this time, the capacity to build more and better weapons was considered vital to defense and national prestige. After the 1890s, the continent was gripped by an arms race, which led directly to the outbreak of World War I in 1914.

For some of Britain's weapons manufacturers, business competition was hardly different from war itself. Hudson Maxim, whose family firm had merged with Vickers in 1897, said in 1899 that "war must be looked upon as a business, and subject, like any other business, to business principles." In consequence, "the chemist, engineer, and inventor find duty as serviceable to their country as does the bleeding soldier; and all the vast industries of a great commonwealth unite to supply the sinews of war." To Maxim, it was obvious that "the most deadly and destructive implements of war are the most humane, and the producers of them may justly be looked upon as humanitarians."[90] His opinion was not shared by everyone, especially after World War I became the bloodiest war in history up to that time. But in the end, Britain and its allies prevailed in that conflict in part because they were able to outproduce the Germans in weapons and ammunition.[91]

For Britain's international trade, on the other hand, the First World War proved to be an unqualified disaster. Before the United States brought its powerful navy into the war in 1917, German submarines almost succeeded in cutting Britain off from the outside world.[92] The British government called the conflict the "great war for Civilization," and Britain was indeed fighting to preserve, if not quite civilization, its dominance of the global economy.

THE WANING OF ECONOMIC IMPERIALISM

In the end, Britain could not hope to win the struggle to preserve its prewar position in world commerce. The nation's all-important cotton industry had reached its zenith in 1913, with more firms producing more cloth than ever before.[93] But the war brought about a collapse. Unfortunately for British textile firms, the wartime disruption of exports and a rise in Indian tariffs stimulated domestic production in India. Meanwhile Japanese firms moved to take over a large share of the vast China market.[94] By 1921, Britain's annual demand for raw cotton had been cut in half, and the trend continued into the next decade. Even though total world consumption of cotton textiles increased between 1914 and 1939, the volume of world trade in cotton goods fell by one-third. By the 1930s British cotton exports had fallen by at least 60 percent from their prewar level, leaving Lancashire's cotton mills little hope for the future (see Table 3.11).[95]

The numbers in Table 3.11 suggest that Britain had no choice but to redirect its economy.[96] In a sense, the First Industrial Revolution was transplanted after World War I to other parts of the globe, especially to southern and eastern Asia. By the 1920s, it was becoming obvious that for British capitalism to remain competitive with other leading western nations, it would have to regain ground it had already lost in the capital-intensive industries characteristic of the Second Industrial Revolution.[97]

BRITAIN'S ROLE IN SECOND INDUSTRIAL
REVOLUTION INDUSTRIES

As Table 3.12 suggests, in 1919 Britain had no giant firms in mass-production staple industries such as steel and chemicals. Each of the top three firms listed was still controlled by families or individual founders.[98] Their companies, though very substantial, were relatively small com-

Table 3.11   The Decline of Britain's Cotton Textile Industry

	% of World Output	Exports (millions of yards)
1830	57	442
1913	20	7,075
1930	12	2,491
1955	5	534

Note: World output percentages are three-year averages incorporating the year listed, except for the 1930 figure, which is for 1926–28.
Source: Adapted from Lars Sandberg, *Lancashire in Decline* (Columbus: Ohio State University Press, 1974), pp. 4, 179.

Table 3.12   Britain's Five Largest Companies in 1919

Company	Industry	Capital
1. J. & P. Coats	Textiles	£45.0m
2. Lever Bros.	Food, Soap	24.3
3. Imperial Tobacco	Tobacco	22.8
4. Vickers	Armaments, Ships	19.5
5. Guinness	Brewing	19.0

Note: This table differs from the tables for 1907 and 1935 owing to a general scarcity of data on employees from this period.

Source: Leslie Hannah, *The Rise of the Corporate Economy* (1976; London: Methuen, 1983), p. 189.

pared with the largest American companies. Many critics took this as a sign of national failure.

In the world of American capitalism, family control of really big businesses had generally given way to the large multi-unit corporation run by hierarchies of salaried managers.[99] One prominent historian has gone so far as to describe the prevailing style of British business as "personal capitalism."[100]

Many British industries continued to be driven by atomistic competition among small firms that resisted amalgamations. Owing to this competitive style of enterprise, the argument goes, the Second Industrial Revolution produced only a handful of British firms on anything like the scale typical of companies in the United States, Germany, and later Japan. British firms were thus at a disadvantage versus companies in these other countries, the argument continues, because large, capital-intensive firms had a superior capacity to innovate and to harness fully the new economies of scale and scope.

This reasoning may be logically valid on its own terms. But one should note that four of the top five companies listed in the table were destined to succeed in the Second Industrial Revolution, in the field of mass-produced, branded consumer goods. The top two, J. & P. Coats and Lever Brothers (which later became Unilever), were particularly strong exporters. Also, in spite of the Great Depression in the 1930s, Britain's manufacturing sector did relatively well, growing by 3.2 percent per year from 1924 to 1937. That figure was substantially higher than Britain's manufacturing growth had been in the half-century before World War I.[101]

Thus, out of the residue of the First Industrial Revolution, Britain managed to find a niche for itself in the Second Industrial Revolution.[102] Between the end of World War I and the beginning of rearmament in the mid-1930s, British firms advanced steadily in a number of Second Industrial Revolution industries (see Table 3.13).

As we shall see below, World War II accelerated this trend. Britain emerged from it as a major exporter of heavy manufactured goods. Ironically, however, Britain's Second Industrial Revolution industries experienced a sharp upturn just as these sectors were themselves becoming less profitable than the more technologically advanced industries of the Third Industrial Revolution.[103]

The economic outlook in Britain was generally pessimistic during the interwar period from 1919 to 1939. The Great Depression caused serious unemployment, which was alleviated only through rearmament beginning in 1936. During these years, many people began to wonder whether Britain had lost its collective soul when, generations before, it had staked its future on industrial capitalism. Statistically, Britons were better off in the 1920s and 1930s than they had been during the First Industrial Revolution, and yet numerous British workers continued to lack basic economic security and comfort.

A great social critic of the thirties and forties, George Orwell, complained that "In a crowded, dirty little country like ours one takes defilement almost for granted. Slag-heaps and chimneys seem a more normal, probable landscape than grass and trees, and even in the depths of the country when you drive your fork into the ground you half expect to lever up a broken bottle or a rusty can."[104] In his short lifetime (1903–1950), Orwell witnessed the two worst wars in human history, both of

Table 3.13 Britain's Five Largest Manufacturing Employers in 1935

Company	Industry	Employees (est.)
1. Unilever	Food, Chemicals	60,000
2. Guest, Keen & Nettlefold	Metals	50,000
3. Imperial Chemical Industries	Chemicals	49,700
4. Vickers	Armaments, Ships	44,200
5. London, Midland & Scottish Railway	Transport	41,300

Source: Adapted from Lewis Johnman, "The Large Manufacturing Companies of 1935," in R. P. T. Davenport-Hines, ed., *Business in the Age of Depression and War* (London: Frank Cass, 1990), p. 33.

which were driven by the efficient organizational systems of the Second Industrial Revolution. In his classic novel *1984*, published in 1948, Orwell warned that mass production could serve totalitarian purposes and lead to wars without end.

The Experience of British Labor in the First Two Industrial Revolutions

MONEY, FOOD, AND SOCIAL CHANGE

Over the three centuries since the Glorious Revolution of 1688, the structure of British society had evolved significantly under the many changes associated with capitalism. Even before the First Industrial Revolution began in the eighteenth century, the British way of life was gradually being altered by market forces. Many English landowners had committed themselves to improving their fields and adopting modern farming techniques. Over a period of centuries, British landowners and their tenants had been permitted to displace peasants from communal lands and hire them instead as wage laborers.[105] Preindustrial England thus became a pioneer in having a large percentage of its working population linked to employers solely through the cash nexus.

The widespread use of cash and credit is one of the defining features of modern capitalism. Using cash instead of barter as the medium of exchange makes it much easier to set and enforce prices, thereby reducing the uncertainty felt by both producers and consumers. The introduction of an efficient market system in Britain and elsewhere no doubt helped to increase the supply of food in the long term. In the short term, however, it could actually hurt consumers. If the price of bread climbed too high (if, say, there was a bad harvest), people became desperate. Sometimes they rioted until merchants were ordered by local magistrates to lower the price. In this context, a necessary precondition for a market-based economy was the capacity of producers and merchants to supply enough bread, and at a low enough price, to prevent riots and make further state intervention unnecessary.[106]

In the long run, England's merchants and farmers were able to keep their end of the bargain. They delivered so well that the population was able to grow rapidly after the mid-1700s (see Table 3.14).

In 1798, the moral philosopher Thomas Malthus warned ominously that the British population was now growing at a faster rate than the

Table 3.14   England's Population (millions)

1701	1801	1851	1901	1951	1991
5	9	17	33	44	51

Sources: For: 1701 to 1851: E. A. Wrigley and R. S. Schofield, *The Population History of England, 1541–1871* (Cambridge: Cambridge University Press, 1989), p. 529. For later years: Central Statistical Office, *Annual Abstract of Statistics, 1996*, p. 16.

Table 3.15   Agricultural Workforce in Britain (% of labor force)

	1700	1800	1870	1910	1995
	61	41	20	12	1

Note: Numbers for 1700–1910 are for male labor only.
Sources: Adapted from Crafts, *British Economic Growth*, p. 62. For 1995: Central Statistical Office, *Annual Abstract of Statistics, 1996*, pp. 126–127.

food supply.[107] The result, he predicted, would be a catastrophic famine. But in fact, England avoided this fate through extensive investments in both farming and infrastructure, and through imports of food.

Not only did the population survive and continue to grow, but by 1800, if not sooner, a majority of British workers were no longer employed in growing food (see Table 3.15).

This stunning decline of agriculture as an occupation was unprecedented in history. Beginning with the Neolithic age, civilizations had always been defined by the social organization of the farm. But by the beginning of the nineteenth century, Britain, along with one or two other countries such as Holland, had become a truly *modern* society with a novel organization of production.

By the late nineteenth century, Britain's food supply was effectively globalized. This process drove domestic prices down and put many British farmers out of work. Such willing dependence on foreign markets for food was unheard of in European history, but for an island nation with a large population, it was the necessary basis for an industrial revolution. Many decades later, Japan would experience a very similar transition. By the mid-twentieth century, a small agricultural workforce would be regarded as one of the main characteristics separating the "developed" nations from the rest of the world.

HUMAN CAPITAL IN THE FIRST INDUSTRIAL REVOLUTION

In the heyday of the First Industrial Revolution, Adam Smith had described the English as a "nation of shopkeepers," which indeed they were. Retail trade was one of England's most common occupations besides farming, and that in itself was a sure sign of economic sophistication.[108] Preindustrial Britain had prided itself on having a strong "middling" element, in between the very rich and the mass of poor people. As Samuel Johnson observed in 1775, "The great in France live very magnificently, but the rest very miserably. There is no happy middle state as in England. The shops of Paris are mean; the meat in the markets is such as would be sent to a gaol in England."[109] Johnson's comment reflects the smug optimism many English people felt during the First Industrial Revolution. Yet many British cities and regions during the First Industrial Revolution were afflicted by extreme poverty, filth, violent crime, and the widespread abuse of cheap gin.

Charlotte Brontë's novel *Shirley,* published in 1849, centered on the economic and social unrest caused by the introduction of power looms a generation earlier. The new looms eliminated jobs in regions such as Yorkshire that were heavily dependent on the textile industry. Brontë described the machines as part of a "moral earthquake." The laborers who suffered most "drank the waters of affliction." Misery bred hate, and the workers "hated the machines which they believed took their bread from them; they hated the buildings which contained those machines; they hated the manufacturers who owned those buildings."[110]

It was no accident that Britain in the 1840s became the chief inspiration for Karl Marx and Friedrich Engels, two German expatriates who spent much time in Britain. Engels himself owned a factory in Manchester. In his landmark book of 1844, *The Condition of the Working Class in England,* Engels described in detail the wretched living conditions in many British cities.[111]

Economists have debated whether Britain's population growth might have retarded the growth of wages, and it is probable that the country's relatively large workforce made labor marginally less expensive than it was in North America.[112] For manufacturers this was a double-edged sword, since low wages stimulate aggregate demand less than do high wages. In Britain's case, real wages did rise during and after the First Industrial Revolution, dramatically in comparison to the trend of the previous thousand years. But even so, the rate of increase was insufficient to relieve mass poverty, until well into the twentieth century (see Table 3.16).

In the 1830s and 1840s, Parliament began to pass effective workplace regulations that eventually banned child labor in factories and improved the overall conditions of work. The Factory Act of 1833 limited children's working hours in textile mills. Those under the age of 9 were prohibited from factory work. Those under 13 could not work more than 9 hours a day, and those over 13 but under 18 no more than 12 hours. The law permitted children to come to the mills in relays, thereby allowing the mills to function 14 to 16 hours a day. This act paved the way for additional factory and mine regulation in the next decade.

By the 1840s, women could no longer be hired to drag coal out of mines. In the textile industry, the workday was reduced from 12 or 13 hours a day to 10, which had long been the norm in other industries. (By the 1870s, trade union pressure would limit the workday to 8 or 9 hours in many industries.)[113] At the same time, health and sanitary regulations were enacted, and these laws made the industrial cities somewhat more livable.

But such efforts did little to alleviate the sheer bleakness of working-class life. In the novel *Hard Times* (1854), Charles Dickens described an archetypal industrial city, which he called Coketown: "several large streets all very like one another, and many small streets still more like one another, inhabited by people equally like one another, who all went in and out at the same hours, with the same sound upon the same pavements, to do the same work, and to whom every day was the same as yesterday and tomorrow, and every year the counterpart of the last and the next."[114]

The factory system was a crude, even brutal mechanism for social engineering, as employers tried to break preindustrial patterns of work.[115] For instance, before the factory system took hold, it had been

Table 3.16 Growth of Real Wages

	% per Year
1780–1851	.80
1856–1973	1.4

Sources: Adapted from Matthews, Feinstein, and Odling-Smee, *British Economic Growth*, p. 171. For 1780–1851: Crafts, *British Economic Growth*, p. 103.

customary for many workers to take Mondays off (often to drink alcohol) and then work harder late in the week to make up the difference. But "Saint Monday," as it was called, ran against the need for strict factory discipline, so it was gradually suppressed.

One way for employers to control the work more effectively was to hire women and children, who in this era enjoyed few rights. In 1862, a manager in the metal trades declared: "it is a pity that females should work in factories at all, as it interferes with their proper life, the domestic. They are, however, very useful. We have employed them [in jobs] which were formerly done by men, who were so much more difficult to keep steady at their work."[116] When they could, some women did observe Saint Monday, though not necessarily to visit the local tavern. Elizabeth Pritchard, a worker in the metal trades during the 1840s, said that she "Don't work much on Monday, don't play, but do washing, and fetch coal, and other work for the home."[117] That was the pattern of life for most working women.

For factory owners, the risks of running a business during the First Industrial Revolution led to a strategy of accumulating no more than the bare minimum of financial, physical, and human capital. Many owners opposed factory legislation on the grounds that it would hurt their ability to compete. One insightful historian has observed that the biggest accomplishment of management in the First Industrial Revolution was "in getting a lot of workers into industry rather than obtaining high productivity from them once there."[118] By eighteenth-century standards, even minimal growth in productivity was likely to boost output and profitability by a substantial margin, as we saw in the chapter on Josiah Wedgwood's experience in the late eighteenth century.

THE RISE OF ORGANIZED LABOR IN THE SECOND INDUSTRIAL REVOLUTION

There was resistance to union activity in Britain throughout the First Industrial Revolution, and well into the Second. Yet organizers persisted in their efforts, and, despite opposition from both business and government, by the late nineteenth century the British union movement was the world's strongest.[119]

At first, British trade unions represented only skilled workers, the "labor aristocracy." During this period the biggest concern of such workers in Britain (and in other countries as well) was to defend their craft against the introduction of mass-production methods. From the beginning, craft unions in Britain were relatively conservative organizations. In many cases the leaders of these unions were more interested in providing social services to their own members than in doing serious battle with the capitalist order. When unskilled workers began to unionize in the 1880s, their leaders did initially call for a radical approach to politics. But within a short time they too became more moderate in their approach.[120]

The trade union movement, with its mostly craft outlook and its sheer numerical strength, became an important factor in Britain's noticeably slow managerial and technical response to the Second Industrial Revolution. The conservative outlook of trade unions was reinforced by the conciliatory approach that most British managers took when dealing with them. Rather than fighting the unions for total control of the shop-floor, as many American employers chose to do, British owners and managers were often willing to concede a share of power in return for labor peace and stability in work practices.[121]

As the Second Industrial Revolution unfolded, British managers continued to see unions more as a threat to wage rates than to innovation. This attitude was a holdover from the old days, when variable costs tended to be much higher than fixed costs as a percentage of total costs, and the only practical way to reduce expenses was by cutting wages or laying off workers.[122]

At the turn of the twentieth century, only the most far-sighted employers understood the concept of organizational efficiencies as a way to lower production costs and raise productivity. In the United States, Henry Ford in 1914 adopted his famous "five-dollar day" policy, in which workers received this princely sum, double the usual wage, in return for accepting whatever work practices Ford's efficiency experts laid out for them. And, of course, they could not so much as speak of joining a labor union. In Britain, innovations such as Ford's were often seen as foolish gimmicks, more likely to upset labor-management relations than to increase company profits.

The relatively conciliatory approach of many British employers did not eliminate conflict between organized labor and industry, however. By the 1900s trade unionists had the power to disrupt production in the most strategic sectors of the British economy: coal, shipbuilding, railways, and cotton. During the decade before World War I there was a steady increase in union membership and an increasing militancy in the face of management efforts to limit union power. In cotton and coal, among other industries, strikes tended to reflect the health of the economy, as workers took advantage of good times to fight for higher wages.[123]

SOCIALISM AND THE LABOUR PARTY

The growing strength of organized labor was accompanied by mounting tensions in British politics. The biggest goal of British socialists was to form a political party to represent the trade unions in Parliament. This effort ultimately led to the creation of the Labour Party, which first took shape in 1900. To most British industrialists, the very presence of a socialist party in Parliament was anathema, especially since the Labour Party by 1918 was officially committed to abolishing the capitalist system.

In practice, it never actually tried to do this. In fact, many socialists in Britain, beginning with Karl Marx himself, agreed with capitalists that free markets were necessary for social progress. In the end, Marx believed, it was the market itself that would destroy the ancient system of private property rights. The old system permitted a small group of nonworkers (landowners, stockholders, and especially bondholders) to exploit the mass of workers who actually added value to goods and services. This belief in the market as an engine of progress sharply divided British socialists as a group from their more radical counterparts in Germany and Russia. There, socialists often argued that progress could only come about by eliminating market forces through a violent revolution and state control of all production.

Ultimately, the British Labour Party decided that what the masses really needed was a labor market that worked better. A noted Marxist historian has written that the reason British workers were exploited in the First Industrial Revolution was simply that they had not yet mastered the "rules of the game." By this he meant that they had been pushed into the factory system without the right to organize and with no received knowledge of how to negotiate with management. But workers gained the necessary experience rather quickly once the law upheld their right to join trade unions and bargain collectively.[124]

Over time the labor movement also benefited from the circumstance that it was never an exclusively working-class phenomenon. In the early days, the leadership of the British socialist movement included a large number of influential, well-to-do, and thoroughly "respectable" members of the educated middle and upper classes. As a group, these leaders believed wholeheartedly in a "scientific" way of reforming industrial capitalism. They emphasized careful research and public discussion, and they abhorred revolutionary violence.

The Third Industrial Revolution, 1940s to the Present

CAPITALISM VERSUS SOCIALISM

The Labour Party gained strength during the 1920s, and, despite an electoral setback in 1931, grew steadily in influence during the 1930s and early 1940s. It finally won a majority in the national election of July 1945. During the Second World War, the need to mobilize the economy for a total war had left Great Britain no choice but to engage in social and economic planning on an unprecedented scale.[125] For example, almost every kind of consumer product was rationed. Even the number of courses in restaurant meals was regulated. To a large extent, civilian control of investment, the heart of the capitalist system, was effectively put on hold.

This entire era proved socially and politically traumatic. In the space of 31 years (1914–1945), Britain experienced two world wars and the Great Depression. In the minds of many Britons, these three crises, taken together, seemed to repudiate the great hope of nineteenth-century capitalists that peace on earth could be achieved through the mechanism of private property and the global market. By the 1940s, many Britons had become convinced that the policy of *laissez faire* had been rendered obsolete, maybe even immoral. In that first postwar election of 1945, the Labour Party's historic victory amounted to a public endorsement of the wartime idea of a "mixed" economy, in which private enterprise was closely regulated by the state, some industries were nationalized, and purchasing power was augmented by public expenditures.[126]

This idea had been developed theoretically during the interwar years, most notably by John Maynard Keynes. An economist trained in the neoclassical tradition, Keynes was deeply concerned by the failure of market mechanisms during World War I. Matters became very much worse during the Great Depression, when a series of bank failures intensified a sharp downturn in the business cycle. With unemployment in Britain at about 25 percent in the early 1930s, Keynes argued that government should act to stabilize the financial system and stimulate demand through increased public-sector employment. Keynes's goal was not to replace market forces with government planning, but rather to restore the health of national and international markets. In practical terms, Keynes's mixed economy represented a compromise between capitalism, as represented by the Conservative Party, and moderate socialism, as represented by the Labour Party.

For Labour politicians, the mixed economy meant two basic policies: first, a welfare state providing "cradle to grave" coverage for health, housing, and education needs; and second, a large and steady pool of trade union jobs, if necessary through the nationalization of heavy industries. For the British masses, this program offered a degree of economic security that past generations of workers had only dreamed of. More Britons belonged to trade unions after 1945 than ever before, and this was both a cause and a consequence of the Labour Party's rise to power (see Table 3.17).

Ironically, the British labor movement reached its historic peak at just the moment when Britain entered the Third Industrial Revolution. In the long run, the Third Industrial Revolution benefited and relied on white-collar workers much more than on the traditional blue-collar trades.

The Conservatives returned to power in 1951, but after Winston Churchill's retirement from government in 1955 at the age of 81, the Party had a weak appetite for ideological conflict with the Labour Party or even with the trade unions. A succession of Conservative Prime Ministers—Harold Macmillan, Alec Douglas-Home, and Edward Heath—dutifully paid lip service to capitalist principles. But they were more than willing to compromise with moderate socialists. Many Conservatives were amenable to some government intervention in the economy, especially if it brought greater stability to markets. It might thereby help to

Table 3.17 Trade Union Membership (millions)

1888	1913	1939	1948	1972	1982	1992
.75	4	6	9	11	12	9

Sources: For 1888: Clegg, Fox, and Thompson, *A History of British Trade Unions since 1889*, vol. 1, p. 1. For 1913 and 1939: Mitchell and Deane, *Abstract of British Historical Statistics*, p. 68. For later years: Central Statistical Office, *Annual Abstract of Statistics*, (London: HMSO), various years.

guarantee the sanctity of private property, the essence of the capitalist system.

The appeal of the mixed economy was reinforced by widespread fears in both political parties that unfettered market forces, which had long been England's great ally, had finally turned against British industry for good. After the mid-1960s, Britain experienced an absolute decline in many of its Second Industrial Revolution industries, most notably automobiles.[127] Throughout the period from 1950 to the late 1980s, and especially in the years after 1965, Britain suffered a sharp fall in total industrial employment, the very thing voters had expected the Labour Party's influence to prevent (see Table 3.18).

This trend in Britain, which reflected a dramatic rise in competition from Asia, was no doubt a victory for market forces. But of course it was a victory neither Labour nor the Conservatives wished to celebrate.

As an overarching public policy, Britain's mixed economy was tested strongly in the 1980s and early 1990s by the Conservative Party, especially under Prime Minister Margaret Thatcher. Her belief, expressed through the privatization of state-owned enterprises, was that Britain could not hope to prosper except through the strict discipline imposed by unregulated market forces, with almost no resort to state planning or public investment. The Labour Party, meanwhile, continued to argue that some form of government intervention (though short of state ownership) would be necessary to revitalize the nation's manufacturing base.

The mixed economy, as a compromise between the historical visions of capitalism and socialism, did not produce a convincing solution to what is perhaps Britain's greatest challenge in trying to compete in the Third Industrial Revolution: steady gains in productivity across leading industrial nations. By historical standards, each of the countries listed

Table 3.18   Industrial Labor (% of workforce)

	Britain	Germany	U.S.	Japan
1950	49	44	36	24
1987	30	41	27	34

Note: Number for Japan is based on 1955.

Source: Adapted from N. F. R. Crafts and N. W. C. Woodward, "Introduction and Overview," in Crafts and Woodward, eds., *The British Economy Since 1945* (Oxford: Clarendon Press, 1991), p. 12.

Table 3.19   Productivity Growth (GDP per employee hour—% increase per year)

	Britain	Germany	U.S.	Japan
1950–73	3.2	6.0	2.4	7.6
1973–86	2.5	3.0	1.2	3.1

Source: Adapted from Angus Maddison, *The World Economy in the 20th Century* (Paris: OECD, 1989).

below achieved a remarkably high rate of productivity growth after World War II. The problem for Britain was that it had trouble keeping up with the growth rates of Japan, Germany, and several other Asian and European countries (see Table 3.19).

THE END OF EMPIRE

For Britain, the political implications of the Third Industrial Revolution have been profound, and continue to be so. More than half a century after World War II, Britain's role in the international community remains ambiguous and open to dispute. The Cold War (1947–1989) effectively divided the world into two spheres led by the USA and the USSR. This conflict reduced Britain to the status of a second-tier power for the first time in several centuries.

Meanwhile, Britain also became comparatively smaller as a commercial center. Its share of world exports fell steadily after 1945, the direct result of increased competition for new as well as existing markets. In 1950, Britain still produced 26 percent of the world's total manufactured exports, but by the late 1980s it produced only around 8 percent.[128] This significant loss of economic power fueled a long public debate in Britain over what might have gone "wrong" with the economy. Nevertheless, in per capita terms Britain has actually continued to be among the world's most successful exporters (see Table 3.20).

Thus, Britain's economic decline has been mostly a relative phenomenon. What *has* declined absolutely is the British empire. World War II robbed Britain and the other European powers of the financial wherewithal and the political will to rule global networks of colonies. Britain's most important colony, India, achieved full independence in 1947. India soon adopted protectionist policies and began to trade more with the Soviet Union than with the West. Britain's African colonies largely fol-

Table 3.20   Manufactured Exports, Performance Relative to Population
(100 = country average)

	Britain	Germany	U.S.	Japan
1913	272	17	53	149
1973	117	87	51	259

Note: The average performance includes Italy and France along with the four countries shown here.

Sources: Adapted, with permission, from a manuscript by Leslie Hannah, 1995. Numbers from Alfred Maizels, *Industrial Growth and World Trade,* and GATT, *International Trade Statistics* (1987); population data from Angus Maddison, *Dynamic Forces in Capitalist Development.*

Table 3.21   Distribution of Britain's Visible Exports (%)

	Western Europe	U.S.	Japan	Settler Colonies	Other Countries
1913	37	9	2	15	37
1951	29	6	0.4	28	37
1983	57	14	1	5	23

Source: Adapted from R. E. Rowthorn and J. R. Wells, *Deindustrialization and Foreign Trade* (Cambridge: Cambridge University Press, 1987), p. 185.

lowed the Indian example, leaving Britain with little influence in the developing world and only a scattering of small colonies, including places as diverse as Hong Kong (until 1997) and Bermuda.

In addition to losing its colonies, Britain also lost its informal commercial empire, as Table 3.21 shows. Note especially the decline in trade with what had been Britain's "settler colonies": Canada, Australia, New Zealand, and South Africa. Through the first half of the twentieth century, these countries had provided relatively secure and lucrative markets for British exports. But by the 1980s, their economies had to a large extent become integrated with regional economic powers—Canada with the United States, Australia and New Zealand with Japan. Meanwhile, South Africa under apartheid had become, along with Rhodesia, more a thorn in Britain's diplomatic pride than a lucrative market. The upshot of all this was that Britain now found itself a regional power only, with most of its visible exports going to Western Europe.

Table 3.22   Britain's Trade Balance (£ million)

	1954	1974	1994
Invisible	+ 325	+ 2,034	+ 8,910
Visible	− 204	− 5,351	− 10,738

Source: Central Statistical Office, *Annual Abstract of Statistics* for 1965, 1975, 1986, and 1996.

FINANCE AND BRITAIN'S ROLE IN THE EUROPEAN
COMMUNITY

During the decades after World War II, Britain maintained its nineteenth-century pattern of being dependent on invisible trade (see Table 3.22). The rapid advance of communications technology during the Third Industrial Revolution created an exceptional opportunity for the City of London, by greatly expanding the international market for financial services. In 1986, the London Stock Exchange adopted an unprecedented series of reforms, accompanied by a broad government deregulation of the financial-services sector. Together these reforms were labeled the "Big Bang," in part because they gave foreign banks and investors essentially unrestricted access to the London market.[129] The changes added to London's natural advantages as a financial center: its location between the New York and Tokyo markets and time zones, and the UK's unbroken 300-year record of political stability and support for private property and financial innovations.[130]

Britain's postwar resurgence as a financial center did not come without a political struggle. After the 1940s British finance became more and more dependent on the European market. And yet, Britain was always a reluctant participant in the European Community (or the European Union, as it came to be called).[131] In the 1950s, Britain first refused to join the European Coal and Steel Community, the direct forerunner of the European Community. Then, in 1957, it backed out of negotiations for the Treaty of Rome, which established the European Community as a formal body. In the early 1960s, Prime Minister Harold Macmillan decided that Britain could no longer avoid joining. But in 1963, French President Charles de Gaulle unilaterally rejected Britain's application. It took two more applications until Britain was finally accepted in 1973. In the 1980s and 1990s, Britain resisted efforts to expand the European

Community into an economic and monetary union with a common currency. Thus, at the end of the twentieth century, Britain was still trying to come to terms with its role as an equal partner with the major European powers and not as their historic adversary.

During the Third Industrial Revolution, Britain has continued to be among the world's richest nations. But in most industries it no longer has the same competitive potential to dominate markets that it had in the nineteenth century. In the developed economies, one of the most striking features of the Third Industrial Revolution has been an acceleration of capital investment. It has been estimated that at the start of the First Industrial Revolution, Britain invested 6 to 8 percent of its Gross National Product in domestic enterprises, and that this number rose to perhaps 12 percent by the 1830s.[132] Compare those estimates with the figures for the top nations of the Third Industrial Revolution (see Table 3.23).

Since the 1960s, many countries have followed the example of Japan, adopting policies favoring a high rate of savings and investment along with an aggressive pursuit of exports. For the most part, Britain has chosen not to imitate Japan's industrial policies. In the 1960s, the Labour Government under Prime Minister Harold Wilson did seek to enhance the nation's technological competitiveness through state planning and large public investments in research and education. But this effort was sharply criticized by Conservatives, for it ran squarely against Britain's centuries-old tradition of letting private interests direct the flow of savings and investment. Even so, in certain very capital-intensive industries such as aerospace, it is questionable whether firms in any country can hope to compete without substantial government assistance in one form or other. This issue will be a focal point of the next chapter of this book, on Rolls-Royce.

In various industries, Britain's domestic investment record has been

Table 3.23   Total Investment (% of GDP)

	Britain	Germany	U.S.	Japan
1950–59	15	21	17	23
1980–87	17	21	18	29

Source: Adapted from N. F. R. Crafts and N. W. C. Woodward, "Introduction and Overview," in Crafts and Woodward, eds., *British Economy since 1945,* p. 10.

something of a mixed bag. Britain fell behind in developing some important new technologies, especially computers and electronics. Nor did its major domestic automobile firms perform well.

Nevertheless, many British managers showed signs of abandoning their "in-built hunger for the status quo," as one American analyst had called it during the 1960s.[133] One of the world's largest oil companies (BP) was British, and another (Shell) half British and half Dutch. Then, too, British business was invigorated by high levels of foreign direct investment, from the United States and, beginning in the 1970s, from Japan as well. By the 1990s, Britain had reemerged as one of Europe's leading automobile manufacturers, its reconstituted industry almost entirely under the control of American, Japanese, and German firms.[134] British companies have themselves invested effectively in some advanced technologies, notably pharmaceuticals. Glaxo, for instance, became a leader in antibiotics during World War II, and then gained a large share of the global pharmaceutical trade.[135] Burroughs-Wellcome, another elite drug firm, went through a similar transition, then merged with Glaxo in 1995 to form one of the world's strongest pharmaceutical companies.

More generally, Britain has long had one of the most effective service sectors of any country. Many individual firms have a tradition of high-quality service, and they have retained and often increased their level of performance during the years of the Third Industrial Revolution. Not only financial services companies, but also retailers such as Marks & Spencer, and transportation firms such as British Airways, have exhibited strength in global markets.

Conclusion

In assessing the long-term significance of British capitalism, it is important to keep in mind two transcendent facts. First, Britain led the world into the First Industrial Revolution. It reaped the benefits of being first, but it has sometimes had to pay the price exacted of the pioneer.

The second important fact is that from the outset Britain's business system has been distinctly international in its orientation. This may seem to be an obvious point, true of all leading capitalist nations at the end of the twentieth century. But it was not true historically of the other three countries covered in this book. All three—Germany, the United States, and Japan—were, for most of their histories, much more inward-looking than was Britain. They were less dependent on imports and exports, less often involved in foreign wars, and less inclined to become entangled in colonial adventures. In part because of their domestic orientations, they were also less influential as models of capitalist development, at least until the twentieth century.

British capitalism, therefore, has historical significance far beyond the British Isles. Its reliance on individual entrepreneurship, its tendency to trade beyond domestic borders, its heavy emphasis on property rights and the rule of law—all of these traditions have reappeared in other settings throughout the world.[136] This should not surprise us. We should be least surprised of all to find British patterns of doing business reappearing in its former colonies. The United States, India, Canada, Australia, New Zealand, South Africa, Hong Kong, Malaysia, Singapore, and other former colonies have all put their own distinctive stamps on what had been British practice. But the outline remains visible. As the German novelist Thomas Mann once wrote, "Very deep is the well of the past," and the British business experience is perhaps the deepest of all wells in the history of capitalism.[137]

One of the subthemes of the preceding chapter was the effect of war on the evolution of British capitalism. That issue becomes central in the next chapter, entitled "Rolls-Royce and the Rise of High-Technology Industry."

The name Rolls-Royce, of course, usually calls to mind not war but luxury automobiles. Throughout much of the company's history, cars were its main product, and the price was always high. Toward the close of the twentieth century, various models were being sold for prices ranging from about $180,000 to $350,000.

But by this time cars were no longer the company's core business, and the reasons why could be traced to the experience of war. Temporarily during World War I and then permanently during World War II, military necessity turned the firm's primary attention away from automobiles and toward aeronautical engines. The transition from making cars to making aero engines was difficult in 1914 and 1915, and even more so between 1939 and 1945, when the urgency of war mobilization changed the business dramatically. During those years, Rolls-Royce was called upon to produce annually not a few hundred or a few thousand cars, but many tens of thousands of aero engines.

In the last part of the twentieth century, Rolls-Royce's primary business became engines for many types of aircraft, notably jumbo jets. At times the manufacture of very high-priced engines required the financial help of the British government, which was forced to develop a national "industrial policy" for this line of products. The same pattern prevailed in the United States for Rolls-Royce's chief competitors in the market for big jet engines, General Electric and Pratt & Whitney.

Somewhat like British industry in general, Rolls-Royce never took to mass-production methods in the way many American firms did. Its main competency had to do instead with the design, manufacture, and constant improvement of very high-quality machines. Luckily, in most of Rolls-Royce's operations, mass-production methods were not absolutely essential, even under the tremendous pressures of World War II. When American-style mass production did become unavoidable during that war, Rolls-Royce figured out a way to shift much of the burden to other firms. One of these was the Ford Motor Company, a symbol of mass production.

The key role in planning and executing this transformation of Rolls-Royce during the 1940s was played by Ernest Hives, a professional manager. Placing himself at the center of a complex network of sub-contractors, Hives accomplished a tour de force of the general manager's art. In the process, he came to exemplify both the best of British management and some of its limitations. In Rolls-Royce's remarkable organization chart, reproduced in this chapter, all lines lead to and from Hives. He became an indispensable person within the company. Is that a desirable condition in business? Or is a charismatic leader like Hives sometimes an essential element in getting teams of engineers to work well together in periods of economic emergency?

4

ROLLS-ROYCE AND THE RISE OF
HIGH-TECHNOLOGY INDUSTRY

Peter Botticelli

The Principal Leaders

The legend began in England with three men: the engineer Henry Royce, the racing driver Charles Rolls, and the professional manager Claude Johnson, who became known as the "hyphen in Rolls-Royce." Later a fourth entrepreneur, Ernest Hives, would lead the company through its most crucial test during the Second World War.

As the firm's chief design engineer, Henry Royce (1863–1933) was the true author of all Rolls-Royce's products from the company's founding in 1906 until the early 1930s. Royce's life was a classic rags-to-riches story.[1] His father died when Henry was still a young boy, and after attending school for less than three years, Henry was forced to leave school and go to work as a newsboy. His engineering career began a few years afterward, with a job as an apprentice for the Great Northern Railway. There he learned to repair locomotive engines. His only other formal instruction came from night classes at a polytechnic school in London. During the 1880s, in his twenties, Royce became a pioneer in the emerging electrical industry. By the early 1900s his firm was making electric dynamos and cranes. The business was a success thanks to Royce's extraordinary work habits and his ingenuity in design engineering.[2]

The background of Charles Rolls (1877–1910) could scarcely have been more different from that of Royce. Rolls was the third son of an aristocrat. He was a romantic figure, a man of wealth and privilege who made a name for himself racing cars. He attended Eton, where his love of machines earned him the nickname "Dirty Rolls." During his undergraduate days, he owned one of the first automobiles in Cambridge. In

1902, Rolls became a car dealer in London, trading on his reputation as a racing driver. He sold mainly French cars, then considered the best in the world.

Rolls's partner in the car business was Claude Johnson (1864–1926), who later played a vital role as General Managing Director (chief executive officer) of Rolls-Royce. As a young man Johnson had been an art student in London. This experience led to a career organizing civic exhibitions for government agencies. Soon he developed an interest in cars, and in 1897 he became the first Secretary for what would become the Royal Automobile Club. In 1903 he joined Charles Rolls's car dealership.

Rolls-Royce Begins as a Car Company

Also in 1903, in the midst of a recession, Henry Royce took his first steps in the automobile business. After purchasing a well-regarded French Decauville car, Royce became convinced that he could design a superior product. In characteristic fashion he tore the Decauville apart and then created a new car that met his personal standards. This new "Royce," with two cylinders and ten horsepower, soon caught the eye of Charles Rolls, who was eager to find a worthwhile English car he could bring to market. In May 1904, a meeting was arranged between Rolls and Royce. The two men agreed to form a partnership in which Royce's firm would produce the cars and C. S. Rolls & Co. would be the exclusive selling agent. This arrangement laid the groundwork for a new corporation, Rolls-Royce, founded in 1906.

Like most fledgling automakers at this time, Rolls-Royce seemed to have none too bright a future. In its first year, the company made at least three different models, yet its total output was fewer than one hundred cars. To have any chance of attaining profitability, Claude Johnson argued, Rolls-Royce would have to increase its capital and then aggressively market a single model in quantity. The board of directors therefore decided in late 1906 to increase the firm's capitalization from £60,000 to £200,000. They hoped that with a new factory Rolls-Royce could produce about 200 cars a year.[3]

These were ambitious plans for an automobile manufacturer in 1906. The industry was still populated by small companies that routinely went bankrupt. *Motor Trader* magazine said of Rolls-Royce that "we cannot help thinking the promoters have made a very weak appeal to the investing public. The price is steep for a name only a few years old, and an estimate of future prosperity [is] about as tangible as the Aurora Borealis."[4] Claude Johnson admitted that neither he nor Rolls nor Royce had any "qualification for the conduct of a large manufacturing undertaking. Frankly I am of the opinion that our names as Directors are more or less worthless."[5]

Nevertheless, by the middle of 1907 the company had raised its share capital to about £100,000, which was enough to allow it to build a new plant at Derby, England, located roughly in the center of the country. With its fresh capital, Rolls-Royce was able to expand production of a new six-cylinder car, which was called the 40/50 model. For tax purposes the engine was rated at 40 horsepower, but in practice it actually ran at 50 and in later models at over 100 horsepower.

The 40/50 model was Rolls-Royce's breakthrough, a legendary automobile that it would sell with incremental changes until the 1930s. As a marketing ploy, Claude Johnson named one of the first 40/50s the "Silver Ghost." The body of the Silver Ghost was painted silver and it had genuine silver-plated fixtures and trim. The car became famous after it completed an unprecedented 15,000-mile endurance test, driving up and down the British Isles and stopping only for petrol. Afterward, the car was thoroughly inspected for signs of wear, and the total cost of repairs came to little more than £2. Soon all the 40/50 cars were being referred to as Silver Ghosts regardless of what color they were painted. In the 1990s, the original Silver Ghost continued to be a valuable marketing symbol for Rolls-Royce Motor Cars Limited.[6] Just as the Model T had shaped Ford Motor Company, the 40/50 model set the standard for all of Rolls-Royce's cars, in some respects even to this day. From the very beginning the model was hailed by the motoring press as the best-made car in the world.

The Rolls-Royce Brand

Claude Johnson in 1908 made a marketing decision that changed the direction of the company. Heretofore Rolls-Royce's reputation as a carmaker had been built mainly on the driving exploits of Charles Rolls. In that era, long-distance road races, along with trials, were a popular although very dangerous sport. Rolls's ability to finish such contests underscored the durability and performance of Rolls-Royce cars. But this form of advertising was expensive, as racing still is today, and so Johnson decided that Rolls-Royce should leave the racing scene altogether.

By this time, Charles Rolls himself had grown tired of the car business and had taken up an exciting new hobby, flying. In 1909 he unsuccessfully lobbied the Rolls-Royce board of directors to acquire a British franchise to build the Wright Brothers' aircraft. Early in 1910, Rolls decided to resign from his day-to-day duties at Rolls-Royce and form a new company dedicated to making airplanes. In July of that same year, however, Rolls was killed when his Wright Brothers biplane crashed during a flying competition.

After Rolls's death, the image of Rolls-Royce cars came to be based primarily on elegance and sheer quality rather than speed and sporting performance. As Rolls-Royce cars became better known, their reputation for exclusivity extended even to the factory floor. A Rolls-Royce employee noted that all of the cars were "custom-ordered and since the job cards bore the customer's names, the cars were referred to by their future owners' names as they progressed along the assembly line. These names read like a page out of Debrett's peerage: His Royal Highness the Prince of Wales, the Duke of Westminster, the Maharajah of Patiala, and so on."[7]

In the early days of the auto business, a car's body and interior were usually made by a different company from the one that made the chassis and engine. In the United States, large-scale carmakers such as Ford and General Motors often bought out such firms and did the bodywork themselves, thereby maximizing their own economies of scale. Yet for Rolls-Royce it made sense to continue making only the chassis and engine, leaving the bodywork to companies whose business had been making horse-drawn carriages. One such firm, Barker & Company, had originated in the early 1700s, and had a long association with royalty in Britain. Another firm, Hooper, had originated in the early 1800s. With the addition of fine coachwork by these companies and others, the finished Rolls-Royce car was a true hybrid of modern technology and old-world craftsmanship.[8]

As luxury cars, most Silver Ghosts were usually driven by chauffeurs rather than by the owners themselves. Thus, taking a test drive meant riding in the back while a Rolls-Royce driver demonstrated the Silver Ghost's exceptionally smooth ride and quiet power. Claude Johnson issued a detailed list of instructions to the chauffeurs, including:

> *Politeness:* When opening a door to allow a passenger to get into or out of a car, [chauffeurs] must touch their hats. They must always address customers as "Sir" or "Madam," unless they be titled people, when they must use the proper appellatives—such as to an Archbishop or Duke, "Yes your Grace," "Your Grace's car is here." To a Baron or Earl, "Yes, my Lord," "Your Lordship's car is waiting."

> *Filling up Petrol:* They must fill up petrol at every opportunity (such as at meal times), so that there may be no possibility of a Rolls-Royce car being seen stopped on the road. The act of filling up at the roadside may be mistaken for a "breakdown"—to the damage of the Company.

> *Over-Lubrication:* Over-lubrication of a Rolls-Royce engine, resulting in a visible smelling exhaust, will immediately indicate gross negligence on the part of the driver, who may in this way be responsible for damaging the high reputation of the car.[9]

Johnson's marketing efforts proved vital in the creation of the Rolls-Royce mystique. Perhaps his most lasting contribution was the famous radiator with the winged-lady mascot, called the "Spirit of Ecstasy." In 1911 Johnson commissioned an artist, Charles Sykes, to design this hood ornament, believing that Rolls-Royce needed a distinguishing mark that would be graceful, refined, and highly visible at the same time. Johnson also successfully resisted Henry Royce's efforts to replace the classically inspired radiator grille with something more aerodynamic and practical. As an engineer who preferred function over form, Royce refused to have the silver statue atop the radiator on his own cars.[10]

The Business Grows

The numbers in Table 4.8 at the end of this chapter reveal that Rolls-Royce was a fast-growing business during its first five years. This growth was in line with the expansion of the British automobile industry as a whole before World War I. Between 1909 and 1913, British car production rose by 300 percent. The industry was risky, however. Between 1901 and 1905, 221 British firms entered the auto business, but by 1914 only about 20 of these companies remained. Still others had entered in the meantime.[11]

Rolls-Royce was founded at about the same time as the Ford Motor Company. At first, both firms emphasized building expensive, high-performance cars for racing. But Henry Ford chose a radically different strategy for his Model T, which appeared in 1908. Ford believed that economies of scale would dictate the future of the car business, so he staked his company on a plan to mass produce a single, standardized model, which would then be sold at the lowest possible price. European carmakers, including Rolls-Royce, typically produced in much smaller volumes and sold at higher prices.

The Ford Motor Company began production in the UK in 1911, and by 1913 it controlled as much as 60 percent of the less expensive car market in Britain. In 1913 Ford was making 200,000 cars per year in the United States, while the largest French company, Peugeot, was making only 5,000, and Britain's largest domestic firm, Wolseley, only 3,000. Rolls-Royce was producing about 1,500 cars annually. Rolls-Royce's first chairman, Ernest Claremont (1864–1921), who had been Henry Royce's original partner, said in 1909 that "a works of excessive capacity is apt to induce excessive production, with the inevitable result of spoiling one's own market, since one in such a case is anxious to employ his works at their full capacity, which can only be done by reducing prices and making goods in large quantity, which is often not to one's advantage."[12] Rolls-Royce was then six months behind in filling orders.

The company's nearly absolute dependence on Henry Royce as engineer-in-chief was a vital feature of Rolls-Royce's culture. As early as 1909, when he was in his mid-forties, Royce's habitual overwork led to serious concerns. Ernest Claremont told the board of directors that the lack of regard Royce showed for his health "constituted such a serious menace to the stability of the company that it was the duty of the board to advise the shareholders of the situation since their subscriptions had been obtained largely on Mr. Royce's personality."[13] The board eventually prodded Royce to relinquish all administrative duties, freeing him to concentrate on engineering design. After 1911 Royce stayed away from Derby, spending winters on the French Riviera and summers in the English countryside, joined after 1913 by his design staff.[14] This odd arrangement did little to lessen his tight hold on the company. Nor did

it prevent him from completing some of his finest engineering work and
dramatically reshaping Rolls-Royce's product line during the First World
War.

World War I: Aero Engines

When war broke out in August 1914, it appeared that the company
might have to close its factory. Even before government rationing took
effect, the demand for new cars fell nearly to zero. Many thought the
company was ruined. As Claude Johnson saw the situation, "a week ago
the business was worth a very large sum of money: I cannot say whether
when the bank opens again the bankers may not take the view that Rolls-
Royce is worth nothing at all."[15]

The only chance to keep running was to convert the plant to making
equipment for the war effort. Rolls-Royce was given some miscellaneous
work, including contracts for shell casings and ambulance wagons. The
Army made some use of the Silver Ghost as a staff car. The Royal Family
preferred Daimler cars, but since Daimler was originally a German company, King George traveled in a Silver Ghost until the end of the war. At
the same time, the Silver Ghost chassis proved strong enough to make
into armored cars. As weapons, these strange-looking vehicles were
praised by none other than T. E. Lawrence, who used them in his famous
desert campaigns in the Middle East.

But the demand for armored cars and other military equipment was
not nearly sufficient to keep the Derby factory running. The logical solution, Henry Royce quickly realized, was to make aero engines. At first,
the Rolls-Royce board of directors balked at the idea of making aero
engines because of the heavy capital investment that would be required—
capital that Rolls-Royce did not have in August 1914. The money, like
the orders, would have to come from the British government.[16]

Fortunately for Rolls-Royce, the government itself had decided that
the Derby plant should be used to manufacture under license aero engines
of existing designs. This was a beginning, but for Henry Royce it was
not nearly enough. Royce began to study the government's various engines, including an air-cooled Renault. He decided they were all inferior,
and then threw himself headlong into the job of designing a new engine
from scratch. By early 1915, Royce's new liquid-cooled 225-horsepower
V-12 "Eagle" was ready for testing. Deliveries to the military were being

made within a year. In the end, the Eagle engine became a mainstay of the British war effort, and its role added immeasurably to the growing reputation of Rolls-Royce.

Of course, from the standpoint of business strategy, there was a vast difference between selling luxury automobiles to wealthy individuals and selling aero engines to the British government. Having the state as sole customer meant that Claude Johnson and the board of directors would have to cope with sensitive issues such as wartime profits. Rolls-Royce was determined to avoid reaping excessive profits from the war and thereby being labeled a "merchant of death." As Johnson said, "I do not believe that it is our duty to use our wits to take out of the taxpayer's pocket the highest possible price for the supply of goods which are devised to bring this war to an end."[17] At the same time, the board could not ignore the interests of Rolls-Royce shareholders. One board member said, "We have no earthly right to tell the shareholders that we propose to adopt a purely patriotic attitude and manufacture stuff for the nation at a loss. Our duty is simply to try and make our orders for national departments work out with a reasonable profit."[18]

By late 1917, Henry Royce's hard work was paying off handsomely. The Eagle was in heavy demand by the British military, and by the end of the war Rolls-Royce was making about 50 engines a week. There were plans to increase production to 100 a week and ultimately to 250 (see Table 4.1). Rolls-Royce's production of aero engines proved to be important to the British war effort.[19]

On the surface, Rolls-Royce's efforts to enter a new business and increase its scale of production had brought about a thorough transformation.[20] But the company's success had depended on a small team of design engineers, again led by Henry Royce. As the journal *Aeroplane* noted in 1918, "the time and money spent on experimental and research

Table 4.1   Rolls-Royce Aero Engines: World War I

Engine	Output	Engine Types
Eagle	4,681	10
Hawk	201	2
Falcon	2,185	3
Total	7,067	15

Source: Rolls-Royce Archives.

work in the Rolls-Royce factory are prodigious. Mr. Royce attains his results by getting a number of little improvements from every part. He scraps and alters until he can squeeze out no further improvement in the design."[21]

By the end of the war, the mystique of Rolls-Royce was firmly implanted in the British national psyche. Meanwhile, the company's internal culture had become all but synonymous with the growing legend of Henry Royce. As the article in *Aeroplane* went on to say, "one of the best things in British engineering is that we have a certain class of man who cares more about getting the best out of an article than he does about getting the most money out of it. These men are artists rather than commercial engineers, and in motor engineering Mr. Royce is a fine example of the engineering artist."[22]

This image of Royce fit perfectly with the reputation Claude Johnson had been crafting for the company. Whether the firm was selling luxury cars to aristocrats or aero engines to the military, Rolls-Royce downplayed the fact that its underlying goal was to make a profit. With the success of the Eagle engine, Johnson publicized Royce's passion for engineering as a unique national asset. This marketing emphasis received a spectacular boost in June 1919, when a Vickers Vimy airplane powered by Rolls-Royce Eagle engines made the first nonstop flight across the Atlantic.

The Question of Mass Production after World War I

As Rolls-Royce executives pondered what would happen when the war was over, they had no doubt that reconverting to peacetime production would be a daunting task. The biggest problem was that Rolls-Royce had become a much larger company. The heavy capital buildup needed to move into aero engines and meet wartime demand led many executives to question whether the company could make cars in the same way it had done before the war.

Claude Johnson and Ernest Claremont were concerned that if the enlarged factory was to run at anything like full capacity, Rolls-Royce might have to mass-produce its cars and sell them at much lower prices. However, within the company there was stiff resistance to the idea of abandoning the luxury price and status of the Silver Ghost. For most, it was a simple issue of quality versus quantity: make too many cars and Rolls-Royce would lose its prized exclusivity.[23]

In April 1917, a secret meeting took place involving three firms: Vickers, a major armaments manufacturer; Daimler, one of Britain's leading carmakers; and Rolls-Royce. The meeting had been called to discuss a broad consolidation of the domestic auto industry. There were widespread fears that British cars would not be able to compete after the war, because too few firms had adopted the American approach of standardizing and mass-producing a few models. Under the proposed merger, weak British firms would be forced out of business, while the rest would each concentrate on only one type of car. As was often the case in such mergers in Britain, each of the companies would continue to be controlled by its own board of directors.

Rolls-Royce executives reacted coolly to the proposal. Claude Johnson thought that "Vickers would probably desire to swallow up Rolls-Royce as part of a combination which they would control rather than face Rolls-Royce in open markets. Personally, I would sooner risk Rolls-Royce going out of business than be a part of a combination in which there would be unholy and dirty elements." Johnson did admit that his views might be nothing more than "short-sighted prejudice," but he was loath to see the company's reputation lose any of its shine.[24]

Henry Royce also disliked the idea of a merger, but he saw the potential benefits of some kind of partnership. He realized that "if we want to stay in government work and be in a strong aero position [after the war] we ought to be associated with one of the bigger armament companies." Nevertheless, Royce was determined to keep the firm independent. "From a personal point of view, I prefer to be absolute boss over my own department (even if it was extremely small) rather than to be associated with a much larger technical department over which I had only joint control."[25]

After World War I, the British car industry went through a protracted consolidation. In 1922 there were 88 British companies in the field, where there had previously been hundreds. By 1929 the number was down to 31, with three firms—Morris, Austin, and Singer—together controlling 75 percent of Britain's total output. In 1932, at its huge new Dagenham works, Ford began to make cars in Britain designed specifically for the British market. With these efforts, Ford brought American-style mass-production techniques to the British car industry. Meanwhile, total production of Rolls-Royce cars remained low, a tiny fraction of the number of Ford and Morris cars sold in Britain (see Table 4.2).

By the late 1920s, Henry Royce clearly saw the need for his company to change. He thought it "astounding that we, charging the very top prices, cannot give as good a scheme [of dashboard instruments] as Citroën and Chrysler."[26] By the 1930s, standardized luxury cars such as Cadillac were fast gaining on Rolls-Royce in quality and appearance, and were selling at much lower prices. Royce knew "that *costs are too high* in Great Britain, and especially *in Rolls-Royce*." The problem was that by focusing "on cost only, *with our high standards* of smoothness, silence, reliability, and *durability*, [we] can only shift the cost some 10%, whereas to compare with USA or even British mass production, we need a 50% reduction."[27]

Likewise, a private consulting firm reported that "the policy of Rolls-Royce in the past has been to design the best car in the world and to base the selling price on the cost at which it can be produced under existing conditions at the Derby factory. It is now proposed that the starting point should be the selling price at which there is a market for a car which will still be accepted as better than any other of its class."[28]

The ultimate problem for all British carmakers was having to compete with the American giants, Ford and GM. Henry Royce had no doubt that Britain's auto industry was going to be revolutionized by competition from the large, vertically integrated American companies. In Royce's words, "all the car trade in Great Britain will combine under 1, 2, or 3

Table 4.2   Rolls-Royce Cars, 1920s–30s

	Model	Total Produced	Avg./Year
1922–29	20 horsepower	2,885	361
1925–31	New Phantom	3,453	493
1929–36	20/25 horsepower	3,827	478
1929–35	Phantom II	1,675	239
1935–39	Phantom III	727	145
1936–38	25/30 horsepower	1,201	400
1938–39	Wraith	491	245
	Grand Total	14,259	792

Source: Adapted from Klaus-Josef Roßfeldt, *Rolls-Royce and Bentley* (Somerset, UK: Haynes, 1991), pp. 260–272.

organizations, and each member will be allotted some section of the work and so get rid of wasteful competition and overlapping (bad times will work this upon all the industries of Great Britain), or like many other industries [the car trade] will leave the country."[29]

Royce did not see his own firm in this light, however. The name Rolls-Royce had become synonymous with superior engineering design and the highest possible quality. Royce believed that a large mass-market-oriented firm could not have achieved the same results as Rolls-Royce, in which the work was carried out by small teams of creative, highly skilled and motivated employees. Thus, the way for Rolls-Royce to compete in the age of mass production was to place even more emphasis on quality while also working to cut costs.[30] Royce believed that design engineering was the function that added the most value to Rolls-Royce's products. Above all else, he was determined to maintain an organization with maximum flexibility, which could make improvements at any stage of the production process.

Henry Royce's strategy was profoundly different from that of contemporaries such as Alfred Sloan at GM, because it involved using a minimum of capital rather than the maximum that could be utilized efficiently. There was one area, however, where Royce was determined to spend as much as possible: research and development. Royce said that "We must spend money in the Experimental Department freely but wisely. It forms the heartbeats of our technical efficiency, without which all will be lost."[31] Given that Rolls-Royce could not hope to lower its per-unit cost of production to mass-production levels, Royce recognized that:

> [the] only hope of continuing to be successful appears to be in the flexibility of our system of production, so that we can improve whenever we know how, and so be without fear of becoming fossilized by the production bug. Had we been low cost specialists in any way on the lines of the Americans, naturally we should have been obliged to have other views, but in England, with our small output, our only chance is that our production shall stand out by all-round perfection, rather than price, and the Company must be satisfied if they can make small and safe profits (safe because they are likely to continue).[32]

In 1930, Royce was made a baronet for his service to the nation. (He was thereafter called Sir Henry.) To mark the occasion, he sent an open letter to the Rolls-Royce works, thanking the employees for their efforts. He expressed his hope that "Great Britain with its fine reputation for [products] of lasting quality will not descend to making low quality goods because prices are too low to meet the cost."[33]

Becoming an Aero Engine Company

In the 1930s the luxury car market practically collapsed under the weight of the Great Depression. Rolls-Royce's fortunes in these difficult years were boosted by its new 450-horsepower aero engine, the Kestrel, named after a bird of prey native to the British Isles. Rolls-Royce would sell almost 5,000 of these engines, accounting for the vast majority of its aero sales during the interwar era.[34] In 1931 Henry Royce said "it would appear that the aero work is our greatest hope for profitable business."[35]

In aero engine technology, 1929 marked another turning point for Rolls-Royce. With government support, Henry Royce designed the "R" engine for racing in an important international flying competition, the Schneider Cup. At 1,900 horsepower, the R was a major step for Rolls-Royce in aero engine design. The R enabled Great Britain to win the 1929 Schneider Trophy by powering a Supermarine S-6 airplane at just under 330 miles per hour. The Schneider Cup race was held again in 1931. To compete, Rolls-Royce undertook still another intensive design effort, which enabled the R to fly at 2,350 horsepower. This was sufficient to win the trophy once more. The R later set a new airspeed record of just over 400 miles per hour, and was also used to break speed records on land and water.

Henry Royce at first had been ambivalent about taking on the R engine project, since it held little apparent commercial potential. But he was glad that "it at once brings some work for Derby in these very difficult times. It is all the time advertisement, and we have another chance of impressing the World that we are good aero engine makers, and even if we lose [the Schneider Cup race] it will be better than not fighting provided we put up a good performance to show that *we are* sound *engineers rather than freak inventors*."[36] A total of only twenty R engines were produced but the work was a crucial step forward in technology. It led directly to the design of the 27-liter Merlin aero engine (1933), which was destined to become the most important product in Rolls-Royce's history.

Organization Building and Ernest Hives

Work is the best fun on earth, and working for Rolls-Royce is even better.

—Ernest Hives [37]

In 1937, Rolls-Royce entered a new era when Ernest Hives (1886–1965) became General Manager.[38] Hives's influence within the company, and maybe his personal legend as well, eventually surpassed even that of Henry Royce.

In 1902, according to company folklore, the 16-year-old Ernest Hives was working in a bicycle shop in his hometown of Reading, just outside London. One day Charles Rolls's car broke down as he was passing through town, and Rolls came into the bicycle shop for assistance. Young Ernest promptly fixed the car, and Rolls was so impressed by Hives's mechanical skills that he hired the boy on the spot as his personal mechanic. In 1908 Hives, now 22 years old, joined Rolls-Royce.

Like Henry Royce, Hives was a tireless and determined worker. He also displayed a remarkable grasp of all aspects of the business, from engineering to administration to sales. After Royce moved away from Derby in 1911, Hives's role in the company grew rapidly. He established and ran the Experimental Department. In Royce's absence, he also became responsible for much of the company's production engineering. This experience proved invaluable during the critical years before and during World War II.

Rolls-Royce was very much in need of Hives's leadership. The growing demand for aero engines under rearmament necessitated a dramatic restructuring and expansion of the firm. The challenge was made more difficult, as Hives noted in early 1937, because for many years Henry Royce had "personally made all the decisions as regards engineering policy and design. Most of our present staff of designers worked with him at his private house, so that for 20 or 25 years they were never asked or expected to take any responsibility. One can see the result of that today."[39] Hives's own keen understanding of aero engine technology enabled him to control the organization thoroughly for twenty years, until his retirement in 1957. Every Monday throughout this entire period he presided over a large meeting of the engineering staff, at which he was famous for asking tough questions and giving detailed orders, which he seldom forgot.

Hives's job during World War II was extremely complex and demanding. Table 4.8 at the end of the chapter gives some idea of how Rolls-Royce grew in *scale* during rearmament after the mid-1930s. What the numbers do not reveal is the dramatically increasing *scope* of Rolls-Royce's activities, which made the company much more difficult to manage. After the war began in 1939, Hives had to coordinate production at Rolls-Royce with several hundred subcontractors in the UK and in America. As we will see below, Rolls-Royce also had to start up and manage operations at two new "shadow" factories, which were built at government expense to mass-produce parts for Merlin engines. In addition, Hives served as Rolls-Royce's liaison with the Royal Air Force and chief negotiator with the Air Ministry.

As a manager, Ernest Hives strongly emphasized teamwork, but with the condition that a strong leader, usually he himself, be firmly in charge.[40] From the viewpoint of a top executive, a company dominated by large numbers of engineers and skilled mechanics was far more complicated to manage than the mass-production firms of the Second Industrial Revolution, which employed thousands of unskilled workers. Hives wrote in 1939 that "the Rolls-Royce factory at Derby has been built and developed around the problem of producing high-class engineering in relatively small quantities with the capacity to change or modify the product quickly. In other words, I should describe the Derby factory as a huge development factory rather than a manufacturing plant."[41]

Within the Rolls-Royce organization, Hives's extraordinary competence gave him nearly unquestioned authority as General Manager (1937–46), Managing Director (1946–50), and finally Chairman (1950–57). The organization chart in Figure 4.1, prepared just after the war, shows Hives at the peak of his influence.[42] Note that three members of the board of directors (identified in boxes) were responsible to Hives and not to the board itself.

Rolls-Royce's hierarchy was relatively informal in this era. Many years later, one of Hives's senior engineers, W. A. Robotham, remarked that "for the first twenty-six years I was with Rolls-Royce, I never had an official title." Robotham recalled that Hives had disliked organization charts: "I think Hives's reasoning was that [a] lack of official titles enabled him to switch personnel about as he thought expedient." Hives's

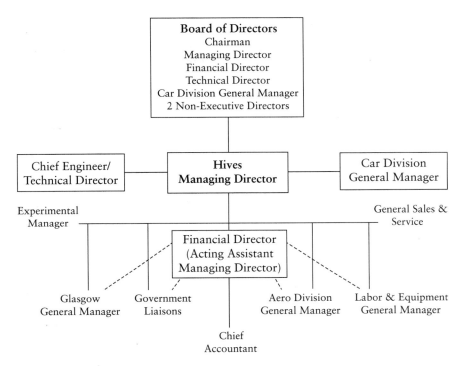

Figure 4.1   Rolls-Royce's Organization, mid-1940s

usual method for dealing with poor performance was "not to demote the man doing a particular job, but rather to bring in someone else at the same time to accelerate progress."[43] In a company of engineers and skilled mechanics, having a title and a spot on the organization chart was less important than knowing one's job on a particular project and making sure it got done properly.

Aero Engines and the Battle of Britain

World War II brought sweeping changes to Rolls-Royce's organization. Between 1939 and 1946 the company made no automobiles at all. But it produced over 80,000 aero engines, four times as many as it had made in all previous years combined. The company's workforce grew from 12,500 in 1939 to almost 60,000 by 1944.

In World War II, military strategy was determined in large part by a nation's capacity for technological innovation. The flexibility Rolls-Royce showed in adapting to wartime demand proved to be a vital national asset. This war was the first in which large military operations hinged on use of the airplane, both as a weapon and for resupplying troops on the ground. In 1939 and 1940, the German Luftwaffe pioneered the use of airplanes in a "Blitzkrieg" ("lightning war") designed to shatter communications and hurt the morale of enemy forces. At first, Britain's Royal Air Force (RAF) was badly outnumbered in the struggle for air supremacy. To survive, Britain needed to increase its output of planes quickly and by a huge multiple. Britain also had to keep up with advanced German technology. Rolls-Royce helped to meet these challenges.

The Battle of Britain (1940) threatened to become the darkest moment in the nation's long history. In the summer of 1940, Hitler's air force launched an all-out assault designed to clear the way for the largest seaborne invasion of Great Britain since 1066. Rolls-Royce, along with the country's airframe manufacturers, found itself squarely on the front lines as Royal Air Force pilots struggled to hold off the attack. The Germans' initial objective was to knock out Britain's air defenses. Thus, the RAF's triumph of 1940 was simply keeping enough planes in the air to harass the Germans and make an invasion too risky to undertake. Between July and September 1940, the number of Merlin-powered fighters in operation rose from roughly 600 to 700, in spite of heavy losses.[44] Once it became clear that Britain was not going to be knocked out of the air, the Germans began to bomb British cities, more to terrorize the population than to gain a strategic advantage. In London, the "Blitz" forced thousands to sleep on Underground (subway) platforms, but it did nothing to weaken Britain's resolve to fight on in the air.

Merlin engines powered some of the most famous aircraft of the war, including the renowned British Spitfire fighter. Rolls-Royce worked closely with the Supermarine company in the development of this plane, which was heavier and better armed than previous fighters, and thus required a much more powerful engine.[45] The Merlin was also used in the Hawker Hurricane, which did even more fighting in 1940 than the Spitfire. In addition, the Merlin was eventually selected for the P-51 Mustang, one of the most effective American fighter planes of the war.

In 1940, during the Blitz, Rolls-Royce operated on 12-hour shifts. Ernest Hives would have asked employees to work even longer hours had he not been bound by wartime labor regulations. During the Battle of Britain, he issued the following message:

> To All Rolls-Royce Workers:
>
> "NEVER IN THE FIELD OF HUMAN CONFLICT WAS SO MUCH OWED BY SO MANY TO SO FEW" said the Prime Minister [Winston Churchill] recently. He was referring to the R.A.F. Pilots, but his words are equally applicable to all who work in the Rolls-Royce factories which turn out engines for Spitfires, Hurricanes and Defiants.
>
> All workers at Rolls-Royce factories have a direct share in the success of the R.A.F. fighters. All free peoples are unanimous in their praise for the work of the R.A.F. fighters—the pilots, the machines and the engines . . .
>
> I am appreciative for all that has been done, and the whole country is grateful for it, but there is such a great responsibility on all Rolls-Royce workers that THERE MUST BE NO LETTING UP, EVEN AT THE EXPENSE OF PERSONAL COMFORT.
>
> "WORK UNTIL IT HURTS" must be our slogan![46]

Manufacturing and Assembling Parts at Rolls-Royce and Its Subcontractors

In Henry Royce's day, Rolls-Royce had nothing like the capabilities needed to produce aero engines on the scale needed in World War II. The British aircraft industry as a whole was in a similar position. When Britain began to plan its rearmament in 1935–36, the immediate task of the Air Ministry was to decide how to increase production in the event of war in Europe. Government officials preferred to build, at state expense, a number of "shadow" factories that would lie dormant until they were needed to mass-produce a particular weapon on short notice. Each shadow factory was tied to a particular company that would provide the necessary management and technical skill.

Ernest Hives, who at that time had just become General Manager of Rolls-Royce, was critical of the Air Ministry's plans. He argued that during the First World War, "all kinds of schemes for expediting the production of aero engines were tried out, but we claim the scheme that gave the most satisfactory results is the one we adopted of [employing] a large number of sub-contractors, controlled by Rolls-Royce."[47] One advantage was cost: "I can promise you that [instead of shadow factories] you would get an infinitely better return for your money by making full use of subcontractors in the USA and Canada to produce Merlin pieces."[48] Rolls-Royce would do the final assembly work and test the completed engines.

Hives believed that the problem of getting aircraft into mass production was easier to solve than the problem of keeping ahead of the Germans in technology. "One is naturally concerned," he wrote in 1937, "because the whole of the Shadow Scheme is built round the production of standardized parts and does not take into account any expansion of technical skill . . . I am firmly convinced in my own mind that where the Germans are well ahead of us is on technical skill."[49] Hives's preferred solution was to let Rolls-Royce concentrate on building *better* engines while other firms worked to build *more* engines. In the end, the RAF's demand for engines was so great that Rolls-Royce had to improvise and do both.

When the Nazi threat became acute in 1938, Rolls-Royce and the Air Ministry agreed to construct shadow factories in order to boost potential output quickly. A new plant would be built at government expense in the town of Crewe, 70 miles northwest of Derby. (After the war the Crewe factory was used to make Rolls-Royce motor cars.) When the war began, another large shadow factory was built at Glasgow, owned by the state but managed by Rolls-Royce. The Glasgow plant began production in September 1940, and by the following year it had over 10,000 employees. This plant was a departure for Rolls-Royce, as it was specifically designed for mass production of parts as well as complete engines, using unskilled labor.[50]

While the Glasgow and Crewe factories were being built, Rolls-Royce was also charged with assembling a network of subcontractors. Early in 1939 company personnel visited about 90 firms in England and Scotland, 25 of which were found to be suitable for building aero engine parts. At the same time, the Engineering and Allied Employers Federation canvassed almost 500 firms, and at least 100 of these companies needed only small modifications in order to do subcontract work for Rolls-Royce. After some negotiating, it was decided that the Air Ministry would supply the necessary machine tools at no charge. Ultimately over 120 companies received machine tools from the state in the effort to increase Rolls-Royce's output.[51]

Hives's faith in subcontracting as a way to raise output was justified by results. The value of labor employed by Rolls-Royce at the Derby and Crewe factories grew by 271 percent between 1939 and 1944. During these same years the value of labor employed by subcontractors producing for Derby and Crewe grew by 252 percent. On average the total value of subcontract labor used was about two-thirds as large as that employed by Rolls-Royce itself.[52]

In addition to its dramatic increase in total shop floor employment during the war years, Rolls-Royce greatly expanded its management staff. The company had employed only 39 managers at the departmental or staff level in 1938, but by 1942 that number had grown to 246. Many of the new managers were promoted from within the firm. The wartime staff at Derby included no outside hires at all, but at Glasgow and Crewe almost 60 percent of the managers were recruited from outside. In addition to hiring more managers, Rolls-Royce had to strengthen its accounting procedures, partly to satisfy the Air Ministry and also to enable Hives to maintain his grasp on the affairs of a company that was now spread around much of the UK.[53]

Production Engineering at Ford and Packard: Mass Production of Complete Merlins

Despite Rolls-Royce's efforts to increase its output through subcontractors and shadow factories, the huge demand for Merlins made it necessary to license the engine to two large mass-production-oriented firms: Ford (UK division), and Packard, a carmaker in the United States. In dealing with Packard, Hives was concerned about the choice of which official would be responsible for insuring the quality of the engine. He argued that "difficulties are bound to arise unless the final inspection is carried out by someone fully conversant with the Merlin engine. In other words, the Merlin engine at present fitted to Hurricanes and Spitfires which are destroying Germans are [sic] not made theoretically to the drawings."[54]

Not following the technical drawings exactly was a normal practice at Rolls-Royce, which before the war had employed highly skilled machinists who could fit parts by hand. This method was well suited to a company whose business was producing high-quality goods in small numbers. But for Packard and Ford, large-scale producers relying heavily on unskilled labor, it was essential that all parts fit together without having to be cut or planed on the shop floor.

One of Rolls-Royce's leading engineers in this period, Stanley Hooker, later acknowledged that his company had much to learn about mass production:

> I considered the Rolls-Royce designs the *ne plus ultra*, until the Ford Motor Co. were invited to manufacture the Merlin in the early days of the War. A number of Ford engineers arrived at Derby, and spent some months examining and familiarizing themselves with the drawings and manufacturing methods. One day their chief engineer said "You know, we can't make the Merlin to these drawings." I replied loftily, "I suppose that is because the drawing tolerances are too difficult for you, and you can't achieve the accuracy." "On the contrary," he replied, "the tolerances are far too wide for us. We make motor cars far more accurately than this. Every part on our car engines has to be interchangeable with the same part on any other engine, and hence all parts have to be made with extreme accuracy, far closer than you use. That is the only way we can achieve mass production."[55]

All of Rolls-Royce's technical drawings had to be re-drafted to meet Ford's more precise tolerances. The job took a year to complete, but mass production made it possible to turn out Merlins in unprecedented quantities (see Table 4.3).

In motor cars the company had always counted its annual output in hundreds rather than thousands. In aero engines, the firm produced 1,700 engines in 1938, 7,100 in 1940, and 17,150 in 1942. Likewise, the value of spare engines and parts delivered to the RAF rose from just over £615,000 in 1938 to about £5,200,000 in 1942. The average building time for each engine dropped from 4,100 hours per engine in 1937 to 2,600 in 1942.[56]

Ernest Hives could have viewed the superiority of Ford and Packard in production engineering and mass-production capabilities as a threat, but in fact he did not see these companies as direct competitors. In his view, Rolls-Royce's business was centered on design engineering and the production of new engine types, which required an unusual degree of flexibility to make changes on the shop floor. "It has got to be realized," Hives wrote, "that with the planned production of 4,000 engines a month from the USA plus Fords plus Glasgow plus Crewe, the whole of the engineering is dependent on Derby. The only reason the Merlin production has gone up, and the only reason the USA are willing to produce 4,000 engines a month is because they are the best engines to be produced."[57] Ford made only five types of Merlins during the war, while Rolls-Royce made 101.[58] Hives was determined that Rolls-Royce would earn its keep by being the best at research and development.

Rolls-Royce's basic strategy in the making of aero engines was to control the two ends of the production process shown in Figure 4.2: *design engineering* along with *testing and installation* and *service and repair.* For aero engines, these three functions were the most technically demanding and the highest in value added, and they were the ones in which Rolls-Royce had the skills and experience to lead rather than follow. Rolls-Royce's competence in these three areas was all the more important given that the field service functions provided a critical stream of information for the design engineers back in Derby, as indicated by the feedback lines at the bottom of the diagram. In the end, it was the design engineers at Derby who set the quality and reliability standards for the Merlin, while many companies participated in the manufacturing process.

Table 4.3   Rolls-Royce Merlin Engines, 1935–1951

	Total Engines	Engine Types
Derby	32,376	63
Crewe	26,065	18
Glasgow	23,647	20
Rolls-Royce	82,088	101
Ford (U.K.)	30,428	5
Total U.K.	112,516	
Packard (U.S.)	55,523	
Grand Total	168,039	

Note: Figures include the 37-liter Griffon engine, which was a Merlin design scaled up by 24 percent. The table does not include spare engines, along with others that were repaired or overhauled. Also not included is the unsupercharged model, the Meteor, which was used in the Cromwell tank. Finally, a substantial but unknown number of Merlins were built in the United States by Continental Motors Corporation.

Source: Rolls-Royce Archives.

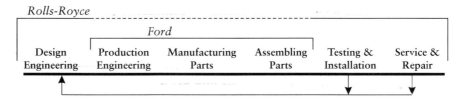

Figure 4.2   Functional Steps in the Output of Merlins

The lines at the top of Figure 4.2 indicate which functions were performed by Rolls-Royce and which by Ford. The Rolls-Royce line shows that it performed all functions. However, in *production engineering, manufacturing parts,* and *assembling parts,* Hives's preferred strategy, as the dotted line shows, was to put Rolls-Royce at the center of a large network of subcontractors who would make parts in quantity while Rolls-Royce itself concentrated on the final assembly. In fact, the wartime demand for Merlins was so great that Rolls-Royce had no choice but to invest heavily in all stages, including *production engineering* and *manufacturing parts.* Ford, in turn, concentrated on the manufacturing processes it had pioneered as a mass producer of automobiles.

Design Engineering: Small Changes, Not Radical Innovations

World War II was a war of technologies, in which both sides invested vast resources in an attempt to build superior weapons. The Allies prevailed in part because they had the benefit of a large network of private firms willing to cooperate with government agencies, academic institutions, and each other. This kind of partnership made possible not only the large output of Merlin engines but also a whole series of other major efforts, most notably the huge Manhattan Project in the United States, which developed the atomic bomb.

As Rolls-Royce's strategist and chief salesman, Ernest Hives understood that what the company could offer most was engineering skill and experience, even more than the finished engines it delivered. Its great service to the British war effort came from Rolls-Royce's ability to improve the engine continually and to keep up with the constantly changing demands of the RAF. In Hives's mind it was highly inefficient to require every change in the Merlin to be cleared with the Air Ministry officials in London before it could be implemented. Ultimately, he preferred that all final decisions on equipment be left to the RAF pilots themselves. Thus, Hives wrote that "we—Rolls-Royce—find there is far too much delay in getting [engine] improvements through all the technical departments. We want to modify a machine and get the criticism or approval from the man who is going to use them against the enemy."[59]

As anxious as Hives was to make changes and improve the Merlin, he recognized that Rolls-Royce's biggest advantage was its long-standing policy of carefully improving an existing design rather than attempting to make radical innovations that might lead to a catastrophic setback. On many occasions Hives warned the Ministry not to base its production plans on new aircraft and engine types that had not yet been proven. In 1941, for example, he claimed that if official plans were to be believed, "next year the whole of our fighter production is going to be changed over to new types. This in my view is criminal. The only safe thing to bank on quantity production for next year is something which exists today. This is not an original idea as far as Rolls-Royce are concerned— our whole policy has been framed round the development of existing types rather than radical changes in design, and there is no sign so far that we have come to an end of the possible improvements by development."[60]

Hives observed that "consistently every few years we have been faced with some wonderful new engine, which was the last word in performance and efficiency, and that it was only a matter of time before Rolls-Royce would be out of business."[61] In the long run, Rolls-Royce had survived because "there is no short cut in getting a complicated mechanism like an aero engine or an aircraft into quantity production. We know that there is a minimum time in which these things can be done."[62] Rolls-Royce's incremental improvements to the Merlin yielded dramatic results over the course of the war. The company's 101 engine types were fitted onto over twenty different airplanes. The Merlin doubled in power during the course of the war, from about 1,000 horsepower to just over 2,000. In all, at least a thousand changes were made to the original Merlin design.[63] The Spitfire's top speed increased from about 340 miles per hour in 1939 to over 420 in 1944. A similar increase in speed was achieved in the P-51 Mustang.[64]

Hives's resourcefulness and determination to cut through red tape paid off in many ways for Rolls-Royce and the British military during the war.

A prime example was the Cromwell Tank, which, with Rolls-Royce's help, became the British Army's most effective tank in the war. As Merlin production was scaled up, it was inevitable that a growing volume of parts would have to be rejected, since, then as now, aero engines had to meet much higher quality standards than engines used for any other purpose. Rolls-Royce believed that it could manufacture a substandard Merlin rated between 500 and 600 horsepower which would make a powerful tank engine, as opposed to 1000 + horsepower for planes.[65]

However, it was evident that the Army's tanks, which were being developed by the Leyland company, were not equipped to handle a 500–600 horsepower engine. So in September 1941 Hives proposed to Lord Beaverbrook, one of the highest-ranking officials in the mobilization effort, that Rolls-Royce should take over the technical development of the Cromwell tank chassis as well as the engine. As a condition for taking on this new responsibility, Hives insisted that Rolls-Royce would need an open credit of one million pounds and "no interference." The answer came in a telegram from Lord Beaverbrook: "The British Government has given you an open credit of one million pounds. This is a certificate of character and reputation without precedent or equal."[66]

Testing and Repair Service: Rolls-Royce
and the Military

The service and repair function was especially important to Rolls-Royce because it provided a stream of information that helped the design engineers make improvements in future engine types. Hence, there was much consternation at Derby when officials in London decided that the Royal Air Force should use more of its own technicians instead of relying on Rolls-Royce employees at the RAF bases. Hives wrote in protest that "We [Rolls-Royce] like to consider ourselves an essential part of the RAF."[67] Along with Hives, Arthur Sidgreaves, the managing director of Rolls-Royce, was determined to fight this policy. He informed the Ministry that "our chief concern in the matter is to ensure the MAXIMUM SERVICEABILITY of Rolls-Royce engines." This goal could hardly be met when "the majority [of RAF mechanics] are not only newcomers to the RAF but also to engine practice in general. It must be of great value to have a specialist available to assist with unusual problems." Moreover, "from the Rolls-Royce point of view the various reports of engine failures sent in by our representatives are most valuable. These reports often play an important part in determining the detail design of new engine types."[68]

The pattern of production for Merlin engines shown in Figure 4.2 above represents an early example of the technology-intensive production processes associated with the Third Industrial Revolution. The design and service functions, at the beginning and end of the production process, were the areas most vital to the success of Rolls-Royce in the war effort, because the Merlin had to be improved constantly in order to stay ahead of German aero technology. Rolls-Royce's great advantage was its specialization in the learning- and technology-based functions that would dominate many industries during the Third Industrial Revolution.

Entering the Jet Age

The Merlin was a mechanical triumph, but even before the war ended piston-driven aero engines were becoming obsolete. The future of both civil and military aviation clearly belonged in jets, and Rolls-Royce now found itself at the forefront of their development.

In 1939, Germany and Britain were the only countries with the technical capability to develop and build a practical jet engine. By 1942 the German Messerschmitt 262, powered by a Junkers engine, became the world's first operational jet airplane. BMW also developed a jet engine for this plane. Had the Germans pushed the plane into quantity production sooner, it could have severely hurt Britain's air defenses and even forestalled the Allied invasion of Europe in 1944.

A young RAF engineer named Frank Whittle developed the first practical jet design outside of Germany. Whittle was still in his twenties when he patented his original design in 1930, but the government chose not to develop his engine. In 1935, Whittle founded a private company, Power Jets, to develop the engine on a commercial basis. But the project failed to attract sufficient private investment, and so the firm was unable to make real progress until 1939, when the British government responded to the threat posed by the Messerschmitt 262. Thereafter Power Jets was able to proceed with technical development, but the company was too small to undertake quantity production.

Rolls-Royce had begun research on its own jet engine in 1938, but by 1940 Hives realized that the Whittle engine, which had a simpler design, was likely to be first to reach the production stage. Thus, to help the war effort, Hives directed his engineers to concentrate on the Whittle project, and in 1940 Rolls-Royce volunteered to make engine parts for Power Jets. But Hives also made it clear to the Air Ministry that, in his words, "Rolls-Royce would not be satisfied just to become a maker of bits. To take full advantage of the full resources of Rolls-Royce we should want to be brought into the problem and have access to any data which was available."[69]

Nonetheless, in 1941 the Rover corporation was chosen to manufacture the Whittle engine in quantity for the RAF. Rolls-Royce agreed to help Rover for the good of the war effort. But then, in November 1942, Hives proposed a ingenious swap with Rover. Rolls-Royce would get the jet in exchange for the Merlin-derived tank engine Rolls-Royce had designed. The offer was accepted over dinner in a pub, with only three people in attendance: Hives, Rover's chairman, and a Rolls-Royce engineer named Stanley Hooker, who later became the firm's chief engineer on jets. In Hooker's words, "there was no talk of money, and no talk of getting government agreement to the arrangement."[70] In hindsight, the deal was an excellent strategic move by Hives, but what made it possible was the extraordinary sense of cooperation and trust that existed in British industry during the war. Firms that had been fierce competitors suddenly found themselves working together at all levels and sharing their most carefully guarded secrets.

The Whittle engine proved useful to the Allied war effort, as Figure 4.3 indicates. When the United States entered the war in 1941, the Whittle engine was far ahead of any US designs, so a copy of the technical drawings was secretly flown to General Electric's facility in Lynn, Massachusetts. Until then GE had made industrial turbines but had no experience in aero engines, so this project became the genesis of GE's aerospace division. In 1944, the Gloster Meteor, powered by the Rolls-Royce Welland engine (the first production model derived from Whittle's original design), became the Allies' first jet airplane to enter military service. A year later it set a new speed record of just over 600 miles per hour.[71]

As Figure 4.3 also shows, in 1947 the American firm Pratt & Whitney was given a contract to produce two different Rolls-Royce military engines under license.[72] Pratt had done experiments on jets before, but the license from Rolls-Royce gave the company valuable experience in man-

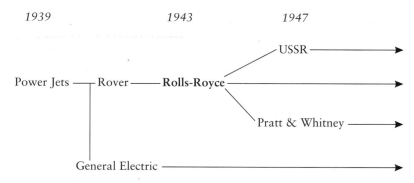

Figure 4.3   International Diffusion of Jet Technology

ufacturing jet engines. Ironically, within a decade Pratt & Whitney became Rolls-Royce's biggest competitor in civil jet engines. Also, at the
same time that Pratt got its license, the British government sold a number
of Rolls-Royce engines to the USSR, which similarly boosted its efforts
to get jet engines into quantity production.

Competitive Pressures in Aerospace

After 1945, Rolls-Royce had both the technical skill and the desire to
compete globally in the emerging aerospace industry. Given the massive
increase in capital spending and employment during the war years, it was
almost inconceivable that the firm could revert to being mainly a small-
scale carmaker, as had happened after the First World War.

Although the future appeared bright for Rolls-Royce's aero engine
business, the Cold War, which began in 1947 and did not end until 1989,
created a serious competition problem for all non-U.S. aerospace firms.
The Soviet threat all but guaranteed that American companies would
receive huge, long-term military contracts that would enable them to
produce on a much larger scale than that of any foreign competitors. A
British government report in the late 1960s showed that between 1945
and 1963, the U.S. aircraft industry was approximately three times more
productive in value added per employee. The report concluded that this
disparity was this direct result of the American manufacturers' greater
production volume.[73]

Great Britain was also heavily involved in the Cold War, but its military spending paled in comparison with that of the United States. If Rolls-Royce was to compete with the Americans on an international scale, it would have to depend heavily on civil applications for its jet engines. The Rolls-Royce Conway engine, for example, was designed in 1952 for an RAF bomber. It later appeared on the Boeing 707, the Douglas DC-8, and the British-made VC10.[74] Other Rolls-Royce projects, notably the Spey engine, were designed for the civil market from the start. By 1965, 67 percent of Rolls-Royce's turnover was in civil engines.[75]

To succeed in the market for civil jet engines, Rolls-Royce knew it would have to break into the U.S. domestic market, which in the decade after 1945 had quickly grown into the world's largest. In 1965, a British government panel noted that the American demand for civil aircraft "accounts for 80% of world production in terms of value. The aerospace industry in Britain accounts for 8% and the French 5%." At the same time, the United States market was absorbing half of the world's output of civil aircraft, with the UK again in second place with 8 percent. All of Western Europe's aircraft purchases equaled one quarter as much as the Americans'.[76]

Building a New Generation of Jet Engines

The level of competition in the civil aero engine market increased dramatically in the late 1960s, as a new generation of "jumbo jets"—the Boeing 747, the Douglas DC-10, and the Lockheed L-1011—moved from the drawing board to the production line. In 1968, Rolls-Royce won an exclusive contract with the American company Lockheed to develop the RB211 engine for the L-1011. The contract called for a total of 540 RB211-22s to be delivered by the summer of 1971. The deal was hailed as a giant step toward preserving Great Britain's competitiveness in aerospace, although the terms of the contract heavily favored Lockheed. Rolls-Royce was to be paid a fixed price for each of its RB211 engines, with no provisions for cost overruns and heavy penalties for late delivery. Such a deal was unquestionably risky, as the RB211 design involved dramatic and hugely expensive advances in technology.[77] Jet engines of the new generation not only had to be twice as powerful as before, they also had to be quieter, more reliable, and more fuel-efficient.

Given these challenges, it was understood from the start that the RB211 could not be built or sold without heavy government support. In the mid-1960s, the Labour Prime Minister, Harold Wilson, had put forth a national industrial policy to strengthen Britain's competitiveness in exports and high technology. Such a policy was almost bound to help Rolls-Royce, both as an exporter of high-value-added goods and as one of the nation's most technologically advanced companies. Anthony Wedgwood (Tony) Benn, Labour's Technology Minister at that time, later said that his decision to back the RB211 was directly affected by the historic stature of Rolls-Royce: "I was dealing with not only the most famous British engineering company, but a company that had a blue-chip reputation. I am afraid those factors influenced me. I would not have done this with any tin-pot company."[78]

The absolute scale of the RB211 project was unprecedented for Rolls-Royce, but in relative terms it was consistent with the company's aggressive pursuit of new markets in the past. As Table 4.8 (pp. 130–132) shows, Rolls-Royce's fixed assets had risen significantly in every decade. The RB211 project actually called for a smaller rate of increase in fixed assets than the company had undertaken in the 1950s, when it first moved into turbofan aero engines (see Table 4.4). By the 1960s Rolls-Royce had become an industrial "national champion," with a significant role in the nation's commercial prestige and balance of trade.

The only difficulty was that Rolls-Royce had become such a national champion in aerospace, one of the most cyclical and risk-plagued of all industries. Indeed, by the summer of 1970 technical setbacks had raised the cost estimates for launching the RB211 from £65 million to at least £170 million.[79] The company argued that the project was still commercially viable, but only because of profits it would make from the sale of replacement parts over the two-to-three-decade life of the engines.[80] The same rationale was adopted by Pratt & Whitney and General Electric in their own efforts to build large jet engines. By the 1990s, an aero engine company could expect its sales margins on new engines to be as low as 3 percent, whereas spares could generate more than 20 percent.[81]

Table 4.4 Growth in Fixed Assets by Decade, From Exhibit 4.1 (%)

1910s	1920s	1930s	1940s	1950s	1960s	1970s	1980s
320	70	60	250	950	430	360	230

Rolls-Royce under Government Ownership

The long-term potential of the RB211 notwithstanding, the engine's start-up costs proved to be staggering. By the end of 1970, Rolls-Royce's credit and cash flow were severely depleted, and it appeared that the engine might not be delivered on time. In early February 1971, the firm was forced into receivership, declaring that it was financially insolvent and unable to continue in business. This development came as a great shock to Lockheed, which was itself reported to be in serious financial trouble. It was a surprise to the London financial community as well, for until this time Rolls-Royce had never before reported a loss, even in the depths of the Great Depression.

The timing of Rolls-Royce's financial crisis was not fortuitous. The Conservative Government elected in 1970 was under pressure in Parliament to curtail state investment in industrial projects. It therefore took months of heated debate before Government ministers agreed that neither the RB211 project nor Rolls-Royce as a company could be allowed to die.[82] In the end, it was a matter of jobs, for Rolls-Royce at the time employed, directly or indirectly, well over 80,000 people. It was also a matter of national prestige, as Rolls-Royce was the only enterprise outside the United States or the Soviet Union capable of developing large jet engines by itself. Then, too, it was a matter of national defense. Many RAF planes, including the famed Harrier "jump-jet," carried Rolls-Royce-built engines. The Royal Navy also depended on Rolls-Royce marine engines to power much of its surface fleet and the submarines that provided Britain's nuclear deterrent.

Under the plan to keep Rolls-Royce in business, the firm was financially reconstituted as a new limited liability company, with the British government as sole shareholder. In September 1971, negotiations involving both the British and the American governments led to a new contract between Rolls-Royce and Lockheed, enabling all sides to complete the L-1011. The terms were reported to be more favorable to Rolls-Royce than before. Even so, the British government had to contribute at least £120 million to complete the project.[83] The United States government also had to provide a $250 million loan guarantee to Lockheed.[84] In the end, the RB211 had proved to be much more than "a purely commercial deal," as the chairman of Lockheed had originally called it.[85] The aerospace industry had become so expensive and so dependent on international collaboration that no government in any participating country could safely avoid the risks.

As owner of Rolls-Royce, the British government decided to sell off those parts of the business that, while profitable, were not considered strategic to the national interest. Thus, the car division, plus another unit that made diesel engines, was spun off as an independent firm which came to be known as Rolls-Royce Motor Cars Limited. The new firm was eventually acquired by Vickers.

In some respects the car business was little changed from the glory days of the Silver Ghost, although the thoroughly nonstandard models of the prewar era did give way to a more standardized car after World War II. In any case, output remained small (see Table 4.5).

By the 1990s Rolls-Royce cars were still among the world's most exclusive and certainly most expensive cars, and were still built with many custom features and options. The Rolls-Royce name continued to be one of the best known and most valuable brand names in existence. In the mid-1990s, a Rolls-Royce Silver Spur was priced at almost $180,000, while a Bentley Azure convertible sold for over $300,000. After 1971 the original firm centered in Derby maintained exclusive rights to the Rolls-Royce name and logo. Rolls-Royce Motor Cars in Crewe used the

Table 4.5   The Best-Selling Rolls-Royce Automobiles

	Model	Total	Avg./Year
1965–80	Silver Shadow (I & II)	29,030	1,814
1980–89	Silver Spirit/Silver Spur	14,493	1,449
1906–26	Silver Ghost	7,876	375
1971–89	Corniche (I & II)	5,658	298

Source: Adapted from Roßfeldt, Rolls-Royce and Bentley, pp. 256–258, 300–310

Table 4.6   Rolls-Royce Automobile Output

	1983	1984	1985	1986	1987	1988	1989	1990	1991	1992	1993
Rolls-Royce	1,345	1,933	2,118	1,847	1,665	1,780	1,631	1,530	709	451	459
Bentley	223	268	470	684	905	1,188	1,623	1,744	911	807	804

Source: Motor Industry of Great Britain: World Automotive Statistics, 1987–1993 (London: Society of Motor Manufacturers and Traders, Ltd.)

name only by permission, although it was given the rights to the "Spirit of Ecstasy" statue, the famous radiator design, and all the trademarks of Bentley, a firm Rolls-Royce had acquired in 1931.

As a state-owned company, Rolls-Royce Limited enjoyed some distinct benefits, as Table 4.8 shows. It was entirely free from the pressures of the stock market. It was not required to pay dividends, so all profits were reinvested in the business. Fifteen years after the government takeover, the firm's fixed assets had risen by over 900 percent in current pounds sterling. This growth made it possible to launch a host of new engines based on the RB211 design (see Table 4.7).[86] Rolls-Royce thereby upheld its status as one of the world's "big three" aero engine firms, along with Pratt & Whitney and General Electric.

Privatization and Beyond

In 1987, the government privatized Rolls-Royce Limited by simply placing its shares back on the market. Looking to the future, Rolls-Royce plc ("public limited company" as it was called after 1985) decided it would be unwise to depend entirely on military contracts and the civil jet business. Demand in these markets was extraordinarily cyclical, while also requiring huge investments in research and development. In order to manage these risks, Rolls-Royce plc chose a policy of extending its product line to other types of engines and power-generating systems that would complement Rolls-Royce's traditional competency in aero engines and high-integrity engineering.

Thus, in 1989 it acquired a holding company called Northern Engineering Industries, a cluster of firms involved in power generation and distribution systems and in a wide variety of materials-handling equip-

Table 4.7   The RB211 Family

	Engine	Airplane	Thrust (lbs.)
1968	RB211-22	Lockheed L-1011	42,000
1976	RB211-524	L-1011 (long-range); Boeing 747, 767	58,000
1978	RB211-535	Boeing 757	37,400
1993	Trent 700	Airbus A330	72,000
1995	Trent 800	Boeing 777	90,000+

Source: Rolls-Royce Archives.

ment. The holding company was reorganized as the Industrial Power Group, which included existing Rolls-Royce divisions that made industrial and marine engines (usually aero engine derivatives), and nuclear propulsion units for the Royal Navy. All of these activities made use of Rolls-Royce's aero engine technology base, while also giving the firm a presence in markets with demand cycles different from that in aero engines.

At the same time, Rolls-Royce plc remained firmly committed to the aero engine market, both civil and military. In 1995 it acquired the Allison Engine Co. of Indianapolis, a long-established firm specializing in engines for small jets and helicopters. Allison was a significant contractor with the United States military. In the 1990s, Rolls-Royce was also involved in a number of joint ventures for aero engines. Among these was International Aero Engines, a five-nation consortium that developed the V2500 engine for medium-range airliners.[87]

As a group of companies specializing in design engineering, Rolls-Royce continued to emphasize its historic reputation for superior quality and reliability.[88] The company founded by Rolls and Royce had changed tremendously over the years, but the example set by Henry Royce had not been lost.

Table 4.8   Rolls-Royce Statistics, 1906–1949

	Net Profit (£000s)	Dividend (%)	Share Capital (£000s)	Fixed Assets (£000s)	Personnel
1906–07	5	6	104	60	400
1907–08	9	6	104	79	
1908–09	20	8	117	89	
1909–10	38	15	136	104	
1910–11	51	15	136	112	800
1911–12	71	20	200	144	
1912–13	91	20	200	145	
1913–14	77	10	200	153	
1914–15	44	5	200	161	1,650
1915–16	83	10	—	—	
1916–17	142	10	200	288	
1917–18	153	10	400	321	
1918–19	193	15	787	317	8,000
1919–20	203	10	804	333	
1920–21	107	8	811	420	
1921–22	149	8	812	469	
1922–23	157	8	814	461	4,000
1923–24	164	8	814	455	
1924–25	166	8	814	467	
1925–26	101	8	814	468	
1926–27	157	10	814	473	3,400
1927–28	186	10	814	483	
1928–29[a]	202	10	819	473	
1930	147	10	826	482	
1931	144	10	826	464	3,000
1932	151	10	829	463	
1933	217	17	839	475	
1934	292	20	847	441	
1935	350	22.5	850	626	7,800
1936	390	22.5	852	643	
1937	393	22.5	1,096	784	
1938	480	25	1,110	788	
1939	464	20	1,132	850	12,500
1940	500	20	1,132	797	
1941	514	20	1,136	650	38,600
1942	556	20	1,136	540	
1943	514	20	1,138	785	55,600
1944	590	20	1,146	795	57,100
1945	590	20	1,150	865	
1946	671	20	1,150	1,507	
1947	669	20	1,150	1,571	30,500
1948	837	20	1,150	1,561	
1949	1,219	20	1,150	1,849	

Continued on next page

Table 4.8 (continued)

	Net Profit (£m)	Dividend (%)	Share Capital (£m)	Fixed Assets (£m)	Personnel
1950	1.2	25	1.5	2	
1951	1.6	15	3	3	33,600
1952	2.2	15	4	4	
1953	3.6	17.5	4	5	36,000
1954	5.3	17.5	6	6	36,400
1955	4.6	17.5	6	8	37,500
1956	5.3	20	8	11	42,300
1957	5.4	20	10	15	43,900
1958	4.6	20	10	16	41,700
1959	4.9	10	20	16	44,000
1960	5.2	11	20	19	48,100
1961	2.5[b]	8	20	22	51,900
1962	1.8	6	20	23	44,500
1963	5.9	10	20	21	43,500
1964	6.5	10	25	21	47,100
1965	6.9	11	25	22	49,700
1966	8.4	11	48	43	84,400
1967	11.8	11.385	56	55	88,100
1968	15.9	11.784	66	70	88,300
1969	6.4	6	66	82	87,100
1970	—	—	—	—	
1971	6.5	0	30	47	64,000
1972	18.4	0	30	44	63,300
1973	22.8	0	60	62	64,000
1974	16.7	0	60	69	65,200
1975	4.5	0	137	88	64,100
1976	−21.9	0	175	96	61,000
1977	16.6	0	196	97	59,200
1978	11.7	0	203	108	59,400
1979	−58.4	0	234	137	60,700
1980	−22.4	0	328	299	62,000
1981	18	0	458	303	56,000
1982	−91	0	508	312	48,800
1983	−114	0	508	312	42,300
1984	26	0	508	302	40,900
1985	81	0	127	383	41,700
1986	120	0	127	405	42,000
1987	156	5.25[c]	160	438	41,600
1988	168	6.3	160	459	40,900
1989	233	7	192	658	64,900

Continued on next page

Table 4.8 (continued)

	Net Profit (£m)	Dividend[c]	Share Capital (£m)	Fixed Assets (£m)	Personnel
1990	176	7.25	192	676	64,200
1991	51	7.25	193	721	
1992	−184	5	194	874	51,800
1993	76	5	244	882	45,800
1994	101	5	245	836	41,000

a. November 1928 through December 1929.

b. Change in reporting method from previous year.

c. Dividend figures for 1987–1994 are in pence per share—all previous years are percentage figures.

Source: Rolls-Royce Archives and Annual Reports.

PROLOGUE TO CHAPTER 5

The next chapter, "German Capitalism," provides a contrast to the British experience, and in so doing highlights aspects of the business systems of both countries. So the comparison in itself pays big dividends.

On the other hand, one of the dangers of comparative analysis is a temptation toward stereotyping. We have all heard remarks like these: "British people are articulate but ineffective." "Germans are stolid and humorless." "Americans are boorish and naive." "Japanese are clannish and obsessive."

How useful are such stereotypes? Different national styles of capitalism do exist, of course. We've seen in the preceding chapters how British ways of doing business are deeply rooted in Britain's political, social, and economic history. But stereotypes can't get us very far, except along the road to costly miscalculation.

So it is with Germany. An understanding of German capitalism must take account of some exceptionally complex historical circumstances: the forced creation of the country itself out of numerous small and medium-sized kingdoms plus dozens of tiny principalities; Germany's powerful traditions of craft guilds, scientific education, and concern for social welfare; its tendency toward military adventurism, from the late nineteenth century to the mid-twentieth; its experience with almost every form of government, from near-absolute monarchy under the Kaiser, to weak democracy during the Weimar period, to totalitarian fascism under Hitler, then to dictatorial communism in East Germany and strong democracy in West Germany.

Merely to list these aspects of Germany's national history is to suggest that its style of doing business is likely to be quite different from Britain's—within the broad patterns common to all capitalist economies. In this chapter, you will read of Germany's preoccupation with *Wirtschaftsordnung* (economic order). You will discover its pre-1945 habit of using cartels to organize some of its industries and tariffs to protect them from foreign competition. You will encounter such characteristics as the tendency toward *Selbstverwaltung* (self-government) in business and industry. You will see other distinctively German institutions such as the *Mittelstand* (small and medium-sized businesses with powerful regional identities). You will encounter universal banks in the realm of finance, codetermination in industrial relations, and two levels of governing boards in corporate management. You will find that the institutional structure of German business and finance makes it almost impossible for corporate raiders to accomplish hostile takeovers.

Why did German capitalism develop these characteristics and institutions? What did they have to do with the country's outstanding long-term economic performance? Did they perhaps bring advantages during the Second Industrial Revolution that might prove to be handicaps in the Third?

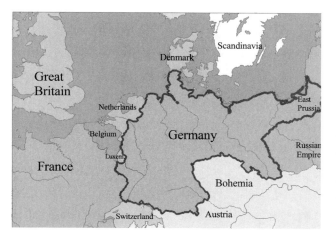

Germany at the time of the initial unification of the country in 1871.

(© 1992–1997, Clockwork Software, Inc., Chicago, IL/Harvard Map Collection, 1997)

Germany after its defeat in World War I, with its national boundaries redrawn according to the terms of the Treaty of Versailles.

(© 1992–1997, Clockwork Software, Inc., Chicago, IL/Harvard Map Collection, 1997)

Germany after its defeat in World War II and before the reunification of East and West Germany in 1990.

(© 1992–1997, Clockwork Software, Inc., Chicago, IL /Harvard Map Collection, 1997)

August Thyssen Sr., founder of major German steel, coal, and machinery companies.

(Courtesy Thyssen AG Archive and Franz Steiner Verlag Wiesbaden GmbH, Stuttgart, Germany)

August Thyssen Sr. in 1895, age 53, nearing the height of his power and influence.

(Courtesy Thyssen AG Archive and Franz Steiner Verlag Wiesbaden GmbH, Stuttgart, Germany)

August's younger brother and partner, Josef Thyssen.

(Courtesy Thyssen AG Archive and Franz Steiner Verlag Wiesbaden GmbH, Stuttgart, Germany)

August's estranged wife, Hedwig, with their children, August Jr., Fritz, Heinrich, and Hede.
(Courtesy Thyssen AG Archive and Franz Steiner Verlag Wiesbaden GmbH, Stuttgart, Germany)

Henrich Thyssen-Bornemisza, his aristocratic Hungarian wife, Margit, and their children, Stephan, Margit, and Gabriele.

(Courtesy Thyssen AG Archive and Franz Steiner Verlag Wiesbaden GmbH, Stuttgart, Germany)

Georg von Siemens, Spokesman of the Deutsche Bank's Managing Board from 1870 to 1900, and the chief architect of the bank's early growth.

(Courtesy Deutsche Bank AG)

Headquarters of the Deutsche Bank in Berlin, 1929, in the Mauerstrasse.

(Courtesy Deutsche Bank AG)

Georg Solmssen, Spokesman of the Deutsche Bank's Managing Board in 1933. Born to Jewish parents, he protested at the government's and the bank's treatment of Jews in one of the most eloquent letters ever written by a German businessman. He was removed from office late in 1933, but he survived the Nazi period by escaping to Switzerland.

(Courtesy Deutsche Bank AG)

Hermann J. Abs, the key leader of the Deutsche Bank during the 1940s and 1950s, when it was first split up by Occupation authorities, then reconstituted as a single bank. Abs spent three months in prison in connection with his activities during the Nazi regime.

(Photo by Holtmann, Stuttgart-Vaihingen, Courtesy Deutsche Bank AG)

The Frankfurt headquarters of the Deutsche Bank in the 1990s. The bank's "twin towers" at the right and their complementary Trianon skyscraper at the left seem to overshadow the official German central bank (Bundesbank) in the foreground.

(Photo by Jutta Hofmann, Courtesy Deutsche Bank AG)

❋ 5 ❋

GERMAN CAPITALISM

Jeffrey Fear

The fall of the Berlin Wall in 1989 and the reunification of East and West Germany in 1990 were episodes typical of the wrenching political changes common in German history for the past 200 years. These political changes were often accompanied by sudden modifications in the "economic order" *(Wirtschaftsordnung),* the collection of customs and institutions that frame the production and consumption of goods and services.[1]

In Britain and America, the economic order is usually seen as a product of slow evolution over many centuries. In Germany, by contrast, the rise and fall of political economies has often been a revolutionary process. In part because of the more abrupt transitions in their history, Germans tend to view politics, society, and business as interdependent spheres, not separate ones.

The Political Unification of Germany, 1871

Germany did not become a centralized state until 1871, by which time its rivals Britain, France, and Russia already had been more or less unified for hundreds of years. German unity before 1871 had rested mainly on a common literary language, and "Germany" as a consolidated country was only a vague idea promoted by ardent nationalists, many of whom hoped that a unified Germany might also be a democratic one.[2]

What brought "Germany" together? As one historian has said, "In the beginning, there was Napoleon."[3] Before Napoleon's conquest of central Europe in 1806, "Germany" consisted of hundreds of principalities. There were ecclesiastical and lay territories, estates of the Holy Roman

Empire, Imperial cities, free cities, and noble lands filled with myriad counts, knights, and princes. The most powerful single states were Prussia and, under the Habsburg monarchy, the Austrian Empire. The Empire was centered in Vienna but comprised a diverse set of territories. Prussia itself was so splintered that the Prussian General Legal Code of 1794 spoke of the "Prussian states." When the Prussian monarchy tried to introduce free trade among its royal lands in 1797, it failed.[4] The heterogeneous collection of German states at the center of Europe was no match for the unified French under Napoleon, who crushed both the Austrians and Prussians. Prussia and the Austrian Empire remained independent, but severely weakened.

In order to rule and to collect taxes more effectively, Napoleon consolidated most of the German lands into the Confederation of the Rhine, which eventually had 39 member states. Napoleon introduced French commercial laws, modern state bureaucracies, public education, and new freedoms of trade, citizenship, and religion. In response, some German states, Prussia in particular, began to introduce thoroughgoing political, economic, and educational reforms designed to modernize their economies and improve their positions against the French. The resistance against French rule also unleashed German nationalism.[5]

After Napoleon's defeat at Waterloo in 1815, the gathering of European diplomats at the epochal Congress of Vienna tried to create a strategic balance among the great powers of Europe. The Congress decided that Napoleon's consolidation of the German states would be maintained. Prussia, as one of the major allies in the war against France, was given additional territory in the Rhineland and Westphalia, including the Ruhr valley and the important cities of Cologne and Düsseldorf. Thus, the fight against Napoleon became a decisive step in the rise of Prussia as a great power.[6]

Until the 1860s most of the German states counted on a rough balance of power between the growing influence of Prussia and the slowly declining strength of the Habsburg Empire. When Prussia went to war with Austria in 1866, most German states allied themselves with the Habsburgs. But the Prussian army's decisive victory allowed the Prussian Minister-President, Otto von Bismarck, to weld many states into a North German Federation. Just four years later, the "Iron Chancellor" Bismarck provoked a war with France, and once again the Prussian army won a surprisingly easy victory. Bismarck induced the rest of the German states to join a unified German Empire, which also annexed the former French province of Alsace-Lorraine. Bismarck admitted that this outcome had been neither inevitable nor initially desired by most "Germans." Instead it had been won by "blood and iron." Indeed, victories depended less on popular national support than on strategic planning by the Prussian general staff and the swift movement of troops by railway.[7]

After unification, the "German question"—how to deal with a powerful new country in the heart of Europe—became the number one problem for European politics.[8] German unification altered the military and economic balance and increased the probability of a continental war. This new nation, with its capital at Berlin, was essentially a federal and constitutional system with a powerful monarch at its head. National policy and legislation were formulated in a complicated bargaining process among the Emperor *(Kaiser),* the Chancellor, the Federal Council *(Bundesrat),* which was made up of the federal princes or their state representatives, and the majority parties in Parliament *(Reichstag).* The Emperor, and the Chancellor he appointed, were the ultimate centers of power. This was particularly true with regard to the higher civil service, foreign policy, and, most important, the military. In theory the Emperor and Chancellor could rule without a voting majority, but Parliament did have some power over the national budget.

Germany's federal states *(Länder)* were at first more powerful than they are today. Before 1919, direct taxation was controlled by the Länder and the municipalities, not by the central Imperial state *(Reich).* Revenues for the Reich came from tariffs, indirect consumption and stamp taxes, redistributive transfers from the states, and inheritance taxes. The state of Prussia had a unusual tax system in which most of its revenue (75 percent in 1913) was drawn from entrepreneurial activities such as government-owned railroads. The state of Bavaria raised about 40 percent of its revenue through a consumption tax on beer.[9] Today the central government and federal states jointly share revenues from the most important forms of direct taxation. The states retain considerable responsibilities that grew out of Germany's traditional regionalism. They still have powers of self-government *(Selbstverwaltung)* over the police, education, social services, culture, and the development of regional and urban infrastructure.[10]

The political system of Bismarck's Reich left a number of important legacies, some of which still shape modern-day Germany. The major opposition party simultaneously demanded social welfare measures (for example, improved working conditions and wages, a strengthening of working class organizations, and a fundamental redistribution of property) and greater democracy. Hence they named their party the Social Democrats, and it remains today the oldest existing party in Germany. Then, too, although the central state bureaucracy was able to expand, it was hampered by its dependence on the tax revenues of the states, a situation that would come to haunt Germany as it attempted to finance the costs of the First World War.

Economic Development before the 1871 Unification

Until the mid-nineteenth century, the various German states had been relatively poor and backward compared to Britain and France. But by 1900, the unified nation of Germany had become a major economic force. Five key institutions that had been in existence even before 1871 helped to make possible Germany's rapid industrial development.

The first was the *Zollverein,* or customs union, which was a free-trade area with a joint commercial policy and a common external tariff. Founded in 1834, the Zollverein involved nearly three dozen states, led by Prussia. It was a patchwork unification at best. Trade did not move easily across state lines. Weights, measures, and coinage varied from one German state to the next. A unified commercial code, first proposed in 1836, was not ratified by the member states until 1861. Nevertheless, the customs union constituted a first step toward a common "German" market.[11]

A much bigger factor behind the nation's industrialization was the development of railroads. These played an even greater role in Germany than in Britain, France, or the United States. The rail networks were constructed first on a regional basis, and were connected to form a national network around 1850, after which they grew enormously. Before they were nationalized in 1879, railroads consistently paid the highest dividends in German business, more so than firms in mining, ironworking, or textiles.[12]

One effect of the railroads was to spur the rise of banking. Some of the German "universal banks" got their start in the railway business, particularly in the issuing of securities. A universal bank was (and still is) a combination of commercial bank, investment bank, and investment trust. Because of highly localized and imperfect capital markets, it was relatively difficult to pool capital for large projects. The need for large investments quickly outgrew the funds available from small banks or wealthy families. As a result private banking houses formed joint-stock or limited-partnership banks that were better able to channel funds from diverse investors into large-scale industrial and commercial ventures. Some of these institutions quickly evolved into universal banks. (One such evolution is explained in detail later in Chapter 7, on the Deutsche Bank.) Most of the directors of the leading joint-stock banks were active as promoters or directors of railroads.[13]

The demand for railroad equipment provided huge new markets for the German coal, iron, and machine-engineering industries. Tariffs on iron and steel aided domestic manufacturers, beginning in 1844, and the universal banks quickly became involved in iron and steel ventures as well.[14] In the 1850s, a large number of coal, iron, and steel companies were founded or greatly expanded in the region around the Ruhr River. These included the Stinnes coal trading company, the Good Hope Mining and Smelting Company (GHH, now Haniel), Krupp, Phoenix, and the Bochumer Verein. The German machine-engineering industry (companies such as Borsig, Henschel, Maffei, and Harkort) also expanded quickly by building locomotives. Krupp, with the financial guidance of the universal bank Schaafhausen, moved extensively into rails, rolling stock, and military hardware.[15]

A third key factor in Germany's drive to industrialize—in addition to the customs union and the railroads—was its strong craft tradition, which to this day allows for a swift transfer of new technical processes and less managerial supervision of production. Skilled workers had considerable pride in their crafts. They were the labor elite, and before 1914 most German factories remained collections of workshops. The pride and dignity found in identification with craft skills still underlies the system of German vocational training today.[16]

A fourth key institution that promoted rapid industrialization was a comprehensive educational system, ranging from primary to vocational school, and from polytechnical to university courses. The principle (though not quite the reality) of a general education for everyone between 6 and 13 years of age was established in Germany by the end of the eighteenth century. By comparison, Britain introduced it only in the late nineteenth century. German universities incorporated a strong research orientation, especially in physics, chemistry, and mathematics.

Of particular importance for industrial development were the polytechnical schools, which institutionalized applied research as well as education. Such schools had been established in many German states by the 1830s, long before their appearance in most other countries. The Berlin Institute, for example, offered a two-year course in how to set up and manage factories. All of the institutes became technical universities *(Technische Hochschulen)* after 1868. By 1872, the University of Munich alone had more graduate research chemists than did all of England. Because commercial arts such as engineering were still considered too practical, unscholarly, and insufficiently scientific, these schools in their curricula placed a strong emphasis on applied theory, which is still a hallmark of German vocational training today.

By 1870, academically trained engineers became key participants, even executives, in major Ruhr iron and steel companies such as Krupp and the Bochumer Verein. Most of the large Ruhr works employed chemists to analyze inputs and control for quality, again long before such scientists worked in the industries of most other countries. German-language textbooks for bridge building, machine engineering, and the making of iron and steel became widely available. As Bismarck once put it, "the nation that has the schools, has the future."[17]

All four of these institutions—the customs union, railroads, the craft tradition, and the educational system—were distinctive aspects of German economic life. And there was (and still is) a fifth major factor, Germany's numerous business associations. These associations tend to blur the boundaries between private and public affairs, between markets and politics. In the early years the most important of these associations were the Chambers of Commerce and Industry, which also grew out of Napoleonic reforms and were modeled on French associations. These Chambers acted as quasi-public institutions for the "self-government" of the economy. The Chambers were organized by region and tended to reflect the interests of small and medium-sized businesses. But they were not just interest groups. They also developed basic standards for com-

mercial transactions across regions and became increasingly involved in
programs for training workers. Their responsibilities went well beyond
those of American chambers of commerce.[18]

Overall, it is striking how many of the basic features of modern German capitalism had already begun to take form by 1871. The subsequent
decades of rapid industrialization saw them coalesce into a distinctive
variety of capitalism, a "German" way of doing business.[19]

Reasons for Germany's Rapid Economic Expansion, 1871–1914

German capitalism became increasingly competitive in world markets
after political unification in 1871. Whereas Great Britain produced over
half of the world's pig iron in 1870, by 1913 its share had dropped to
14 percent. Germany's had risen to 21 percent and that of the United
States to 40 percent.[20] An intense Anglo-German trade rivalry had begun,
and it would eventually affect the strategic military balance in Europe.
At its roots was steel, which had become the foundation of modern military power. By 1913 Germany had assumed its place as one of the world's
leading exporters, particularly in machinery and other heavy industrial
products. It was the world's largest exporter of iron and steel goods. It
also manufactured 90 percent of all dyestuffs sold on world export markets, 30 percent of pharmaceuticals, 35 percent of electrical goods, 27
percent of chemicals, 29 percent of machine-tools, and 17 percent of
internal combustion engines.[21]

The rapid expansion of the German economy occurred in a distinctive
political and ideological environment. Most important, a dramatic boom
and bust in the early 1870s had discredited laissez-faire liberalism. A
general shift toward protectionism ensued, symbolized by the reintroduction of tariffs for iron, steel, and agricultural goods.[22]

LEGAL REFORM

During the economic boom of 1870, Germany had instituted a free incorporation law. This same law made obligatory, for joint-stock companies, a two-tiered division between the executive or managing board
(*Vorstand*) and the supervisory board (*Aufsichtsrat*). Numerous bank
and industry failures after 1873 made further corporate legal reforms

necessary. In the interests of investors, a law revised in 1884 strengthened the control of the supervisory board over the managing board. The supervisory board's key power was (and still is today) its ability to appoint members of the managing board. Shareholders and representatives of large banks still sit on the supervisory board, and the whole two-tiered system is one of the hallmarks of German business.[23]

BANKING SYSTEM

In 1876, the old Prussian Bank was transformed into the Reichsbank, Germany's central bank. At the same time the Reichsmark (RM) became the official currency of the empire. The Reichsbank built up branch offices all around Germany. It also developed close financial and personal relations with the great universal banks, which increasingly relocated to Berlin. The Reichsbank followed liberal discounting policies, a practice that allowed the universal banks to operate with low liquidity ratios. Banking analysts have spoken of an implicit "liquidity guarantee" by the Reichsbank during this period.[24]

In Germany's era of rapid economic growth, the universal banks played a central role. Institutions such as the Deutsche Bank (formed in 1870) and Dresdner Bank (1872) concentrated on financing the development of large-scale industry. This left the financing of small and medium-size businesses, the agricultural sector, and construction activity mostly to other types of banks, including regional savings banks, private banking houses, and credit cooperatives. Especially during the difficult period of the 1870s, German universal banks were able to increase their direct influence over some capital-intensive firms. One historian has aptly described the great banks' behavior as "development assistance to the strong."[25]

Total bank assets rose from RM 600 million to over RM 17.5 billion between 1870 and 1913, that is, from 6 to 20 percent of total estimated industrial capital in Germany. Half of these assets were held by the 5 largest Berlin banks. In 1913, the 3 largest joint-stock companies in Germany in total assets and share capital were banking corporations. Among the top 25 firms ranked by assets, 17 were banks. Banking representatives also sat on corporate boards in every major industrial sector, and credits from universal banks helped to finance almost half of all net investment. Although the direct power of the banks over industry has been greatly exaggerated in many interpretations of German business history, the universal banks remain to this day distinctive, powerful features of the German economic landscape.[26]

German universal banks exercised influence over industry through four basic levers, which still operate today. First, the banks held significant long-term investments in a number of important firms. They played a crucial mediating role in the issuing and trading of these firms' securities on the stock market. Second, they routinized their financial transactions with leading firms, particularly through current-account credits that could be rolled over, effectively making them long-term credits. Third, because bank executives sat on supervisory boards, they took part in strategic decisionmaking, especially the approval of future investments. Close financial and personal relationships between banks and industry cemented these institutional ties. Georg von Siemens, for example, a cousin of the famous inventor and industrialist Werner von Siemens, occupied a seat on the managing board of the Deutsche Bank. Fourth, the universal banks' voting power in the supervisory boards was enhanced by proxy voting rights, which gave the banks the right to vote all shares deposited by other shareholders with that bank. These rights ("bearer shares" as they are called in English) were increasingly used after 1887, when they were first employed in the establishment of the General Electric Company of Germany (AEG).[27] This practice, which is not followed in most other countries, by itself makes German corporate governance different from that of the United Kingdom or the United States. For one thing, it makes hostile takeovers almost impossible to execute.

Although banks thus could exercise much influence, particularly in periods of crisis, the influence was not a one-way street. The banks' relations with industry were marked by a dense web of interdependency that varied by industrial sector, firm—and even person, as is shown in Chapter 6, on the steel magnate August Thyssen. The levels of financing needed by firms, especially after the 1890s, often outstripped the capabilities of any one bank. Banking consortiums rapidly became the norm. Industrialists explicitly encouraged consortiums, to avoid dependence on any one bank. After 1895 many firms, especially in heavy industry, were sufficiently profitable to rely on retained earnings for long-term investment. Some, such as Krupp, Thyssen, and Siemens, formed investment strategies specifically designed to limit bank influence. Even so, the universal banks did alter the strategic environment for capital-intensive firms.

INDUSTRIAL PRODUCTION

Yet it was not only the power of the universal banks that characterized Germany's path of capitalist development. Germany's long-term strength also rested on the classic industries of the Second Industrial Revolution: deep-shaft coal mining, new mass production steel processes (Bessemer, Siemens-Martin), chemicals, electrical products, heavy industrial machinery, and machine tools. The distinctive aspects of German industry were its strong export orientation and its concentration on investment goods such as machinery. In particular, German firms demonstrated an outstanding ability to commercialize engineering and scientific discoveries. Many of the first movers in these fields would dominate German (and European) markets well into the twentieth century.[28] Table 5.1 lists some of these first movers.

Some German industries remained well behind the pace set in other nations. The production of automobiles, for example, was minuscule compared to that in the United States. In 1913, Germany manufactured just over 17,000 motor vehicles, while the United States turned out over 460,000. Each of the German producers built cars and trucks in a craft-based, labor-intensive manner. Like Rolls-Royce in England, Daimler concentrated on luxury automobiles and, after 1911, aircraft engines. Not until the mid-1920s did Adam Opel, by then Germany's largest car producer, begin to introduce American-style assembly methods.[29]

CORPORATE ORGANIZATION

Beyond its strong roots in craft production, German industry after 1871 developed other characteristics that proved enduring. Although families continued to play an important role in strategic decisionmaking in many large companies, they now worked with and through a managerial hierarchy. People with strong technical skills usually rose to the top. Before 1950 German companies, compared to American ones, tended to have flatter hierarchies, less middle management, and less standardized administrative procedures. They grew more "organically." Because of specialization, diversified product lines, and the necessity to compete in foreign markets, authority was often pushed downward. Responsibility was given to technically competent people in particular product areas, not to American-style middle managers or general managers. The German reputation for excessive bureaucracy, therefore, is largely unjustified.[30]

Table 5.1   The 25 Largest Manufacturing Companies in Germany in 1913, Ranked by Assets

	Company	Founded	Industry	Total Assets (RM millions)
1	Krupp	1812	Coal/Steel/Mechanical Engineering	587.2
2	Thyssen (Consolidated)	1871	Coal/Steel/Fabricated Metal/Mech. Eng.	504.2
3	AEG	1883	Electrical	462.8
4	GBAG	1873	Coal	394.9
5	Siemens-Schuckert	1903	Electrical	313.6
6	Deutsch-Luxembourg	1901	Coal/Steel	278.2
7	(Thyssen) GDK	1891	Coal/Steel	249.9
8	Phoenix	1851	Coal/Steel/Fabr. Metal	223.9
9	Siemens & Halske	1847	Electrical	187.3
10	Harpener Bergbau	1856	Coal	185.9
11	Hohenlohe	1905	Coal	134.0
12	Hibernia	1873	Coal	131.9
13	GHH (Haniel)	1810	Coal/Steel/Mech.Eng.	130.4
14	Bayer	1881	Chemicals	127.5
15	BASF	1865	Chemicals	126.3
16	Loth. Huettenverein	1897	Coal/Steel	116.0
17	F&G Carlswerk	1900	Fabricated Metal	114.8
18	Mannesmann	1890	Steel/Fabricated Metal	114.7
19	Hoechst	1880	Chemicals	114.3
20	Deutsche Solvay	1885	Chemicals	112.7
21	MAN	1898	Mech. Eng.	112.3
22	Rombach	1884	Coal/Steel	111.5
23	Mansfeld	1851	Mining	110.4
24	Zellstoff Waldhof	1884	Paper	109.7
25	Bergmann	1900	Electrical	103.9

RESEARCH AND DEVELOPMENT

German firms pioneered internal laboratories and a commitment to R&D even in such basic industries as coal, iron, and steel. Whereas many British firms tended to rely on trial and error, German companies built upon theoretical science.[31] At its root, German capitalism has long been characterized by science-based commercialization, facilitated by formal information sharing and intra-industry cooperative arrangements. As mentioned earlier, the formation of German business associations was well under way even before the nation's political unification of 1871. This continuing movement was closely linked to research and development. Over the years, a number of cooperative groups such as the Association of German Engineers (1856), the Association of German Iron and Steelmakers (1860), and the Association of German Machine Engineering Firms (1890) were formed to disseminate technical knowledge. Such associations became highly respected consulting organizations for industry and government. They had their own statistical services and published their own magazines.

In 1887 Werner Siemens helped to found the Imperial Institute of Physics and Technology (now the Federal Institute of Physics and Technology). This institute played a role similar to that of the National Physical Laboratory in Britain (1900), the National Bureau of Standards in the United States (1901), and the Institute of Physical and Chemical Research in Japan (1917). Germany was a model for these other institutes, as it was for post-graduate education in the American university system. This whole web of shared knowledge, commitment to science and research, and self-interest was exemplified by the founding of the Kaiser-Wilhelm-Society in 1911 (today called the Max Planck Society). The Society sponsored research and scientific seminars and was funded by both private industry and the government.[32]

OTHER FUNCTIONS OF ASSOCIATIONS

German associations did not limit their activities to the production and dissemination of technical knowledge. They also became important political interest groups. As early as 1876, German steel and textile manufacturers founded the Central Association of German Industrialists. A little later, a similar group called the Federation of Industrialists began to represent many other manufacturers, as well as wholesalers. These two big associations merged in 1913.[33] After having been a member of the Central Association, the chemical industry established an independent association after 1890 to preserve its special interests. Banks too set up their own national organization. Often strongly anti-union, the associations developed long-term plans, coordinated industry strategies with government policy, and negotiated with other sectoral associations.

For smaller firms, the regional Chambers of Commerce provided a policy forum. The state of Württemberg had set up a Central Office for Trade and Commerce in 1848, which became an industrial policy model for other German states. It concentrated especially on workforce education, regional social policy, and improving the economic health of the *"Mittelstand."*[34]

MITTELSTAND

This broad class of small and medium-sized businesses was the heart and soul of German capitalism. It was and continues to be heterogeneous— a mixture of handicraft trades, small craft shops, small and medium-sized industrial firms, agriculture-associated businesses, and small and medium-sized retailers and wholesalers.[35] Mittelstand firms are often strongly identified with their particular regions. Württemberg and Saxony especially turned into hotbeds of industrial activity built on Mittelstand businesses. By 1895, Württemberg showed the most explosive growth in industrial employment, and by 1925 it was, together with Saxony, the leading industrial area in Germany, even more so than the famous Ruhr.[36]

The remarkable dynamic of Mittelstand businesses was usually based on strong family involvement and local or regional orientation. Tapping into a large reservoir of skilled craftsmen, these entrepreneurial firms were able to focus on finished manufactures for niche markets, most notably products requiring fine mechanical work, such as watches, clocks, cameras, optical and musical instruments, but also sophisticated turbines and engines.

Much of the story of the Mittelstand had to do with its slow, uneven integration into the national and international economy. The Mittelstand had to learn how to compete alongside large capital-intensive businesses. It was here that the regional Chambers of Commerce played an important role in initiating and supporting constructive changes that could not be undertaken by small businesses alone.

Despite the central role of the Mittelstand in the process of industrialization, many businessmen in this sector felt increasingly squeezed by large corporations. They opposed those cartels and tariffs that drove up prices for steel, coal, or basic foodstuffs. Their economic anxiety was directed against big business, financial speculation on the stock market and in real estate, as well as against the growing influence of socialism and trade unions. Epitomizing this resentment were small retailers who felt threatened by department stores and retail chains, both of which grew rapidly after the 1890s. Years later, the Nazis tapped these resentments by attacking department stores (in general), and especially those whose owners happened to be Jewish.[37]

CARTELS

In their many forms, cartels were pervasive features of German cooperative capitalism from the 1870s until 1945. The goals of these cartels were usually threefold: (1) to ensure producers and financiers an "adequate" return on their investments by avoiding "excessive" competition; (2) to coordinate supply and demand in the face of business cycles by regulating competition through production quotas or sales quotas; and (3) to represent the marketing interests of the industrial sector as a whole. Acceptance of interfirm agreements took away many aspects of competitive strategy, but at the same time it gave German managers a range of strategic, market-ordering options not available to Americans. In structure, the cartels ranged from oral "gentlemen's agreements" to well-organized syndicates. The "model cartel" was the coal syndicate, which governed production quotas and prices, and which operated in various forms between 1893 and 1945, counting among its members as many as 90 companies before 1914.[38]

Even an IG (*Interessengemeinschaft,* or "community of interest"), which resembled an American holding company, was a coalition of firms that gave up part of their entrepreneurial autonomy. IGs could be relatively weak profit-pooling arrangements or strong rationalizing institutions, depending on the terms of the particular agreement.

Overall, the existence of horizontally aligned cartels tended to encourage vertical integration of production, forcing a change in the strategy and structure in particular of German heavy industry. Unlike American oligopolies, which showed a high degree of market concentration among a few large firms, Germany's integrated combines generally had smaller market shares, but attained a greater degree of vertical integration and a more extensive product line.[39]

The strength of most cartels should not be exaggerated. In actual practice, they were neither monopolistic nor particularly solid. The cartels slowed but did not eliminate concentration. Nor did they prevent competition altogether. Rather they changed its nature. Even within cartels, industrialists could still attempt to increase the differential between cartel-set prices and production costs through greater economies of scale and scope, or higher technical efficiency, or both. Cartel members haggled over quota shares, chased after productive efficiency, and attempted to reduce transaction costs arising from the cartels that they had erected themselves.

German industrialists and bankers largely considered cartels "children of necessity" designed to save entrepreneurs from "ruinous competition." One of Germany's leading liberal thinkers, Lujo Brentano, saw them as "parachutes" that softened landings after a high-flying business cycle. Cartels moderated the price-cutting practices of individual firms in the interests of the industrial branch as a whole. These attitudes were affirmed by a famous Imperial Court decision of 1897, which upheld the legality of cartels in Germany. Said the Court:

> If the price of products of a given trade sinks too deeply such that the healthy operation of the trade is made impossible or endangered, then the resulting crisis would be ruinous not only for the individual, but also for the economy in general. It is therefore in the interests of the whole that inappropriately low prices do not continue to exist in a branch of industry. Commensurately, legislative bodies have often and up to the present day undertaken to exert pressure to raise the prices of certain products by means of protective tariffs. In this sense, it also cannot be considered simply and in general against the interest of the public welfare if the participating entrepreneurs in a trade join together to prevent or moderate the mutual undercutting of prices and the resulting decline in the prices of their products. In addition, if prices remain so low that economic ruin threatens entrepreneurs, their union appears not merely as a rightful exercise of self-preservation, but rather as a measure serving the interests of the whole as well. [The cartel contract] does not violate the principle of freedom of trade, insofar as the interests of the whole should be safeguarded against the self-interest of the individual . . . A contract of such sort can therefore only be objected to . . . if it is obviously intended to bring about an actual monopoly and the usurious exploitation of the consumer, or if such consequences actually are achieved through the contractual agreement and institution.[40]

The Imperial Court justified cartels as a form of "cooperative self-help." Unlike the situation in America, where cartels were illegal, or even in Britain, where they were tolerated but not enforced, German cartel agreements were both legal and enforceable.[41]

The distinction between giant American firms ("trusts") and German cartels is critical to an understanding of the positive assessment of cartels in the eyes of German economists and the German public. They found "trusts" (a derogatory term in Germany) to be far more dangerous than cartels. Cartels were contractual associations of legally independent firms. American-style trusts and mergers, by contrast, dissolved the legal and economic independence of individual firms into one big corporation under a single management.

The cartels were thus viewed by many Germans as a "dike" against further trustification. They were favored because they reduced the level of industrial concentration and allowed smaller firms to stay in business. Cartels, it was argued, could help to provide a steady source of employment in comparison to the "unbelievably ruthless" American practice of "throwing workers into the streets."[42] The Social Democrats also realized that freedom of association was critical for legitimizing workers' unions, a belief borne out by the frequent early use of the Sherman Antitrust Act of 1890 against the American union movement. In addition, some Social Democrats found cartels a necessary stage toward a socialized economy.

Unlike American oligopolies led by huge firms such as U.S. Steel, which alone accounted for 45 to 77 percent market share of various iron and steel product lines in America in 1901, the 10 largest German companies produced only about 50 percent of German crude steel. The 10 largest German mining firms (often the same as the steel companies) had just under a 30 percent market share in 1913.[43] Cartel-administered price collusion kept German steel companies relatively small compared to American firms in any given product line. Hence, the cartels proved quite successful as a means of avoiding excessive concentrations of property and keeping ownership in the hands of family members.

In the words of Gustav Schmoller, Germany's leading economist before World War I, cartels were a form of "cooperative competition" that only "fanatics of individualism" would want to ban. At bottom, German economists of the late nineteenth and early twentieth centuries were skeptical of Adam Smith's arguments that the unlimited pursuit of private gain always served the public interest. They did not believe that a host of uncoordinated decisions automatically added up to a superior economic order.[44]

LABOR AND THE GOVERNMENT

The major outsider to this producer-oriented, cooperative capitalism was labor. Unlike the American labor movement, which focused mainly on wages and hours, the German labor movement made sweeping calls for political and economic change. Its main actors embraced Marxism and called for a transformation to socialism. A significant minority advocated a communist revolution. In practice, however, the Social Democrats, along with the unions, focused on pushing for greater democracy in government and in business firms.[45]

At the start of the twentieth century, as now, unions in Germany were built on a core of highly skilled workers. The strength of organized labor in Imperial Germany, together with the paternalist traditions among economic and political elites, resulted in a peculiar system of industrial relations that combined progressive reforms "from above" with outright repression. Labor relations inside the firm were characterized by a top-down, military model of command, but were softened by strong welfare policies. Krupp, for example, provided about 6,000 homes for its employees in 1906. Far in advance of their American counterparts, major German companies in all industrial sectors introduced sickness, accident, and disability insurance, as well as retirement benefits for white-collar employees. Some of these policies were mandated by the imperial government, but others were voluntarily introduced by the companies.[46]

Most significant of all was Chancellor Bismarck's successful push for comprehensive social insurance, which became the basis of what Germans still call the "social state" *(Sozialstaat)*, the first state-administered insurance scheme in the world and more than a generation in advance of most such developments in the United States.[47] Between 1883 and 1889, a compulsory health insurance law, a worker compensation scheme, and pension and disability insurance laws were passed. It was the responsibility of the employer to bear all worker compensation costs. Employers and employees shared health insurance payments, and the state added to the pension and disability funds. The insurance boards consisted of both managers and workers, and they became a forum where workers could have their voices heard about company policy. In 1891, worker protection laws were inserted into a new set of trade regulations, and industrial courts were formed to mediate and inspect conditions in the factory. The factory insurance plans were the seedbeds for modern "codetermination," or worker representation, in German firms. Altogether, Bismarck's initiatives began to build an influential model of social reform around the principle of insurance, rather than the principle of welfare, which built on poor relief and charitable help for those who fell onto hard times.[48]

Yet the advanced German welfare state went hand in hand with political repression. The so-called Socialist Laws outlawed the Social Democratic Party and made trade unions illegal from 1878 to 1890. Despite the ban, the Social Democrats became more and more popular both before and after 1890, their brand of Marxist agitation being tempered by a firm commitment to pragmatic reform. By 1912, they received 34.8 percent of the vote, and by 1914, Germany had the largest organized socialist party in the world.[49] The growth of support for socialism in Germany went hand in hand with that for democracy, and this situation generated tremendous political tension.

World War I, 1914–1918

World War I changed the face of German capitalism. The war created new relationships among industry, labor, and the government, resulting eventually in greater power for labor. Labor sought a stronger role in microeconomic and governmental decisionmaking, and at the same time the war transformed the government into a new, more powerful macroeconomic force. For 45 years after 1914, many of the most serious problems of business involved both labor and government, and were as much political as economic in nature.[50]

In 1914, as the demand for war production increased, the state took on new roles. There was already a tradition in German history that industrialists would take the lead in organizing themselves on behalf of the state, and they did so now. Walther Rathenau, the son of the founder of the electrical giant AEG, and himself a leading businessman, urged the government to set up a central office to manage raw materials and important foodstuffs. Government officials found the cartel system to be a natural intermediary through which to regulate the war economy. These private organizations thus came to fulfill a public function, one that could be easily extended as the need arose. "War committees" in the name of industrial self-administration were established.[51]

By 1916, however, it had become clear that such efforts were not sufficient, especially since industry took advantage and reaped tremendous profits. The "Battles of Materiél" on the Somme in the summer of 1916 made it apparent that far higher levels of production and economic mobilization were necessary. The Hindenberg Program (named for a leading general in the army) and the Auxiliary Service Law for the Fatherland, passed in 1916, proved to be major turning points. They were designed to maximize war production with little regard for cost. No caps on war profits were imposed. With prominent industrialists in its advisory council and technical staff, a new War Office was established for the mobilization of manpower resources and the centralization of military procurement. The Auxiliary Service Law also mobilized most German civilian men for war-related work and allowed the state to shut down small firms in order to transfer labor to high-priority factories.

But the Auxiliary Service Law also forced employers to recognize worker representation in those factories. It introduced collective bargaining and affirmed unions' right to organize. Worker committees were established to help mediate disputes. The military often intervened on the side of workers in issues such as cost-of-living raises. Industrialists insisted (unsuccessfully) that all these reforms were temporary wartime measures and they increasingly derided this government intervention as a type of "war socialism" or as "concessions to the street."[52]

By 1916, the war had become an all-out contest of attrition, requiring an unprecedented mobilization of the whole society.[53] Between 1916 and 1918, the German business system, for all practical purposes, operated under a command economy. For German consumers, the war years meant severe shortages caused by an Allied sea blockade. Price controls and regulations were established, but their main effect was to create a flourishing black market and hide the real rate of inflation.

The war also radicalized the middle classes, who increasingly felt squeezed by the organized interests of big business on one side and of labor on the other. Retailers and farmers—some of the strongest supporters of the government—found themselves the target of hostility by their fellow Germans who were angry about rising prices. The middle classes felt increasingly impoverished and disenchanted. The war began a "decade of hell" for small retailers, who were especially squeezed by inflation. Tensions rose quickly among Germans and were often released against Jews and against so-called speculators.[54]

In many large firms, especially the mines, a radical communist movement gained strength. Wildcat strikes became a common feature throughout the "turnip winters." Ironically, it was the Social Democratic unions and workers' committees that staved off a broader strike movement in the interests of peaceful and democratic change.[55]

The war permanently changed the relationship of the state to the economy. Notions of a planned economy, which had been embraced by those on the political left, now also found adherents on the right.[56] These ideas were generally opposed by business, but they continued to resonate throughout the twentieth century in the notion of a "Third Way," situated somewhere between free-market capitalism and communism, between models represented by the United States on one side and the new Soviet Union on the other.

The Weimar Republic, 1919–1933

The war left a legacy of impoverishment and a sense of social decline, especially among the middle classes. The sudden and surprising military defeat of November 1918 brought Germany to the brink of a full-scale revolution. General Erich Ludendorff, the Chief of Staff, had asked for an armistice while the German army was still deep in the heart of France. Germany had not been invaded, and German public opinion was completely unprepared for the news of defeat. Because of press censorship, many Germans thought the army had been undefeated in the field. This myth paved the way for the stab-in-the-back legend propagated by Generals Ludendorff and Paul von Hindenburg, both of whom viewed Germany's defeat as having resulted from socialist agitation.

In November 1918, the monarchy collapsed, along with the old Prussian military order, leaving parliament the unpleasant task of negotiating peace terms with the victorious Allies. On November 9, 1918, a new German republic was proclaimed, accompanied by an air of revolution, strikes, and power wielded by left-wing soviets (councils). Reluctantly, industrialists had to rely on labor unions and the Social Democrats to maintain order. When in January of 1919 the first fully democratic parliament in German history was elected, the Social Democrats garnered the largest number of votes. The new Weimar Republic, as it came to be called, got its name from the small town where the first parliamentary proceedings were held, by delegates escaping the violent situation in Berlin. The Social Democrat–led government sent troops into the cities to quell left-wing strikes and communist agitation, and these troops often used excessive violence.[57]

Even so, the new republic was built on a social compromise between employer and union associations, and it gave Germany the most advanced system of industrial relations and social welfare in the world. German industrialists met labor halfway in order to head off more radical threats to the rights of private property. The symbol of this cooperation was the Central Working Association, which had been formed in November of 1918. Hugo Stinnes, representing the employer position, and Carl Legien, representing the unions, signed an agreement that institutionalized collective bargaining, guaranteed returning soldiers their old jobs, confirmed the status of worker's committees in companies, established wage arbitration courts, and introduced the eight-hour workday.[58]

Along with the new democratic constitution, the Weimar Republic introduced important reforms to Germany's "economic order." Parliament gained control over economic policy. The central government acquired tax sovereignty over the states. A central finance ministry was formed, and historians have spoken of it as the "first comprehensive nonmilitary executive organ in [the history] of the Reich."[59] Public spending as a proportion of national product rose dramatically. A Factory Council law was ratified in 1920, allowing worker representatives to sit in on supervisory board meetings, as they still do today in Germany's largest firms.[60] Unemployment insurance was enacted in 1927, and before the depression of the 1930s Germany allocated proportionally more public funds to social expenditure than did any other industrialized nation.[61]

FROM REPARATIONS TO HYPERINFLATION

Simultaneously with those reorganizations, however, the 1919 Treaty of Versailles had delivered a sharp blow to the German economy. Half of Upper Silesia, most of Posen and East Prussia, the Saar, the left bank of the Rhineland, and Alsace-Lorraine were not returned to German control. These border changes meant the loss of roughly 80 percent of German iron ore supplies, 44 percent of pig iron capacity, 36 percent of steel capacity, and 32 percent of rolled steel product capacity. The treaty required Germany to deliver 25–40 million tons of coal yearly and 25 percent of its pharmaceutical and dye production to France, Belgium, and Italy until 1925. All overseas assets of German companies in Allied countries were lost, without compensation. Tariff sovereignty was denied to Germany until 1925. France, Belgium, and Luxembourg imposed inside Germany a five-year tariff-free zone for all of their own iron and steel products. At the same time, a wave of international protectionism followed the war, and tariffs were raised against German exports.[62]

For ordinary Germans, the most hateful and humiliating aspect of the Versailles Treaty was the "war guilt" clause, which blamed Germany for starting the war and thus purported to justify reparations of over 132 billion gold marks. Over the next decade, the questions of if, when, and how the Germans would pay became one of the most controversial points of international politics. John Maynard Keynes and many other economists denounced the treaty, which they believed would ruin European economic recovery. On the domestic front, the reparations question poisoned Weimar politics almost irreparably. Right-wing nationalists viciously attacked those in government who supported a policy of fulfillment of the terms of the treaty, which under the circumstances was the only responsible policy.[63]

Already severely strained, the German economy was hit in the early 1920s by a spectacular financial crisis. The war had been financed largely by bonds and by the printing of money. Although this generated some inflation, monetary problems had remained manageable through the war years. Inflation turned sharply upward from 1919 to 1922, however, and then broke into hyperinflation in the summer of 1922 because of the domestic and international stalemate over the reparations issue. Hyperinflation accelerated in 1923, when the French invaded the Ruhr to confiscate coal and steel goods in lieu of reparations. In response to this seizure, the Germans began a campaign of passive resistance, whereby workers were paid with newly printed marks for not working. This step destroyed the Reichsmark altogether. Whereas in January 1919 the American dollar was worth an average of 8.2 Reichsmarks, four years later one dollar bought 17,972 RM. After ten more months one dollar equaled 4 trillion RM.[64]

Political tensions remained high throughout the course of the inflation. Finance Minister Mathias Erzberger, who was trying desperately to stabilize the finances of the Republic, was murdered in 1921 by two right-wing assassins. Foreign Minister Walter Rathenau, who was attempting to put the reparations on some stable basis, was submachine-gunned to death in June 1922. The left-wing governments of Saxony and Thuringia armed themselves against fascist movements in Bavaria. And on November 8–9, 1923, Adolf Hitler attempted a *Putsch* (coup d'état) in Munich. The Putsch failed, and Hitler went to jail, where he began to write *Mein Kampf.*

Meanwhile, in November of 1923, a new currency, the Rentenmark, was introduced, a step that ended the hyperinflation almost overnight. (The term *Rentenmark* derived from the successful *Rentenbriefe,* which were state-guaranteed bonds issued in the nineteenth century to compensate landlords after the peasants were emancipated.) The Rentenmark was backed by mortgages on the lands and industrial assets of the "productive classes," that is, the top strata of German capitalism.[65] The new currency also introduced into public life the mercurial figure of Reichsbank President Hjalmar Schacht. Schacht's policy of tight credit paved the way for extensive American loans to German firms. These loans allowed the Germans to turn the Rentenmark into a gold-backed currency and then into Reichsmarks.[66]

These economic and political crises resulted in structural changes for German industry. Steelmakers went on a binge of mergers and acquisitions to reconstruct their vertically integrated structures, and to diversify into machine engineering. The entrepreneur Hugo Stinnes, nicknamed the "Inflation King" for having profited exorbitantly from the monetary crisis, offered the most dramatic vision of empire-building. He formed the Siemens-Rheinelbe-Schuckert Union (SRSU) as an Interessengemeinschaft (IG), uniting coal, steel, and electrical-engineering firms.[67] In the end, big business was considered the "winner" in the losing game of inflation. The banking sector in particular underwent a major wave of consolidation to compensate for the depreciation of its assets.[68]

The big losers of the great inflation were elderly pensioners, small savers, students, and the owners of small and medium-sized businesses. All of these groups saw their savings devalued. They also felt left out of the political process. Partly as a result of the great inflation, many disaffected voters drifted to splinter parties on the right, and eventually to Hitler. An increasing number of people vented their anger and, with their rabid anti-semitism, found a scapegoat in the Jews. Another legacy of the hyperinflation was a type of fiscal conservatism that later hindered the government's attempt to deal with the Great Depression of the 1930s. Nervousness about the stability of the currency discredited many potential counter-cyclical measures until it was too late.[69]

THE BRIEF "GOLDEN YEARS"

But before the crash of 1929 there were a few years of prosperity. These years saw the flowering not only of the economy but also of cultural life, years that indeed brought the stamp of modernism with which Weimar Germany has been generally associated. Modernism implied a more rational organization of society and also of business. Some companies became more "American," using time-and-motion studies, assembly lines, piecework practices, and even *Psychotechnik* (experimental psychological studies designed to put the right person in the right place).[70]

Meanwhile, detailed business norms and standards were created by what, in English translation, was called the German Standards Committee. An earlier Standards Committee of German Industry had been established in December 1917 as a subcommittee of the Association of German Engineers. By 1926, it was closely affiliated with the central efficiency commission organized by industry associations in the interest of "self-administration" of the economy. At this time it was renamed the German Standards Committee. This shift in title was characteristic of the practice of German industry at this time to speak for the good of the nation as a whole. Nor was the practice an empty gesture. The total number of standards created by the committee went from 66 by early 1920, to 125 by May 1921, then to 1,100 by the beginning of 1925, 2,000 by 1927, 2,900 by 1929, and 4,500 by 1932.[71] These norms still underlie product standards in Germany today.

"Trusts" also began to appear in the 1920s, among them the chemical giant IG Farben, consisting of Bayer, Hoechst, BASF, Cassella, and four others. In automobiles there was Daimler-Benz. In steel there was the Vereinigte Stahlwerke (VSt), that is, in English, the United Steelworks. This huge combine included Thyssen, Phoenix, Rheinische Stahlwerke, Dortmunder Union, Gelsenkirchen, and the Bochumer Verein. The VSt was explicitly modeled on U.S. Steel. It introduced new methods of "American" accounting and installed an extensive Hollerith (IBM) information system.[72]

Meanwhile, the number of small, regional, and medium-sized cartels exploded into the thousands. Even international cartels appeared. A whole series of transnational agreements were formed in the chemical industry, which included firms in the United States and Japan. The most important international cartel was the one set up in the steel industry in 1926, which included Germany, France, Belgium, Luxembourg, and Czechoslovakia.[73]

Surprisingly, union leaders and Social Democrats were often the most enthusiastic proponents of business rationalization. They envisioned a future of increased productivity, high wages, and a consumer society. Industrialists often tended to be skeptical. They believed that Germany lacked a strong consumer market appropriate to American-style mass-production methods. They cited the traditional German emphasis on "quality work." Moreover, the broad base of Mittelstand businesses made assembly-line techniques less attractive. Many Germans preferred instead a system of industrial and vocational apprenticeship, a form of technical training that also indoctrinated the workforce with obedience, patriotism, and pride in the national and regional community.[74]

The short breathing space enjoyed by the German economy in the 1920s derived ultimately from the willingness of the Allies to ease the burden of war reparations. A triangular system of debt payments emerged: American credit flowed to Germany, the Germans used the money to pay reparations to Britain and France, and the British and French sent the money back to the United States to service their own huge wartime debts. This system was a life preserver for Germany and for the international economy. By 1928, Germany's Gross Domestic Product finally surpassed that of 1913.[75]

The debate about social policy and the limits of the new welfare system continued throughout these "golden" years. Industry expanded its social welfare measures in the 1920s, but wanted them to be in the hands of private firms, not the central state. Still, German capitalism's distinctive emphasis on some sort of social policy remained unquestioned. The real issue was how much German business could afford, and who was going to require what. As employers in the Reich Economic Council (a top business group), emphasized in 1924:

> We do not need to follow the "like it or lump it" policy of the Americans in the area of social policy, which is simply "work or you die." In America, there is no social welfare policy at all. We certainly don't

want that. But insofar as questions of how far we want to go in our social legislation and welfare are concerned, the outside world has a voice today. We need foreign credit, and the outside world asks: what are you going to do with the credit? We cannot afford things they cannot afford.[76]

Following up on such thinking, the Ruhr iron and steel industry in 1928 engaged in a massive lockout that called into question the implicit labor-management compromise undergirding the industrial peace of the Weimar Republic. Steel firms refused to accept a wage decision handed down by a government arbitration board. The ensuing mixture of economic and political conflict seriously damaged the shaky Weimar democracy.[77]

THE GREAT DEPRESSION AND HITLER'S RISE TO POWER

The level of stabilization that had been attained by the mid-1920s was devastated once the Great Depression hit. In 1928, exports, the lifeblood of the German economy, began to slow. Business investment dropped significantly. World market prices for agricultural goods fell, and the reparations monster reared its ugly head again. Then the Wall Street crash in October 1929 sank the life preserver of American money. The ensuing depression affected Germany even more than most other countries because of its strong export orientation and weak consumer market. Unemployment rose from 10 percent in 1929 to 25 percent by 1931, and to the astronomical figure of 33 percent in the winter of 1932–33. Numerous banks became insolvent.[78]

The political fallout from the economic crisis now began to threaten Germany's fragile democratic institutions. From March 1930 on, Germany was governed by an ad hoc presidential regime using emergency decrees. The Chancellors of the Republic ruled with little support from Parliament, but were backed by an aged, near senile President (former Field Marshal Paul von Hindenburg) and by many conservatives, including a large number of businessmen.[79]

It was in the context of this crisis that the National Socialists (Nazis) were able to take power. Historians have disagreed on which factor was decisive in moving Germany onto the road that led to Hitlerian barbarism. Some argue that traditional and still powerful military and business elites turned against democracy by backing a group of conservative politicians, who eventually embraced Hitler and appointed him Chancellor on January 30, 1933. Other historians emphasize that popular support for the presidential cabinet and the entire Weimar "system" evaporated as a result of the economic crisis.

Statistics provide at least some indication of what was happening. Voters on the left gravitated toward the Communist Party (10–17 percent in the late 1920s and early 1930s), while those on the right moved toward the National Socialist party. In May 1928, the Nazis received only 2.6 percent of the national vote; but in September 1930, 18.3 percent; then in March and April 1932, 30.2 percent in the first presidential election and 36.8 percent in the second; in July 1932, 37.4 percent; and in November 1932, 33.1 percent. In March 1933, after Hitler's appointment as Chancellor, the party polled 43.9 percent of the vote, but this was not a free election. Hitler already had suspended civil liberties, rounded up and harassed his political enemies, and ransacked opposition parties' headquarters. Tragically, Hitler had been appointed Chancellor just as his popularity was waning, his party treasury nearing bankruptcy, and the German economy showing signs of recovery. The horrors of Nazi Germany, therefore, were not inevitable.[80]

The role of businessmen in Hitler's rise has been the subject of heated controversy, but it is clear that big industrial interests did not put Hitler into power. His party rode into power on a wave of strong popular support, even though not majority support, which no party had. Although some prominent industrialists, such as Fritz Thyssen, did support Hitler early on, others showed a profound ambivalence toward the Nazi party. Its "socialist" goals included the abolition of interest, nationalization of many business enterprises, profit-sharing by large industrial firms, expansion of old-age pensions and social benefits, and immediate government seizure of huge department stores, which were to be leased to small shopkeepers. Yet many businessmen, challenged by a strong labor movement and a disintegrating economy, had become disenchanted with democracy. By January 1932, when Hitler delivered an important speech at the Industry Club of Düsseldorf, many powerful figures in German business had become convinced that they could do business with him.

Big industrial firms and lobbies gave money mostly to the conservative nationalist parties, but these parties' popular support dwindled. A good deal of Nazi financial support came from disenchanted leaders of Mittelstand firms and from grassroots donations.[81] Overall, the abandonment of the Weimar Republic by most of the country's elites, together with the popular support for Hitler, put an end to democracy in Germany after only 14 years' experience with it.

The Third Reich, 1933–1945

The assumption of power by the National Socialists ushered in a new "economic order" that was designed principally around rearmament and war. Though official economic ideology explicitly denounced "liberal capitalism," the cooperation of German industry was needed for rearmament. Hitler downplayed the more radical elements of his economic policy program, and essentially tried to divorce liberalism from capitalism. The Third Reich exercised greater state control over foreign trade and exchange, wages and prices, raw material supplies, and investment. It circumscribed the rights of private property, but did not dissolve them. Private interests had to orient or subordinate themselves to the "common interest" as set by Hitler and the Nazi Party. In the end, the Nazis were able to harness private capitalism and individual ambition to its larger goals.[82]

The government's macroeconomic approach went through three distinct phases: general economic recovery supported by large public works programs from 1933 to 1936, accelerated rearmament under the auspices of Hermann Göring until the army's failure in Moscow in the winter of 1941, and massive rationalization of the war economy under Albert Speer thereafter.

PHASE 1: ABSOLUTE POWER AND ECONOMIC RECOVERY

In 1933, Hitler's first moves to consolidate power were political. He suspended civil liberties and destroyed the Communist Party. The first concentration camps, for political prisoners, were set up. Party leaders and organizations unsympathetic to the Nazis were terrorized. On March 24, 1933, the Weimar constitution was disabled. Harassment of Jews, liberal or socialist intellectuals, some Catholics, and Social Democrats followed. By the summer of 1933, the Nazis had dissolved all other political parties, making Germany a one-party state.[83]

An ominous policy of "synchronization" (Gleichschaltung) subsumed public and private associations under Nazi party organization, including the top industrial association, the Reich Association of German Industry.

The state forced all major industries to cartelize. The cartels then became not a means of self-government, but an instrument of the state. Price controls were introduced. The Nazis also eliminated union organizations and seized their property, replacing them with the "German Labor Front." A new industrial relations law ended collective bargaining and factory councils, substituting the principle of unconditional subordination of workers, who were now termed "followers."

As he took power, Hitler's domestic popularity depended on whether or not he could provide jobs. The Nazis therefore used a welter of macroeconomic policies to overcome slack demand and reduce unemployment. The "battle for work" was masterminded by the opportunistic Reichsbank President Hjalmar Schacht, who became Hitler's Minister of Economics.[84] Hitler particularly liked grandiose public undertakings such as the building of monumental architectural projects in Berlin and Nuremberg. He promoted the People's Radio (the better to hear Hitler), the Autobahn, and a new "people's car" (Volkswagen). All of these projects were designed to make the new Nazi order appear powerful, efficient, and modern.[85] Many public works projects, including the Autobahn, had already been suggested under previous governments. But Nazi propaganda skillfully credited Hitler for all of them and for the subsequent recovery of the German economy.

The scale of these undertakings was sometimes vast, as exemplified by the plans to build a low-priced family car—the VW. The designer Ferdinand Porsche received unprecedented financial support for working on the new car. The Nazi German Labor Front took over control of erecting an immense new plant at Wolfsburg, a plant even larger than Ford's huge Willow Run factory near Detroit. The Wolfsburg facility was built entirely on the principles of Fordist mass production, a stunning exception to the traditional manner of German shopfloor organization. Like so much of the Nazi regime, however, the VW project turned into a colossal scam. By 1945 not one German had a VW delivered, although several hundred thousand people had submitted advance monthly installment payments over a period of years.[86]

Full employment in Germany was reached by 1936, but at the cost of vanishing civil liberties, low living standards, wage and price controls, low productivity, and a loss of union bargaining power. Businesses recorded higher profit rates, but at the cost of greater state regulations and interference by Nazi party organizations. In spite of the recovery, real earnings never reached the peak levels that had been achieved under the Weimar system.[87]

PHASE 2: PREPARING FOR WAR

The announcement in 1936 of the Four Year Plan under General Hermann Göring, Hitler's deputy and a World War I flying ace, marked a turning point in Nazi preparations for war. Just as the Olympic games were being held in Berlin, Hitler issued a top-secret memorandum calling for an "autarkic" (self-sufficient) economy capable of waging war within four years. The Four Year Plan put special emphasis on the development of iron ore, synthetic rubber, synthetic fuel oil, synthetic textiles, and oils and fats for explosives, and on the production of all kinds of military equipment.[88]

How did business react to these preparations for war? The huge chemical combine IG Farben naturally played a central role in the Four Year Plan. Its executives' responses to government initiatives were typical for those businessmen who sought to preserve the long-term interests of their companies at any cost. When IG Farben at first objected to raising its production of synthetic textiles, Nazi economic planners simply established five new regional companies, using government funds. The Nazis then forced local textile firms to buy stock in the new companies and to use at least 20 percent synthetic fibers in their fabrics. It did not take long for IG Farben to scramble more actively into the synthetic textile field in order to preserve its own market share. IG Farben's Chief, Carl Krauch, joined the staff of Göring's Four Year Plan and became one of its most important architects. This form of weak resistance and eventual involvement sent business executives ever deeper into active accommodation with the Third Reich, and placed them on a slippery slope that ran all the way to Auschwitz.[89]

Hitler's treatment of leading executives, whom he once called "gullible fools," was exemplified by the confrontation between the new Nazi steel company (the Reichswerke Hermann Göring) and the giant VSt.[90] VSt executives feared that the Reichswerke, engaged in an ever-increasing number of industrial ventures, would simply add an unnecessary competitor in the industry. But when they objected, Göring threatened to arrest them for conspiracy, and they caved in. So the Nazis quickly defeated the steel industry, which had once fielded Germany's most powerful industrial lobby. Such defeats became easier for business to bear as rearmament provided a welcome source of contracts for German indus-try. Daimler-Benz, Krupp, the machinery giant MAN, Rheinmetall, BMW, and Henschel all expanded quickly. Daimler-Benz's Munich sales director delivered Mercedes automobiles to top Nazi officials at special prices. He himself was a longtime personal friend of Hitler's.[91]

Nazi labor policy manifested the same combination of incentives, ac-commodation, and repression that characterized the regime as a whole. The Nazi-sponsored German Labor Front helped to improve working conditions in factories, initiated cheap holiday excursions, and drew up plans for a comprehensive social policy. The Nazis promised full em-ployment, a performance-based wage system, medical care (including preventive medicine), housing, and social insurance.[92] On the other hand, the German Labor Front absorbed the old working-class unions, disem-powered workers, and brutally suppressed dissent.

ANTI-SEMITISM

The feverish escalation of rearmament was matched by the radicalization of Hitler's other war, the one against the Jews. Up until 1938 the Nazis followed a simple strategy of making discrimination legal. For example, they implemented the "Nuremberg Laws" (1935) which deprived Jews (also Gypsies, homosexuals, and the mentally ill) of their political rights. The law also forbade "mixed" marriages.[93]

The Four Year Plan contemplated the expropriation of all Jewish busi-nesses. In 1938, new laws defined any firm with just one Jewish super-visory board member as "Jewish," and thus ineligible for government contracts. IG Farben's CEO, Carl Bosch, confronted Hitler directly with the Jewish question, sending the Führer into a rage. Bosch was curtly turned away, as understanding nothing about politics. IG Farben then proceeded to transfer many of its Jewish executives to overseas posts, removing them from harm's way. But at the same time it accepted the Nazi party line. It tried to compensate for its "Jewish" reputation. In its public statements it downplayed the actual extent of anti-Semitic activ-ities in Germany in an effort to save its foreign sales. About one-fourth of the members of IG Farben's 24-member supervisory board at the end of 1937 were Jewish. With the Aryanization laws of 1938, all of these Jewish board members were forced to resign.[94]

By the end of 1938, Jews were officially excluded from German eco-nomic life altogether. Hundreds of Jewish-owned businesses, including a number of major department stores, were sold off at bargain-basement prices, often to the great benefit of non-Jewish competitors and with their strong support.

The path from exclusion to deportation and extermination was short. In November of 1938, Nazi stormtroopers burned synagogues and destroyed thousands of Jewish businesses, in a rampage that became known as "Crystal Night." At this time about 25,000 Jews were sent to concentration camps.[95] Bereft of their civil rights, without means of support for their families, and lacking any sense of their future in a country where they had deep roots, thousands of Jews emigrated. After Germany invaded Poland in 1939, however, escape became increasingly difficult. Rapidly the Nazis' net grew tighter. Jews were forced into ghettos in 1941 and 1942, and eventually were deported to the factories and gas chambers of Auschwitz, Treblinka, Majdanek, and Sobibor.

Mass murder went hand in hand with war. Indeed, it was the military success of the German army that enabled the Nazis to get hold of most of Europe's Jewish population. As the war began, Germany fielded a fighting machine that seemed unstoppable. The devastating *Blitzkrieg* ("lightning war") on Poland and France quickly subdued two major military opponents. Rearmament under the Four Year Plan, despite its vast inefficiencies, stood on the brink of success.

PHASE 3: THE WAR ECONOMY

Hitler's strategy of winning in a short war was rooted in military thinking as well as in the specific shape of Germany's war economy. Resources were tight. Conflicting priorities and the lack of coordination led to a Darwinian struggle between regular army procurement offices and Heinrich Himmler's growing SS military empire. "Combing out" actions transferred workers from firms of low priority to armaments-related companies, but often hurt important subcontractors. Inefficiency and low productivity resulted. But the war itself would soon supply from conquered countries the raw materials and labor necessary to expand production.[96]

The haphazard nature of the war economy began to improve in early 1942 when Hitler appointed Albert Speer, who had previously served as his architect and urban designer, as Minister of Armaments. With Hitler's support, Speer formed a command economy with relatively clear lines of responsibility. Speer involved industry more directly in committees (so-called product rings), which set targets and designed simplified but robust weapons that could be made in long production runs. Speer called this principle of business involvement "industrial self-responsibility." Scientific management principles, best-practice pricing, volume production, and faster throughput, combined with the exploitation of foreign workers and concentration camp inmates, all became hallmarks of Speer's administration. In the end, Speer and other managerial technocrats made Nazi Germany even more murderous.[97]

One short-term result of these efforts was a quadrupling of aircraft production between 1941 and 1944 with the same number of workers, and a 250 percent increase in the production of tanks between 1941 and 1943. Despite a shortage of steel, production of weapons rose by roughly 200 percent in most sectors, and German armaments production actually reached a peak early in 1944, at the height of the Allied bombing offensive. Only at the very end of 1944 did ceaseless bombing begin to thwart the regular supply of materials and the delivery of finished products to the military. At that point, the German economic infrastructure gradually began to crumble. But German production facilities continued to turn out armaments.[98]

The demands of the war caused wide-ranging structural changes in the German economy, and these changes are important for understanding the postwar economic miracle and even the economy as it was at the end of the twentieth century. Overall, the war economy under Speer became a Mittelstand affair. It moved away from the predominance of heavy primary materials (steel, coal) to the finished manufacturing industries: automobiles, engines, aircraft (including jet fighters and rockets), mechanical engineering and machine parts, machine tools, electronics, and radar. The armament boom transformed the German economic landscape by integrating older small and medium-sized firms into large networks of subcontractors on a strongly regional basis. It allowed a great number of new Mittelstand businesses to blossom. Almost half of the armament firms around the Augsburg area in Bavaria employed fewer than 100 employees. Over 80 percent of the subcontractors for the aircraft company Messerschmitt employed fewer than 250 employees.[99]

Much of the war economy operated on the backs of millions of slave laborers who were brought into Germany or forced to work at factories located in German-occupied areas of Europe. At about the same time that Speer became armaments czar, Hitler appointed Fritz Sauckel to a position as the plenipotentiary of labor allocation. Sauckel's position gave him full authority to round up, kidnap, and force foreign workers into the armament factories of the Third Reich. Sauckel set up quotas that encouraged his men to ship people into Germany. Some were kidnapped as they were standing in line at the movies in Warsaw or attending church in Minsk or celebrating in Ukrainian villages. Himmler's SS set up work camps around factories, viewing labor as the "spoils of conquest." At the Messerschmitt aircraft works 50 percent of all workers employed were foreigners, at Daimler-Benz about 45 percent, at the machinery giant MAN about 32 percent, and at Siemens about 26 percent. They received very low wages or none at all. Their treatment varied but it was generally poor and often brutal. Foreign workers wasted away in the mines and factories from malnutrition, overwork, sickness, and mistreatment.[100]

Until late in the war, the armaments industry as a whole did not resort to employing concentration camp inmates, although the SS had exploited them in its own camps and enterprises. Early in 1944, however, Speer requested that Himmler "assist armaments production to a greater degree than previously by deploying concentration camp inmates in functions that I regard as especially urgent [since] the inflow of foreigners has been on a considerable decline for some time now."[101] The SS then used concentration camp inmates for private industry, especially to build underground sites for relocating the all-important aircraft industry. Overall, about 600,000 concentration camp inmates were employed, just over one-third in private industry. Most of them did not survive the war.

BETWEEN FOLLOWER AND ACCOMPLICE

How did so many German businessmen become accomplices in such barbarism? Their narrow focus on company profits and the jockeying for improved positions in the Nazi "New European Order" resulted in a complete ethical and moral collapse. Superficial legality went hand in hand with crimes, and managerial responsibility fed into political immorality.

In retrospect, many businesspeople argued: "We did not know." "We were just following orders." "We just built the planes." "We would have been sent to the Gestapo."

The unique aspect of Nazi economic ideology and practice was its ability to align private self-interest with its radical goals of conquest and plunder. For example, in 1941 the industrialist Gustav Krupp stated in a company memorandum that because no consistent business strategy was possible under the Nazi regime, "Krupp's interests must be pursued as an opportunity arises."[102] Opportunities did arise, professional self-interest came to the fore, and German business sank ever deeper into complicity. The Nazi party steered Germany's economic order and let the engine of capitalist production motor it along.

The ethical collapse, defined by a sort of conscienceless professionalism, led some businesses into direct involvement in the most heinous crimes of the Nazis, including the Holocaust. IG Farben's synthetic rubber plant, for example, was constructed only three miles outside the extermination camp at Auschwitz. It used a revolving supply of camp inmates, who wasted away at a rate of 32 deaths per day. The Italian author Primo Levi, who wrote an eyewitness account, probably survived only because he worked in the polymerization laboratory there.[103] Its Zyklon-B product was the gas used in the chambers of Auschwitz.[104]

In the spring of 1945, Allied troops finally liberated the death camps and crushed the German armed forces. Hitler ordered Germans to leave their country a scorched earth for the Allies, essentially asking them to commit suicide along with him. Hitler's war had almost destroyed Germany, and the Holocaust had left behind a huge moral mortgage.

For most Germans, though, the immediate postwar concern was simply survival. After that, they tried to return to normal life, reestablish a credible government, and come to terms with the horrors of the Third Reich. By the 1990s, only the last issue remained a touchy question.[105]

Occupation, 1945–1949

For the Allies, the top priority was making the world safe from German aggression. Between 1945 and 1948, they divided Germany into four occupation zones: French, British, American, and Soviet. The first three became West Germany, the last East Germany. The capital, Berlin, though located in eastern Germany, was also divided into four zones.

At first, all of the Allies worked to dismantle German industry, the French and Soviets being the most aggressive. Henry Morgenthau, the U.S. Treasury Secretary, even floated the idea of de-industrializing Germany and turning it into an agrarian buffer zone. The Soviets, having lost 20 million people in the war and having borne the brunt of German attacks, seized almost anything that could be shipped back to Russia. The British, in control of the Ruhr industrial region, seemed on their way toward nationalizing the coal and steel industries. The Allies were genuinely concerned about the concentration of economic and political power represented by cartels, IG's, and universal banks. So all cartels were declared null and void, and the Allies confiscated outright the assets of IG Farben, Krupp, and the Reichswerke. Major business figures were put on trial for war crimes. Overall, the Allies followed a policy that became known as "the four D's": deconcentration, decartelization, denazification, and democratization.[106]

Practical problems overwhelmed some of these plans. Germany's currency had become all but worthless, and the controlled economy had collapsed into underground black markets. Some minimal economic recovery was absolutely essential if Germans were to be able even to feed themselves. And the British and Americans concluded that if the country was ever again going to run itself, then those involved in managerial positions had to be reinstated despite their often questionable reputations.

The spread of Soviet-style communism was forcing the western Allies to reconsider much of their occupation policy, just as they were having to do at the same time in Japan. The Soviets continued to dismantle German factories and to insist on stiff reparations payments. This policy was interpreted by the western Allies as a means of weakening and destabilizing eastern Germany so that communists could take over. The British and Americans favored free elections and market economies based on private property, measures which they thought would expedite economic recovery. In June 1947, the European Recovery Plan (better known as the Marshall Plan), was announced. The Soviets read these new policies as signals of an escalating American imperialism. The Cold War began to heat up.[107]

In Germany, reversals in occupation policy were tightly linked to rising international tensions. The British and Americans merged their two zones and consolidated the zones' public finances. They strengthened a series of public banks and later the Bank of German States in Frankfurt, the predecessor of today's Deutsche Bundesbank (central bank). Simultaneously, they allowed Germans to participate in the formation of economic policy. In June 1948, a new Deutsche Mark (DM) was introduced in the three western zones, and price controls were lifted for most goods.

The new Deutsche Mark had a quick and beneficial effect. Overnight, goods that merchants had been holding back because of price controls appeared in shop windows.[108]

The political effect of the currency reform was no less dramatic. The Soviets prohibited their occupied zone from participating. They blockaded West Berlin in 1948, and the Allies began a dramatic 15-month airlift of supplies. Germany turned into a divided nation. The division was dramatized by concrete and barbed wire when East Germany began erecting the Berlin Wall in 1961 to stop the flood of emigration. For the next 40 years, East and West Germany went their separate ways. Each gradually developed the strongest economy in its European bloc: communist East Germany, capitalist West Germany.[109]

The Federal Republic of Germany, 1949–1990

As the Cold War intensified, the Allies decided that West Germany would have to be rehabilitated as an industrial power, integrated into the European economy, and made a military partner in the North Atlantic Treaty Organization (NATO). The three western zones were therefore united to form the Federal Republic of Germany under a democratic constitution. In 1949, Konrad Adenauer of the Christian Democrats was elected Chancellor by a bare majority. Adenauer placed the Federal Republic firmly on a path of integration into the western alliance.

The new government, with its capital in Bonn, in some respects followed in the footsteps of the Weimar Republic. But it had a stronger constitution, the Basic Law, sponsored by the Allies and aimed at preventing another breakdown of the state. The new republic reemphasized the long German tradition of federalism. National policy was formed by legislative compromise among the parliament *(Bundestag),* the Federal Council *(Bundesrat,* representing the states), and the executive (the Chancellor and his Cabinet). Eleven states were established, each with a "self-supporting" budget.[110]

Just what democracy and federalism were to mean in actual practice was worked out by the two major parties, the Christian Democrats (CDU) and the Social Democrats (SPD). Between 1949 and 1983, the CDU, together with its Bavarian sister party, received roughly 45 percent of the vote in national elections, and the SPD between 30 and 46 percent. Neither party consistently received a solid majority. So they regularly tried to ally themselves with the Free Democratic Party (FDP), a free-market-centered party that typically received between 6 and 12 percent of the vote. After 1983, these three parties were joined in Parliament by the Green Party, an anti-nuclear and ecologically oriented group that usually attracted between 5 and 8 percent of the vote.[111]

THE SOCIAL MARKET ECONOMY

The Federal Republic developed a stable democratic polity. The notion of a "social market economy" became central to national stability. The concept represented a fusion of demands for economic freedom on the one hand and social security on the other. It represented a compromise between advocates of totally free markets and those of a "social state." Christian Democrats as well as Social Democrats chartered an economic "third way" based on the social market economy.[112]

The policies that took shape after 1948 were based on high savings and an extensive safety net of social security and medical insurance. Unions and special-interest groups played a large role in formulating economic policy at the firm, sectoral, regional, and national levels. Companies and individuals came to be taxed at a much higher rate than was the case in the United States. Yet Germany managed to compete and export even more successfully than it had done before the war, in spite of also being one of the highest-wage economies in the world.[113]

ECONOMIC MIRACLE

In contrast to the images one sees in war footage of a devastated Germany, the Third Reich oddly enough left behind a permanent economic legacy. The "capital buildup" of 1936 to 1942 was left largely intact at the end of the war. Despite bombing damage, Germany's industrial capacity in 1945 was actually about 20 percent larger than it had been at the onset of the war. Human skills and organizational capabilities built up during the war also remained.[114]

The government guided investment policies in the interest of restarting the economy. Business received generous tax concessions for investment. As a result, investment levels remained high throughout the 1950s and into the mid-1960s. By the early 1950s, a policy of reconstruction, re-investment, reconcentration, and reintegration had been firmly established.[115]

Public and private investments were also helped by West Germany's international rehabilitation. Beginning with the Marshall Plan, West Germany was reintegrated into an American-sponsored multilateral trading system.[116] The establishment of supranational organizations embedded the country in the new international trading regime. The Organization for European Economic Cooperation (OEEC, now the OECD, the D being Development) was formed to liberalize trade. In 1950 the European Payments Union was initiated to facilitate the transfer of credits among European countries. At the same time, Chancellor Konrad Adenauer situated his country firmly under the American nuclear umbrella. West Germany joined NATO in 1955 and was permitted to rearm just 10 years after it had been disarmed.

The idea of a single European market was the most vital innovation of this period. In 1950, under the leadership of French Foreign Minister Robert Schuman, the establishment of a European Coal and Steel Community was begun, in part to bind the economic potential of the Ruhr to French interests. Essentially a free trade zone that limited the imposition of tariffs and quotas, this organization became the forerunner of the European Economic Community (EC), which was established in 1957 with the Treaty of Rome.[117] Altogether, the spectacular success of this new postwar economic order became known in Germany as the *Wirtschaftswunder* ("economic miracle"). "Supergrowth" exceeded even pre-1913 patterns, and German capitalism once again became a force to be reckoned with on the world stage.[118]

BANKING

The German banking system played an especially important role in the nation's rapid economic growth. In 1957, the Deutsche Bundesbank was created and molded into a fully autonomous central bank. Its overriding aim was to safeguard the currency, and its stabilization policies have now become almost legendary. They have enabled the Deutsche Mark to become one of the strongest currencies in the world, sometimes even to the detriment of German exports.[119]

After an initial Allied breakup of the banking system, the universal banks were fully reestablished by 1957. (See Chapter 7 for details.) They continued to play a vital role in industrial financing. Recovery would have been much slower without the long-term investment horizons of the big banks and their moderate dividend demands. The Big Three

banks were heavily represented in prominent large-scale firms, and these
firms themselves had extensive cross-shareholdings in other major companies. In the 1990s, for example, Siemens was still represented on the
supervisory board of the Deutsche Bank, continuing a 100-year relationship.[120]

ASSOCIATIONS

Germany's rich associational life was also reconstituted in the 1950s,
under the cherished notions of freedom of association and self-regulation
that underlay the entire German system of capitalism. In 1949, an umbrella organization called the Diet of German Industry and Commerce
was formed. The regional Chambers of Industry and Commerce quickly
made themselves invaluable to the Allies. Membership in these Chambers
became mandatory, and they continued at the close of the century to
represent the diverse interests of small and medium-size businesses.[121]

   In the 1950s, a new Federation of German Industry (BDI) provided a
top-ranking business association to lobby and help coordinate national
economic legislation. Unlike its predecessor, the BDI was organized not
on a purely regional basis, but on the basis of about 35 regional industrial
branches. The BDI directed most of its lobbying effort at ministries and
government agencies. The Federation of German Employers' Associations (BDA) organized the collective bargaining process, in cooperation
with the leading associations for labor. BDA members included employer
associations from industry, banking, transport, insurance, commerce,
handicrafts, and agriculture.[122]

THE CARTEL OFFICE

The one pillar of German capitalism that the social market economy had
to remove if it was to be more than mere rhetoric was the cartel system.
Naturally, the idea of outlawing cartels met with stiff resistance, especially in the steel industry and among small-to-medium-sized businesses.
The Federation of German Industry and the Diet of German Industry
and Commerce each fought hard with Economics Minister Ludwig Erhard, who advocated full prohibition of all cartels. A heated 10-year
debate climaxed in 1957 with the Act Against Restraints on Competition.
Most cartels were made illegal, but by no means all, and a new Federal
Cartel Office (1957) guarded the economic order against harmful busi-

ness collusion. As a result many of the formerly cartelized parts of the economy became characterized by oligopolistic competition.[123]

All in all, the Cartel Office acted pragmatically. It developed a model of "workable competition" that took into account the life cycles of particular industries, their periodic expansion and contraction. (Even in the mid 1990s, almost 200 legal cartels existed in Germany, assisting rationalization or downsizing in particular industries.)[124] In the social market economy, competition was not an end in itself, but a means to the prosperity necessary to pay for desired social security (and now environmental) programs.

LABOR RELATIONS

In contrast to the experience under the Weimar government of 1919–33, the Federal Republic successfully integrated labor into economic decisionmaking.[125] Throughout the postwar years, about 40 percent of the West German labor force was unionized, as compared with about 15 percent in the United States during the 1990s. Unions were specifically protected by the constitution. Particular collective bargaining agreements were hammered out between employers and employees on factory, industrial branch, local, regional, and federal levels.

One scholar estimates that about 300,000 such agreements existed in various degrees of detail and geographical breadth. Regionally negotiated agreements often ended up influencing national developments. Local, state, and federal labor courts mediated disputes. The ensuing system of labor relations was very stable, and the Federal Republic became the industrial country with the fewest strikes and days lost from the 1950s until the 1980s, with the exception of Switzerland and Austria. This negotiated cooperation between unions and employers, with its emphasis on collective bargaining, arbitration instead of strikes, and contracts which included an explicit "no strike" clause, was called "social partnership" *(Sozialpartnerschaft)*.

The labor counterpart to the employers' BDA was the German Trade Union Federation (DGB), a nationwide union with 17 affiliated subunions organized by industrial branch, the most important being the IG Metall. The unitary nature of the DGB allowed it to overcome the previous splits within the labor movement, which had traditionally been divided among Socialist, Christian, and liberal wings. The branch unions, however, allowed it to maintain a degree of negotiating flexibility among different industrial sectors and regions. (The DGB proved to be a critical actor in integrating former East German workers into the West German system after the unification of 1990.)

In general, unions and management representatives negotiated wage rates, fringe benefits, and the length of the work week. In 1955, the average work week in Germany was 49 hours; in 1965, 45 hours; in 1975, 41 hours. In the 1980s unions embarked on a road toward the 35-hour week, and they were approaching success in the 1990s. Unions and management groups also negotiated holiday entitlements, which at 6 weeks per year became one of the highest in the world.

The most innovative change in labor-management relations in the Federal Republic was the policy of "codetermination." Under pressure from labor, a codetermination law for the coal and steel industry was passed in 1951 with the blessing of the conservative Chancellor Adenauer. Under codetermination, the supervisory board of any coal or steel company with over 1,000 employees consisted of equal numbers of labor and industry representatives. An additional "neutral" member could cast the deciding vote in the event of a tie.

A labor representative also filled the role of personnel director on the managing board. In 1952, the Works Constitution Act gave labor a one-third representation on supervisory boards of firms employing 500–2,000 workers, but with no right to a personnel director on the managing board. Then the Codetermination Act of 1976 extended the principle of parity representation to firms outside coal and steel with more than 2,000 employees, albeit on a more limited basis. Codetermination did not extend to smaller (Mittelstand) companies, and as a result about 80 percent of firms with over 5 employees did not get this form of labor representation.

In addition, labor influenced company management through works councils. The 1952 Works Constitution Act, which was modeled on the 1920 works council law, anchored works councils in firms by law and extended works councils' powers in personnel and social matters. Works council representatives were also required to cooperate with the employer, employers' associations, and the unions. In 1972, a revised Works Constitution Act strengthened works councils' powers in personnel matters. In 1994, and effective after September 1996, the European Union adopted the European Works Council Directive—over mainly British resistance—which required the establishment of some form of consultative forum along the lines of codetermination or works councils.[126]

MACROECONOMIC POLICIES, 1961–1973

Except for the strong governmental promotion of investment and of monetary and price stability, the 1950s were characterized largely by free market–oriented policies. Economic growth was so strong that there was tremendous growth even during periods of cyclical downturns. One such downturn occurred in 1966–67, but it was soon over. For the most part, as a prominent analyst has argued, the Federal Republic was a "conservative welfare state centered around distributing the dividends of economic growth as they trickled down."[127] These trickle-down dividends were impressive, and real wages rose steadily.[128] The cumulative gains gave birth to a strong consumer culture and rising living standards, and allowed an affluent society to arise for the first time in German history. By the late 1950s, Economic Minister Ludwig Erhard began speaking of a "mature society."

A symbol of the fundamental changes was the Social Democrats' Bad Godesberg reforms of 1959, which committed it to becoming a "people's party" rather than a class-based workers' party. This change allowed the Social Democrats to break out of their mid-30 percent range of support and reach a broader array of voters, peaking at 46 percent in 1972. In 1966, a "Grand Coalition" of Christian Democrats and Social Democrats took over. Then, in 1969, the Social Democrats were able to form a coalition with the Free Democrats, and Willy Brandt, a Social Democrat who had been Mayor of West Berlin, became Chancellor.[129]

During the 1960s, an activist macroeconomic policy in the tradition associated with the late British economist John Maynard Keynes became the order of the day. In 1963, the important Council of Economic Experts was established and given the task of writing a critical annual report on the state of the economy. The Council advocated greater labor-management cooperation and a stronger Keynesian policy of demand management. In 1967, Parliament passed the Law for Promoting Stability and Growth of the Economy, often called the Magna Carta of managed growth. For the first time, fiscal policy had the official goals of stabilizing swings in the economy and distributing wealth more equitably. A "magical rectangle" of four goals was codified into law: (1) currency stability,

(2) economic growth, (3) full employment, and (4) a positive trade balance.[130]

This 1967 Stabilization Law also contained measures to coordinate national, state, and local budgets more effectively in the interest of macroeconomic stability. A consultative Fiscal Planning Council was created to work out consensus among the federal and state governments, the Bundesbank, and political party representatives. As a 1969 extension of the Stabilization Law, important constitutional reforms went into effect. Their goal was to secure uniform living standards throughout the Federal Republic by redistributing revenue from stronger to weaker regions. Another central part of the Stabilization Law was the notion of "Concerted Action," designed to integrate labor's wage demands and management's investment policies into macroeconomic policymaking.[131]

CONFRONTING STRUCTURAL CHANGE

Although the Social Democrat–led "global steering" appeared to pull the economy out of the 1966–67 recession, it ran headlong into massive changes in the global economy after 1973, marked by increasing international competition. During the worldwide "stagflation" of the 1970s, Germany's economic policy, spearheaded by the Bundesbank, moved toward a less interventionist, more free-market position.

After the 1970s, the major problem in Germany as in other European countries was persistent structural unemployment combined with slowing growth. German unemployment rose from under one percent to about 5 percent in 1975, then to over 9 percent in 1985. Although Germany had fewer unemployed workers than many other European countries, joblessness remained a burning political issue into the late 1990s.[132]

With the 1982 election of Helmut Kohl of the conservative party (CDU), West Germany moved toward the political right. Kohl promised to cut back on state intervention and regulations, bring wage pressures down, and increase flexibility in the labor market. He wished to create greater monetary stability and to cut expenditures and taxes. He also pressed for greater privatization. Although Kohl's election could be placed alongside those of Ronald Reagan and Margaret Thatcher as evidence of a general rightward shift, there was no real assault on the welfare state. The conservatives professed to be cutting the level of subsidies to industry, but these actually rose during the 1980s. Reduction of the German social safety net and of vacation time remained a politically sensitive issue, comparable to raising taxes or cutting social security in the United States.[133]

In addition, the 1980s saw the "greening" of German politics and business. A Federal Environment Ministry was created in 1986, and Germany led Europe in its commitment to improving the environment. Environmental training was emphasized within the vocational system. Consumers developed a strong preference for ecologically friendly products and packaging, and the Environment Ministry's blue angel seal became commonplace in German stores. Recycling became mandatory, and German business increasingly moved into environmental protection and waste management technologies, in which they led the world.

On the whole, West German industry met the challenge of international competition by moving into higher-value-added products and using flexible production methods, particularly in niche markets. Industrial associations played a critical role in this adaptation process.[134] The associations acted as a link between the macroeconomic decisionmaking of the government and the microeconomic decisionmaking of individual firms. The dense associational bargaining system, which placed a premium on consensual action, helped to coordinate change between individual firms among industrial sectors, and between business and government. Consensus emerged not from some warm, fuzzy feeling of togetherness, but from hard bargaining under a sense of interdependency.

In conjunction with the many national industrial associations, the Chambers of Commerce tried to coordinate vocational programs, retraining initiatives, and new technologies. The Chambers actively reshaped vocational training and standards of certification, especially for the important machine-tool industry. Even general marketing functions were partially provided by regional agencies or associations. Regional governments, such as that of Baden-Württemberg, took an active role in economic development. They sought market contacts overseas for their industries, much as a salesforce does for a company.[135]

While the United States and Britain moved more quickly into service-sector employment, the German economy continued to rest solidly on the core manufacturing industries of the Second Industrial Revolution. In the mid-1990s, 38 percent of workers were employed in manufacturing, nearly twice the ratio in the United States. Most German companies retained a strong sense of tradition and of regional identity—a sense of their history and of where they now stood. These characteristics tended to make German companies slower moving, but also more solidly placed once they decided to enter a new field or to change strategic direction.[136] German bankers and top executives were more frequently seen on factory floors than were English or American bankers and executives. Germans still tended to believe that business was about "making things." Not until the 1980s, for example, was a nonchemist permitted to join the managing board of a Big Three chemical company.[137]

Though economic policy in postwar Germany was to some extent a departure from pre-1945 patterns, most of the companies that came to flourish under the new order looked back on a long history. This continuity was remarkable, considering that Germany in only a little more than one century became a unified nation, lost two major wars, was occupied twice, saw its borders shift every few decades, and experienced political systems ranging from a monarchy to state socialism, and from fascism to liberal democracy. Despite these upheavals, those firms that played a crucial role in the late nineteenth century still tend to play a central role today. Most of Germany's largest industrial companies near the end of the twentieth century were major players at the start of the century as well, as Table 5.2 shows.

MITTELSTAND

Behind Germany's strength in the domestic economy and on world export markets stood a vibrant Mittelstand. According to official statistics, the Mittelstand accounted in the 1990s for about 50 percent of all private-sector GDP, 40 percent of total investment, and two-thirds of all private-sector employment. It trained 80 percent of all apprentices. But statistics cannot capture the attitudes that permeated Mittelstand business, attitudes exemplified within companies strong in niche markets in the global arena. Such companies included Baader (fish-processing machines), Heidelberger Druckmaschinen (offset printing machines), Heidenhain (measurement and control instruments), Körber/Hauni (cigarette-making machines), Krones (labeling machines for beverages), Märklin & Cie. (model railways), Stihl (chain saws), TetraWerke (tropical fish food, with an 80 percent share of the world market), and Webasto (car sunroofs). Each of these Mittelstand companies ranked number one in the world market for its products.

Being Mittelstand was perhaps more an attitude than a statistical category.[138] Sales representatives could roll up their sleeves and fix machines.

Table 5.2   The 30 Largest Manufacturing Companies in Germany, 1994, Ranked by Turnover (Sales) in Millions of Deutsche Marks

	Company	Founded	Industry	Turnover
1	Daimler-Benz	1890/1926	Conglomerate	97,737
2	Siemens	1847	Electrical Engineering	81,648
3	Volkswagen	1938	Automobiles	76,586
4	VEBA	1926	Energy	66,349
5	Mercedes-Benz	1890/1989	Automobiles	64,696
6	Telekom	*1990	Telecommunications	58,988
7	RWE	1898	Energy/Engineering/Chemicals	53,094
8	Hoechst	1863	Chemicals/Pharmaceuticals	46,047
9	Bayer	1863	Chemicals/Pharmaceuticals	41,007
10	BASF	1865	Chemicals	40,568
11	Thyssen	1871/1891	Steel/Fabr. Metal/Mech. Engineering, Trading, Services	33,502
12	Robert Bosch	1886	Auto. Supply/Electr. and Mech. Eng.	32,469
13	BMW	1916	Automotive	29,016
14	Mannesmann	1890	Mech. Eng./Trading/Electr. Eng./Telecommunications	27,963
15	Metalgesellschaft	1881	Metallurgy/Engineering/Chemicals/Trading/Mining	26,094
16	Haniel & Cie.	1756	Engineering/Trading/Services	24,417
17	VIAG	ᵃ1988	Energy/Metallurgy/Chemicals/Packaging/Trading/Glass	23,734
18	Ruhrkohle AG	1968	Coal	23,408
19	Preussag	1923	Energy/Engineering/Conglomerate	23,290
20	Adam Opel	1862	Automotive	23,007
21	Ford-Werke	1925	Automotive	21,189
22	Krupp-Hoesch	1811	Steel/Mech. Eng./Auto. Supply/Trading/Services	20,504
23	MAN	1898/1986	Mech. Engineering/Automotive	18,972
24	Deutsche Aerospace	1989	Aviation (subsidiary of Daimler-Benz)	18,626
25	Aral	1898	Petroleum	17,449
26	Bertelsmann	1835	Publishing/Printing/Media	17,170
27	RWE Energie	1989	Energy	16,549
28	VEBA Oel	1935	Petroleum	15,390
29	Degussa	1873	Metallurgy/Chemicals/Pharmaceuticals/Trading	14,901
30	Ruhrgas	1926	Energy/Gas	14,349

a. Year of full privatization.
Source: Germany's Top 500: A Handbook of Germany's Largest Corporations, 1995 ed. (Frankfurt: Frankfurter Allgemeine Zeitung Information Services, 1994).

Many had engineering degrees. Customer service, tight product focus, and high-quality engineering and design were the hallmarks of these firms. They tended to compete on quality instead of price. Many remained deeply committed to the culture and well-being of their local communities.

Some Mittelstand entrepreneurs made names for themselves in consumer products. Hugo Boss, located in a little town south of Stuttgart, built an international network in upscale menswear. Jil Sander, a self-made entrepreneur, became a star in the fashion world in the 1980s and 1990s. Her success was based on the classic simplicity of her designs. Surprisingly for a high-wage economy, Germany in the 1990s still produced more clothes than any other country in Europe, and was the second-largest exporter of apparel in the world.[139]

Epilogue

The sudden collapse of the Berlin Wall on November 9, 1989, illustrated once more why politics and economics are never considered very distant from each other in German life. For eastern Germans, unification meant a shock conversion, after 44 years of communism, to the West German economic order. Five new states were added to the now-united Federal Republic of Germany. Many people all over the world hoped that this new expanded nation, firmly embedded in the international structures of the postwar era, would finally find a peaceful, secure place in the heart of Europe.[140]

The process of unification and the pressures resulting from a more internationalized world economy would affect the German business system for many years to come. Even before political unification, a number of economic research institutes had questioned whether Germany could still be an attractive industrial site or could continue to have a competitive capital market in the new context of the Third Industrial Revolution. Others pointed to the "fading miracle" of the German economy, with its slowly declining growth rates. The very heavy economic costs of unification exacerbated these long-term problems.

But one should not underestimate the ability of the system as a whole to change. During the last 130 years, Germany has undergone more changes, and more profound adjustments, than perhaps any other country in the world. During that tumultuous period, German capitalism has shown many times its remarkable strength and flexibility.

PROLOGUE TO CHAPTER 6

The impressive performance of German capitalism during the Second Industrial Revolution is illustrated in the next chapter, "August Thyssen and German Steel." The history of the Thyssen company, which continues down to the present time, is almost exactly concurrent with the history of Germany as a unified country. We can therefore deepen our knowledge of German capitalism in general by following the company through the revolutionary political and economic changes Germany has experienced. In addition, we encounter here the first really big business of the Second Industrial Revolution covered in this book. We also meet one of the book's most memorable characters.

August Thyssen built his iron, steel, coal, and machinery companies from almost nothing. In the beginning he had few assets, no long-term strategy for horizontal or vertical integration, and no clear idea of how a large and diversified set of companies should be managed. The kinds of challenges he faced lay at the heart of managerial problems in many countries during the Second Industrial Revolution.

But German capitalism at the end of the nineteenth century was different in some ways. It was hemmed in with protectionism, cartels, and other pervasive regulations. In such a system, how might an obsessive competitor like August Thyssen be predicted to behave? How might he deal with the restrictions imposed by the government and by industry agreements? How would we expect him to function, given his intense drive for control and his powerful wish to expand his operations? In the larger sense, How much of this story is distinctively "German"? How much is universally "capitalist"?

Clues to answering all of these questions can be found in the specific pattern of growth exhibited by the Thyssen companies. Constrained in one direction, they moved forward in another. Hemmed in by cartel quotas, they sought loopholes, which they promptly found and exploited. One result was that Thyssen's companies, like many other German firms, tended to have more diversified product lines than their British and

American counterparts, to be more export-oriented, and to be more vertically integrated. It is important to grasp why this was so, and what the general implications are for managing in any highly regulated environment. The lesson is that the nature of competition will shift in response to changing regulations. But competition itself will never disappear.

Like nearly all big businesses, Thyssen & Co. originated as a small family firm. As often happens with successful companies, its rapid growth created havoc within the family of the founder. August Thyssen's relationships with his wife and children could not stand the strain, and periodically the drama erupted into episodes reminiscent of a soap opera. Here too the history of August Thyssen and German Steel typifies some elements that extend beyond a story of one company in one country.

6

AUGUST THYSSEN AND GERMAN STEEL

Jeffrey Fear

Rast' ich, so rost' ich. (If I rest, I rust.)
—*August Thyssen*

August Thyssen (1842–1926) was Germany's version of the American steel tycoon Andrew Carnegie, his great contemporary. Like Carnegie, Thyssen (pronounced approximately TISS-en) was renowned for his energy and ruthlessness. Among Germans, he was legendary for the aggressive way in which he expanded his steelworks, and for his success as an investor on the stock market. In German business circles, he earned such nicknames as "the American" and "the trustmaker."[1] After Thyssen's death, the *New York Times* dubbed him "the Rockefeller of the Ruhr."[2] By World War I only Krupp and Siemens, Germany's largest industrial firms, rivaled the Thyssen firm in total assets. Yet Thyssen for a long time issued hardly any shares of his own company's stock. He preferred complete family control, and until 1925 he managed to retain it.

But after the end of World War I in 1918, the company's finances slid downhill. The postwar loss of August Thyssen's immense steelworks in Alsace-Lorraine, the need to modernize worn-out equipment, constant problems with labor, and increasing international competition left his firm in urgent need of cash. When August Thyssen and two of his sons, Fritz and Heinrich, launched a major capacity expansion, the firm was even more strapped for money. In 1924 the 82-year-old Thyssen along with other German steelmakers turned to Wall Street for loans, but by 1925 he was slowly reaching the end of his financial capabilities.

At that time, a number of industrialists advocated a merger of all or most German steel firms into a gigantic company along the lines of U.S. Steel. Like Andrew Carnegie before him, Thyssen and his sons had to decide whether to join this new venture and thereby end his family dynasty after 54 years of hard-fought independence. They decided to join, and the resulting giant company took shape just before August died. But the Thyssen name has continued near the top of German industry in one company after another for the rest of the twentieth century. In the 1930s and 1940s Fritz Thyssen became even better known than his father had been; but it was August who founded and built the enterprise.

Early Years

August Thyssen was born in 1842 outside the Rhineland city of Aachen, near Belguim and the Netherlands.[3] In contrast to later myths, he came from an established and modestly wealthy Catholic family. He acquired an unusually good education for that time, attending a leading technical university in Karlsruhe and then studying at the renowned Institut Supérieur du Commerce de l'Etat in Antwerp, Belgium. Next he returned to Aachen for a two-year apprenticeship in a bank owned by his father. This business experience gave August access to one of the densest entrepreneurial webs of small merchants and industrialists in Germany. Drawing on these contacts, he entered into a partnership with the wealthy Bicheroux family, and in 1867 opened a small hoop-iron mill in Duisburg on the Rhine. Here August Thyssen learned the steel business.

The mill was profitable, but he left it after a few years, because he did not find "enough freedom."[4] In 1871, the year Germany was politically unified, Thyssen, backed by his father, founded his new hoop-iron mill, Thyssen & Co., just outside the town of Mülheim on the Ruhr River. (Hoop-iron was medium-width strip steel, used as the hoops for barrels, crates or wheels. Now it is simply called strip steel. The thinnest strips were used for binding items such as cotton bales or crates. The widest strips of steel, called tubing strips or skelp, were also used for fashioning welded pipes and tubes.) After the father died in 1877, another son, Josef, closed the family banking operations and joined the hoop-iron mill. The company was then transformed into a general partnership, although the division of assets reflected the dominance of August Thyssen, who received a 75 percent stake.

In 1872, when August was 30, he married 18-year-old Hedwig Pelzer, whose dowry found welcome use in the new company. Typically, the marriage was as much a business arrangement as a romantic liaison. Over the next six years, four children were born. August Thyssen devoted himself singlemindedly to his business affairs, while Hedwig yearned for a more aristocratic lifestyle. August, who was sober-minded, ambitious, and immersed in the dirty and busy world of ironworking, was not the right match for her. When Hedwig miscarried a child whose paternity August denied, they divorced. This was an unusual and scandalous event for the Germany of 1885. Even Josef's wife, who took over the strenuous social task of entertaining bankers and businessmen for both brothers, thought that August's treatment of young Hedwig had been unduly stern and unfair.[5]

The divorce soured Thyssen's relationship with his children, and it also affected the future of the business. Hedwig had agreed to the divorce only with the proviso that ownership be transferred to their three sons and one daughter. August Thyssen, however, could determine when possession and control over the firm would pass into the children's hands. The agreement left property rights unclear as between Thyssen and the four children. German law distinguishes between ownership *(Eigentum)* and possession *(Besitz)*. August Thyssen retained lifelong possession and thus control over the firm. His children became owners, but without a legal voice in decision-making for the company. Not until 1907 was it absolutely clarified that the transfer of possession remained dependent on Thyssen's approval or his death. The original 1885 divorce agreement was then ruled to have been a mere statement of intent. Thyssen never remarried. Hedwig remarried a number of times, eventually entering into upper-class Belgian circles. She lived out her life in Brussels.[6]

Early Growth and Diversification of Thyssen & Co.

The founding of Thyssen & Co. in 1871 came in the midst of a feverish economic boom, but after a Vienna stock market crash, a deep European recession began in 1873 and prices for iron and steel products dropped dramatically. Thyssen & Co., however, expanded production, employment, and sales, emphasizing the importance of "running full." By 1882 employment had risen to about 1,000. August traveled as far as Russia to find markets for his products, exporting 20 to 30 percent of his production.[7]

The crucial period in the development of Thyssen & Co. was the early 1880s, when August both diversified his products and integrated related product lines. In 1884, Thyssen also moved into distribution by opening in Berlin a branch sales office that eventually became his main trading company. This subsidiary attempted to crack the most lucrative urban market in Germany by undercutting the strong wholesalers then dominating the iron and steel trade. The office also served as an excellent training ground for Thyssen's future sales directors.

By 1886, the shape of the firm was set. It consisted of the hoop-iron mill, a small steel mill, a plate and sheet mill with a pressing works for railway rolling stock, a pipe and tube mill, a tin-plate mill, and a machine-engineering shop. Later a welding shop was added for the manufacture of marine and stationary boilers, high-pressure tanks, and furnaces.

The company's policy was to offer a full range of iron goods, especially in the pipe and tube markets. August Thyssen moved into pipe production to ensure a steadier demand for his hoop-iron, then into plates and sheets to produce pipes of wider diameter. Because he exported heavily, his output had to conform to many different national standards. He manufactured pipes denominated in both inches and centimeters. His advertising manuals were written in English, French, and German. Because of his segmented markets and his export orientation, Thyssen's product line was much more diversified than those of many American companies, which tended to concentrate on one or two lines of standardized products. Thyssen & Co. also offered very specialized products, made in the welding and pressing works and the machine-engineering shop. This pattern of specialization in Europe versus standardization and high-volume production in North America was typical of the contrast between the two areas at that time, and in some ways it still is today.

The machine-engineering operation began as an internal repair shop. Thyssen rapidly transformed it into an in-house R&D station and a supplier of rolling-mill equipment for all of his departments. Later it became an R&D center for his various other companies. Thyssen expanded into machine construction primarily in order to maintain secrecy, fearing that independent machine-engineering contractors would convey his expansion plans to his rivals.[8] He did not begin to sell machinery in significant quantities on the open market until after the turn of the century. By then his shop was producing pumping equipment and steam and gas engines, as well as entire rolling mills.

Thyssen developed a general policy of maintaining the highest technical standards in both products and production techniques. He relentlessly emphasized to his department heads the importance of developing a solid reputation for quality and prompt delivery. August Thyssen also formulated his charismatic managerial style during the early 1880s. More than just a classic entrepreneur, he became a modern corporate executive at the head of a hierarchy of professional salaried managers. Throughout his life, he generally identified more with his managers than with members of his own family.

Thyssen's Organizational Structure

Thyssen organized his company into a series of departments, each of them responsible for both production and trade.[9] The four main departments of the rolling mill, for example, had their own sales, shipping, and production offices (see Figures 6.2–6.3, pp. 221–222). Throughout the company, the department heads were responsible for hiring and firing workers and for setting wages, albeit within a given range. In conjunction with the central accounting office, each department kept track of its own inventories and appraised its own capital assets. The goal of this system was to decentralize authority while maintaining tight supervision from above, one of the salient principles of modern management.

Beginning in that same decade of the 1880s, Thyssen standardized management procedures and defined what he expected from his managers. The ideas became leitmotifs of Thyssen & Co.'s corporate culture for decades to come. They included:

the ability to work with ambition, energy, and vigor;

the ability to work with care and conscientiousness;

the ability to think ahead and to deal with complex problems;

the ability to maintain authority over workers;

the practice of basing employee evaluations on performance, not on personal favor or social status;

the practice of maintaining collegiality and politeness with others, including subordinates;

above all, the practice of "self-sufficiency" and independence of judgment.

Thyssen understood managerial performance as commercial success and departmental profitability, rather than technical competence and productive efficiency. In one instance, the first manager of the Thyssen pipe and tube mill was abruptly fired because he did not satisfy the delivery needs of customers, and in spite of his having developed some very innovative technical processes. As far as Thyssen was concerned, the manager had damaged the company's reputation. Eventually, "department results" were sure to suffer. In another case, Thyssen fired an engineer who spent too much time with new designs and theoretical questions instead of with customers. He fired still another manager for mistreating a subordinate and for being too worried about the proper line of authority rather than the job at hand. Thyssen often had trouble with the academically trained engineers of the machine-engineering department. They tended to look down on the master craftsmen of the rolling mills, who had only apprenticeship training. Thyssen actively tried to stamp out the bureaucratic, civil-servant culture that sometimes crept into German business firms of this era.

Most important, Thyssen judged his managers by what he called their "results." He focused on commercial success. For him, marketing was as important as manufacturing. He viewed his departments as "widely diverse," but he monitored them by using monthly reports with standardized accounting procedures. The financial statements themselves had been constructed by Thyssen's chief accountant in consultation with department heads. Beginning in the 1880s, the monthly departmental reports became the cornerstone for assessing managerial performance. Bonuses and salaries depended on them. The statements strictly separated renewal and operating costs, and they even took into account a percentage of overhead and depreciation, on a monthly basis. This type of internal financial accounting was more advanced than corresponding American practices. In the nineteenth century, many American firms did not depreciate, even on a yearly basis.[10]

Within the Thyssen system of management, the departments were treated as semi-autonomous commercial centers, not just production workshops. One Thyssen manager put it this way: "delegate as much as possible but supervise."[11] Unlike American functional models, the departmental units required managers to combine both commercial and technical responsibilities. The principles of these managerial reforms underlay Thyssen's business operations for the rest of his life.

Tariff Protection and Vertical Integration

The modern German steel industry grew up behind tariff walls. After a brief experiment with free trade during the early 1870s, the imperial government in 1879 imposed almost prohibitively high tariffs on iron, steel, and many other products. The government also permitted internal cartels in coal, iron, steel, and a wide variety of other goods, and actually sponsored one in potash.

In economic theory, a combination of tariff protection with internal cartels is a formula for industrial inefficiency. But from the late 1870s until the outbreak of World War I in 1914, many German companies, including those run by August Thyssen, achieved outstanding performance records. Tariff walls kept out British and Belgian steel, and gave the infant German industry time to develop. Cartels smoothed out the business cycle for steel and other industries especially sensitive to the boom-and-bust pattern common in the early years of a nation's capitalist development. German steel came to be dominated by a handful of powerful companies, which competed with each other for low-cost production and domestic market share. (See Figure 6.1 at the end of the chapter for a list of some of these companies.) Negotiations for larger market shares within the cartels went on almost continuously. And export markets grew especially fast, in part because German companies' market shares in other countries were not covered by the cartel agreements. German steel's strong export performance was impressive evidence of the industry's efficiency, even though a significant amount of "dumping" (selling abroad for lower prices than at home) was involved.

The strong presence of cartels in Germany after 1887 also forced August Thyssen to integrate upstream into coal mining, iron smelting, and crude steelmaking in order to maintain his independence. Thyssen & Co. had been what the Germans called a "pure" rolling mill, largely dependent on outside sources for its coal, pig iron, and crude steel. (A small existing Thyssen & Co. steel mill satisfied only the immediate needs of the plate mill.) To help insure his supply of raw materials, August Thyssen had bought shares in a number of regional mining companies and ironmaking firms. But the growing cartelization movement in coal jeopardized his fuel supplies. As he later stated, secure control over his own coal became a "matter of survival."[12]

So by 1890, Thyssen had bought all 1,000 shares of the mining company Gewerkschaft Deutscher Kaiser (GDK). The name translates to "Mining Company German Emperor." A Gewerkschaft was a special type of company for mining operations, usually with 100 or 1,000 shares. It differed from a joint-stock company in that the owners were liable not only for their equity stakes but also for any losses incurred or capital expenditures needed by the company. A Gewerkschaft was not required to disclose its financial statements publicly, only to its owners. Thyssen's GDK was a large firm located directly on the Rhine and Ruhr rivers, providing a superb location for shipping coal to south German and export markets. The core steelmaking capabilities of today's Thyssen AG (*Aktiengesellschaft,* or joint-stock company), still rest on this site.

August Thyssen rushed to integrate each stage of the steelmaking process, situating the GDK's steel mills directly on top of its coal reserves. The company sank numerous coal shafts right next to the Rhine, in territory highly dangerous for miners. Coking ovens were added immediately after the mines began producing coal. In 1890, Thyssen began constructing at the GDK a Siemens-Martin open-hearth steel plant and heavy rolling mills for rails, blooms, billets, and structural steel. Later, Thomas steel converters were added for mass-production goods. All of these innovations represented the latest technology. When bottlenecks arose in Thyssen's pig iron supply—and just before a stronger pig iron cartel could be formed—the GDK added blast furnaces on the recommendations of Franz Dahl, Thyssen's 35-year-old plant director. Dahl was a first-class plant designer who knew how to blend the peculiar technical demands of individual processes with the layout of the plant as a whole. By the turn of the century, Dahl had turned Thyssen's GDK into the largest producer of crude steel in Germany. The GDK was also mining over one million tons of coal annually. By 1913, its yearly coal output reached 4.5 million tons.[13] At that time it was still a separate organization from Thyssen & Co., but August Thyssen was very much its boss.

In order to restore some balance to his product line and to secure downstream demand, Thyssen built a GDK strip steel and pipe mill in the town of Dinslaken, on the Rhine north of Duisburg. He sent a new company director, 27-year-old Julius Kalle, to America to study the latest techniques. On the advice of Kalle, Thyssen bought the license to construct an American-style cold-rolling strip steel mill, which remained the only one of its type in Europe for over 25 years and was especially profitable.[14] Kalle had complete control over both sales and production at the entire GDK plant at Dinslaken. Altogether, the GDK had several advantageous characteristics: a favorable situation on the Rhine, at the head of the largest inland river harbor in Europe; a first-class staff of (often young) plant managers; integrated state-of-the-art facilities; and a policy of careful laboratory testing of its metals. These characteristics made the GDK plant one of the premier steel works in the world.

The vertical integration was a great success, but it stretched company finances to the limit, and a turn-of-the-century recession caught Thyssen in the middle of his expansion plans. At one point his finances became so tight that the "equity" of the GDK had to be covered by short-term credits from his other firm, Thyssen & Co., which had taken out extensive loans from large banks. Such financing practices earned August Thyssen a notorious reputation in banking circles.[15] In 1901–02, he had to ask some of his creditors to delay payments. Josef Thyssen's wife had to dip into her private funds to help pay the wage bill.[16] Inadvertently, the Prussian Mining Authority now came to Thyssen's rescue by purchasing some of his important mines, although the sale was not conceived as a bailout of Thyssen. Instead, the Prussian state was attempting to penetrate into the Ruhr coal business in order to gain influence over the coal cartel.[17]

Characteristically, August Thyssen took the profits from this sale of mines and invested in still more expansion, establishing in 1901 the Aktiengesellschaft für Hüttenbetrieb (AGHütt, or Ironworks Joint Stock Company) in Meiderich, near Duisburg. The AGHütt supplemented the pig iron production of the GDK, whose own production primarily covered what it needed in steelmaking. The AGHütt supplied Thyssen & Co. and the open market with pig iron of special qualities.

Few people outside August Thyssen's companies appreciated the tremendous capacity he had assembled, nor the resulting cost advantages. He was now the fifth-largest coal producer in Germany, and he owned more mining rights to untapped coal fields than did any of his German competitors. When he joined the steel cartel in 1904, his quota surpassed that of Krupp, a circumstance that caused quite a press sensation.[18] Krupp had dominated the German steel industry in the nineteenth century, but Thyssen came to hold the top position for most of the twentieth.

By integrating his companies vertically, Thyssen outraced the cartelization movement in German heavy industry at the turn of the century. Had he failed, Thyssen & Co. might have been destroyed along with many other independent rolling mills and steelworks. Integrated com-bines such as Thyssen's developed tremendous cost advantages over the independents. Thyssen himself took over two other steelworks, the Kre-felder Stahlwerke and the Oberbilker Stahlwerke. He eliminated pro-duction overlap with his core firms and moved the new companies into high-quality steel goods.

At this point the only real gap in Thyssen's vertical integration was in iron ore. The search for a secure supply took him far afield, to France, Spain, the Caucasus, Norway, British India, and Morocco. By purchasing an iron ore mine, Thyssen hoped to gain near total independence from potential competitors or cartels. He revealed this desire in a 1902 letter to his close friend Carl Klönne of the Deutsche Bank:

> After we have succeeded in making the GDK one of the greatest com-panies on the continent, [there] remains still one great job left to do and that is the creation and securing of our iron ore supply . . . If the iron ore question is not regulated, the GDK and the Meiderich iron works could probably expect difficulties, which could cost our entire position in the iron business. If the few Lorraine mines which are still free for us fall into others' hands, then our position would become untenable because we would have to fear at any point that a strong syndicate of iron ore mine owners [would move] against us.[19]

In 1910, Thyssen established the Stahlwerke Thyssen AG next to the iron-ore mines of Alsace-Lorraine, near Germany's border with France. Its construction took more than three years, and Franz Dahl's work made it the best-designed, most modern, most "American" steel factory on the continent. The establishment of this works marked the apex of Thyssen's expansion. Most impressive was the fact that the 550,000-ton-per-year blast furnace could be run by only eight people. Individual batches were 35 to 40 percent larger than any produced thus far on the continent. But the main purpose of building the steel works on this spot—next to a regular supply of iron ore—was only partially fulfilled. The Lorraine ore proved to be of relatively low quality, and Thyssen still needed to pur-chase some high-quality Swedish ore.

All told, by 1914, the Thyssen empire stretched from coal and steel to machinery and waterworks (see Figure 6.6, p. 225). In the years before World War I, Thyssen also put more resources into distribution. On the initiative of the top commercial executive in the GDK, a Thyssen shipping enterprise with five steamers was set up to ply the Rhine, and a number of coal and steel trading companies were established both at home and as far away as Argentina.

Thyssen discussed a crucial element of his strategy at a GDK board of directors meeting in December 1905: "If we have succeeded in building our works over the last fifteen years to its present height, then we have to attribute this above all to the fact that we have never distributed one penny."[20] Not once during Thyssen's 40-year ownership of the GDK were dividends paid out to shareholders. The long-term survival of the GDK clearly depended on a heavy reinvestment of profits.

Thyssen and the Cartels

After the turn of the century, August Thyssen began to wonder whether the German cartel system might soon give way to even larger consolidations, like U.S. Steel. In 1902, he wrote Carl Klönne that:

> the time of syndicates [cartels] is past and we must move on to the time of trusts [huge mergers] . . . German syndicates performed well in the beginning. Now they are obsolete, because they continually multiply the competition [i.e. the number of firms, because new ones arose outside the cartel] and raise the production costs. Also the coal and coke syndicate has reached its high point and will be very weakened by the building of the syndicate collieries. German industry cannot bear over the long term the burdens of its expensive railway monopoly, the coal and coke syndicate, the pig iron, semi-processed and finished product syndicates. We have to work cheaper and nevertheless make money, which will only be possible by fusing the works, creating larger companies and by a better division of labor.[21]

It was a radical idea, one that did not sit well with German public opinion or with Thyssen's competitors. He was labeled an "enemy of cartels" and an "American-style" entrepreneur—a robber baron as opposed to a civilized steward of the nation's industry. It was widely believed that Thyssen's ultimate goal was an industry-wide monopoly under his own leadership.[22]

But in contrast to Thyssen's predictions, the cartel movement in German steel actually grew stronger than ever, with him ironically playing a leading role. The GDK joined the reorganized coal syndicate and pig iron syndicate in 1903. Thyssen & Co.'s plate department executive became a major figure in various plate and sheet cartels. Thyssen himself was also an active member of the gas and boiler pipe cartels. He followed the strip steel cartel with particular interest because he felt that strip steel was his specialty. For years he shadowed the cartel price without undercutting it, and eventually he joined the cartel.[23] In 1904, just two years after he had predicted the demise of cartels, Thyssen was actively promoting the formation of the most powerful German steel cartel of all, the Steel Works Association. Although banks have been held responsible for forcing one large but reluctant steel firm, Phoenix, into the cartel, there was little question who was the driving force: August Thyssen.[24]

Without the entry of Phoenix, the Steel Works Association would have been ineffective. Phoenix managers thought they would be better off outside the cartel, but, as one of Phoenix's bankers wrote at the time,

> Thyssen is greatly interested in the establishment of the Steel Works Association because on one hand he has completed his production facilities and runs them full, and would gladly see hoisted on the shoulders of his competition the burdens of helping to supply his large export business. He is going through the fire for it with his renowned energy and does not spare those who stand in his way. Unfortunately our [bank] President does not have as much courage and endurance as the other . . . You will have already gathered by which means Thyssen has influenced our President and has frightened him.[25]

Thyssen had threatened to cut out of the cartel's financial transactions any bank that did not promote Phoenix's entry into it. These heavy-handed maneuvers gave Phoenix's bankers little choice. The banks called an extraordinary meeting of Phoenix shareholders, who overrode the objections of the Phoenix executive board, thereby forcing Phoenix into the cartel. As one of Thyssen's pet sayings went: "It may not be pretty but it is practical."[26]

Thyssen and the Banks

Perhaps the most striking fact about August Thyssen's business career was that he financed one of the largest and most capital-intensive industrial complexes in Germany by his own personal wealth and credit alone. This made him remarkably independent of bank executives and supervisory boards. Thyssen did, however, borrow heavily, and he worked closely with banks when they offered him special advantages or services, such as help in issuing long-term bonds. Oscar Schlitter, director of the Deutsche Bank, commented years later on the unusual nature of Thyssen's financial strategy:

> Thyssen operated a lot with credit, but he apprehensively avoided committing himself to an overly close relationship with a single bank. He played them off of one another, and when the banks at the time criticized the abuse of acceptances [loans], that criticism was directed above all at Thyssen. In the construction of his financial transactions, he was a master. Bonds, loans, personal credit—it was all arranged in that way [i.e., intermingled, so that] he would not feel restricted in his leadership.[27]

Unlike other German steel companies, which issued shares to raise capital, Thyssen paid for his expansion largely through retained earnings. When his firms needed short-term cash, he had his accountants sell off parts of his own extensive stock portfolio. He used his securities as a type of defensive reserve fund as well as an offensive weapon against his competitors. Since so much of Thyssen's internal financing was private, his actions on the stock market received a lot of outside attention. Many investors timed their own stock purchases to coincide with Thyssen's. His efforts to conceal transactions only heightened the speculation.

Thyssen's financial standing was seriously questioned only twice before the onset of World War I in 1914. In 1901–02, there was little secret that Thyssen's firms were granting credits to one another, a sure sign of financial strain. To make matters worse, a family disagreement led one of his sons, August Thyssen Jr., to cast doubt publicly on his father's creditworthiness. The financial crisis, though not the family crisis, was averted by the sale of mining fields to the Prussian state. Doubts about August Sr.'s credit arose a second time in 1912, when the massive steel works in Alsace-Lorraine was under construction. This plant seemed to be financed out of thin air. The financial press questioned August Sr.'s ability to pay, so he ostentatiously placed an advertisement in a trade journal requesting that any creditors feeling uneasy about his financial condition meet him in Mülheim, where they would receive payment in full. After this public relations coup, no one again questioned his financial condition.[28]

Organizing the Thyssen-Konzern

Having achieved a relatively self-sufficient vertical integration as well as diversified product lines, Thyssen, along with many of his contemporaries, had to cope with the problem of organizing and running a very large operation. His solution was a form of the distinctively German *Konzern:* a multisubsidiary organization with a parent company that controlled the financial and strategic direction of legally independent subsidiary firms. Usually, a Konzern was run by a family or a single powerful entrepreneurial figure. In this sense, the Konzern resembled a Japanese *zaibatsu.* But unlike the zaibatsu, it tended to remain committed to related product areas.[29] The parent company also could take many different forms: it could be an official holding company, a "community of interest" (*Interessengemeinschaft* or IG), or simply the strongest firm in the group.[30]

The evolution of the Thyssen & Co. machine-engineering company and of the GDK steel plant at Dinslaken illustrates the strategic advantages that a decentralized Konzern had over one giant corporation. The machine-engineering department, since its founding in 1884, had acted as an in-house contractor and research arm. Outside sales grew rapidly after the turn of the century, with the development of an engine capable of recycling burned-off gas from coking and blast furnace operations, and then transforming this "waste" into power and energy. The machine-engineering department's gas engine proved to be the key element in an integrated energy economy for the Thyssen-Konzern. The gas engine not only furthered August Thyssen's general strategy of diversification, but also proved to be the "catalyst" for the "German path" of rationalization through economies of energy. This process culminated in the co-generation of steam for heating and electric power, and co-generation is a well-known element of German heavy industry even today.[31]

By 1911 the machine-engineering department had become a large entity in itself, and it was spun off as an independent firm. The new Maschinenfabrik Thyssen AG (Thyssen Machine Company, as it was called in English) began life with the expressed intention to "conquer the world market."[32] Within a few years, the company had become a huge success, and a powerful rival to the most renowned machine-engineering firm in Germany, the Maschinenfabrik Augsburg-Nürnberg (MAN). In typical German fashion, a syndicate for high-powered gas engines was soon established, in which MAN received a quota of 22.8 percent and Thyssen 20 percent. No other company came close to these high market shares.[33]

Similarly, the GDK Dinslaken plant was managed as a "profit center," or division of the GDK. Its year-end balances, capital accounts, and all of its commercial and financial transactions were calculated independently from those of the rest of the GDK. It even extended credits to other firms as if it were a separate firm. Its physical separateness from the main GDK works and the strong personality of its director kept it relatively autonomous. But it too was part of the Thyssen-Konzern.[34]

The Konzern structure itself was a departure from the typical pre-1914 German management system. Most other heavy industrial firms preferred to incorporate their holdings into a single large corporation. But Thyssen kept his core companies (GDK, AGHütt, Stahlwerke Thyssen AG, Thyssen & Co., and Maschinenfabrik Thyssen AG) legally separate. Siemens & Halske and Siemens-Schuckert followed a similar Konzern strategy.[35] And after the war, tighter alliances and stronger measures promoting rationalization led to a boom in Konzern-building. The structure of the Thyssen-Konzern reflected not only a strategy of vertical integration and product diversification, but also the autonomy Thyssen gave to his top executives, which became a cherished part of the company's culture. But there were other reasons that impelled Thyssen to embrace the Konzern structure:

FINANCIAL ADVANTAGES

The decentralized Konzern allowed Thyssen companies a great deal of flexibility. They could extend and receive credits through their current accounts with one another and with outside firms. Sometimes the resulting financial maneuvers were a bit irregular, as mentioned before. But since the companies were formally independent, these maneuvers were legally permissible. The GDK and Thyssen & Co. were entirely private companies, so August Thyssen could move funds quickly from firm to firm without outside oversight. In addition, this technique helped to identify and remedy financial weaknesses of individual Thyssen firms.[36]

ENHANCED INTERNAL COMPETITION

The Thyssen-Konzern used market transfer prices for deliveries between manufacturing and marketing offices. The trading companies bought from the manufacturing works at the most favorable market price for nonsyndicated goods and at cartel prices for syndicated goods. Transfer prices were set in a process of internal negotiation according to an organizational rule of thumb. Thyssen trading companies had to give the most favorable deals to Thyssen manufacturing works, while the manufacturing works had to offer the trading firms the most favorable prices and conditions on their products.[37]

In addition, Thyssen directors could freely tender outside offers for new equipment, forcing the Thyssen Machine Company to outbid or outclass other suppliers.[38] Moreover, a great part of all directors' yearly income was based on the financial success of their companies.[39] It was as if Thyssen had institutionalized his favorite saying: "If I rest, I rust."

STREAMLINED MANAGEMENT

The top executives of each company in the Konzern acted with great authority and autonomy. Thyssen firms had small corporate boards and only a few people with power of attorney (executive authority to act for the company). Other German industrial firms at this time typically had a supervisory board of twenty people, a managing board of ten, and perhaps thirty executives with power of attorney, all of whom received some form of directors' fees or dividends. By contrast, the GDK operated with nine to ten board members and four executives with power of attorney, and the Stahlwerke Thyssen in Alsace-Lorraine was even leaner.[40]

The decentralized organization with its numerous firms did multiply the total number of board of directors' chairs, however. In fact, when the question arose in the early 1920s as to whether or not to unify the Konzern, the most controversial question was which directors would be appointed to oversee the centralized firm. This was an even more heated question than the decision about which firm should become the central holding, or which Thyssen family member would be named to head a centralized firm. None of the Thyssen companies' board members was willing to be subordinated to any of the others. In the end, the extreme independence of the Thyssen directors made a centralized organization almost unthinkable.[41]

BEATING THE CARTELS

The legal structure of the Konzern proved extremely useful to Thyssen in his off-and-on battles with the cartels. By setting up new companies,

Thyssen found that he could expand production, since the new firms were not part of any existing cartel agreement. Thus, around 1910, Thyssen established two new mining companies, Gewerkschaft Lohberg and Rhein, for purely tactical reasons vis-à-vis the coal syndicate. He could now expand coal production beyond the terms of the 1909 coal cartel agreement. Since the GDK, which was bound by the cartel, technically stayed below its production quota, no one could argue that Thyssen had illegally violated the cartel agreement.[42]

SUPERVISION

The defining characteristic of the Konzern system was not just the legal independence of its constituent firms, but rather the high degree of supervision and interlocking controls which made a Konzern a unified economic and administrative unit. For the Thyssen-Konzern, family property relations were an important source of cohesion, but just as important was a series of formal corporate offices which administratively bound the separate companies into a coordinated and systematic whole. Here Thyssen reinvented his principle of "delegate, but supervise."

In 1906, Thyssen set up a Central Auditing Office to provide an overview of Konzern finances. It began to standardize cost accounting and audit the cash accounts for all the Thyssen firms. It consolidated the individual firms' balances into a Konzern balance, and created investment budgets that used return-on-equity ratios. It audited and intervened in member firms' accounts. It became the prime authority on the effectiveness of the firms' management. It carried out "organizational studies" (Organisationsarbeiten), and made extensive recommendations for the internal structure of Thyssen firms. The independence of the Central Auditing Office ensured a degree of objectivity in setting standards. The office constantly mediated internal cost and pricing disputes.[43] After 1918, it was empowered to decree organizational and financial changes in the firm's operations as though the orders came from August Thyssen himself.[44]

In addition to the auditing unit, three other offices were established in the superstructure of the Thyssen-Konzern: an office (called the Centrale) that dealt with complicated financial and transfer pricing questions, a legal department, and, in 1918, a central advisory board for Thyssen marketing operations.

Thyssen firms formed a cohesive Konzern because they had a unified central direction, formal institutional arrangements, and a more or less uniform set of financial standards. (Cost accounting moved forward less quickly). They also had a coherent manufacturing and marketing strategy, best expressed as a balanced vertical integration with little or no overlap between firms. The central corporate offices mentioned just above marked the beginning of a centralized-decentralized structure as sophisticated as that of Siemens in Germany, Mitsui in Japan, or any company in the United States at the time.[45]

Thyssen and His Managers

August Thyssen became legendary in his own time—a symbol of German entrepreneurship and one of the richest men in the country. He came to epitomize the image of the magnate who commanded as a master of his industrial house. He was essentially a creature of Bismarckian Germany. He looked like an aged Lenin, with his little white goatee and black frock coat. He preferred to wear stiff, rolled collars, and appeared quaint and old-fashioned. He had to have his shirts specially made because they were no longer in style.[46]

When dining alone, Thyssen ate simple fare such as sausage and red cabbage. He did not smoke or drink beer, though he did take an occasional glass of white wine.[47] Yet when he had people over for business, Thyssen knew how to set a grand table.[48] He enjoyed lavish and rich meals with the elite of the German business and political communities. Thyssen was very form-conscious. When guests were present, dinners became black-tie affairs. Overall, however, he was notably unostentatious.

For over 30 years, Thyssen lived in a medium-sized house right next to his original steel factory, a practice that had been typical for German entrepreneurs in the mid-nineteenth century. This proximity allowed Thyssen to be the first and last person on his factory grounds every day. The house was increasingly squeezed between the railroad tracks, the factories of Thyssen & Co., and the Friedrich Wilhelms-Hütte, one of the large steel mills in the Ruhr. The house was therefore drowned in constant rumblings of freight cars and enveloped in black smoke. Thyssen's butler called the area flat-out "ugly."[49] Thyssen did purchase a manor near the Rhine river, but he permitted the family of one of his factory directors to live in it.[50] Not until 1903, at the age of 61, did

Thyssen himself move to a nearby castle. His old house could no longer accommodate the constant stream of visitors who came for social and business purposes. In addition, his sons had put pressure on him to move. They did not think his living situation appropriate for one of the most important men in Germany.

Many contemporaries thought that with the purchase of his castle Thyssen was attempting to match Friedrich Krupp's luxurious Villa Hügel. Yet Thyssen compared himself with Krupp only in terms of business, not personal lifestyle. He repeatedly refused the German government's offer of ennoblement, under which he might have become a baron and had his name changed to von Thyssen.[51] His own castle was filled with fine, high-quality furnishings, but they were conservative and modest, not gaudy.[52] He was proud to have outdistanced Krupp in steel production, and especially proud that he was able to match Krupp in stature without recourse to the production of armaments. This feeling had little to do with any anti-militaristic stance. Rather it derived from Thyssen's knowledge that he had competed on the market, not for favors and high prices from the Reich bureaucracy or the Emperor. Nor had he enjoyed monopolies in any product lines.[53]

Thyssen gained a somewhat unfair reputation for miserliness. (His brother, Josef, was the true miser of the partnership.) Reichsbank President Hjalmar Schacht liked to relate how August Thyssen carried his own bags, traveled in third-class coaches, and stayed in "second-rate" hotels, even bargaining about the price of a room. In fact, Thyssen simply preferred to stay in hotels with other merchants, not in those catering to high society. He generally adhered to standards appropriate to a respectable businessman of the time.[54]

But there was just enough truth in all the myths to make them plausible. Thyssen did habitually walk across the Ruhr River bridge, not to save the toll as rumor had it but for the exercise. Once when he was buying a large mine worth several million Reichsmarks, he pointed out to the seller that the envelopes used for the contracts were so heavy that they had to pay double the postage.[55] He constantly hounded his managers about their travel expenses. The top sales executive of the plate department once received a letter from Thyssen complaining that expenses (a minuscule 8.10 RM) charged to the firm for a conference sponsored by the foremost iron and steel association in Germany should be a private expense, not a company one.[56] Thyssen would steam off stamps that had not been invalidated and reuse them. He never did own an automobile.

In business Thyssen was extremely secretive, private, and often cold and hard-hearted.[57] But in person he seemed a rather polite and modest man, so long as he was not crossed. He sternly admonished his executives if they gloated about victories over rivals or if they acted disrespectfully toward subordinates.[58] Politically, he was a nationalist, deeply conservative, and a devout Catholic.

Thyssen obsessively protected himself against outsiders, a habit that fed his reputation as an autocrat. Yet inside his firm, and especially among his leading executives, he acted more as first among equals than as an autocrat whose orders were to be followed unquestioningly. Although he had veto power, at times he let himself be overridden by majority vote of his managers.[59] He rarely summoned people to his office, but called on them in their own spaces, usually after giving prior notification. He liked to walk around his production facilities and talk informally with managers and workers.[60] All of his top managers agreed that he genuinely listened to their recommendations.[61]

Thyssen was generous with new investment funds to keep his firms on the cutting edge of technology and high productivity. He listened carefully to even his most junior managers when they presented suggestions for improvement. But he always required that his engineers and managers submit detailed calculations on projected costs and returns for their new proposals. In this way he again underscored his general commercial orientation. Few engineers and managers ever saw Thyssen scrutinize mechanical designs, but he could almost daily be observed checking costs.[62]

Thyssen retained ultimate decisionmaking power, but an elite group of salaried managers actually ran the Konzern. Thyssen's competitive edge was his ability to choose good, often strong-willed people, and then to take their advice. If he gained trust in their abilities, he swiftly approved new projects. If they failed: "I have great companies for which I am responsible, therefore I throw people out who do not perform."[63] All of his managers attested to his leadership capacity. He had a sixth sense in choosing capable young managers and putting them into positions of great authority.[64] Franz Dahl was 35 when he took over as chief plant engineer. Julius Kalle of the GDK Dinslaken was only 27. The top administrative and marketing director of the GDK, Carl Rabes, was 34.

The chief accountant of the Thyssen machine company, Heinrich Din-kelbach, was 27.

Thyssen and his Children

Thyssen's family relationships were not as solid as his business ones. He never really trusted his children and they never warmed to him. He had a "coldness" about him that made him an effective businessman but a difficult father.[65] When August's brother Josef died in 1915, Josef's sons entered Thyssen & Co. as new proprietors, but they were expressly excluded from the direction of the firm.[66] August Thyssen usually relied on the advice of his managers, and his and Josef's sons knew it. They were at least 40 years old before they began exercising leadership roles in the firm. Even then, they remained in the shadow of August Thyssen Sr., whom the divorce agreement had given lifelong control over his companies. Meanwhile, the children remained emotionally close to their mother, Hedwig. Like her, they had aspirations to nobility and the corresponding lifestyle, a circumstance Thyssen Sr. found horrifying. They urged him to accept ennoblement, but he repeatedly refused the offer from Berlin. At times they united against him, but they squabbled incessantly among themselves.[67]

August's oldest son, Fritz (1873–1951), worked most closely with him inside the GDK, but relations between the two remained tense. When Fritz was learning the ropes of the firm, Thyssen Sr. treated him more strictly than the lowest trainee. He tried to block Fritz's marriage, by rather unsavory means. (August thought Fritz's fiancée carried a hereditary disease.) When Thyssen Sr. could not change Fritz's mind about the marriage, he placed humiliating conditions on the bride's parents, hoping to change their minds. Fritz's wedding went forward anyway and the marriage proved a lasting one.[68] After 1914, father and son often argued about the direction of the Konzern, and Thyssen executives found Fritz moody and difficult. In the end, Thyssen Sr. felt that Fritz's character was "unpredictable and easily influenced," a judgment that during the early part of the Nazi period in Germany proved to be correct.[69]

The second son, August Thyssen Jr. (1874–1943), was his father's favorite. He inherited much of Thyssen Sr.'s cunning ruthlessness, but none of his interest in business. In training at the firm's Berlin office,

August Jr. soon became seduced by the capital city's aristocratic culture. In an attempt to become an aristocrat himself he purchased noble lands outside Berlin. He bought his way into a feudal Potsdamer guard regiment and entered into numerous romantic liaisons and near marriages. Meanwhile, he ran the Berlin business into the ground in 1910, taking an affiliated bank with it. August Jr. attempted to fight a duel with the managing director of the bank, whom he blamed for its failure, but August Sr. whisked him back home. Naturally, these escapades cost a good deal of money, and August Jr. and his sister, Hedwig (named for her mother), continually came up with new schemes to have their allowances raised. Both of them took out extensive loans based on the inheritance provisions outlined by their parents' divorce agreement. August Jr. was not above blackmailing his father by writing to banks and insinuating that Thyssen Sr.'s credit rating was not what it should be. He even offered a rival steel industrialist a share of his inheritance. In 1902, August Sr. wrote in despair to his friend Carl Klönne of the Deutsche Bank:

> My sons should be striving wholeheartedly with me and my brother to develop our ventures into really great and independent enterprises. Our future does not lie in Potsdam; our greatness and significance lies in our coal and soon in our iron ore mines. Only these factors will secure us for a long time the justified influence and the great reputation that a world-class firm must achieve in order to create and sustain, freely and independently, and with all its power, a great, flourishing export industry for the Fatherland.[70]

The statement illustrates Thyssen Sr.'s goals for business and life, which wrapped family, enterprise, and country together.

Eventually, Thyssen Sr. tried to declare his favorite son legally incompetent. At a reception he attempted to place August Jr. in a straitjacket, but the son escaped, and his mental incompetence could not be proven. Thyssen Sr. had to hire a lawyer to help settle the myriad legal claims arising from his son's 1910 bankruptcy. August Jr. insulted the lawyer and tried to provoke him into a duel.[71] Eventually the lawyer, a director of the Thyssen Machine Company, advised August Sr. to dissolve the 1871 Thyssen & Co. partnership and incorporate its assets into the machine company in order to void any claims by August Jr.'s creditors. This was done, and in 1918 the original partnership ceased to exist as an independent company.

A third son, Heinrich Thyssen (1875–1947), appeared only formally on Thyssen company boards before World War I. He wisely avoided most of the family feuds by moving to Budapest, where he married into and was adopted by an aristocratic family. He thus became entitled to carry the name Baron Heinrich Thyssen-Bornemisza. Thyssen-Bornemisza inherited his father's broad streak of independence. After the communist revolution in Hungary in 1919, he moved to The Hague in the Netherlands, basing his operations in Rotterdam and taking over primary responsibility for Thyssen's foreign financial transactions.

Before the war, the children of both August and Josef had minimal influence on the strategic direction of the Thyssen-Konzern. Josef's children tended to defer to management, then suffered from various maladies that kept them from becoming more active after the war. Leadership fell to Fritz Thyssen and Heinrich Thyssen-Bornemisza. But the two turned out to have very different personalities and ideas about the future of the business.

The Impact of War, 1914–1925

The First World War was highly profitable for the Thyssen-Konzern, but it also caused severe financial strains. All of the firms converted to wartime production, which radically altered the size and scope of the business. In 1913, for example, the Thyssen Machine Company had employed just over 3,000 workers. By 1917, it employed almost 22,500 (including 8,000 women), more than the entire workforce of the prewar rolling mills.

Coping with such changes demanded a new financial structure, so in 1915 the Thyssen companies formed a "community of interest." This unique German form of business, called an IG (Interessengemeinschaft), pooled the profits of member companies and redistributed them according to the amount of wages and salaries paid by the individual firms. The IG was designed to support the GDK, and it formalized the financial relationship among Thyssen firms in the event of the now 73-year-old August Thyssen's death.[72]

The Allied victory over Germany in 1918 left the national economy and the Thyssen-Konzern in disarray.[73] The Versailles Treaty required that the Germans pay reparations and transfer the Alsace-Lorraine region back to France. (The Germans had taken it by force in 1871.) The treaty cost Thyssen his steel works in Lorraine, which many analysts considered to be the most modern plant of its kind on the continent. The Lorraine works was taken over by a consortium of French industrial consumers of iron and steel products, including Renault, Peugeot, and a number of heavy equipment and electrical machinery firms. They divided the plant's production among themselves according to a specified percentage.

The Versailles Treaty also tore down the tariff walls protecting German steel goods. At the same time, many countries, including Great Britain and the United States, raised their own tariffs against German exports. In addition, the German steel industry now became dependent on Swedish iron ore, which had to be imported and paid for with depreciating marks. International competition became fierce, as countries struggled to adjust to peacetime production levels.

As if this were not enough, German politics tumbled into chaos. The spread of the Bolshevik revolution out from Russia seemed quite possible. Indeed, some of the "reddest" pockets in Germany were found within the GDK and the Thyssen Machine Company.[74] For a while it appeared certain that Germany's mines would be socialized. So, on the advice of his top legal counsel, August Thyssen took preventive measures. He divided the GDK, giving its mining operations over to a new company, the Gewerkschaft Friedrich Thyssen, named after his father. After long discussions, his managers convinced Thyssen to rename the steel operations the August Thyssen-Hütte (ATH).

In the midst of this chaos, the Thyssen-Konzern had to convert back to peacetime production. All facilities needed extensive renovations because of high usage and poor maintenance during the war. Central to August Thyssen's postwar outlook was the reconversion of his machine engineering company. Taking advantage of its engineering skill, the Thyssen Machine Company bought out a troubled electrical machinery producer and began manufacturing heavy electric dynamos. These products successfully penetrated into Siemens-Schuckert's traditional markets.[75]

At the same time, Thyssen began a massive expansion program to offset the loss of the Lorraine steelworks. Government compensation for this loss helped to finance the expansion, but because of high inflation, the funds were worth only about 6 percent of the original cost of building the Lorraine plant.[76] Nevertheless, the steelmaking capacity of the ATH grew immensely over the next six years.

The sometimes erratic Fritz Thyssen played an active role in ensuring the expansion of the ATH. (Thyssen Sr. increasingly retired to his castle and was often disoriented during the hyperinflation period by discussions of money in orders of magnitude that bore little relation to anything in his experience.) State-of-the-art equipment was installed, with a heavy emphasis on energy regeneration economies. By 1925, the ATH did not need a single ton of coal for the crude steelmaking stage of production, because it used the ample gas energy coming from the coking and blast furnace processes.[77] Many of the Thyssen rolling mills converted to electricity drawn from the regional electric company, which itself was partially owned by the Thyssen-Konzern.

Following the stabilization of the German Mark in 1924, the Thyssen-Konzern turned to the United States investment bank Dillon Read & Co. for help. After intense negotiations, Thyssen's chief commercial director managed to acquire a large loan, based on "Assets and Reputation," with no public disclosure of Thyssen's financial condition. Decisive for this favorable result was a glowing report from the Chicago-based steel consulting firm H. A. Brassert, Inc.:

> Giving due consideration to all important steel plants in the various countries, there are in my opinion none more favorably situated for the long pull, in regards to raw material supply, assembly manufacturing costs, than this August Thyssen plant. I make this statement because combined with its favorable geographical location, it is one of the most modern and best equipped steel plants in the world. Competition from German or other plants can therefore be successfully and profitably met . . .
>
> Mr. August Thyssen who with members of his family owned and still owns the entire interests, has consistently followed the policy of reinvesting his large earnings in plant improvements, it being a matter of personal pride with him to have at all times the most advanced and best equipped plant. I personally know Mr. Thyssen and have been well acquainted with his son and his chief executives, who made frequent visits to the United States and kept themselves well informed as to our progress. They were at all times eager to exchange technical information and were first in Europe to adopt our ideas of large production and labor saving. In respect to fuel economy, they were always in advance of the industry and today they lead the world in heat economy in the production of steel . . .

[On blast furnaces] These furnaces produce more iron than any foreign furnaces and are very well equipped with labor saving machinery, and particularly well equipped for fuel economy . . . [On the gas power station] This plant is only surpassed in magnitude by that of the United States Steel Corporation at Gary, Indiana . . .

The Rolling Mill Plant of the August Thyssen Works has a capacity of 1,120,000 tons of finished product per year. It is more elaborate than plants of equal capacity in the United States, owing to the greater diversity of sizes and specifications required in the German trade and the world's market . . .

[On housing] A considerable amount of the company's assets is represented by houses of which the company owns many thousands, having supplied a house for every four of its 10,000 employees at the steel plant and a house or living quarter for every one of its 20,000 miners. This is in accordance with the German law and the houses are very substantial and attractive, in marked contrast to our usual workmen's colonies [in America] . . . In conclusion I beg to state that the August Thyssen Steel Concern have as modern a type of plant as can be found anywhere and I consider them, all in all, the most efficient steel manufacturers of Europe.[78]

Founding the Vereinigte Stahlwerke AG

By 1925, Germany's steelmaking capacity had climbed back to its prewar level, thanks to American loans, government subsidies, and the economics of inflation, which made it easier to pay off debt. But German steel still suffered from a number of structural problems. It had too much vertical integration, too much scope, too many niche products, and not enough scale. In large measure these characteristics had resulted from the cartel system.

August Thyssen saw the situation clearly, as did Albert Vögler, the General Director of Deutsch-Luxembourg, a large heavy-industry combine. As early as 1919, Vögler had written a memorandum outlining an alternative strategy for steel. This document launched a serious debate about the future among German steel producers. And this debate ultimately led to the founding in 1926 of the huge and famous VSt, which stands for Vereinigte Stahlwerke AG or, in English, United Steelworks.[79]

Echoing Thyssen's own analysis of nearly 25 years before, Albert Vögler argued that "the time of syndicates has passed." The only sure way to raise productivity and reduce overcapacity, he said, was through an "Alliance" of the steel industry in a community of interest (IG), something the chemical industry had already initiated with IG Farben. According to Vögler, the strategic goal for steel should be a thorough rationalization: improvement of productivity ratios, a better division of labor, pooling of research capabilities, and reduction of administrative and marketing costs. The current organization of the German steel industry did not allow the best use of technical improvements, because of low-volume production and frequent changes in product types. A strategy of relatively small-scale vertical integration had made German Konzerne mirror images of one another, with low productivity and low capacity utilization in all lines. Vögler's memorandum offered a vision of standardized mass production geared to enhance international competitiveness.

Initially, Vögler's memorandum found little favor. Only August Thyssen and some of his executives agreed that the proposed consolidations should be supported.[80] Most other steel industrialists continued to extend further their vertically integrated Konzerne. However, in the autumn of 1925 the German economy entered a sharp recession, and in this new situation even American credit was no solution to overcapacity and poor productivity (see Table 6.1, p. 226).

Six large German steel firms now began negotiations to form a "union of steel." But the talks that ultimately led to the VSt turned out to be torturous. Two firms, Krupp and Hoesch, dropped out (and stayed independent until their own merger in 1991). Their withdrawal left the Rheinelbe Union, Phoenix, the Rheinische Stahlwerke (Rheinstahl), and the Thyssen-Konzern to carry on. Negotiations among these four nearly collapsed several times, but were always brought back on track by Albert Vögler, with the strong backing of August Thyssen. Thyssen even made the merger of his Konzern contingent on Vögler's being named General Director of the VSt for at least five years.[81]

The VSt negotiations forced the elderly Thyssen to make a choice between two of the most cherished principles of his corporate strategy since 1871: the desire to be number one in the steel industry in scale and reputation versus the desire for independent family control. The negotiating position of the Thyssen-Konzern was further complicated by sibling rivalry. Fritz Thyssen was nationalistic; Heinrich Thyssen-Bornemisza was cosmopolitan. Fritz was blunt in manner; Heinrich was diplomatic. Fritz controlled the fixed assets of the Konzern in the Ruhr stronghold; Heinrich controlled the liquid assets of the Konzern from Rotterdam. A large proportion of these liquid assets had drifted into foreign currencies during the time of hyper-inflation, and therefore into Heinrich's hands. Heinrich often threatened to block further credit to Fritz. This kind of activity dismayed Thyssen Sr., who sometimes derided Heinrich as "only a banker," not a real industrialist.[82]

The tensions among the three reached their climax in 1925–26. The family debated joining the VSt while Thyssen Sr. lay on his deathbed. Heinrich Thyssen-Bornemisza simply refused to join. In a letter of September 1925 he declared:

> This trust [the VSt] will shatter a broadly conceived and extensive family enterprise. The factories and companies I am responsible for do not need this trust. Even in times of crisis these factories and companies have made it through without any significant outside help and hope to survive in the same manner in the future. In case the condition of the ATH is such that it must seek merger in this trust, then the board of directors and other authorized parties must assume exclusive responsibility for it. I will not accept such a responsibility. My warnings have not been heeded for years. My ideas were not taken into account.[83]

Until the last minute, even August and Fritz Thyssen, as well as many managing directors, had second thoughts about the merger. Some Thyssen executives even offered to reduce their salaries to help alleviate the financial straits of the Konzern if it could remain independent.

All resistance was finally overcome, and in May 1926, the shareholders of companies merging into the VSt approved the consolidation. The withdrawal of Thyssen-Bornemisza's support had meant that roughly half of the assets of the Thyssen-Konzern would never enter the new VSt, but the core steel facilities did join.

The official founding date of the VSt was 1 April 1926, and the Thyssen-Konzern came to an end on that day. But August Thyssen, who had done so much to promote the fusion, never saw its first general assembly. He died on 4 April 1926, at the age of 84. Thyssen's children, who now inherited one of Germany's largest fortunes, had to pay only a stamp tax of three Marks. On the old issue of the divorce, Prussian tax lawyers agreed that August Thyssen's death had brought no actual transfer of ownership to his children, because ownership had already been transferred to them in 1885 by the original divorce agreement. Thus there was legally no inheritance and no inheritance taxes.[84]

Operating the Vereinigte Stahlwerke AG

The Vereinigte Stahlwerke was explicitly modeled on the United States Steel Corporation. Fritz Thyssen chaired the VSt's supervisory board and Albert Vögler its managing board. The VSt held market shares in German steel similar to those U.S. Steel held on the American market. In 1927, it mined about 18 percent of all German coal and produced just under 50 percent of all German pig iron and crude steel (see Table 6.2, p. 226). It also embarked on a rationalization program, closing down obsolete plants and concentrating production in the most efficient facilities. The Thyssen factories, being the most modern, were the least affected by these measures. The VSt centered its production for export at the Thyssen works on the Rhine.[85]

The VSt also built on the financial relationship the Thyssen-Konzern had developed with American bankers. It had a share capital of RM 800 million, a figure chosen primarily to attract American capital. The government also gave the VSt a one-time tax break on the costs of the merger and allowed it to defer payments. The VSt and Dillon Read closed another major loan. Price Waterhouse became the VSt's chartered accountant.

In order to make the giant merger successful, the VSt had to take into consideration a number of competing interests in the German economy. Many manufacturers, including potential competitors, feared that the huge company would exercise a disproportionate influence within cartels and on the national economy. The VSt therefore signed a special agreement limiting itself to coal mining and iron and steel production. It promised not to follow the prior logic of "vertical trust building" that had been so predominant in German steel. As a result, the VSt sold the Thyssen Machine Company to DEMAG, a competing firm, which immediately shut it down and sold its electric dynamo production to Siemens-Schuckert. This sale helped to define the new spheres of interest between crude-steel producers and other manufacturers.[86]

The VSt itself, however, turned out to be a lumbering, bureaucratic dinosaur. The problems of combining everything from coal mines to pipe production into one large, functionally organized corporation became overwhelming. The fusion of former rivals made internal decisionmaking unwieldy and highly politicized. In 1926, when the VSt was created, the managing board was made far too large, with 40 regular members and 12 vice-board members. When the Great Depression hit a few years later, the VSt proved incapable of reacting quickly to the crisis and nearly went bankrupt.[87]

Heinrich Dinkelbach, a high-ranking Thyssen accounting and control officer, now proposed that the VSt be reorganized into a Konzern structure, with all its competitive advantages. Dinkelbach invoked the principles underlying the Thyssen-Konzern. He found a sponsor in Albert Vögler, who supported a complex redesign of the firm into a much more decentralized structure. The reorganization was similar to that of the earlier Thyssen-Konzern, and of 1920s American firms such as Du Pont and General Motors as well. Standardized accounting and organizational procedures were retained, but operations were decentralized into profit centers. Of great importance was the establishment of independent subsidiaries that would again carry the former companies' traditional and still well-known names. In 1934, the VSt formed a number of fully owned subsidiaries, most of which carried the old names, among them the August-Thyssen Hütte (ATH). A new VSt subsidiary, whose name in English was the German Pipe and Tube Company, comprised several firms, including the former Thyssen & Co., August Thyssen's first firm, organized back in 1871.[88]

The fortunes of the VSt and its subsidiaries mirrored those of the German economy, which improved during the 1930s before Nazi Germany plunged into war. Though the VSt profited from the armaments boom, tensions with the Nazis grew as well. The VSt's second in command, Ernst Poensgen, retired in disgust. Fritz Thyssen, after first supporting the Nazis, turned against the regime. But, for the most part, VSt executives played a role in keeping the mills going. One important VSt executive, Walther Rohland, who succeeded Ernst Poensgen, also headed mobilization chief Albert Speer's organizational "ring" for tank production, thereby earning the nickname "Panzer Rohland." He was one of Speer's closest colleagues and was one of the few German steel industry managers permanently purged from business after the end of the war.[89]

The VSt and its subsidiaries struggled to produce coal, steel, and many other materials throughout the war. Like other German firms, it used forced labor and prisoners of war. By 1944, crude steel production at the

ATH plant of the VSt had sunk to two-thirds of its prewar level, mostly because of constant interruptions of work by air-raid sirens and Allied bombing. Serious damage from the bombing was felt by the autumn of 1944, and production at the ATH was stopped entirely in January 1945.[90] When the Allies marched into the Ruhr, they arrested the leading executives of the VSt. Albert Vögler, the General Director, committed suicide just before he could be captured.[91]

August Thyssen's Sons

Fritz Thyssen had belonged to a set of industrialists who supported Adolf Hitler before 1933. Yet his enthusiasm for the Nazis quickly waned. Fritz turned away from the party during the 1930s and the Gestapo put him under surveillance. When Germany began World War II in 1939 by marching its troops into Poland, Fritz telegraphed Hermann Göring protesting the war. The next day he escaped to Switzerland. In Germany, meanwhile, all of his assets were confiscated. During his period of flight, Fritz prepared a manuscript that was later published with the title "I Paid Hitler"—that is, helped finance his rise to power.

Fritz planned to flee to Argentina, but first wanted to visit his ailing mother in Brussels. He arrived there just as the Germans were invading Belgium. He escaped to France, but the Gestapo caught up with him. He and his wife were then confined for two years in a sanitarium, and later in concentration camps, including Buchenwald and Dachau. At the end of the war, the Americans detained Fritz as a potential war criminal and a witness for an intended case against the VSt. After 1948, he was ruled to be a free man. He moved to Buenos Aires and died there in 1951, at the age of 78. He was buried next to his father at the castle home in Mülheim.

No one knows where August Thyssen Jr. is buried. He never married, and he had no children. He died in 1943 at the age of 69 at a hotel in Munich. But when his doctor tried to perform an autopsy, he found only the body of a young soldier, and the disposition of August Jr.'s remains is a mystery to this day.

Heinrich Thyssen-Bornemisza lived outside Germany and remained politically neutral during the war. When the Germans invaded Holland, they confiscated his assets and securities. After the war, the Dutch tried to seize his properties as "enemy assets," but Heinrich's Hungarian citizenship saved them. In addition, the complicated interrelationship between Fritz's and Heinrich's assets proved hopelessly confusing both to the Nazis and later to the Allied authorities. Not until 1953 were all questions clarified. Meanwhile, Heinrich had died in 1947, at the age of 72.[92] Heinrich had been an ardent collector of art. With the money from his inheritance and his business, he built up one of the world's greatest private art collections. His children continued his extensive dealings in art, and the entire collection was eventually purchased by the government of Spain and transferred to a museum in Madrid.

Postwar Reconstruction

With the advice of Price Waterhouse, the British occupation authorities appointed Heinrich Dinkelbach, who had been the chief accountant of the Thyssen Machine Company and then of the VSt, to be trustee *(Treuhand)* of the entire Ruhr steel industry. Dinkelbach had been the only VSt executive not to be interned at the end of the war. He now designed plans to break up the German steel industry. He was also the decisive figure on the employer side in the establishment of labor-management "codetermination" for German steel, and he lost many of his industrialist friends in the process. Dinkelbach divided the VSt into 23 companies. The last to be reestablished was the August Thyssen-Hütte AG, in 1953.[93]

With Fritz Thyssen's death in 1951, the Allies ordered that the Thyssen family's 21 percent of the former VSt share capital be divided equally among Fritz's heirs: his wife, Amélie Thyssen, and his daughter, Countess Anita Zichy-Thyssen. Through private investment trusts, their share portfolios came to be concentrated in firms that had once been parts of the old Thyssen-Konzern: the Rheinische Röhrenwerke AG (the former Thyssen & Co.); the Hüttenwerke Phoenix AG (the former AGHütt); the Deutsche Edelstahlwerke (the former Krefelder Stahlwerke); the Handelsunion AG (the former Thyssen and VSt trading companies); and the August Thyssen-Hütte AG or ATH. The Thyssen family stock portfolio not only provided a secure capital base for the new companies, but also facilitated the merger of these former Thyssen-Konzern companies into a new consolidated firm, which went by the old name ATH.

During the 1950s, with the help of "counterpart" (foreign aid) funds and generous state investment programs for coal and steel, the new ATH invested heavily in new plant. Within a few years, it began to pay out dividends and expand through retained earnings. When the ATH's new hot rolling mills went into production in 1955, it was considered such an event that Chancellor Konrad Adenauer and Economics Minister Ludwig Erhard participated in the ceremony. Adenauer reminisced about how he had toured the original ATH plant years before with August Thyssen Sr.[94]

The ATH rebuilt its position in the German steel industry through a policy of expansion and acquisition. The old company's desire to be number one in steel reasserted itself. In 1964–65, a mere dozen years after its reestablishment, it produced 8.6 million metric tons of steel, the largest single-company total in Europe and the fourth-largest in the world. Facilitated by the Thyssen family investment trusts, the ATH by 1965 had managed to reunite many of the old Thyssen firms, reversing the effects of the Allied deconcentration program. The former GDK, GDK Dinslaken, AGHütt, and Thyssen & Co. were now once again parts of the Thyssen organization. By 1967, the ATH's revenues made it the third-largest company in Germany, behind only Volkswagen and Siemens.[95] The German steel industry as a whole was again led by the ATH, Krupp, Hoesch, Klöckner, and Mannesmann, a constellation of firms very similar to the group that had led the industry 50 years earlier.

The Thyssen-Bornemisza Group

After clearing up all of its property questions in 1953, the Thyssen-Bornemisza group headquartered in the Netherlands could begin operations again. According to the terms of the final settlement, the Dutch government had to be represented on the supervisory board, along with a number of Dutch banks, for at least 15 years. The mayor of The Hague held the chair position on the board. Belonging to the group were a number of specialty steel firms in the Ruhr, the private August Thyssen Bank, the Thyssen gas and waterworks, a Dutch bank, a few trading companies, and parts of two major shipbuilding companies.

The Thyssen-Bornemisza group developed a long-term strategy of diversifying its investments internationally and moving into consumer-oriented sectors. The group retreated out of shipbuilding and gas, and later gave up private banking. For the most part, the group had little central coordination and was run as a financial portfolio operation. By 1970, a somewhat more centralized organization was administering about 50 enterprises around the world, through four geographically oriented business sectors. In the mid-1990s, the European sector was specializing in the production and sale of pumps and light agricultural equipment, and the transport of liquid gas and chemicals. The American branch concentrated on information technology through Indian Head, Inc., based in New York. In 1971, the central holding was renamed the Thyssen-Bornemisza Group N.V., with headquarters first in Amsterdam, then in Willemstad on the island of Curaçao in the Netherlands Antilles. In the mid-1990s, annual sales of the group averaged about 3 billion U.S. dollars.[96]

Epilogue: Reorganization and Diversification of Thyssen AG

Until 1973, the August Thyssen Hütte, or ATH, concentrated on its core steel operations. In 1968, coal operations that had come with some of the acquired companies were sold to the newly formed Ruhrkohle AG. In 1970, the Thyssen firm and its steel competitor Mannesmann exchanged certain assets, in order to focus on their core competencies. Thyssen transferred its pipe and tube operations to Mannesmann, thereby moving August Thyssen's first venture in Mülheim out of the Thyssen orbit. Mannesmann, in return, gave up its plate production to Thyssen. Thyssen maintained a 25 percent cross-shareholding in the Mannesmann Pipe Works subsidiary.[97]

The year 1973 marked a turning point in the history of the ATH. In response to a worldwide structural crisis in the steel industry, the ATH began to diversify into technology-related sectors, particularly mechanical engineering. The ATH also took over Rheinstahl, in one of the largest mergers of this period. Rheinstahl had operations in machine engineering, elevators, and steel-framed construction. In 1978 Thyssen strengthened its holdings overseas by acquiring the Budd Company of Troy, Michigan, a manufacturer of auto parts and body panels. In addition, Thyssen acquired a host of smaller firms, ranging from producers of machine tools to service and logistics operations.

To signal these changes, the ATH in 1976 renamed itself Thyssen AG, a holding company. Thyssen AG then grew from 186 companies in 1978 to 318 by the middle 1990s.

Thus, by the 1990s, Thyssen AG had become a widely diversified firm. Its product lines included steel, capital goods, automotive parts, mechanical engineering, elevators and escalators, defense contracting, ship-building, plastics, energy, waste disposal, industrial engineering, and en-vironmental technology, plus trading and services. Thyssen Stahl AG, the steel subsidiary, was the direct successor of the original GDK and ATH. In the middle 1990s, Thyssen Stahl AG was the twelfth-largest crude-steel producer in the world and the fourth-largest in Europe. But steel accounted for less than 30 percent of Thyssen AG's total sales. The company later engaged in a joint venture with VEBA and Bell South to build a second nationwide cellular phone network in Germany, called E-plus.[98]

Altogether, the long story of Thyssen steel had exemplified Germany's encounter with the Second Industrial Revolution. It remained to be seen how the company's successor firms, and the larger German economy, would adapt to the Third Industrial Revolution. In the 1990s, Thyssen AG's chairman, Heinz Kriwet, announced that the time might have come to "think the unthinkable" and exit steel, though no quick action was taken. In September 1995, the Commerzbank announced that it had purchased the largest single package of Thyssen shares, 15.5 percent owned by Count Frederico and Count Claudio Zichy-Thyssen, in a deal worth about $1 billion.[99] The Fritz Thyssen Foundation still retained about 9 percent of the company, and several family members also held small percentages. But, for the first time in the company's tumultuous 120-year history, the Thyssen family was no longer its largest shareholder.

Figure 6.1 Germany's Twelve Largest Industrial Enterprises in 1913 and 1924 according to Balance Sheet Totals, in Millions of Reichmarks (1 $U.S. (1913) = 4.2 RM)

1913			**1924**				
Company	Industry	Total Assets 1913	Company	Industry	Total Assets 1924	1913 Rank
1. Krupp	Heavy	RM 587.2m	1. Phoenix	Heavy	RM446.2m	8
2. ªThyssen, Consolidated	Heavy	504.2	2. Krupp	Heavy	369.2	1
3. AEG	Electrical	462.8	3. ᵇThyssen, Consolidated	Heavy	335.3	2
4. GBAG	Coal	394.9	4. GBAG	Coal	327.3	4
5. Siemens-Schuckert	Electrical	313.6	5. BASF	Chemicals	301.6	14
6. Deutsch-Luxembourg	Heavy	278.2	6. AEG	Electrical	285.6	3
7. GDK	Heavy	249.9	7. Siemens-Schuckert	Electrical	264.0	5
8. Phoenix	Heavy	224.0	8. Rheinische Stahlwerke	Heavy	257.2	30
9. Siemens & Halske	Electrical	187.3	9. Bayer	Chemicals	242.8	13
10. Harpener Bergbau	Coal	185.9	10. Gew. ᶜThyssen	Heavy	235.1	7
11. Hohenlohe	Coal	134.1	11. Deutsch-Luxembourg	Heavy	230.5	6
12. Hibernia	Coal	131.9	12. Hoechst	Chemicals	226.6	18
13. GHH	Heavy	130.5	13. Siemens & Halske	Electrical	205.1	9

a. Thyssen Consolidated = ATH, AGHütt, Thyssen & Co. and Machine Company and Stahlwerke Thyssen in 1912.
b. Thyssen Consolidated = ATH, AGHütt, Thyssen & Co. rolling mills and Machine Company in 1924.
c. Gew. Thyssen = same as former GDK.

Source: Adapted from Wilfried Feldenkirchen, "The Concentration Process in the Entrepreneurial Economy since the Late 19th Century," in Hans Pohl, ed., *Zeitschrift Für Unternehmensgeschichte* (Stuttgart, 1988).

IMPORTANT NOTICE!

In order to insure prompt attention to enquiries, commands etc., Correspondents are respectfully requested to indicate in the address of every letter the number of the department, for which its contents are intended and consequently to entertain all their correspondence separately with each of the below named departments.

DEPARTMENT I
Hoops
plain and galvanized of all dimensions and for all purposes, especially for Cotton Ties and Barrels, splayed and nosed, cut and cornered.

DEPARTMENT II
Steel Plates
of largest sizes up to about 12′ wide for all purposes, especially
Boiler Plates
for Marine and Land Boilers, plain as well as planed and bent, Pressing, Flanging and Welding Work
of every description for Marine Boilers and all other purposes,
Pressed Boiler Heads, flat and dished,
Flanged and Dished Boiler Ends with flanged Flue Holes
for Cornish and Lancashire Boilers, Corrugated Furnaces
Fox's and Morison's Type, Adamson's Flanged Flues,

Universally Rolled Flat Bars up to about 32″ wide,
Tube Strips,
Wrought Iron and Soft Steel, Pulley Strips
Welded Steel Pipes
of largest diameters for Water Mains and other Conduits, etc.
Pressed Steel Trough Flooring Plates,
Pressed Steel Underframes and Bogies
for Railway Rolling Stock,
Patent Pressed Steel Coke Oven Doors.

DEPARTMENT III
Lapwelded and Weldless Steel Tubes, especially for Boilers and other purposes,
Field Boiler Tubes,
Perkins' Hot Water Tubes,
Artesian Well boring Tubes,
Oil Well Tubing and Oil Line Pipes, etc.
Buttwelded Iron & Steel Tubes and Fittings
of every description for the Conveyance

of Oats, Water, Steam, Air, etc. plain and galvanised.
Coils
to any shape and of any length, plain and galvanised for
Steam Superheaters,
Refrigerating and Heating Plants, etc.
Tubular Steel Poles
for Lighting, Traction and Telegraphy.

DEPARTMENT IV
Galvanising
of Hoops, Bars, Sheets, Tubes, Rivets, etc.
Corrugated Sheets
and heavy Corrugated Plates, plain and galvanized.

DEPARTMENT V
Iron Foundries and Engine Works Specialty:
High Class Steam and Gas Engines, Gas Producers
Kerpely-Turk's System,
Pumping Machinery
for Rolling Mills, Collieries, Water Works, etc.

Besides the above named Iron and Steel Products, as they are made at our Mülheim Works, we are also producing

at our Bruckhausen Works, viz. The works of our sister firm
Gewerkschaft Deutscher Kaiser,
Bruckhausen am Rhein (Rhenish Prussia)
Billets, Sheet Bars,
Joists, Channels, Angles, Tars, Zeds, Bulbs, Rounds and Flats and all others Section Bars, especially for Shipbuilding Purposes,
Rails, Sleepers, rolled and Stamped, Fish Plates and other Railway Material,

and at our Dinslaken Works, viz the works of our sister firm
Gewerkschaft Deutscher Kaiser,
Walzwerk Dinslaken, DINSLAKEN, (Rhenish Prussia)
Wire Rods, round and square,
Hoop Steel, cold rolled and bright rolled,
Weldless Steel Tubes for Boilers, Shafting, etc.

All correspondence on behalf of the Gewerkschaft Deutscher Kaiser Products to be set direct to these firms.

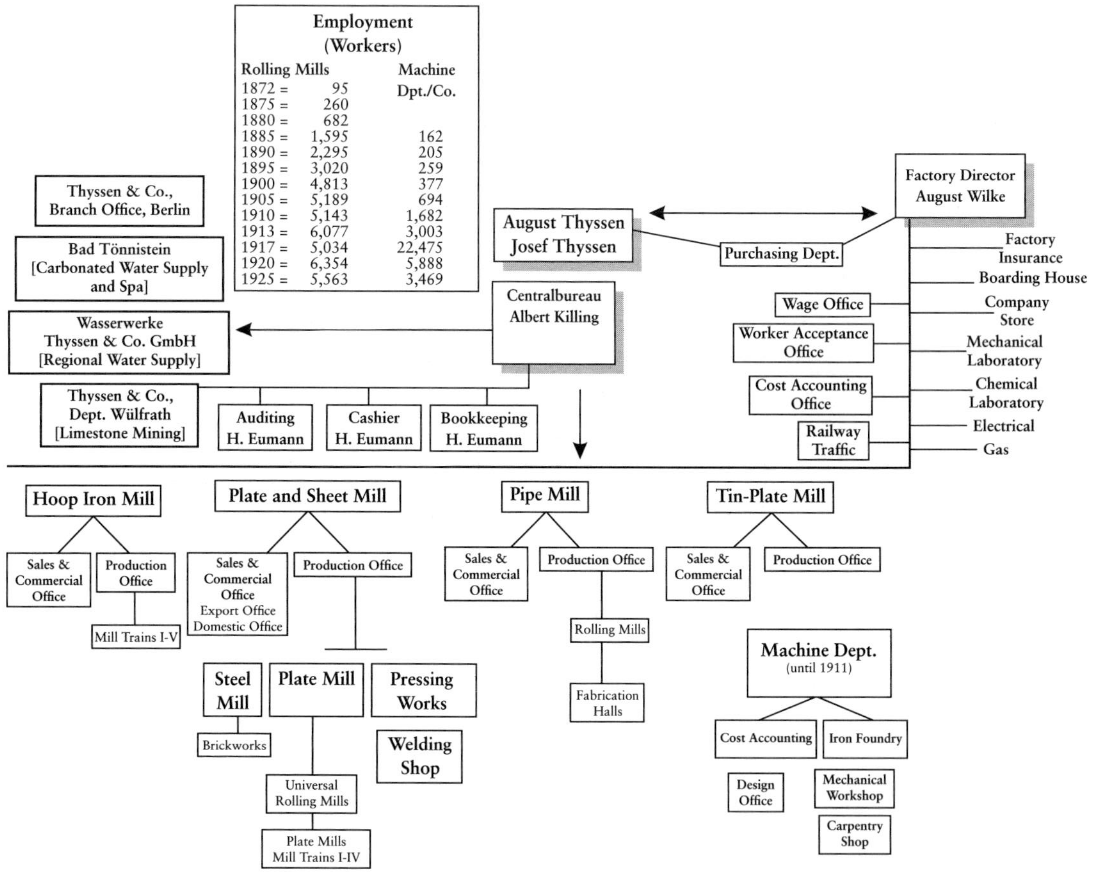
Employment (Workers)
Rolling Mills
Machine Dpt./Co.
1872 = 95
1875 = 260
1880 = 682
1885 = 1,595 162
1890 = 2,295 205
1895 = 3,020 259
1900 = 4,813 377
1905 = 5,189 694
1910 = 5,143 1,682
1913 = 6,077 3,003
1917 = 5,034 22,475
1920 = 6,354 5,888
1925 = 5,563 3,469
Thyssen & Co., Branch Office, Berlin
Bad Tönnistein [Carbonated Water Supply and Spa]
Wasserwerke Thyssen & Co. GmbH [Regional Water Supply]
Thyssen & Co., Dept. Wülfrath [Limestone Mining]
August Thyssen Josef Thyssen
Centralbureau Albert Killing
Auditing H. Eumann
Cashier H. Eumann
Bookkeeping H. Eumann
Purchasing Dept.
Factory Director August Wilke
Wage Office
Worker Acceptance Office
Cost Accounting Office
Railway Traffic
Factory Insurance
Boarding House
Company Store
Mechanical Laboratory
Chemical Laboratory
Electrical
Gas
Hoop Iron Mill
Sales & Commercial Office
Production Office
Mill Trains I-V
Plate and Sheet Mill
Sales & Commercial Office Export Office Domestic Office
Production Office
Steel Mill
Brickworks
Plate Mill
Universal Rolling Mills
Plate Mills Mill Trains I-IV
Pressing Works
Welding Shop
Pipe Mill
Sales & Commercial Office
Production Office
Rolling Mills
Fabrication Halls
Tin-Plate Mill
Sales & Commercial Office
Production Office
Machine Dept. (until 1911)
Cost Accounting
Iron Foundry
Design Office
Mechanical Workshop
Carpentry Shop

Figure 6.3 Organization of Thyssen and Co., oHG (partnership), 1903

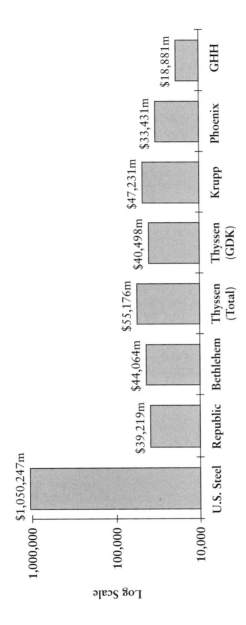

Figure 6.4 Comparison of U.S. and German Steel Companies, 1911 (adjusted fixed assets in millions of 1914 U.S.$)

Sources: Wilfried Feldenkirchen, *Die Eisen- und Stahlindustrie des Ruhrgebiets 1879–1914: Wachstum, Finanzierung und Struktur ihrer Großunternehmen* (Wiesbaden: Franz Steiner, 1982), Table 83 a/b; Gertrude G. Schroeder, *The Growth of Major Steel Companies, 1900–1950* (Baltimore: Johns Hopkins Press, 1953). Thyssen (Total) is based on the Konzern balance created by the CAO in 1912 from TA: A/814/3.

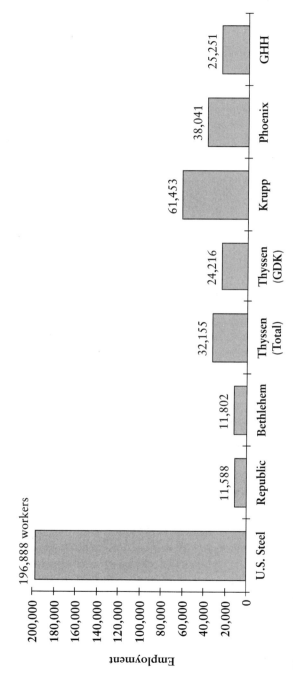

Figure 6.5 Comparison of U.S. and German Steel Companies, 1911 (total employment)

Sources: Same as for Figure 6.4, except Feldenkirchen, *Die Eisen- und Stahlindustrie,* Table 104 a/b.

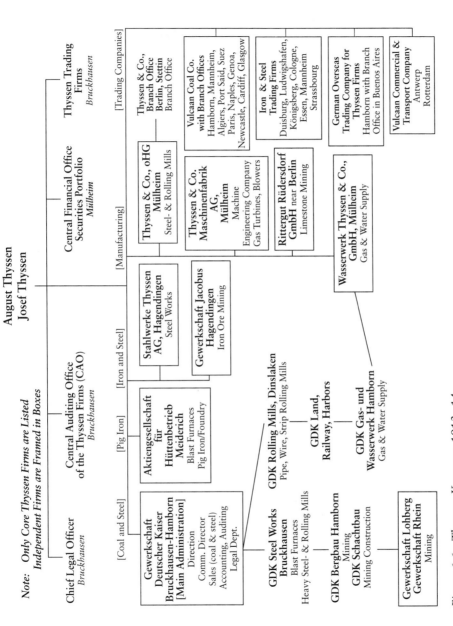

Figure 6.6   Thyssen-Konzern, 1913–14

Table 6.1 Capacity and Production (Capacity Utilization) in 1925 of the Four VSt Groups before Founding of the VSt (in millions of tonnes)

VSt Group	Firms	Coal Capacity	Coal Prod.	Coke Capacity	Coke Prod.	Pig Iron Capacity	Pig Iron Prod.	Crude Steel Capacity	Crude Steel Prod.
Rhein-Elbe Union	Gelsenkirchener Bergwerks AG	11.7M	58.1%	2.2M	75%	1.0M	39.1%	.1M	50.3%
	Deutsche-Lux	6.0	59.8%	2.4	60.5%	1.3	61%	1.2	68%
	Bochumer Verien	2.5	60.9%	.9	51.1%	.8	51.1%	.9	48.1%
Thyssen-Konzern		8.0	66.9%	1.5	91.6%	2.2	63.5%	2.1	63.4%
Phoenix-Group	Phoenix van der Zypen	9.0	62.4%	2.0	84.3%	2.2	45.1%	2.1	60%
		—	—	—	—	.3	49.3%	.3	53.3%
Rheinstahl		—	—	.3	80.4%	1.2	52.2%	1.1	71%
Total Capacity		37.2M		9.2M		9.0M		7.9M	

Source: Mannesman Archive: R 5 35 28 (1) "Handbuch für die Anleihen des Jahres 1926, Mit Anlage: Brassertsche Bewertungszahlen, Vereinigte Stahlwerke Aktiengesellschaft."

Table 6.2 Comparison of the VSt, U.S. Steel, and Bethlehem Steel: 1925 Production, Revenues, and Employment (production numbers are in millions of tonnes)

	VSt	U.S. Steel	Bethlehem
Coal Production	22.9	32.0	6.4
Coke Production	6.8	16.6	4.5
Pig Iron Production	4.8	15.0	4.1
Bessemer Steel	4.9	19.2	5.4
Rolling and Finished Products (incl. self-consumption	3.6	13.5	3.9
Revenues (incl. internal *Konzern* deliveries)	RM 1,502 million	RM 5,907 million	RM 1,147 million
Salaries + Wages	RM 467 million	RM 1,918 million	RM 453 million
Avg. Salary/Wage per Person per Year	RM 2,241	RM 7,678	RM 7,531
Total Employment	208,546	249,833	60,098

Source: Mannesmann Archive: R 1 35 28 (2)

As mentioned in Chapter 1, the widespread use of credit is one of the defining characteristics of a capitalist economy. Credit has been crucial. The chief instruments for its creation, and by extension the creation of money, have been banks. The Deutsche Bank was closely involved in the development of credit instruments and, beyond that, in the shaping of its country's business system.

Banks developed along similar lines in most capitalist economies, but there were some noteworthy differences. As we saw earlier, commercial banks in Britain tried to maximize their own liquidity, and so they tended to avoid long-term commitments. A few German banks, by contrast, evolved into "universal" banks. They came to combine the functions of commercial and investment banking, and they also served as investment trusts. This blend of functions gave universal banks a bigger role in the German business system than banks customarily played in either Britain or the United States.

That role was especially evident in the realm of corporate governance, and German banks wielded broad influence inside many industrial companies. In the years just after World War II, the American and other Occupation authorities judged that this influence was unhealthy, and they broke up the universal banks. What happened next, as you'll discover, tells a good deal about both the nature of German capitalism and the imperatives of the Cold War.

The entire history of the Deutsche Bank is surveyed here, and you will see how it acquired, step by step, all of the functions of a modern universal bank. There was no initial master plan for the evolution of this kind of structure. As is nearly always the case with even the biggest businesses, growth occurred because of a series of discrete and incremental decisions by the firm's management over a long period. Each step was taken in response to changing needs of the economy and related opportunities to deploy the firm's resources in new ways.

To say it that way may sound a bit trite, but we should remember that most new businesses do not succeed and many established ones fail. Even the best entrepreneurs can misread the needs of the economy, the perceptions of consumers, the resources of their own firms, or all three.

This chapter, in addition to showing the details of how the Deutsche Bank's management shaped its strategy over time, contains an unforgettable episode from the period of the Third Reich. At the moment when Hitler came to power in 1933, several of the bank's most capable leaders happened to be Jewish, and at least one of them immediately sensed the full implications of where the Nazi dogmas of anti-Semitism might lead. An internal letter from a high-ranking Deutsche Bank executive to his board of directors, excerpted here, expresses this sense of doom with poignant eloquence. The letter itself is one of the most memorable documents in the history of German business; and because of what it reveals about the evil side of ambition and human nature irrespective of country, it has significance far beyond Germany alone.

7

THE DEUTSCHE BANK

David A. Moss

The history of the Deutsche Bank is marked by many pitfalls and turning points. And yet, through it all, the bank's managers have pursued an almost continual strategy of expansion. As early as 1896, Georg Siemens, the first spokesman of the bank's managing board, had worried about the size of the firm. "To my mind, the Deutsche Bank has now grown too big," he wrote to his wife. "I'd have made quite a good Elector of Brandenburg, but Chancellor of Europe would be too large a task even for me."[1] At that time, the Deutsche Bank was not only the largest bank in Germany, it was also a strategic actor in the broader European market and, indeed, in the world economy.

Founded in 1870 to help finance surging German exports and imports, the bank soon moved into domestic banking. Georg Siemens aimed to create both a commercial bank and an investment bank under one roof, and he succeeded. The Deutsche Bank fulfilled its commercial role by taking deposits and offering short-term loans. As an investment bank, it managed the long-term credit needs of its customers by underwriting stock and bond flotations. Most of its private clients were big industrial firms, including still-familiar enterprises such as Krupp and BASF. The bank also underwrote the securities of national governments and railroads, many of which were publicly owned. Often the bank held significant equity stakes in its corporate clients, and it typically placed representatives on their supervisory boards.

Because it combined so many different financial functions, the Deutsche Bank has been described as a "universal bank." By the outbreak of the First World War in 1914, it stood as the most powerful financial institution in Germany. Over the next three decades, the Deutsche Bank faced a series of national crises: defeat in the war of 1914–18, revolution in 1919, hyperinflation in 1923, economic depression in the early 1930s, the rise of Hitler in 1933, another world war in 1939, and then total defeat in 1945.

After the Second World War, the Soviets closed the Berlin headquarters of the Deutsche Bank as part of their denazification effort and their broader strategy of converting eastern Germany to a Soviet-style economy. Meanwhile, the United States, Britain, and France, occupying the western portion of Germany, attempted to implement a policy of economic decentralization. They therefore broke what remained of the bank into small pieces.

The history of the Deutsche Bank could have ended there, in the late 1940s. But the bank soon reconstituted itself and set out on another extraordinary growth path. The so-called German economic miracle of the postwar era was certainly miraculous for the Deutsche Bank, creating an environment for it to consolidate and expand its operations both in Germany and abroad. By the mid-1990s, it ranked both as the largest bank in Germany and as the ninth largest in the world in terms of assets. (The top eight were all Japanese. The biggest British bank, HSBC Holdings, ranked eighteenth in the world, and the largest American bank, Citicorp, ranked thirtieth.)[2] The Deutsche Bank and other big German banks offered both commercial and investment banking services, unlike their counterparts in most other industrialized countries.

As the preeminent universal bank in Germany and perhaps the world, the Deutsche Bank in the mid-1990s managed assets worth more than $350 billion, and underwrote securities for many of Germany's most important companies. It held equity stakes ranging from 6 to 35 percent in 7 of Germany's 50 biggest firms as well as shares in many smaller firms. It controlled voting blocks of 15 percent or greater in 8 of Germany's 20 biggest firms. And it held more than 110 seats on the supervisory boards of a wide variety of German corporations.[3] The bank now aspired to be a major player in the evolving global economy.[4] Georg Siemens's fears from 1896 had not disappeared, but a century later they did not seem of primary concern to the Deutsche Bank's top management.

The Making of a Universal Bank

THE EARLY YEARS: TRADE FINANCE AND GERMAN NATIONALISM

The year of the Deutsche Bank's founding was a momentous time in central Europe. In July 1870, Prussia went to war with France to assert its dominant position on the continent. Although Germany was not yet a unified country, Prussia was the strongest force in a loose confederation of independent German states. With the support of most of these smaller powers, Prussian forces quickly crushed the French army and compelled France to give up the precious territories of Alsace and Lorraine and to make huge reparations payments. Prussian Minister-President Otto von Bismarck, who had masterminded the isolation and defeat of France, now induced the other German states to unify under the leadership of the Prussian King, Wilhelm I. The establishment of a new German Empire *(Reich)* was proclaimed on January 18, 1871.

The intense nationalism evident in Bismarck's drive for German unification was also a factor in the emergence of the Deutsche Bank. On the eve of unification, German businesses and individuals could count on domestic banks for a wide range of financial services, from short-term credits to transfers of funds. But firms that wished to obtain financing for foreign trade generally had to turn to London bankers for assistance. German banks lacked the requisite sophistication and organizational reach to handle such international transactions.

Among those who found this humiliating were Adelbert Delbrück and Ludwig Bamberger, the two original promoters of the Deutsche Bank. Delbrück had founded his own private bank in 1854, and Bamberger, also a banker, had been elected to the parliament of the pan-German Customs Union (Zollverein) in 1868. Together with five like-minded colleagues, they pointed out in an 1869 memorandum that the "German flag now bears the German name to every corner of the world," and they declared that the establishment of a German trade bank "would be a further step towards doing honour to the name of Germany in more distant lands and carving out at last for Germany a position in the sphere of financial intermediation commensurate with that already occupied by our country in the fields of civilization, science and art."[5]

Of course, nationalism was not the only motivation behind the founding of the Deutsche Bank. Money was also at issue. Since German exports and imports had surged in the 1850s and 1860s (see Table 7.1), Delbrück and Bamberger saw trade finance as a huge growth field.[6]

The Deutsche Bank opened for business in Berlin on April 9, 1870, just one month after King Wilhelm I personally approved its charter as a joint-stock bank. Joint-stock companies, which divided ownership among shareholders whose liability was generally limited to the extent

Table 7.1   German Exports, Imports, and Gross National Product (average annual % change, in real terms)

Period	Exports	Imports	GNP
1840–50	3.2%	1.8%	n.a.
1850–60	5.2	5.0	2.1%
1860–70	6.1	4.8	2.0
1870–80	2.4	2.9	2.2

Note: For GNP data before 1870, the Prussian per capita GNP was multiplied by the population of the area that made up the Deutsche Reich in 1870. Export and import data are for the area of the German Customs Union (Zollverein).

Source: Walther G. Hoffmann, *Das Wachstum der deutschen Wirtschaft seit der Mitte des 19. Jahrhunderts* (Berlin: Springer-Verlag, 1965), tables 129 (pp. 530–31), 131 (pp. 538–39), and 103 (pp. 454–55).

of their investment, were relatively rare in Prussia. Joint-stock banks were almost unheard-of. No such bank had ever been established in Berlin and only one had ever been chartered in Prussia. At its inception, the Deutsche Bank had 76 shareholders, who together contributed capital of 5 million thalers. (This sum amounted to 15 million marks, or about $3.6 million. Corrected for inflation, $3.6 million in 1870 is equivalent to about $42 million today.)[7]

The founders of the Deutsche Bank set up two executive bodies to run the institution, the supervisory board and the board of managing directors. Adelbert Delbrück chaired the supervisory board while Georg Siemens and Hermann Wallich dominated the managing board. In the early years, Delbrück's supervisory board maintained tight control over bank operations and even day-to-day affairs. Since Delbrück ran a separate, private bank of his own, he wanted to assure that the Deutsche Bank would not emerge as a competitor. Ultimately, however, the board of managing directors took control of management functions, assisted by the German corporation law of 1884 which explicitly limited supervisory boards to oversight functions.[8]

Although decisionmaking on the managing board was based on a consensus style, one figure on the board, the spokesman *(Vorstandssprecher),* stood out as the first among equals. From 1870 until 1900, that position was held by Georg Siemens (who became Georg von Siemens when he was ennobled in 1899). Before joining the bank, Georg Siemens had worked for his father's cousin, Werner von Siemens, at the electrical firm of Siemens & Halske. That firm was propelled to the forefront of the

German electrical industry when Werner von Siemens invented the electrical generator in 1866. Georg, whose father was a lawyer and who himself had studied law at Heidelberg, served as a negotiator for Siemens & Halske in a major telegraph deal.[9] When he accepted Adelbert Delbrück's offer in 1870 to join the Deutsche Bank, Siemens was only 30 years old. He was a very talented young man, but he knew little about banking.

Siemens's new associate Hermann Wallich, by contrast, was already well schooled in international finance. Born in Bonn in 1833, the son of a Jewish merchant, Wallich had begun to work in the banking industry at the age of 16. Several years later he left for Paris to work for his uncle's bank and subsequently for Comptoir d'Escompte, a prestigious French financial firm with strong international connections. In this job Wallich spent a good part of his time in China, Japan, and India. He was well suited to help the Deutsche Bank's effort to finance the growing international trade of German companies.[10]

According to Hermann Wallich, he and Georg Siemens complemented each other well, although Siemens remained the dominant figure. Years later, Wallich looked back on the nature of their collaboration:

> Frequently Siemens and I disagreed over one or other of the audacious proposals he came up with. More often than not, however, sometimes even against my better judgment, I let him have his way, an unconscious instinct telling me: "You can't allow this fellow to go. He is an enormous asset to the bank and possesses qualities you yourself lack." In moments of crisis, on the other hand, my experience and conservative principles prevailed. Siemens called me the bank's conscience. Anyhow, a large firm like ours had room for more than one man of talent. In good times, possibly my younger colleague's fire was more useful than my own perhaps over-cautious, if not downright old-fashioned, style of management.[11]

Wallich was not exaggerating when he described some of Siemens's proposals as "audacious." Even as the supervisory board approved new Deutsche Bank branches in Germany's two leading trading centers, Bremen (1871) and Hamburg (1872), Siemens decided to establish branches in Shanghai and Yokohama as well. These cities looked especially attractive because the directors at the Deutsche Bank anticipated enormous growth in German trade with the Far East. At about the same time, the

bank also secured representation in New York, Paris, and, most important, London.[12]

These branches were set up to facilitate international trade transactions. Because of the long delays involved in shipping a product from
one nation to another, and then actually selling the product, exporters
and importers looked to banks to tide them over. But bankers wished to
extend such credit only when they were sufficiently familiar with the
specific transactions and the parties involved. This was an important
reason for locating branches in major trading centers. In addition, the
business of trade financing, which paid high commissions, normally went
to institutions that were on site and had connections to trading centers
worldwide.

In the late 1860s and early 1870s, many Germans thought the idea of
challenging the British in trade finance was foolhardy. About a month
before the Deutsche Bank's founding, a German newspaper had predicted that the project would be a "splendid fiasco."[13] As it turned out,
the bank's experiment with branches in the Far East did in fact fail. With
losses mounting in Shanghai and Yokohama, Siemens was forced to close
both branches in 1874.

The bank's annual report attributed this outcome to Germany's adoption of a gold standard in 1873. As the German Mark appreciated relative to Far East currencies, the branches' foreign-currency remittances
and assets lost value, and the volume of German exports declined.[14] Some
outside observers, on the other hand, thought that the bank's problems
were the consequence of an unworkable business strategy. One newspaper asserted that the bank's closing of its branches in the Far East
constituted an admission of failure and that the "question of the liquidation of the bank is now being seriously considered."[15]

ENTRY INTO DOMESTIC BANKING

Siemens and Wallich were not deterred, however. From the beginning,
Siemens had insisted that a healthy international business had to be built
on a solid domestic foundation.[16] The core of the Deutsche Bank's domestic business was the so-called current account, a vehicle for managing
short-term deposits and short-term loans for firms. Industrial enterprises
that maintained current accounts could deposit excess cash at low rates
of interest and withdraw the funds whenever necessary. The current account also provided them with a flexible line of credit, allowing them to

overdraw the account up to a specified limit. Naturally, the rate of interest on loans was higher than on deposits. Both deposits and loans were short-term. Their purpose was to stabilize normal fluctuations in a firm's liquidity position. A company might use its line of credit to meet its payroll, for example, and then pay back the loan and build a deposit after receiving payment for a large sale. The current account tended to facilitate close ties between banks and their business customers.[17]

Although extremely important, the current-account business was not the only domestic opportunity open to the Deutsche Bank, particularly during the economic boom of 1870–73. French reparations after the Franco-Prussian war totaled 5 billion francs, or three times Germany's money supply. This extraordinary injection of liquidity into the German economy pushed down interest rates and sparked an economic expansion based on easy credit. At the same time, changes in German corporation law reduced restrictions on the establishment of joint-stock companies. Some 843 public companies were founded between 1871 and 1873, including 103 joint-stock banks. In the 44 years prior to 1870, only 397 new joint-stock companies had been founded.[18]

Many German banks got caught up in the excitement, but the Deutsche Bank steered its funds in a conservative direction. In Hermann Wallich's words, "company 'promotions' [i.e., the launching of new companies] of every conceivable kind and color became all the rage. To my untutored mind this unsavory business, more akin to blood sports, was utterly repugnant, and I would have none of it."[19] As scores of banks were forced into liquidation following a financial collapse in 1873, the directors of the Deutsche Bank saw a golden opportunity. Between 1873 and 1876, they took over five failing banks, including two large ones, and this expansion, said Wallich, "put us into the big league in a single stroke." By 1876, the Deutsche Bank held more assets than any other bank in Germany.[20]

Increasingly after 1875, Georg Siemens worked to expand the bank's domestic role by moving into new product lines. One of the most important was the acceptance of individuals' short-term deposits, unconnected to any current account.[21] Other banks had shunned this business because they worried about getting caught without sufficient funds. Whereas current accounts tended to be fairly predictable (subject to the standard rhythms of business operations), individual depositors sometimes acted erratically. If a bank's depositors wanted their money back when all or most of the funds were loaned out, the bank could easily fail. German banks, therefore, typically relied on their own paid-in capital and their current-account liabilities to make loans. But Siemens was not one to follow the crowd. Through Wallich, he knew that British banks carried on a successful deposit business. Moreover, the establishment of the German central bank (Reichsbank) in 1876 reassured Siemens that traditional ideas about liquidity constraints in German banking were now obsolete. One of the hallmarks of the Reichsbank was its willingness to "rediscount" liberally. This meant that the Deutsche Bank could make a short-term loan (also known as a discount) to a customer and then sell (or rediscount) the loan to the Reichsbank for cash, if necessary. Generous Reichsbank rediscounting thus guaranteed the viability of a bank taking short-term deposits and then lending them out.[22]

The Deutsche Bank accepted short-term deposits for fixed periods of time (somewhat like today's certificates of deposit). Depositors, who were normally wealthy individuals, could place their funds with the bank for one day, two weeks, one month, or three months. The interest rate that the bank paid was generally between 2 and 3 percent, and it rose with the duration of the deposit. The bank's involvement in the deposit business grew rapidly through the 1870s. By 1880, the bank managed more than twice as many deposit accounts as current accounts, and by 1900 almost eight times as many (see Table 7.2). Still, the total value of current accounts always exceeded that of deposits because, on average, deposit accounts were much smaller than current accounts.[23]

FORAYS INTO INVESTMENT BANKING

As Siemens was moving the Deutsche Bank into the deposit business and enlarging the institution through the acquisition of failed banks in the mid-1870s, he began contemplating the merits of expanding into investment banking. One group of bank shareholders opposed this idea, proposing instead that the bank's share capital be reduced by one-third. But Siemens and Wallich were not swayed. Warning that a reduction of capital would constitute "the biggest policy mistake it would be possible to make," they insisted on piloting the bank into the unfamiliar waters of investment banking.[24] In doing so, they transformed the enterprise into a true universal bank, which serviced both the short-term and long-term financing needs of its customers.

For the Deutsche Bank, long-term financing involved the flotation of

Table 7.2 Vital Statistics for the Deutsche Bank, 1870–1919

Year	Assets, Berlin Office and Its Branches (mil. Marks)	Net Income, Berlin Office and Its Branches (mil. Marks)	Dividends (%)	Turnover, Berlin Office and Its Branches (mil. Marks)	Number of Current Accounts, Berlin	Number of Deposit Accounts, Berlin	Staff	Branches
1870	27.7	0.7	5.0	239.3	176	0	~50[a]	1
1880	169.4	6.0	10.0	10,484.5	2,015	4,812	~550	3
1890	423.3	11.2	10.0	28,304.1	3,733	11,554	~950	4
1900	897.0	20.4	11.0	49,773.5	6,585	51,622	2,063	5
1910	2,158.2	32.6	12.5	112,101.3	172,995		5,816	10
1919	15,791.9[b]	64.5[b]	12.0	428,878.5[b]	601,921[c]		13,529	108

a. For the year 1871.

b. Because of wartime inflation, the nominal-mark figures for 1919 represent overstatements as compared to the prewar nominal-mark figures. In order to compare "real" values (i.e., controlled for inflation), the 1919 figures may be divided by a deflator equal to 4.79 (to convert them to 1910 equivalents). Prices were generally stable in Germany prior to 1914.

c. Total accounts for Berlin office and its branches.

Sources: Manfred Pohl and Angelika Raab-Rebentisch, *Deutsche Bank: Dates, Facts and Figures, 1870–1993* (Mainz: Hase & Koehler, 1994); and assorted Annual Reports of the Deutsche Bank, 1870–1919.

stocks and bonds and, at times, the direct purchase of such securities from industrial firms. The bank made almost no long-term loans.[25] By the time the Deutsche Bank was founded in 1870, German banks already had a good deal of experience placing government bonds. But the first industrial bond in Germany was not issued until 1874. The issuer was the steel firm of Friedrich Krupp, which raised 30 million marks ($7.1 million) at a 6 percent rate of interest. Although the Deutsche Bank did not handle this flotation, five years later it underwrote a new debt issue for Krupp worth 22.5 million marks at an interest rate of 5 percent.[26]

Placing a new security issue was a delicate operation. Because most industrial firms did not go to the capital market often, they were inexperienced in finding enough buyers at a given price. Potential investors might prove unwilling to buy a new security because they felt insufficiently familiar with the issuing firm. Or they might be unaware of the flotation because of inadequate advertising. In either case, the price of the new security might end up being lower than the earnings potential of the issuing firm would warrant.

Industrial firms therefore looked to specialists such as the Deutsche Bank for assistance. The bank would advise a firm on how to structure a deal: what type of security to issue, in what quantity, and at what price. The bank would advertise the new issue and prepare the necessary information for potential investors. Ultimately, it would bear most of the risk by underwriting the whole operation. That is, the bank would pay the firm a fixed price for the entire issue in advance and thus accept the responsibility for finding secondary buyers. Because underwriting was a risky business, it was also a lucrative one. Underwriting new issues brought in high fees, and underwriting shares (which were considered riskier than bonds) brought in the highest fees of all.

The Deutsche Bank managed placements of industrial securities for some of the most prominent names in German business. Besides the Krupp bond placement already mentioned, the bank underwrote a share issue for BASF (Badische Anilin & Soda-Fabrik) in 1886. The following year it helped to float new shares for the electrical giant AEG (Allgemeine Electricitäts-Gesellschaft). In the late 1890s it helped to convert Siemens & Halske from a limited partnership into a joint-stock company.[27] Often the Deutsche Bank preferred to work in concert with other banks, mainly to minimize underwriting risks. In 1885, it headed a consortium that placed the shares of Friedrich Bayer & Co. on the Berlin Stock Exchange. Similarly, the AEG flotation of 1887 was managed by a consortium led jointly by the Deutsche Bank and Delbrück Leo & Co. Such consortia were often referred to as syndicates, and they were typically led by big institutions.[28]

In its 1890 annual report, the bank presented a list of new syndicates in which it was participating. The list detailed twelve debt issues but only two share issues. More than half of the debt issues appear to have been government bonds, including the German Imperial Loan, municipal loans to numerous German cities, the Swiss Federal Loan, and the Roumanian Gold Loan. There were also syndicates for debt-financing the Central Pacific Railroad in the United States, the Italian Railway, and the Ottoman Railway Company. The two share issues listed were for AEG and a Cologne gunpowder mill. Table 7.3 provides an overview of the Deutsche Bank's investment banking business. Significantly, industrial stock and bond issues comprised only a small fraction of total new issues. Placements for governments and for railroads, many of which were publicly owned, dominate the list.

In its investment-banking role, the Deutsche Bank served mainly as an intermediary between its clients and the capital market. It was not un-

Table 7.3   Security Flotations by the Deutsche Bank and by Syndicates in Which the Deutsche Bank Participated, 1882–1908 (in millions of marks)[a]

	Value of Securities Issued and Listed on German Stock Exchanges	German Public Securities (Bonds)	Foreign Public Securities (Bonds)	Foreign Railway Shares	Foreign Railway Bonds	German Industrial Shares	German Industrial Bonds	Other Flotations
1882–1896[b]								
DB Alone	2,744.9	178.2	115.7	0.0	2,131.0	26.7	8.7	284.9
DB Syndicate	5,253.9	1,229.8	2,259.6	40.4	997.4	92.4	160.0	474.1
1897–1908								
DB Alone	4,849.1	541.4	417.4	2,027.9	0.0	316.9	185.1	1,360.5
DB Syndicate	21,612.6	5,376.5	12,899.1	234.0	0.0	1,000.1	745.5	1,357.3

a. Throughout this period, the exchange rate was approximately 4.2 marks to the dollar.

b. Securities issued and listed on Berlin Stock Exchange only.

Source: Adapted from Jakob Riesser, *The German Great Banks and their Concentration* (Washington: Government Printing Office, 1911), 3d ed., Appendix V and VI.

common, however, for the bank to hold on to some part of a new issue itself, and it thereby built up a substantial inventory of stocks and bonds. In some cases, the bank held such securities only because it had been unable to place an entire issue at the desired price. But often it wanted to hold a stake in the enterprise it was financing. In 1890, for example, when the Deutsche Bank floated the steel-tubing company Mannesmann with a starting capital of 35 million marks ($8.3 million), it chose to retain in its own portfolio shares amounting to 3.5 million marks.[29]

Because it was involved in both the short-term and long-term financing of its industrial customers, the Deutsche Bank tended to establish close relationships with them. After managing the incorporation of Siemens & Halske in 1897, the Deutsche Bank placed one of its own managing directors on the firm's supervisory board. The bank also obtained several million marks' worth of Siemens & Halske shares, and it positioned an ally of the bank as spokesman of the firm's managing board.

The Deutsche Bank subsequently served as the "house bank" for Siemens & Halske. This meant that Siemens & Halske not only maintained its current account at the Deutsche Bank but also relied on it to place new issues of debt and equity. One problem here was that the bank already had close ties to Siemens & Halske's chief competitor, AEG. Forced to choose between the two so as to avoid conflicts of interest, the Deutsche Bank chose Siemens & Halske. Family loyalty through the Siemens connection no doubt played a role, but the decision could also be justified on business grounds. Annual sales of Siemens & Halske were one-third larger than those of AEG in 1896. In any event, Georg Siemens resigned as the chairman of AEG's supervisory board, and allowed another institution to replace the Deutsche Bank as AEG's house bank.[30]

Besides owning equity in many of its corporate customers and placing bank officials on their supervisory boards, the Deutsche Bank also influenced its customers' development through the control of proxy voting rights. In Germany, owners of stock typically deposited the share certificates at their banks. Increasingly after 1900, the bank not only provided a safe place for customers to store their certificates but became the voting proxy for their deposited shares. Often the Deutsche Bank controlled big blocks of votes at the annual meetings of Germany's most powerful industrial companies, both through its own shareholdings and its proxies. The practice of proxy voting by banks was not followed in Britain, the United States, or Japan.

Because it combined so many different banking functions, and on such an enormous scale, the Deutsche Bank became known as one of Germany's "great banks" *(Großbanken)*. As of 1913, there were eight great banks headquartered in Berlin, with total assets of 7.8 billion marks ($1.9 billion). Germany's 352 privately owned banks had assets of 20.4 billion marks, and the assets of the entire German banking system (about 22,000 publicly and privately owned banks and credit unions, many of them tiny) totaled 50 billion marks. Against this backdrop, the Deutsche Bank's assets of 2.2 billion marks in 1913 stand out as extraordinary.[31] It held 10.8 percent of private bank assets and 4.4 percent of the assets of all banking institutions in Germany.[32]

Already by the turn of the century, the Deutsche Bank had been called "Germany's most powerful institution." In 1909, one of the bank's managing directors claimed that the Deutsche Bank was the biggest bank not only in Germany but in the world.[33] Although Georg Siemens had ended his reign as spokesman of the managing board in 1900 (only one year before his death), the bank continued on a strong upward trajectory until the First World War.

WAR AND THE CONSEQUENCES OF DEFEAT

The most immediate impact of the war on the Deutsche Bank was that the government's demand for loans expanded enormously. Although the bank permitted only a modest increase in its own holdings of government debt, its involvement in placing government securities with the public grew dramatically. All told, the Deutsche Bank floated almost 6.5 billion marks worth of wartime loans, which represented a large portion of its entire investment-banking business. According to one historian, "the private business of the bank in commercial bills and stock market transactions had virtually disappeared" by the end of the war.[34]

The early success of the German army created opportunities for bank expansion, particularly into eastern Europe. But these opportunities turned out to be short-lived. By 1918 the German army was in disarray and its leaders were suing for peace. The English-language version of the Deutsche Bank's annual report for 1918 shows management's astonishment at the very severe Allied terms for a peace settlement: "The German nation in any case has not deserved to have imposed upon it terms of peace destroying the innermost roots of its national and material existence."[35]

By 1919, the country was falling into chaos. The Kaiser had abdicated on November 9, 1918, and the war had ended two days later. That winter, communists launched a revolution against the new republican government. Oscar Wassermann, one of the Deutsche Bank's managing directors (and soon to become its top executive), reported to a prominent Hamburg banker in January 1919 that these were "rather unsettled times, but one gets used to the fact that, when one goes to the bank or comes out of it, a bullet occasionally strikes very near by, and that one's ears are mistreated by infantry fire, machine guns, and periodically also by mine throwers and artillery."[36]

The government quickly put down the communist revolution, but unrest on both the political left and the right continued. In April of 1919, many of the Deutsche Bank's own workers went out on strike, and the strike quickly turned violent.[37] Eleven months later, Wolfgang Kapp initiated the so-called Kapp Putsch and briefly took control of the government in Berlin. Kapp, a right-wing nationalist, himself had served on the Deutsche Bank's supervisory board until the first day of the coup (March 13, 1920), when he was dismissed by the bank. Although the Kapp Putsch quickly failed, no one associated with it was ever punished.[38]

Even apart from the social and political turmoil, the strain of the war years and Germany's defeat left the Deutsche Bank in a severely weakened condition. As the bank's 1919 annual report put it, "The war has upset the regular course of our economic life and shaken German trade and industry to their foundations. Through paralyzing the activity of our foreign branches it also severely interfered with our Bank's organization."[39]

The bank's foreign operations proved especially vulnerable. For example, one of the bank's prize foreign investments from the late nineteenth century, the Baghdad Railway, nearly collapsed during the war. The railway had been intended to serve both as an economic lifeline linking Europe and the Middle East and as a symbol of German imperial strength. Under wartime conditions, however, the Deutsche Bank had found it hard to maintain the operation on a business footing. Not only did the railroad take on new strategic significance during the war, but the Turkish government, which was allied with Germany, became ever more impervious to bank pressure. The bank thus continually looked to the German Reich for guarantees. Finally, in July 1917, the bank prevailed on the Reich to take over a majority of the shares of the Baghdad Railway Company and to buy 100 million marks in Railway bonds.[40]

The bank's international position deteriorated even further once the war ended. Many of its most valuable foreign assets disappeared. Given Germany's military defeat, there was no opportunity for appeal. These foreign assets were gone, and the bank had no choice but to reconstruct its balance sheet accordingly.[41]

HYPERINFLATION AND "THE DEATH OF MONEY"

The postwar crisis reached a climax in 1923. Since the end of the war, prices in Germany had been rising rapidly. The Deutsche Bank's annual reports complained regularly about the "depreciation of money." Whereas in June 1918 it had cost about 8 marks to buy one American dollar, in December 1921 it cost 192 marks. Twelve months after that the price was 7,600 marks. In December 1923, the exchange rate reached the incomprehensible figure of 4.2 trillion marks to the dollar. Domestic prices followed a similar path. At the end of 1923, wholesale prices in Germany were 656 billion times higher than in 1918.[42]

The hyperinflation resulted mainly from the German government's simultaneous policies of stimulating its economy to reduce unemployment and resisting the huge reparations burden imposed by the Allies after World War I. As the government printed ever greater numbers of bonds, the Reichsbank printed ever more money in order to buy them. The government used this money for such purposes as paying idle German coal workers in the Ruhr region who were "passively resisting" the French occupation force that was there to collect in-kind reparations. Prices skyrocketed and the exchange rate collapsed because the money supply was growing at an uncontrollable rate. One analyst described the result as "the death of money."[43]

The impact of the 1922–23 crisis on the Deutsche Bank was immense. The economic environment was so chaotic that planning for the future proved almost impossible. Equally troubling, the bank was drowning in administrative work. The 1922 report commented on the enormous "strain of unproductive work on everyone concerned."[44] As prices surged, the bank had to process transactions immediately or face huge penalties. It was vital that the bank avoid holding cash for any length of time, and yet it had to hold enough to pay depositors who were clamoring for their funds. Borrowers recognized that they could pay back their debts in vastly depreciated currency, so credit demand was increasing "geometrically from day to day," in the words of one managing director. In August 1922, the bank began issuing orders to its branches to restrict the availability of credit. About a year later, it began insisting on "valorized" credits, to be repaid on the basis of real values such as foreign exchange or commodities, as opposed to mere paper marks. By September of 1923, the value of money was changing literally by the hour.[45]

To handle this administrative nightmare, the Deutsche Bank hired thousands of new employees. Between 1913 and the end of 1918, when prices in Germany roughly doubled, the bank's staff increased from 6,638 to 13,529, and the number of accounts increased from 290,000 to 513,000. The number of employees reached 17,800 in 1920 (739,000 accounts) and 26,286 in 1922 (804,000 accounts). Deutsche Bank personnel peaked at 37,000 near the end of 1923, when the great inflation was at its height. Mainly as a result of these increases in staff, the proportion of gross profits devoted to operating costs increased from 57 percent in 1920 to 76.5 percent in 1923. In 1913, by comparison, the proportion had been just 38.1 percent.[46]

By 1924, when the German currency finally stabilized as a result of tough new government policies, the Deutsche Bank's staff was thoroughly exhausted. The bank's balance sheet and its business standing had been severely damaged as well. Because of the enormous cost of servicing small deposits, the bank had been forced to reduce its total number of accounts from 804,000 in 1922 to 281,000 in 1924. Meanwhile, its underwriting business had nearly collapsed as industry increasingly found alternative (especially foreign) sources of investment funds. The bank's capital base also appears to have eroded substantially. According to official currency conversion rates, the Deutsche Bank reduced its capital by 25 percent and its reserves by 43 percent from 1913 to the end of the inflation in 1924. In the meantime, the Deutsche Bank slipped from being the largest corporation in Germany in 1913 to being the ninth-largest in 1926 (behind eight industrial firms). In the words of one historian, "It almost seemed as if the great age of the German universal banks had come to an end."[47]

PICKING UP THE PIECES

Much as it had done in the mid-1870s, the Deutsche Bank implicitly addressed the ongoing crisis of 1914–23 with a strategy of expansion through acquisition. Beginning with only 15 branches in 1913, the bank grew to have 108 branches by 1919 and 142 by 1924. The additions came mainly from mergers with smaller banks that had numerous branches of their own. In most cases, the Deutsche Bank began the acquisition process by purchasing a minority share of the target bank's stock, thereby establishing a community of interest. Merger often followed, but only after the banks got to know one another.

The Deutsche Bank continued its expansion through the 1920s. It used the stepping-stone strategy to acquire three important regional credit banks in 1924, 1925, and 1929. Significantly, the bank reduced its staff even as it enlarged its branch network through these acquisitions. The number of bank personnel fell from the peak of 37,000 in 1923 to just 13,261 at the beginning of 1929.[48]

Particularly through the period of high inflation during and after World War I, takeovers proved attractive to the Deutsche Bank because they involved the acquisition of real assets. Unlike paper money, which the Reichsbank was printing at an unprecedented pace, assets such as buildings, land, and brand equity held their value over time. Even more important, the directors of the bank believed that larger size would translate into increased strength and stability. Beginning in 1908 and culminating in 1924, the deregulation of savings banks in Germany created several thousand aggressive new competitors in the credit markets. This competition became particularly intense in the mid-1920s. Meanwhile, another reason for the Deutsche Bank's continued expansion was that it faced increasing competition from abroad, as foreign banks began lending directly to German firms. By 1927, short-term lending by German credit banks to German non-bank firms was only 37 percent greater than that by foreign banks.[49]

Of course, the logic of expansion through consolidation was not limited to banking. Through the war and postwar years, integration within the industrial sector proceeded even faster than within the financial sector. This movement led to the creation of such giants as I.G. Farben in chemicals and the Vereinigte Stahlwerke (United Steel Works), both in 1926.[50] In general, the Deutsche Bank strongly endorsed consolidation in industry as well as banking. Oscar Wassermann, the spokesman of the bank's managing board from 1923 to 1933, was a vigorous advocate of rationalization in business.[51] Wassermann believed that it was imperative in the 1920s for bankers to resume their role as coordinators of business activity within Germany. The Deutsche Bank performed that role on numerous occasions. In 1926, it orchestrated the merger of Aero Lloyd, Junkers, and numerous smaller firms into a powerful single entity, Lufthansa. Significantly, one of the Deutsche Bank's managing directors assumed the chairmanship of Lufthansa's supervisory board.[52]

Within the banking industry, the greatest merger of all came in October 1929, when the Deutsche Bank itself fused with its biggest rival, the Disconto-Gesellschaft, and four smaller banks. According to Oscar Schlitter of the Deutsche Bank's managing board, this huge merger was designed to counterbalance the rapid consolidation taking place in industry. Otherwise, the two big banks risked being dwarfed by the rapidly emerging industrial giants. "In order to meet the challenge of industry," he declared in anticipation of the merger, "it is necessary to create a banking block of such dimensions that its placement capacity will dominate the domestic market and that underbidding of opposition groups which go beyond the reasonable would be pointless." The new institution, Schlitter maintained, would "be in a position to develop a force of such magnitude that it could not be circumvented in the securities business and in the reconstruction of the German economy at home and abroad."[53]

The new institution was named the Deutsche Bank und Disconto-Gesellschaft. Because the new name was so cumbersome, the nickname "Dedi Bank" arose, much to the chagrin of management. Altogether, the Dedi Bank held 800,000 accounts worth almost RM 5 billion ($1.2 billion). It operated 289 branches and 77 urban subbranches all over Germany. Its total assets were about 70 percent greater than those of the Deutsche Bank alone, and the increase in human capital was at least as great. In addition to the Deutsche Bank's own capable executives, the Dedi Bank inherited the financial genius of Georg Solmssen from the Disconto-Gesellschaft.[54] Solmssen would later rise to become spokesman of the bank's managing board, and he would be sorely tested during the period of Nazi ascendance in 1933.

Economic, Political, and Moral Collapse

After the great merger of 1929, the Deutsche Bank und Disconto-Gesellschaft targeted savings deposits as a desirable new market. Most savings accounts were held by individuals who deposited small amounts of money. Customers earned interest and could withdraw their money with some notice, though not immediately on demand. Until the late 1920s, savings banks had dominated this market segment. But as the savings banks became increasingly involved in the short-term credit markets as a result of deregulation, credit banks such as the Deutsche Bank und Disconto-Gesellschaft decided it was time to invade their turf. The Dedi Bank therefore introduced savings certificates that would pay interest if held for at least a year, and began marketing them aggressively.[55]

Another reason that the Deutsche Bank und Disconto-Gesellschaft began to seek savings deposits was that it needed the funds. Foreign deposits, which had flooded into Germany in the mid-1920s, were now rapidly flowing out. In 1928, foreign deposits at all German credit banks had made up 43 percent of total deposits, as compared to 20 percent in 1925. The enormous inflow of foreign funds had seemed to indicate a high level of international confidence in the German economy. But after the Wall Street crash of late 1929, foreign deposits began to leave Germany. The ratio of foreign to total deposits at credit banks fell to 34 percent in 1930 and to 18 percent in 1931. This outflow was likely exacerbated by political events. In September 1930, Adolf Hitler's National Socialist (Nazi) Party made big gains in the parliamentary elections, winning 107 seats, 20 percent of the total. Nine months later, Berlin issued its "reparations declaration," announcing that the German people would not tolerate much more in the way of reparations payments.[56]

Closely associated with these financial and political developments was the rapid deterioration of the German economy, which had fallen victim to the deepening worldwide depression. Real Gross National Product stopped rising after 1928 and began falling sharply in 1931. Particularly troubling for Germany was the collapse in world trade, which had been triggered by the United States' imposition of extremely high tariffs in the middle of 1930. By 1931, the volume of German exports had fallen by 14 percent as compared to the 1928 level, and over the next year exports fell by an additional 31 percent.[57]

At the Deutsche Bank und Disconto-Gesellschaft, deposits fell from RM 4.7 billion in 1929 to RM 3.0 billion in 1931.[58] At the same time, many of the firms to which it lent money were themselves at risk of failing. In response to these ominous developments, the Deutsche Bank und Disconto-Gesellschaft wrote down its share capital and reserves from RM 445 million in 1929 to RM 169.2 million in 1931, and cut its dividends from 10 percent to zero.[59]

The German banking system broke down entirely in the summer of 1931. By July, one of Germany's great banks, the DANAT-Bank, was on the verge of collapse because some of its big loans had gone bad. The Reichsbank, which had traditionally injected liquidity into the banking system whenever necessary, was no longer in a position to do so. Constrained by international agreements associated with war reparations, the Reichsbank was desperately trying to maintain its own foreign-exchange reserves and could be of little help to the DANAT-Bank.

On July 8, one of the DANAT-Bank's top officials, Jakob Goldschmidt, went to talk to Oscar Wassermann about a possible merger with the Deutsche Bank und Disconto-Gesellschaft. But Wassermann resisted. He had never approved of Goldschmidt's bold banking style, and he worried that such a merger was too risky a proposition. Without substantial help from either public or private sources, the DANAT-Bank was finally forced to suspend payments on July 13. The following day, the government declared a general bank holiday, which lasted until August 5. Government and bank officials feared that without such a holiday, bank runs could break out all across the country and destroy the entire banking system. Like all banking systems, Germany's was built on little more than faith, and by the summer of 1931, faith seemed to have disappeared.[60]

After declaring the bank holiday, the government began moving aggressively to stabilize the financial system. Currency controls were imposed on July 15 and progressively tightened thereafter. Perhaps most important, the Reich injected cash directly into the system by purchasing equity in the banks. The DANAT-Bank was merged with another troubled bank, the Dresdner Bank, and the government ended up taking over 91 percent of the merged institution's share capital. The government even acquired 35 percent of the shares of the Deutsche Bank und Disconto-Gesellschaft, which remained one of the nation's strongest banks.[61]

During the crisis of 1931 and soon thereafter, many critics attacked the banks and even the banking system itself. The State Secretary made reference to "a crisis of confidence in capitalism" and argued that the "banking system is overly concentrated." The Finance Minister even contemplated separating commercial from investment banking, as had long been the practice in Britain. Georg Solmssen of the Deutsche Bank und Disconto-Gesellschaft answered with a powerful defense of universal banking. Dismissing the crisis as an "act of God," he insisted, "This unification of financing and deposit banking is a system of which one can say without being arrogant that it built Germany's economy. The hallmark of this system, as it exists today and for whose retention I would like to work for and fight for in the interest of the economy, is its elasticity."[62]

Although deposits at the credit banks continued to fall through 1932, mostly because of continued foreign withdrawals, they finally stabilized in 1933.[63] The banking system appeared to be back on its feet. In the meantime, however, the economy had continued to deteriorate and the political landscape had been severely scarred, as if struck by a fire bomb.

By 1932, Germany's unemployment rate reached 17 percent. In the national elections of July, the Nazi Party won 38 percent of all seats in the Reichstag (parliament), more than any other political party. In the November presidential election, Adolf Hitler challenged the incumbent, Paul von Hindenburg, an 80-year-old former general and war hero. Hitler lost the election, but he received 30 percent of the popular vote. Hindenburg now felt that he had no choice but to appoint Hitler Chancellor of Germany. After the Reichstag building mysteriously went up in flames in February of 1933, Hitler declared emergency powers. He formally established himself as dictator of Germany in March by appropriating the power to make laws without the approval of the Reichstag. The Nazi seizure of power was nearly complete.

Through 1933, the German economy began growing again and was soon surging ahead. The Deutsche Bank und Disconto-Gesellschaft said in its 1933 annual report, "The first year of National Socialist leadership in the Reich saw a definite change for the better in Germany's economic life. This was the result of energetic governmental measures in regard to employment and economic policy together with reawakened enterprise, based on a revival of confidence due to the new political constellation."[64]

The bank's directors were probably sincere in their praise of the new regime's economic policies. But the Nazi impact on the bank, and particularly on its managing board, went far beyond the upturn in economic conditions. Because the spokesman of the managing board, Oscar Wassermann, was Jewish, pressure quickly mounted for his resignation. Significantly, suggestions for his removal came directly from the Reichsbank president, Hjalmar Schacht. The justification for action against Wassermann within the Dedi Bank itself was the allegation that he had faltered during the banking crisis of 1931. "Whether Herr Wassermann was a Jew or a Christian," an internal bank memorandum asserted, "had nothing to do with all this."[65] Of course, nothing could have been further from the truth. Wassermann was targeted only because he was a Jew.

With political pressure intensifying, Wassermann agreed to leave the Deutsche Bank by the end of 1933. Despite this extraordinary concession on his part, the bank's management unexpectedly announced his resignation on May 20. Wassermann had served on the managing board for 21 years, since 1912, and he had run the bank as its spokesman since 1923. But now, just four months after Hitler took power, Wassermann was gone. The other Jewish member of the bank's managing board, Theodor Frank, also resigned under pressure. Promises were made that both men would later be moved up to the supervisory board, but these promises were never kept. Wassermann died the following year at the age of 65, presumably of natural causes. Frank moved to Zurich, where he died in 1953.[66]

The man who took over as spokesman of the managing board in 1933 was Georg Solmssen. Although himself born to Jewish parents, Solmssen was not an immediate target in the spring of 1933 because he had been baptized as a baby. Solmssen was disgusted by his colleagues' willingness to appease Nazi anti-Semitism, and he seems to have recognized quite early that his own days at the bank were numbered. On April 9, 1933, Solmssen wrote a stunning letter to the chairman of the bank's supervisory board:

The exclusion of Jews from state service, which has now been accomplished through legislation, raises the question of what consequences this measure—which was accepted as self-evident by the educated classes—will bring for the private sector. I fear that we are only at the beginning of a conscious and planned development which is aimed at the indiscriminate economic and moral destruction of all members of the Jewish race living in Germany. The complete passivity of the classes which do not belong to the National Socialist Party, the lack of any feeling of solidarity on the part of those who have up to now worked in business shoulder to shoulder with Jewish colleagues, the ever more evident pressure to draw personal advantages from the free positions created by the purges, the silence about the shame and humiliation imposed on those who, although innocent, see their honour and existence destroyed from one day to the next: all this is evidence of a position so hopeless that it would be wrong not to confront facts straightforwardly, or to make them appear harmless. In any case, those affected have apparently been abandoned by those who were professionally close to them, and they have the right to think of themselves. They should no longer let the enterprise to which they have devoted their lives determine their actions—unless that enterprise treats them with the same loyalty that it expected of them. Among our colleagues too, the question of solidarity has been raised. My impression was that this suggestion met only a lukewarm response in the managing board . . . and that if it were to be realized it would take the form of a gesture rather than complete resistance, and as a result would be doomed to failure. I recognize that in the decisive deliberations, differences will be made between different members of the managing board who happen to be on the list of proscription. But I have the feeling that, although I am viewed as someone whose activity is thought of positively, and although I may be honored as the representative of a now seventy-year-long tradition, I too will be abandoned once my inclusion in a "cleansing action" is demanded by the appropriate authorities. I must be clear about this . . .[67]

By the end of that fateful year, Georg Solmssen had been removed as spokesman of the managing board. He was subsequently moved to the bank's supervisory board, on which he officially remained until 1938. In the meantime, he had departed for Switzerland to find safe haven from the Nazis. He died there in 1957.[68]

Besides the question of Jewish personnel, the bank's directors also had to deal with many other problems and challenges that emerged as a result of the Nazi takeover. For one thing, they had to decide how best to establish and maintain connections to the Nazi Party. Early in 1933, two bank employees who were members of the National Socialist Factory Cell Organization were appointed to the supervisory board. In addition, a former managing-board member who had close ties to the Nazi Party, Emil Georg von Stauss, was elevated to the powerful "Working Committee" of the supervisory board. This development would not have been unusual except that Stauss previously had been regarded as a rather careless adventurer, and the Working Committee had been created to prevent people like him from gaining power. Ironically, the supervisory-board member who had created the Working Committee and whom Stauss effectively replaced in 1933 was Paul Silverberg, a Jew who fled Germany that same year.

Overall, Nazi officials were never very comfortable with the Deutsche Bank (which changed its name back from the Deutsche Bank und Disconto-Gesellschaft in 1937). Since four Catholics sat on the institution's managing board, some Nazi Party members derisively labeled it the "Catholic bank." No Nazi Party member was appointed to the bank's board of managing directors until 1938. After that, only two more were appointed—both in 1943, immediately following Stauss's death.[69]

Meanwhile, the nature of the Deutsche Bank's business was radically transformed. Its holdings of government bonds increased from about 3 percent of assets in 1929 to 11 percent in 1937 and then to 70 percent in 1944. The Nazis imposed strict capital-market controls, virtually prohibiting the flotation of private securities. The purpose of these policies was to reduce the government's cost of borrowing. Similarly, the Nazis encouraged banks to transform private deposits directly into state loans, without going through the capital market at all. As one economic historian has noted, this "so-called noiseless financing . . . thus [eliminated] the public signal of a market valuation of Reich debt."[70]

In December 1938, one month after a night of anti-Jewish violence known as Kristallnacht,[71] the Nazis promulgated new laws restricting the bank accounts of all Jews. Jewish account holders were permitted to withdraw small amounts each month to cover necessities, but additional withdrawals had to be approved by the state. The Deutsche Bank was thus forced to keep meticulous records on its Jewish clients and to seek approval from state authorities for almost every transaction. Whenever the bank's Jewish customers left the country, either because they were deported to concentration camps or because they succeeded in emigrating to a friendly country, the state immediately ordered the bank to turn over their assets. Under recently enacted German law, the state had the right to seize the assets of any Jewish person who left the country. The Deutsche Bank often delayed the process by arguing that it could not turn over a client's assets until directly instructed to do so by the Gestapo. Many of the bank's surviving files on Jewish customers end with just such an order, properly signed by the Gestapo.[72]

The bank also became heavily involved in the so-called Aryanization of property, that is, the sale of Jewish property to non-Jews. In most cases, Jewish sellers entered into such deals only because of the implicit threat of future state expropriation. In July 1943, a member of the Deutsche Bank's supervisory board who ran a subsidiary bank in occupied Czechoslovakia complained bitterly in a letter about the devastating impact of Aryanization. He asserted that

> the extension of the German business [in Czechoslovakia] depended entirely on the Aryanization of previously Jewish businesses, which, unfortunately, have been taken over in many cases by persons who have only political recommendations, but who lack technical knowledge and especially the necessary financial resources. Even if the state is selling these firms at drastically reduced prices, it is unavoidable that at first the loans will have the character of an equity stake . . . [These] loans are especially risky. Consequently we will try to restrict our business. But we cannot avoid every risk since otherwise we would inevitably lose contact to the development of this business.[73]

As this passage suggests, Nazi anti-Semitism imposed not only a crushing moral burden, but substantial economic costs as well.

As the Nazi war machine rolled through Europe, the Deutsche Bank took control of the Czech bank just mentioned, and numerous other foreign banks as well. Indeed, the government pressed the big private banks to expand along with the Reich. Although the Deutsche Bank participated more reluctantly in such takeovers than did its major competitors, the Dresdner Bank and the Commerzbank, it nonetheless accepted the spoils of war.[74]

Meanwhile, the political challenges facing the bank intensified. The Nazi Party had long condemned the high degree of concentration in German banking and occasionally had singled out the Deutsche Bank for special criticism. Government officials finally began to take action against the bank in 1942 and 1943, ordering the closure of numerous branches and placing limits on the number of outside supervisory boards on which bank directors could serve. Under this pressure, the Deutsche Bank closed over 80 branches and significantly reduced its representation on other firms' supervisory boards. Political assaults on the bank occasionally turned violent. Two directors of Deutsche Bank branches were executed in 1943 for uttering "defeatist remarks." One was alleged to have referred to Hitler as a "swindler." The other supposedly had predicted that German fascism would ultimately fade away—that "National Socialism was in any case nothing more than a fart."[75]

In 1945, when the end finally did come for National Socialism, many at the Deutsche Bank worked furiously to shift their operations from Berlin much farther west to Hamburg. They feared that the Soviets, who were invading from the east, would destroy private banking in the parts of Germany they occupied. And indeed, when the Soviets took control of Berlin in May 1945, they quickly arrested many of the Deutsche Bank's remaining employees, blasted open the vaults, and shut down the institution.[76]

The Occupation

Unlike the Soviets, the three Western occupying powers—the Americans, British, and French—accepted the concept of a private banking system. The three differed, however, on how such a system should be structured in the defeated Germany. They disagreed not only about what type of banking structures would be most efficient, but also about the extent to which the old German banking system was implicated in Nazism and Nazi atrocities. As the Western Allies worked to resolve their own differences regarding occupation policy, the former directors of the Deutsche Bank understood that their personal and professional futures hung in the balance.

Once the three Western powers took control of their occupation zones, they removed the managing directors of the big banks from positions of power. The day-to-day operations of the Deutsche Bank were left to 12 executive vice-presidents, dubbed "the twelve apostles" by former managing-board member Hermann J. Abs. After conducting extensive investigations of the big German banks, the Financial Division of the American Occupation began transmitting its findings and recommendations in late 1946. "Investigation of the Deutsche Bank," it reported, "has revealed it to be an excessive concentration of economic power and a participant in the execution of the criminal policies of the Nazi regime in the economic field." The Division went on to recommend that the bank be liquidated, that those most responsible for its conduct be prosecuted as war criminals, and that the "leading officials" of the bank be prohibited from obtaining high-level economic or political positions in Germany.[77]

This, of course, was an enormous blow to the Deutsche Bank. But its chief rival, the Dresdner Bank, came in for even harsher condemnation. The Financial Division identified the Dresdner Bank itself as a war criminal, and recommended that nearly every member of its management structure, including the entire managing board and supervisory board, be indicted and tried.[78]

As it turned out, no "war crimes" case from the Deutsche Bank ever went to trial. However, one of the bank's leading figures, Hermann J. Abs, did end up spending three months in prison. In 1945, when the American occupation authorities wanted to try him as a war criminal, Abs was living in the British occupation zone. The British had worked with Abs before the war, and they thought highly of him. According to one British official, "The Americans wanted to be rough with him. They didn't appreciate his banking experience. They believed him to be a Nazi. But he wasn't a member of the party, so we gave him protection." Ultimately, however, the Americans prevailed. Especially after a court in Yugoslavia sentenced Abs, in absentia, to 10 years of hard labor, the Allies felt compelled to act. Abs was divested of his 45 supervisory board seats and subsequently interned. His cellmate was a member of the Dresdner Bank's managing board. Once released, Abs was dismissed from the Deutsche Bank at the instruction of British authorities, who themselves were under pressure from the Americans. Though subjected to a denazification trial in Nuremberg, Abs was exonerated in February 1948. Less than a year later, he was appointed spokesman (chairman) of the newly created Reconstruction Loan Corporation, the postwar institution responsible for distributing Marshall Plan aid in Germany. By all appearances, Abs had now won the confidence not only of the British but also of the Americans in Germany and Washington.[79]

At about the same time that the Allies were settling Abs's fate, they were also contemplating the future of the German banking system. The biggest question concerned what to do with the three great banks—the Deutsche Bank, the Dresdner Bank, and the Commerzbank.

On May 6, 1947, the Americans announced a plan for bank decentralization in their zone. Each of the three great banks would be broken up into a number of smaller pieces. The various "successor" banks were actually former branch offices of the three parent banks, and their formal legal relationship to the parent banks remained unchanged. But the decentralization plan dictated that the successor banks act as independent enterprises, regardless of their legal status. Through this scheme, the Americans sought to provide a temporary solution to their concerns about excessive concentration. The French soon followed with a similar bank-decentralization plan for their zone. The British delayed announcing their own decentralization plan for nearly a year. In the end, the Deutsche Bank was broken into ten successor banks, spread across the three western zones.[80]

Although the delay by the British reflected some discomfort with the American approach, they nonetheless shared American suspicions about universal banking. In both the United States and Britain, commercial banking and investment banking were conducted separately by specialized institutions. After the enactment of the Glass-Steagall Act in 1933, this separation had the force of law in the United States, whereas in Britain the division was mainly a matter of tradition. Both the British and the Americans worried that combining commercial and investment banking under one roof created potential conflicts of interest.

The Americans worried in addition about substantial concentrations of financial power, concentrations which they regarded as economically inefficient and politically dangerous. As a result, they moved to restrict the German banks' control over proxy voting rights and to limit their representation on other firms' supervisory boards. In the words of Joseph M. Dodge, an American banker and advisor to the occupation authorities, such policies "would eliminate the excessive concentration of economic power in banking and destroy the intimate relationship between German banks and large corporations." These proposals, Dodge said, "are an integral part of our program to ensure that the German financial hierarchy will never again play any part in disturbing world peace"[81] (see Table 7.4).

Though the Americans and British agreed that excessive scope in the banking industry was a problem, they disagreed sharply over the issue of scale. In Britain, each of the big commercial banks had a vast network of branches serving the entire country. But in the United States, branch banking was illegal in most states, and those branch networks that did exist never crossed state boundaries. The fear of large agglomerations of financial power and the preference for "unit banks" had deep roots in America's history.

Table 7.4 The Power and Influence of the Deutsche Bank, 1945, 1986, and 1994

Total Voting Shares of the Deutsche Bank as a Fraction of Capital Present at the General Assemblies of Selected Large Firms (%)

	1945	1986
I.G. Farben Industrie	38.1	
BASF		28.1
Bayer		30.8
Hoechst		15.0
Mannesmann	53.9	20.5
Siemens	>16.0	17.8
Daimler-Benz	>50.0	41.8

Number of Seats Held by Officials of the Deutsche Bank on the Supervisory Boards of Other Firms

	1945	1994
Seats held by members of DB Managing Board	197	78
Seats held by members of DB Supervisory Board	328	36
Total	525	114

Note: Total voting shares include Deutsche Bank's own holdings, shares held by Deutsche Bank investment companies, and proxy votes of shares deposited with the Deutsche Bank.

Sources: For 1945: Finance Division—Financial Investigation Section, Office of Military Government for Germany, United States, *Ermittlungen gegen die Deutsche Bank, 1946/1947* (Nördlingen: Franz Greno, 1985), pp. 367–368, 366. For 1986: Gottschalk, "Der Stimmrechtseinfluß der Banken in den Aktionärsversammlungen von Großunternehmen," *WSI Mitteilungen,* 1988, pp. 295–296. For 1994: Deutsche Bank Press Office.

Although British officials ultimately bowed to American pressure and announced a bank decentralization plan within their zone, they were never satisfied with the result. They may even have worked quietly to undermine it. Besides their philosophical preference for big banks with extensive branch networks, the British also believed that large German banks would be better able to honor prewar debts to British creditors.[82]

Representatives of the German universal banks objected vehemently to the concept of decentralization. In a November 1949 report entitled "The Decentralization of the Great Banks," former directors of the Deutsche Bank insisted that there were substantial economies of scale in banking. Small banks, they argued, were unable to spread risks effectively. Nor could small banks finance large projects. "Large firms need large loans," said the report, "and large loans can only be issued by banks with a commensurate loan potential and capital basis." The same was asserted about investment banking services. Large banks were necessary in order to float large security issues. The report acknowledged that small banks might form consortia (syndicates) on a regular basis, but argued that such a solution was slow, clumsy, and costly. Another complaint outlined in the report was that because the successor banks had been forced to give up the Deutsche Bank name, they had lost an immense amount of goodwill. Without the Deutsche Bank name, the authors insisted, it was nearly impossible to attract foreign capital.[83] The report also highlighted the great advantages of branch banking. A bank with numerous branches could clear transactions quickly. It required smaller total reserves than did an equal number of unit banks. And it was well equipped for collecting essential information about creditors and debtors and about the overall economy.[84]

Another report drafted by representatives of the Deutsche Bank in December 1945 had taken an explicitly historical approach to the whole subject of universal banking in Germany. The authors explained that both the Deutsche Bank and the Disconto-Gesellschaft

> have since their foundation in 1870 and 1856 favored the financing of industry. The industrial development in Germany was necessarily followed by a corresponding development of the banks, inevitably leading to a branch-system as the local and regional banks could not fulfill the financial demands of a modern economy. It was only the branch-system that enabled [the banks] to balance [those] districts [with] a surplus of deposits [against those with a] demand [for] credits. At the same time

the branch-system facilitated the placing of instruments of financing, bonds and shares, and established the necessary partition of risks.

Through this development the big banks especially Deutsche Bank came into close touch with most of the industrial companies. It was only a natural consequence that the industrials asked the leading bankers to join their Supervisory Boards after having obtained their financial advice for longer periods. The mutual relations resulting therefrom having proved to be valuable for both parts have established a tradition still prevailing. This tradition is based on grounds of suitability and friendly relationship.[85]

There is perhaps no more concise defense of the practice of universal banking than this one, written by Deutsche Bank officials in 1945.

As the German economy recovered, particularly after the important national currency reform of 1948, the successor banks began coming together like so many beads of mercury. At first their cooperation was informal, and sometimes covert. Despite orders from the occupation authorities not to work together, many of the managers of the Deutsche Bank's successor banks met privately to coordinate their activities. A director of one successor bank explained at a supervisory board meeting in 1949, "We continued to consider it our duty to the German economy as a whole to maintain the solidarity between the ten sister banks in West Germany, naturally while abiding by military regulations . . . What we are operating is the collective business of banks."[86] A report prepared in 1950 by the three big German banks described a "continued intimacy between the incorporated Successor banks of each Pre-war bank." It suggested that "there seems no way to stop or prevent such intimacy without seriously harming the banks as well as the German economy."[87]

German banking leaders now began to push for recentralization. Hermann J. Abs of the Deutsche Bank played a crucial role in formulating their strategy and orchestrating their lobbying campaign. Along with representatives from the Dresdner Bank and the Commerzbank, Abs drafted a proposal in 1950 calling for the partial reconstitution of the great banks. The proposal defined three banking districts within West Germany, and suggested that each of the three big banks establish one regional bank in each district. Under this proposal, the Deutsche Bank's ten successor banks would be reduced to three.

Abs and his compatriots insisted that at least this degree of recentralization was imperative. "Decentralization down to a level on which successor banks cannot operate profitably is wholly inadmissible," they wrote. "During times of recession and depression, the failure of only one joint stock bank can easily pull down the entire banking structure. The banking system of a country is only as strong as its weakest joint stock bank."[88] The Allied powers accepted the proposal in 1951, and the new German legislature enacted it into law the following year. The Americans moderated their hard line on decentralization largely because of the threat they perceived from the Soviet Union. Once the containment of communism became their chief objective, a strong German economy and the prospect of strong German banks began to look better and better.

By the end of 1952, the managing directors of the three Deutsche Bank successor banks were holding joint sessions on a regular basis. The leading historian of the subject argues that by this time "the separation and autonomy imposed on the banks by the Allies no longer existed in reality." Just one year after the Federal Republic of Germany gained full sovereignty in 1955, it enacted a law removing all limitations on the regional scope of credit institutions. The Deutsche Bank formally reconstituted itself into a single banking enterprise on May 2, 1957. The man who had done more than anyone else to advance this process of recentralization, Hermann J. Abs, was elected spokesman of the bank's managing board.[89]

The Deutsche Bank since 1957

After becoming whole again in 1957, the Deutsche Bank resumed its historic path of growth. The bank benefited from Germany's extraordinary economic performance through the postwar years, and by some measures even outperformed the economy. In 1994, German GNP (nominal) was ten times larger than it had been in 1960. Over the same period, the annual net income of the Deutsche Bank had increased by a factor of 15, and the bank's total assets by a factor of 51 (see Table 7.5).

Throughout these years, the bank maintained and strengthened its core competencies in domestic business financing. Its expansion was based primarily on three new conditions: dramatic growth in the retail-banking market, revolutionary changes in banking technology, and extraordinary opportunities in the international arena. These developments

Table 7.5 Vital Statistics for the Deutsche Bank, 1924–1994

Year	Assets (mil RM to 1944; mil DM, 1952–)	Net Income (mil RM to 1944; mil DM, 1952–)	Dividends (%)	Number of Accounts	Staff	Branches
1924	1,091	19	10	281,000	20,474	271
1929	5,534	34	10	800,000	21,600	466
1937	3,301	8	6	839,000	17,282	442
1944	11,374	10	6	na	na	na
1952	3,758	6	6	na	12,080	254
1960	11,222	90	16	na	19,106	410
1967	22,133	140	8[b]	na	28,800	812
1975[a]	91,539	391	10[b]	na	40,839	1280
1985[a]	237,227	1,101	12[b]	6,500,000[c]	48,851	1410
1994[a]	573,022[d]	1,360	16.5[b]	>6,500,000[c]	73,450	2483

a. Data from 1975 onward are for the Deutsche Bank Group.

b. Dividend (in DM) per DM 50 share, par value.

c. Approximate number of customers (not accounts).

d. In 1994, total assets for the Deutsche Bank Group were worth approximately $379 billion at market exchange rates.

Sources: Annual Reports of the Deutsche Bank, 1924–1994; and the Historisches Archiv der Deutschen Bank.

had a profound impact on the bank. According to its 1994 annual report, the Deutsche Bank "saw greater change [during the period 1970–1994] than in the entire century that preceded it."[90]

RETAIL BANKING

Wages and salaries began rising rapidly in Germany during the 1950s and 1960s. As more and more workers attained middle-class incomes, their need for bank accounts increased. In 1957, the Deutsche Bank managed 550,000 savings accounts. But these were the only small personal accounts that the bank offered, and most of them probably belonged to relatively wealthy people. In the 1960s, therefore, the Deutsche Bank began moving aggressively into retail banking. It created a variety of deposit accounts for individuals, and began offering small personal loans as well as home mortgages. At about the same time, the bank started to work more extensively with Mittelstand (small and medium-sized) companies, a departure from its previous policy of attending only to the nation's largest corporations.

The Deutsche Bank's success in the retail sector proved phenomenal.

By 1993, it had several million retail customers, and retail operations accounted for 60 percent of all its business with nonbanks. As the former chief economist of the Commerzbank put it, "Retail banking is now the strongest leg of every big bank [in Germany]." Remarkably, retail banking had barely existed at any of the big banks prior to 1960.[91]

TECHNOLOGICAL REVOLUTION

Although the Deutsche Bank's total assets increased 51-fold between 1960 and 1994, its staff increased less than fourfold (see Table 7.5). Part of the reason was that technological advances radically increased the efficiency of processing transactions. (By way of contrast, total assets had increased only slightly faster than total bank staff between 1880 and 1910.) The most critical technological change, of course, was the advent of the computer. The Deutsche Bank first adopted a punch-card system in 1958 and moved into electronic data processing beginning in 1961. From then on, productivity increased substantially with each new generation of computers.[92] In the early 1980s, the bank began to experiment with direct computer interfacing with the customer, which was called "intelligent bank automation." Increasingly, customers could obtain a wide range of banking services directly from computer terminals 24 hours a day. By the early 1990s, automated teller machines had been installed in every Deutsche Bank branch.[93]

In addition to the computer revolution, the related communications revolution also exerted a profound impact on the Deutsche Bank. By the late 1980s, bank personnel were able to conduct trades in real time almost anywhere in the world. Through fax machines and computers, they could collect huge quantities of information from the far reaches of the globe. The bank's directors could dispatch instructions to agents abroad with comparable ease. Within this context, the prospect of the Deutsche Bank's large-scale entry into foreign financial markets finally became a real possibility.

BECOMING A "GLOBAL PLAYER"

By the standards of the early twentieth century, the Deutsche Bank had already become a global player on the eve of World War I. Even that early it had branches located in major money centers, and it was involved in financing large projects on several continents. The two world wars, however, dealt devastating blows to the bank's international operations. By 1957, it had no foreign branches. It held almost no foreign assets of any kind, and few if any of its employees worked abroad.

As had been the case in the 1870s, the Deutsche Bank's international activity after World War II began with the financing of exports and imports. By 1957 its market share in German trade finance and payments was about 30 percent. In the early 1960s, it started to reacquaint itself with international underwriting. It floated two large Japanese bond issues in Germany in 1962 and 1964, and it helped to found the Eurodollar bond market in 1963.[94]

The bank soon began taking minority holdings in foreign banks, and it subsequently participated in a number of joint ventures abroad. In the mid-1970s, the bank's leadership finally decided that it was time to obtain foreign branches of its own.[95] As was by now its custom, the Deutsche Bank executed a successful strategy of expansion through acquisition. It acquired 12 foreign branches by 1980 and 65 more by 1990.[96] By the mid-1990s, one out of every four Deutsche Bank employees lived and worked outside Germany. Almost 30 percent of the bank's branches were located abroad, and about a third of its gross income was generated outside Germany.[97]

Through the late 1980s, the spokesman of the managing board, Alfred Herrhausen, had articulated a global vision for the Deutsche Bank. In 1988 he declared, "We have to position ourselves globally . . . We are not bent on global conquest. We are simply considering, in a rational and businesslike manner, the global financial networks which, visible to all, will develop towards the end of this century, and are trying to adjust our own strategies accordingly." Widely respected as a business strategist, Herrhausen hoped to transform the bank into a true "global player." His core idea was to extend the universal bank concept from the national to the international level.[98]

Herrhausen was assassinated by left-wing terrorists in late November 1989. Over the next few years, the Deutsche Bank's directors had to grapple with his vision for the future. In many ways, they continued on the course that Herrhausen had chartered. Soon after his death, they completed the purchase of Morgan Grenfell of London for about 2.7 billion DM ($1.7 billion). Five years later, the bank's directors decided to shift the nucleus of their global investment banking operations from Frankfurt to London.[99]

Although the bank's early steps toward internationalization were impressive, serious questions still remained. The new spokesman, Hilmar Kopper, and his colleagues had to decide which universal-banking services to extend to the rest of Europe and which to extend to financial markets overseas. Most analysts agreed that there were economies of scale and scope in banking. But no one was quite sure about the extent to which these economies would traverse national, cultural, and linguistic boundaries.

Conclusion

It is probably fair to say that by the mid-1990s, the Deutsche Bank had reached another turning point. Its leadership certainly faced an extraordinary combination of challenges. German reunification had become official in 1990, and the European monetary union was scheduled to be complete in 1999. In the meantime, the world's capital markets continued to develop and integrate so rapidly that some analysts predicted the emergence of a single global market for financial services.

With so many opportunities before them, the bank's leaders had to choose which ones to exploit and, more generally, how best to position the firm for future growth. After all, rapid but carefully controlled growth had always been one of the defining characteristics of the Deutsche Bank. The big question now concerned direction. Were Georg Siemens's worries from 1896 about excessive international expansion still relevant? Or, a full century later, were they finally obsolete?

The next chapter, our first on the American economy, introduces two of the most important figures in the business history of the United States and indeed the world. One of them, Henry Ford, became practically a living emblem of the core features of the Second Industrial Revolution: machine mass production, economies of scale, the combination of mass production with mass marketing, and the rise of purchasing power for consumers.

The Model T Ford revolutionized the automobile industry, and it came to symbolize the profound implications of mass production in general. Similarly, the Ford Motor Company's five-dollar day for some of its production workers came to symbolize the potential of mass consumerism. Henry Ford himself became one of the most famous people in the world. Like most celebrities, he enjoyed the attention.

The second figure introduced here, Alfred P. Sloan Jr., was the very model of the salaried general manager. Whereas Ford was obsessed with manufacturing, Sloan implemented a broader view at General Motors. With remarkable clarity, he saw that sustainable business success required constant attention to both manufacturing and marketing, and that the issue of organizational design had to be kept at the top of the general manager's priorities.

Like the chapter on Josiah Wedgwood, set in the eighteenth century, this one on Ford and Sloan set in the twentieth highlights the importance of both marketing and manufacturing and emphasizes the strategic relationship between the two. The chapter presents a three-phase model of the evolution of marketing, a model not confined to the American automobile industry but generalizable across many other consumer products in all countries.

As you think about the battle for market supremacy between the Ford Motor Company and the General Motors Corporation, you might try to assess the importance of first-mover advantages. Those advantages can arise in many different forms: innovations on the assembly line, the pro-

motion of installment purchasing, the annual styling of the product, and
the designing of the business organization itself. The history of the car
industry is especially revealing here. It demonstrates that a first-mover
advantage can pop up anywhere, but it also shows that no innovation,
by itself, can bring long-term business prosperity. The quest for success
has to be an unending one.

In the latter part of the chapter, we see the American automobile industry in seemingly excellent shape in the years after World War II. We
see both General Motors and Ford making record profits. We see company executives taking permanent American supremacy for granted. But
at just that moment, the "Japanese invasion" begins, and the very survival of the American car industry suddenly comes into question.

❧ 8 ❧

HENRY FORD, ALFRED SLOAN,
AND THE THREE PHASES OF MARKETING

Thomas K. McCraw and Richard S. Tedlow

The automobile has been the signature product of the twentieth century. For many people it has almost come to rank with food, clothing, and shelter as one of the necessities of life. How and why did the market for cars and trucks become so immense?

One reason has to do with population growth. At the start of the century, there were about 1.6 billion people in the world, and about 76 million in the United States. By the 1990s, these numbers had more than tripled: world population to 5.6 billion, U.S. population to over 250 million.[1]

During these same years, the most developed parts of the world became exceedingly rich. Purchasing power multiplied manyfold. For most of the twentieth century, consumer spending in the American economy outpaced that in all others. In constant dollars, per capita income in the United States grew by a factor of about five over the course of the century. Beginning in the 1960s, the economies of Germany, Japan, and a few others began to catch up to the American economy and in some sectors to overtake it.[2]

For mass-production industries, this fantastic growth in the 15 or so "rich" industrialized countries had tremendous implications. Over the course of the Second Industrial Revolution, potential markets for almost any useful item became huge. New products proliferated. Production runs stretched far beyond previous lengths. Continuous improvements of products and processes became routine. Immense economies of scale and scope resulted. Prices fell accordingly.

The single product that best embodied these trends was the motor vehicle. This industry's backward linkages into steel, glass, and rubber, plus its lucrative symbiosis with the petroleum industry, put the motor vehicle at the core of the twentieth-century economy. By the 1970s, one out of every six business establishments in the United States was involved in the manufacture, distribution, or operation of automotive products.[3]

The automobile's social and environmental consequences have been incalculable: liberation of the human spirit through instant and autonomous mobility, the individual elation of joyriding and road trips, the end of solitude for farm families, the evolution of suburbs, and the phenomenon of commuting. These developments transformed the life of almost everyone who had access to a car.

The automobile came of age in the 1920s, the first decade of a full-blown consumer economy, and American carmakers were far in the lead. In 1927, four out of every five automobiles in the world were located in the United States, where there was one car for every 5.3 people. In both France and Great Britain, the most mechanized countries in Europe, there was only one car per 44 people in 1927.[4]

By the mid-1990s, those same ratios were as follows: China, one car per 680 people; Brazil, one per 14; Poland, one per 6; Japan, one per 3; the countries of the European Union, one per 2.5; the United States, one per 1.7.[5]

In every country the coming of the automobile had high costs as well as benefits. The twentieth century's toxic air, its clotting of streets and freeways, and its carnage from accidents were just as unprecedented as the automobile's positive consequences. Over two and a half million Americans have been killed in car crashes during the twentieth century. This is about twice as many deaths as the combined total in all the wars in which the United States has ever participated.

Yet few people in any country have expressed even a hint of willingness to give up their cars. For some, driving can be a mystical experience of liberation and self-fulfillment, of being one with the machine. For many, it is simply a necessity of life.

The Beginnings

The question of who made the first car is still a matter of dispute, but the Germans Karl Benz and Gottlieb Daimler were probably first, with gasoline-powered vehicles in 1885. Later Armand Peugeot built another workable car in France, and by the 1890s the European auto industry had begun. France was in the lead and Germany second. Britain was hamstrung by its "red-flag" rule, requiring that self-propelled vehicles on public roads could not exceed four miles per hour and had to be preceded by a person carrying a red flag. This law, passed by Parliament at the instigation of rail and stagecoach companies fearful of competition from buses, was repealed in 1896. Far more important to the course of the British and European auto industry was the powerful and deep-seated assumption that cars would remain playthings for the wealthy, beyond the reach of the mass market.

In the United States, the auto era dates from 1893, when the Duryea brothers of Springfield, Massachusetts, who were bicycle mechanics, built a carriage driven by a one-cylinder motor. By 1899, many individuals and about thirty American companies had built some 2,500 automobiles, and the race was on. Important entrepreneurs of the next two decades included Ransom Olds, father of the Oldsmobile; the twin Stanley Brothers, whose boiler-powered "Steamer" was produced until 1910; the Dodge Brothers, Horace and John, who made transmissions for Ransom Olds and later became partners with Henry Ford; the five Mack Brothers of New York, who made their first truck in 1900; John North Willys, whose Overland company later produced the Jeep of World War II; the Studebaker Brothers of South Bend, Indiana, who had manufactured top-of-the-line wagons before going into the car business; and Walter P. Chrysler, who left General Motors in 1919 and later started the company that still bears his name.[6]

But the two giants of the American automobile industry were Henry Ford, who became the most famous industrialist in the world, and Alfred P. Sloan Jr., who with the backing of the du Pont family built General Motors into the world's largest manufacturing company. In the 1920s, the fight for market leadership between the Ford Motor Company and the General Motors Corporation became one of the epic struggles in the history of business.

The Three Phases of Marketing

Before we take a closer look at Ford and Sloan, a word is in order about the evolution not only of the automobile but of consumer products in general. The characteristic sequence of mass marketing of products to consumers has been called the "Three Phases of Marketing."[7]

The first phase is one of market fragmentation. For example, in 1900 no automobile firm had a broad market reach, a well-known name, or a heavy capital investment. None had a national dealer network. Each was confined to a small geographical area. Each had a different product design and different production and marketing strategies. In 1909, at the peak of proliferation, some 274 companies were manufacturing cars in the United States, mostly with low volumes of production, high margins, and high prices.[8] These characteristics are typical of the first stage in the development of many consumer products.

In the second phase, the market becomes defined and united by a superior brand or product configuration. The key characteristics of Phase II marketing are high-volume production, low margins, low prices, and national (and perhaps international) mass distribution. In the automobile industry, the classic Phase II product was the Model T Ford. Shortly after its introduction in 1908, this car established a dominant design for the industry. Soon a gigantic Ford factory and an international system of dealerships made possible an undreamed-of volume.[9] The Model T represented Phase II marketing carried to a phenomenally successful extreme.

Confronted by Henry Ford's mastery of Phase II, Alfred P. Sloan Jr. of General Motors adopted a different strategy, and took the industry into an early version of Phase III. During the 1920s, Sloan boldly segmented the car market on the basis of price and product policy. The ultimate consequences of Sloan's move into Phase III during the 1920s were profound not only for General Motors and Ford, but for the automobile industry worldwide.

Some two decades later, after World War II, American automakers pioneered a more comprehensive form of Phase III market segmentation. Consumers were now targeted not only on the basis of demographics (age, income, and education) but also "psychographics" (lifestyle). Using the new medium of television and exploiting the "generation gap" between those who grew up before versus after World War II, the new Phase III marketers came up with novel ways in which to differentiate products and create market segments. The high-performance "muscle" and "pony" cars of the 1960s and 1970s were sold by designers and marketers who were making a statement about the kinds of people who bought these cars, and thereby attracting their attention and allegiance.

The idea of Three Phases of Marketing is a generalizable proposition. Table 8.1 provides an outline of the content and timing of each phase, for automobiles and most other consumer products.

Table 8.1 The Three Phases of Marketing

Phase	Characteristics	Approximate Dates	
		Automobiles	Most Consumer Goods

I	Fragmentation
	  High margin per unit
	  Low volume of unit sales
	  Limited geographic market
	  Slow and expensive flow of transportation
	    and information
	  Commodity products
		1890s–1908	To the 1880s

II	Unification
	  Low margin per unit
	  High volume of unit sales
	  National mass market
	  Faster and less expensive flow of transpor-
	    tation and information
	  Branded products
		1908–1920s	1880s–1950s

III	Segmentation
	  Value-pricing to capture as much margin as
	    brand loyalty allows
	  Volume of unit sales high enough to achieve
	    scale economies in manufacturing and
	    marketing
	  Global market with numerous demographic
	    and psychographic segments
	  Enhanced research capabilities leading to
	    more precise segmentation
	  Brand proliferation with brands targeted at
	    specific segments
		1920s–Present	1950s–Present

The evolution of the automobile is an apt illustration of the Three Phases of Marketing, but there are many others. The soft-drink industry, for example, follows the pattern in much the same way, though the key dates for both Phase II and Phase III come a little later. During the late nineteenth century, when the soft-drink industry began, there were hundreds of brands, offered mostly in fragmented local markets. That was Phase I.[10]

Then, for several decades in the early and middle twentieth century, a single product, Coca-Cola, redefined the industry so thoroughly that it practically became the industry all by itself. During that period Coca-

Cola was offered in a single formula. It was delivered to the customer through soda fountains, but much more widely in a standard, take-home, six-and-a-half-ounce returnable bottle. The bottle itself had a distinctive shape, and the standard Coca-Cola formula in its "hobble-skirted" bottle dominated the soft-drink market of the world for almost 40 years. It was a preeminent Phase II product.

Not until the 1960s did Phase III come to soft drinks, first through the "Pepsi Generation," then by an extraordinary multiplication of products from both Coke and Pepsi. For Coca-Cola, which had long marketed one product in one size, Phase III meant a sudden proliferation of offerings: Classic Coke, Caffeine Free Coke, Tab, Diet Coke, Caffeine Free Diet Coke, Cherry Coke, Sprite, Diet Sprite, Fresca, and Minute Maid orange drink, among others—each offered in bottles, cans, and plastic containers of many different sizes.

In the movement of soft drinks from Phase II to Phase III, one standard product was thus subdivided into dozens of stockkeeping units. The Coca-Cola Company, PepsiCo, and other firms made finely calculated segmentations of the soft-drink market through demographic and psychographic targeting accompanied by massive advertising expenditures.

Not all consumer products went through each of the three phases at the same time, and a few do not fit the model well at all (milk and eggs, for example, which are not nationally branded). Nor are the Three Phases of Marketing exactly congruent with the Three Industrial Revolutions discussed throughout this book. Some significant correlations with the industrial revolutions can be seen, but they vary according to industry, country, and product. Within these limits, the Three Phases of Marketing idea is a useful way of thinking about the changing nature of consumer products over time.

The automobile went through its transition from Phase II to Phase III in the 1920s, earlier than most products. In the car wars of that decade, the principal combatants were the industrial titans Henry Ford and Alfred Sloan.

Henry Ford (1863–1947)

Born in the month of the Battle of Gettysburg, during the presidency of Abraham Lincoln, Ford survived until the year of the Marshall Plan, during the presidency of Harry Truman. Throughout his life he had one foot planted in the American past of a supposed agrarian simplicity, while the other strode forward, leading the world into the modern industrial era. Ford himself was never able to reconcile his conflicting impulses about modernity, and throughout his life he remained a figure of extreme paradox.[11]

He grew up on the family farm in Dearborn, Michigan, and he loved all things mechanical. Cutting his education short, he took a job in a Detroit machine shop at the age of 16, then moved to a drydock firm, and then to a job at the Westinghouse company. After a brief return to farming, during which he married Clara Bryant of Dearborn, he returned to Detroit. He worked in a large electric utility company and ultimately became its chief engineer.

Meanwhile, he constantly tinkered with machines. He was never able to sit still, and was always talking with fellow mechanics and engineers about better ways to do things. Ford was the classic American mechanic, but several orders beyond the average because of his remarkable intuitive flashes about how machines could be made to work better. Prowling about the shop, his skillful hands in perpetual motion, he gave the impression of a confident, handsome, supremely fit middleweight boxer waiting for the fight to start.[12]

Ford's first automobile was his "quadricycle" of 1896, an impractical though distinctively lightweight vehicle. His first company, launched in 1899, was a failure, although he was making a name for himself as a racing car driver. A second company also went nowhere. In 1903 he made a third try, this time with a firm called the Ford Motor Company, which had 12 investors and a paid-in capital of $28,000. The company brought out a series of models identified by letters of the alphabet, such as the A, B, C, F, K, N, R, S, and finally in 1908, the Model T. Henry Ford assembled a talented team of young executives, including the astute and determined business manager James Couzens (who left after a dozen years, eventually to become a U.S. Senator); the capable production man Charles Sorenson, who stayed until the 1940s; and, beginning in the 1920s, his only son, Edsel Ford. Edsel had first-rate talents, and at an early age was given major responsibilities, but he was never allowed to fulfill his potential.[13]

Henry Ford had great difficulty in delegating authority to anyone, even his son. With some justification, he regarded himself as a seer, a prophet of mass production. In 1906, he published the following letter in a trade journal, and its text catches the brilliance of his intuition about the American market and about the nature of a car for the masses:

> There are more people in this country who can buy automobiles than in any other country on the face of the globe, and in the history of the automobile industry in this country the demand has never yet been filled . . . The greatest need today is a light, low-priced car with an up-to-date engine of ample horsepower, and built of the very best material. One that will go anywhere a car of double the horsepower will; that is in every way an automobile and not a toy; and, most important of all, one that will not be a wrecker of tires and a spoiler of the owner's disposition.[14]

Ford was exceptionally bull-headed, and at this point in his career his stubbornness served him well. He saw that the proper *design* of the car must precede all considerations about inexpensive manufacture, but that the key to success was the manufacturing process. Ford evangelized about the wonders of mass production. As early as 1903, when cars were still being built in small batches of numerous individual models, he had said that "The way to make automobiles is to make one automobile like another automobile, to make them all alike, to make them come from the factory just alike—just like one pin is like another pin when it comes from a pin factory or one match is like another match when it comes from a match factory."[15]

As one of Ford's closest friends put it, "Standardization is his hobby. He would have all shoes made on one last, all hats made on one block, and all coats according to one pattern. It would not add to the beauty of life, but it would greatly reduce the cost of living." Ford himself, writing in 1931, put it this way: "Machine production in this country has diversified our life, has given a wider choice of articles than was ever before thought possible—and has provided the means wherewith the people may buy them. We standardize only on essential conveniences. Standardization, instead of making for sameness, has introduced unheard-of variety into our life. It is surprising that this has not been generally perceived."[16]

The Model T was the ultimate standardized machine. It was simple in the extreme—small, light, and strong. It contained the barest minimum of moving parts. In contrast to today's complex cars, it could be repaired by almost anyone with a smattering of mechanical sense. It was far more durable and reliable than anything else on the market near its price range. And when Ford was finally satisfied that he had the basics right, he concentrated all of his company's resources on this one model and no other. That decision to focus on just the T made possible a cycle of ever-improving product at ever-higher volume and ever-lower price. In 1908, a Model T sold for $850. By 1912 the price had dropped to $600, by 1920 to $440, and by 1924 to only $290.[17]

As the price fell, the production of Model T's shot forward at an accelerating rate. It took the company 7 years to reach its millionth unit, but only 18 months to reach the 2 millionth, and so on: the 4 millionth came in 1920, 6 millionth in 1922, 8 millionth in 1923, 10 millionth in 1924, and 12 millionth in 1925.[18]

By the early 1920s, the Ford Motor Company was producing more than 60 percent of all motor vehicles made in the United States, and about half made in the entire world. This unprecedented scale led to, and then depended on, a series of radical changes in the production process. These culminated in the moving assembly line, which became fully operational by 1914. In October 1913, it had taken 12 hours, 28 minutes to assemble a chassis. In the spring of 1914, with the assembly line, it took 1 hour, 33 minutes.[19]

In 1915, two knowledgeable analysts visited Ford's huge factory and wrote up for an engineering magazine their impressions of the assembly line and other innovations:

> Beyond all doubt or question, the Ford Motor Company's plant at Highland Park, Detroit, Michigan, U.S.A., at the time of this writing is the most interesting metalworking establishment in the world—because of its size (something over 15,000 names on the payroll) [eventually there were more than 65,000]; because it produces one single article only (the Ford motor car) for sale; because the Ford Motor Company is paying very large profits (something like $15,000,000 a year); and because, with no strike and no demand for pay increase from its day-wage earners, the Ford Company made a voluntary and wholly unexpected announcement January 5, 1914, that it would very greatly increase day-pay wage [to the astronomical figure of five dollars per day, more than twice the prevailing rate] and would at the same time reduce the day-work hours from nine to eight.[20]

When Henry Ford introduced the five-dollar day in 1914, he became an almost instant hero throughout the world. An unprecedented spotlight of press coverage focused on his generosity, his vision in promoting consumer buying power through high wages, and the new era of enlightened industrialism that the five-dollar day seemed to symbolize.

Ford's motives for the five-dollar day had more to do with reducing the unacceptable turnover in his plants than with any other impulse. The annual turnover rate, which sometimes reached 300–400 percent, derived from the strength-sapping and mind-numbing character of the work. The five-dollar day did little to reduce those problems, but Ford's simultaneous reduction of the workday from nine and ten hours to eight did help somewhat. In the mid-1920s he again pioneered, reducing the workweek from six days to five.[21]

For these changes, in combination with his miracles of production, and for the sheer quality of his product, Ford was lionized. He became a kind of international saint, a glorious symbol of the new potential for freedom from toil, the most famous American in the world. "Fordism" (*Fordismus* in German) came to be synonymous with machine mass production of standardized products. In Aldous Huxley's satirical novel *Brave New World,* Henry Ford is the deity of the new society. The calendar is calculated in "the year of our Ford." Exalted persons are addressed as "your Fordship."

The Bolshevik revolutionary Vladimir Lenin became one of Ford's greatest admirers. In 1926, a South American writer said of Ford that in Brazil he now ranked alongside Moses and Columbus. A poll of American college students in the 1920s placed Ford as the third-greatest person in the history of the world, after Napoleon and Jesus. In 1967, a national survey by researchers at the University of Michigan rated Ford the greatest business person in American history. A similar survey in 1971 sponsored by *Nation's Business* also ranked Ford first.[22]

During the 1920s, more articles were published in general periodicals on Ford and the Ford Motor Company than on the combined total of the next ten most publicized corporations. One scholar has calculated that more words have been written about Henry Ford than anyone could possibly read in a lifetime devoted to no other task.[23]

Why this public fascination? What, exactly, was Ford's contribution? A perceptive French analyst wrote that "What Marx had dreamed, Ford achieved." In the five-dollar day, Ford had seen the "vast role that mechanization can play in emancipating human society." This French writer concluded that Ford had grasped and acted on the insight that "A man is a customer on the market when he has purchasing power, just as he is a citizen of the republic when he has the power to influence affairs of state. In the last analysis, the customer controls the market and is therefore a free citizen of it. With Ford, the American worker became a customer." All over the world, Ford's name came to represent the promise of abundance from mass production and mass consumption.[24]

With unlimited renown came unlimited opportunity for Ford to demonstrate his naiveté and ignorance along with his wisdom. During World War I, he sponsored a noble but predictably futile "Peace Ship" expedition to Europe, designed to persuade the warring nations to stop fighting. As the years passed, his abundant eccentricities became more and more conspicuous. Although he hired thousands of African-Americans, for whom he expressed sympathy and respect noteworthy for that period, he remained hostile to Jews. For years, his company-sponsored newspaper, the *Dearborn Independent,* published anti-Semitic articles and editorials.

One of Ford's many biographers, whose book contains a chapter entitled "Genius Ignoramus," listed some of Ford's eccentricities and outlandish comments: "Ford told newsmen that 'this globe has been inhabited millions of times, by civilians having airplanes, automobiles, radio, and other scientific equipment of the modern era.'" In 1919, he proposed that horses, cows, and pigs be eliminated. "The world would be better off without meat," said Ford. According to the biographer, "Ford challenged scores of people, particularly reporters, to footraces, and only the most fleet-footed could stay with him over 100 yards. [He] was still racing when he was eighty years old."[25]

A friend of Ford's once wrote, "His mind does not move in logical grooves. It does not walk, it leaps. It is not a trained mind. It does not know how to think consecutively . . . He does not reason to conclusions. He jumps at them."[26]

Ford's philosophy of business turned out to be remarkably simple. Assuming high quality, which his cars nearly always had, then everything else resolved into a question of price. He liked to say that for every dollar he cut from the price of the Model T, he gained a thousand new buyers.[27] In 1916, he told an interviewer that many people "will pay $360 for a car who would not pay $440. We had in round numbers 500,000 buyers of cars on the $440 basis, and I figure that on the $360 basis we can increase the sales to possibly 800,000 cars for the year—less profit on each car, but more cars, more employment of labor, and in the end we get all the total profit we ought to make."[28]

During a lawsuit brought against him by the Dodge brothers, who were minority stockholders upset with his low-dividend policy, Ford said from the witness stand that "The only thing that makes anything not sell is because the price is too high." On cross-examination, he went on to state his larger views of the purpose of business:

Q. You say you do not think it is right to make so much profits? What is this business being continued for, and why is it being enlarged?

A. To do as much [good] as possible for everybody concerned.

Q. What do you mean by "doing as much good as possible"?

A. To make money and use it, give employment, and send out the car where the people can use it.

Q. Is that all? Haven't you said that you had money enough yourself, and you were going to run the Ford Motor Company thereafter to employ just as many people as you could, to give them the benefits of the high wages that you aid, and to give the public the benefit of a low priced car?

A. I suppose I have, and incidentally make money.

Q. Incidentally make money?

A. Yes sir.

Q. But your controlling feature, so far as your policy, since you have got all the money you want, is to employ a great army of men at high wages, to reduce the selling price of your car, so that a lot of people can buy it at a cheap price, and give everybody a car that wants one?

A. If you give all that, the money will fall into your hands; you can't get out of it.[29]

This testimony received wide publicity, almost all of it favorable to Ford. Millions of people seemed to like him, to imagine that they knew him personally, and to trust him as an exemplar of the common man. In fact he was probably the richest person in the world. Yet writers often commented that his fortune of more than a billion dollars had been earned "cleanly," in contrast to the wealth of bankers and speculators, and even to that of other industrialists such as John D. Rockefeller.

Ford himself fed this feeling. He had strong prejudices about conventional business. He hated financiers. He referred to stockholders as "parasites." In 1919, he purchased all outstanding shares of the Ford Motor Company and took the firm private. That proved to be a fateful move. It put this vast company entirely under the personal control of one eccentric individual, at the very moment when it was about to confront the newly reorganized General Motors Corporation.[30]

Alfred P. Sloan Jr. (1875–1966)

Whereas Henry Ford grew up on a farm, the man who guided General Motors was distinctly a city person. Alfred Sloan was the son of a prosperous importer of coffee and tea, based in New Haven, Connecticut. In 1885, the family moved to Brooklyn. Alfred went to public schools and to Brooklyn Polytechnic Institute, where he distinguished himself as a brilliant student. He then attended the Massachusetts Institute of Technology, graduating in three years with a B.S. in electrical engineering, at twenty the youngest member of his class. "I had been a grind," Sloan recalled of his college days. "I had worked every possible minute." Like Ford, he was married early (at 23) to Irene Jackson of Roxbury, Massachusetts, whom he met while attending MIT.[31]

After Sloan graduated ("I was thin as a rail, young and unimpressive"), he went to work at the Hyatt Roller Bearing Company in New Jersey. John Wesley Hyatt was the inventor of celluloid, a plastic used in collars and billiard balls. Besides celluloid, the company also made roller bearings, which were needed in growing volume by automobile manufacturers. When Sloan first joined Hyatt, the firm had 25 employees and $2,000 in monthly sales. Sloan's salary was $50 per month. Frustrated by the company's lack of progress, he left for what proved to be a brief and unsuccessful fling in the refrigeration business. When he returned to Hyatt, his father, Alfred P. Sloan Sr., became one of the company's major backers.[32]

A profile of Sloan Jr., published in *Fortune,* described the next phase of his career. He became president of Hyatt at the age of 24. He did everything from supervising the company's engineering and production to going on the road as a salesman of its roller bearings. "But many Saturdays," said the *Fortune* article, "Hyatt's workers had to wait until Father Sloan, in his Manhattan office, had written a check and young Alfred had rushed it through the bank to meet Hyatt's payroll." Eventually the two Sloans came to own a majority interest in the firm.[33]

As the car industry grew, so did Hyatt Roller Bearing. Propelled by

Sloan's energy, Hyatt sold bearings to more and more manufacturers, and Sloan came to know the automobile industry intimately. He met and sold to most of the important pioneers, including Ransom Olds, Henry Ford (his biggest customer by far), and the flamboyant William C. Durant.

"Blue-eyed Billy" Durant had formed the General Motors Corporation in 1908, the same year that Ford brought out his Model T. One of the great visionaries in the industry, Durant was primarily a sales and finance person who bought and sold entire automobile and parts companies. He speculated in their shares and liked to consolidate them into bigger groups. In 1918, when GM bought what became the Frigidaire company, Durant paid for it by writing out his personal check for $56,366.50.[34]

Durant was a plunger, not a systematic planner. Under his direction, the General Motors Corporation remained a motley agglomeration of independent firms with little common purpose. Many GM companies competed directly with each other. The star performer, Buick, which was guided by the extraordinarily capable executives Charles W. Nash and Walter P. Chrysler, provided profits that Durant spread around to other companies, several of which chronically operated at a loss. Impatient with Durant's methods, first Nash and then Chrysler left, eventually to form their own firms. GM had no common accounting system, no clear way to tell exactly how much money each company was making or losing, and no coherent plan for the future. As Alfred Sloan later wrote, "Mr. Durant was a great man with a great weakness—he could create but he could not administer."[35]

Durant habitually overextended himself. In a liquidity crunch of 1910, bankers ousted him from GM, which was then only two years old. In 1915, he regained command through his control of Chevrolet, but then in 1920 was expelled by the du Ponts, this time permanently. The du Pont company had acquired a one-quarter interest in GM beginning in 1918, and had insisted on a determining voice in finance. GM, despite its problems, seemed an attractive investment because, as du Pont's John J. Raskob put it, "our interest will undoubtedly secure for us the entire Fabrikoid [artificial leather], Pyralin [plastic], paint and varnish business of those [GM] companies."[36] The stake du Pont took in GM became one of the most lucrative investments in American business history.

Despite Billy Durant's failures in finance and administration, he made vital contributions to General Motors. He saw much earlier than did

most other pioneers that some kind of vertical integration of parts manufacturers, body companies, chassis works, and assemblers was going to
be necessary before the industry's economies of scale could be fully realized. Henry Ford, an even more determined apostle of vertical integration, had built his own company into a giant through internal expansion.
Durant did it for GM through merger and acquisition.

That strategy brought him together with Alfred Sloan. In 1916, Du-
rant consolidated a series of accessory companies into a new entity called
United Motors, into which he wanted to absorb Hyatt Roller Bearing.
By this time Hyatt had become a booming company of 4,000 employees.
Sloan, who with his father owned 60 percent of the firm, now sold it to
Durant for $13.5 million, taking half his payment in United Motors
stock. Durant then made Sloan president of United Motors.[37]

In 1918, when Durant merged United with General Motors, Sloan
became a GM vice president and member of the Executive Committee.
In 1920, when Durant was again forced out, Pierre du Pont reluctantly
took the GM presidency himself. However, as Sloan wrote in his autobiography, "Mr. du Pont continued to feel that he was acting as president
under duress. He loved his home in Wilmington [Delaware] and disliked
the obligation to travel all over for General Motors."[38] So Pierre du Pont
made Sloan his own chief assistant, with broad executive power. Sloan
was then 45 years old, and he faced a very uncertain future. GM was in
serious trouble, and not only because of Durant's financial escapades.
The deep economic recession of 1920–21 had pulled the rug from under
the market for automobiles.

As *Fortune* later described it, Pierre du Pont's choice of Sloan as his
chief assistant "was obvious for several reasons. He was an engineer, and
engineers were rising in popularity. He stood out as an 'organization
man' in contrast to Durant." In 1923, Sloan himself became president of
GM, succeeding Pierre du Pont. The *Fortune* article went on to describe
Sloan's management style:

> [He] devotes himself to getting all views out in the open, laying par-
> ticular emphasis on the positive views. He throws his weight to those
> who point out what good the proposal may bring, knowing well, as
> one pessimist has put it, that men in committee "tend only to confirm
> each other's fears" . . .
>
> In all the committee work Mr. Sloan displays an almost inhuman
> detachment from personalities, a human and infectious enthusiasm for

the facts. Never, in committee or out, does he give an order in the ordinary sense, saying, "I want you to do this." Rather he reviews the data and then sells an idea, pointing out, "Here is what could be done." Brought to consider the facts in open discussion, all men, he feels, are on an equal footing. Management is no longer a matter of taking orders, but of taking council . . .

[General Motors] has escaped the fate of those many families of vertebrates whose bodies grew constantly larger while their brain cavities grew relatively smaller, until the species became extinct. It has escaped because Mr. Sloan has contrived to provide it with a composite brain commensurate with its size.[39]

Whereas Henry Ford courted reporters and received blanket coverage, the homely and shy Sloan remained elusive. The same *Fortune* article contained a vivid description of Sloan, and it is one of the few first-hand reports available:

This lively, wiry, slightly built [six feet, 130 pounds] man in the dapper clothes has for years been among the country's highest paid executives—in 1936 he topped them all—and has been responsible, in so far as any one man could have been, for the consolidation of its second biggest manufacturing enterprise, outranked in assets by Big Steel alone. Yet the public and even the automobile industry itself know little or nothing about his private life, little or nothing more about his contribution to General Motors . . . In his rare leisure moments he is restless. He has given no time to culture in the old fashioned sense. When he goes to Europe, most of the trip is business. Even the choosing of his well-tailored clothes is delegated to a valet. He has no children to absorb his time or attention. Everything has gone into the job.[40]

Sloan had almost no private life and few friends. He and Pierre du Pont had assembled a talented management team at General Motors, including the financial wizard Donaldson Brown, the inventor Charles F. Kettering, and the production managers William S. Knudsen and Charles E. Wilson. But Sloan's closest comrade remained his business rival Walter P. Chrysler. Sloan believed that no CEO should try to have real friends within his own company. He liked to point out that Abraham Lincoln and Franklin D. Roosevelt had held themselves aloof from associates, whereas less effective presidents such as Ulysses S. Grant had been betrayed by their friends. An associate of Sloan's once compared him to the product he had earlier manufactured at Hyatt Roller Bearing: "self-lubricating, smooth, eliminates friction and carries the load."[41]

Ford Motor Company versus General Motors

During the industry-wide crisis of 1920–21, Henry Ford was simultaneously taking his company private, producing at nearly full throttle, and building a vast new facility at the River Rouge.[42] This combination of activities placed heavy cash demands on the company. Ford responded by ruthlessly requiring his 6,400 dealers to accept and pay him cash for 90,000 new cars for which there was no ready market. The choice for individual dealers was to pay or lose the franchise. The episode typified Ford's attitude toward a group that should have been his closest allies. GM's Sloan, by contrast, always went out of his way to accommodate the company's dealers. He offered financing for startup dealers, and through the General Motors Acceptance Corporation managed to finance their wholesale purchases as well as individual buyers' retail purchases. Ford was very slow to convert to installment buying.[43]

By 1925, the auto industry, which had not even existed during the previous generation, ranked first among all American industries in cost of materials, wages paid, value of products, and value added in manufacturing. The contest for supremacy between Ford and General Motors, played out against a backdrop of robust macroeconomic growth, exhibited all the basic themes of modern corporate strategy: the shifts in consumer tastes, the imperatives of a particular industry structure, the force of personality, and the decisive role of leadership and management.[44]

The basic strategic situation was concisely captured by Figure 8.1, which first appeared in 1926 in a leading trade publication, and which depicts the early evolution of the American car market. This rather complicated-looking chart had a simple message, and its meaning is explained in the note below the diagram. Had the full implications of the data that went into Figure 8.1 somehow penetrated the mind of Henry Ford, the contest with General Motors might have turned out differently. The outcome of the great contest between Ford and General Motors is summarized in Table 8.2.

How did General Motors win such a spectacular victory in so short a time? The principal reason was that Henry Ford's product policy remained so inflexible: Keep building the Model T with better materials,

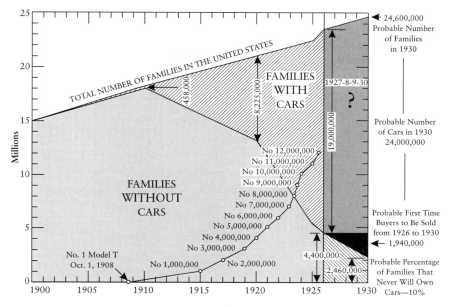

Figure 8.1   The U.S. Auto Market in 1926

Note: Families without any car at all were big buyers of the Model T. Today (1926) few families have no car at all and the business is largely one of replacement. The "2,000,000" locates the date when the 2,000,000th Model T was built, etc.

Source: James Dalton, "What Will Ford Do Next?" *Motor* (May 1926), rpt. in Alfred D. Chandler, Jr., ed. and comp., *Giant Enterprise: Ford, General Motors, and the Automobile Industry* (New York: Harcourt, Brace, and World, 1964), p. 107.

constant improvements, and reduced cost to the consumer. It had been a classic example of Phase II marketing, and it worked miraculously well for almost 20 years. The aphorism that customers could buy a Model T in any color so long as it was black derived not from Henry Ford's contempt for customers but from the imperatives of the production line. Before the advent of du Pont's colored lacquer, black paint dried much faster than any other, and the line could be kept moving. The larger point, however, was Henry Ford's almost maniacal commitment to a single product. That kind of commitment was the core principle of Phase II marketing.

By 1927, a combination of forces finally caused Ford to abandon his beloved Model T. These forces were the rising consumer preference for enclosed cars, the proliferation of new models from Chrysler, General

Table 8.2   Market Shares, 1911–37

Year	Passenger Motor Vehicles Sold by All Manufacturers	Chrysler	Ford	General Motors	
	THOUSANDS OF UNITS				
1911	199		40	35	
1917	1,746		741	196	
1925	3,735	134	1,495	746	
1929	4,587	375	1,436	1,482	
1933	1,574	400	326	652	
1937	3,916	996	837	1,637	
	PERCENT [market share]				Subtotal: Chrysler, Ford, GM
1911	100%		19.9%	17.8%	37.7%
1917	100		42.4	11.2	53.7
1921	100		55.7	12.7	68.4
1925	100	3.6%	40.0	20.0	63.6
1929	100	8.2	31.3	32.3	71.8
1937	100	25.4	21.4	41.8	88.6

Source: Adapted from Chandler, *Giant Enterprise,* pp. 3–4.

Motors, and other manufacturers, and—most important—the advent of annual model changes, which amounted to a revolution in styling. GM exploited all of these changes, plus other kinds of appeals, through ingenious advertising campaigns. Nor did GM surpass Ford in marketing alone. It also had copied Ford's state-of-the-art production methods, and had taken them a step further. By making parts that could go into several different makes and models, it had converted large economies of scale into economies of scope as well.[45]

In 1927, Henry Ford responded to the competitive pressures by shutting down his works for many months, retooling his factories, and producing a new Model A. This car was a quantum improvement over the T, but in the last analysis it amounted to another standardized, unvarying product.[46] After a few years at number one, the Model A was overtaken by Chevrolet. Not until 1933 did Ford follow the industry trend and convert to annual model changes. Not until 1938 did the company introduce the Mercury, a midsize car designed to compete with GM's Pontiac, Oldsmobile, and Buick. The Mercury seldom sold well. Ford's luxurious Lincoln, made in small lots, had been a weak competitor of Cadillac since the early 1920s.

Meanwhile, Henry Ford had alienated almost every one of his promising young executives. Many of them were snapped up by Sloan at General Motors. They could not tolerate Ford's eccentric behavior, his playing favorites, his increasing reliance on the tough ex-boxer Harry Bennett, whom he installed at the very top of his company. Bennett, with no appreciable automotive training and a well-deserved reputation for underworld connections, ultimately became the second-most-important person at the Ford Motor Company. Henry Ford himself, who was 70 years old by 1933, grew ever more querulous and less flexible. Had his product not been of such high quality, and his brand name of such extraordinary value, his company might well have perished.[47]

While Henry Ford was slowly destroying his organization, Alfred Sloan was honing General Motors into an ever more efficient industrial colossus. Whereas Ford hated even to think about organizational issues, Sloan reveled in their subtleties and nuances. One of the great organizational innovators in American business history, Sloan created an early version of what came to be called the "multidivisional structure." Of crucial importance in the governance of large organizations, this "M-form," as economists have named it, is one of the signal achievements of the twentieth-century corporation.[48]

Sloan's careful design of the M-form for General Motors in 1925 is reproduced here as Figure 8.2. Note in this chart how complex the structure is, yet how clearly the lines of responsibility and reporting are worked out. In later years the design proved to be so structurally sound that it accommodated the immense growth of the company past total employment of more than half a million people.

In an M-form organization, division heads may be called managing directors, presidents, or vice presidents, as they are in Figure 8.2. Whatever their titles, they have full profit-and-loss responsibility for the products or services in their bailiwicks.

This one change in the locus of responsibility amounted to a revolution in business thinking. Older forms of organization had tended to allocate managers' responsibilities not according to product but according to function: the sales function, the manufacturing function, the purchasing

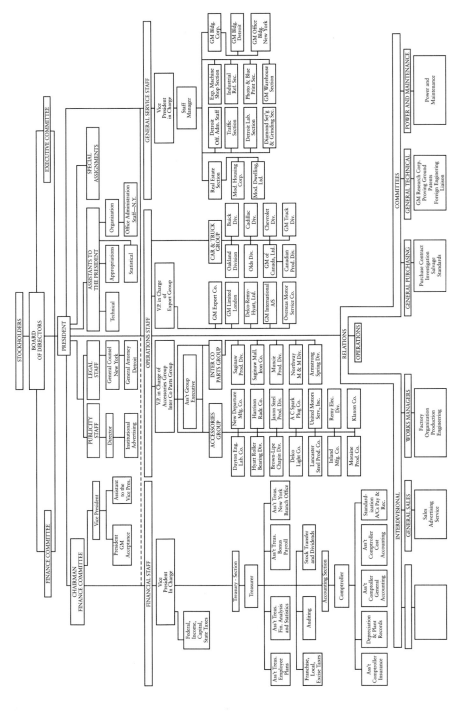

Figure 8.2   General Motors Organization Chart, 1925

function, and so on. Functional department heads reported to a single chief executive officer, who maintained central control of the organization. That kind of "centralized, functionally departmentalized structure" worked nicely in small organizations, and it still does today. It can also work well in a large corporation, provided the products being sold are all of one type, such as the products of a coal company or a steel company.

But in a firm such as General Motors, with its huge divisions making separate models of cars and trucks, not to mention the parts divisions making batteries, bearings, and sparkplugs, a centralized, functionally departmentalized structure could produce disaster. If profits fell, there was no one to blame except the person at the very top. There was no way to figure out exactly where the problems might be. That was what had happened at the Ford Motor Company.

At General Motors, it was Alfred Sloan's particular genius to figure out all of these crucial organizational issues.[49] At its best, the M-form combined the virtues of centralized control with those of decentralized decisionmaking. It matched power with responsibility up and down the organization. In so doing it addressed and often solved the perennial management problem of maximizing individual autonomy without creating hopeless disorder.

Sloan, together with members of the elite team he assembled, had created a system for managing human relationships that was just as rationally planned and as efficient for business organization as Henry Ford's assembly line had been for production. What Ford could do with physical machines, Sloan could do with human organizations. And just as Ford's greatest innovation was the assembly of separate mechanical parts into the Model T through the assembly line, Sloan's was the assembly of organizational parts into one smoothly functioning whole through the M-form.

Among its other virtues, the new GM structure provided a framework for motivating large numbers of managers to work together. Sloan himself resolutely ruled by persuasion, almost never by fiat. He instituted a series of cross-divisional committees and had many top managers serve on multiple committees of different makeups. (An early version of this committee system appears at the bottom of Figure 8.2.) Sloan thereby forced almost all executives of importance within the organization to communicate regularly with each other.

The contrast between Henry Ford and Alfred Sloan captures an essential tension within the American business psyche. Their dissimilar styles and radically different ways of thinking are illustrated in Appendixes A and B of this chapter, which contain brief excerpts from their autobiographies. These excerpts bear careful reading. Each man can be seen to be revealing perhaps more of himself than he intended.

Henry Ford, with his mechanical genius, homespun individualism, and impulsive entrepreneurship, is perhaps the more arresting character study, and in some sense the more typically "American" type. But it is Alfred Sloan, the patient, persuasive, and systematic organization man, who probably better symbolizes the essence of the many American triumphs in the Second Industrial Revolution. Certainly the outcome of the struggle between their two great companies could hardly be much clearer or more conclusive. For six decades, in every single year from 1925 to 1986, the profit performance of the General Motors Corporation surpassed that of the Ford Motor Company.

The American Automobile Industry during the "American Century"

The Ford Motor Company staggered through the 1930s, but, like General Motors, it was the beneficiary of large military contracts during World War II. Even so, the company emerged from the war in feeble condition. Edsel Ford, Henry's son, died in 1943 at the age of 49, never having received the chance to demonstrate the full range of his formidable talents. Henry Ford, who had become ever more irascible and eccentric, was finally forced from an active role in the firm in 1945, when he was 82 years of age.

The revival of the Ford Motor Company began on September 21, 1945, when Edsel's son, Henry Ford II, became CEO. Henry II, then only 26 years old, acted decisively. With courage, energy, and open-mindedness, he set about remaking the once-great company. He banished his grandfather's crony Harry Bennett. He instituted a strict meritocracy, and sought management talent wherever he could find it. He pirated executives from General Motors, reversing the old pattern that had been exploited by Alfred Sloan. He also hired bright young men who, like himself, were veterans of World War II. Ten of them, including Tex Thorton and Robert S. McNamara, came in one package—the famous "Whiz

Kids" from the Office of Statistical Control of the Army Air Corps. Over-all, the new Ford team replicated in the 1940s and 1950s the multidivi-sional structure and management system that Alfred Sloan had installed at General Motors in the 1920s. In so doing, they masterminded one of the greatest corporate turnarounds in American business history.[50]

In 1950, Ford overtook Chrysler to regain second place in the Ameri-can market. In volume of sales, however, General Motors continued to stand alone at the head of the class. In 1950, it sold more automobiles than the combined total of its two largest rivals. Sloan had stepped down as chief executive officer in 1946, but he stayed on as chairman of the board until 1956. After that he became honorary chairman until his death in 1966 at the age of 90.

In 1941, Henry R. Luce, the publisher of *Time, Life,* and *Fortune,* had christened the coming era the "American Century."[51] After the war, the American automobile industry quickly began to make Luce's label look accurate. In 1946, still hindered by war-caused shortages, the American industry sold 1.8 million automobiles. But in 1950 it sold 6.3 million. This figure represented an increase of almost a third over the previous year, which itself had been a record high. Of all the automobiles manu-factured in the world in 1950, 85 percent were produced in the United States.[52] At this time imports held less than 0.3 percent of the U.S. mar-ket.[53]

With the dramatic postwar spike in demand, new domestic firms en-tered the market. Cars with names such as Kaiser and Frazer began to appear on the American road. Sears even tried a private-label automobile called the Allstate. But none of these challengers made much of a dent. General Motors, Ford, and Chrysler controlled nearly 87 percent of the domestic market in 1950.[54]

The apogee of the American automobile industry in the "American Century" was reached in 1955. Rebounding from the Korean War and from a recession shortly thereafter, the industry sold more than 7 million automobiles in the United States, still another new record. Chrysler had about 17 percent of the market, Ford 28 percent, and General Motors 51 percent. Imports accounted for a minuscule 0.7 percent.[55]

Time magazine's "Man of the Year" for 1955 was Harlow H. Curtice, CEO of General Motors. In January 1956, the same month when Cur-tice's portrait appeared on the cover of *Time,* the Ford Motor Company went public. Its initial stock offering was the biggest in the history of

Wall Street. Coming on the heels of a record-breaking sales year, the offering was a spectacular success.

No one knew it then, of course, but the "American Century" was not going to last very long, and the American automobile industry would never be quite so heady again. Sales did not reach 1955 levels again until 1963. And in that year, foreign cars, mostly Volkswagen Beetles, accounted for more than 5 percent of total sales in the American market. Four years later, in 1967, when total sales were 8.4 million units, the foreign share exceeded 9 percent.[56]

STYLE AND SUBSTANCE

For Henry Ford I, with his artisan mentality, the automobile had been an appliance that took its owner from place to place. "It takes you there and it brings you back," was old Henry's favorite slogan about the Model T. An important reason why General Motors was able to overtake Ford during the 1920s was that Alfred Sloan understood that the market was changing. He was able to introduce an element of fashion into his cars through an investment in styling and color. He brought a brilliant young designer named Harley Earl from Hollywood to Detroit, and gave him ample authority. Instead of a single vehicle type like the Ford Model T, GM offered "a car for every purse and purpose." Chevrolet became the plainest and least expensive car in the GM line, Cadillac the fanciest and most expensive. In between, in ascending order of price and stylishness, Sloan and his colleagues slotted Pontiac, Oldsmobile, and Buick. They took the industry from Phase II marketing, typified by the standardized Model T Ford, to the segmentation of Phase III, typified by five nameplates, annual model changes, and a wide range of colors.[57]

During the 1950s, and even more intensely in the early 1960s, the industry began to segment markets into ever smaller niches. In 1965, ten different lines of cars were marketed under the nameplate Chevrolet: Corvair, Chevy II, Chevelle, Biscayne, Bel Air, Impala, Caprice, Camaro, Corvette, and Station Wagon.[58] Each one of these lines came in numerous variations. Nor was this pattern of wild escalation confined to General Motors. The 1982 Ford Thunderbird, one consulting firm estimated, "offered 69,120 possible option combinations." This was Phase III marketing run amok.[59]

Lost in the blizzard of product proliferation was the question of whether the American car was being improved or merely made more elaborate. Before the era of computer-assisted engineering, which began to mature in the late 1980s, it was much more difficult to design and produce such a wide variety of vehicles. As variety increased, so did the potential for flaws in manufacturing. Variety also raised difficulties at the point of sale. Salespeople, in order to discuss all the options intelligently, needed an enormous amount of knowledge. Few actually had it.

The consequences for the dealer's service department were equally severe. Each one of the new options could fail, and the poorer their design and manufacture, the greater the likelihood of failure. So the proliferation of options created a parade of unhappy purchasers into the service areas. And a serviceperson had to be very skilled to be able to handle the many problems to be confronted. Variety, the industry discovered, could be costly, especially in an era of increasing government regulation. A long sequence of expensive recalls underscored the point.

Meanwhile, the powering and styling of American cars had begun to reach new extremes. Within the industry, the 1950s and 1960s became decades symbolized by the "horsepower war" and the "tail fin." Horsepower reached 300 and even 400 in some models. Progressively more "souped-up" engines seemed to be useful selling points in the dealer's showroom, but they proved to be positively dangerous on the open road. Speedometers registered 120 miles per hour. Many models actually could go that fast, even though the speed limit in most states was 60.

The automotive historian James J. Flink has noted that for the styling of cars, designers now seemed to be trying to emulate the airplane. "The nonfunctional tail fins introduced on the 1949 Cadillac grew in proportion to set a styling trend to be emulated eventually even by stodgy Chrysler with what became known as the 'Forward Look.' By 1958, the Chrysler, Dodge, and even the lowly Plymouth had fins so outlandish that they appeared to have been stolen from the drawing boards of Boeing Aircraft."[60] These sharp tail fins were not only extravagant, they were dangerous. Even at low speeds they could cause great harm to pedestrians and to other vehicles, thus contributing to the growing carnage on American streets and highways.

The frills were costly in other ways as well. Heavy and high-powered cars achieved notoriously low fuel efficiency, a departure from the recent past. A large 1949 Cadillac had run for 20 miles on a gallon of gasoline. But in 1973, the year of the first oil shock, the average American automobile got only 13.5 miles per gallon, and large models typically got fewer than ten.[61] In the 1960s, Detroit had begun marketing "muscle" and "pony" cars such as Ford's Torino Cobra, the Mercury Cougar Eliminator, the Ford Mustang with its 260-cubic-inch engine, the Pontiac GTO with a 389-cubic-inch V-8, and the popular Plymouth Fury. The ultimate muscle car was the 1968 Plymouth Road Runner, with its stupendous 426-cubic-inch engine.[62]

DESIGN PROGRESS ABROAD

Meanwhile, almost unnoticed by the American Big Three auto companies, foreign manufacturers were making steady progress. For the most part, the domestic markets they served were less wealthy than the American market. Their customers were generally more demanding of core product quality than of souped-up toys. The result was that during the 1950s and the 1960s, these foreign companies were innovating technologically. The car industry in the United States, which viewed itself as impregnable, was beginning to fall behind.[63]

By way of illustration, James J. Flink has compared the 1967 Cadillac Eldorado to the Mercedes-Benz 250 of the same year. The sticker price for the Eldorado was $6,277. For this, the consumer purchased an automobile that weighed 5,000 pounds and got ten miles to the gallon. The Eldorado was the epitome of the "road cruiser," featuring the kind of "feather pillow" ride that its designers believed the American consumer wanted. This ride was made possible by a suspension system that was too soft for the car to take corners well or to handle easily on rough roads. Adding to that problem were the old-fashioned bias-ply tires that came as original equipment, along with old-style hydraulic drum brakes. An Eldorado could attain high speeds very quickly, but stopping it was another matter. No fewer than 386 feet were required to bring an Eldorado to a halt from 80 miles per hour, a not uncommon speed well under the Eldorado's top capability.[64]

As for the German-made Mercedes-Benz 250, its 1967 price was almost a third less than that of the Eldorado. The Mercedes weighed 4,000 pounds and got 20 miles to the gallon. It had a fuel injection engine that reduced exhaust emissions and increased mileage at no cost to performance. It had as original equipment disc brakes, which were lighter, simpler, and far more efficient than drum brakes in stopping the car quickly. The fully independent suspension of the Mercedes provided a better ride on rough roads than the ride of a Cadillac, and better control of the car. The Mercedes also had other important safety advantages, including unitary body construction, a rigid passenger compartment for protection in the event that the car rolled over, and a front end designed to protect the passenger compartment in a head-on collision. Steel-belted radial tires were provided as standard equipment. These tires, which the French company Michelin had begun mass-producing as early as 1948, lasted twice as long as the bias-ply tires coming out of Akron, Ohio, the center of the American tire industry. They provided a slightly rougher ride, but a far better feel for the road, and they saved on gasoline.[65]

THE CHALLENGE OF JAPANESE IMPORTS

A threat even greater than the one from across the Atlantic Ocean was beginning to appear from across the Pacific. The first entry of Japanese manufacturers into the U.S. market took place, coincidentally, at about the same time that the Ford Motor Company introduced the Edsel, perhaps the most comically ill-fated of all American automobiles.

Toyota Motor Sales, at a cost of a million dollars, opened its first American sales subsidiary in October of 1957, one month after the introduction of the Edsel. That same year, Nissan tried out the Datsun 210 in California. Toyota's Toyopet Crown and the Datsun 210 were both displayed at the imported car show in Los Angeles in January 1958. These cars, it turned out, were not ready for the American market. The Datsun 210, with its tiny engine, was capable of a top speed of only 59 miles per hour. When the car reached about 50, it began to shimmy and vibrate. This symptom worsened the longer the car was on the road. Running at top speed, the 210 overheated and burned oil. On any major American highway, this car was in danger of being run over.[66]

The Japanese firms beat an embarrassed retreat back across the Pacific. But it was a strategic withdrawal, not a surrender. When they returned, they did so with a vastly improved product aimed directly at the heart of the American mass market. In 1967, the United States imported some 82,035 Japanese cars. That number leaped to 182,547 the following year.[67]

By 1980, a year when Chrysler lost $1.7 billion and had to turn to the federal government for financial assistance, Toyota, Nissan, and Honda had captured more than 16 percent of the American market. Ford, which lost $1.5 billion in 1980 and seemed to be next in line behind

Chrysler for bankruptcy, had only a 17 percent share. General Motors, with its 46 percent share, alone seemed robust.[68]

But by 1990, the combined share of the three most important Japanese firms had climbed to more than 22 percent. Mazda and Mitsubishi were heavily involved in the American market as well, and the addition of their sales to those of Honda, Nissan, and Toyota brought the share held by major Japanese producers to 26.5 percent, compared to 9.3 percent for Chrysler, 21 percent for the resurgent Ford, and a startlingly low 35.6 percent for slumping General Motors.[69] From 1986 through 1990, the cumulative U.S. bilateral trade deficit in automobiles and parts with Japan amounted to over $120 billion and had long since become a major political issue.[70]

In 1980, Japan, with a population only half that of the United States, became the world's leading producer of cars and trucks. The United States had held this distinction since 1908, the year of the introduction of the Model T. In 1994, after years of corporate reorganization and "re-engineering" (which often meant massive layoffs), the United States regained the top position—but not without the help of Japanese "transplant" factories located in Tennessee, Kentucky, Ohio, Illinois, and Michigan.[71]

One key to Japan's success had been a corporate strategy that favored outsourcing over vertical integration. This strategy was coordinated through a carefully crafted set of supplier relations. Quality was the goal, and it was achieved partly through the introduction of the "Toyota Production System." Those aspects of Japanese production technology, and numerous others as well, are covered in detail in the chapter on Toyota later in this book.

Toward the Future

At the close of the twentieth century, additional major changes seemed in store for the world motor vehicle industry. In the long term, severely constraining environmental issues would have to be faced. The supply of oil was finite, and the limits of the ability of the atmosphere to absorb pollution might already have been reached.

A whole range of decisions by individual companies necessarily became international in scope. The abolition of many trade barriers made it essential to manage automobile firms as genuinely global enterprises rather than merely multinational ones. At the end of the twentieth century, major auto companies of all nationalities struggled to capture all possible economies of operation.

Another pressing issue was worldwide overcapacity. Facilities were in place for building far more cars and trucks than the market seemed able to absorb. The kind of industry shakeout that had occurred a hundred years earlier in the United States and Europe, at the beginning of the twentieth century, loomed as a possibility on a global level at the beginning of the twenty-first. Forced exits from the industry seemed more likely than entry by new companies.

On the other hand, in the era of the Third Industrial Revolution, the practice of consumer marketing in general was moving in the direction of customizing products to the specific tastes of individual consumers. The growth of information technology made this customization progressively more possible. Motor vehicle manufacturers thus faced the conundrum posed by the oxymoron "mass customization." The industry might even have been entering an as yet undiscernible Phase IV of Marketing. Every major company awaited the insights of some new Henry Ford or Alfred Sloan to point it in a profitable direction.

Appendix A: Henry Ford's Comments on Business and Other Subjects

At the height of his career, Ford prepared three volumes of autobiography and assorted thoughts, reliably ghostwritten by his longtime collaborator Samuel Crowther. These books sold well all over the world. Here are some excerpts:

Business men believed that you could do anything by "financing" it. If it did not go through on the first financing then the idea was to "refinance." The process of "refinancing" was simply the game of sending good money after bad . . . I determined absolutely that never would I join a company in which finance came before the work or in which bankers or financiers had a part.[72]

Repetitive labor—the doing of one thing over and over again and always in the same way—is a terrifying prospect to a certain kind of mind. It is terrifying to me. I could not possibly do the same thing day in and day out, but to other minds, perhaps I might say to the majority of minds, repetitive operations hold no terrors. In fact, to some types of mind thought is absolutely appalling . . . I have not been able to discover that repetitive labour injures a man in any way. I have been told by parlour experts that repetitive labour is soul- as well as body-destroying, but that has not been the result of our investigations . . . The most thorough research has not brought out a single case of a man's mind being twisted or deadened by the work. The kind of mind that does not like repetitive work does not have to stay in it . . . If he stays in production it is because he likes it.[73]

To my mind there is no bent of mind more dangerous than that which is sometimes described as the "genius for organization." This usually results in the birth of a great big chart showing, after the fashion of a family tree, how authority ramifies. The tree is heavy with nice round berries, each of which bears the name of a man or of an office. Every man has a title and certain duties which are strictly limited by the circumference of his berry . . . And so the Ford factories and enterprises have no organization, no specific duties attaching to any position, no line of succession or of authority, very few titles, and no conferences. We have only the clerical help that is absolutely required; we have no elaborate records of any kind, and consequently no red tape.[74]

The right sales price is always the lowest price at which, all things considered, the article can be manufactured, and since experience in making and volume of sales will bring about lower costs, the sales price can as a rule constantly be lowered. It is the duty of a manufacturer constantly to lower prices and increase wages.[75]

Not a single item of equipment can be regarded as permanent. Not even the site can be taken as fixed. We abandoned our Highland Park plant—which was in its day the largest automobile plant in the world—and moved to the River Rouge plant because in the new plant there could be less handling of materials and consequently a saving. We frequently scrap whole divisions of our business—and as a routine affair.[76]

In 1916, during an interview with a writer from the Chicago Tribune, *Ford delivered his views on the uselessness of history. His comments were misleading in a sense, because he had a deep streak of nostalgia that ultimately expressed itself in numerous historical philanthropies. Some of these were expensive: the gigantic Henry Ford Museum in Dearborn, comparable to the Smithsonian Institution as a museum of industry; the adjacent Greenfield Village, containing dozens of original buildings from the American frontier; Ford's restoration of the Wayside Inn in Sudbury, Massachusetts, near Boston; and a multitude of other projects such as the sponsorship of folk music and folk dancing. Here, however, is what he told the* Tribune *interviewer in 1916:*

Say, what do I care about Napoleon. What do we care what they did 500 or 1,000 years ago? I don't know whether Napoleon did or did not try to get across there (to England) and I don't care. It means nothing to me. History is more or less bunk. It's tradition. We don't want tradition. We want to live in the present and the only history that is worth a tinker's dam is the history we make today.

That's the trouble with the world. We're living in books and history and tradition. We want to get away from that and take care of today. The men who are responsible for the present war in Europe [1914–18] knew all about history. Yet they brought on the worst war in the world's history.[77]

Appendix B: Alfred P. Sloan's Comments on Business Administration*

Sloan was president or CEO of GM from 1923 to 1946. He wrote two autobiographies. The second, entitled My Years with General Motors, *was published in 1963, when the author was 88 years of age. It is widely regarded as the most important business autobiography ever written, and one of the two or three most important works on business in any literary genre. Here are some excerpts:*

FROM CHAPTER 3, "CONCEPT OF THE ORGANIZATION"

At the close of the year 1920 the task before General Motors was reorganization. As things stood, the corporation faced simultaneously an economic slump on the outside and a management crisis on the inside.

It has been supposed by some students that General Motors took its decentralized type of organization from the du Pont Company . . . But they proceeded from opposite poles. The du Pont Company then was

*Copyright 1963 by Alfred P. Sloan Jr., © renewed 1991 by Alfred P. Sloan Foundation. Reprinted by permission of Harold Matson Co., Inc.

evolving from a centralized type of organization, common in the early days of American Industry, while General Motors was emerging from almost total decentralization . . .

The two types of operating problems, one arising from too much centralization (du Pont) and the other from too much decentralization (General Motors), were soon to be met by many large American manufacturing enterprises.

The principles of organization got more attention among us than they did then in the universities. If what follows seems academic, I assure you that we did not think it so.

The "Organization Study". . . began as follows:

1. The responsibility attached to the chief executive of each operation shall in no way be limited. Each such organization headed by its chief executive shall be complete in every necessary function and enabled to exercise its full initiative and logical development.
2. Certain central organization functions are absolutely essential to the logical development and proper control of the Corporation's activities.

. . . I am amused to see that the language is contradictory, and that its very contradiction is the crux of the matter . . . The language of organization has always suffered some want of words to express the true facts and circumstances of human interaction. One usually asserts one aspect or another of it at different times, such as the absolute independence of the part, and again the need of co-ordination, and again the concept of the whole with a guiding center. Interaction, however, is the thing . . .

The primary object of the corporation, therefore, we declared was to make money, not just to make motor cars . . . We proposed in general that General Motors should place its cars at the top of each price range and make them of such a quality that they would attract sales from below that price . . . This amounted to quality competition against cars below a given price tag, and price competition against cars above that price tag . . .

In 1921 Ford had about 60 per cent of the total car and truck market in units, and Chevrolet had about 4 per cent . . . it would have been suicidal to compete with him head on. No conceivable amount of capital short of the United States Treasury could have sustained the losses required to take volume away from him at his own game. The strategy we devised was to take a bit from the top of his position.

FROM CHAPTER 8, "THE DEVELOPMENT OF FINANCIAL CONTROLS"

The big gap in our information system at headquarters and in the divisions was at the retail level . . . We were not in touch with the actual retail market . . .

In a certain very important sense, this [planning system] involved the reconciliation of the work of two kinds of persons in General Motors—essential, I should think, in any corporation with a nationally distributed consumer product. One kind is the sales manager with his natural enthusiasm . . . The other is the statistical person who makes his analyses objectively on broad general evidence of demand . . .

It was on the financial side that the last necessary key to decentralization with co-ordinated control was found. That key, in principle, was the concept that, if we had the means to review and judge the effectiveness of operations, we could safely leave the prosecution of those operations to the men in charge of them . . . The basic elements of financial control in General Motors are cost, price, volume, and rate of return on investment.

FROM CHAPTER 9, "TRANSFORMATION OF THE AUTOMOBILE MARKET"

Seldom, perhaps at only one other time in the history of the industry—that is, on the occasion of the rise of the Model T after 1908—has the industry changed so radically as it did through the middle twenties. I say luckily for us because as a challenger to the then established position of Ford, we were favored by change. We had no stake in the old ways of the automobile business; for us, change meant opportunity.

These new elements I think I can without significant loss reduce to four: installment selling, the used-car trade-in, the closed body, and the annual model. (I would add improved roads if I were to take into account the environment of the automobile.)

[Mr. Ford's] precious volume, which was the foundation of his position, was fast disappearing . . . yet not many observers expected so catastrophic and almost whimsical a fall as Mr. Ford chose to take in May

1927 when he shut down his great River Rouge plant completely and kept it shut down for nearly a year to retool, leaving the field to Chevrolet unopposed and opening it up for Mr. Chrysler's Plymouth. Mr. Ford regained sales leadership again in 1929, 1930, and 1935, but, speaking in terms of generalities, he had lost the lead to General Motors. Mr. Ford, who had had so many brilliant insights in earlier years, seemed never to understand how completely the market had changed from the one in which he made his name and to which he was accustomed . . .

By the mid-twenties, the product engineer had begun to feel the influence of the sales people . . . Now he devotes much of his skill to solving the problems created by the stylist . . . Automobile design is not, of course, pure fashion, but it is not too much to say that the "laws" of the Paris dressmakers have come to be a factor in the automobile industry— and woe to the company which ignores them.

We employed women as automobile designers, to express the woman's point of view. We were the first to do so, I believe, and today we have the largest number of them in the industry.

PROLOGUE TO CHAPTER 9

The American economy is the biggest and by most measures the most successful in the world's history. What made the United States such an economic juggernaut? Was the country simply lucky? Did it somehow get the political and economic "basics" right, with its Constitution of 1787? Was its rich endowment of natural resources the key?

This chapter emphasizes certain factors while necessarily relegating others to the background. Highlighted here are the capitalist origins of the United States, the diversity and rapid growth of its population, its quick and attentive response to market signals, and its particular mix of public policies, which gave strong encouragement to entrepreneurs.

In thinking about reasons for American success, you might also ask yourself two questions that are posed specifically at the end of the chapter: Was individualism carried too far in the United States? Was the nation's economic success worth the social cost that it exacted in the daily lives of the American people?

These questions lead to others: Was there, at some point in American history, a golden age when that social cost was not so severe? Or are Americans actually living in a golden age today? Was the United States a meritocracy through most of its history? Is it one now? If the rich in America become richer and the poor poorer, does that situation, in itself, threaten the tradition of broad opportunity that lies at the core of the nation's experience? If income distribution is very uneven, then does a country's level of per capita income accurately reflect the quality of most of its people's lives?

Like the earlier "country" chapters on British and German capitalism, this one on the United States is merely an introduction. Because it emphasizes the elements of successful economic growth, it does not provide adequate coverage of some other important topics. These include slavery, the dispossession of American Indians, and other issues rooted in race, gender, and class. We can't cover these topics well, but we can ask some questions about them: How intricately were both the "good" and the "bad" elements of American life interwoven into the fabric of American business history? To what extent did the prosperity of white Americans as a whole derive from the exploitation of nonwhite Americans? Was the country's relentless territorial expansion inevitable?

Many Americans tend to regard the United States as *the* model of capitalist development—the base case, the one good way. But that line of thinking is not only parochial, it is seriously mistaken. The history of American capitalism is extraordinarily significant, but it offers only one among many models of successful development.

Growth of the United States

OREGON COUNTRY 1846

MEXICAN ACQUISITION 1848

LOUISIANA PURCHASE 1803

AREA OF THE ORIGINAL UNITED STATES 1783

GADSDEN PURCHASE 1853

TEXAS ANNEXATION 1845

ALASKA PURCHASE 1867

1813

1810

FLORIDA 1819

HAWAII ANNEXED 1898

During the nineteenth century, the United States purchased or took (mostly from Mexico) vast territories, until it became one of the largest countries in the world.

(Harvard Map Collection, 1997)

Henry Ford and his son Edsel, posing in the late 1920s beside Henry's original "quad-ricycle" of 1896 and the 15 millionth Model T.

(Courtesy Ford Motor Company/Historical Collections, Baker Library, Harvard Business School)

The Model T assembly line in about 1914. This innovation fundamentally changed the process of mass production for consumer durables, and it came to symbolize many aspects of the Second Industrial Revolution.

(Courtesy Ford Motor Company/Historical Collections, Baker Library, Harvard Business School)

Alfred P. Sloan Jr. in his office in 1924, shortly after he became President of General Motors. Sloan was the chief architect of GM's victory over Ford, and one of the greatest professional managers in modern business history.

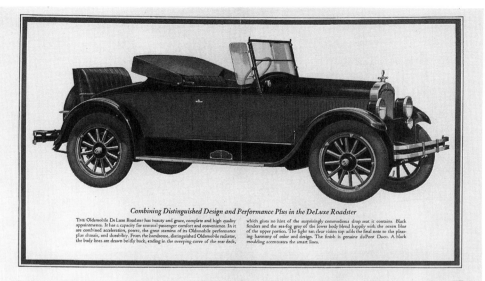

Combining Distinguished Design and Performance Plus in the DeLuxe Roadster

THE Oldsmobile De Luxe Roadster has beauty and grace, complete and high quality appointments. It has a capacity for unusual passenger comfort and convenience. In it are combined acceleration, power, the great stamina of its Oldsmobile performance plus chassis, and durability. From the handsome, distinguished Oldsmobile radiator, the body lines are drawn boldly back, ending in the sweeping curve of the rear deck, which gives no hint of the surprisingly commodious drop seat it contains. Black fenders and the sea-fog gray of the lower body blend happily with the ocean blue of the upper portion. The light tan clear vision top adds the final note to the pleasing harmony of color and design. The finish is genuine du Pont Duco. A black moulding accentuates the smart lines.

High in Quality – Low in Price

The 1925 Oldsmobile De Luxe Roadster. The original photograph was in color, and the ad copy in the center informs the reader that "black fenders and the sea-fog gray of the lower body blend happily with the ocean blue of the upper portion." The whole composition captures GM's strategy of marketing and of Phase III market segmentation.

(Courtesy General Motors Corporation/Historical Collections, Baker Library, Harvard Business School)

CHEVROLET

℘HROUGH Chevrolet, the world's largest builder of automobiles, General Motors offers both economical transportation and quality at low cost—a six in the price range of the four . . . from $525 to $725

More segmentation of the market. The 1929 Chevrolet, as it appeared in a trade catalogue. The original of this photograph was also in vivid color—the car green, the flowers red, yellow, and lavender.

(Courtesy General Motors Corporation/Historical Collections, Baker Library, Harvard Business School)

T. J. Watson in the 1890s, early in his career as a traveling salesman. His first sales job was peddling sewing machines off the back of a wagon. He and his son built IBM into one of the world's most important companies, and he remained focused on the marketing function throughout his life.

(Courtesy IBM Archives)

The two Thomas J. Watsons in 1917. Already they seem to feel the tension that always characterized their relationship.

(Courtesy IBM Archives)

This picture of T. J. Watson beneath his famous motto "THINK" hung in IBM offices all over the world during the early 1950s. It typified the cult of personality that dominated this patriarchal "family" company.

(Courtesy IBM Archives)

Handing over the reins in 1956. Tom Watson Jr. commented about this picture that his father seemed a little nervous about the transfer of power, while he himself was full of confidence.

(Courtesy IBM Archives)

The IBM System/360, 1964. The sleek design of this phenomenally successful product expressed the modernist aesthetic that form should follow function.

(Courtesy IBM Archives)

9

AMERICAN CAPITALISM

Thomas K. McCraw

Capitalism came in the first ships.

Carl N. Degler, *Out of Our Past* [1]

No nation has been more market-oriented in its origins and subsequent history than the United States of America. The very settling of the country, from the Atlantic to the Pacific and onward to Alaska and Hawaii, was one long entrepreneurial adventure. Even down to the present day, more Americans have probably made fortunes from the appreciation of real estate values than from any other source. But land is only the starting place for the epochal drama of American capitalism. That story, in comparison with the long-term business histories of all other large countries, has been one of intense and incessant competition. Americans have persistently shown themselves willing to follow market forces with relatively little hesitation.

In the early years, Americans' ravenous appetite for land was born of European deprivation confronting New World opportunity. Demand, which had been pent up for centuries, suddenly encountered plentiful supply. The settlers' hunger for more and more territory thrust them relentlessly westward, where they could establish farms and ranches that they themselves could *own*. This was the American Dream in its earliest form, and for the people living the dream, it had an aura of double-edged incredulity. There was disbelief not only at their own good fortune, but also at the backbreaking work required to capitalize on it.

From the colonial period through the early national years, and on into the nineteenth century, everything seemed up for grabs in the new country. Vast, apparently unlimited tracts of land were given away by the government or sold at irresistibly low prices. To get the best land, neither the first colonists nor the pioneers pressing across the frontier had much compunction about dispossessing Native Americans or each other. Sometimes they resorted to outright murder. The movement west constituted a great epic, but in its details was not a pretty story.[2]

Land was available in prodigal abundance in early American history, but it is only one of the classic economic "factors of production." The others are labor, capital, and entrepreneurship. As the earlier chapters of this book have shown, modern capitalism fuses these four factors into operational systems for the conduct of economic life, most notably through the ingenious device of the business corporation.

There are several million corporations in the United States today, and a handful existed at the nation's official birth in 1776. The device became integral to the American economy only in the middle nineteenth century, but it was actually present at the creation 250 years earlier. In 1607, the settlers at Jamestown arrived under the charter of the Virginia Company of London. Puritans founded Boston in 1630 under the auspices of another English corporation, the Massachusetts Bay Company.

The proprietors of the Virginia Company soon were interested primarily in revenues from tobacco. Those of the Massachusetts Bay Company cared less about profit than about setting up what their leader John Winthrop called a "City upon a Hill." They wanted to demonstrate for all humanity the virtues of clean Christian living. If some of the Puritan merchants among them became moderately wealthy, then that might be a sign of God's grace, so long as customers were not cheated or overcharged. The line between virtuous profit and damnable avarice was blurry then, as it remains today. But the Puritans had an unmistakably capitalist turn of mind.[3]

So did William Penn and his community of Friends. Persecuted in England for their religious beliefs, they acquired in 1681 a royal grant of land in America, and proceeded to develop their new colony on both religious and commercial principles. The Quaker merchants of Pennsylvania became prosperous international traders. Like the Puritan merchants of New England, they used their familial and religious connections to form a tight network of trustworthy relationships stretching over long distances.[4] This kind of system for making credible business commitments is one of the essential conditions of strong economic development. In most capitalist economies today, it is embedded in the intricate law of contracts enforced by governments through courts.

Still another English corporation instrumental in populating the New World was the Royal African Company. Chartered in 1672, this company proceeded to take a significant though not dominant part in the slave trade. For the profit of shareholders, it brought to the western hemisphere masses of men and women who had been taken from Africa against their will. Eventually, many thousands of white merchants and seamen on both sides of the Atlantic participated in this commerce, including several hundred from Massachusetts and Rhode Island. The total number of Africans transported to the New World was about 10 million. Their destination was usually Brazil or one of the Caribbean sugar islands, but some 596,000, or about one of every 17, went to areas that became part of the United States.[5]

In 1776, the 13 colonies that made up the original United States declared their independence after almost 170 years of British colonial status. Even at that early date, the new country's population of 2.5 million included plentiful examples of capitalism's many faces. Then as now, capitalism could serve despicable ends, noble ones, or some mixture of the two.

In between the oppressed slaves on the one hand and free yeoman farmers and entrepreneurs on the other stood a large number of whites who had come to America as indentured servants. Between one-half and two-thirds of all white immigrants before the Revolution arrived under these terms. They flocked to America mainly from England, but also from Scotland, Ireland, and Germany. (Germans tended to come in family groups, the others as single adults.) A few were abducted and taken aboard ship by force, but most made the trip voluntarily. They exchanged four to seven years' labor for passage to the New World.[6]

So capitalism did come in the first ships, and in many different forms: legitimate commerce, legal cover for religious freedom, the slave trade, and individuals' exchange of labor for a ticket to America. Yet none of these examples represented *modern* capitalism. Few had much to do with the First Industrial Revolution, let alone the Second or Third. Each concerned farming, commerce, and trading, not technology and manufacturing. But all contained powerful elements of capitalism, and that proved to be momentous for the nation's future.

The Contours of American Capitalism

In the 200-odd years since the writing of the Constitution, some of the most striking attributes of American capitalism have been:

1. the systematic development of the North American continent's rich natural resources;
2. the deliberate diversification of the national economy away from agriculture and into manufacturing, mining, and services;
3. the exceptional heterogeneity and energy of the American people;
4. the effectiveness of public policies in promoting growth.

None of these conditions, either alone or in combination, entirely accounts for the American record of sustained economic progress. Most obviously, rich soil and mineral deposits cannot suffice by themselves. Many lavishly endowed countries, both old ones (China, Russia), and new (Argentina, Zaire) have never approached the long-term growth record of the United States. By contrast, some meagerly endowed countries (Japan, Switzerland) have taken their places among the richest nations of the world. They have usually done so through the education of their people and careful attention to the quality of their products.

If resource endowments are to generate long-term advantage, then value must be added to the raw materials. The final products must become plywood and paper, not just trees; steel beams and sheets, not just coal and iron ore; gasoline and petrochemicals, not just crude oil. More than any other economy, American capitalism has added tremendous value to its natural resources. Some famous corporate names underscore the point: Weyerhaeuser, Champion, Georgia Pacific; USX, Bethlehem, Republic; Exxon, Mobil, Du Pont.[7]

A pattern of systematic development also characterized American agriculture. In the year 1800, 74 percent of the American labor force worked on farms. (The figure today is under 2 percent.) There were some prosperous tobacco plantations in Virginia and Maryland, but most farmers and their families, which is to say most Americans, grew crops primarily for their own consumption. They had already started to barter with each other, and to buy and sell produce in significant quantities. So some specialization had begun. This shift in farming patterns was the real inauguration of American capitalism on a broad scale, at least outside the major (but still small) commercial cities of the eastern seaboard. From the rising productivity of agriculture, including the lucrative slave-based cotton economy, came the burst of growth that engendered mass capitalism in the United States.[8]

The American People

Throughout the nineteenth century, the population grew dramatically in both numbers and diversity. In 1800, there had been only 5.3 million people in the United States, less than half as many as in the U.K. at that time, and only a fifth as many as in France. This population was mostly of British, German, and African descent.

A century later, in 1900, the American people had become much more numerous and very much more diverse. The population had multiplied by a factor of almost 15, from 5.3 million to about 76 million, a total larger than that of any European nation except Russia. No other country had ever grown this fast over so long a period. During most individual *decades,* the American population increased by about one-third. If that nineteenth-century growth rate had continued through the twentieth century, the population of the United States today would be well over one billion, or four times what it actually is.

Even more striking was the diversity of the people. By the start of the twentieth century, fewer than half of all Americans were both white and the children of two native-born parents. Put another way, most Americans at that time were either nonwhite, immigrants, or the children of at least one immigrant parent. Applied to a mass population of 76 million, this was an almost unbelievable degree of racial and cultural heterogeneity, something new in the world. The situation differed radically from that in Britain, France, Germany, Italy, and Japan, all of which were ethnically homogeneous. The one notable exception in those countries was the multicultural makeup of the business community in London. But even so, only 6 percent of London's total population in 1890 had come from outside the British Isles. By contrast, 80 percent of New York's citizens were immigrants or the children of immigrants, 87 percent of Chicago's, and 84 percent of Detroit's and Milwaukee's.[9] By 1900 there were likely more people of Italian descent in New York than in any Italian city except Rome, and probably more Jews than in any other city anywhere. More people of Polish descent likely lived in Chicago than in any Polish city except Warsaw. Four-and-a-quarter million Irish people had emigrated to the United States between 1820 and 1920, which was more than the total remaining in Ireland itself in 1920. Substantial numbers of Asian and Hispanic immigrants had begun to arrive as well, though not yet in the large totals that would come late in the twentieth century.[10]

Of course, immigrants would not have continued to pour into the country had the economy not been growing. Nor would the economy have grown so fast without the immigrants, most of whom were vigorous and hard-working young adults. So the relationship was reciprocal from the beginning. The diversity that resulted from immigration paid off economically because of the ability of American society to absorb and exploit the best that each contributing culture had to offer, without falling into fatally divisive ethnic conflicts. This accomplishment has not come easily, and it constitutes one of the distinguishing triumphs of the United States.

Even so, by the middle of the nineteenth century there was passionate disagreement about what the country's ethnic makeup and immigration policy should be, just as there would be at the close of the twentieth century.[11] This disagreement folded into larger questions of how the American national character should be shaped and how the economy should be developed. Arguments over those issues had been going on since the time of the Declaration of Independence.

Public Policies, Economic Diversification, and Nineteenth-Century Growth

Thomas Jefferson, 1780: "Those who labour in the earth are the chosen people of God, if ever he had a chosen people . . . While we have land to labour then, let us never wish to see our citizens occupied at a workbench. . . . The mobs of great cities add just so much to the support of pure government, as sores do to the strength of the human body."[12]

Alexander Hamilton, 1791: "Manufacturing pursuits are susceptible to a greater degree of the application of machinery, than those of Agriculture. If so, all the difference is lost to a community which, instead of manufacturing for itself, procures the fabrics requisite to its supply from other Countries. The substitution of foreign for domestic manufactures is a transfer to foreign nations of the advantages accruing from the employment of Machinery."[13]

As it turned out, the American people enjoyed the best of both worlds. They fulfilled Jefferson's dream of a vast land populated by yeoman farmers. And they brought to fruition Hamilton's vision of a diversified economy that took full advantage of manufacturing and production by machine. Whereas in 1800 the national economy had been overwhelmingly agricultural, by the 1880s it had become remarkably diverse. And by 1890, barely a hundred years after its founding, the United States was the world's leading agricultural *and* industrial country, as it remains today.[14]

The bitter fights at the nation's birth between the followers of Hamilton and those of Jefferson centered on the creation of an appropriate infrastructure for economic growth. Hamilton argued in favor of what he called "energetic" government. As the nation's first Secretary of the Treasury, he wished to convert an underdeveloped farming economy into a diversified modern one. An energetic government would help build roads and canals, sponsor a national banking system, and offer protective tariffs and cash bounties to manufacturers. In addition, as Hamilton rather tactlessly put it, public officials should do everything they could to tie "the monied interest" to policies of the national government.[15]

Jefferson, a Virginia planter, saw nothing but trouble in Hamilton's plans. The nation's first Secretary of State, Jefferson was one of the greatest apostles of personal liberty in the annals of history, even though he himself owned slaves. He opposed "energy" in government, and argued for minimal interference in citizens' lives. It horrified him that the "monied interest" Hamilton was wooing included avaricious speculators along with honest merchants and planters. He was convinced that Hamilton's program to encourage manufactures would create in unspoiled America the kind of urban squalor and moral decay that Jefferson had seen in Europe during his years as Minister to France. Hamilton, who had grown up poor on the Caribbean island of St. Croix and had come to the United States at the age of 15, had no experience with Europe and no fear of cities. But he did have an extreme aversion to poverty, and a matching conviction that government must be active in economic development.

The bickering between Hamilton and Jefferson, two supremely talented public servants, made early debates over American economic policy exceedingly contentious. That situation has persisted down to the present time, and for the same reason that got it started between Hamilton and Jefferson: the tradeoff between government "energy" and private liberty.

When Jefferson became President in 1801, he began to see things a bit differently, and to act with considerable energy himself. In 1803 he went after the Louisiana Territory and secured its purchase from Napoleon. At one stroke, he thereby doubled the size of the United States, which was already a big country. Jefferson and his brilliant Secretary of the Treasury, the Swiss-born Albert Gallatin, began to appreciate the need for government action in creating a transportation infrastructure. In 1803, Jefferson signed legislation that included a provision for building a "National Road" across the Allegheny Mountains. This key east-west route formed a link between the Potomac River, which flows into the Atlantic Ocean, and the Ohio, which flows westward into the Mississippi and thence to the Gulf of Mexico. Many Americans opposed even this kind of federal activity. But the virtues of the National Road were so obvious that all objections were overcome. The road was constructed and periodically upgraded. It is still in use today as U.S. Highway 40 and Interstate 68.

"The American System"

Federal aid for "internal improvements"—roads, canals, bridges, and, over the next 200 years, railroads, interstate highways, and airports—remained controversial. Federal support rose and fell according to party politics, the need to supplement private capital, and the question of whether the national government or the states had primary authority. One of the greatest of all internal improvements, the Erie Canal from Albany to Buffalo, was built with New York state funds. The financing of this huge project, which cost ten times as much as the authorized capital of the largest manufacturing company then in existence, gave birth during the 1820s to a substantial bond market in New York City. It thereby boosted the development of Wall Street as a money center.[16]

Soon Pennsylvania, Ohio, Indiana, and Illinois were sponsoring their own elaborate canal projects. Often states depleted their treasuries in futile attempts to duplicate New York's success. After several embarrassing debacles, some states enacted new constitutions forbidding further bond issues of this kind. Some required that budgets be balanced annually, a provision that still survives in many state constitutions. But a great deal of public support for economic development came from state and local funds rather than federal ones, and that is still true today.[17]

Even so, the United States Congress, like most national legislatures, has usually acted to stimulate development. At an early date, Congress decided that domestic producers must enjoy some protection from manufactured imports. During the first few decades of the American nation's existence, its manufacturing sector was not very competitive, as productivity in Britain during the First Industrial Revolution outstripped that of any other country. British-connected merchants proved willing to "dump" on the American market cargoes of ironware, pottery, and textiles, at prices that undercut those of local manufacturers.

Nascent American producers, together with their political representatives, acted to remedy this situation. The result was a long series of tariff acts, starting with the first Congress in 1789. As it happened, import duties on foreign goods also were the main source of revenue for the federal treasury. So the tariff question became a staple of rancorous political discourse. Policy evolved on an ad hoc basis, then became explicitly protectionist with the Tariff of 1828. The whole issue remained heated throughout that century, largely because of the regional diversity of the nation's economy. Manufacturers in such states as Pennsylvania and New Jersey wanted tariff protection. But in the South, planters who sold their tobacco and cotton on world markets saw no reason why they should pay inflated prices for manufactured imports, just to benefit producers living in the North.[18]

Today it is hard to recapture the fervor or even the mind-set behind the acrimonious debates over protectionism. Americans born after World War II became accustomed to thinking of the United States as a bastion of open markets. They tended to take the virtues of free trade as self-evident. They often forgot that historically, American policy was not one of free trade at all. Instead, it was consistently protectionist. Some of the most famous American leaders of the nineteenth century spoke out in favor of encouraging domestic manufactures, protecting the home market, or both:

> *James Madison* (congressman, principal author of the Constitution, Secretary of State, and President from 1809 to 1817): "The meaning of the phrase 'to regulate trade,' must be sought in the general use of it . . . when the phrase was inserted in the Constitution. The power has been understood and used by all commercial and manufacturing nations, as embracing the object of encouraging manufactures. It is believed that not a single exception can be named."

Abraham Lincoln (congressman, President from 1861 to 1865, and emancipator of the slaves): "I do not know much about the tariff, but I know this much, when we buy manufactured goods abroad we get the goods and the foreigner gets the money. When we buy the manufactured goods at home we get both the goods and the money."

William McKinley (congressman, Governor of Ohio, and President from 1897 to 1901): "We lead all nations in agriculture; we lead all nations in mining; we lead all nations in manufacturing. These are the trophies which we bring after [several decades] of a protective tariff."[19]

One of the greatest of all nineteenth-century statesmen, Henry Clay, provided the first full articulation of a thoroughgoing program for economic development. With his ear for a good slogan, Clay entitled his plan "The American System." In speeches and legislative bills, he proceeded to sketch out an overall blueprint for internal improvements, tariff protection, and encouragement of manufactures. In 1824, when Clay was Speaker of the House of Representatives, he delivered what became a famous oration on the subject: "We must speedily adopt a genuine American policy. Still cherishing the foreign market, let us create also a home market, to give further scope to the consumption of the produce of American industry. Let us counteract the [protectionist] policy of foreigners, and withdraw the support which we now give to their industry, and stimulate that of our own country."[20]

In modern terminology, Clay was outlining a strategy of "import substitution" as a route to economic development—a substitution of home manufactures for imports. Like Hamilton, Clay was an ardent nationalist. His plan for a network of canals and turnpikes was aimed at promoting harmony in a country rife with sectional discord. Under his "American System," the industrializing Northeast and Middle Atlantic states would secure new markets in the South. The South itself would keep its vast international market for cotton, which made up more than half of all American exports in the decades before the Civil War and almost that much long afterward. Under Clay's plan, the South would purchase fewer imports from Europe and more products made in America.

The Middle West and Upper South, meanwhile, would be opened for development by a transportation system designed to penetrate the Allegheny Mountain barrier in many places. As for the tariff, it would not only protect American manufactures, but would also generate revenues for the new network of internal improvements. The salient aspect of Henry Clay's American System was that it *was* a *system,* not just a convenient marriage of unrelated policies.

Like Abraham Lincoln, who as a young politician idolized him, Clay had been born in the "western" state of Kentucky. He thought of himself as neither a "Yankee" nor a Southerner, but a Westerner and a prophet of economic development. As a committed nationalist, he was determined to tie the Union together economically and prevent it from splitting apart over the agonizing issue of slavery. Yet Clay and his entire generation failed in this effort. The institution of slavery was too morally corrupt to be offset by economic forces. So the Union broke apart during the Civil War, which lasted from 1861 to 1865. It was one of the bloodiest conflicts in human history up to that time.

More than half a million American soldiers died in that war, almost as many as the combined total for all other wars in the nation's history down to the present time. But, as President Lincoln said in 1864 in his second inaugural address, the goal of emancipation was worth whatever price might be required. If God willed that the war must go on "until all the wealth piled by the bondsman's two hundred and fifty years of unrequited toil shall be sunk, and until every drop of blood drawn with the lash shall be paid by another drawn with the sword," then the country would have to pay that price. Slavery was a malignancy, a curse to America's existence as a nation. It had to be eradicated.[21]

The Civil War ended legal bondage for 4 million people, but the abolition of slavery did not by any means confer equal bargaining power upon those who had been liberated. Racism and oppression continued, and progress toward equality was painfully slow. Even so, African Americans took a steadily increasing role in economic life, and the nation profited commensurately. The war's other main economic effects were the integration of the Middle West more tightly into the business system of the East, and the direct promotion of industrial development by the federal government. With southern representatives out of Congress during the war and less influential afterward, legislation to promote growth became easier to pass. And in the very long run, the war also reduced sectional discord between North and South. In all of these ways the war helped to fulfill Henry Clay's plans for a unified national economy.[22]

The American System as a full-blown industrial policy, however, was never implemented in the sweeping way Clay had envisioned. It smacked of a more powerful and directive national government than many American voters were prepared to endorse. Before the Civil War, it had been vigorously opposed by Andrew Jackson and other leaders of the Democratic Party.

Even so, in the decades before 1870 federal aid continued in the form of substantial land grants to railroads. Just as important, individual cities and states stepped into the breach with their own assistance programs to banks, canals, and railroads. So the dream of an integrated, diversified, and booming national economy—the aspiration of Hamilton, Clay, Lincoln, and many others—eventually came true.

As for the keystone of the American System, the protective tariff, no other public issue with the exception of slavery proved to be more divisive. Debates over trade policy constituted a hardy perennial not only of American politics but also of academic economics in the years when that discipline began to be taught. In the 1880s, the University of Pennsylvania required that its new economics professor not support free trade. Cornell met the problem by appointing two lecturers, one on each side of the controversy. The free traders usually won the academic debates, and they still do so today. But for more than a century, from the 1820s to the 1930s, political forces advocating the protection of infant, adolescent, or ailing industries triumphed in Congress. So the American economy grew to maturity behind tariff walls averaging close to 30 percent of the value of all imports, and much more than that on dutiable imports.[23]

Whether such a high degree of protection was necessary for healthy growth is not at all clear. Most economists believe that the enormous size and thorough integration of the American market, which spurred domestic competition, lessened the harmful effect that protection from foreign competition would otherwise have had. But there can be no question that the United States protected its home market, just as Germany did during the key period of its economic growth (1879–1914), and as Japan did during and after its own "miracle growth" era (1951–73). The wisdom and efficacy of these policies remain open to question; but their systematic implementation is a settled historical fact. In America throughout the nineteenth century, the law was on the side of producers who were protected, not consumers who paid higher prices as a result. The immediate impact of tariffs unquestionably damaged consumer interests. But the long-term dynamic effect may have promoted a staged development of some industries from infancy to adolescence to healthy adulthood.[24]

Hospitality toward Business

Besides tariff policy, American law evolved in many additional ways that favored the interests of producers and other entrepreneurs over those of consumers. Nineteenth-century banking regulations, for example, were either nonexistent or quite liberal. For several decades around the middle of the century it remained possible in some states for almost anyone to operate a bank and issue paper currency. (That practice ended during the Civil War.) Over the years, it also became easier to form a limited liability corporation for any legitimate business purpose. This development was crucial for the Second Industrial Revolution, when big new companies needed unprecedented amounts of capital. Formerly, a special enactment of law had been required to "charter" each individual firm, and such an unwieldy system retarded growth because legislatures could not keep up with the demand for corporate charters. Like other elements in the evolution of modern capitalism, this one was gradual and cumulative. It was a complex process, and it did not happen all at once.[25]

The law helped to accelerate growth in still other ways, sometimes at a heavy human price. There were practically no regulations at all for environmental protection, and cities such as Pittsburgh and Chicago grew so dirty from the burning of coal that sunlight could hardly pierce their smoky air. Industrialization also pressed hard on workers. Throughout American history until the 1930s, the government often hindered union organizing, and sometimes it directly assisted corporations in their battles against striking employees. In all kinds of disputes, courts tended to side with employers. The law seemed to encourage businesses to treat their workers however they wished, exempting companies from damages from most deaths and injuries suffered on the job. The justification for this policy lay primarily in the doctrine of freedom of contract, which is so important to capitalist development. In the early years of industrialization, the principle was used to justify the "freedom" of workers to contract for dangerous jobs and toil 72-hour weeks.

Meanwhile, American bankruptcy law was being interpreted more and more leniently, so as to favor business debtors over creditors. The practice of imprisonment for debt was abolished in the United States long before it disappeared from Europe. Many American entrepreneurs whose names became household words, such as R. H. Macy and H. J. Heinz, suffered repeated business failures before achieving breakthrough success. The law encouraged them to try again. More broadly, the lenient American attitude toward bankruptcy changed the burden of risk-sharing in new ventures, allowing owners to pursue ever-riskier projects. This is one of the hidden reasons why the American business system has tended to be more entrepreneurial than that of other countries.

From the beginning, American capitalism exhibited many elements of what later came to be called the "mixed economy." Government activity at every level was energetic, though often chaotic. As a perceptive historian once wrote about nineteenth-century American government, "King Laissez Faire" was "not only dead; the hallowed report of his reign had all been a mistake."[26] The policies followed by American city, state, and national governments toward business during the nineteenth century were haphazard and uncoordinated. But in the aggregate, they constituted a reasonably coherent formula. In the awkward syntax of modern academic jargon, that formula today would be called an import-substitution but still market-conforming and entrepreneurially oriented strategy for rapid economic growth in a developing country.

For most of its history, the United States has been the nation in the world most open to entrepreneurial opportunity, the one whose laws best encouraged rapid economic growth. All of the ideas and movements mentioned above—the American System, the law of corporations and contracts, lenient bank and bankruptcy laws, and the freedom of employers to damage the environment and exploit their workers (freedoms later curtailed)—added up to a hothouse for the growth of business. The flowers of private enterprise did the actual growing and made up the final bouquet. But without the hothouse, and without close attention to the provision of plentiful sunlight, warmth, and moisture, the flowers could never have blossomed so spectacularly.

The Evolution of Big Business

The same generalization about the United States is valid not only for the nineteenth century, but for most of the twentieth as well. As a rough guide, imagine four broad categories of potential government intervention in capitalist economies:

1. laissez faire, with minimal intervention;
2. frequent, uncoordinated intervention in a mostly free market;
3. systematic state guidance of private decision-making;
4. thorough state management and decision-making for the whole economy.

The record throughout American history hovers around category 2. In this sense, events interacting with the national temper resulted in a compromise between the ideas of Thomas Jefferson and those of Alexander Hamilton. Whereas Jefferson, especially before he became president, favored the least possible government and therefore preferred category 1, Hamilton with his "energetic" and coordinated policies embraced category 3. But the actual record of the United States places it in neither 1 nor 3, but squarely in category 2.[27]

Residence in category 2 is one of the salient constants of the nation's 220-year existence. The American experience has shifted around within this category, but has never left it for long. As a nation, the United States has spent no time at all in either category 1 (laissez faire) or category 4 (thorough state management). And only during periods of major war (1861–65, 1917–18, 1941–45) has it taken up temporary residence in category 3.[28] Category 2, frequent but uncoordinated intervention in a mostly free market, has been the real "American System." That was certainly true during the last half of the nineteenth century, when big business began to flower.

During the years of the First Industrial Revolution in America, most businesses had been conducted as proprietorships or partnerships. A small number of banks, turnpikes, and canals were incorporated as joint-stock companies, as were a handful of factories. A few of these early companies still survive and prosper today, as members of the *Fortune* 500. Such companies include the Bank of New York and BankBoston (then called Massachusetts Bank), both of which appeared in the 1780s. In the 1790s came the Insurance Company of North America, known today as Cigna, and Providence Bank, now known as Fleet Financial Group. Today's Du Pont chemical firm was founded in 1802 as a small gunpowder company. In 1812 came the City Bank of New York, now called Citicorp. In 1827 appeared the Baltimore & Ohio Railroad, now part of the huge CSX system. All of these companies remained small-scale in their early years. At most they employed a few hundred people. By far the majority of American business was still done by much smaller enterprises involving individual merchants and artisans.[29]

After the Second Industrial Revolution began in the 1840s, however, companies in a few industries quickly grew much bigger. The corporate form now proved to be an essential device for mobilizing the unprecedented amounts of capital required to construct large-scale railroads, telegraph lines, factories, and pipelines.

The first big businesses in America, the railroads, were organized in the 1830s and 1840s. By the 1850s a few rail corporations had grown to very substantial size, their tracks connecting cities and towns hundreds of miles apart. And during this crucial development of the nation's transportation network, a formidable array of new management challenges suddenly surfaced.[30]

The operation of a railroad required innovative techniques in finance, accounting, engineering, labor relations, and general management. It called for an endless variety of *decisions,* ranging from the immediate (when to take a locomotive in for repair) to the very long term (when, where, and how to finance and build a transcontinental line). An almost overwhelming roster of problems bedeviled managers: whether to build expensively for the ages (the engineering style in most of Europe), or quickly and cheaply for immediate needs (the usual American choice); how to market the large volume of stocks and bonds necessary for construction (the answer here was to sell securities everywhere, including Britain and Continental Europe); how to monitor the handling of cash by hundreds of employees; how to schedule train departures and arrivals; whether to mix freight and passenger traffic in the same train; and, most difficult of all, how to price—that is, how to calculate freight rates and passenger fares in a situation where the absence of competition took away the traditional regulator of price levels.[31]

On top of all these issues loomed the troubling problem of safety. Into a society accustomed for centuries to the speed of the dray horse and the mass of the wagonload, railroads introduced terrifying new conditions of random death and destruction. Locomotive smokestacks emitted flurries of sparks, which often set fire to houses, barns, fields, and prairies.

The coming of railroads also meant that hundreds of tons of metal were suddenly hurtling at phenomenal speeds through unfenced towns, countrysides, and grade crossings. Deaths of tramps, pedestrians, horseback riders, passengers, and railroad employees became all too commonplace. The grisly toll increased year by year, until by the 1890s trains were killing some 7,000 Americans annually.[32]

The key management challenge here was an organizational one: how to fix authority and responsibility so that railroad firms could operate safely, efficiently, and profitably. For many years, railroads seemed simply too big to manage. In the 1840s, the largest factories in the United States were employing perhaps 800 people. But railroad companies quickly came to employ several thousand, and by the end of the nineteenth century a few employed over 100,000.[33]

The only precedent for managing such enterprises was the kind of organizational structure designed for the huge "citizen armies" of Europe that had fought the Napoleonic Wars. So, in the United States, many graduates of West Point began to gravitate toward work on the railroads. As engineers and managers, they adapted to their new setting the line-and-staff distinctions between types of assignments for military officers. But armies do not have to show a profit. They usually shrink or disband when the war ends. So the central problems were quite different. And for several decades the search for solutions to what was called "the railroad problem" taxed the ingenuity of the brightest people in American business and government. As the writer Henry Adams (1838–1918) put it, his entire generation was "mortgaged to the railways."[34]

The spread of railroads occurred swiftly. There were only 23 miles of track in 1830, but 208,152 by 1890. Altogether, this was probably the largest and most sustained construction program in the world's history up to that time. And once the national railroad system began to emerge, the American economy was poised for a big leap forward.[35]

Commercial agriculture took off. Farms in the "breadbasket" regions of the Middle West grew to gigantic size. In the 1840s and afterward, new firms such as the Deering Company and the McCormick Perfected Reaper Company sprang up to supply harvesting machinery. (McCormick and Deering merged in 1902 to form International Harvester, which is now Navistar International.) Milling companies such as Pillsbury and Washburn-Crosby (Gold Medal Flour) followed in the 1880s and 1890s.

Soon the Middle West was producing at a volume far beyond national needs. It was exporting wheat and flour of greater value than the South's exports of tobacco, and in some years approaching that of cotton.[36]

Industrialization grew even faster than did agriculture. The $2.7 billion invested in American manufacturing in 1879 shot up to $8.2 billion in 1899, and to $20.8 billion in 1914. Capital invested per worker in manufacturing almost tripled between 1869 and 1899, going from about $700 to $2,000. The annual increase in total factor productivity, which had held steady at about 0.3 percent for most of the nineteenth century, now skyrocketed to a rate of 1.7 percent for the years 1889–1919. This was an almost unbelievable *sixfold* rise. Changes of such magnitude explain why historians and economists use the term "Second Industrial Revolution."[37]

Before the 1880s, even the largest manufacturing firms seldom had been capitalized at more than $1 million. But by 1900, John D. Rockefeller's Standard Oil Company had grown into a multinational corporation capitalized at $122 million. By 1904, James B. Duke and his colleagues had built the American Tobacco Company into a behemoth capitalized at $500 million. And in 1901, when the financier J. Pierpont Morgan engineered a merger of leading steel firms, including the giant company already built up by Andrew Carnegie, he capitalized the new United States Steel Corporation at $1.4 billion. At that time the nation's Gross National Product was about $21 billion. A similar deal done in the 1990s, expressed as the same proportion of GNP, would approach half a trillion dollars.[38]

U.S. Steel, American Tobacco, and Standard Oil were the three biggest manufacturing companies in the United States at the start of the twentieth century. Remarkably, almost half of the largest American firms at the *close* of the twentieth century (manufacturing and other types as well) originated during the period 1880–1930. These were the key years of the Second Industrial Revolution, and the growth of big business was the central trend of the American economy. Two hundred forty-seven of the *Fortune* 500 firms of the middle 1990s were founded during those fifty years: 53 companies in the 1880s, 39 in the 1890s, 52 in the 1900s, 45 in the 1910s, and 58 in the 1920s.[39]

Successive changes in the nature of the national economy can be traced through shifts in the kinds of companies that emerged from one decade to the next. Table 9.1 gives some examples from the *Fortune* 500 of the middle 1990s, with the companies' original names in parentheses where they differ substantially from present-day names. As the baseball player Yogi Berra is supposed to have said, "You can see a lot just by looking," and that maxim applies to this table. A visitor from another planet could make some accurate guesses about the evolution of the economy just by scrutinizing this roll call of companies. This visitor might ponder the nature of these firms, speculate about the rate and sequence of their establishment, tote up what industries they do and do not represent, and hypothesize about why they have proved so durable.

The decades listed are those of the companies' founding, not necessarily the time when they became large. Many firms remained small for a number of years, then became giants when demand for their products

Table 9.1   Founding Dates of *Fortune* 500 Companies, 1880s–1920s

Founded in the 1880s:
  Eastman Kodak
  Chiquita Brands International (Boston Fruit Co.)
  Johnson & Johnson
  Coca-Cola
  Westinghouse Electric
  Sears Roebuck (R.W. Sears Watch Co.)
  Avon Products (California Perfume Co.)
  Hershey Foods (Lancaster Caramel Co.)

Founded in the 1890s:
  General Electric
  Knight-Ridder (Ridder Publications)
  Ralston Purina (Robinson Danforth Co.)
  Reebok International (J.W. Foster and Sons)
  Harris Corp. (Harris Automatic Press Co.)
  Pepsico
  Goodyear Tire and Rubber

Founded in the 1900s:
  Weyerhaeuser
  USX (United States Steel)
  Ford Motor
  Gillette (American Safety Razor Co.)
  Minnesota Mining and Manufacturing
  United Parcel Service (Am. Messenger Service)
  General Motors
  McGraw-Hill

Founded in the 1910s:
  Black & Decker
  IBM (Computing-Tabulating-Recording Co.)
  Merrill Lynch
  Safeway (Skaggs United Stores)
  Boeing (Pacific Aero Products)
  Cummins Engine
  Reynolds Metals

Founded in the 1920s:

Chrysler	Delta Air Lines (Huff-Deland [Crop-]Dusters)
Time-Warner	Ace Hardware (Ace Stores Inc.)
Marriott Corp.	Fruit of the Loom (Union Underwear Co.)
Walt Disney	Northwest Airlines

Source: Selected from Harris Corporation, "Founding Dates of the 1994 *Fortune* 500 U.S. Companies," *Business History Review,* 70 (Spring 1996), pp. 69–90.

mushroomed or when they introduced an attractive new item into the market. Several companies mentioned, especially some that appeared during two periods of intense merger activity (the 1890s and 1920s), represent consolidations of smaller firms. Many companies listed for the period 1880–1910 grew big right after they went through a crucial phase of vertical integration. Typically, they integrated forward from manufacturing into marketing. Then, in a second step, they integrated backward into the sources of parts and raw materials supply.[40]

Other patterns can be deduced from the table, especially when it is combined with names of the companies mentioned earlier, such as the Bank of New York (1780s) and the Baltimore & Ohio Railroad (1820s). In the first few decades of the nineteenth century, as the First Industrial Revolution took root in the United States, commerce and finance began to be overshadowed by transportation and textile manufacturing. Then, toward the close of the nineteenth century, industries of the Second Industrial Revolution became dominant: steel, rubber, electrical machinery, and branded and packaged consumer goods. Finally, by the 1950s, the Second Industrial Revolution began to give way to the Third, with its emphasis on computer technology, information systems, and the service economy.

Table 9.2 gives a similar enumeration of firms for the most recent period.[41] A far lower proportion of the present-day *Fortune* 500 was created in recent decades than during the explosive period 1880–1930. And the companies created have tended to be to be quite different from the kinds of firms most characteristic of the Second Industrial Revolution. Just as Table 9.1 embodied the Second Industrial Revolution and its array of new goods manufactured for mass markets, Table 9.2 captures the essence of the Third Industrial Revolution. That movement was organized around information technology and the service economy. Computer firms are most conspicuous on the list, but health insurers, HMOs, and retail firms such as Wal-Mart, The Gap, and Office Depot grew rapidly as well. These innovative retailers depend on sophisticated information technology to manage their inventories and inform their managers about emerging consumer trends.

There is much that lists of the largest companies *cannot* tell us about the American business system. For one thing, regardless of century or decade, giant firms have never dominated the entire economy. Large companies appeared only in certain kinds of industries, and most industries

Table 9.2   Founding Dates of *Fortune* 500 Companies, 1930–1990s

Founded in the 1930s:	*Founded in the 1940s:*
Texas Instruments	Blue Cross/Blue Shield (Associated Ins. Co.)
Polaroid	Mattel
Hewlett-Packard	Wal-Mart (Walton 5 & 10)
Sara Lee (Consolidated Grocers)	Kelly Services (Russell Kelly Office Services)
Founded in the 1950s:	*Founded in the 1960s:*
Eckerd (Eckerd Drugs of Florida)	Nike
Digital Equipment	Turner Broadcasting System
National Semiconductor	Intel
Service Merchandise	The Gap
Founded in the 1970s:	*Founded in the 1980s:*
Microsoft	Compaq Computer
Apple Computer	Sun Microsystems
Home Depot	Dell Computer
U.S. Health [HMO]	Office Depot
Founded in the 1990s:	
None so far	

Source: Selected from Harris Corporation, "Founding Dates of the 1994 *Fortune* 500 U.S. Companies."

were never controlled by big businesses. For example, except for Marriott in the 1920s, no hotel or food service companies appear anywhere on the list. In the aggregate, hotels and restaurants employ millions of people, but they typically operate as small businesses. (Beginning in the 1960s, franchising brought a type of big/small business to both the hotel and the restaurant trades, but this was not "big business" in the usual sense.)[42]

The overall point is that in the United States, as in all capitalist countries, most people do not work for big companies. Only certain kinds of industries lend themselves to large operations. Such industries either have major economies of scale (electric utilities, steel, oil refining, chemicals, automobile manufacturing) or economies of scope (pharmaceuticals, discount retailers, branded snack foods). Throughout American history, entrepreneurs have tried, sometimes desperately, to create big businesses out of naturally small-scale operations. It has not worked. Everyone knows about National Biscuit (RJR Nabisco), but few people have ever heard of National Novelty, National Salt, National Starch, National Wallpaper, and National Cordage, all of which perished soon after they were incorporated. Standard Oil became one of the world's largest companies, but Standard Rope and Twine quickly dropped from sight. United States Steel prospered, but United States Button came and went in a flash.[43]

The structure of different industries does not seem to vary by much across capitalist economies. Table 9.3 shows a selective breakdown by industry of manufacturing companies worldwide that employed more than 20,000 persons as of 1973 (communist countries excluded). Of the 401 such companies, 210, or a little more than half, were American. The 191 non-American firms included 50 British, 29 German, 28 Japanese, and 24 French companies. A remarkable similarity of industry structure becomes evident.[44]

Of all major twentieth-century economies, that of the Soviet Union was the one most dominated by big enterprises. And the ultimate failure of that country's economic system derived in substantial part from the government's attempts to fuse into giant integrated enterprises a series of activities best done on a small or medium scale. The huge Soviet companies were government-owned, of course. But in the end that circumstance proved perhaps less decisive in their failure than was the sheer inappropriateness of their scale to the industries in which they were operating.[45]

Big Business, Antitrust, and Industry Structure

The rise of big business in the United States has often been called, somewhat misleadingly, the "trust movement." A trust is a legal device designed to vest custodianship of assets in a trustee or group of trustees, who act in the interests of the owner of the assets. The trustees' work is usually not subject to public scrutiny, and this characteristic is one reason American businesspeople found the device attractive.

Table 9.3   Companies with More than 20,000 Employees in 1973

Industry	U.S. Firms	Non-U.S. Firms
Chemicals	24	28
Electrical Machinery	20	25
Transportation Equipment	22	23
Tobacco	3	4
Furniture	0	0
Printing and publishing	0	0

The first American "trust," Standard Oil, appeared in 1882. Operationally, it amounted to an administrative consolidation of 40 existing companies that had been loosely allied. John D. Rockefeller and his associates decided to use the trust device because of its legal convenience. No state yet permitted formal holding companies, and thus it was illegal for one company to own another. When that situation changed, as it did during the late 1880s, the trust form was generally abandoned. Firms such as Standard Oil then reorganized themselves as holding companies. Their legal headquarters, though not their actual ones, were usually moved to either New Jersey or Delaware, both of which had enacted lenient incorporation laws.

The real purpose of trusts and holding companies was to facilitate centralized management. After the formation of the Standard Oil trust in 1882, Rockefeller and his colleagues, now in complete control, proceeded to "rationalize" their operations. In only three years' time, these executives concentrated Standard Oil's production in the 21 most efficient of the company's existing 53 refineries. They increased the refining capacity of these 21, and shut down the other 32 plants. This rationalization of production reduced the company's average cost of refining by two-thirds, from 1.5 cents per gallon to 0.5 cents.[46] Proprietors of some of the shut-down refineries watched as their names disappeared from plant gates and business letterheads. During this period family names became much less conspicuous in American big business, in contrast to the practice in British companies even down to the present day.

Like Standard Oil, the American Tobacco Company consolidated and rationalized several smaller firms during the 1880s, abolishing most of those firms' prior names. Meanwhile, American Tobacco reduced the average wholesale price of its cigarettes from $3.02 per thousand in 1893 to $2.01 in 1899. Many other big new companies rationalized in similar ways, riding technological changes and what came to be called the "experience curve" to ever-lower prices.[47]

Perhaps the most spectacular price reductions in American business history up to that time came in one of the most expensive of all consumer goods, the automobile. As shown in Chapter 8, Henry Ford's Model T, which in its first year of production (1908) sold for the comparatively low price of $850, could be purchased in 1916 for only $360. By 1924, 10 million Model T's had rolled off the assembly line, and the Ford Motor Company had achieved vast economies of scale. Exploiting its long production runs for ever-greater efficiencies, Ford rode the experience curve to remarkably low costs. In 1924 the Model T was selling for only $290, and the 1924 Ford was a much better car than that of 1908 or 1916.[48]

Sharp price cuts in automobiles, cigarettes, oil, and many other items came as wonderful news for consumers. But the news was not uniformly good for these same consumers in their roles as traditional producers, marketers, and workers. Despite its benefits for industrial efficiency, the Second Industrial Revolution brought in its train some severe political and cultural dislocations.

This was especially true in the short run, as different business sectors battled for advantage in an atmosphere of radical change. Railroads fought shippers, wheat farmers fought mortgage bankers, and small retailers and wholesalers fought big new companies whose marketing divisions threatened their existence. As for ordinary workers, they were exploited by nearly everyone who had power over them. Again the American situation differed from that in Britain and Germany. Whereas in much of Europe the typical political battles pitted a fairly united business community against a powerful labor movement, in the United States the fight was more often between one group of business interests and another.

Economically speaking, the success of the Second Industrial Revolution depended on the integration of mass production with mass marketing, and the mechanization of work that for centuries had been done by skilled craftsmen.[49] One result was a partial disempowerment of individual artisans. Overall, their incomes tended to rise while their sense of autonomy shrank. Other segments of American society also saw themselves losing ground as production and marketing functions came together within the same companies, and as these companies grew ever larger. Wholesalers, who had long been powerful players in the American economy, began to see their functions made obsolete as big companies started marketing directly to retailers. Retailers lost much of their own bargaining power, as producing companies became larger and more autonomous. Even producers, if they happened to be small operators of oil refineries, iron works, and cigarette factories, could not begin to compete with the new giants. So they often faced the prospect of either selling out or going under. Again, however, the movement toward large size applied only in certain sectors, not to most of the American economy.[50]

In the sectors that did move toward big business, there came a dramatic wave of consolidation. During the period 1897–1904 alone, 4,227 American companies were merged into 257 combinations, sometimes forcibly. By 1904, some 318 large firms were alleged to control about 40 percent of the entire nation's manufacturing assets.[51]

Nothing like this sudden concentration of economic power had occurred anywhere during the First Industrial Revolution. Nor had it yet happened during the Second Industrial Revolution in any country besides the United States. Both British and German firms remained relatively smaller and more specialized than the new American giants. A few powerful German companies such as Thyssen and Siemens did integrate vertically. But, as the chapters on Thyssen and German capitalism in this book show, those companies remained much smaller than United States Steel and General Electric, their American counterparts.

There were several reasons why American companies were the first in the world to become gigantic. One was the tiny size of the American government, together with the absence of a landed aristocracy, an established church, or a large standing army. Without these institutions, a vacuum of power existed in America, and no countervailing force emerged to array itself against the forward thrust of market forces.[52] Another reason was that European companies did not have ready access to an open, unified market comparable in size to the immense American market. The European Economic Community, formed during the post–World War II era (and later renamed the European Union), was a successful attempt to emulate the huge, integrated, and open market of the United States. But that development lay many years in the future.

As the Second Industrial Revolution unfolded, neither Europeans nor Americans understood very clearly what was happening. In the United States, and even more so in Europe, many people regarded the new corporate titans of American business as dangerous and unnatural mutations of the natural order. Firms such as Standard Oil and American Tobacco seemed to be Frankenstein monsters. Some people even predicted that one huge trust would come to dominate the entire American economy.[53]

There was almost no perception at this time that big companies were prospering in only a few industries. Practically nobody drew the appropriate lesson from failed attempts to create corporate giants in the manufacture of clothing, shoes, wallpaper, leather, and salt. The proper lesson was that none of these industries had production processes that lent themselves to powerful economies of either scale or scope. But even the entrepreneurs who made valiant attempts to create big companies in these industries chalked up their failures to poor financing, bad marketing, or ill luck. Today we know that they never had a chance. They had picked the wrong industries to consolidate.[54]

But the sudden appearance of big companies in even a few industries seemed a stark, immediate, and generalized threat to American traditions of entrepreneurial opportunity. Even more ominously, the big new companies were now wielding conspicuous and unprecedented political power. Their lobbyists swarmed over Washington and roamed the halls of every state capitol. To many contemporaries, therefore, the "trusts" seemed to represent a frontal challenge to the country's democratic institutions, a dagger pointed at the heart of the American national character.[55]

John D. Rockefeller, whose Standard Oil Company might have been revered as a national treasure had it arisen in Japan, became in America one of the most vilified persons of his time. Angry farmers spoke of Rockefeller, Carnegie (steel), James B. Duke (tobacco), and Jay Gould (railroads), as "Robber Barons." The very fact that the name stuck signaled a widespread conviction that nobody could get this rich this fast without stealing from the public. And the Robber Barons did become almost unimaginably wealthy. When Rockefeller retired, early in the twentieth century, he was worth nearly a billion dollars. At that time, the Gross National Product was about $30 billion.[56]

Rockefeller had entered the oil business in the mid-1860s. The movement toward big companies in oil refining and other industries began to gather steam during the 1870s and broke through in the 1880s. Adverse public opinion soon began to crystallize, and it became clear that something had to be done about the new giants. Courts started paying more attention to common-law prohibitions against collusive price-fixing. State legislatures began to pass laws designed to curb cartels and tame mammoth corporations.

In 1890, the United States Congress enacted the milestone Sherman Antitrust law, which declared illegal "every contract, combination in the form of trust or otherwise, or conspiracy, in restraint of trade or commerce." The Sherman Act exposed to criminal prosecution "every person who shall monopolize, or attempt to monopolize, or combine or conspire with any other person or persons, to monopolize any part of the trade or commerce among the several States, or with foreign nations."[57] In 1911, after several years of investigation and prosecution under the Sherman Act, Standard Oil was broken apart by the Supreme Court. Some of the 34 pieces into which it was divided became very big companies themselves, with now-familiar brand names: Exxon, Mobil, Chevron, Marathon.

In the long period since the original passage of the Sherman Act in 1890, federal and state governments have expended vast resources in defining and implementing antitrust policy. The Department of Justice, after a sluggish start, eventually came to employ several hundred full-time lawyers dedicated to ferreting out business offenders. The Federal Trade Commission was supposed to devote itself to the prevention of what the FTC Act of 1914 called "unfair methods of competition in commerce."[58]

The task has not been easy. The American economy has always been extremely competitive, and seldom has it been clear at just what point "unfair methods" depart from fair ones. Nor is it entirely plain when "monopoly" may be said to exist. Often the legal definition of monopoly has depended on whether the "relevant market," as antitrust authorities have come to call it, is construed by courts as local, regional, national, or international.

Most troublesome of all, there has been persistent disagreement over exactly what "competition" means. Is competition keenest when the number of competitors is maximized? If so, then small businesses should be protected even if consumers have to pay higher prices. Or, does maximum competition imply the lowest prices for consumers? If that is the case, then big companies sometimes must be allowed to squeeze out smaller ones.

As the twentieth century progressed, the whole subject of antitrust grew increasingly technical. Decade by decade, its abstruse minutiae moved further beyond the ken of ordinary citizens. Much like environmental policy later on, antitrust became the purview not of the general public but of highly trained lawyers and economists.[59] Most college courses in microeconomics came to have a component on antitrust. Yet many students emerged from their encounter more confused than when they started. American law schools routinely instituted courses on antitrust, which soon became among the most technical in the curriculum.

Thousands of lawyers made careers of the subject, and nearly all large American firms today have antitrust specialists on their legal staffs.

Considering that there are more big companies in the United States than in the rest of the world combined, the entire antitrust effort might be regarded as an obvious failure, or even some kind of historical joke. That would be an incorrect conclusion, for two reasons. First, American companies became so big primarily because the national economy itself was so much larger than any other. Second, antitrust law was not synonymous with anti-bigness law. It is true that the most conspicuous targets of antitrust have been giant companies, and suits brought against them have been a staple of newspaper headlines. But the majority of prosecutions have been against groups of small firms engaging in collusive behavior.[60]

Whatever the identity of the target companies, antitrust policy over the years has had powerful effects in controlling collusion, stopping cartels, preventing anti-competitive mergers, eliminating resale price maintenance, and encouraging entrepreneurship.[61] Then, too, the antitrust laws have constituted a formal expression by the American government that the interests of the people come before those of any company, however powerful. Although this might seem to be an unnecessary precaution in an era of vigorous international competition, not every industry is exposed to such competition. And for many that are, the exposure is only a recent phenomenon. For most of American history, companies in the domestic economy were either protected by tariff laws or were so much stronger than non-U.S. firms that they could act pretty much as they pleased, subject to domestic competition.

During the post–World War II years, most national governments in western Europe passed laws resembling America's Sherman Act. The European Community in particular instituted stringent regulations designed to break down trade barriers and maximize interfirm competition within and across national boundaries. Tough antitrust laws are also on the books in Japan, although their enforcement is more casual and selective than in the United States and Europe. Even so, the most telling tribute to the wisdom and efficacy of the American antitrust system has been its widespread emulation abroad.[62] The task of defining effective competition may be difficult, and U.S. antitrust enforcers have made a great many mistakes over the years. But in general they have managed to move toward outcomes that have been economically effective.

Where the Money Came From

Whether companies are small, medium, or large, one of their perpetual problems is how to pay for current operations and how to finance future development. It is not by accident that all business schools have required courses in finance, just as law schools do in contracts.

Financial capital is of course related to the other three factors of production. In the United States these factors were out of balance, not only in the early years but well into the nineteenth century. There was a superabundance of land and a healthy spirit of entrepreneurship, but also a scarcity of labor and a severe shortage of gold and silver. This situation had numerous effects. The shortage of labor put a high premium on inventions and other ways to mechanize work. In addition, real wages rose to levels higher than those in Europe, a difference that encouraged immigration.[63] Another effect of the factor imbalance was that both the government and private entrepreneurs made land do the work of money. When new territories and states were added to the Union, their public lands became federal property. (The only exception was Texas, which was allowed to keep its lands.) Almost two billion acres of public land were acquired by the federal government in this way between 1781 and 1867. By the last quarter of the twentieth century, more than one billion acres had been disposed of. About a fourth of this total was sold to citizens, and another fourth sold or given away to settlers under the Homestead Act of 1862. Eleven percent more went to railroad companies or to states for the construction of railroads. An additional 7 percent was allocated to states for the support of common schools. The remainder was given over to a variety of uses such as veterans' bounties and the reclamation of swampland. All together, sales and donations of federal lands served to provide both the government itself and an assortment of chosen recipients with an endowment of capital, a convenient substitute for money.[64]

During the middle and late nineteenth century, with successive discoveries of gold and silver in California, Colorado, Nevada, and Alaska, the nation began to overcome its historic shortage of specie (hard money). But there could never be enough specie to finance modern economic development, either in the United States or any other industrialized country. Reliance on precious metals, which had been the preferred medium of exchange for thousands of years, proved inadequate to finance even the First Industrial Revolution, let alone the Second and Third.

Credit therefore became vital to capitalist development. It appeared in many ingenious forms: bills of exchange, currency backed by fractional specie reserves, bank loans, and common and preferred stocks. Financial officers in both the public and private sectors also developed a very broad range of bonds: city, county, state, and federal bonds, corporate "full faith and credit" bonds, mortgage bonds, debentures, convertibles, junk bonds, and so on.

Most important of all in the Second and Third Industrial Revolutions, major firms relied on retained earnings to finance their growth. That is, they did not pay out all their profits as dividends, but kept strong reserves for future investment.

As shown in the other chapters of this book, methods of finance varied across countries. Nineteenth-century British firms relied on family fortunes and bank overdrafts, with little or no government participation. German "universal banks" underwrote and marketed stocks and bonds for private firms, in addition to granting them loans. Japanese companies of the post–World War II "miracle growth" years received funds from private banks, which themselves were indulging in "overloans" supported by the Bank of Japan and the Ministry of Finance. In general, two characteristics set American practice apart from those of other countries.

One of these characteristics was a stronger willingness of individuals to gamble on their future ability to pay bills. This penchant to use personal credit may be observed even today. Americans buy "on time" more than citizens of other countries do, and they use their credit cards with sometimes reckless extravagance, even in the face of high interest rates.

The other characteristic, which incidentally helps to explain why credit cards came into such wide use, was the decentralization and competitiveness of the American banking system. Whereas in most industrialized countries the banking sector came to be organized around a few very large banks with widespread branches, the American system evolved quite differently. Most banks were chartered by the states, not the national government, and until recently the practice of branching was restricted even within states. This was a formula for the emergence of a very large number of banks.

The ideology behind these unusual banking rules was the American people's pronounced individualism and their emphatic distrust of concentrated economic power—the same principles that lie behind the anti-trust laws. In the case of finance, the distrust surfaced at an early date. In 1791, Secretary of the Treasury Alexander Hamilton had difficulty getting his bill for the First Bank of the United States passed by Congress. President Washington had to overrule the strident objections of Thomas Jefferson and others, who held that such a bank represented unwise policy and in any case was unconstitutional. Hamilton got his bank, but when its 20-year charter expired in 1811, Congress voted down a renewal.[65]

Financial exigencies connected with the second war with Britain (1812–15) soon made it clear that the nation in fact needed a central bank to help with public finance, note issue, and management of balance-of-payments problems. Even more important, a powerful bank might serve as a disciplining force against loose practices by proliferating state-chartered banks. Such institutions had grown in number from three in 1790 to about 250 in 1815. So in 1816, Congress created the Second Bank of the United States, again with a 20-year charter. The Second Bank, under its talented president Nicholas Biddle, performed excellent service both for its own stockholders and for the nation. But Biddle overreached himself and grew too powerful. So once more political forces were mobilized to thwart any recharter of the Second Bank.[66]

President Andrew Jackson's spirited veto of the Bank's recharter bill is one of the most memorable and revealing state papers in American history. Jackson declared: "Many of our rich men have not been content with equal protection and equal benefits, but have besought us to make them richer by act of Congress. By attempting to gratify their desires we have in the results of our legislation arrayed section against section, interest against interest, and man against man, in a fearful commotion which threatens to shake the foundations of our Union." Jackson's veto message was an ingenious political manifesto. But its rhetoric displayed the common American misunderstanding of the functions of banks and financial systems.[67]

After Jackson's veto, the United States went without a central bank for 77 years (1836–1913). Since tremendous economic growth took place during these years, it cannot be argued that central banks are essential for capitalist development. On the other hand, the whole period was punctuated by regular financial crises: 1837, 1857, 1873, 1893, 1907. Each financial "panic," as it was called, was accompanied by such severe reactions from the public that new terms began to be used. But as time passed, words that had become successive euphemisms for "panic"—first "recession" and then "depression"—themselves became scare terms.[68]

By the turn of the twentieth century, the nation's economy had become so complex that it could no longer function well without a central bank. In 1913, therefore, Congress created the Federal Reserve System. Again the American penchant for decentralization became evident in the new organization's design. The System was headquartered in Washington, but it included 12 regional branches in such cities as New York, Atlanta, St. Louis, and San Francisco. A Board of Governors would run the System, and eventually the Chairman of this Board would in fact behave much like the central bankers of other countries.[69]

But all of this took many years to work out, and in the meantime banks continued to proliferate. Whereas most modern industrialized countries counted their banks by the score or the hundreds (some with many branches), Americans could count theirs by the tens of thousands. Unaffiliated "country banks" sprang up everywhere, until by 1920 there were 30,909 banks in the United States. When more than 7,000 of these institutions failed during the period 1931–33, wiping out the savings of millions of depositors, it became clear that further reforms were necessary.[70] During the 1930s a sound method of deposit insurance was put into place, and the Federal Reserve System was strengthened. But even then the principle of decentralization remained powerful, as investment banking was separated from commercial banking by the Glass-Steagall Act of 1933. It was at this time that the Morgan bank, for example, had to split into parts that went on to become Morgan Stanley, J. P. Morgan, and Morgan Guaranty. To this day, there is no American "universal bank" of the Deutsche Bank variety.

Not until the middle and late twentieth century did the "Fed" begin to function well. Only then could there emerge powerful and effective chairs of the System, such as Marriner Eccles, Paul Volcker, and Alan Greenspan. Toward the end of the century, during the 1980s and 1990s, a deregulation movement produced a welter of rationalizations. After a series of mergers, acquisitions, and downsizings, the American banking system began to take on the shape of a modern financial sector. Some disastrous mistakes in policy were made during this period of deregulation, and the savings and loan crisis of the 1980s added several hundred billion dollars to the national debt. The long-term effects of banking deregulation remain unpredictable, but there is no question that the system was made leaner and more competitive.[71]

Over the course of the Second and Third Industrial Revolutions, American companies relied more on banks for their financing than did British firms, but less so than either German or Japanese ones. The primary source of money, especially for big business, was retained earnings.

Securities Markets

In early nineteenth-century America, when Wall Street began to emerge as the principal money center, most of the stocks and bonds offered for sale were those of banks themselves. Then came a brief period when turnpikes and canal companies issued significant amounts of securities. But a really modern market for securities did not came into existence until the advent of large-scale railroad finance during the 1840s and especially the 1850s.[72] Railroad stocks and bonds dominated the American markets for the next 60 years, well into the twentieth century. What we know today as the Dow-Jones averages were first quoted in 1884, but only for railroads. The separation of the Dow into rails and industrials was begun in 1897, by which time a broad market for industrial securities had finally begun to develop.[73]

Meanwhile, regional stock exchanges arose in many cities. A few of these became important, such as the San Francisco Mining Exchange and the Chicago Board of Trade, which became the center of an immense international grain market. But none of these other centers rivaled Wall Street, where the major investment banks established their headquarters and where the New York Stock Exchange reigned supreme. By the flush days of early 1929, a seat on the Exchange was selling for $625,000, the equivalent of several million dollars today.[74]

Then, late in 1929, came the catastrophic crash of the stock market. The ensuing Great Depression, which lasted until 1941, was the longest and worst economic crisis in American history. Unemployment reached 25 percent in 1932, and recovery throughout the decade was uneven and erratic. By 1942, during the first months of World War II, the Exchange seat that had sold for $625,000 brought only $17,000.[75]

Gyrations in the price of an Exchange seat mirrored the violent ups and downs in securities prices and volume of trading. When the twentieth century began, only about half a million Americans owned stocks of any kind. By 1929 that figure had multiplied by a factor of 20, to 10 million. The daily volume of shares traded topped 3 million in 1929, only to fall by almost 60 percent by 1932. So severe was the impact of the Great Crash that this 1929 volume of shares traded was not again reached until 1963, some 34 years later.[76]

Since that time, activity in the securities markets has skyrocketed. The average daily share volume had been only half a million in 1900, and was only 3 million in the early 1960s. But it reached 12 million in 1970, 45 million in 1980, and 157 million in 1990. A big reason for this explosion in volume was the rise of huge pension funds and the movement of institutional investors into the market. Whereas the average number of shares per trade in 1965 was only 224, it was 2,082 by 1990.[77]

How have investors fared? In the years since 1900, real returns from bonds and commercial paper have averaged a little under 2 percent annually, while those on stocks have averaged over 6 percent.[78] So the stock market proved to be an excellent place in which to invest one's money. Just as important, the exchanges supplied a constant barometer of American business. Price quotations from the exchanges gave daily, even instantaneous valuations of thousands of publicly traded companies. In so doing, they classified the present condition of firms and provided explicit comparative odds for the future. That, together with concern about personal portfolios, is why American managers paid so much attention to the stock market.

Management

Throughout the twentieth century, management played an ever more influential part in the evolution of business. The American economy grew rapidly in size, but the complexity of its operations increased even faster. The need for managers therefore rose more quickly than that for other kinds of workers. At the end of the twentieth century, several million men and women could legitimately call themselves "managers."[79]

American managers generally had more autonomy than their German or Japanese counterparts, but not necessarily their British ones. They were freer from oversight by financial institutions and government agencies. Apart from a brief period of "financial capitalism" during the heyday of J. Pierpont Morgan around the start of the twentieth century, there were few American parallels to the active supervision practiced by German universal banks.[80] Nor did America's Treasury Department historically have quite the potency of Japan's Ministry of Finance. Nor did any American agency, at least in peacetime, exercise the broad planning power sometimes wielded by Japan's Ministry of International Trade and Industry.

Managers were also remarkably insulated from the interference of owners. The separation of management from ownership (stockholders), which first became conspicuous with the rise of big companies during the nineteenth century, grew in the twentieth to be a hallmark of major firms throughout the world. This trend had mixed results, but on the whole it was a beneficial development.

On the positive side, managers acquired the power to make quick decisions without consulting owners. Even more important, they gained the authority to make crucial choices about the disposition of corporate earnings. At their own discretion, they were able to retain within the firm significant amounts of money for reinvestment. They could therefore concentrate on the long-term good of the company. They could ignore plaintive pressures from family owners for high dividend payments. Many scholars believe that this long-term perspective by professional managers is an important reason why German, American, and Japanese firms have sometimes out-performed British ones. British companies remained comparatively more dominated by families, and paid out higher percentages of their earnings as dividends.[81]

There was a downside to the separation of ownership and control, however. Autonomous managers sometimes overinvested in unpromising initiatives. They could, if they chose, indulge in lavish perquisites. And they could pay themselves exorbitant salaries even if their companies were not performing well.[82] But whether or not the positive elements of professional management exceeded the negative elements, one thing remained clear. Throughout the twentieth century, in the United States and elsewhere, professional managers with little equity ownership made most of the strategic decisions for major companies.

At the beginning of the century, there were not very many American "managers" in the modern sense of that term. They probably numbered in the low hundred thousands among a total population of 76 million. American firms had grown big enough to need hierarchies of salaried managers only in the mid-nineteenth century, and even then only in the case of railroads. Soon enough, however, a few thousand big firms, plus tens of thousands of other companies within the big firms' networks of suppliers and subcontractors, began to require active, self-conscious management in order to prosper within the competitive marketplace. So did several hundred thousand medium-sized companies operating in the industries not dominated by big business. By 1938, the management scholar Chester Barnard estimated that "not less than 5,000,000 individuals are engaged in the work of executives, of whom 100,000 occupy major executive positions."[83]

Managers' functions included the use of increasingly sophisticated tools of information retrieval, cost control, and financial accounting.[84] Costing techniques were pioneered by such innovators as Albert Fink, the "father of railway economics," who in the 1870s perfected a system for separating fixed and variable costs.[85] Even more influential was Frederick Winslow Taylor, who in the 1880s began to develop for manufacturing companies a system of controls and motivational devices which he called "scientific management." Taylor's short book *Principles of Scientific Management* (1911) became an international bestseller, admired by readers as different as the Russian revolutionary Vladimir Lenin and the French premier Georges Clemenceau.[86]

Other management pioneers included the young financial officer F. Donaldson Brown of Du Pont, who in 1914 invented the concept "return on investment." This useful tool spread quickly through American business after Brown took it to General Motors in the early 1920s.[87] By the late twentieth century, statistical controls of all kinds (net present value calculations, breakevens, inventory ratios), had become routine elements in complex information systems.

With the arrival of the computer, these systems could be shared much more widely and used cooperatively by management and the workforce. The story of IBM, told in Chapter 10, traces the spread of information management through American business.

From the primitive punch-card systems of the 1890s to the invention of the computer in the 1940s, both the utility and the burdens of information management grew at only a moderate pace. Then, starting with mainframes in the 1960s and then exploding with the arrival of personal computers in the 1980s, the use of integrated-circuit technology thrust the American business system into a new era. The spread of computers to desktops, workstations, and home offices all over the country meant an unprecedented degree of access to information. For individual firms, it implied constant flux. The technology changed so fast that today's hardware and software might become obsolete tomorrow.[88]

In the midst of all the technological upheaval, professional management remained as much art as science. Executives spent most of their time in the tedious but rewarding task of convincing others to pull together in developing new products, increasing market share, and seeking steady profits. As one of the greatest managers in American history, longtime General Motors president Alfred P. Sloan Jr., put it, "I got better results by selling my ideas than by telling people what to do."[89] Chester Barnard expressed the same kind of point in his classic book *The Functions of the Executive* (1938): "The fine art of executive decision consists in not deciding questions that are not now pertinent, in not deciding prematurely, in not making decisions that cannot be made effective, and in not making decisions that others should make."[90]

For managers in the Third Industrial Revolution, the availability to all employees of almost unlimited amounts of data made possible the flattening of hierarchies and the broadening of management's "span of control." Yet even toward the end of the twentieth century the full implications of the change had not become wholly clear. And the trend was not just an American phenomenon but a full-fledged global movement.[91]

Globalization

In part because of the information explosion, the late twentieth century became a time of rapid multinationalization of business. This was not a completely new kind of activity, of course. Even at the beginning of the century, a few American companies such as Standard Oil, International Harvester, and Singer Sewing Machine already had been operating abroad for many years.[92] Companies' foreign operations grew significantly after World War I, but faltered during the Great Depression. Then, in the period after World War II, American business activity abroad leaped forward, inaugurating a trend followed by firms in other countries. This movement altered the structure of the world economy.[93]

The United States, despite its protectionist past, also led the postwar movement for free trade. Two discrete forces interacted to produce this result. The first originated in the 1930s, when the Franklin D. Roosevelt administration wrested primary control of trade policy from Congress and lodged it in the White House. That transfer of power curtailed the time-honored congressional process of "logrolling," in which blocs of legislators would support each others' protectionist policies: Louisiana sugar growers allied themselves with Pennsylvania wool manufacturers, and so on.

The second force promoting free trade was American policy during World War II and its aftermath. By 1945, the economies of Germany, Italy, Japan, and other nations on the losing side lay in ruins. Even the economies of victorious powers such as Great Britain and the Soviet Union were more or less exhausted from the war effort. But the United States, where no fighting had occurred and no bombs had fallen, was in better economic shape than at any other time in its history. By the final years of the war, the American industrial machine was turning out about 40 percent of the total of war material produced by all belligerents on both sides. This was a colossal, almost unimaginable performance. No other country could come near matching American industrial might at this time.

For a variety of reasons, the United States now proceeded to sponsor a series of steps aimed at reorganizing the world trading system. The Americans led a coordinated movement to slash tariff rates and to develop and liberalize national economies throughout the world. Policymakers promoted new transnational institutions such as the General Agreement on Tariffs and Trade, the World Bank, the International Monetary Fund, and the United Nations. Washington, D.C., became the headquarters of this drive to open world markets and develop a new trading system. There was considerable opposition to these moves from powerful interest groups within the United States. But the outcome was unambiguous: a much freer world trading system.

The U.S. government deliberately opened up the American market itself, which became by far the richest single destination for other countries' exports. European producers and, even more so, Asian ones took full advantage of the invitation. By the 1950s a trickle of imports had begun. By the 1960s it turned into a stronger stream, and by the 1970s and 1980s an absolute flood. The result, toward the end of the twentieth century, was a chronic American trade deficit, but also world economic integration on a scale hardly conceivable only a short time earlier.

American policymakers from the 1940s onward promoted economic integration in pursuance of several objectives. For one thing, they feared a return of the Great Depression, and they wanted to develop strong foreign markets for American products. Unless the devastated economies of Europe and Asia could somehow be rebuilt, such markets would never materialize. Second, and of much more importance, the specter of Soviet expansion called for strengthening the economies of Western Europe and Japan as barriers against the spread of communism. In 1947, the Truman administration announced its Marshall Plan for systematic economic aid to Europe. Events soon seemed to justify the immense expenditures contemplated. The Soviet Union's Berlin blockade (1948), the triumph of the communist revolution in China (1948), the successful test of a Soviet atomic bomb (1949), and the communist invasion of South Korea (1950) confirmed the resolve of the Americans to "contain" the spread of communism. This would be done through economic means as well as military ones.

Then, too, there was an altruistic impulse among many citizens of the United States to share what in the 1950s came widely to be called "the American way of life." This way of life rested on a fusion of democracy with capitalism—a marriage of "liberty" with "the free market." A powerful ideology, it amounted in substance to an emphasis on materialism, unlimited economic growth, a high degree of peacetime military spending (which had been unknown in America before the 1950s), and a new level of prosperity for everyone. It was all symbolized by the "American Dream" of individual prosperity, home ownership, suburban living, and the freedom of the open road.

Of course, some of these things were not altogether new. The United States had been the world's leading industrial and agricultural power since the 1890s. Its people had been more prosperous than those of almost any other country for even longer. Yet nineteenth-century living standards, striking though they were, gave little hint of the tremendous growth that lay ahead. Toward the end of the twentieth century, real gross domestic product per capita reached a level about five times what it had been at the end of the nineteenth century.

The Waning of the American Dream?

With the conspicuous exception of slavery, one of the great things about the United States had always been its openness and egalitarianism. At the time of the country's founding in 1776, there had been few of the trappings of Old World caste and privilege: no feudal tradition, no established church, no hereditary aristocracy, no standing army. The authors of the Constitution had gone so far as to forbid the creation of titles of nobility by the federal government or the states. From the beginning, America had developed as the quintessential middle-class country.[94]

Wealth was respected and honored, of course, but only if it was earned. Even men such as Washington and Jefferson, who inherited small fortunes in land and slaves, were expected to work hard on their plantations, and they did. Many European visitors remarked that the general American preference for earned wealth contravened that of Old World society, which tended to revere leisure and "old money" while holding the *nouveaux riches* in contempt. As the German philosopher Hugo Münsterberg wrote in 1904, after spending time as a professor at Harvard, an American "who does not work at anything, no matter how rich he is, can neither get nor keep a social status." This was something of an overstatement, as was made clear in the novels about American society at that same time written by Edith Wharton and Henry James. But Münsterberg had a valid point. He went on to say that in contrast to Americans' embrace of business, "the European of the Continent esteems the industrial life as honest, but not as noble."[95]

Decade by decade, American affluence increased, interrupted in a serious way only by the Great Depression. The prosperity of the post–World War II "Baby Boom" generation seemed to bring American economic progress to a kind of climax. Not only did most families come within reach of home ownership, but many began to build two-car garages. The historian David M. Potter, in his provocative book of 1954, *People of Plenty,*[96] explored both the virtues and the problems of abundance. But he seemed to take its indefinite continuation for granted. In another influential book, *The Affluent Society* (1958),[97] the economist John Kenneth Galbraith lamented the loss of public spirit as suburbanites became so self-sufficient that they no longer cared enough about public works.

In the 1960s, under Lyndon Johnson's Great Society, the federal government instituted a smorgasbord of public programs designed to help almost everybody become prosperous. These new measures, ostensibly targeted for the poor, ended up subsidizing the American middle class most of all. But that seemed not to matter, since plenty of money was available to pay for every program. "Guns *and* butter," President Johnson said in a prominent speech, arguing that the United States could fight the Vietnam War and fund the Great Society at the same time.

But the nation's potent growth record during the long period from 1940 to 1973 turned out to be something of a historical aberration, not any kind of permanent norm. As the final decades of the twentieth century began, an inauspicious trend became evident. The rich were getting richer, faster than ever. But the middle class was stagnating, and the poor were starting to get poorer.[98]

Statistics told an ominous story. Throughout the twentieth century up to 1973, real wages in the United States had grown at an annual rate of about 2 percent. Compounded over the years, this meant that average pay, and by implication average living standards, doubled every 35 years. But in 1973 the trend came to a halt, and the average real wages of production and nonsupervisory workers began to decline. By the middle 1990s, the average hourly real wage of a worker in manufacturing was less than 90 percent of what it had been in 1973.[99] By itself, that might not seem so terrible. But looked at another way, it was quite a striking change. If the longstanding prior trend of 2 percent annual growth had continued, the figure for the middle 1990s would not have been less than 90 percent of the 1973 level, but more than 150 percent.

So the long upward movement of wages for skilled workers in manufacturing appeared to have ended. Meanwhile, the average pay of unskilled workers had dropped even more rapidly. Analysts began to refer to a "permanent underclass," something new in American history. The entire trend threatened to undercut the egalitarianism and entrepreneurial opportunity that had long been at the core of American culture.[100]

Meanwhile, the pay of "knowledge workers" had continued to grow at the old pre-1973 rate. Professionals such as lawyers, physicians, engineers, accountants, and consultants experienced little or no relative loss of income. Corporate executives, especially those in top management positions, paid themselves higher salaries and bonuses than ever before. By the 1990s, chief executive officers of large American firms were commonly earning 200 times the compensation of the lowest-paid members of their companies. In Europe and Japan that multiple was very much lower. In the United States itself as recently as the 1970s, the multiple had stood at about 40.[101]

Nor were American CEO's the only beneficiaries of the new patterns

of income distribution. During the 1980s and 1990s, American investment bankers reaped profits and fees from mergers and acquisitions that
would have been inconceivable even in the buccaneering nineteenth-century days of Jay "Mephistopheles" Gould and John W. "Bet-a-Million"
Gates. By the 1990s, the wealthiest 0.5 percent of the American people
found themselves in possession of a higher portion of the national wealth
than had been the case at perhaps any other time in the nation's history.
The only likely exception was the year 1929, just before the market crash
and the onset of the Great Depression.

Between 1962 and the 1990s, the average net worth of the least
wealthy 20 percent of American households actually shrank. Meanwhile,
that of the top 20 percent increased by 88 percent, and that of the top
0.5 percent by 118 percent. The richest one percent of Americans had
owned less than 20 percent of the national wealth as recently as 1976,
but they held over 40 percent by the mid-1990s. None of this constituted
good news for the nation as a whole. At the very least, it represented
powerful seeds of social division. If the trend continued, it threatened to
split the country into the House of Have and the House of Want, a
condition that the United States had mostly avoided during its first 200
years.[102]

There had been plenty of class conflict in American history, but not
nearly as much as in Europe. Until the 1930s, organized labor remained
weaker in the United States than in Germany or Britain. But the passage
of the National Labor Relations Act of 1935, followed by several Supreme Court decisions favorable to labor, reversed a century-long trend
in which American law had favored employers. Union membership
promptly shot up. Whereas it had been less than 3 million in 1933, it
reached 7 million in 1937 and nearly 15 million by 1945. Measured as
a proportion of the workforce, union membership peaked at 23.6 percent
in 1960.[103] For a variety of reasons, it then began a gradual decline.
Employer hostility, the pressures of foreign competition, and a general
shift of the labor force from manufacturing into less easily unionized
service industries caused a drop in union membership. Whereas about
one worker in four had belonged to a union in 1960, only about one in
seven did by the middle 1990s. This was a low percentage compared to
those in other advanced industrial economies. White-collar workers are
heavily organized in some European countries today, but that has never
been the case in the United States.[104]

In the late twentieth century, the partitioning of America's national wealth and income was all the more frustrating because of its apparent intractability. Its complex causes included the internationalization of labor markets, which benefited production workers abroad as well as consumers in the United States; advancing technology, which automated some high-paying jobs while making others obsolete; and the flattening of the progressive income tax, a measure apparently favored by most Americans. Because these causes ran so deep, there was no quick way out.

The American government itself was to blame for part of this maldistribution problem, though not most of it. Over the span of the twentieth century, total public expenditures at all levels, measured as a percentage of GDP, had grown by a factor of about four. By the end of the century, they stood at well above 20 percent. An additional 10–12 percent of GDP was funneled through government as transfer payments such as Social Security and Medicare. Even so, the total tax bite in the United States continued to be substantially lower than that in comparable industrialized countries such as Britain, France, and Germany. One reason for many Americans' inaccurate view to the contrary was that most taxes in the United States were so visible. They were paid directly to the government as personal and corporate income taxes rather than indirectly as value-added or sales taxes, the practice prevalent in most other countries.[105] At the close of the twentieth century, the American "welfare state" was still not as highly developed as its European counterparts.

Government's influence on the economy had grown during the two world wars and in three periods of domestic "reform": the Progressive Era (1901–16), the New Deal (1933–38), and the Great Society of the 1960s. This growth of government's presence in everyday life was common throughout the industrialized world. In America rather more than elsewhere, it represented a change from the situation that existed during the late nineteenth century. Both the federal and state governments had been active during the first half of that century, then less so during the second half.

This was particularly true of the federal government, which until the twentieth century was of minuscule size. Property rights remained secure, and throughout the nineteenth century the legal framework of business was being shaped by decisions within state and federal courts. But even so, in the early years of the Second Industrial Revolution the federal presence was all but invisible.

As late as 1871, only 51,071 civilians worked for the federal government, of whom 36,696 were postal employees. The remaining 14,375 constituted the entire working national government for a country whose population exceeded 40 million. This was a ratio of one nonpostal employee per 2,858 people. As the Second Industrial Revolution surged forward, that ratio grew to one per 751 people in 1901. The ratio continued to climb during the twentieth century, spurred by increases in governmental functions during the three reform periods, two world wars, and two other wars in Korea and Vietnam. In 1970, the ratio peaked at one federal employee per 91 people. After that, the relative size of the federal government shrank. By 1980 the ratio had declined to one employee per 102 people, and it slid slowly downward in subsequent years.[106]

By the 1980s, government in America was widely seen as part of the economic problem, not of the solution. Chronic budget deficits became endemic after the Reagan Revolution cut and flattened income tax rates during the 1980s. With increased spending on defense, the size of the federal debt grew rapidly during the 1980s, so that by the middle 1990s the United States faced the prospect of a national debt exceeding $5 trillion. During these years, the electorate seemed reluctant to accept either tax increases or reductions in middle-class entitlements such as Social Security, Medicare, and mortgage interest deductions. So huge federal deficits became locked in.

As with so many other recent developments, here too there were ample precedents in American history. More than 200 years earlier, in 1795, retiring Secretary of the Treasury Alexander Hamilton had written ruefully about the problems of taxation in a republic:

> To extinguish a Debt which exists and to avoid contracting more are ideas almost always favored by public feeling and opinion; but to pay Taxes for the one or the other purpose, which are the only means of avoiding the evil, is always more or less unpopular . . . Hence it is no uncommon spectacle to see the same men Clamouring for Occasions of expense . . . [and also] declaiming against a Public Debt, and for the reduction of it as an *abstract thesis,* yet vehement against every plan of taxation which is proposed to discharge old debts, or to avoid new [ones] by defraying the expences of exigencies as they emerge.[107]

In the history of American capitalism, it would be difficult to find a comment more pertinent to the fiscal dilemma in which the country found itself during the closing years of the twentieth century. But the nation's 200-year record of preeminent economic performance gave reason for hope that this latest set of problems might be managed, even if not altogether solved. The dynamics of capitalism have been traditionally underrated, and it would be a mistake to perpetuate that custom.[108]

In the 1990s, the American business system showed some tentative signs of renewed growth in investment and productivity. After investing only about 7 percent of GDP in producers' durable equipment during the 1980s, American business started an upward trend in 1992 that reached about 11 percent by the middle 1990s. Productivity growth, which had languished at about one percent per year during the 1970s and much of the 1980s (about half the figure for most of American history up to that time), seemed to be recovering in the 1990s to something close to the long-term figure of 2 percent.[109] Productivity growth is difficult to measure, and its causes are hard to unravel. Pessimists attributed this latest round of growth to massive layoffs, as American companies pursued strategies of "downsizing" and "re-engineering." Optimists proclaimed a new era of aggressive national "competitiveness." Some analysts doubted whether much of anything had changed.[110]

It is too early to assess the historical significance of the possible business revitalization of the 1990s, or even the long-term significance of the merger and acquisition mania of the 1980s.[111] What both of these movements did show is the characteristic American willingness to go where the market seems to direct. More than the citizens of other large industrialized countries, Americans always have been ready to accept the consequences of business upheavals. As the economist Joseph Schumpeter once wrote, the essence of capitalism is precisely this kind of disruption. Schumpeter saw capitalism itself as a "process of industrial mutation— if I may use that biological term—that incessantly revolutionizes the economic structure *from within,* incessantly destroying the old one, incessantly creating a new one."[112]

Schumpeter's oxymoronic metaphor, "Creative Destruction," has applied historically more to the American economy than to any other. The sweeping out of old products, old enterprises, and old organizational forms by new ones has been the hallmark of the American business system. Such changes have often been brutal, with excruciating consequences for many participants. But in the long run the changes have promoted a sustained record of remarkable economic growth.

"Creative Destruction," wrote Schumpeter, "is the essential fact about capitalism. It is what capitalism consists in and what every capitalist concern has got to live in." Businesspeople directly involved cannot lead a quiet, contemplative life. They must innovate relentlessly or be overtaken by competitors. "Every piece of business strategy," Schumpeter concluded, "must be seen in its role in the perennial gale of creative destruction; it cannot be understood irrespective of it."[113] Of all peoples of the world, Americans have shown themselves to be the most thoroughgoing Schumpeterians.

As the *Economist* commented in its mid-1990s "Survey of American Business":

> Underpinning all of this [recent productivity growth] is something distinctive in American society and politics. No other rich country gives companies quite such a free hand to lay off workers and shift resources from declining industries into growing ones. No other country refreshes itself in quite the same way by continuous waves of immigration . . . For as long as Americans are willing to put up with the mass lay-offs and accompanying social dislocation, these are incomparable wealth-creating advantages.[114]

For 200 years, the American people have revealed an overwhelming preference for an extreme form of competitive individualism, even as they have tried desperately to dodge its harsh penalties to themselves and members of their families. This ideology has proved to be invaluable for unleashing economic energy and achieving wondrous entrepreneurial performance. But its social costs have been very severe. To mention only the most conspicuous of many such costs, the persistent violence that has dogged the United States, from cowboy shootouts in the nineteenth century to drive-by shootings in the twentieth, cannot be unrelated to American society's glorification of individual autonomy above the collective needs of the community. The question for the future of American Capitalism, as it has been for the past, is how best to balance the economic gains against the social costs.

PROLOGUE TO CHAPTER 10

The story of IBM is an epic in the business history of the United States. Through it run some of the main currents of twentieth-century American life: the Great Depression, the administration of the welfare state, World War II, the antitrust movement, and the Cold War. For several decades starting in the 1940s, IBM's evolution as a company was profoundly affected by a complex pattern of cooperative research and development that arose among companies, universities, and the federal government.

In its particulars, this story introduces some unforgettable characters involved in bet-the-company gambles. In so doing, it presents arresting questions about the mechanics of corporate culture. Under Thomas J. Watson Sr., the firm's first great leader, IBM was preeminently a marketing company. Would one expect this kind of company to become a pioneer in the highest of high-tech products? How did the marketing-oriented top executives manage their relationships with the scientists and engineers on whom the company's future depended? How did the scientists and engineers learn to influence the managers who were making the big decisions?

In the early 1960s, when IBM was already the market leader in computers, its top executives made one of the biggest gambles in the history of business. They allocated a sum equal to three times the company's annual revenues to the development of one new product, which they called System/360 because it was intended to cover all 360 degrees of the market circle in computers. The System/360 decision is described in some detail here and is elaborated in an appendix to the chapter.

Besides thinking about this episode in hindsight, you might also try to imagine what things were like within the company as the decision unfolded in real time. As you do so, you might ask yourself a series of questions. Was the decision to go ahead with System/360 a responsible one? Is any company, at a time when it is far and away the market leader, justified in taking such a dangerous gamble? Would you yourself, as an investor in the company at that time, have supported the decision? Had you been managing a mutual fund heavily invested in the company's shares, would you have sold the shares, or bought still more? As a consultant to IBM, would you have advised the company to take a more conservative course?

As it turned out, System/360 was a huge triumph. And for many years during and after the 1960s, IBM was consistently listed by business magazines as one of America's ten best-managed companies. Often it was ranked number one.

But during the 1980s, when personal computers became the high-growth sector in information technology, IBM began to fall from grace. As you think about that fall, try to evaluate how much of it was attributable to external forces, and how much to mistakes by the company's management. If, in reviewing the IBM story as a whole, you find yourself regarding the company as a failure, then how are you defining business success?

❧10❧

IBM AND THE TWO THOMAS J. WATSONS

Rowena Olegario

From the 1920s to the mid-1950s, the International Business Machines Corporation dominated the market for data processing technology under the leadership of Thomas J. Watson Sr., one of the great business managers of the twentieth century. From the mid-1950s until 1971, his equally able son and namesake maintained the company's preeminence, as the name IBM became almost synonymous with the new computer technology. The Watsons and IBM set the industry standards in technology, financial performance, and personnel policies, in much the same way that Henry Ford had dominated the automobile industry earlier in the century. Despite serious problems during the 1980s and early 90s, IBM was still in the mid-1990s the overall industry leader, a position it had held since the beginnings of the market for commercial computers more than four decades earlier.

Such long and consistent success is rare in business, and the story of IBM invites us to take a long-term perspective on both the company and the industry it helped to define. Why was IBM's leadership so decisive and enduring? What features of American capitalism might help to explain the company's early and continuing success?

The Computer Industry

Americans coming of age in the last part of the twentieth century would find a world without computers difficult to imagine. The machines that seemed remote and exotic to that generation's parents now perform the mundane tasks of sending memos around the world, making bank transactions, and accessing the almost limitless information available through public databases. Yet as recently as the 1950s, the computer's commercial uses were not at all clear-cut. Private companies, including IBM and RCA, were reluctant to invest in computer research and development, and in the United States, the Department of Defense financed most of the necessary R&D. The government's heavy investment allowed the United States to take the lead in the information-techonology industry. That industry has since become one of the world's largest, with estimated annual worldwide revenues in the mid-1990s of about $400 billion.[1]

The computer industry in the United States was the creature of two historical developments. Beginning in the late decades of the nineteenth century, the federal government as well as many large American companies systematically started to gather an ever-burgeoning amount of data that had to be filed, sorted, and analyzed. A steady progression of new methods and technologies evolved, which contributed both to the information explosion and the attempt to manage it. Pencils, pens, and ledgers gave way to adding machines, cash registers, and manual typewriters. In the 1880s, electro-mechanical punchcard machines, the forerunners of modern-day computers, first made their appearance. Tasks involving the gathering and manipulation of data began to be a much larger part of the American economy. In 1880, only 10 percent of all workers were in the information sector, but that figure grew to 25 percent by the late 1940s and to over 30 percent by the early 1980s.[2] In many ways, the computer was only the latest entrant in a long and continuing attempt to manage the information explosion that accompanied the Second Industrial Revolution.

The other historical development was the larger role that defense-related industries and the U.S. military played in the American economy, especially during World War II (1941–1945) and the Cold War (1947–1989). The government's new investments in R&D spurred technological innovations, primarily in electronics, communications, advanced materials, and aerospace. In 1940, when total U.S. spending on R&D was $345 million, the federal government had provided only 20 percent of it. But by 1961, when total R&D spending had risen to $14.6 billion, no less than 64 percent was paid for by the government, including 85 percent of all electronics R&D.[3] A case in point was semiconductor research, to develop tiny chips containing integrated electrical circuits. From the late 1950s to the early 1970s, companies involved in national defense paid for nearly half of all semiconductor R&D.[4] Table 10.1 il-

Table 10.1   Expenditures on Research and Development, by Source of Funds, 1930–61

Year	Federal	Industry	Other
1930	14%	70%	16%
1940	20	63	17
1941–45 (avg.)	83	13	4
1947	54	39	7
1955	56	40	4
1961	64	33	4

Source: Adapted from Kenneth Flamm, *Targeting the Computer: Government Support and International Competition* (Washington: Brookings Institution, 1987), p. 7.

lustrates the federal government's much larger role in funding the nation's R&D beginning in World War II.

Most of the research was done under contract by scientists and engineers at American universities such as the Massachusetts Institute of Technology and the Moore School of Electrical Engineering at the University of Pennsylvania. The innovations they produced trickled down into the business and consumer markets and gave a huge boost to the computer and consumer-electronics industries.[5]

But it was the private sector that refined computer technologies in order to make them commercial. Many individuals who had worked on projects for the government established their own firms to meet the increased demand for business applications. These companies were largely behind the development of computer languages and commercial software. Thus, after the early 1960s the private sector took on a much larger share of the costs of innovation. In 1990, IBM alone spent nearly $7 billion on R&D.[6]

The governments of other industrialized countries also played crucial roles in developing their own industries for information technology. In the years after World War II, however, no other country was in the advantageous position of the United States. The war had devastated the economies of Japan and the leading countries of Europe—the U.K., Germany, Italy, and France. These nations were confronted with the immediate problems of rebuilding their infrastructures and providing economic security for populations grown weary of sacrifice. Their governments made desultory attempts to develop information-technology industries after the war. But only in the mid-1960s, when their own much smaller industries were gravely threatened by IBM's new System/ 360, did they seriously attempt to challenge the American lead in commercial markets.

These governments used different tactics. Japan chose a flexible approach that mixed cooperation and competition among its private firms. The European countries tended to focus on developing one firm as a national "champion." Both the Japanese and the Europeans used a combination of government subsidies, preferential procurement policies, and tax incentives to build up their computer industries.[7] No other government, however, approached the level of R&D funding provided by the American public sector in the 1950s and 1960s. Nor did any other country have the ready supply of private venture capital that was available to U.S. computer entrepreneurs. The other countries were highly dependent on U.S. technology, which they attempted to access through local firms' partnerships with American firms. The number of electronic digital computers in the United States far outpaced those of all other countries, as shown in Table 10.2.

As late as 1971, American firms accounted for half of the computers in the U.K. and France, 78 percent of those in West Germany, and 32 percent of those in Japan.[8] American companies had a 92 percent share of the world computer market, and IBM alone accounted for 62 percent.[9] In the years afterward, the firms most successful in challenging U.S. hegemony were Japanese. Fujitsu, NEC, Hitachi, and Toshiba became major players in the global market for information technology.

In the United States itself, the spread of computer use went through three stages: first the military market, then business applications, and finally the household market. In 1960, fewer than 6,000 mainframes were in operation, mostly in businesses. By 1968 the number had increased to 67,000.[10] (Before the mid-1960s, all computers were mainframes. Now the term refers to the largest, fastest, and most expensive class of computers.)[11] Minicomputers—smaller, less expensive machines used primarily for scientific and academic purposes—were introduced in the mid-1960s. By the early 1970s, these new machines accounted for nearly 30 percent of all installed computers. Total industry revenues rose from $1.3 billion in 1960 to $12.8 billion in 1972.[12]

The microcomputer, also called the personal computer or PC, was introduced in the late 1970s. The number of PCs shipped by U.S. pro-

Table 10.2   Total Number of Electronic Digital Computers in Use, 1950–74

Year	U.S.	U.K.	France	W. Germany	Japan
1950	2	3	0	0	0
1960	5,400	217	165	300	85
1970	74,060	6,269	5,460	7,000	8,800
1974	165,040	14,400	16,100	18,800	26,100

Source: Adapted from Kenneth Flamm, *Creating the Computer: Government, Industry, and High Technology* (Washington: Brookings Institution, 1988), p. 135.

ducers rose from 344,160 in 1981 to 10,182,500 in 1991—a nearly thirtyfold increase in only one decade.[13] By the mid-1990s, the worldwide PC market totaled about $80 billion annually. Some 50 million PCs were sold each year, compared to 35 million passenger cars and 100 million color television sets.[14]

Part of the PC's success came from rapidly declining costs. The microchip, a vital part of the machine, provides a striking example. The number of transistors that can be put in a microchip doubles around every eighteen months, without a corresponding increase in price.[15] This represents the most radical sustained efficiency gain for any product in industrial history. Intel's Pentium chip of 1995 was 300 times faster than the Intel chip inside IBM's original PC. A PC based on the Pentium chip had a thousand times the processing power per dollar of an IBM *mainframe* of the mid-1980s.[16] The PC's popularity also surged when the industry achieved compatibility—that is, when uniform standards were set so that consumers could mix and match components bought from different makers. IBM's profoundly important decision of 1981 to go with an open architecture went a long way toward making compatibility a reality, as its smaller competitors decided to go with the new standards IBM set.[17]

IBM to the Late 1940s: The Leadership of Thomas J. Watson Sr.

The company that became IBM was first established in 1911. Christened the Computing-Tabulating-Recording (C-T-R) Company, it was the product of a merger of several small firms. The deal was put together by the financier Charles R. Flint, who ran the new company from his offices near Wall Street. The constituent firms manufactured scales, coffee grinders, meat slicers, time clocks, and a line of punchcard tabulating machines.

In 1914, Flint hired a 40-year-old unemployed executive named Thomas J. Watson to run C-T-R. Watson was born in 1874 in the Finger Lakes district of upstate New York, the youngest of five children and the only boy. His father, a Scots-Irish immigrant, supported the family by farming and cutting lumber. By the time Watson joined C-T-R in 1914, he had over two decades of selling experience. In his first job at age 17 he had sold pianos, organs, and sewing machines to farm families. "Everything starts with a sale," he liked to say. "If there's no sale, there's no commerce in the whole of America."[18] That obsessive focus on the marketing function was Watson's most distinctive trait, and it remained with him throughout his long and distinguished business life.

In 1903, Watson joined the National Cash Register Company, headquartered in Dayton, Ohio, and quickly rose to become its second in command. The company's CEO, John Henry Patterson, was himself an important figure in the history of modern salesmanship. He was a charismatic individual who could be demanding and even sadistic. Patterson once let an NCR executive know he was fired by dragging the man's desk outside, dousing it with kerosene, then setting it alight. When office politics led to Watson's own fall from grace, he decided to resign rather than endure Patterson's brand of humiliation. But apparently he never spoke harshly about the treatment he had received. He always maintained that Patterson taught him more about salesmanship than anyone else he had ever known.[19]

"T.J.," as Thomas J. Watson Sr. came to be known, took from his experience at National Cash Register a heightened sense of what marketing could accomplish, as well as an enduring love for field salesforces. At C-T-R he re-created many of Patterson's innovations, such as providing professional training for all new sales recruits, giving sales people exclusive rights to their territories, and implementing sales quotas. T.J. also tied the manufacturing and engineering organizations closer to the salesforce so that customer information gathered from the field could be used in developing new products.[20]

T.J. Watson's visions for C-T-R were grandiose. In 1924, he renamed the C-T-R Corporation the International Business Machines Company, even though at the time the firm was actually not very international. In

1939, T.J. used his salesman's charm to have IBM included in the New York World's Fair alongside the two corporate giants General Motors and General Electric. At that time, IBM's annual revenues were around $40 million, compared with GM's $1.4 billion and GE's $305 million. The World's Fair gambit, T.J.'s son Thomas J. Watson Jr. later recalled, resulted in an exhibition that consisted of "two elephants and a gnat."[21] At the fair, T.J. hired the Philadelphia Orchestra to play the "IBM Symphony," which he had commissioned several years earlier. The exhibition cost IBM $1 million, or 2.5 percent of its entire sales for the year. But T.J. achieved his goal: he conveyed to the world an image of IBM's potential.

T.J. conceived of himself as something of a statesman and opinion-maker. He sent the company magazine, *Think,* to everyone whose goodwill he thought might be helpful, including all members of the U.S. Congress and all of the country's college presidents. According to Tom Jr., "He would work on his editorials for *Think* magazine as though it were *Time* and he were [*Time*'s editor] Henry Luce and millions of people were waiting to hear what he had to say."[22]

T.J. loved to preach, but he was also a shrewd listener. A marketer at heart, he hammered on the theme of paying scrupulous attention to customer needs. Although not himself an engineer, T.J. played the key role in developing new products. "Many, many times, the engineers [were] reasonably satisfied with a machine development," recalled an IBM laboratory manager, "and it [was] only because of the dissatisfaction and the criticism which Mr. Watson . . . presented that the engineers renewed their efforts and came out with something far superior."[23] Throughout the 1920s and 1930s, T.J. gradually moved IBM's focus away from low-tech machines and into that period's state-of-the-art tabulating instrument, the punchcard machine.

Punchcards had originally been designed by a man named Herman Hollerith to help the U.S. Census Bureau tabulate the results of the 1890 census.[24] Hollerith had founded the Tabulating Machine Company, one of the firms in the merger that created C-T-R. His basic idea was simple: rather than write data into ledgers, clerks could punch holes into cards. Each hole would represent one piece of data. Once the datum was entered, there was no need to write it again, and information could be electro-mechanically tabulated and sorted. Later, T.J. Watson realized that by adding printers to the tabulating machines, he could automate record-keeping and eliminate much of the drudgery entailed by manually entered data. In this way, the Census Bureau machines could be adapted for use in every large office in America.

An IBM executive who worked with T.J. over many years described his boss's conviction "that information, just like cash registers and rifles and cotton gins, could be made of interchangeable parts." Watson Sr., this executive recalled, "believed that a human choice to record a number could be made once, and that number, encoded on a card, could be available, reclassifiable, and printable by a machine, forever—or at least as long as the card was not bent, folded, or mutilated. I heard him say a hundred times, 'You can punch a hole in a card . . . and you'll never have to write it down again. Machines can do the routine work. People shouldn't have to do that kind of work.' "[25]

By the end of the 1920s, IBM and its competitor Remington Rand dominated the U.S. tabulating equipment market. Remington Rand, a leading manufacturer of typewriters, was three times the size of IBM in 1928. But by 1939, the two companies were roughly equal in size, each with sales of about $40 million.[26]

The stock market crash of 1929 and the subsequent Great Depression put intense pressure on the profits of most American companies. IBM, however, turned out to have both history and new legislation on its side. In 1933, President Franklin D. Roosevelt pushed through the National Industrial Recovery Act, and other legislation important to IBM followed in quick succession. These new laws necessitated data gathering and tabulation by government and industry on a scale the country had never seen before. The Social Security Act of 1935, for example, obliged businesses to supply the government with information on all their workers. IBM's revenues, which had suffered in the early years of the Depression, quickly recovered as orders for its punchcard machines poured in from both business and government.[27]

When the United States entered World War II, the entire military establishment began to use IBM cards. The company's total sales went from $40 million in 1939 to $142 million in 1945. When the war ended, the demand for U.S. manufactured goods boosted supporting industries such as banking, retail, and insurance—all of them big customers of IBM. By 1947, IBM's revenues were once again on the upswing.[28]

The space and arms race with the Soviet Union increased the U.S.

government's demand for research on computer technology. Beginning in the late 1940s, IBM and other high-tech companies reaped windfalls from the government's much larger outlays for R&D. The government did not have a coordinated procurement policy. Instead, the different federal agencies and organizations independently put out contracts for bid. They then worked closely with their high-tech suppliers to develop computers that would meet their specific goals. IBM thrived in that environment. As one authoritative historian has written, "The company's entire culture was dedicated to the task of meeting specific data-processing problems in the field." In this regard the punchcard system was not so different from the larger, more expensive computers.[29]

IBM eventually lived up to its grandiose name. By the end of World War II, the company had offices in 78 countries. But IBM's foreign operations generated less than one-eighth of the company's profits. Dissatisfied with these results, T.J. in 1949 formed IBM World Trade, a subsidiary that contained all of the company's non-U.S. operations. He adopted a decentralized approach by establishing wholly owned national companies that were managed and staffed primarily by local citizens. T.J. installed his younger son, 30-year-old Arthur K. (Dick) Watson, as vice-president and director of World Trade. Under Dick Watson, World Trade shrewdly capitalized on Europe's postwar revival. IBM's punchcard business soon dominated all major European markets except that of Britain.[30]

Until the late 1940s, IBM's punchcard machines accounted for 85 percent of its revenues. These machines assured the company a solid source of cash flow because T.J. had implemented a leasing strategy, with the field salesforce pitching the complete service that customers could expect from IBM. This full-service leasing system, which had earlier been used by Hollerith to promote his tabulating machines, proved tremendously popular with IBM customers, most of whom could not afford to buy the machines outright.

Just as important, leasing became the basis for the stability of IBM's own revenues. Although the rental system required IBM to put a lot of cash up front, as well as to manage a big field salesforce, the company was able to capitalize the equipment. On IBM's balance sheet, the machines appeared as an asset, which the company could then depreciate. The leasing system also strengthened the ties between IBM and its customers. Replacing or returning a major piece of equipment such as a punchcard machine—or, later, a mainframe computer—was too disruptive a step for most customers to contemplate. As a result, many customers renewed their leases year after year.[31]

Leasing thus became a virtuous circle for IBM. It allowed members of the salesforce to hit about 80 percent of their annual targets automatically. They could spend the bulk of their time pleasing existing customers and were able to bind those accounts even more tightly to IBM. The large initial investment required to compete with IBM in the leasing business deterred potential rivals. And the cash flow from operations became large and predictable, a circumstance that made IBM's business stable and almost depression-proof. The company could then confidently gear its rate of growth to a predictable cash flow.[32] IBM maintained this leasing system until the late 1970s, although a 1956 Department of Justice consent decree required it also to offer its hardware for sale.

By the late 1940s, IBM held 90 percent of the U.S. market for punchcard machines. T. J. Watson saw no reason to change the company's core business, even when the evidence suggested that electronic computers were becoming increasingly attractive to customers. Many years later, Tom Watson Jr. defended T.J.'s stubborn adherence to the older punchcard technology, while admitting that his father could make costly blunders:

> Without [T.J.'s] devotion to punch cards, IBM would have lost its focus; it might have become a hodgepodge conglomerate like Remington Rand. Sometimes Dad stuck to his last a little too closely—we came close to missing the computer business, for example, and in 1941, Dad turned down the chance to buy the patents for xerography. The inventor Chester Carlson came over from Queens and offered them to Dad before founding the company that eventually became Xerox. That was the biggest opportunity my old man ever missed.[33]

IBM *from the 1940s to 1971: The Leadership of* Thomas J. Watson Jr.

Thomas J. Watson Jr. (1914–1993), or "Young Tom," as he was called until well into middle age, was instrumental in overruling his father and pushing IBM into the computer age.[34] By the late 1940s, young Tom had proved his ability to take over the reins at IBM, but his relationship with his charismatic and demanding father remained difficult. In his autobiography, Tom Jr. wrote: "We fought about every major issue of the business—how to finance IBM's growth, whether to settle or fight a federal antitrust suit, what role in IBM other members of our family ought to play." Young Tom's uneasy relationship with his father had begun in childhood, and the tensions between father and son continued until T.J.'s death in 1956 at the age of 82.[35]

Tom Jr. had been born when T.J. was 39, perhaps too old and certainly too obsessed with business to be the kind of father most children hope for. By the time Tom Jr. was 13, the tall and awkward boy was attending IBM sales conventions. Painfully aware that he was not his father's favorite (that honor belonged to his sister, Jane), young Tom expended a good deal of energy alternately fighting with his father and seeking his approval. At the age of 23, with some misgivings, Tom Jr. entered the family business.

His first few years as an IBM salesman seemed to confirm his doubts. During the mandatory training session, he needed a personal tutor to teach him how to program the punchcard machines. As a young salesman, he was never able to shake off the feeling that his successes had been handed to him by his father. In 1940, for example, he was named the company's top salesman when U.S. Steel Products, a major account that had been given to him to enhance his performance, placed a large order that fulfilled his entire annual sales quota on the first day of the year. The pressure of being T. J. Watson's son simply overwhelmed him. He began to shirk his responsibilities and often spent half his days flying airplanes and most of his evenings carousing in nightclubs.

World War II, however, proved to be as beneficial for Young Tom personally as for IBM in general. In 1940, at the age of 26, he became an officer in the Army Air Corps. For the first time in his life, Tom Jr. felt he had escaped his father's long shadow. Even then, however, he was unable to escape from IBM's presence altogether. Reminders were everywhere. The military used the company's punchcard machines to tabulate its payroll, personnel, supplies, bombing results, and casualties. But under the tutelage of Major General Follett Bradley, to whom he later dedicated his autobiography, Tom Jr. acquired the confidence to go back after the war and aim for IBM's top job.

By the time Tom Jr. came back in 1946, IBM was on the verge of entering the computer age. But T.J. still hesitated on the threshold, although IBM had been supporting the work of Howard Aiken of Harvard on the Mark I computer. Even Tom Jr. was skeptical. When he went to the University of Pennsylvania to see one of the country's most advanced computers, the Electronic Numerical Integrator and Computer (ENIAC), he saw little potential in it. Instead, IBM introduced the 603 Electronic Multiplier, essentially a fancy calculator but much faster than the old punchcard machines.

In 1947, driven in part by competition from ENIAC, T.J. charged IBM's engineers with developing an alternative. The following year they came up with something called the Selective Sequence Electronic Calculator (SSEC), a hybrid of the modern computer and the punchcard machine. It was 120 feet long. It was also the first big calculator ever to run on software. IBM displayed the SSEC in its huge glass-front showrooms on Manhattan's Fifty-Seventh Street and attracted a lot of attention from pedestrians. The SSEC soon became popularly associated with the machines of the future. To the new generation of electronics engineers, however, IBM continued to seem old-fashioned, a step behind the times.

The big insurance companies, eager to move on to the next level in data-processing machines, backed the inventors of ENIAC, Presper Eckert and John Mauchly, who were developing magnetic tape to replace cumbersome punchcard technology. Meanwhile, T.J. continued to resist changes to the punchcard system. He distrusted magnetic tape because information could be erased from it. But some of IBM's largest customers, including Metropolitan Life, began to complain about the great amounts of physical space the punchcard machines were taking up. In response, Tom Jr., who had been named an executive vice president in 1949, reviewed all of the company's development projects. He learned that RCA, GE, and other successful companies were spending 3 percent of their revenues on R&D whereas IBM was spending only 2.25 percent.[36] Tom Jr. came to the inescapable conclusion that IBM was still in the electronic Dark Ages.

The competitive pressures grew stronger when Remington Rand bought Eckert and Mauchly's next project, the Universal Automatic Computer (UNIVAC), in 1950.[37] (Antitrust laws prevented IBM from buying UNIVAC.) Tom Jr.'s in-house evaluation, the enthusiasm of IBM's scientists and engineers for the new technology, customer demand for faster and less cumbersome tabulating machines, and intensifying competition finally convinced T.J. that IBM had to take the big step. In June

1950, right after the outbreak of the Korean War, IBM finally began producing computers.

From 1950 onward, Tom Jr. provided strong support for those executives within the company who were pushing IBM into computers. This strategy became his top priority when he was named the company's president in 1952.[38] From a marketing point of view, IBM's dominance in punchcard machines greatly facilitated its move into computers. Metropolitan Life and other companies that were already using IBM's tabulating instruments were receptive to the new technology.

In 1950, IBM's annual sales totaled $215 million. By 1955, when IBM became the world's leading producer of computers, revenues had more than doubled to $564 million. In the 1950s, two projects for the U.S. military, the "Bomb-Nav" guidance computer in the B-52 bomber and the SAGE air defense system, contributed more than half of IBM's domestic electronic data processing revenues. These projects for the military benefited IBM in other ways. The company gained access to computer technology that was being developed in universities such as MIT. And IBM learned how to mass-produce key components such as magnetic core memories and circuit boards.[39]

With the aggressive push into the computer market, IBM grew so quickly that in some years the company had to train 20,000 or more new employees. R&D was dramatically strengthened. From 1950 to 1954, the number of R&D employees grew from 3 percent to 9 percent of the domestic workforce.[40] Continuing his father's emphasis on marketing, Tom Jr. put the whole weight of the salesforce behind the new technology. As he later wrote:

> In the history of IBM, technological innovation often wasn't the thing that made us successful. Unhappily there were many times when we came in second. But technology turned out to be less important than sales and distribution methods. Starting with UNIVAC [the rival product], we consistently outsold people who had better technology because we knew how to put the story before the customer, how to install the machines successfully, and how to hang on to customers once we had them. The secret of our sales approach was the same thing that made Dad so successful in punch cards: systems knowledge. That was where IBM had its monopoly. No competitor ever paid enough attention to it, not even the people at Remington Rand, who should have known better because they were in the punch-card business too.[41]

IBM was opportunistic in its pursuit of market share. The company considered both the scientific and commercial markets equally fair game, and it often applied what it learned in one market to the other. This certainly was the case with the Defense Calculator, or what was later called the 701.[42] Originally designed for use by the military, it eventually became IBM's first computer for the commercial market. The company's willingness to commit $3 million to the project, the equivalent of IBM's entire research budget two years earlier, presaged a pattern of risk-taking that was to characterize the younger Watson's entire tenure as head of the company. There was as yet no clear market for the new technology. But Tom Jr. felt pressured by competition from UNIVAC. By his own admission, he was "terrified" when he learned that UNIVAC had made inroads at the Census Bureau, where Hollerith's punchcard machines had been launched and which traditionally had been an IBM client.[43]

Tom Jr. and his allies within the company responded by keeping teams of engineers working three shifts to design, simultaneously, the 701 and what became the 702, another machine for business applications. T.J. gave the project his blessing, and the first IBM 701 was delivered in December 1952. The customer response to the project was eye-opening. When IBM announced that the monthly rental price would be double the $8,000 that the company had originally quoted, not a single customer bailed out. "That was when I felt a real *Eureka!*" Tom Jr. later wrote. "Customers wanted computers so badly that we could double the price and still not drive people away."[44]

Unlike the UNIVAC, which was the size of a small truck, IBM's 701 was made up of a number of smaller parts, each of which could fit into a freight elevator. Assembling the machine took only three days, compared with a week for UNIVAC. From the customer's perspective, the 701 was clearly a step up from IBM's SSEC. The new machine took up 75 percent less space and operated 25 times faster than the older machine. Just as important, IBM designed a set of high-quality peripherals for the 701, such as printers and magnetic tape drives. The availability of these add-ons convinced many customers to choose the 701 over its rivals.[45]

Even before the initial shipment of the 701, IBM had planned its next major product. The 650 Series of electronic computers was launched in 1954 and was the first to be mass-produced by the company. These machines, which ran on punched cards, became the country's best-selling first-generation computers, surpassing UNIVAC. Sperry Rand (formerly Remington Rand) rapidly fell behind IBM. Managerial and organizational difficulties slowed its ability to bring new technologies to market, and many UNIVAC customers migrated to IBM's more advanced products.[46] Meanwhile, IBM's revenues reached the $1 billion mark in 1957, the year after T.J.'s death. In 1960, over two-thirds of its revenues came from computers and peripherals, the remaining third from electric typewriters and other office equipment. By the early 1960s, it was clear that IBM had achieved what few other firms of its size had ever managed to do: it had exited a thriving business and shifted into a new and risky technology. And it had made the gamble pay off.[47]

IBM's performance in the international arena mirrored its domestic success. Because of the competitive disadvantages World War II and its aftermath had imposed on Europe and Japan, the company faced little significant foreign competition when it moved into electronic computers. In some years, World Trade grew at double the rate of the U.S. business. In 1954, it passed the $100 million sales mark. By 1960, it was a $350 million-a-year business, accounting for 20 percent of IBM's total sales. From the 1960s onward, foreign markets were very important contributors to the revenues of IBM and its American rivals (see Table 10.3).

Until the late 1960s World Trade remained subordinate to U.S. headquarters and had little say in product and pricing strategy. Nevertheless, the various countries within World Trade had a large degree of autonomy. IBM's offices and plants abroad were staffed almost exclusively by local citizens, and very few of the company's American executives inter-

Table 10.3   Importance of Foreign Markets to American Computer Firms (foreign revenues as % of total revenues)

Firm	1960	1969	1979	1990
IBM	20	35	54	61
NCR	41	41	54	n.a.
Control Data	n.a.	26	32	32
Digital	n.a.	24	36	56
Hewlett-Packard	n.a.	n.a.	49	61
Wang	n.a.	n.a.	33	51

Note: Sales figures are for all of the companies' products, not just computers.

Sources: Adapted from Kenneth Flamm, *Creating the Computer,* p. 101. Figures for 1990 from company reports.

fered with World Trade's day-to-day operations. IBM maintained T.J.'s vision of making the two halves independent of each other and restricting the imports and exports between them. Thus World Trade eventually had its own manufacturing plants and a large proportion of its workforce outside the United States. This strategy helped to make IBM a "local" company in its foreign markets. The approach paid off most impressively in Japan, traditionally a market closed to many U.S. products. In the mid-1960s, IBM had 75 percent of the computer markets in West Germany, Italy, and France; 50 percent in the United Kingdom; and about 40 percent in Japan.[48]

By the 1960s, IBM's dominant position in the computer industry and its strong commitment to R&D placed formidable constraints on the technological options open to competitors. In 1963, IBM's $1.2 billion in revenues from electronic data processing was nearly nine times that of its closest rival, Sperry Rand ($145.5 million). IBM's competitors were so comparatively small that they were nicknamed the "Seven Dwarfs." Those seven manufacturers—Sperry Rand, Control Data, Burroughs, General Electric, National Cash Register, Honeywell, and RCA—had combined electronic data processing revenues that were only about half of IBM's.[49]

Even so, not all was well at IBM. For one thing, there were some serious compatibility problems with IBM's hardware. In 1960, the company's sales catalog offered eight computers, each with a different internal architecture. Customers who wanted to upgrade were often required to lay out money for altogether new systems. The lack of compatibility also prevented IBM from achieving optimum scale efficiencies in engineering, manufacturing, and sales. In 1961, an in-house task force concluded that IBM's products were aging. The task force warned that IBM would have to move faster or risk being overtaken by rival companies, several of which were poised to enter the market with new and cheaper technologies.[50]

In response, IBM used its tremendous scale and scope to develop System/360 and its successors, which became the company's flagship products from the late 1960s through the 1970s. Here the company's long experience in designing computers for the Department of Defense proved advantageous. One project in particular, the Stretch computer that IBM completed in 1962, helped lay the technological foundation for System/360's flexible architecture. IBM had designed Stretch for two agencies, the Atomic Energy Commission and the National Security Agency, which had very different computer needs. In trying to meet both agencies' requirements, IBM developed for Stretch many of the features that later made System/360 such a huge success.[51]

Introduced in 1964, System/360 turned out to be one of the most important products of the Third Industrial Revolution. System/360 consisted of a broad line of compatible computers. The initial set included five computers, the operating system, and a new line of peripherals: disk, tape, card input/output equipment, and the most popular printer of the next two decades, the 1403 N1. The new compatibility enhanced the appeal of computers by giving customers greater flexibility. They could easily trade up to a better machine or move laterally to a compatible one. Compatibility drove down the price of computing, largely because customers saved on software costs. Those savings, in turn, whetted customers' appetite for more hardware—which they bought from IBM.[52]

The company invested $5 billion in System/360, about three times its revenues in 1960. It hired more than 60,000 new workers, bringing total employment to 190,000 in 1966 and 325,000 by 1970.[53] Developing System/360 put the company under tremendous pressure. It was an all-or-nothing gamble. IBM aimed to replace existing computers, including the 1401, its bestselling product at the time, with a technology that had never before existed in the marketplace.[54] In addition, the new machines were targeted at both the scientific *and* business markets, which had very different computing needs. The whole 360 strategy alienated many of IBM's own employees, who had a stake in the company's older technologies. Tom Jr. and Vin Learson, the executive in charge of the 360 project, had to whip all divisions into line to support the new strategy. Learson, writing to a reluctant colleague, laid down the corporate policy thus: "By 1967 the 1401 will be dead as a Dodo. Let's stop fighting this."[55]

The 360 project changed the company's structure in several ways. For one thing, the 360's proprietary circuitry forced IBM to become the world's largest manufacturer of computer components, and this was a major change. The company's backward integration into componentry production ultimately led to its becoming the world's largest producer of semiconductors, by far. The resulting scale economies lowered the cost of memory, thus opening the door to greater programming flexibility. In addition, IBM began relying more heavily on its foreign R&D and manufacturing facilities. The company integrated its overseas divisions and gave international managers responsibilities that were equal to those of their U.S. counterparts. IBM's foreign divisions, under the leadership of Dick Watson, had sales in 1969 that accounted for 35 percent of total revenues, up from 20 percent in 1960. And finally, the 360 necessitated three significant corporate reorganizations, carried out between 1960 and 1966.[56]

System/360 proved to be the most successful big-ticket product introduction in American business since the Model T Ford. With System/360, IBM set the standard and brought about unprecedented growth in the use of computers throughout the world. The company's revenues began to grow by nearly 30 percent per year, an almost unheard-of rate for a multibillion dollar corporation. Sales were $2.5 billion in 1965 and $7.5 billion by 1970. No other modern industry had ever grown so quickly.

Related industries experienced parallel growth. These included makers of software, leasing companies, and "service bureaus" that provided computer services to customers who did not wish to do the work themselves. (One such company was Electronic Data Services, which made a billionaire out of its founder, former IBM salesman H. Ross Perot.) System/360 also spurred governments abroad to step up their investment in computer technology in order to remain competitive. Japan, for example, launched a series of joint research projects linking major electronics manufacturers with NTT and MITI laboratories.[57]

After System/360, writes one authoritative student of the industry, "it was no longer the era of atomic energy: it was the information age. IBM had neatly reinforced what economists such as Kenneth Galbraith or social critics such as Alvin Toffler would variously label a postindustrial or service-oriented economy. What Henry Ford had done for automobiles and [the] industrial economy, Tom Watson, Jr., had done for data processing and the American economy of the late twentieth century."[58] The story of System/360 is such a vital part of IBM's history that additional details about its development within the organization are provided in an Appendix at the end of this chapter.

IBM's proprietary, internally controlled standard for System/360 further consolidated the firm's dominance. Rivals General Electric and RCA, unable to compete in mainframes, exited the market. IBM's remaining competitors became known as BUNCH, an acronym for Burroughs, UNIVAC (owned by Sperry Rand), National Cash Register, Control Data, and Honeywell. However, in a scenario that was to recur during the PC wars two decades later, IBM's success in establishing the industry standard made possible the rise of new competitors who rode the wave of System/360's success. A number of companies began to market their own versions of the System 360/370 peripherals. The makers of these "plug compatibles" (equipment that could be plugged into the IBM machines) did not have to incur the first mover's R&D costs. Nor did they have to invest as heavily to market new products. Among the companies that moved aggressively into plug-compatibles were Telex (which manufactured tape drives), Memorex (magnetic and tape drives), Amdahl (disk drives and core memories), and Control Data (a full line of peripherals).[59]

Many plug-compatible manufacturers prospered by reacting nimbly to IBM's moves. Control Data followed each IBM announcement of a new peripheral by quickly introducing its own lower-priced version. By retroengineering and making slight modifications in its knockoffs, Control Data could compete without infringing on IBM's patents. IBM also found itself competing with firms set up by its own former employees. The first true IBM-compatible machine was designed by Gene Amdahl, who had been one of the chief architects of System/360. Amdahl left IBM in 1970 to found a company that bore his name and that produced high-end computers and peripherals. When Amdahl left his company nearly ten years later, its 360/370 plug-compatible was the largest competitor to the IBM 360/370 original. The Amdahl firm was also the crucial channel through which Fujitsu (which became a part-owner of Amdahl in 1972) obtained information on System/370's architecture. Thus, System 360/370 created and nurtured many of its own rivals.[60]

But the increased competition hardly seemed to matter. By 1971, when Tom Watson Jr. took early retirement at age 57, the demand for computers had penetrated most of American business. IBM had established itself as the leading-edge supplier and servicer of commercial mainframe computers. That reputation for top-notch systems knowledge served IBM well. As early as the 1950s, Tom Jr. had discovered that "getting a computer was a major investment that required approval by the board of directors in most companies, and for the executive in charge of picking the right machine, IBM became known as the safe choice." As an article in *Fortune* magazine put it: "Boards of directors may know little about machinery, but they know about IBM." The company became a fertile training ground for individuals who later headed the information technology departments of major corporations throughout the world. A study in the late 1970s found that more than half of the chief information officers at *Fortune* 500 companies were IBM alumni. More than 60 of the *Fortune* 500 companies either had someone on IBM's board or had an IBM-er on their own boards.[61]

When Tom Watson Jr. retired in 1971, the company had a 62 percent share of the world computer market. Other American firms combined had 30 percent, and European and Japanese makers accounted for the rest.[62] IBM's market dominance, and the inbred networks that developed between IBM and its customers, added long-term reinforcement to an already spectacular success story. In 1979, IBM's annual revenues reached $23 billion. Only six years later, they had more than doubled, to $50 billion.

The Evolution of IBM's Corporate Culture

Under Thomas J. Watson Sr., IBM had developed into a model paternalistic company. Although he was not quite a household name in America, T.J. Watson was for many years actually more famous than IBM, which as a company dealt primarily with other businesses rather than directly with consumers. Although T.J. owned only a small portion of the company's stock, he succeeded in imprinting his personality so thoroughly on the firm that it became impossible to think of IBM apart from Watson himself.

But the cult of personality that T.J. encouraged among IBM workers sometimes seemed extreme, even to his son. Tom Jr. wrote in his autobiography that his father had "the biggest and most successful one-man show in American business, with something like twenty-two thousand people working as if they were an extension of his personality. To Dad it seemed perfectly natural that his photograph should hang in everybody's office. It didn't embarrass him in the slightest when his men organized a worldwide IBM celebration on the thirty-third anniversary of his employment."[63]

T.J. filled IBM factories and offices around the world not only with his photograph but also with a steady progression of company slogans: "Give full consideration to the individual employee." "Spend a lot of time making customers happy." "Go the last mile to do a thing right." The most famous sign of all simply urged everyone to "THINK." In addition, T.J. encouraged trainees to sing company songs. "Ever Onward" was among the most popular:

> There's a thrill in store for all,
> For we're about to toast
> The corporation in every land.
> We're here to cheer each pioneer
> And also proudly boast
> Of that "man of men," our friend and guiding hand.
> The name of T.J. Watson means a courage none can stem:
> And we feel honored to be here to toast the "IBM."
> *Chorus:* EVER ONWARD—EVER ONWARD!
> That's the spirit that has brought us fame!
> We're big, but bigger we will be,
> We can't fail for all can see
> That to serve humanity has been our aim!
> Our products now are known in every zone.
> Our reputation sparkles like a gem!
> We've fought our way through—and new
> Fields we're sure to conquer too
> For the EVER ONWARD IBM.[64]

Lou Mobley, an executive who worked closely with both Watsons, re-called: "I'd come to work at nine in the morning and hear that song rolling through the hills of Endicott [New York]. A new class of salesmen would be singing it, so loud the people over in the factory could hear it. I remember how inspiring I found it."[65] The conservative IBM "look"—dark blue suits and stiff-collared white shirts—amounted to a kind of uniform, and strongly reinforced the company's culture.

T.J.'s autocratic style was matched by his keen sense of what was appropriate for the times. With the New Deal and the rise of labor unions in the 1930s, the public began to expect more out of large corporations. T.J.'s sensitivity to the prevailing climate of opinion, his genuine support of Roosevelt's New Deal principles, and the company's great prosperity helped deter any serious threats from labor unions. During the Great Depression, T.J. refused to curtail output or to lay off employees. Instead, he stored new machines in warehouses until they could be sold. That decision proved fortuitous. IBM won the contract with the Social Security Administration partly because the company already had a large number of machines that were ready to be delivered.[66]

T.J. established an Education Department in 1932, and by 1937 one-half of the 3,200 factory employees were taking courses on 24 subjects.[67] IBM earned a reputation for providing perhaps the best pay and benefits of any large firm in America. The company had a number of unique perks, including the IBM country club in Endicott, which any employee could join for $1 a year. The club served dinner three times a week to give IBM wives a break from cooking. T.J. even delivered FDR-like "fireside chats" to his employees via microphones installed in the offices and factories at Endicott. Because his own employment contract paid him a percentage of IBM's profits, T.J. became the highest-compensated executive in America. In 1936, newspapers dubbed him the "thousand-dollar-a-day man." But in fact, T.J. had already adjusted his percentage downward to avoid earning an even higher amount.[68]

Lou Mobley summed up the significance of IBM's culture and personnel policies:

> Watson [Sr.] provided a company that promised his employees the safety and security of a lifelong career and the feeling of belonging to a family. As the head of the family, Watson expected commitment, loyalty, and obedience. Looking back on Watson through the lens of today's values, we label him an autocratic, paternalistic leader. He was. And he was precisely what his followers wanted . . .
>
> Once the sales job was defined as managing a relationship with the customer, the salesman had all of IBM's resources at his fingertips to keep the customer happy. Every IBM sales class listened to talks by the manufacturing manager, the R&D director, the marketing manager, the service manager, even the editor of *Think* magazine. All would tell the class, "If you have any problems with a customer, pick up the phone and call me" . . .
>
> Because IBM salesmen became IBM executives, the company's dedication to the primacy of the customer was self-perpetuating. Those who rose through the ranks serving the customer insisted that all of their employees be similarly dedicated. Even the financial breakthroughs of IBM grew out of Watson's dedication to serving the customer.[69]

IBM's facilities in Endicott, New York, a factory town near the Pennsylvania border, reinforced the interdependence of the firm's departments. Although the company was headquartered in Manhattan, its most important activities all took place in Endicott. IBM manufactured its punchcard machines there, and its sales training facilities and major laboratories were located near the factories. Customers learning how to use the company's products were housed in the IBM Homestead, an elegant mansion that had belonged to the town's founder. In the 1940s, IBM held the Hundred Percent Club convention in Endicott. The "Club" was composed of salesmen who had met their yearly quotas. T.J. erected a huge "tent city," complete with wooden floors and sidewalks, to accommodate them. (Endicott continued to be the focal point of IBM's activities until the 1950s, when the company built a number of plants throughout the United States, including one of the first factories in what later became Silicon Valley. In 1964, IBM relocated its headquarters to Armonk, New York.)

When Tom Jr. took over in the 1950s, he did not want to abandon either IBM's distinctive internal culture nor its orientation toward the customer. But he knew that he had to reorganize the company. His father had not liked organization charts because he thought them too restricting. Instead, T.J.'s method consisted of calling managers at random into his office, where he deliberately unsettled them by asking questions about the company he knew they could not answer. Shortly after Tom Jr. took over, he and another top executive put together an organization chart. They discovered that between 30 and 40 divisions were reporting directly to T.J.! Something had to be done.[70]

As Tom Jr. himself put it, "Every entrepreneurial company, if it succeeds, must eventually face the transition to professional management. In our case, Dad had been so good at his job that this maturing process was long overdue. As big as IBM now was, it had almost none of the things that corporations count on to keep small problems from ballooning into big ones—such as a clear chain of command, large-scale decentralization, a planning process, or formal business policies." Tom Jr. went on to say, "Our way of getting things done consisted mostly of wisdom carried in a few people's heads. If we kept growing and tried to run a billion-dollar business that haphazardly, IBM would probably not survive. It would explode like a supernova and end up a dwarf."[71] The ensuing reorganization took several years. But during Tom Jr.'s tenure, IBM emerged with a modern, systematic, and bureaucratic leadership.[72]

Tom Jr. began to rethink the company's strategy and structure in other ways. He stopped the singing of IBM's songs and overhauled its general "look." In 1956, he sliced the company into four semi-autonomous divisions, each with its own general manager. He insisted that the company develop position descriptions, formal appraisals, and a standardized wage and salary administration.[73] He explicitly based the company's strategy on continuous R&D investment, a step which all but guaranteed that IBM would remain a market leader in technology. In the early 1960s, internally financed R&D jumped from about 15 percent of net income to just under 50 percent.[74] "What we created," Tom Jr. wrote, "was not so much a reorganization as the first top-to-bottom *organization* IBM ever had":

> We took the product divisions that we'd already established, tightened them up so that each executive had clearly defined tasks, and then turned the units loose to operate with considerable flexibility. These were IBM's arms and legs, so to speak. At the head of the corporation, to oversee plans and major decisions, we set up a six-man corporate management committee . . . I gave each man responsibility for a major piece of IBM, while leaving myself free to roam across the whole company. Finally we superimposed a corporate staff that included experts in such areas as finance, manufacturing, personnel, and communications. Their task was to work as a kind of nervous system and keep our adolescent company from tripping all over itself, as had happened a few months earlier when we had two divisions unwittingly bidding against each other on the same tract of land for a factory.[75]

DuPont and GM had applied this kind of system as early as the 1920s. IBM, like most other large American companies, adopted the practice for the first time in the 1950s.

In reflecting on IBM's new structure, Tom Jr. articulated the basic philosophy that T.J. had instilled in the company—the emphasis on individuals, the careful listening to both employees and customers, and the policy of fierce personal competition among managers within IBM itself. As Tom Jr. put it, "I never thought the proper place for a senior executive was sitting behind a bare desk looking at the ceiling, dreaming up great deeds for the future, and drawing new lines on the organization chart." Instead, he liked to wander around the company. "I asked what was right and, more important, what was wrong. You don't hear things that are bad about your company unless you ask."[76]

Despising the "yes-men" who had kowtowed to his dictatorial father, Tom Jr. tried to surround himself with people who did not tell him what they thought he wanted to hear. He implemented a system of internal competition that became known as "contention management." In Tom Jr.'s view, "The best way to motivate people is to pit them against one another, and I was constantly looking for ways to stir up internal competition." He said that "when you have separate units competing against one another, to a large extent they discipline themselves."[77] Even this was not entirely new. Contention management of a kind had grown out of T.J.'s informal method of giving the same assignment to several people within IBM, forcing them to compete, and then choosing the results he liked best. As is described in the appendix to this chapter, the contention management system was instrumental in pushing IBM into computers. It also made possible the development of the immensely complex System/ 360.

Despite the new bureaucratic structure, IBM in many ways remained the paternalistic company that T.J. had made it. Tom Jr. was dedicated to job security and to promoting from within, so people would not be fired for taking risks and failing. He also distributed the profits broadly among top management. During his tenure, IBM continued its generous retirement plans and was one of the first companies in the United States to offer major medical insurance. When Tom Jr. discovered that employees joked about IBM standing for "I've Been Moved," he encouraged managers to decrease the number of employee relocations, which were disruptive to family life. In 1958, IBM became the first major U.S. industrial company to put all of its employees on salary. Tom Jr. looked for ways to increase employee ownership of the company. Also in 1958, he implemented an employee stock purchase plan. The plan had mixed results. Employees often felt demoralized whenever the stock price dipped, so Tom Jr. decided instead to increase benefits such as major medical coverage and scholarships. He wrote: "I knew exactly the attitude I wanted to cultivate in ordinary IBM employees: I wanted them to feel a proprietary interest, and to have some knowledge of each other's problems and goals. I also wanted them to feel that they had access to top management and that no one was so far down the chain of command that he couldn't be kept aware of where the business was heading."[78]

Tom Jr. also was careful to continue his father's tradition of the personal touch. "Probably an efficiency expert would have condemned these practices as a gargantuan waste of time for a chief executive," he wrote. "But in a service-oriented business like ours, these seemingly minor details of courtesy and style were too important to let slide."[79] Overall, IBM by the 1970s had developed one of the strongest and most distinctive corporate cultures in American business history.

IBM's Problems with Antitrust

IBM consistently battled a problem that had long been unique to American companies: the Justice Department's aggressive antitrust surveillance. In contrast to the practice in some other industrialized countries, the U.S. government tended not to devote its resources to building up national "champions." Instead, federal policy was to level the playing field for smaller and newer companies. Antitrust policy was not always clear-cut or consistently enforced. And it sometimes had the ironic result of handicapping the dominant and best-run companies in order to achieve a vaguely defined ideal of fairness.

Thomas J. Watson Sr. was no stranger to antitrust suits. He had figured in one of the most sensational of the early cases brought by the federal government, *U.S. v. National Cash Register* (1912). The court had actually sentenced T.J. to a year in prison for engaging in a scheme, proposed by CEO John Henry Patterson, to buy out secondhand dealers of NCR's cash registers—a flagrant violation of the spirit of the antitrust laws. The conviction was thrown out on a technicality when the case was appealed, and T.J. never served time in prison. But the experience shocked and embittered him. For the rest of his life he harbored what Tom Jr. described as an "irrational hatred of the Department of Justice."[80]

With IBM, much as in its later battles with AT&T, the Justice Department objected to the company's practice of selling all of its supplies and services as an integrated *system*. This made even the punchcards themselves a distinctive item that only IBM could supply. Even in the 1930s, T.J. Watson had had to settle a case brought by the Department on this basis.[81]

During the Truman administration (1945–1953), the Justice Department and the Federal Trade Commission vigorously went after several dominant firms, including the United Shoe Machinery Co. and the aluminum giant Alcoa. The Watsons knew that it would only be a matter of time before IBM caught the attention of the federal trustbusters. The company held 90 percent of the punchcard market, and its machines could be found in every federal agency. "The thing Dad could never accept about monopoly law," Tom Jr. later wrote, "is that you don't have to *do* anything wrong to *be* in the wrong. The Department of Justice was coming after us entirely because they didn't think there was enough competition in our market."[82]

When the Justice Department began investigating IBM after World War II, the Watsons tried to argue that their company was only a small part of a much larger market defined as "the entire world of business calculations," which included adding machines, posting machines, bank-teller machines, and even pencils and ledger-books. T.J. himself insisted that he had declined to buy out or merge with others in the industry, including Underwood Typewriter and his former employer, National Cash Register. Yet the Watsons' arguments failed to sway the regulators. The Justice Department declared that punchcards were a separate industry altogether, and that IBM's market share put it in a monopoly position. Since the 1930s, the federal government had won about 90 percent of its antitrust cases. Knowing this, Tom Jr. tried to convince his father that IBM should settle the complaint by consent decree so that it could focus its attention on the emerging computer market. T.J. refused, however.[83]

In 1952, the government filed suit against IBM. After four years of fighting the suit, Tom Jr. succeeded in convincing the extremely reluctant and combative T.J. to settle out of court. In 1956, IBM signed a consent decree that required the company to offer its equipment for sale as well as for lease. The decree also required that IBM sell its data-processing services separately from its manufacturing and sales business, and to make parts available to other service organizations. After the decree, and especially after the introduction of System/360, a vibrant market sprang up consisting of independent service and leasing businesses, as well as dealers in used IBM equipment. For many years afterward these competitors acknowledged that they owed their existence to the Justice Department's intervention. "If you don't regulate IBM," one executive of a large independent computer-leasing company said in 1994, "it will put handcuffs on companies like ours to compete effectively. And that will cause consumers to suffer."[84] Despite this kind of increased competition, Tom Jr. believed that settling the case "was one of the best moves we ever made, because it cleared the way for IBM to keep expanding at top speed."[85]

In 1967, the Justice Department again began investigating IBM, and in 1969, it filed a major antitrust suit accusing the company of monopolizing the computer market. (IBM's U.S. share was about 70 percent.) This time, the proposed remedy was far more serious: the Justice Department asked the courts to break the company into seven $1 billion companies rather than allow it to continue as one $7 billion entity. Tom Jr. refused to consider such a move. His resolve strengthened when growing competition from Japanese firms such as Fujitsu and NEC convinced him that IBM needed size to preserve its competitive advantage.[86]

Tom Jr. had spent most of his management years under the threat of antitrust suits. He had lived with the knowledge that T.J. had once been sentenced to federal prison for violating antitrust law. So he was especially sensitive to the potential for conflict brought about by IBM's size and market dominance:

> In spite of all our efforts, we often found it hard to pull our punches, especially against companies who jumped into the business to piggyback on our success. In the late '60s a whole crop of new businesses sprang up, specializing in cut-rate disk drives, terminals, and other peripherals designed to plug into System/360 equipment. These so-called plug-compatible manufacturers, or PCMs, took business away from some of the most lucrative segments of our product line, and were a constant annoyance. Because they were parasites, they were terribly vulnerable to any move we made, and we faced a legal and customer-relations dilemma whenever it was time for us to update our designs or lower our prices. Say, for example, IBM's engineers wrote an improved piece of software—could we introduce it if, as a side effect, it would cause our computers to reject data that were being stored on a Brand X disk? Could we introduce it even if this, in turn, might put the Brand X Disk Corporation out of business? It was a very gray area of the law.[87]

The lawsuit of 1969 had at least one immediate effect. Six months after it was filed, IBM abandoned the practice of "bundling," in which the company included a set of services such as engineering help, maintenance, and training sessions in the price of its hardware and software. The practice was an old one. It had been used by Herman Hollerith, the inventor of the punchcard machine, as an incentive for potential users to try the new technology. According to the Justice Department, however, bundling made IBM guilty of "restraint of trade," forbidden by the Sherman Antitrust Act. The regulators reasoned that other companies selling software and support services would have difficulty entering these markets because they had already been sewn up by IBM. Thus, a practice that IBM saw as providing value for its customers was deemed illegal by regulators. In forcing IBM to abandon its bundling practice, the federal government opened the way for numerous companies to enter the software and computer services markets. Thereafter, IBM machines would function as a platform for a diverse array of software applications, generated by a collection of highly competitive small firms.[88]

In addition to litigation filed by the federal government, IBM was hit with suits filed by other companies. Several of these suits seriously threatened IBM's future. The most important was started by Control Data Corporation, a Minneapolis company specializing in supercomputers—the fastest and most expensive mainframes. Founded in 1957 by a small group of ex–Sperry Rand engineers, Control Data reached annual sales of $60 million by 1963. (IBM's revenues that year were $2.1 billion.) In a scenario that prefigured the PC wars of the 1980s, Control Data's development staff of only 34 people developed the 6600, a supercomputer far superior to any developed by IBM. Furious, Tom Jr. blasted IBM's managers for allowing a small upstart to beat them in a market he felt should have been IBM's. In an attempt to dampen enthusiasm for Control Data's 6600, IBM announced that it would soon unveil a technology that would make the 6600 obsolete. The announcement had its desired chilling effect. Control Data, which until then had appeared invincible, suddenly seemed destined to lose its market to an IBM machine that did not yet exist.

Control Data eventually recovered. Tom Jr. decided that the supercomputer market was too small and specialized to present much of a threat to IBM, which never succeeded in surpassing its smaller rival's technology anyway. But Control Data's CEO, William Norris, now demanded compensation for the ordeal his company had suffered. In 1968, Norris filed an antitrust lawsuit that closely resembled the 1969 suit of the Justice Department. As the parallel suits went forward, Control Data's lawyers worked closely with public antitrust authorities, and the company developed a computerized index to document all of IBM's alleged abuses. Some 80,000 key documents were indexed, the first time computer technology had been used on such a scale in an antitrust suit. Norris's deep antagonism toward IBM greatly benefited the understaffed and underfunded Justice Department, which relied heavily on Control Data's resources. Meanwhile, IBM spent tens of millions of dollars fighting the suits. Perhaps more important, the scale and importance of *U.S. v. IBM* affected the company's strategic decisionmaking. According to Tom Jr.:

> For years every executive decision, even ones that were fairly routine, had to be made with one eye on how it might affect the lawsuit. To keep damning evidence to a minimum, the lawyers even dictated what we could and couldn't say at meetings . . . This sort of mealymouthing went against my instincts. I wanted IBM to be the best in everything and recognized as such, which meant making no apologies and capturing more market share than anybody else. Instead we were slowly tying ourselves in knots. In 1969 and 1970, because of the double drag of the lawsuits and a recession, IBM's annual growth slumped to less than five percent—down from the nearly thirty percent we'd achieved in each of the two previous years.[89]

Control Data Corp. v. IBM remained deadlocked from 1969 to 1972, when IBM finally settled out of court. As part of its agreement, IBM sold to Control Data its Service Bureau Corporation subsidiary, a $63 million-a-year business which did data processing work for customers. IBM also simply gave Control Data a $101 million package of cash and contracts. In return, IBM received Control Data's computerized index, which had proved so useful to the Justice Department's case. On the advice of IBM's lawyers, Tom Jr. promptly ordered the files to be burned. The Justice Department finally dropped its suit in 1982, 13 years after the complaint was initiated.

Epilogue: *IBM after the Watsons*

Tom Watson Jr. lived on for 22 years after his retirement in 1971. He died in 1993 at the age of 79. He remained active in public life, serving as ambassador to the USSR from 1979 to 1981 under President Jimmy Carter. But his proverbial golden years closed on a somber note. At the end of his life, Watson silently looked on as the company that he and his father had built over the span of six decades reeled under the relentless attack of its American and Japanese rivals.

New industry dynamics and some management mistakes precipitated IBM's decline. Beginning in the 1970s, faster and cheaper semiconductor technology shifted the center of gravity away from large mainframes, IBM's core product. Minicomputers began to cut into the mainframe market, and in the 1980s, the minicomputers were themselves increasingly replaced by microcomputers and office workstations.[90]

The new semiconductor technology broke IBM's hold on the industry for several reasons. For one thing, the semiconductors were standardized, a circumstance that allowed independent suppliers to provide parts to a host of new computer makers. Barriers to entry fell, and competition proliferated. Product cycles shortened. Young entrepreneurs, unhindered by bureaucratic corporate structures, exploited the new growth segments and brought their products to market with a speed that IBM could not match.[91]

Then, too, the advent of personal computers drastically changed the customer-supplier relationship. PCs were easier to understand than were their "black box" predecessors. Power shifted to the end-user, and sales of application software began to grow faster than sales of hardware. Customers became much more savvy about comparison shopping. Gone were the days when IBM could simply take its customer base for granted.

The world market for computers also began to look very different. By 1990, the market for computers and computer parts was $98 billion for the U.S., $90 billion for Europe, and $71 billion for Asia. Those figures represented a larger overall pie, but one in which the U.S. slice looked much smaller. American makers now competed more fiercely not only with one another, but with foreign makers as well. Fujitsu, NEC, and Hitachi, partly supported by policies of the Japanese government, collectively became the world's largest semiconductor producers. In 1990, their combined market share in computers was larger than IBM's. Although the United States continued to be the largest exporter of computers and parts, especially to Europe, it imported a large amount of these goods from Japan and the newly industrialized countries of Asia.

In 1990, the U.S. ran a $4 billion trade deficit in computer goods with those countries.[92]

The new industry dynamics had serious implications for the way IBM did business. The company continued to spend generously on R&D. But the complex task of responding to a more global and technically sophisticated customer base, served by a growing number of rivals, strained IBM's large and centralized organization. As early as the mid-1980s, industry growth clearly lay in software, and in markets outside of North America. But IBM's product mix in 1988 consisted of 71 percent hardware, and most of its assets, labor force, and R&D activities were in the United States.[93]

The swift rise of the personal computer drove home the lesson that IBM was competing in a different world. When IBM entered the PC market in 1981, it immediately defined a new market segment in the same way that System/360 had done almost two decades earlier.[94] But this time, in order to reach the mass computer market more quickly, IBM outsourced the machine's most important parts to two much smaller producers. Seattle-based Microsoft, run by William H. Gates III, who was then in his early twenties, developed the machine's disk operating system (DOS). Intel, a firm in California's Silicon Valley, provided the microprocessor, a technology it had invented in 1971. These two elements together made up the "heart and brains" of the IBM PC.[95]

Although IBM was not the first to venture into the PC market, it quickly became the industry leader, with PC sales in 1984 of $4 billion.[96] That figure was large enough to have qualified IBM's PC unit, by itself, for the *Fortune* 100 list. But the PC division was still much smaller than IBM's mainframe computer business, which had sales of $14 billion in 1985.

IBM's early success in PCs established the Microsoft/Intel combination as the industry standard. But because IBM did not have exclusive rights to these parts, Microsoft and Intel prospered by selling their proprietary technologies to the fast-growing IBM clone market. By 1986, more than 200 clone suppliers had emerged. Startups such as Compaq, Dell, AST, Northgate, and Gateway thrived by undercutting IBM's prices. They exploited new distribution channels such as mass retailers. They even sold computers over the phone. IBM, too, used mass marketers such as ComputerLand and Sears to sell its PCs. It also built a network of international franchised dealers and allowed the salesforces of its other divisions to sell and service the company's PCs.

The shift in emphasis to microcomputers occurred so quickly that many in the industry referred to it as a "revolution" or as the "second wave" in the computer industry's history. By the mid-1990s, PCs accounted for 80 cents out of every dollar spent on information technology. The Microsoft/Intel combination was by then a standard feature in more than four-fifths of the world's 176 million PCs. The standard became so entrenched that not even IBM could challenge it. IBM's OS/2 disk operating system, introduced in 1987 and developed with Microsoft, never succeeded in establishing a new industry standard. In the mid-1990s, it was unclear whether IBM's PowerPC chip, based on more powerful "reduced instruction-set computer" (RISC) technology and developed jointly with Apple and Motorola, could unseat Intel's "x86" microprocessor architecture, the one that is inside all of the IBM clones.[97]

The income statements of Microsoft and Intel reflected their remarkable success in the PC market. Microsoft's revenues and profits rose at an average annual compound rate of over 40 percent from 1989 to 1994. Intel's revenues rose by an average of 26 percent per year during that period, and its annual profit gain was an even more impressive 45 percent. The net profit margins of both companies hovered at 25 percent, a figure that put them among the world's most profitable publicly quoted companies.[98]

The open standards, and the combination of falling prices and rising capabilities, made the PC market more ruthlessly Darwinian than anything IBM had faced before.[99] The company often misjudged its market. IBM's inexpensive PCjr, introduced in 1983, did not catch on with consumers. In 1992, the company unveiled its own cheaper "clone," Ambra, which did little except dilute IBM's own brand name. IBM's products took a relatively long time to reach the market. Unlike the loyal mainframe customers of the previous generation, impatient PC consumers declined to wait and simply bought other brands.

Instead of the 15 percent annual growth that management had come to expect, IBM was jolted by something entirely new. In 1991, the company's sales fell for the first time since 1946, when it was adjusting to the post–World War II economy. In 1993, the year of Tom Watson Jr.'s death, the company posted a loss of $8 billion, the largest one-year loss of any firm in American history. Also in 1993, IBM formally scrapped its fabled no-layoff policy. By 1994, the company had cut a total of 170,000 jobs worldwide, a drastic reduction from its 1986 peak of 406,000 employees.[100]

In the mid-1990s, after the drastic downsizing, IBM showed strong signs of renewed health. But the long-term significance of the company's problems, and its attempts to resolve them, will become clear only in the future. Whatever the verdict, those who pronounce it will analyze the difficult decades of the 1980s and 1990s within the larger context of IBM's entire history. They will examine, too, the history of the industry that IBM, more than any other single company, helped to define.

Appendix: The System/360 Decision*

Editor's Note: In the antitrust lawsuits that ran from 1969 until 1982, IBM defended itself by presenting to the courts an enormous quantity of information, far more than practically any judge or jury could reasonably hope to understand. The trial transcript in United States v. IBM *reached 100,000 pages before the Justice Department finally called off the suit. Much of the direct testimony by IBM executives concerned technical information about computers and data processing. These witnesses from IBM also said a great deal about the company's corporate strategy and its financial structure. So the trial records provide a rare source on the history of IBM in the 1950s and especially the 1960s, when the company developed its revolutionary System/360. The information and quoted material in this appendix are drawn from these trial records.*

THE IBM ORGANIZATION

During the 1950s and 1960s, IBM's managerial hierarchy faced the critical problem of building consensus between two very different groups of people: engineers on one side, marketers and professional managers on the other. In the early 1950s, when IBM first entered the electronic computer market, the two sides had come into direct conflict. The marketers and managers, led by Thomas J. Watson Sr., resisted computers because

---

*This Appendix was written by Peter Botticelli.

they represented such a heavy capital investment that the company's financial health might be endangered. Also, should computers be a success, the lofty position of marketers within the firm might be rendered less influential. On the other side were a group of electrical engineers, who were able to convince Thomas J. Watson Jr. that computers would revolutionize the data processing industry. What emerged out of this struggle was a company with a powerful culture of both engineering and marketing, and very strong *collective* leadership.

By the mid-1950s, IBM had begun to develop what became known as the "contention system," which guided the company's decisionmaking during the development of System/360. At the antitrust trial, one IBM executive explained that IBM's organization "is based on checks and balances, which provide a structure to insure the representation and confrontation of staff, line, product division, subsidiaries and headquarters viewpoints." The big point was that "checks and balances act as a limitation on the exercise of authority." When a proposal was made for a new product, "both line units and staff units . . . must concur with the part of the proposal which relates to their function."[101]

Frank Cary, who in the 1970s became Chairman of the Board, President, and CEO, explained in his testimony that the decisionmaking function on major issues at IBM was carried out first by staff officers, who numbered about 2,500, and only then by top management. Cary emphasized that staff functions were vital to a company with over 300,000 employees. The staff level was "where the people are that understand the product, understand the marketplace, do the product development, do the pricing, do all the work and really present a final proposal that has been reviewed and checked and balanced against Manufacturing, Engineering, Service, [and] both the Domestic and the World Trade Marketing Divisions, before they come forward to have it further reviewed by the Corporate Staff and the Management Review Committee."[102]

The Management Review Committee was the ultimate mediator in the contention system. It met about twice a week and was made up of the three or four highest-ranking IBM executives. According to Cary, "the philosophy of operation in the IBM Company is that the Chief Executive Officer delegates just as much responsibility and authority as he possibly can," while the Management Review Committee considered "only those things that it really believes that it must."[103] Cary was asked whether, in considering proposals for new products, "the Management Review Committee and Chief Executive Officer put some degree of reliance on the fact that [new] products have been reviewed by all these divisions and have been reviewed by separate staff?" He replied, "Oh, absolutely. That is why this system is designed the way it is."[104]

IBM's complicated decisionmaking process would be severely tested in an industry affected by exponential changes over time. It was retained because, in Cary's words, "we are managing a lot of risks. And so I think that one of the things that has been very, very important to the success of the Company is that we've had a system of management that is prudent, that has taken into consideration the kinds of risks that we are making."[105]

MAKING THE SYSTEM/360 DECISION

Contention management was actually a major reason the System/360 was built. On the engineering side, the staff review process gave the 360 team a chance to argue their case on a company-wide basis, rallying its supporters against those who wanted to kill it. By the time the proposal reached the Management Review Committee, the 360 had generated sufficient momentum that top executives, especially Thomas J. Watson Jr., could make a strong case to investors and the financial community that the new machine justified the enormous expenditures required to bring it to market.

At the time the 360 decision was made in December 1961, the Management Review Committee included the Chairman, Thomas J. Watson Jr.; his brother Arthur K. Watson, who was Vice President in charge of IBM's overseas operations; the company President, Al Williams; and T. Vincent Learson, a Vice President assigned as "group executive" in charge of all the product development and manufacturing divisions.[106] Each member of the Management Review Committee originally had been trained as a salesman or professional manager, not as an engineer.

In the case of the 360, however, the contention system enabled IBM's top managers and sales personnel to find common ground with the engineers. To lay the groundwork for the 360 decision, John Opel, a senior manager with a sales background who later would succeed Frank Cary as Chairman of the Board, chaired a staff committee whose job was to compare the 360 design with that of a less ambitious alternative. In his antitrust testimony, Opel explained that there were people who thought that there ought to be machines designed to optimize towards . . . scientific computing problems . . . There were others who said, "you ought to have a line of machines that is optimized around commercial data processing." The conclusion we came to was that we should generalize the architecture even though we recognized there was a possible degradation in scientific performance. We did that in the belief and in the conviction that the customer did not try to make those distinctions in the way he did data processing work.[107]

What mattered most to Opel was not the technical question of whether the 360 could be developed at a reasonable cost, but rather the marketing question of whether it was the company's best response to anticipated customer demand.

In the early 1960s, there was apparently little doubt among the marketers that a new product was needed to replace IBM's model 1401, which was facing tough competition from Honeywell's model 200. During this period, Frank Cary was Vice President of Field Operations in the Data Processing Division, responsible for IBM's sales efforts. In his testimony, Cary was asked whether or not he put "pressure on the Development organization to announce the 360 because of the announcement by Honeywell of its Model 200." He replied: "Well, I would say that I wanted a competitive product just as rapidly as the Product Development people could give it to us. We were certainly telling them that Honeywell had a product that had better price/performance than ours and that we wanted a product answer. That was my function, that was my role. I was expected to tell the corporation what the field needed in the way of products to compete."[108]

Thomas J. Watson Jr. was equally concerned about IBM's competitors. He recalled that at the time the 360 was announced in 1964, "I thought that our position in the marketplace was degrading, and would continue to degrade. It was bound to, no matter how hard I worked at the leadership of the corporation. The degrading process would continue simply because of the people [other firms] who were coming into our field."[109]

Given the extraordinary degree of risk involved, the decision to go ahead with System/360 could not have been made without a firm consensus among the company's top managers on both the engineering and marketing sides. The 360 not only had to *be* the right machine for the times, but the company also had to *believe* it was good enough to spend the colossal sum of $5 billion on it. Frank Cary said in his testimony that IBM's basic strategy "is a leadership strategy, an innovative strategy, a growth strategy. It's a way of bringing out new products that grow the business. It's a more exciting kind of a business to be in, I think. I think people like to be in that kind of company as opposed to a follower kind of company."[110]

This is not to say that IBM's top managers did not consider the problems that were likely to be involved in bringing the 360 to market. Cary recalled in hindsight:

> I certainly felt that we had accepted a very, very challenging set of objectives . . . I have at times said that, in a way, it was like drinking out of a firehose or it was like trying to swallow an elephant or something of that kind [given] the complexity and the magnitude of the job that we had undertaken. But I don't think any of us had any doubt we were going to succeed, and, of course, we did and it was just a tremendous success.[111]

SYSTEM/360'S CHIEF ADVOCATE: BOB EVANS

The 360 decision was the victory of a lifetime for Bob O. Evans, IBM's Vice President of Development. An engineer who had joined the company in 1955, Evans emerged in 1960–61 as leader of those who wanted to build a revolutionary line of general-purpose computers. The opposition was led by Frederick Brooks, a brilliant young engineer who wanted to build the 8000 series, a less radical successor to the model 1401. Evans was a remarkably confident and forceful advocate for the 360 within the framework of the contention system. He overwhelmed the opposition, killing the 8000 series outright in 1961. Afterward he even convinced the defeated Fred Brooks to serve as the 360's chief design engineer.[112]

As the project took shape, Evans's job was to coordinate the development efforts on System/360 as they were carried out at a number of different laboratories around the world. The actual work began in mid-1961. As Evans later recalled, "the most important task was to conceive and design this family [of computers] that we wanted to be interrelated. So I selected several of IBM's most experienced and brightest engineers and programmers and we set out to specify and lay out the design concepts, the functions and the plans for this whole family. It had never been done before."[113]

It was decided at the outset that the new family of machines should be equipped to compete in both the business and scientific markets. The overarching goal was one single and completely compatible system. However, "it wasn't clear at all," said Evans, that a computer could be designed to do both science and business calculations efficiently. "As a matter of fact, it haunted us. The question was whether we really [would] be building mediocrity and someone could come along . . . and build better scientific machines, better business data processors, and in the process negate our plans and our aspirations."[114]

The 360 engineering team faced huge obstacles in the early stages of development. According to Evans, the design concepts that were being examined were "often failing, increasing our concerns whether we could even do it, until some time in mid-1962 it coalesced to the point that we had a feeling that we were on the way."[115] At this point, "certainly by mid-1962, we believed that we could be ready to announce this family [the 360 product line] in the first quarter of 1964."[116]

By September 1963, Evans himself had no doubt that the 360 could be announced on schedule, by May or June of 1964. But he sensed wavering support from the top. In a memo, he wrote:

I suspect I have gotten the dub of radical but I am certainly baffled by executive management's failure to champion [the 360]. It is true the top men in IBM finally took the step which allowed the plan to be set but since that time support has been tacit and accomplishment has been by and large "in spite of" rather than under the leadership of our executives. The project has continually been viewed with suspicion and doubt. In a most incredulous [sic] manner there have been established "checks and balances" reviews, audits, etc. which have only kept the company moving in circles. The very hesitation with which management has approached [the 360] may become its obituary. [The 360] is good—it is simple and powerful—it is ready enough—proven enough.[117]

But top management had reason to worry. At the antitrust trial, Evans was asked: "Had the System/360, as of September 1963, been successfully tested?" (Prosecutors in cases such as this one try to show premature announcement, that is, a company's strategic positioning in a potential market it was not in fact ready to serve.) Evans replied "No. We tested thousands of things . . . each and of themselves, but we hadn't completed testing [on the system as a whole.]" The judge then asked Evans: "It was also the most complex and innovative [system]?" Evans said "Oh yes, sir, by a longshot."[118] Later in his testimony, Evans was asked, "prior to April 1964, had IBM introduced any product line that had been developed from the start [with] a pre-defined architecture applicable to the whole product line?" Evans replied "No. The 360 was by any measure the biggest, nothing was even in its league in terms of scope."[119] He acknowledged that "more than three-quarters of the products that went with the System/360 were all new."[120]

Nevertheless, by late 1963, Evans had begun to press the company to begin marketing the 360 to some of its technologically advanced customers. "I was anxious to get IBM committed to the new product line and I was anxious to show that the users would accept it."[121] However, when asked whether he thought users would "readily accept" the new architecture, Evans admitted, "No, indeed we were frightened to death they might not."[122] Evans explained that "we had put all of our eggs in this basket hoping, expecting that the 360 would be accepted by the users. We didn't have any alternative. We had no other design plans under way, and if the users had decided that what we had in the 360 was not what they wanted, then IBM today would be a radically different company, if even in the computer business."[123]

In general, Evans believed that IBM would experience little or no difficulty in selling the 360 line once it was ready to ship. In December 1963, he wrote a memo saying "it would be unwise for us to announce the system sporadically in an effort to optimize market penetration or profit. It is proper that IBM announce [the 360 machines] in a group because our customers . . . must better understand the abilities of the architecture . . . [while it also] requires a greater depth of understanding by our systems engineers, salesmen and customer engineers."[124] He was then asked whether the introduction of the Honeywell Model 200 was spoken of within IBM as a challenge by the marketing organization to the development organization. Evans replied, " 'Challenge' is a word that the marketers use all the time so they probably were using that in connection with the Honeywell 200 and lots of other things." He noted that the April 1964 announcement of the 360 was "right on the schedule we had set back in 1961."[125]

Evans was also asked whether the risks taken with the whole project "helped explain the ultimate success of the System/360." He replied, "Yes. Because we were reaching out to achieve the highest heights we could find, we could strive for, we could attain. We didn't take the easy course. We tried to break the sound barrier in computer systems design and it was very risky . . . in the labs it was [said that] 'you bet your company'" on the 360.[126]

Bob Evans's forceful optimism notwithstanding, System/360 experienced a rocky start because of repeated delays in shipping OS/360, the operating system designed for high-end models. The 360s could run on a less powerful operating system, but this hurt the line's commercial viability. In Evans's words, "it's true that by late 1964 we knew we were in trouble" with the 360's high-end operating system. At that time Evans wrote a letter admitting that "we have even heard the senior VP's say we are a laughing stock in a sense. I fear that any announcement of delay at this point would cast such a tower of gloom over OS/360 as to make it impossible to recover fully. I believe that any [announcement] of late delivery would spread uncontrollably like wild fire across [the Data-Processing Division] and our customers."[127]

Evans recalled that as the company labored to solve the 360's software problems, Tom Watson Jr. "wrote a letter saying that the whole series had been announced at least a year before it was ready, and some of the machines were two years early." Evans was asked whether he agreed with Watson's assessment. "No," he answered, "I think the record proves it was wrong. The status of the design . . . the flow-charting in detailing the programs"—in other words, the *theory* behind the 360 architecture and its applications—had boosted "our teams' confidence that we could deliver as we said we were going to do."[128] However, transforming flow charts into working applications for the 360 would prove to be a far more difficult feat than Evans realized at the time. He later admitted "that as we got deeper into the applications work . . . [there were] more intricate things that we had to solve than we had foreseen."[129]

VIN LEARSON'S PERSPECTIVE ON SYSTEM/360

As group executive for product development and a member of the Management Review Committee, Vin Learson was Bob Evans's boss during the 360's development. As "tie-breaker" in the battle between the 8000 and the 360, Learson had a heavy stake in the 360's success. (He became

Chairman of the Board in 1971, after Tom Watson Jr. retired.) The following is an excerpt from an October 1966 speech he gave to a group of Systems Engineers, who were software programmers assigned to IBM's branch sales offices. They were regarded as integral members of the company's sales force, pursuing the same quota objectives as the marketers. One can detect both the triumph and the strain Learson and others had felt in trying to deliver on the promises made when the 360 was announced in April 1964:

> I want very much to thank you personally for your vast and continuing contributions to System/360 . . . contributions made despite the workload and despite the obvious shortcomings in our current programming capability. I know it has been mighty rough out there . . . Behind you is a team of thousands, working around the clock in many places to find solutions to the problems which exist—solutions which, before too long, will enable you to do the kind of job for your customers which meet their total needs and your own high standards of performance.
>
> When we introduced [the 360,] 36 months ago, IBM had been in the market for a long time with the old circuitry and the old architecture . . . put together back in the early 1950's, data processing's distant past. It was time for a change. But we made two miscalculations. We were off on our assessment of 360's potential reception, and we were off on our assessment of IBM's production capability to meet the demand. And programming System/360 presented a particularly formidable challenge. We did what Charles Kettering, an engineering genius and president of the General Motors Research Division, always advised against: we put a delivery date on something yet to be invented.
>
> Observers have characterized the 360 decision as perhaps the biggest, in its impact on a company, ever made in American industry— far bigger than Boeing's decision to go into jets, bigger than Ford's decision to build several million Mustangs. Because 360's circuitry is the proprietary item which makes IBM machines different, we felt that we could not contract this job out. Hence we had to become, in a very short time, the largest component manufacturer in the world—and we had trouble learning how to make these microcircuits.
>
> The fact is, IBM has been built on problems. Each of them, at one point or another seemed to defy solution. Each of them cost a lot of good men plenty of sleep. Yet solve them we did, and because of them

this company has been able to increase its size 15 times in the last 16 years. It is no exaggeration, in my mind, to say that data processing is an agent of social revolution. Every installation on which you work moves this society forward in some significant and demonstrable way . . . [It is] a pioneering effort, which, little by little, is advancing man's efficiency, expanding his capabilities and widening his horizons.[130]

Table 10.4 IBM's Revenues, Earnings, and Workforce, 1914–94

Year	Revenue ($ million)	Earnings ($ million)	Earnings/ Revenue	Year-end Workforce (thousands)
1914	$ 4.2	$ 0.5	7.6%	1.3
1930	20.3	7.3	36.0	6.3
1940	46.3	9.4	20.3	12.7
1950	214.9	33.3	15.5	30.3
1960	1,436.1	168.2	11.7	104.2
1970	7,489.0	1,017.0	13.6	269.3
1980	26,213.0	3,562.0	13.6	341.3
1985	50,056.0	6,555.0	13.1	406.0
1990	69,018.0	6,020.0	8.7	373.3
1994	64,052.0	5,155.0	8.0	256.2

Sources: David Mercer, IBM: How the World's Most Successful Corporation is Managed (London: Kogan Page, 1987); Emerson W. Pugh, Building IBM: Shaping an Industry and Its Technology (Cambridge, MA: MIT Press, 1995); company reports.

Table 10.5 Top Ten Computer Firms Worldwide, 1975 vs. 1994

1975	1994	1994 IT revenues ($ billions)
IBM	IBM	$64.1
Burroughs	Fujitsu	21.3
Honeywell	Hewlett-Packard	19.2
Sperry	NEC	18.7
Control Data	Hitachi	13.7
NCR	Digital	13.5
Bull	AT&T	11.5
Digital	Compaq	10.9
ICL	EDS	10.1
Nixdorf	Toshiba	10.0

Sources: McKinsey & Co. and Gartner Group; Yardstick Worldwide; Datamation, June 1, 1995.

Table 10.6   The Five Leading American Vendors by Market Segment, 1994

Rank	Company	Worldwide Revenue ($ Mil)
Large Systems		
1	IBM	$5,956.8
2	Unisys	1,243.2
3	Amdahl	819.3
4	Cray	571.4
5	Intel	460.8
Mid-range Systems		
1	IBM	$5,764.7
2	AT&T GIS	5,042.0
3	Hewlett-Packard	2,688.0
4	Tandem	1,538.9
5	Digital	1,174.5
Workstations		
1	Sun Microsystems	$3,262.0
2	IBM	3,206.6
3	Hewlett Packard	2,880.0
4	Silicon Graphics	1,223.2
5	Digital	1,080.0
PCs		
1	Compaq	$9,018.8
2	IBM	8,775.1
3	Apple	7,161.8
4	Dell	2,870.0
5	Gateway 2000	2,700.0
Peripherals		
1	IBM	$8,583.0
2	Hewlett-Packard	6,336.0
3	Seagate	3,465.0
4	Quantum	3,286.0
5	Xerox	3,126.8
Softwares		
1	IBM	$11,529.4
2	Microsoft	4,464.0
3	Computer Associates	2,454.7
4	Novell	1,918.1
5	Oracle	1,901.6

Source: Datamation, June 1, 1995.

PROLOGUE TO CHAPTER 11

The story of the Toyoda Automatic Loom Company and its lineal successor Toyota Motor is exceedingly rich in what it reveals about a whole series of business issues. Those issues include the commercialization of invention, the transfer of technology between industries and countries, the involvement of the workforce in making improvements, the role of government in economic development, and the nature of two Japanese "economic miracles"—the one that occurred during the 1920s and 1930s, and the much more familiar one after World War II.

The story starts in the late nineteenth century with a lone inventor, Sakichi Toyoda. (The family name Toyoda was changed to the brand name Toyota for reasons detailed in this chapter.) Sakichi was determined to build an indigenous Japanese loom that would help his country prosper in textiles and textile machinery, two major industries of the First Industrial Revolution. After numerous setbacks, Sakichi was finally successful. But he was so obsessed with his business that, as was the case with August Thyssen in Germany at about the same time, his personal life suffered and his first marriage collapsed. Also like Thyssen, he brought the next generation into the business. It was Sakichi's son Kiichiro Toyoda who, on the advice of his dying father, took the company into motor vehicles. This happened in the 1930s, just before Japan as a country took the first fateful steps that led to the Pacific War and defeat at the hands of the United States.

The militarization of Japan during the 1930s brought the expulsion of foreign manufacturers of vehicles, and this opened a window of demand, especially for Toyota's trucks. In a series of business-government interactions similar to those we saw in the histories of Rolls-Royce and IBM, the fortunes of Toyota were strongly affected by the military policy of the country. In fact, some analysts of the postwar economic miracle believe that the key to Japan's overall economic success was the government's intervention in business affairs, especially during the 1950s and

1960s. Other analysts disagree, arguing that private-sector performance was the key, as exemplified in rivalries among strong companies.

The Toyota story brilliantly illuminates this issue. As you read it, you might make a list of the ways in which Japan's government intervened in the motor vehicle industry from the 1930s through the 1960s. You might ask yourself how the fate of Toyota and the other Japanese car companies would have been different without these interventions.

After thinking through your list of interventions, you might then address the equally compelling question of competition for market share within the Japanese economy. Why did the rivalry between Toyota and Nissan become so extraordinarily intense? What kinds of management decisions determined the outcome? How important was the Toyota Production System, led by the mechanical genius Taiichi Ohno? And, after Toyota and other Japanese car companies became strong in their home market, how did they mount their invasion of the United States, the world's "automobile kingdom"?

11

TOYODA AUTOMATIC LOOMS AND TOYOTA AUTOMOBILES

Jeffrey R. Bernstein

In 1929 the Japanese inventor and entrepreneur Sakichi Toyoda signed a licensing agreement with Platt Brothers of Britain. Platt Brothers paid £100,000 for the right to manufacture and sell Toyoda's G-type automatic loom everywhere except Japan, China, and the United States. For seven decades, Platt Brothers had been the world's preeminent maker of textile machinery. It was especially dominant in Japan.[1] Sakichi Toyoda, by contrast, had spent most of his career simply trying to create a loom that could compete with Western models. For him, the 1929 agreement with Platt Brothers was the crowning achievement of a life's worth of inventive effort.

More generally, the fact that a British firm was buying Japanese technology at this time indicated the remarkable technological progress Japan had made in the early decades of the twentieth century. Much of this progress was concentrated in textiles and textile machinery, and Japan's international ascendance in these industries has been called the "first Japanese economic miracle."[2] Thus, this seemingly mundane agreement between Toyoda and Platt Brothers actually represented a significant moment in the history of industrial capitalism.

Half a century later, in 1983, another member of the Toyoda family took part in a similar agreement. Eiji Toyoda, Sakichi's nephew and chairman of the Toyota Motor Corporation, signed a deal for joint production of small cars with General Motors Corporation (GM). GM had long been an American icon and, for nearly 60 years, the world's largest automobile producer. But by the early 1980s, GM was losing market share and bleeding cash. Toyota, on the other hand, was considered the world's most efficient automaker. GM thus turned to Toyota for help in building a small car. Toyota also saw a possible gain from the joint venture. Since 1981, America had limited imports of Japanese cars, and calls for stronger protective measures still resonated. A pact with GM to help modernize the U.S. auto industry might defuse some of this political pressure.

These two agreements testify to the remarkable ability of Japanese companies to catch up to their Western counterparts in two key industries of modern economic development. Textile machinery had helped spark Japan's first economic miracle, and automobiles played an important role in its second economic miracle, the two decades of rapid growth starting in the early 1950s. The two agreements are also part of the story of a single family. The Toyoda family, and those who worked for and with them, overcame what appeared to be almost insurmountable hurdles in two different eras.

Toyoda Automatic Loom Works

SAKICHI TOYODA, "KING OF INVENTORS"

Born in 1867, Sakichi Toyoda was the eldest son of a carpenter.[3] (See Figure 11.1 for the Toyoda family genealogy.) After elementary school, Sakichi learned the rudiments of carpentry by observing his father and then received formal training from a master carpenter in a nearby town. Sakichi was an indifferent and distracted student, whose heart lay not in carpentry but in invention. In his late teens, he heard about Japan's new patent law of 1885, and he resolved to invent something that would promote the nation's economic development.

Having grown up in an area of Shizuoka prefecture known for the production of cotton goods, Sakichi was familiar with looms. The local villagers were mainly farmers, but almost every home had a handloom. At the age of 20, Sakichi began thinking about ways to make looms easier to operate, and thus to lower the cost of producing cotton goods. The Japanese textile industry was then facing powerful pressure from foreign competition, especially inexpensive and high-quality British imports. The Japanese government sought to foster a modern textile industry by building model factories and by selling machinery to entrepreneurs at low prices. Sakichi had the same goal, which he aimed to achieve by building a better loom.

This objective consumed him. Like the American Thomas Edison with his long series of light bulbs, Sakichi built wooden loom after wooden

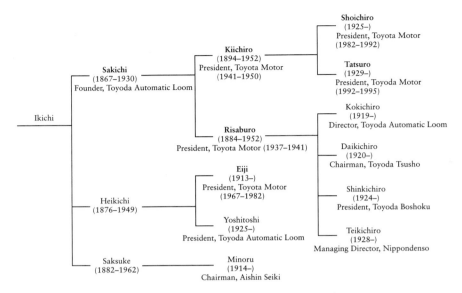

Figure 11.1   Abbreviated Genealogy of the Toyoda Family

Sources: Adapted from Michael Cusumano, *The Japanese Automobile Industry* (Cambridge, MA: Harvard University Press, 1985), p. 183, and Shotaro Kamiya, *My Life with Toyota* (Toyota City: Toyota Motor Sales, 1976), pp. 100–101.

loom, trying to improve the design. His obsession displeased his father, who thought it was distracting him too much from carpentry. The other villagers began to regard Sakichi as an eccentric. But neither parental nor societal disapproval could dissuade Sakichi. His determination was strengthened by a trip to Tokyo in 1890 to see the Third National Industrial Exhibition.

Soon after returning home, Sakichi devised his first invention. Patented in 1891, it was a wooden, manually operated loom that produced better cloth while raising productivity by 40 to 50 percent.[4] Sakichi moved to Tokyo, where he opened a weaving business and tried to sell his new loom. The weaving business did well, but he found few purchasers for his machine. Small textile companies could not afford the new looms, and large-scale commercial weavers opted for more expensive but superior imported power looms. Sakichi hoped to invent his own power loom, but he lacked money for research. In 1893, at the age of 26, he closed his weaving business and returned to his home village.

By this time Sakichi had married, and in 1894 his son Kiichiro was born. Sakichi's preoccupation with work quickly led to the demise of the marriage. His wife's family, upset at his neglect of their daughter, demanded a divorce. Sakichi complied, and in accordance with the custom of the day, he retained custody of Kiichiro.[5] Sakichi then moved to a village near Nagoya, one of Japan's largest cities and a growing industrial center. There, in 1895 he founded Toyoda Company to sell a yarn-reeling machine he had invented. Twice as efficient as existing models, the yarn-reeling machine was a commercial success. Sakichi also remarried in 1897. His new wife, in addition to raising Kiichiro and her own daughter Aiko, helped manage Toyoda Company.

In the meantime, Sakichi perfected a steam-operated power loom. Power looms had been around since the beginning of the nineteenth century, but before Sakichi none had ever been built in Japan. This accomplishment impressed one purchaser of Toyoda's yarn-reeling machine, and in 1898 the two opened a textile mill, using 60 of Sakichi's power looms. Each worker could operate two or three power looms simultaneously, as opposed to just one conventional loom. The result was a fourfold increase in worker productivity, and an overall cost reduction of more than 50 percent.[6]

These remarkable results naturally attracted attention. Managers of the trading company Mitsui & Company, one of Japan's most prominent firms, thought that Sakichi's power loom might prove useful in meeting the enormous demand in China for cotton fabric. In 1899, Mitsui signed a 10-year agreement with Sakichi for the exclusive rights to his power loom. To manufacture the looms, Mitsui established Igeta Company in Nagoya. Sakichi, then 32 years old, became chief engineer of the new company and continued his quest to improve the power loom. At first the company prospered. Its loom, in addition to being lighter than competing products, was priced at 93 yen, only a fraction of the price of the 872-yen German Hartmann loom or the 389-yen French Diedrichs loom.[7] However, a retrenchment in the Japanese textile industry hurt business. As profits fell, Sakichi's research budget was cut, and he resigned in frustration in 1902.

He returned to his original firm, Toyoda Company, where he made a number of important improvements in his looms.[8] With the outbreak of the Russo-Japanese War in 1904, the textile business picked up, as did demand for his latest models. Sakichi, now 37, was contacted by Kane-gafuchi Spinning Co., then one of Japan's largest firms, to see about running some comparative performance tests. Sakichi reluctantly allowed Kanegafuchi to manufacture his looms at its own expense and compare them with several imported models. The tests lasted a year, and the results were discouraging. Looms made by Platt Brothers ran more efficiently and produced better-quality cloth, so Kanegafuchi chose not to purchase any of Sakichi's looms. It was a chastening experience.

However, Sakichi did not give up. In 1907, at Mitsui's urging, he dissolved Toyoda Company and established Toyoda Loom Works. By the standards of the time, it was a huge enterprise, capitalized at 1 million yen, the same as Mitsui & Co.[9] The new company struggled at first, because of a recession following the Russo-Japanese War. Again, Saki-chi's desire to maintain a large research budget led to conflicts with other investors, and in 1910 he resigned from the company. Even after his departure, Toyoda Loom Works continued to bear his name, and it would compete vigorously against the companies he himself subsequently established.[10]

Frustrated and disheartened, Sakichi now traveled to the United States and Europe. He was awed by America's burgeoning industrial prowess, and he was particularly impressed by the new automobiles he saw. In 1910, only two years after the introduction of the Model T Ford, American firms were turning out over 100,000 vehicles a year. Though intrigued by cars, Sakichi remained focused on looms. In tours of American mills, he watched the operation of the famous U.S.-made Draper automatic loom. Believing that his looms compared favorably in reliability and efficiency to the Draper models, Sakichi returned to Nagoya with renewed determination.

By now suspicious of outside capital, Sakichi raised his own financing for a cloth mill, named Toyoda Automatic Weaving. The mill proved profitable, but Sakichi found that the performance of his power looms was hampered by the low quality of Japanese yarn. He called upon Ichizo Kodama, manager of the Nagoya office of Mitsui & Co., to help him establish thread-spinning operations at Toyoda Automatic Weaving.

Sakichi reinforced the business relationship by arranging for his daughter, Aiko, to marry Kodama's younger brother, Risaburo. Following a relatively common Japanese practice, Sakichi then adopted Risa-buro, who assumed the Toyoda family name. Ten years older than Kiichiro, Risaburo became the eldest son. He left his old job to help Sakichi run the family business.

To Kiichiro, then a 20-year-old college student, this was a devastating blow. As a child, he had been neglected by his father, who was totally preoccupied with his looms, and to a lesser extent by his stepmother, who took an active role in Sakichi's businesses. Now Risaburo seemed to be usurping his rightful position as heir. Kiichiro protested vigorously, but he could not prevent his sister's marriage or the adoption of Risaburo. An experienced and worldly businessman, Risaburo turned out to be a much-needed asset to the firm.

The outbreak of World War I in 1914 sparked a massive boom, and Toyoda Automatic Weaving was hardly able to cope with the deluge of orders. It expanded quickly, and in 1918 became Toyoda Spinning & Weaving Company, capitalized at 5 million yen. Sakichi was its president, Risaburo its managing director, and Kiichiro a member of the technical staff. Sakichi also moved quickly to invest overseas, setting up a subsidiary in Shanghai as a means of avoiding high Chinese tariffs on Japanese cotton goods.

These business ventures diverted Sakichi from his research, but in 1921, after a seven-year interruption, he resumed work on the automatic loom. (An automatic loom is a power loom that automatically replenishes the yarn when it runs out, thus eliminating a labor-intensive task.) He was joined in this endeavor by Kiichiro, who turned out to possess outstanding inventive talent.[11] Kiichiro improved his father's design for an automatic shuttle-changing device, and he developed a better mechanism for stopping the loom automatically when a thread broke. In 1923, Sakichi set up a pilot plant with 200 newly designed looms. The following year, Sakichi and Kiichiro perfected their first fully automatic loom. In 1925, they designed the new loom so that it could be mass-produced, and in 1926 Sakichi founded Toyoda Automatic Loom Works, capitalized at 1 million yen. Production of the Toyoda G-type automatic loom began in 1927.

The G-type was an instant success. Although it cost three times as much as a conventional power loom (¥630 versus ¥200), it was far more efficient. One worker could operate 25 automatic looms simultaneously, compared with two or three power looms. The Toyoda automatic loom began to spread throughout the Japanese textile industry, and exports of looms to China and India soon followed. Platt Brothers heard about the

Toyoda G-type loom and commissioned Mitsui & Co., its exclusive agent in Japan, to evaluate it. Mitsui's positive assessment led to the landmark 1929 agreement between Platt and Toyoda.

For Platt, the venture was not the triumph that it was for Sakichi Toyoda. Platt had difficulties manufacturing the Toyoda-licensed looms and made only 271 of them. Receiving no repeat orders, it abandoned production three years after the 1929 agreement.[12] This lack of commercial success was largely the result of British weavers' hostility toward the new automatic looms. Workers were reluctant to welcome the new looms because they feared that jobs would be lost. British capitalists did not want to see their large investments in power looms go to waste, even though the new automatic loom was much more efficient. Their refusal to upgrade technology would prove very costly to the British textile industry, whose dominance was under increasing pressure from none other than the Japanese.

By 1929, Sakichi had created a sizable industrial group around a core of related enterprises: Toyoda Automatic Loom Works, Toyoda Spinning & Weaving, and Toyoda Spinning & Weaving Works in Shanghai. Ranked by assets, Toyoda Spinning & Weaving was Japan's 103rd largest company in 1930, and Toyoda Automatic Loom Works the 191st.[13] Surrounding these two firms were a number of smaller spinning, weaving, and dye works. Sakichi's success had paralleled and supported the development of the Japanese textile industry as a whole.

THE FIRST JAPANESE ECONOMIC MIRACLE

Before 1914, British dominance of the world export market for cotton yarn and finished goods had been almost unchallenged. The British share of world cotton goods exports had been 82 percent in the early 1880s, and it still averaged 70 percent between 1910 and 1913. In less than 20 years after that, however, Japan overtook Britain as the largest exporter of cotton goods. By the late 1930s, Japan accounted for 39 percent of world exports of cotton goods, and the British share had dropped to 27 percent.[14]

The rise of the Japanese textile industry, a part of Japan's "first economic miracle," was a long and complex process. Contrary to the views of many observers at the time, it was not built simply upon a disciplined, low-wage workforce. Such arguments made at that time by British textile magnates and others strongly resemble those made decades later by managers in other industries overtaken by the Japanese, such as automobiles. Before 1914, British textile managers dismissed the possibility of a Japanese threat. In the 1920s, they attributed the first achievements of Japanese firms to low wages and undervaluation of the yen. Further Japanese advances in the market brought forth allegations of unfair trade practices. Finally, once the shift in competitive advantage was clear, resignation set in, and the Japanese were regarded as invincible.[15]

By reacting in this manner, the British failed to perceive the institutions that underlay Japan's strength in textiles. One was the integrated spinning and weaving company. Integrated Japanese firms soon became quite large and began to challenge the leading British firms, which usually did not engage in both spinning and weaving.[16] (U.S. textile firms became integrated much earlier than their Japanese counterparts and were also quite sizable.) Another important Japanese institution was the specialized trading company which, by virtue of its huge volume of purchases, acquired cotton at low prices. The large spinning companies banded together into the Japan Cotton Spinners' Association, whose countervailing bargaining power enabled members to obtain cotton from the big trading companies at favorable prices. The trading companies themselves served as invaluable conduits for marketing Japanese cloth products abroad.

In spinning, Japanese textile managers made an important discovery: how to blend high-priced U.S. cotton with low-priced Indian cotton to make high-quality yarn. Elsewhere, high grades of yarn required the exclusive use of high-priced American cotton, so the Japanese gained an important cost advantage.[17] They enhanced this cost advantage by adopting the newer and less physically demanding ring-spinning technique[18] and by mobilizing a relatively skilled and disciplined female labor force.[19] Meanwhile, their British rivals persisted with mule spinning, and their U.S. competitors were more reliant on relatively expensive male workers.

Of course, the Japanese textile industry also benefited from the development of indigenous power looms and automatic looms. Here Sakichi Toyoda's inventive genius played a vital role, but the willingness of Japanese weaving firms to install the new looms proved equally important. By 1936, automatic looms accounted for 12 percent of Japan's installed base of cotton looms, compared to only 3 percent in Britain. To be sure, the penetration of automatic looms was much lower in Japan than in America (68 percent) or Italy (23 percent), but those two nations were generally competing in higher grades of textiles than were the Japanese and the British.[20]

Sakichi's efforts helped to establish Japan as a textile-*machinery*-producing nation. Though the rapid ascent of the textile industry was impressive in its own right, the making of textiles did not necessarily provide the foundation for further industrial development.[21] In spinning and weaving there would always be new challengers from low-wage countries, but the textile-machinery business was far more difficult to enter. As a result, the world textile-machinery industry consisted of companies from only a few advanced nations. The Japanese government had long understood the importance of textile machinery, and in the early 1880s it had become the first government in the world to keep separate trade statistics for this industry.[22]

When Sakichi Toyoda invented his first loom in 1891, the prospect that Japan would soon become a leading textile-machinery producer was hardly conceivable. The British were the undisputed leaders, and as late as 1922, they still accounted for 67 percent of world exports of textile machinery.[23] After that, Britain's long-standing preeminence was eroded as the Americans, Germans, and Japanese all developed indigenous industries. In 1938, Japan overtook Germany to become Britain's most serious rival as an exporter of textile machinery. As the leading historian of this industry observes, Japan "had made the transition from net import to net export, achieved in 1931, faster than any other state."[24]

The rapidity of this transition owed much to Sakichi Toyoda and his many rival loom inventors. This community of domestic inventors learned much from one another, and their intense competition undoubtedly stimulated Sakichi's own creativity.[25] In the end, however, he outshone all his rivals. His inventions ultimately made him a national hero. In 1927 he was awarded Japan's highest civilian honor, the Imperial Order of Merit. A 1937 Japanese elementary school textbook proclaimed Sakichi the "King of Inventors," and in 1985 the Japanese Patent Office recognized him as one of the 10 most important inventors in Japanese history.[26]

ENTRANCE INTO THE AUTOMOBILE BUSINESS

Sakichi Toyoda had become a phenomenal success, but he did not live long to enjoy it. In 1927 he suffered a mild cerebral hemorrhage, and on October 30, 1930, he died of acute pneumonia at the age of 63. As he lay on his deathbed, Sakichi had achieved all of his life goals. Still, he harbored another promising idea, which he now disclosed to Kiichiro: "The automatic loom business was my life's work. I had nothing but ideas and my two hands when I first started out. You should have your own life's work. I believe in the automobile. It will become indispensable in the future. Why not make it your life's work?"[27]

Even before this exhortation, Kiichiro had toyed with the idea of manufacturing automobiles, but he had been very cautious. After all, the Japanese car market was minuscule, and it was dominated by Ford and GM, which had established Japanese plants for the assembly of knock-down kits beginning in the mid-1920s. By 1929 there were only 81,000 motor vehicles in all of Japan, less than a week's worth of U.S. production. The American companies had an 84 percent share of the Japanese market and had built up nationwide sales and service networks there. They towered over the only three Japanese producers, whose collective output in 1929 was fewer than 450 vehicles.[28] Even the formidable business groups called *zaibatsu* were hesitant to enter an industry so thoroughly dominated by foreign producers.

However, Kiichiro was ready. Along with paternal encouragement, Sakichi gave him some seed money for the automobile venture—the royalty payment he had received from Platt Brothers. Though Risaburo was the formal heir and thus destined to lead Toyoda Automatic Loom, Kiichiro now had an inheritance and direction of his own. The first stone had been laid for the foundation of today's Toyota Motor Corporation.

Toyota Motor: The Early Years, 1930–1953

KIICHIRO'S COMPANY (1930–1938)

Kiichiro Toyoda was well suited to start an automobile enterprise. He had graduated with a degree in mechanical engineering from Tokyo Imperial University, the most prestigious educational institution in Japan. Kiichiro thus took a more scientific approach to invention than his father's trial-and-error methods, but he shared his father's keen mechanical instinct and interest in automobiles. In the early 1920s, on a tour of U.S. and European textile mills, he had been impressed by the growth of the automobile industry in the West. In 1929, he once again went to the United States and Britain, this time explicitly to visit auto assembly plants and parts makers.

In March 1930—even before Sakichi's death—Kiichiro took over a corner of the Toyoda Automatic Loom Works factory to conduct research on automobiles. Drawing on a network of friends from his university days, he solicited advice and information. Most people were pessimistic about his idea, but Kiichiro was determined to create a viable automobile company. He read Henry Ford's autobiography, *My Life and Work,* and recommended it to his small cohort of engineers. Meanwhile he strengthened Toyota Automatic Loom's technological base. He installed a conveyor belt for loom production and imported high-quality German and American machine tools. He introduced an electric furnace for high-grade castings and purchased Japan's first molding machine.[29]

By 1933, Kiichiro had almost exhausted the £100,000 (¥1 million) that Sakichi had given him. At the age of 39 Kiichiro felt ready to launch into automobile production, and he asked Risaburo for more funds. Risaburo initially rejected his request. Kiichiro was the engineer, engrossed in product development and unconcerned about finances. Risaburo was the businessman, entrusted with preserving Sakichi's fortune, and he regarded auto production as too risky. However, he eventually yielded to Kiichiro, and in late 1933 a separate automobile department was established at Toyoda Automatic Loom. In early 1934, the shareholders of Toyoda Automatic Loom voted to triple the capitalization of the company to ¥3 million. In 1935 they doubled this sum, to ¥6 million. Most of the additional capital went to the automobile department, which used it to construct a pilot assembly plant and a steel plant on the grounds of the Loom Works compound.[30]

Kiichiro attracted several talented engineers to his department, but they were inexperienced in automobile construction. It took half a year to cast the first cylinder block for the engine, and the first prototype engine, the Type A, was not finished until September 1934. Kiichiro chose not to rely on a foreign automaker for technological expertise. His engineers did, however, borrow liberally from foreign models, making enough design changes to avoid patent infringement. Their first prototype vehicle, the Model A1 passenger car, blended parts based on several different American makes: the body design of the Chrysler DeSoto, a Ford frame and rear axle, and a Chevrolet engine and front axle.[31] The A1 prototype was completed in May 1935.

Kiichiro then set about choosing a brand name for his new cars. In 1936 the company ran a contest which attracted over 20,000 entries.

The winning entry was "Toyota." In English, this looks like a minor variation on the family name, but in Japanese there is a major difference. "Toyoda" is written in Chinese characters and has an easily identifiable meaning—abundant rice field:

豊田

"Toyota" is written in *katakana,* the Japanese phonetic alphabet used for foreign words:

トヨタ

Sleek and modern compared to "Toyoda," "Toyota" requires eight strokes to write, and in Japan the number eight connotes increasing prosperity.[32]

The brand name was now decided and the prototype complete, but plans to mass-produce the A1 passenger car would have to wait. The reason was that the Japanese military needed trucks instead. What happened was as follows. After ignoring the domestic auto industry for years, the Japanese government suddenly changed its policy and clamped down on foreign cars. Its initial motive was to mitigate its chronic balance-of-payments problems, but soon another motive became paramount: the military's desire to avoid dependence on foreign truck manufacturers. The decisive measure was the 1936 Automobile Industry Law, which required government licensing of all motor vehicle producers with annual output exceeding 3,000 vehicles. Since the government granted licenses only to two domestic firms (Toyota and Nissan), this law effectively precluded GM and Ford, by far the dominant sellers of autos in Japan at the time, from further participation in the Japanese market.[33] The foreign firms now proposed joint ventures with Toyota and Nissan but were blocked by opposition from the Japanese military and by deteriorating U.S.-Japanese relations.

In 1934, the share of imports (both knock-down kits and whole vehicles) had stood at an overwhelming 93 percent of the domestic market. By 1938, imports comprised only 43 percent, and by 1939 Japan's entire supply of motor vehicles was domestically produced.[34] Toyota and Nissan now had the Japanese market entirely to themselves. Though sheltered from foreign competition, the two Japanese automakers were now forced to produce what the military wanted.

In early 1935, Kiichiro had learned of the impending 1936 law and the military's desire for more truck production. He instructed his automobile department to begin the trial manufacture of trucks, using the Type A engine that had been developed for the passenger car. The prototype for the first truck, the model G1, was produced very quickly, in less than six months. It featured some elegant touches, such as a radiator grille patterned after a mask used in Noh, a form of classical Japanese theater.[35] However, the truck performed poorly, especially over rough mountain roads. Its flaws were clearly revealed in 1935 when it was driven to Tokyo for an exhibition. It broke down several times along the way, causing Risaburo to despair, "Will our trucks ever run?"[36] Nevertheless, the truck made it to the exhibition, which marked the public entry of Toyoda Automatic Loom Works into the automobile industry. The company quickly added a number of models to its product line, including the DA (bus), GA (improved truck), AA (passenger car), and the AB Phaeton (open-top model of AA). These vehicles were exhibited in a big automobile show on September 14, 1936. On the same day, the Ministry of Commerce and Industry announced that it had selected Toyoda Automatic Loom Works as one of the licensed automakers.

Even before this authorization was in hand, Kiichiro had moved ahead with his plan to produce motor vehicles, building a plant in Kariya near Toyoda Automatic Loom Works. The plant was completed in May 1936. Kiichiro also purchased 2 million square meters (about 500 acres) of land in Koromo, a town east of Nagoya. At the time, Koromo was undeveloped forest land, but it would eventually become an industrial center famous throughout the world as Toyota City.

Another big step into the automotive world occurred in 1937, when Kiichiro persuaded the board of directors of Toyoda Automatic Loom to create a separate automobile company and to construct a new plant in Koromo. In August 1937, the board spun off the automobile division as Toyota Motor Company (TMC). It was capitalized at 12 million yen, with 26 stockholders, mostly family members, company officials, and Mitsui & Co.[37] Risaburo became its president, and Kiichiro executive vice president. In spite of his nominal title, Kiichiro actually ran the business. In 1941 he became president, while Risaburo assumed the largely ceremonial post of chairman.

TMC had its headquarters in Kariya with offices in Nagoya, Tokyo, and Osaka. It was organized into seven departments: administration, sales, manufacturing, engineering, technical, total vehicle engineering administration, and research. Kiichiro viewed research as vital to TMC's development. Even before Toyota became a separate company, he had established a laboratory in Tokyo. This laboratory was initially under the direction of his cousin Eiji Toyoda, like Kiichiro an engineering graduate of Tokyo Imperial University.

Kiichiro specified that the new Koromo factory be built with a monthly capacity of 500 cars and 1,500 trucks, an enormous volume given that TMC was producing fewer than 350 vehicles per month at the time. Production at Koromo began on November 3, 1938.

THE WAR YEARS (1938–1945)

Stimulated by Japan's war with China, government procurement rendered Toyota profitable almost from the beginning. Its good prospects enabled it to attract outside funding, mostly from large financial and trading concerns, which Toyota used to expand its facilities to meet the rising military demand. Japan's entry into World War II in 1941 brought a powerful surge in demand, all but guaranteeing a period of prosperity for Toyota Motor Company.

Meanwhile, the pressures of war proved devastating to Toyoda firms in textiles. Japanese military authorities began by shutting down small textile firms and confiscating their equipment. Later, they ordered larger textile firms to transform themselves through merger. The Chuo Spinning Company, for instance, was created in March 1942 from the combination of Toyoda Spinning & Weaving, Toyoda Oshikiri Spinning and Weaving, Chuo Spinning and Weaving, and several smaller textile companies. Soon the military converted almost all textile concerns to armaments production. Chuo Spinning, by now a producer of aircraft parts, was absorbed by TMC in late 1943.

World War II thus shifted the balance of power within the Toyoda Group, reducing the importance of the textile business and making motor vehicle production the central focus. In effect, it catalyzed the Toyoda Group's eventual transformation into the Toyota Group.

This shift of power might have been expected to please Kiichiro, but it did not. As the war progressed, successive governmental directives constricted the freedom of automobile manufacturers and parts suppliers. Passenger car production dwindled to almost nothing. Between 1935 and 1945, Toyota produced over 90,000 trucks and buses, but fewer than

2,000 cars. (Nissan, with an earlier start in the business, produced 108,000 trucks and 19,000 cars over the same period.)[38] The military also pressed Toyota to make do with fewer and fewer materials. Shortages forced the firm to produce such abominations as the "one-eyed truck," which had a single headlight and no front brakes. Obsessed with quality and proud of his work, Kiichiro found such restrictions anathema. However, he could offer no more than token resistance: for instance, he had TMC clandestinely continue to pursue research on passenger cars, his own first love. He also pursued other interests. Kiichiro led TMC into the aircraft industry, first directing the research division to study rocket propulsion and in 1943 forming Tokai Aircraft, a joint venture with Kawasaki Aircraft. In general, though, the war years were a frustrating time for Kiichiro.

The war did have one positive and very important long-term consequence for Toyota and the Japanese auto industry: it stimulated the development of close subcontracting relations. The military, by forcing smaller companies to affiliate with a larger firm and by considering these affiliated suppliers to be branch plants of the larger firm, compelled major manufacturers to pay close attention to their suppliers. At Toyota the result was that supplier-purchaser transactions began to take on a more cooperative and permanent tone. In 1939, Toyota formed the Kyoryokukai (Cooperation Council), an association of Toyota suppliers in the region surrounding its headquarters. In late 1943, it renamed that organization, calling it the Kyohokai (Joint Prosperity Association), and expanded its scope to include Toyota suppliers in the Osaka and Tokyo regions.

This association worked to improve the quality of parts made by suppliers, but Toyota still struggled with the poor quality of essential components. TMC therefore established its own suppliers of important parts. It usually began by creating an in-house workshop to build a particular part. Then, once the operation had been launched, it was spun off as a separate company. This process had begun in a limited way even before the war. The steel manufacturing department, which originated within Toyoda Automatic Loom in 1934, had been spun off in 1940 as an autonomous firm, Toyoda Steel Works. Similarly Toyoda Machine Works, started in 1937 as an internal machine-tool shop at TMC, became a separate company in 1941.[39] The aircraft parts producers established and acquired by TMC also became invaluable suppliers of auto parts to Toyota after the war.

During the war, however, the direction of this future evolution was not at all clear. As the war dragged on, TMC seemed less and less like an automobile company. Its workforce became a motley assemblage of regular employees, soldiers, women, schoolchildren, and even criminals.[40] After peaking in 1942 at 16,302 vehicles, its production slumped to just 3,275 in 1945.

On the other hand, at war's end TMC was in far better shape than many other Japanese companies. By 1945 it had six manufacturing plants. It also possessed a number of affiliated firms, including Toyoda Automatic Loom Works, Toyoda Steel Works, Toyoda Machine Works, Tokai Aircraft, and the Toyoda Physical and Chemical Research Institute. Although its main plant at Koromo absorbed significant bombing damage in the last week of the war, its other factories were largely intact. Had the war lasted just a week longer, Koromo (Toyota City after 1959) was apparently scheduled to be destroyed altogether by American bombers.[41]

The start of the Allied Occupation in 1945 raised many questions about Toyota's fate. TMC's connections to the Japanese military raised the possibility that Occupation authorities, under the Supreme Commander of the Allied Powers (SCAP), might close the company down. This possibility was heightened by Toyota's ties to Mitsui, which had already been targeted by Occupation authorities who were intent on destroying the power of the *zaibatsu*. Alternatively, SCAP might seize Toyota's factories and equipment as war reparations. All of these concerns led Kiichiro to consider a variety of activities for Toyota if barred from automobile production: the manufacture of china, prefabricated housing, and *chikuwa* (a type of fish paste), and even the cultivation of loaches (an eel-like freshwater fish).[42]

In the end, Kiichiro's fears did not materialize. The Toyoda family were forced to sell most of their stock in TMC, eliminating their position as significant owners but not their prominent role in governing the enterprise. SCAP seized no TMC facilities, and more important, it did not shut down the Japanese auto industry. At first it permitted only truck production, but in 1947 it began to allow the manufacture of passenger cars.

PERIL AND PROMISE (1945–1953)

Permission to operate was only the first thing Toyota needed. Restructuring its operations was another essential task. One notable change was the shifting of specialty-parts production to affiliates which had formerly produced aircraft parts. Before the war, Toyota had made 45 percent of all parts in-house, because it did not trust the quality of parts made by suppliers. After the war, it began to rely more on outside subcontractors, whose labor costs were considerably lower. In financial trouble, TMC decided to shed a number of its divisions, including a new version of Toyoda Spinning (Toyoda Boshoku) and another firm called Nippondenso, which has become Japan's leading car electronics producer. Between 1945 and 1950, TMC spun off nine major companies both to reduce expenses and to develop better outside suppliers.[43] These companies became parts of the modern Toyota Group, which is illustrated in Table 11.1.

As the table indicates, many of the Toyota Group members arose during the late 1940s and early 1950s. In the long run, these major subcontractors (and a legion of other suppliers to be discussed later) have proved critical to Toyota's performance, since Toyota has outsourced much of its component production. In fact, by the 1980s it produced only 25 percent of its cars' value in-house. (By contrast, GM produced about 50 percent of its cars' value in its own factories.)

In the short run, however, these restructuring measures did not prevent Toyota's financial health from deteriorating. In the midst of postwar economic chaos, with per capita incomes very low in Japan, the automobile industry was not a very promising business. Domestic producers also faced tough competition from American vehicles, which once again were flooding the Japanese market. Toyota's annual production volume did not exceed 10,000 vehicles until 1949, and did not surpass its wartime peak of 16,000 vehicles until 1953. Almost all of the vehicles produced were trucks—fewer than 1,000 cars were built between 1945 and 1950. In fact, as Table 11.2 indicates, cars did not account for a significant share of Toyota's production until the mid-1950s.

Along with stagnant production levels, Toyota confronted another problem: its labor union. The Toyota Motor Koromo Labor Union was founded in 1946, during an initial postwar surge in labor activism. Though more moderate than many other contemporary Japanese labor

Table 11.1 The Toyota Group, 1993

Primary Industry & Company Name	Date Established	Sales ($ mil.)	Employees
Automobiles/Auto Parts			
Toyota Motor	Aug. 1937	81,213	73,046
Hino Motor	May 1942	5,686	8,949
Daihatsu Motor	Mar. 1907	7,059	12,353
Kanto Auto Works	April 1946	3,794	6,818
Toyoda Machine Works	May 1941	1,456	4,939
Toyoda Automatic Loom Works	Nov. 1926	5,140	9,907
Toyoda Auto Body	Aug. 1945	5,443	8,687
Aishin Seiki	June 1949	4,905	11,613
Electronic Parts			
Nippondenso	Dec. 1949	12,208	42,621
Fibers and Textiles			
Toyoda Boshoku	May 1950	449	1,375
Rubber Products			
Toyoda Gosei	June 1949	2,195	7,059
Iron and Steel			
Aichi Steel Works	Mar. 1940	1,475	3,515
Trading and Commerce			
Toyota Tsusho	July 1948	18,739	2,060
Towa Real Estate	Aug. 1953	53	105
Research			
Toyota Central Research and Development Laboratories	Nov. 1960	137	988

Sources: Company names and establishment dates from Toyota Motor Corp., *The Automobile Industry: Toyota and Japan*, 1991 ed., table 1–16. Figures for sales (converted at an exchange rate of $1 = ¥111.2) and employees are the latest available as of September 30, 1993, from *Industrial Groupings in Japan*, 11th ed. (Tokyo: Dodwell Marketing Consultants, 1994–95), pp. 256–257.

organizations, the Koromo union soon developed strained relations with Toyota management. In 1948, the union formally affiliated itself with the All-Japan Automobile Industry Labor Union. This national union was modeled on the United Automobile Workers of America (UAW), and its leaders were far more radical than those of Toyota's union.

Union-management tension was exacerbated by the recession of 1949–50, which followed a series of financial retrenchment measures imposed by SCAP and known as the Dodge Line. Toyota had been using installment loans to sell its vehicles, but the recession made it impossible for many consumers to repay their loans, and Toyota's cash flow dried

Table 11.2   Production at Toyota, 1935–60

Year	Cars	Trucks and Buses	Total Vehicles	Cars as % of Total
1935	0	20	20	0%
1940	268	14,519	14,787	2%
1945	0	3,275	3,275	0%
1950	463	11,243	11,706	4%
1955	7,403	15,383	22,786	32%
1960	42,118	112,652	154,770	27%

Source: Toyota: A History of the First 50 Years (Toyota City: Toyota Motor Corporation, 1988), p. 461.

up. Toyota soon found itself in severe financial difficulty. Investment in new plant and equipment was slashed, and layoffs appeared imminent. Nissan and Isuzu, the two other main auto companies at the time, discharged a total of 3,000 workers in 1949.[44] Kiichiro Toyoda tried to avoid this outcome at his own company by promising no layoffs if the union accepted a 10 percent wage cut. The union consented, but as Toyota's financial condition worsened, this deal proved untenable.

Kiichiro tried to obtain additional loans, and in late 1949, the head of the Nagoya Branch of the Bank of Japan organized a consortium of banks to provide financial support. The banks demanded that Toyota accept a reconstruction plan as a precondition for this aid. Noting Toyota's history of excessive production without consideration of demand, the banks ordered it to create a separate sales company. Thus in April 1950 the Toyota Motor Sales Company (TMS) was born.

The issue of layoffs proved thornier. Kiichiro was ashamed to renege on his promise, but he had little choice, as the banks insisted on large reductions in the workforce. He pleaded with the Koromo union for 1,600 "voluntary" retirements. Feeling betrayed, union officials petitioned for a court injunction to enforce the previous agreement. As the dispute dragged on, production fell to a trickle, further damaging Toyota's precarious financial position.

The labor crisis took two months to resolve. Kiichiro resigned as president of TMC to take symbolic responsibility for the layoffs, and 2,146 employees (26 percent of the workforce) took "voluntary" retirement. Taizo Ishida, then president of Toyoda Automatic Loom Works, became president of TMC. Though Ishida knew nothing about cars, the textile machinery business was thriving after the war, and it was believed that his appointment might restore the banks' confidence in the automobile company. Ishida agreed to take the position, but it was understood that after a suitable interval Kiichiro would return.

One round of labor strife was settled in 1950, but another came in June 1953. The national union presented a list of demands to Isuzu, Nissan, and Toyota, and the auto companies refused to give in. Toyota workers now held a series of strikes, lasting from one hour to one day. After two months of contentious bargaining, agreements were reached at both Toyota and Isuzu.

Nissan, however, was a different story. The Nissan union was much more radical than that at Toyota, and Nissan management took a harder line. Nissan executives formed a second union and then used financial pressure, in conjunction with a systematic campaign of harassment, to destroy the original union. Nissan received assistance from its banks, which provided loans throughout the strike. It was also helped by the restraint of the other Japanese auto companies. Officials from Nikkeiren (the Japan Federation of Employers Associations) won agreements from Toyota and Isuzu not to increase production and steal market share from their temporarily weakened competitor. Nissan's strong-arm tactics worked. By the end of 1953, the second union had triumphed. Nissan's victory in effect sounded a death knell for the national auto union, which dissolved in 1954. There would be no Japanese equivalent of the UAW. Instead, each car company would have its own union, representing not only blue-collar but also many white-collar employees.

The collapse of the national auto union ushered in an era of relative labor peace. The strike threat eliminated, management at Toyota and Nissan were able to extract large wage concessions during the late 1950s. Auto workers, once among the best-paid employees in Japanese manufacturing, saw their wages lag behind those in sectors such as steel and shipbuilding.[45] This taming of labor had long-term implications. Until the appreciation of the yen in the late 1980s, Japanese auto companies maintained a significant labor-cost advantage relative to their U.S. counterparts.

Meanwhile, Toyota's financial difficulties of the late 1940s had been eased by events outside Japan. The Japanese automakers were rescued by the Korean War (1950–53), which led the United States to place large orders for Japanese-made trucks. The very first exports by Toyota Motor

Sales (TMS) were 1,000 trucks for the U.S. military in 1950. To companies on the brink of bankruptcy, the Korean war was "a gift from the gods," in Eiji Toyoda's words. But more than luck was involved. TMC president Taizo Ishida put it this way: "When luck comes your way, you can't sit back and relax, or it will be gone. Luck is something you have to grab through effort when it comes your way."[46] TMC had recorded a large loss for the fiscal year ending in March 1950. By the next term, it was back in the black, where it has remained, year after year, through the mid-1990s.

Japanese automakers were also helped by a shift in the Japanese government's posture regarding the domestic automobile industry. Unlike steel, coal, and shipbuilding, the automobile industry had not been a consensus choice among bureaucrats and business leaders for targeted government promotion. The governor of the Bank of Japan adamantly opposed the creation of any domestic auto industry. "It makes no sense to foster a car industry in Japan," he said in 1950. "Because we live in an era of an international division of labor, we can rely on the United States."[47] Even the Ministry of Transport disapproved of using scarce resources to create a domestic passenger-car industry, although it was more enthusiastic about truck production.[48] However, the Ministry of International Trade and Industry (MITI), concerned about Japan's balance-of-payments problems, thought it unwise to rely on foreign automobile suppliers. MITI put into place a powerful system of protection, imposing a hefty 40 percent tax on imported automobiles and a strict limit on foreign exchange allocations for motor vehicle imports.

The new policies quickly achieved their purpose. Whereas in 1951 imports comprised 45 percent of the Japanese market, by 1956 the import share was down to 7 percent, and by 1966 below 1 percent, where it remained until the mid-1980s.[49] Under pressure from abroad, the government's blunt measures of protection were periodically fine-tuned to give at least the appearance of liberalization. For example, Japan first abolished import taxes on vehicles with small engines, a market segment where domestic firms were very powerful and foreign firms absent. The final government-created barriers were lifted only in the 1980s, after the Japanese auto industry had become the world's largest. As the leading historian of this subject writes, the measures taken to protect Japan's domestic auto industry "turned companies that would surely have been business failures into highly profitable operations."[50]

Toyota Motor: The Making of a World Leader, 1954–1980

SETTING THE STAGE

In the early 1950s, at the same time that MITI was blocking the inflow of imported cars, it was encouraging Japanese firms to form joint ventures with foreign automakers. From MITI's vantage point, the technological gap between foreign and domestic automakers was so vast that only through technical tie-ups could the Japanese auto industry develop. Several such alliances were concluded: Isuzu and Rootes (U.K.), Hino and Renault (France), and Shin-Mitsubishi (later Mitsubishi Heavy Industries) with Willys-Overland (U.S.)

Nissan also engaged in a venture with Austin (U.K.), and this foreign tie-up preserved its prewar strategy of acquiring technical knowledge from abroad. Nissan's first car, marketed in 1933, had been designed by an American, William Gorham. In 1936, it had purchased all the machinery in an idle Detroit auto factory and shipped it back to Japan. In 1939, Nissan had confiscated most of the equipment in Ford's Yokohama plant and shipped it to Manchuria.[51]

By contrast, Toyota in the prewar period had developed its automobile manufacturing capabilities without any direct foreign assistance. But in the early postwar period, having difficulty producing cars that would sell, Toyota turned to the Ford Motor Company for help. Just after Ford had selected the engineers to be dispatched to Japan, the Korean War intervened, and the U.S. government restricted overseas investment and the exchange of technical knowledge.

Though the alliance with Ford never materialized, the negotiations produced one major benefit: Kiichiro's cousin Eiji Toyoda, by now a Toyota managing director, visited Ford for six weeks in 1950. He spent most of his stay touring Ford's manufacturing facilities, including the world-famous River Rouge colossus. At the time Ford was making 8,000 vehicles a day, 200 times Toyota's daily output. Though impressed by the scale of Ford's operations, Eiji was not overawed by the technology gap. In fact, he concluded that "Detroit isn't doing anything Toyota doesn't already know."[52] Eiji's reaction recalled that of his uncle Sakichi upon visiting U.S. textile mills four decades earlier. Eiji did, however, pick up some valuable lessons from the trip. Shortly after his return to TMC, he put into place an employee suggestion system based on Ford's model.[53] In early 1951, he called upon his experience at Ford in drafting a modernization plan which aimed to triple production in five years. It was an audacious proposal, but one that proved apt for the time.

Thus, by the mid-1950s, the stage had been set for Toyota to become a major automobile producer. However, the two men who had struggled so hard to get to this point would never see their dreams fully realized. Kiichiro Toyoda, just as he was poised to return as TMC president, died in 1952 at the age of 57. Risaburo Toyoda died the same year, at the age of 68. On his deathbed, Risaburo implored Eiji Toyoda, "Whatever you do, have Toyota make cars."[54] It was a remarkable conversion for the man who had vigorously opposed entering the auto business.

WINNING THE DOMESTIC MARKET

In the mid-1950s, the Japanese economy surged, and so did demand for motor vehicles, especially for trucks. A large market for passenger cars came a bit more slowly. Between 1955 and 1960, Japanese annual truck production increased tenfold, from 22,000 to 224,000 vehicles. Over the same five-year period, passenger car production increased eightfold, from 20,000 to 165,000 units. It then quadrupled between 1960 and 1965, to 696,000 units.[55]

The explosive growth in demand attracted new competitors. They proceeded in defiance of MITI, which sought to promote economies of scale by consolidating the industry around two or three large producers. By the mid-1960s there were 12 competitors: Toyota, Nissan, Isuzu, Mitsubishi, Honda, Toyo Kogyo (Mazda), Suzuki, Fuji Heavy Industries (Subaru), Daihatsu, Hino, Prince, and Nissan Diesel.

Some consolidation in the industry did occur, but not as the result of MITI's maneuvering. Instead, the main banks of fringe producers brokered arrangements with larger companies to help their clients survive. In 1966 Toyota linked up with Hino Motors, a producer of large diesel trucks and buses, and in 1967 with Daihatsu, a specialist in minicars. Nissan merged with Prince in 1966 and formed business ties with Fuji Heavy Industries in 1968. In spite of the many competitors, leadership of the industry eventually became a two-firm race. Each year beginning in 1950, Toyota and Nissan together accounted for more than 50 percent of domestic production.[56] Smaller producers jockeyed among themselves for third place, and their presence kept the big two honest.

Of the big two producers, Nissan seemed to be the clear industry leader in 1950. It accounted for 54 percent of Japanese motor-vehicle production that year, almost twice Toyota's 29 percent.[57] Nissan was the more experienced producer of autos, and it possessed more sophisticated production equipment. Headquartered in Tokyo, Nissan was considered the smoother, more cosmopolitan firm. Toyota, in Aichi prefecture, was located far from the center of Japan's business establishment.

However, in the early postwar period Toyota enjoyed some advantages of its own. During the Allied Occupation, SCAP purged most of Nissan's senior executives, 20 in all, but no Toyota officials. This difference in treatment in part reflected Nissan's closer ties to the Japanese military. Also important were the arbitrary criteria used by SCAP. According to these rules, Nissan's larger authorized paid-up capital rendered its executives eligible for forcible dismissal, while Toyota was too small to penalize.[58] SCAP dealt Nissan a further blow by requisitioning some of its plants, which were not returned until the mid-1950s. Nissan's plants were chosen because they were conveniently close to the Yokohama and Tokyo wharves. Far from Tokyo or Osaka, Toyota's plants did not interest the Americans.[59] Toyota's rural location offered other benefits. Cheaper land prices enabled the company to concentrate its plants and those of its suppliers geographically, thereby facilitating coordination and reducing transportation costs. Toyota's rural workers tended to be more obedient than Nissan's city-bred ones. Toyota exploited the conservative nature of rustic Japanese citizens. Starting in about 1960, it actually sent individual conduct reports to workers' families, very much like report cards from school.[60]

Nissan was also handicapped by a Faustian deal that its management had struck with the "second union" it had created to crush the radical union in 1953. Top managers were beholden to the second union, and their freedom of action was constrained by what the union considered acceptable. Toyota's union was much weaker. Taiichi Ohno, the man credited with developing the now-famous Toyota Production System (to be discussed later), regarded Toyota's ability to control the union as its foremost advantage over its domestic and foreign rivals.[61]

The Nissan-Toyota battle for market share was fought on many fronts. One of them was distribution. Here Toyota seized the first-mover advantage, building a larger dealer network, and more quickly, than Nissan. The key figure was Shotaro Kamiya, who in 1950 had become the first president of Toyota Motor Sales (TMS).[62] Formerly the highest-ranking

Japanese national at GM Japan, Kamiya took an 80 percent pay cut when he joined the automobile department of Toyoda Automatic Loom in 1935.[63] Before World War II, Kamiya constructed a franchise dealer network by recruiting former GM dealers to sell Toyota cars. His efforts were nullified during the war, when the Japanese military established a single distribution network for all automobile makes. After the war, Kamiya became an adviser to SCAP on the auto industry. In this capacity, he learned that the wartime dealer association would soon be dissolved. Deciding that it would be unethical to poach Nissan dealers after this dissolution, he strove frantically to recruit former Nissan dealers before the scheduled date. His efforts paid off, and Toyota's larger dealer network provided an early and powerful advantage over Nissan.[64]

Organizing parts suppliers was another battlefront. As mentioned earlier, Toyota had created a suppliers' association in the late 1930s. In the 1950s, it reorganized its suppliers into three geographic branches and, in conjunction with MITI's Small and Medium-Sized Enterprise Agency, conducted comprehensive evaluations of them. By the early 1970s, Toyota had fashioned close ties with its largest subcontractors and presided over an extensive subcontracting hierarchy: 168 first-tier suppliers reporting directly to Toyota, 5,437 second-tier suppliers in turn producing parts for the first-tier suppliers, and 41,703 third-tier suppliers—including many small family workshops—serving the second-tier suppliers.[65] In forging this network, Toyota was helped by the fact that many of its largest suppliers had once been parts of the main company. Nissan, by contrast, did not even attempt to organize its primary subcontractors until 1949. It had more trouble cultivating close relations with its suppliers, most of which were preexisting firms with no historical connection to Nissan. Nor could Nissan, with its urban location and geographically scattered factories, hope to emulate Toyota's policy of clustering its main suppliers close to its manufacturing facilities.

In the race to invest, both companies tended to be reactive, building capacity to meet existing demand rather than adding facilities in anticipation of future sales growth.[66] However, Toyota proved bolder than Nissan. A key turning point came in 1959 when Toyota opened a new plant with an initial monthly capacity of 5,000 cars and additional space to double output. This plant was considered enormous at a time when Toyota's monthly production was only 2,000 vehicles. In the rapidly expanding economy of the early 1960s, however, the new plant became indispensable for Toyota to meet the demand for its cars. Nissan, which recognized the need for a new factory at the same time Toyota did, had more difficulty finding land. Nissan also encountered much more disagreement among its own managers over the scale of the operation. Consequently, its plant came on line three years after Toyota's and proved far too small, with monthly capacity of only 5,000 units and no room for expansion. Eiji Toyoda later called the decision to build such a large plant one of his most memorable moves at TMC and the moment when "Toyota suddenly rose head and shoulders above its domestic competitors."[67]

Of course, a superior dealer network, better supplier relations, and more production capacity did not guarantee that Toyota would surpass Nissan. The crucial issue was the quality of the product itself. Here Toyota's relative performance was initially less impressive. Its trucks sold well, but its cars in the early postwar period were disappointing. They tended to be awkward and improvised, featuring a car body mounted on a truck chassis.

The Crown, marketed in 1955, involved no such compromises and was a true passenger car. Carefully targeted at the booming market for taxis and hired cars, the large-size Crown sold well. Its success led Toyota to give many of its passenger cars names associated with the word "crown." Corona, for example, means "crown of the sun." Corolla denotes "crown of the flower." Even the Camry derives its name from *kanmuri*, the Japanese word for crown.[68]

After the Crown came the Corona. Debuting in 1957, the mid-size Corona was pitted against Nissan's Bluebird, which dominated the market segment. Unreliable and underpowered, the Corona did little to change the conventional wisdom at the time: "Nissan for passenger cars, Toyota for trucks." Toyota went back to the drawing board and introduced a new version in 1960, thereby starting the second battle in what the Japanese media called the BC (Bluebird-Corona) wars. Again the Corona proved to be riddled with flaws, and Nissan's Bluebird remained the best-selling car in Japan. In 1965, Toyota brought out a third incarnation. Displacing the Bluebird as Japan's best-selling car that year, the new Corona became the decisive salvo in the BC wars.

Even so, Toyota's most convincing triumph in the Japanese market was yet to come. In late 1966 it introduced the Corolla, a compact car aimed at the mass market. The Corolla arrived six months after the Sunny, Nissan's product in this class, and thus appeared to be at a disadvantage. However, Toyota cleverly positioned the Corolla as an up-market alternative. Priced a bit higher than the Sunny, the Corolla offered a number of features its competitor lacked. With a 1,100-cc engine, the Corolla had a little more power than the Sunny with its 1,000-cc engine. In the largest advertising campaign in Japan's history up to then, Toyota proclaimed that "the extra 100 cc gives extra comfort." This message struck a chord with Japanese consumers, who were seeing their incomes more than double in a decade. The car was a key consumer durable, the most important of the so-called three C's—car, color television and cooler (air conditioner). Vastly outselling the Sunny, the Corolla became a smashing success. By 1974 it was the best-selling car in the world, and by the end of 1994 Toyota had produced 18 million Corollas, making it the best-selling car of all time.

The Corolla propelled Toyota to unquestioned leadership in the Japanese market. In 1966 the company moved ahead of Nissan on all fronts to become the top Japanese automaker in production, domestic sales, and exports.[69] Toyota's annual output soared, doubling from one million to two million vehicles between 1968 and 1972 (see Table 11.3). By the early 1970s, Toyota Motor Company had displaced Matsushita Electric as Japan's most profitable corporation.[70]

FURTHER CHANGES OF THE 1960S AND 1970S

In 1961, Taizo Ishida stepped down as TMC president after 11 years at the helm. Eiji Toyoda seemed the natural choice to replace him, having been with Toyota from the start and having served as one of the two

Table 11.3   Production at Toyota, 1960–94

Year	Cars	Trucks and Buses	Total Vehicles	Cars as % of Total
1960	42,118	112,652	154,770	27%
1965	236,151	241,492	477,643	49%
1970	1,068,321	540,869	1,609,190	66%
1975	1,714,836	621,217	2,336,053	73%
1980	2,303,284	990,060	3,293,344	70%
1985	2,469,284	1,196,338	3,665,622	67%
1990	3,345,885	866,388	4,212,273	79%
1994	2,769,359	739,097	3,508,456	79%

Source: Toyota Motor Corp., *The Automobile Industry: Toyota and Japan,* 1995 ed., p. 3.

executive vice presidents under Ishida. However, at 48 years of age, Eiji was considered too young to become president. Instead, the post went to the other executive vice president, Fumio Nakagawa, who had joined Toyota in 1950 when he was dispatched from Mitsui Bank to oversee the company's financial reorganization.

When Nakagawa died in 1967, Eiji, then 54 years old, succeeded him as president. Eiji's appointment marked the return of a "car man" to the top post. When Taizo Ishida had said "my company," he meant Toyoda Automatic Loom Works. For him, cars were just a side business. His successor Nakagawa had come from a bank. Eiji, though, had been working with cars ever since his days as a university student. More conspicuously, Eiji's promotion meant that a Toyoda family member again presided at TMC. For the next 15 years, Eiji served as TMC president and watched it become one of the world's leading automobile producers. He considered himself the "lucky Toyoda," actually experiencing what his cousin Kiichiro had only dreamed about.[71]

Even so, Eiji's tenure was not without challenges. One new development was that Japanese auto companies, like their U.S. counterparts, now found themselves subject to more stringent regulatory oversight. In June 1969, Toyota was forced by the Ministry of Transport to recall 700,000 vehicles because of safety defects. All Japanese manufacturers were affected by mass recalls, the first of their kind in Japan. But Toyota, as Japan's largest auto manufacturer, had the largest number of cars recalled. Then, in the early 1970s, the Japanese government established much stricter vehicle emission standards. Smaller Japanese automakers, including Honda, met the new requirements relatively quickly, but Toyota struggled. It was forced to concentrate on developing pollution-control devices. New-model development became a secondary concern, and Toyota's share of the Japanese market declined for three consecutive years after 1975. Chastened by the experience, it went on to become a pioneer in the development of advanced pollution-control devices. In the end, neither the recalls nor the trouble meeting pollution standards seriously damaged Toyota's position as Japan's premier automaker.

THE TOYOTA PRODUCTION SYSTEM: A NEW MANUFACTURING PARADIGM

Underlying Toyota's success in the product market was a system that later became famous as "lean production." At its heart was the Toyota

Production System, a manufacturing approach developed over a 20-year period. (Lean production also encompassed innovations in car design, quality control, and sales promotion. Less unique to Toyota, they are discussed in the Appendix to this chapter.)

The Toyota Production System had its roots in Kiichiro Toyoda's notorious aversion to waste. In the mid-1930s at Toyota's first plant, Kiichiro had posted a banner proclaiming "just in time." He explained, "What I mean by 'just in time' is not simply that it is important to do something on time, but that it is absolutely essential to be precise in terms of quantity and not, for example, produce something on time but in excess, since excess amounts to waste."[72] Kiichiro tried to implement his vision in the design of the Koromo factory in the late 1930s, when he ordered that warehouses for spare parts be kept to a minimum. He directed plant engineers to develop machines flexible enough to perform many different tasks, and he told them to locate machinery so as to facilitate the smooth flow of work. Kiichiro created a manual 4 inches thick detailing work rules and procedures. He assigned lot numbers to each batch of 10 vehicles, so as to monitor the manufacturing process better.[73] All of these initiatives were interrupted by World War II, when material shortages and a largely untrained labor force made it impossible to operate this system.

Many of Kiichiro's ideas were revived in the postwar era by Taiichi Ohno, who became famous in Japan as a manufacturing genius.[74] Unlike Kiichiro, Ohno lacked a university education. But he shared Kiichiro's loathing of waste and had a keen aptitude for identifying unnecessary or inefficient practices. Ohno had begun his career at Toyoda Spinning & Weaving and had moved to TMC in 1943 when it absorbed Toyoda's textile firms. He had no experience in the auto industry, but his outsider's perspective allowed him to see some of the inefficiencies in Toyota's car factories.

Ohno relied on his background in the textile industry to distill one of what became the two pillars of the Toyota Production System: *jidoka* (self-working). The Toyoda automatic loom was designed to stop immediately if it ran out of thread or if it encountered some other problem. Otherwise, it operated smoothly with little need for monitoring. Ohno believed that this distinction between "normal" and "abnormal" operations could be applied to auto manufacturing as well. Under normal circumstances, machines should operate with minimal supervision. In the event of a problem, a machine should clearly indicate a malfunction, and any worker should be authorized to shut it down and fix the problem.

The second pillar of the Toyota Production System had to do with inventory replenishment. Ohno's development of this pillar in the late 1940s amounted to a resurrection and broad implementation of Kiichiro Toyoda's "just-in-time" system of the 1930s. Shortly after the war, Ohno read that American supermarkets replaced items only as they sold them. He reasoned that, in the same way, workers should provide parts only when the next station on the assembly line needed them. This was in line with Kiichiro's ideas but was the antithesis of the prevailing system, in which workers were expected to perform their tasks as quickly as possible, stockpiling parts in front of the next station if necessary. To make the new system practical, Ohno developed a tool called a *kanban,* meaning "signboard." A kanban is a card showing the type and quantity of parts needed. When a worker anticipated a need for more parts, he would pass the kanban to the station responsible for their manufacture. Then, and only then, would the parts be assembled.

In 1948 Ohno, by now 36 and head of a TMC engine shop, began testing his ideas. His first step was to implement the jidoka (self-working) concept by rearranging equipment so that one worker could oversee multiple machines. Later he trained each worker to operate the several different machines required to produce a component. He also developed monitoring switches that stopped a machine when it was finished processing, plus signal lights that indicated a malfunction. Ohno then tried out the kanban (just-in-time) system and found that it greatly reduced inventories.

In 1953, Ohno became Toyota's general manager of manufacturing. In this post, he could try his ideas on the main automobile assembly lines. In 1955 he empowered assembly-line workers to stop the line in the event of a problem. This was a radical change from decades of conventional worldwide practice in the industry. Ohno also attacked the problem of how to change dies more quickly. Dies are heavy metal forms used to stamp body panels from sheet metal. By redesigning them and developing better ways to move them, Toyota reduced its average setup time from two or three hours in 1955 to 15 minutes in 1962, and then to a mere 3 minutes by 1971.[75]

With these kinds of results, Taiichi Ohno's ideas gained attention, both positive and negative. They elicited strong resentment from union officials, who interpreted them as a sneaky way to increase the workload. Indeed, Ohno's reforms in the engine shop became one of the main issues in the 1950 strike at Toyota, and his production system as subsequently implemented has been criticized for exacting too much effort from workers.[76] In addition, many skilled workers resented having to learn how to operate several different kinds of machines. Workers gave Ohno the unflattering nickname "Mustache," because of his facial hair, unusual for Japanese men in the early postwar period. They derided his ideas as the Mustache's Methods.[77] However, having served on the union's executive committee, Ohno was personally close to many union leaders. He also had the unwavering support of Eiji Toyoda, who helped spread Ohno's ideas throughout TMC.

By 1963 the Toyota Production System was in place at all TMC plants, and by the mid-1960s, Toyota's first-tier suppliers had been integrated into the production flow of the main company. After the worldwide oil shock of 1973, Toyota insisted that all suppliers, not just first-tier ones, employ its Production System. Toyota's first-tier suppliers became, in effect, mini-Toyotas, teaching their own subcontractors about the Production System. The second-tier suppliers, in turn, instructed their own suppliers, spreading Ohno's gospel throughout Toyota's vast network.

Other Japanese automakers, battered by the oil shock, began to experiment with their own versions of Ohno's ideas in the 1970s. But none achieved a comparable degree of efficiency. Nissan adopted a loose adaptation of the kanban idea, but it failed to achieve a more rigorous "just-in-time" system, in part because of its strong union, but also because, in the words of a former Nissan official, it lacked "a fanatic, a Taiichi Ohno."[78]

ENTERING THE "AUTOMOBILE KINGDOM"

By the middle of the 1960s, the Japanese auto industry's most explosive growth had already occurred. Most of this growth was confined to the domestic market, although Japanese automakers had some modest success in exporting, most notably to Southeast Asia. As late as 1970, domestic consumers purchased 80 percent of Japan's domestic motor vehicle production.[79] In the huge U.S. market, Toyota and other Japanese firms had little presence (see Figure 11.2).

In Japanese eyes, America remained the "automobile kingdom." It was the place where Henry Ford had begun the mass production of auto-

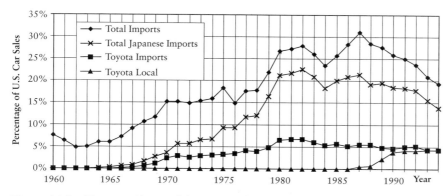

Figure 11.2   Toyota's Share of the U.S. Passenger Car Market

Note: Total Japanese imports refers to all imports of Japanese passenger cars, including those of Toyota. It does not include cars produced in the United States by Japanese automakers.

Source: American Automobile Manufacturers Association, *AAMA Motor Vehicles Facts and Figures 1994; Ward's Automotive Yearbook,* various issues; Toyota Motor Sales, U.S.A.

mobiles, and where both mass production and mass marketing had reached perfect realization in Alfred Sloan's General Motors. The Big Three automakers, GM, Ford, and Chrysler, dominated world production. In 1955 their share of the U.S. market was 95 percent. Overall, U.S. firms accounted for about 99 percent of the domestic market and 60 percent of world production.[80] The first attempts of Japanese companies to export to America were laughable. In 1958 Toyota began exporting its Crown model, which proved completely unsuitable for American driving conditions. The Crown vibrated terribly at speeds over 60 miles per hour, and it had problems with overheating. In 1960, Toyota suspended car exports to the United States. Nissan never engaged in a full-scale retreat, but its U.S. dealers called its first cars "mobile coffins" because of their propensity to overheat.

The dominance of the U.S. automobile industry obscured what would later be revealed as a major weakness of American automakers: the lack of genuine competition among the Big Three, aside from cosmetic model changes. For a long time after the introduction of automatic transmissions in the 1930s, no technical improvements of major significance came from U.S. auto firms. By contrast, in the 1960s and 1970s European automakers developed such innovations as front-wheel drive, disc brakes, fuel injection, and five-speed transmissions.[81] American companies were capable of innovation, as GM's rapid development of the catalytic converter during the early 1970s demonstrated. However, they seemed to focus on styling changes and "comfort features" such as air conditioning and stereos. Devising new technology was simply not a high priority.[82]

On the other hand, the dramatic growth of the domestic automobile market in Japan, contested vigorously by a large number of competing firms, demanded continuous improvement in product quality, production efficiency, and marketing. At Nissan and Toyota, car prices fell every year between the early 1950s and 1973, even before adjusting for inflation.[83] The American Big Three imagined that they were engaged in this kind of fierce competition, when they were actually enjoying the quiet life of secure oligopolists. One former Ford executive likened Detroit to an exclusive suburban tennis club where the Big Three were the three best players. Then one day the world's top tennis pros, the Japanese, stepped onto the court.[84]

American auto executives were also slow to recognize the need for smaller cars. The cheap gasoline of the 1950s and 1960s lulled them into thinking that big cars, filled with more and more gadgets, were the way to go. No doubt they were also swayed by the lavish profits from big cars laden with optional equipment.[85] Their reluctance to produce small cars left a void, first exploited in the 1950s by Volkswagen with its Beetle. In penetrating the American market, Volkswagen, like the Japanese automakers who followed, was helped by U.S. antitrust policy. Fearful of violating antitrust laws, the Big Three did not write contracts forbidding their dealers from handling other automakers' vehicles. (In Japan and Europe, by contrast, auto manufacturers have had more latitude in writing and enforcing such exclusive-dealing provisions.)

The Japanese were not major players in the U.S. market until the 1973 oil shock, but even earlier they showed signs of becoming a long-run competitive threat. Toyota resumed its exports to America in 1964. Over the next three years its U.S. exports rose tenfold to 39,000 vehicles, and in 1967 the United States became Toyota's largest single export market.[86] In 1975, Toyota displaced Volkswagen as the best-selling import brand in America.

Even then, U.S. automakers were slow to recognize the vast improvement in the quality of Japanese cars and the extent of the potential damage. Detroit executives remained convinced that they could make better small cars than their Japanese rivals, and they joked that if you scratched the body of a Japanese car, you could still see Budweiser labels.[87] The joke, however, was on them. Japan's automakers had secured a beachhead in the U.S. market, and they were not to be dislodged.

U.S. sales of Japanese automobiles skyrocketed following the second oil crisis in 1979. As the 1980s began, imports from Japan made up over 20 percent of all vehicles sold in America, and an astonishing 67 percent of U.S. imports.[88] Toyota sold over 700,000 vehicles in America in 1980, three and a half times its 1970 sales figure. In the meantime, the Big Three all lost money in 1980, GM for the first time since 1921. Chrysler had to be bailed out with loan guarantees from the U.S. government. On top of all this, in 1980 Japan surpassed the United States as the world's leading producer of motor vehicles. As with textiles in the 1930s, Japan had risen from obscurity to become the world leader. Once again, the Toyoda family had played a key role in an economic "miracle."

Toyota Motor Corporation: The Challenge of Leadership, 1980–1995

THE 1980S: PROSPERITY, PROTECTIONISM, AND OFFSHORE PRODUCTION

In 1982 Toyota Motor Company (TMC) and Toyota Motor Sales (TMS) merged to form the Toyota Motor Corporation. To lay the groundwork for the merger, Eiji in 1981 appointed his nephew Shoichiro Toyoda as president of TMS. The next year Shoichiro at 57 became president of the new Toyota Motor Corporation, and Eiji, by then 69, its chairman. A grandson of Sakichi, Shoichiro had earned a doctorate in mechanical engineering and then worked his way up TMC. His term as Toyota president, lasting until 1992, coincided with tranquil and prosperous times at the company.

During the early 1980s, Toyota widened its lead over Nissan in the Japanese market. Toyota's share of that market surpassed 40 percent and stayed there.[89] In addition, a rise in the value of the dollar, with a corresponding weakening of the yen, enhanced the already strong demand for Toyota's exports (and those of other Japanese automakers). Toyota generated such large cash flows that some were calling it "Toyota Bank." Although its profits in the 1980s were unprecedented, Toyota had long been profitable enough to fund its investments largely with internally generated funds. Its debt-to-equity ratio, which stood at 1.1 in 1973, was unusually low for Japanese manufacturers, whose average debt-to-equity ratio at the time was close to 4.

In the second half of the 1980s Toyota, like other Japanese companies, faced more difficulty exporting as the dollar exchange rate plunged from ¥240 in 1985 to ¥120 at the start of 1988. Yet Japanese automakers continued to register strong sales in the U.S. market. Meanwhile the buoyant Japanese economy of that period caused domestic car purchases to rise at an annual rate of 16 percent during three straight years beginning in 1988.[90] Toyota, with its dominant share of the Japanese market, reaped benefits from the economic expansion.

Toyota's increasing technological prowess became apparent during the 1980s. Along with its Japanese competitors, Toyota introduced cars with multi-valve engines, electronically controlled fuel injection, superchargers, antilock brakes, and other innovations. Although the basic technology underlying these features had been developed elsewhere, Toyota and other Japanese firms pioneered the application of this knowledge to commercial products.[91]

Even more impressive was Toyota's move into luxury cars. After six years of development, in 1989 it introduced a new brand, Lexus. The Lexus received high plaudits from car aficionados and from its owners, capturing the top position in the annual J. D. Power and Associates Customer Satisfaction Survey for an unprecedented five straight years. It demonstrated that Toyota could make cars ranking with the world's best, not just in economy and reliability but in styling and handling.

The initial responses of the Big Three to the Japanese challenge were generally ineffective. Instead of cutting prices to gain market share, they raised prices to boost short-run profits. (U.S. automakers could increase their prices because of a quota on Japanese car imports, as discussed in the next paragraph.) They then used these profits to invest in unnecessary automation and unrelated diversification. GM alone spent $70 billion on investment and R&D in the 1980s. This sum was over three times the combined market value of Toyota's and Honda's equity in 1985.[92] GM also purchased Electronic Data Systems for $2.5 billion and Hughes Aircraft for $5 billion. Nevertheless, its share of the U.S. market declined from 45 percent in 1984 to 35 percent in 1991.[93]

Troubled Detroit also strove for a political solution, which was achieved in 1981 when the Japanese government accepted a "voluntary" export restraint (VER). The VER limited imports of passenger cars from

Japan to 1.68 million units, a significant reduction from the 1.9 million Japanese cars imported in 1980.[94] The VER, initially set to run for three years, was extended for more than a decade, though the import ceiling was raised periodically. (European countries generally subjected Japanese imports to far more stringent quotas.) The VER limited Japanese firms' share of the U.S. market, but it allowed them to collect a scarcity premium on the cars they did sell. It also induced them to move upscale in the market, from economy cars to higher-priced ones.

In addition, Japanese automakers evaded the export restrictions by locating production facilities in the United States. These Japanese-owned factories became known as auto "transplants." Here the pioneer was Honda, which opened a car factory in Ohio in 1982. (It had established a motorcycle plant at the same site in 1979.) Nissan soon followed with a Tennessee plant.

Toyota management, concerned about possible difficulties in operating its production system abroad, had already decided to test the waters with a joint venture. The company had approached Ford in 1980 with a proposal to build cars together in America, but it had been rebuffed. This brought General Motors into the picture and led to the historic agreement mentioned at the outset of this chapter. In early 1983, Toyota and GM agreed to establish a joint venture called New United Motor Manufacturing, Inc. (NUMMI). Using a shut-down GM plant in Fremont, California, they planned to build a Toyota-designed car to be sold as the Chevrolet Nova. Toyota and GM had equal ownership in NUMMI, but Toyota directed the plant's operations.

Tatsuro Toyoda, younger brother of Toyota President Shoichiro Toyoda, became NUMMI's first president. Tatsuro faced a number of obstacles. The Fremont plant had been one of GM's worst, with abysmal labor-management relations and high absenteeism. When NUMMI opened in 1984, former Fremont employees comprised over 80 percent of its workforce. However, in atmosphere and performance, NUMMI could hardly have been more different from the old GM plant. Tatsuro eliminated detailed labor contracts, rigid job classifications, and many perquisites that had sharply distinguished labor from management. He flattened the hierarchy, organized workers into teams, and trained them to perform multiple jobs. Absenteeism, near 25 percent under GM, fell to 2 percent. Productivity and quality numbers almost matched those of Toyota's Japanese factories (Table 11.4).[95]

Table 11.4   NUMMI's Performance in Comparative Perspective

	GM Framingham	Toyota Takaoka	NUMMI Fremont
Assembly Hours per Car	31	16	19
Assembly Defects per 100 Cars	135	45	45
Average Parts Inventories	2 weeks	2 hours	2 days

Note: The figures for assembly hours per car reflect adjustments for differences in vehicle sizes and option packages.

Source: James P. Womack, Daniel T. Jones, and Daniel Roos, *The Machine That Changed the World* (New York: HarperCollins, 1990), p. 83.

Its experience at NUMMI smoothed the way for Toyota to build a new, wholly owned plant in the United States. In December 1985, it announced plans to construct a plant in Georgetown, Kentucky.[96] The plant, with an initial annual capacity of 200,000 vehicles, was intended to produce the entire Camry supply for the U.S. market. The first car rolled off the line in July 1988.

By then, Honda, Nissan, and Mazda were already operating factories in America. Isuzu, Fuji Heavy Industries, and Mitsubishi soon followed. Overall, the speed and scale of Japanese automakers' investment in America had been extraordinary. The authors of a major study of the world automotive industry marveled that in one decade the Japanese had built in America "an auto industry larger than that of Britain or Italy or Spain and almost the size of the French industry."[97]

THE 1990S: CONTINUING CHALLENGES

The 1980s had been golden years for Japanese automakers, but they failed to realize that good times could not last forever. Like their Detroit counterparts two decades earlier, they began to believe in the myth of their own invincibility. They overinvested in sparkling new Japanese plants, and they overextended themselves by introducing too much product variety. Even Toyota, devoted to the notion of continuous improvement, succumbed to the sin of excessive self-satisfaction. Success in the 1980s made it difficult to adjust when circumstances changed.

In the 1990s, Japanese automakers were hit with a double blow. On the one hand, the dollar's value, after rising to ¥150 in late 1989, fell during the next six years, momentarily tumbling below ¥85 in 1995. The

rising yen made production in Japan relatively more expensive and necessitated price increases for Japanese cars sold abroad.[98] This adverse
development was accompanied by a prolonged domestic recession. Motor-vehicle sales in Japan decreased for four consecutive years beginning
in 1991. The recession was hardest on the smaller producers, such as
Mazda and Isuzu, but even large producers suffered. Nissan racked up
losses and was forced to close its Zama plant in 1993, the first Japanese
automobile plant to close in the postwar era. Toyota remained profitable,
but its operating profit declined for four straight years starting in 1990.
In response, the company took decisive cost-cutting measures. It reduced
the number of parts and available options for its vehicles, and it placed
severe pressure on its suppliers to lower costs.

Compounding the domestic recession was continued political tension
in the auto market. Automobiles and auto parts constituted between one-
half and two-thirds of the U.S.-Japan bilateral trade imbalance. This sector thus became the center of many trade disputes. Though the focus in
the early 1980s had been the flood of Japanese exports into America, it
later became the low level of Japanese auto imports. U.S. officials argued
that the Japanese had erected a systematic series of barriers to foreign
vehicles. Their Japanese counterparts contended that the problem was a
lack of American effort. As evidence, they pointed to European car producers, whose share of the Japanese auto market in the late 1980s was
similar to their share of the U.S. market.[99] Unimpressed by these arguments, the Americans urged Japanese companies to purchase more U.S.-
made auto parts. Some minor agreements (such as the Toyota-GM deal
mentioned below) notwithstanding, the issue remained unresolved and
highly divisive as of the mid-1990s.

At the same time, the Big Three eventually began to learn from their
Japanese counterparts and thus posed yet another challenge to the Japanese auto producers. Ford had been the most eager student, dispatching
executives to Japan in 1981 to study Mazda's production methods. By
1989 Ford's North American assembly plants were as productive as the
average Japanese transplant.[100] Chrysler overcame two brushes with
death in the 1980s to generate record profits by the mid-1990s. Even
GM seemed to improve, although its U.S. market share continued to drift
downward. In late 1993 it signed a deal with Toyota to sell a few thousand GM-built cars in Japan.[101] Though strongly motivated by politics,
this agreement hinted that GM's quality was improving.

The best indication of the U.S. resurgence in automobiles came in 1994 when, for the first time in 14 years, American motor-vehicle production surpassed that of Japan. To be sure, Japanese transplants accounted for one-fifth of U.S. production, and Japanese automakers' share of the U.S. market still exceeded 25 percent.[102] Productivity also remained higher at Japanese transplants than at other U.S. auto factories.[103] However, Japanese automakers had lost their aura of invincibility.

Tatsuro Toyoda was the one who confronted the problems of the 1990s. He became president of Toyota Motor Corporation in 1992, at the age of 63. Unlike his older brother's prosperous and lengthy tenure, Tatsuro's reign was turbulent and lasted only until 1995. His successor was Hiroshi Okuda, the first company chief in 28 years to come from outside the Toyoda family. Tatsuro's departure marked the retirement of the second generation of Toyodas after Sakichi, although Shoichiro retained the largely ceremonial post of chairman. It remained to be seen whether another Toyoda, from the next generation, would someday lead the company.[104]

Of course, the late 1990s were a new and different age. In the 1930s, the family automobile business had been a struggling upstart, financially dependent on its parent, the very successful Toyoda Automatic Loom Works. Sixty years later, this relationship had long since reversed. The Loom Works now was deriving 95 percent of its revenues from assembling cars, car air-conditioner parts, and industrial vehicles. A mere 5 percent came from textile machinery. Toyota Motor Corporation had become the acknowledged world leader, with a production system celebrated around the globe. In the short term, it would remain one of the world's top auto producers. Its long-term future was less assured, however. Japan was becoming an almost prohibitively expensive place to manufacture cars, and the Japanese market showed signs of saturation. Toyota also had to fight complacency, the curse of almost every successful company in any industry. Those who had helped to build the Toyota Motor Corporation into its present form could justifiably be proud of what they had accomplished. But they were in no position to be complacent.

Appendix: Other Dimensions of Lean Production

Lean production not only improved the manufacturing process but also made car design more efficient. Under the traditional method, each functional department worked in sequence. First the marketing department determined the desired characteristics of the car. Then engineers drew sketches and constructed models, often without considering very thoroughly whether their designs could actually be manufactured. That job was the responsibility of production engineers, who sometimes found that designs were tough to mass-produce. Suppliers were not consulted at all until the parts had been designed, at which time the lowest-cost supplier was sought. This entire procedure was long and costly, and it often produced unsatisfactory results.

Toyota, however, formed cross-functional teams to design a car. Under a project leader, people from marketing, engineering, and production all worked together. Suppliers of key parts were consulted early in the project, and they often were given responsibility for designing the components they would make. Simultaneous development was far more efficient than the traditional sequential process. By the mid-1980s, the average Japanese automaker required 45 percent fewer engineering hours and 24 percent less time overall to introduce a new car than did its U.S. rival.[105]

Toyota also struggled to raise the quality of its cars. These efforts fell under the rubric of quality control (QC).[106] Narrowly construed, QC meant using statistical tools to monitor the production process and to identify and eliminate sources of defects. More broadly, it meant fostering worker responsibility for improving quality, not just in manufacturing but in all areas.

Much of the inspiration for the QC movement had originally come from the United States. The ideas of American QC experts, including W. Edwards Deming, A. V. Feigenbaum, and Joseph Juran, became very influential among Japanese companies in the early 1950s. Deming was particularly revered. In 1950 he donated the royalties from one of his books to establish an annual award, the Deming Prize, for the outstanding QC program at a Japanese company. Deming's picture, along with portraits of Toyota's founder and its current chairman, is displayed in the lobby of company headquarters in Toyota City. Of the three portraits, Deming's is the largest.[107]

Nissan, however, was the first Japanese automaker to establish a formal QC program, and in 1960 became the first to capture the Deming Prize. Toyota did not even begin formal QC efforts until 1961, and to do so it called on the expertise of its supplier, Nippondenso, which had won the Deming Prize that year. Toyota chose two company heavyweights to oversee the QC program's implementation: Eiji Toyoda and his nephew Shoichiro Toyoda. The internal pressure to attain the Deming Prize became severe. One engineer even inquired if he would be fired in the event that Toyota failed to win. Shoichiro responded that if this subordinate was fired, then he himself would leave as well.[108] This hypothetical situation never arose, as Toyota triumphed in 1965. It then worked to establish QC programs at its top suppliers.

Toyota also undertook a series of new sales tactics, which sprang from the fertile marketing mind of Shotaro Kamiya at TMS. Like Taiichi Ohno in production management, Kamiya was constantly generating new ideas and eagerly trying them out. Under his leadership, Toyota became the first Japanese automaker to offer a monthly installment program. He encouraged Toyota dealers to hire college-trained salesmen, and he professionalized their training programs. Toyota dealers dispatched representatives to sell cars door-to-door. This "aggressive selling," as it became known, enabled sales reps to collect a great deal of information on Toyota customers. Toyota compiled this information into a massive data base, which its marketing staff and design engineers used in planning new models. Aggressive selling also smoothed production over time. When orders were down, sales reps worked longer hours, and when the factory was overburdened, they worked less. This built-in stabilization pleased Ohno, who was a strong advocate of level production.

PROLOGUE TO CHAPTER 12

"Japanese Capitalism" is the last country chapter in this book. Since we've examined three other countries in some detail, we now have a solid basis for cross-national comparison. What exactly is "Japanese" about Japanese capitalism? How does it resemble or differ from other varieties?

As with Great Britain, another island nation with a long history, some of the most obvious aspects turn out to be the most important. Japan has a very large population, most of it living near the sea. The country's interior is a rugged land mass, a significant portion of which is uninhabitable. Japan's population density per habitable square mile is among the highest in the world.

As measured by Gross Domestic Product per capita at current exchange rates, Japan is the richest of the four countries we have examined, and it has been so since the late 1980s. Its people are among the world's best educated and most urbanized. Yet Japan is an expensive place to live, and measured by purchasing power parity its per capita income still lags behind that of the United States by about 18 percent. And substantial numbers of the people who still live in rural areas follow ways of life that haven't changed for many decades. Of the four countries covered in this book, Japan presents the strongest contrasts with the other three.

Historically, the most striking thing of all about Japanese capitalism is how rapidly it developed. For centuries before the Meiji Restoration of 1868, the country had sealed itself off from the rest of the world. It had preserved an essentially feudal society even during the years when the other three countries were passing through the First Industrial Revolution and getting well into the Second. (Germany was a partial exception in that the country itself was not unified until 1871.) So Japan became, in the argot of economic historians, a "late industrializer."

Like many other latecomers, it used the power of government to try to accelerate development. Unlike most, it achieved spectacular success. You should ask yourself why that was so. Why was Japan able to develop a modern industrial sector so fast, while so many other countries (China,

Russia, Mexico) were trying but failing? How did Japan's companies organize themselves? Just how old are the characteristics the world now associates with Japanese ways of doing business, such as lifetime employment, dedicated "salarymen," close interfirm ties, and enterprise unions?

Any rapid shift from traditional to modern ways of living is traumatic for the people living through it—even though emotional stress does not show up in economic numbers. So you might think about the social costs of Japan's fast economic growth, and try to imagine which groups in different periods bore the brunt of those costs. Also, given that Japan's industrialization was so focused and deliberate, might it be a better model for developing nations today than are the other three countries covered here? Or were Japanese conditions so unusual that its experience would be impossible to duplicate?

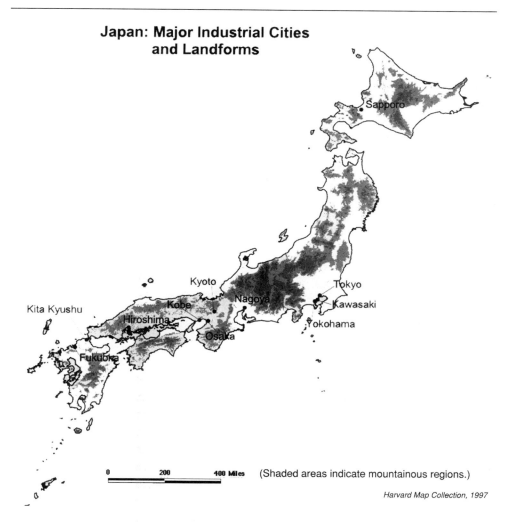

Japan: Major Industrial Cities and Landforms

(Shaded areas indicate mountainous regions.)

Harvard Map Collection, 1997

Japan is a relatively large country, but much of its land mass is so mountainous as to be almost uninhabitable. So the majority of its people live in only a small part of the total territory.

(Harvard Map Collection, 1997)

Sakichi Toyoda, "King of Inventors," whose automatic looms symbolized Japan's first economic miracle and provided the seed capital for Toyota's entry into motor vehicles.

(Courtesy Toyota)

Kiichiro Toyoda, Sakichi's talented son and a technological wizard in his own right. He led Toyota into its
intense competition with Nissan.

(Courtesy Toyota)

Kiichiro Toyoda (seated, fourth from left) and Toyota's dealers. The year is 1936, the Model Toyota's AA.

(Courtesy Toyota)

Masatoshi Ito, the innovative founder of Ito-Yokado, honorary chairman of Seven-Eleven Japan, and in the 1990s one of the three or four wealthiest men in Japan.

(Courtesy Seven-Eleven Japan)

Toshifumi Suzuki, chairman and CEO of Seven-Eleven Japan in the 1990s. An entrepreneurial visionary, Suzuki encountered 7-Eleven convenience stores on a trip to the United States during the 1970s, and after his return home convinced his reluctant colleagues at Ito-Yokado to introduce them into Japan.

(Courtesy Seven-Eleven Japan)

The rundown liquor store that would become the very first 7-Eleven in Japan. (Courtesy Seven-Eleven Japan)

The same store after its transformation—modernized inside, redecorated with new colors outside.

(Courtesy Seven-Eleven Japan)

A hand-held graphic order terminal, part of Seven-Eleven Japan's fourth-generation
information system and one of the keys to its remarkable business success.

(Courtesy Seven-Eleven Japan)

12

JAPANESE CAPITALISM

Jeffrey R. Bernstein

The Enigma of Japan

Japan is essentially a country of paradoxes and anomalies, where all, even familiar things, put on new faces, and are curiously reversed. Except that they do not walk on their heads instead of their feet, there are few things in which they do not seem, by some occult law, to have been impelled in a perfectly opposite direction and a reversed order.

—*Sir Rutherford Alcock, the first British minister in Tokyo, in 1863*[1]

I don't know whether the Japanese system is good or not. I just don't understand it.

—*Bob Horner, an American baseball player who played in Japan, in 1987*[2]

To many Western observers, Japan is mysterious and enigmatic.[3] Its economic system is often portrayed as different from and even diametrically opposed to more familiar types of capitalism. A prominent American economist has concluded that "market capitalism, Japanese-style, departs so much from conventional Western economic thought that it deserves to be considered a different economic system."[4] Others have concocted terms such as "human capitalism," "competitive communitarianism," and "non-capitalistic market economy" to describe Japan.[5] A group of scholars and journalists known as "revisionists" argue that one cannot begin to understand Japan's economic system without recognizing its obvious distinctiveness.[6]

Yet Japan is clearly "capitalist" in the sense that its economy is based on private property and relatively free markets. According to this standard, it was a capitalist country as early as the 1890s. By that time it had a written constitution, a commercial code with limited liability for corporations, and a nascent indigenous capitalist class. Some analysts insist that contemporary Japan largely conforms to Anglo-American notions of capitalism.[7] They ascribe Japan's development more to conventional factors (freely operating markets, secure property rights, a well-educated populace, and so forth) than to any particularly Japanese policies or institutions.

This chapter considers Japan to be a capitalist economy but acknowledges that Japanese capitalism differs significantly from the three varieties described in previous chapters. The main differences involve: (1) the governance and employment structures of large firms; (2) the extent and variety of interfirm linkages; and (3) the perceived role of the government. The importance of these differences is much disputed. Indeed, this issue lies at the heart of a vigorous, long-standing, and often acrimonious debate, in which revisionists are labeled "Japan-bashers," and those emphasizing the similarity of Japan to other advanced capitalist nations are branded "apologists."

Though Japanese capitalism's distinctiveness is open to question, its remarkable performance is not. In the space of 100 years, it transformed a preindustrial nation into an economic superpower. Why has Japanese capitalism succeeded? Will it continue to do so? What lessons does it hold for other countries? In providing an overview of Japan's economic development, this chapter is intended to inform the reader's own answers to these questions.

The Foundations for Japanese Development: The Precapitalist Era

[The Japanese] are very capable and intelligent, and the children are quick to grasp our lessons and instructions. They learn to read and write our language far more quickly and easily than children in Europe.

—*Alessandro Valignano, a Jesuit missionary in the late sixteenth century*[8]

The Japanese did not suddenly [after 1868] acquire that energy and restless ambition that have so disturbed the Western nations. Throughout their history they have shown a gift for rapidly assimilating new ideas and new practices, a boldness in executing large projects and, above all, a trained and frequently exercised capacity for organization.

—*G. C. Allen, an economic historian, 1981*[9]

EARLY CONTACTS WITH THE WEST (1543–1639)

For many centuries before the year 1543, Japan had engaged in trade and cultural exchange with China, from which it took its system of writing and much of its religion, art, culture, and technology. An important Chinese innovation adopted in Japan was the notion of bureaucratic government, in which civil servants were chosen on educational merit rather than simply on their family's standing. Although this principle was for a long time honored more as an abstract ideal than in actual practice, its influence cannot be denied.[10] Even today Japanese government, business, and society retain a strong meritocratic emphasis. In borrowing from China, Japan had been careful to remain outside the Chinese sphere of control. Japan would take the same approach when it encountered Westerners: learning from them, but limiting their influence.

The first Westerners to arrive in Japan were Catholic missionaries from Spain and Portugal, who sought to convert the Japanese to Christianity. Some Japanese quickly embraced this new religion, leading one Jesuit to describe Japan in 1572 as "famous for its fine silver and soon to be famous too through the spreading of Christianity among its own people."[11] By the start of the seventeenth century, there were around 300,000 Japanese Christians, most of whom lived on the southern island of Kyushu.

Missionaries were soon followed by traders, who came from Holland and England as well as Spain and Portugal. Some of them made inroads in Japan. A group of Portuguese shipwrecked on a Japanese island in 1543 were able to sell matchlocks (primitive rifles) to the local feudal lord for 1,000 gold taels apiece, or 14 times the average Japanese worker's annual wage. Commercial success proved fleeting, however, as the Japanese soon learned how to make guns and even improved upon their design. Before long, they were mass producing matchlocks. The price of a firearm fell to 1.2 taels by the beginning of the seventeenth century, and Japanese battles came to involve tens of thousands of guns, while contemporaneous European battles typically had a few hundred.[12]

When Westerners first arrived in Japan, the country was in the midst of a prolonged civil war. In 1603, however, the warlord Ieyasu Tokugawa established control over all of Japan. For the next 265 years, until 1868, his family ruled Japan. They presided over an elaborate feudalistic system. A member of the Tokugawa clan served as *shogun*, head of the central government *(bakufu)* in Edo (now Tokyo). The shogun directly ruled a quarter of the country's agricultural land, and the remaining area was divided into about 260 domains *(han)*, which were governed by lords *(daimyo)*.

The Tokugawa rulers, as they consolidated their power, increasingly viewed foreigners and their practices as threats. They actively suppressed Christianity, culminating in the massacre of more than 20,000 Japanese Christians in 1637–38. Though the British left voluntarily, the Spanish were expelled in 1624 and the Portuguese in 1639. Shortly thereafter the shogun forbade all but a tiny amount of contact with the outside world. A few Dutch and Chinese traders were allowed to conduct business from a small island off the coast of Nagasaki, but nothing more. Japan thus became a "closed country," but with the help of Dutch writings, a few scholars were still able to accumulate scraps of Western knowledge in such fields as gunnery, navigation, mathematics, and astronomy.[13]

TOKUGAWA SOCIETY (1640–1868): THE BUILDING OF SOCIAL INFRASTRUCTURE

The Tokugawa rulers also imposed a hierarchical class structure, dividing the people into four groups. At the top were the *samurai* (military retainers), making up around 7 percent of the population and holding all of the top government offices. Next came the peasants, who made up 80 percent of the population. They were followed by artisans and craftsmen. At the bottom of society were merchants, regarded as a necessary evil in a largely agrarian society.

In spite of this social rigidity, the Tokugawa era was far from a period of complete stagnation.[14] The major cities of Tokugawa Japan—Edo, Osaka, and Kyoto—were among the largest cities in the world at the time, and each boasted a lively urban culture. Though pervasive guilds stifled much entrepreneurial activity, there was considerable trade across the various han, with Osaka functioning as the center of commercial activity. A particularly important business was the management of daimyo income, the bulk of which came from rice taxes on peasants. After setting aside a portion of this rice for their own consumption and for compensation to their subordinate samurai, many daimyo shipped their rice to Osaka for storage and sale. Over time, the financial position of many daimyo deteriorated, and using the next tax delivery of rice as collateral, they borrowed from merchants. By the early 1700s, a futures market for rice had been established in Osaka. The market was surprisingly similar to modern ones, with such features as a clearing house, a membership system, expiration dates, and margin requirements.[15]

The big cities of Tokugawa Japan also featured money exchange shops *(ryogaeya)*, which supplied commercial credit, and merchant houses *(ie)*, which sold goods such as clothing, tea, iron, paper, and *tatami* (woven straw) mats. The merchant houses were family enterprises, but larger ones typically employed a staff of apprentices, assistants, and head clerks. The head clerk was often entrusted with managing the operation. Most merchant houses aimed for continuity and thus tended to be conservative. Managerial ability was, however, highly valued, and it was not uncommon for a merchant family to adopt a competent manager as heir, in place of less able children.

In the rural areas, too, Tokugawa Japan also exhibited surprisingly developed commercial networks. Farmers marketed a significant portion of their crops, and many of them were engaged part time in nonagricultural occupations.[16] In agricultural production, too, there was progress, however slow and incremental. In fact, by the 1860s, Japan's productivity in rice cultivation was higher than that of many other Asian countries as late as the 1960s.[17]

Such advances were possible because Japan had a relatively well-educated population. The educational system of Tokugawa Japan encompassed over 12,000 schools scattered throughout the country. By the end of the Tokugawa period, 43 percent of boys and 10 percent of girls attended these schools, attendance rates comparable to those in the more technologically advanced Western nations at the time.[18] This early emphasis on education remains apparent in contemporary Japan, which boasts one of the best-educated citizenries in the world.[19]

Tokugawa Japan also had a slow-growing population. The annual rate of population growth was about one percent in the first half of the period, and it was even lower during the second half.[20] Some have attributed this slow growth to the effects of poverty, disease, and famine. Others portray it as the outcome of conscious family planning (through abortion and infanticide) by farm households seeking to improve their standard of living. Whatever its cause, low population growth gave Japan a distinct advantage over developing countries today, where high population growth rates (sometimes exceeding 3 percent) have impeded economic development.

Although Tokugawa Japan featured a relatively advanced society and culture for its time, its technological and military weakness proved decisive when it encountered Western nations directly. In 1853, Commodore Matthew Perry of the United States Navy sailed into Edo Bay with his "black ships," demanding that Japan open its ports and allow trade. Faced with the military might of the West, the shogun had no choice but to assent to American demands. Once the door had been opened, European powers rushed in as well. By 1859, Japan had signed treaties with the United States, Great Britain, Russia, France, and the Netherlands, and it had opened three commercial ports for trade. Subsequent treaties with these nations, signed in 1866, gave their citizens extraterritoriality in Japan and prevented Japan from levying tariffs of greater than 5 percent. Of course, the Japanese gained no such concessions, leading them to resent these "unequal treaties."

The shogun's feeble acquiescence to foreign demands outraged many samurai, who, adopting the slogan "revere the emperor and expel the barbarians," carried out sporadic attacks on Westerners and Western property. The shogun himself soon became a target of this discontent and in 1868 was overthrown by a coalition composed mainly of warriors from the Satsuma and Choshu clans of southern Japan. These warriors portrayed their coup d'état as a movement to restore power to the imperial family, which throughout the Tokugawa period had been cloistered in Kyoto. They established a new government in Tokyo and installed as nominal ruler the 16-year-old emperor, who chose the name Meiji (Enlightened Rule) for his regime. This event, known as the Meiji Restoration, led to radical changes in Japanese politics, society, and economics.

EARLY MEIJI JAPAN (1868–1885): GROWTH OF TRADITIONAL INDUSTRIES

The Meiji emperor reigned in name only. Actual power resided in a small circle of oligarchs, drawn mainly from the ranks of lower-tier samurai. At the outset, these officials faced two waves of insurrection. The first, arising from clans which still supported the Tokugawa shogun, was put down by 1870. The second series of rebellions were instigated by samurai initially supportive of the Restoration but subsequently disillusioned with it. The last of these revolts was the Satsuma Rebellion of 1877; with its suppression, the Meiji government achieved true political unification.

Its position was secure domestically, but the Meiji government still felt threatened by the power of the advanced Western nations. Catching up with the West economically and militarily became its highest priority, as attested by the well-known slogan "rich country, strong army." To achieve that goal, the Meiji government instituted an astonishing array of reforms.

In the political sphere, the han and their independent administrations were abolished and replaced by a prefectural system modeled on the French example. The outward form of a democratic government was created with a bicameral legislature and quasi-independent judiciary, but as noted above, power remained in the hands of an elite few. Yet the aristocratic Meiji government was a liberalizing force. It abolished the caste system, guilds, and restrictions on occupational choice and domestic travel, prompting a large migration of workers from agriculture to industry. It also stripped the samurai of their warrior status and established an army based on universal conscription.

The old Tokugawa rice tax was replaced by a land tax, which not only reduced fluctuations in government revenues but also constituted the bulk of these revenues in the early Meiji period. Of course, before the new tax could be collected, the government had to determine who owned the land. In so doing, it established modern property rights in Japan.

The government enacted universal compulsory primary education for both boys and girls in 1872, earlier than in Britain. Also established in 1872 was Tokyo Institute of Technology, which had become the world's largest technological university by 1877.[21] That year, the government founded Tokyo University, which, along with the private universities Keio and Waseda, played an important role in cultivating the nation's elite.

Of all Meiji reforms, the most remarkable were the extensive efforts to learn from abroad. The last years of the Tokugawa era had already featured some deliberate attempts to absorb Western knowledge by the shogun and various dissident daimyo. During the first decade of the Meiji era, the pace of Japanese institutional borrowing accelerated. More than 2,400 foreigners came from 23 different nations to provide instruction in Western methods of organization, administration, and production.

Employment of foreign experts accounted for 2 percent of government expenditures.[22] At considerable expense to the state, Japanese students were dispatched to universities in Europe and North America.[23] Virtually all of them returned to Japan. The most famous study trip was the Iwakura Mission of 1871–73, when many prominent government leaders toured several Western nations, seeking revision of the unequal treaties and trying to determine which institutions should be introduced in Japan. Table 12.1 illustrates the variety of institutional borrowing undertaken in the early Meiji period.

In business, too, the Japanese government took the initiative in trying out foreign models. It introduced Western agricultural techniques and built model factories, using Western technology in silk spinning, shipbuilding, cement, and glass. These attempts were generally failures. The capital-intensive agricultural techniques used in the West proved uneconomical in Japan, given its abundant supply of cheap labor and scarcity of land. The model factories were unprofitable under government management and were sold off to private entrepreneurs in the early 1880s.

The government thus withdrew from direct ownership of firms, but it continued to play an important role in the economy. It made crucial investments in infrastructure, including roads and bridges and modern forms of communication and transportation; telegraph service between Tokyo and Yokohama commenced in 1870, postal service began in 1871, and the first railway line was built in 1872. Government investment amounted to 66 percent of total Japanese investment in 1884, and until the outbreak of World War I usually exceeded private-sector investment.[24]

The government did not just invest in large projects. In organizing trade fairs, establishing quality certification programs, and promoting trade associations, it coordinated and supported the small-scale enterprises that comprised the bulk of the nonagricultural Meiji economy. Many of these activities were proposed in a 10-year economic plan entitled *Kogyo Iken* (A Proposal for Economic Development), which was published by the Meiji government in 1884. Thirty volumes long, this document represents one of the world's first comprehensive national development plans.[25]

When this plan was being compiled, however, Japan was in the midst of a serious economic crisis. By 1881, it faced runaway inflation, spiral-

Table 12.1 Examples of Institutional Borrowing in Meiji Japan

Source	Organization	Year Initiated
Britain	Navy	1869
	Telegraph System	1869
	Postal System	1872
	Postal Savings System	1875
France	Army	1869
	Primary School System	1872
	Police	1874
	Judicial System	1872
U.S.	Primary School System*	1879
	National Bank System	1872
Germany	Army*	1878
Belgium	Bank of Japan	1882

Note: Asterisks denote a reorganization based on a new model.
Source: D. Eleanor Westney, *Imitation and Innovation* (Cambridge, MA: Harvard University Press, 1987), table 1.

ing government debt, and a rapidly deteriorating trade balance. Under the guidance of Finance Minister Masayoshi Matsukata, the government responded with a drastic stabilization program.[26] It sold off its model factories, levied taxes on *sake* (rice wine) and tobacco, and slashed government spending. This hard medicine worked, arresting the furious inflation and shoring up the government's revenues. Along with the establishment of the Bank of Japan in 1882, the Matsukata deflation provided a secure financial base for subsequent economic growth. At the same time, this episode, which has been called the first historical case of "shock therapy," inflicted considerable pain. Many fledgling enterprises went bankrupt, and a large number of farmers were forced to sell their land and become tenants.

Even before the Matsukata deflation, some segments of the population had found it difficult to adapt to the new era. Highly dependent on the old order, many merchant houses were devastated by the abolition of the guild system, the opening of trading ports, and other Meiji reforms. Some of the best-known merchant houses went bankrupt, and others barely survived. At the same time, a few merchant houses, including Mitsui, rose from the ashes to become business leaders.

During this early period, Japanese economic growth came largely from the expansion of the traditional farm sector. In 1880, 45 percent of the real increase in Japan's GDP came from primary industry (agriculture, forestry, and fisheries), compared to 30–40 percent in Germany, 19 percent in the U.S., and 11 percent in the U.K. This result can be attributed to the large magnitude of Japan's primary sector, as shown in Figure 12.1. Two agricultural products, silk and tea, were Japan's main exports during this period. Without them, Japan's chronic balance-of-payments problems would have been even more severe. Raw silk alone accounted for more than 30 percent of all Japanese exports between 1868 and 1900.[27]

The Japanese Economy from the 1880s to the 1940s

Wealthy we [Westerners] do not at all think [Japan] will ever become . . . The Japanese are a happy race, and being content with little, are not likely to achieve much.

—*Japan Herald, then Japan's leading English-language newspaper,
April 9, 1881*[28]

The industrial structure of Japan is a new edifice . . . The overwhelming fact about the industry so created is its efficiency. It is so efficient that it sells beer to Germany and American flags to the American Legion.

—*Fortune, September 1936*[29]

THE EMERGENCE OF THE ZAIBATSU

The late 1880s marked a turning point for Japanese industry, as a modern business sector began to arise alongside the traditional economy. In this development, the *zaibatsu* were a key institution. *Zaibatsu,* whose literal meaning is "financial clique," refers to a diversified group of businesses which are owned by a family.[30] The Big Four zaibatsu were Mitsui, Mitsubishi, Sumitomo, and Yasuda. Second-tier zaibatsu included Furukawa, Okura, Asano, and Fujita. The great capitalist families that controlled these enterprise groups have been likened to Japanese versions of the Rockefeller, Vanderbilt, and Ford families in the United States.[31]

Some of the zaibatsu had long histories. Sumitomo began in 1590 as a copper refinery, and Mitsui in 1673 as a clothing retailer. Most, however, arose in the early Meiji period and owed their initial growth to political patronage. Mitsubishi, for instance, received 11 iron steamboats from the Meiji government in 1874. This gift doubled the assets of the

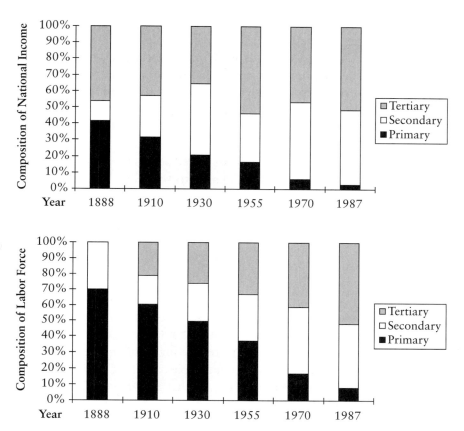

Figure 12.1 National Income and Working Population by Type of Industry

Note: Primary sector = agriculture, forestry, and fisheries. Secondary sector = mining, manufacturing, construction, transportation, communication, and public utilities. Tertiary sector = commerce and services. For 1888, the secondary sector region includes both the secondary and tertiary sectors; i.e., it constitutes the non-primary sector.

Source: Ryoshin Minami, *The Economic Development of Japan,* 2d ed. (New York: St. Martin's Press, 1994), pp. 85, 212.

company and allowed it to take business from the foreign shipping lines that had been handling the bulk of Japanese trade. Even the more established zaibatsu benefited from political patronage. Mitsui bought the Miike coal mines from the government in 1888, an acquisition that turned out to be very profitable.[32]

As these above examples suggest, the zaibatsu initially concentrated on non-manufacturing activities such as shipping, mining, and banking.

Only later did they diversify into new businesses. The Mitsubishi zaibatsu clearly illustrates this pattern. Starting with a shipping company, an ex-samurai named Yataro Iwasaki launched an insurance company (Tokio Marine and Fire Insurance Company) and then a foreign exchange and discount bank (Mitsubishi Bank), so that his group of firms encompassed not just the physical transport of goods but also the associated financial services. Subsequently shipbuilding, mining, and foreign trade were added to the Mitsubishi empire.

The ownership structure of zaibatsu varied across groups and evolved over time. Ultimately each zaibatsu came to be led by a family-owned holding company that controlled other firms in the group through share-holdings and interlocking directorates. (Figure 12.2 offers a graphical representation of zaibatsu and post–World War II keiretsu.) The zaibatsu form expanded the scope of a business while retaining a decentralized management structure. In contrast to big U.S. corporations in the early twentieth century, which generally internalized related functions, the zaibatsu tended to create new firms to conduct peripheral operations, while retaining coordinating links between these spin-offs.[33]

Thus, diversification into new industries took place at the group level of the zaibatsu, with individual firms remaining small and relatively undiversified compared to their U.S. counterparts. Unlike their American rivals, hardly any Japanese companies, whether zaibatsu-affiliated or not, integrated forward into distribution or backward into the purchase of their supplies. Instead, as a Japanese business historian writes, "Almost all of the modern industrial corporations which appeared at the end of the 19th century depended on external retail or wholesale organizations to market their products."[34] These features of Japanese corporations can be seen even today.[35]

The zaibatsu played a large role in some industries, such as shipping and foreign trade.[36] In these sectors, Japanese firms were able to displace formerly dominant Western competitors before World War I. In shipping, Japanese ships handled 7 percent of Japan's exports and less than 9 percent of its imports in 1893, but in 1913 the corresponding figures were 52 percent and 47 percent. Over this period, Japan's largest shipping company was Mitsubishi's Nippon Yusen Kaisha. By 1900, Mitsui & Company alone handled one-third of Japan's foreign trade volume, having largely supplanted the foreign merchants who had commanded a 90 percent share in 1887.[37]

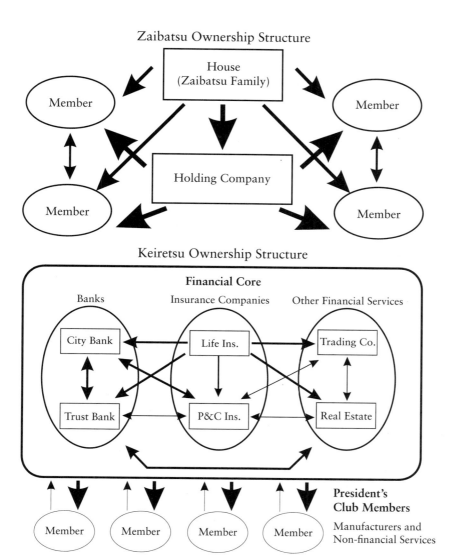

Figure 12.2 The Ownership Structures of *Zaibatsu* and *Keiretsu*

Note: Arrows indicate ownership, with the thickness of the arrow indicating the approximate magnitude of share ownership, as follows:

Source: Modified version of two slides provided by Professor David Weinstein of the University of Michigan Business School.

We will return to the zaibatsu later, but it should be emphasized that zaibatsu firms were not the only companies venturing into modern industries. Most of the textile industry lay outside their confines, and independent companies ventured into such industries as watchmaking and clocks (Hattori Seiko), soy sauce (Kikkoman), and pharmaceuticals (Takeda).[38]

THE RISE OF TEXTILES AND THE BEGINNING OF HEAVY INDUSTRY (1886–1913)

The spectacular growth of the prewar Japanese textile industry is discussed in detail in the chapter on Toyota, but three points deserve mention. First, the textile industry occupied a sizable share of the Japanese economy: its share of manufacturing output rose from 10 percent in 1877 to 26 percent in 1900 and then 28 percent in 1920. The textile industry's share of Japanese exports was even larger, reaching 56 percent between 1910 and 1920.[39]

Second, the performance of this industry owed little to promotional efforts by the Japanese government. In fact, the unequal treaties, by preventing the Japanese government from setting high protective tariffs, may have forced Japanese entrepreneurs to invest in accordance with their comparative advantage at the time, thus contributing to the dynamism of the textile industry.[40] The privately owned Osaka Spinning Mill, founded in 1882, was Japan's first successful modern mill. Powered by steam, run by a Japanese manager trained in Manchester, and five times larger than the typical government-built mill, the Osaka Spinning Mill was an overnight financial success that paved the way for other entrepreneurs to establish textile mills.

Third, the development of the textile industry both reflected and contributed to the emergence of the corporation as Japan's predominant form of business organization. The joint-stock company did not appear in Japan until 1872, three centuries after the first emergence of the corporation in Europe. A commercial code defining the legal rights and obligations of Japanese corporations was not formulated until 1893. The largest companies in Japan were initially textile mills, though in time they would be eclipsed by corporations from heavy industries. As Table 12.2 reveals, in 1918, 4 of Japan's 10 largest industrial firms came from the textile industry. Textile companies made up one-quarter of the 200 largest industrial firms in 1918 and one-third in 1930.[41]

Table 12.2 Japan's Largest Industrial Corporations, Ranked by Assets
(thousands of yen)

1918		1954	
Company	Assets	Company	Assets
1. Kawasaki Shipyards	140,347	1. Yawata Steel	105,544
2. Kuhara Mining	103,610	2. Fuji Steel	85,415
3. Mitsubishi Shipyards	89,327	3. Japan Steel (NKK)	66,671
4. Kanegafuchi Spinning	69,936	4. Hitachi	49,420
5. Toyo Spinning	61,705	5. Toyo Spinning	44,690
6. Dai-Nihon Spinning	59,209	6. Toshiba	41,799
7. Taiwan Sugar Manufacturing	55,930	7. Mitsubishi Heavy Industries	35,895
8. Mitsubishi Steel	46,942	8. Kanegafuchi Spinning	34,827
9. Fuji Gas Spinning	40,057	9. Dai-Nihon Spinning	34,321
10. Japan Steel (NKK)	39,374	10. Sumitomo Metal Industries	34,199

1973		1987	
Company	Assets	Company	Assets
1. Nippon Steel	2,270,889	1. Toyota Motor	6,024,909
2. Mitsubishi Heavy Industries	1,891,257	2. Nissan Motor	3,418,671
3. Japan Steel (NKK)	1,371,319	3. Matsushita Electric	3,277,613
4. Hitachi	1,198,053	4. Japan Tobacco	2,946,881
5. Ishikawajima Harima	1,111,154	5. Hitachi	2,919,539
6. Sumitomo Metal Industries	1,084,556	6. Toshiba	2,682,781
7. Kawasaki Steel	1,033,610	7. Honda Motor	2,650,077
8. Nissan Motor	1,005,063	8. NEC	2,304,392
9. Toshiba	1,001,285	9. Nippon Steel	2,147,038
10. Kobe Steel	887,039	10. Mitsubishi Electric	1,954,187

Note: The book value of assets is not a wholly satisfactory measure of company size. (Other possible indices include total sales, total employment, and market capitalization.) Book values are affected by accounting rules and therefore may present a somewhat distorted picture of true economic worth.
Source: W. Mark Fruin, *The Japanese Enterprise System* (New York: Oxford University Press, 1992), appendix.

Starting in the late 1800s, Japanese enterprises also began to move into heavy industries.[42] Here government intervention, sparked by military needs, played a vital role, as the cases of shipbuilding and steel illustrate. In shipbuilding, the government passed two important laws in

1896: the Shipbuilding Promotion Act, which provided subsidies for the construction of large iron and steel vessels, and the Navigation Subsidy Law, which granted special subsidies for the purchase of Japanese-built ships. In steel, the key measure was the establishment of the government-owned Yawata Iron Works in 1897. It was Japan's largest enterprise at the time and Asia's first integrated modern iron and steel works.

These efforts produced mixed results. Though the Yawata Works accounted for a large share of domestic iron and steel production (73 percent and 78 percent respectively in 1913), it was not a financial success. Moreover, Japan remained a net importer of iron and steel products, with domestic production of iron and steel constituting 48 percent and 34 percent respectively of home consumption in 1913.[43] In shipbuilding, Japan came closer to achieving self-sufficiency. By 1913, its shipyards were able to construct large cruisers and battleships. Still, production of ships and other heavy industrial goods at this time was modest compared to that of leading Western nations.[44]

Moreover, the Japanese economy remained largely traditional. In 1910 the primary sector still accounted for 60 percent of the labor force. Even so, the trend toward industrialization was clear. Figure 12.1 (p. 451) shows the shrinkage of the primary sector between 1880 and 1910, as well as the growth of the secondary sector (manufacturing and mining, construction, transportation, and utilities). Japan had passed through the First Industrial Revolution in less than 50 years, about one-third of the time it had taken Britain, the first country to make this transition.

MILITARY POWER, WORLD WAR I, AND THE INTERWAR PERIOD
(1914–1931)

Japan had made another important transition, going from a potential colony of the West to a budding imperialist nation. In 1876—only eight years after the Meiji Restoration—Japan sent its own version of the "black ships" to pry open the Korean market. This aggressive action foreshadowed future Japanese conflicts with its neighbors. Building on its new economic strength, Japan emerged victorious in two major military campaigns. It routed China in the Sino-Japanese War of 1894. From China it received an enormous indemnity, the equivalent of one-quarter of its national income at the time. Then in 1905 it defeated Russia, shocking the world with its triumph over a European power. Through its military victories, Japan acquired two important colonies, Korea and Taiwan, and earned some respect from Western nations. In 1899, the unequal treaties were revised in part. In 1902 Japan signed a military alliance with Great Britain, and in 1911 it regained full tariff autonomy. When the Meiji emperor died in 1912, Japan was at least a regional force to be reckoned with, if not a great power.

The son of the Meiji emperor assumed the throne in 1912. He took the name Taisho (Great Rectitude) for his reign, which lasted just 14 years. It was a time of liberalization, termed "Taisho democracy." Tight political control by a small oligarchy gave way to party politics, and Western ideas and culture enjoyed a fleeting burst of popularity. The Taisho era witnessed economic boom and bust, as well as the emergence of some of the major institutions of Japanese capitalism.

Two years into the Taisho period, World War I began in Europe. As Britain's ally, Japan soon became a belligerent, capturing German colonies in China and the North Pacific. World War I proved an economic boom for Japanese industry, which faced increased demand from the warring nations and from the Asian markets whose trade with Europe was disrupted by the war. Japan's trade volume increased by more than 2.5 times between 1914 and 1918. Over the same period, the composition of its exports also changed dramatically, going from 50 percent raw materials and 30 percent finished goods to 35 percent raw materials and 50 percent finished goods.[45]

This increase in trade stimulated the growth of trading companies. The leading trading company, Mitsui & Company, had been established well before the war, but new competitors grew quickly. In 1917, for instance, Mitsubishi Corporation was spun off from the holding company as an independent firm.[46] Naturally, the growth of trading companies boosted shipbuilding, and Japanese steamship tonnage doubled during the war.[47] Japanese companies also began to produce industrial goods such as chemicals, dyestuffs, steel, and machinery, whose importation was interrupted by the war. The wartime boom made many entrepreneurs rich almost overnight. One notable example was Naokichi Kaneko, who managed a business empire that included Suzuki Company (a large trading company), Kobe Steel, Harima Shipbuilding, and Imperial Rayon. Suzuki Company grew so fast during World War I that at one point its trading volume exceeded that of Mitsui & Co., the traditional leader.

However, some firms which expanded rapidly during World War I were devastated by the postwar recession. Suzuki Company, for example, eventually collapsed. Kaneko's fledgling zaibatsu was then dismembered, with its constituent firms absorbed largely by the Mitsui and Mitsubishi groups. Taking over failed firms in this manner, the zaibatsu expanded in scale and scope even during this economic downturn.

A similar consolidation occurred in the banking sector. The Great Kanto Earthquake of 1923, which killed more than 91,000 people in the Tokyo area, also wrought havoc on a financial system already shaken by the postwar recession. Many Japanese banks, especially small ones, found themselves in severe financial straits. Suzuki Company alone had outstanding loans amounting to one-quarter of Japan's national budget when it went bankrupt in 1927, and that event shook confidence in the financial system. An indiscreet remark by the Japanese Finance Minister set off a full-fledged banking panic, which in turn led to the demise of many prominent banking institutions.

In response, the Japanese government instituted far more stringent banking regulations. These new rules substantially increased the capital requirements of banks and, in conjunction with the shake-out of many vulnerable banks, led to a dramatic consolidation of the whole industry. There had been about 1,700 banks in Japan at the end of 1924, but by 1932 only 651 still survived.[48] Again, the zaibatsu were the prime beneficiaries of this consolidation. By the end of 1928, the five largest banks, four of which belonged to zaibatsu, controlled 34 percent of bank deposits.[49]

Still, the influence of the zaibatsu must not be exaggerated. They constituted a substantial but not overwhelming share of the Japanese economy: probably between one-quarter and one-third of Japan's GDP before 1930.[50] In 1930, the eight largest zaibatsu controlled 15 percent of total joint-stock capital but wielded somewhat greater influence in practice because of their control over partially owned subsidiaries and their dominant position in finance and foreign trade.[51] Most Japanese industrial workers, however, were employed at small and medium-sized firms. In 1930, 58 percent of the industrial labor force worked in factories with four or fewer employees.[52]

The zaibatsu and other large companies were significant for reasons other than size. Productivity was much higher at large companies. While 79 percent of the Japanese labor force worked in small and medium-size firms (those employing fewer than 100 employees), such firms accounted for only 25 percent of total industrial production. Wages were also much lower at small and medium-size firms, averaging only 40 percent of those in large firms in 1930.[53] Thus, it was said that Japanese industry at this time exhibited a "dual structure," with a small number of large, modern companies coexisting with a large number of small, traditional firms.

The Japanese Enterprise System: Some Early Developments

Large firms also were the place where, in the decade following World War I, several institutions that later would be seen as the essence of Japanese capitalism first appeared. Indeed, Japan's corporate sector more closely resembled those of Western nations in the very early 1900s than it does today.[54] Some of the distinctive features of Japanese firms, such as an emphasis on in-house training, seniority wage and promotion systems, permanent employment, and profit-sharing bonuses emerged between 1910 and 1930.

By providing internal company training, managers wrested power in the workplace from traditional foremen, who were unable to provide the technical skills needed by workers and who might have posed an obstacle to the introduction of more modern production methods.[55] In-house training programs were established in shipyards in the 1890s and in other large industrial firms in the early 1900s, so that by 1920 most large companies had some form of internal training system.[56]

Permanent employment and seniority wage scales were introduced in the 1920s. It is important not to misunderstand the nature of these practices. "Permanent" or "lifetime" employment has never meant that all workers remain with the same firm until they retire. Rather, it signifies a dual commitment: by the company to make its best effort not to fire the worker before a designated retirement age, and by the worker to stay at the firm for the long term. Nor is permanent employment extended to all workers. It applies to about 20 or 30 percent of the Japanese workforce and is heavily concentrated among male employees.

Similarly, a seniority-based wage and promotion scale does not mean that a worker's salary and advancement are determined solely by seniority. An employee's pay is based mainly on age, but it also reflects individual merit, overall company performance, and other factors such as the family obligations of the employee. Promotion is based largely on age, but over time the more able employees are promoted at a faster rate than others who entered at the same time. The ability of exceptional performers to leap quickly to the top of the corporate ladder is, however, much more circumscribed in Japan than it is in the United States or in European countries.

These practices are often attributed to "traditional" paternalism on the part of Japanese managers, but the history of their adoption suggests a very different story. Management was often reluctant to extend job security because it did not want to lose the ability to fire unneeded workers during downturns, but it did so in order to prevent job hopping by skilled workers whom it had taken the trouble to train. Workers, by contrast, wished to preserve their own mobility in good times while retaining their jobs in bad times. They also sought to obtain higher status and better treatment by firms. Out of these opposing interests emerged permanent employment and seniority-based wages. Thus, these practices were not gifts bestowed by management but rather emerged over time as the outcome of conflicts and compromises between workers and management.[57]

Permanent employment and seniority wages were not widely applied to blue-collar workers, even at large Japanese companies, before World War II.[58] However, these two practices have proven quite enduring. Along with enterprise unions—a postwar phenomenon to be discussed later—they have become known as the "three pillars of the Japanese employment system."

Another important development of the 1910–30 period was a shift in operational control from shareholders to managers. This was especially common in the zaibatsu, which, as they expanded in scale and scope, became much harder to govern effectively from the top. As the most prestigious and best-paying companies, the zaibatsu were able to employ the highest quality managers. In general, the leaders of large Japanese corporations were very well educated. A 1924 survey of the largest 181 Japanese companies found that 64 percent of top executives held a college degree or equivalent, a higher percentage than in the United States at that time.[59]

The Plight of Small Business and Agriculture

Small business struggled during the 1920s and 1930s. Even in retailing, a sector largely outside the confines of zaibatsu control, traditional Japanese shops found it difficult to compete with the modern department stores appearing at this time. The agricultural sector suffered even more.

Food shortages in Japan during and immediately after World War I led to increased production of rice in Korea and Taiwan, Japan's colonies. This expansion depressed produce prices on the home islands. Prices of agricultural products fell by 15 percent between 1926 and 1929. Then the onset of the Great Depression in the United States caused the silk market to crash, and agricultural prices fell by a whopping 40 percent between 1929 and 1931. Over the same two-year period, farm household incomes dropped by over 50 percent.[60]

The prosperity of the zaibatsu made them an obvious political target for dissatisfied rural workers, who still made up half of the labor force in 1930. Even before the agricultural depression, there had been a vast gap between the traditional and modern sectors in prewar Japan. The collapse of commodity prices led impoverished farmers to commit desperate measures, such as selling their daughters to brothels, to fend off starvation.[61] Many farmers thought that the zaibatsu were enriching themselves at the nation's expense. Their suspicions intensified with the "dollar-buying scandal" of 1931, in which large Japanese banks made huge profits by speculating that Japan would abandon the gold standard. Mitsui Bank reportedly made $50 million when Japan went off the gold standard late that year.[62] The general public was outraged. Right-wingers took up arms, assassinating the head officer of the Mitsui zaibatsu in 1932. This incident spurred all of the zaibatsu to make public "conversions," whereby they offered donations to public causes and refrained from criticizing the government. The discrediting of the zaibatsu as well as of politicians associated with them contributed to the fateful ascendance of the Japanese military.

THE WARTIME ECONOMY (1932–1945): TOWARD GOVERNMENT CONTROL

The Taisho emperor died in 1926, and his son Hirohito succeeded him. Hirohito chose the name Showa (Enlightened Peace) for his reign, which lasted until 1989. The Showa era had a turbulent start. A banking crisis in 1927 was followed by a severe economic recession, which deepened existing social rifts in Japan and aided the rise of Japanese militarism. In September 1931, some middle-ranking Japanese army officers stationed in Manchuria, a northeastern Chinese province, sabotaged a small section of the South Manchurian Railway, which Japan owned. The Japanese army used this event as a pretext for overrunning all of Manchuria and there establishing Manchukuo, a puppet state more than three times as large as Japan itself. The conquest of Manchuria led to widespread condemnation of Japan by the international community, but it emboldened the Japanese military. Over the next few years young army extremists assassinated a number of high-ranking government officials and several prominent industrialists who were opposed to the military. One group of officers even staged an attempt to take control of the government by force. Though they failed, the military's grasp on the reins of power was strengthened.

Military control was further bolstered after the 1937 Marco Polo Bridge Incident, in which clashes between Japanese and Chinese soldiers erupted into all-out war. Confronted with Japan's invasion of China, the United States and several European nations imposed severe economic sanctions. The Japanese military argued that the Western nations were using these measures to cut off Japan's access to raw materials and to maintain Western colonial empires in Asia. Resentment of this economic pressure contributed to Japan's surprise attack on Pearl Harbor in December 1941, which ignited a war that few, even in the Japanese military, thought could be won.[63] Japan initially scored some astonishing victories—in six months occupying Burma, Malaya, Singapore, the Philippines, and much of the Dutch East Indies. But by 1945, after an unusually bloody war, it had to bow to overwhelming American military and industrial power.

Economic Recovery and Trade Friction

Though the 1932–45 period of Japanese history is beclouded by militarism, economically it did not begin badly. Japan recovered from the Great Depression faster than most other countries. Against a 1929 index of 100, mining and manufacturing production in 1935 was at 142 in Japan, 106 in Britain, 94 in Germany, and 76 in the United States.[64] Expansionary fiscal and monetary policy, as well as yen depreciation, stimulated the Japanese economic recovery.

The fall in the yen's value (from ¥1 = $0.50 in 1930 to ¥1 = $0.25 in 1933) led to a vast expansion of Japanese exports. At a time of constricting trade worldwide, this increase in exports led to widespread complaints about Japanese trade practices. An otherwise sympathetic 1936 *Fortune* article called Japan's export boom "aggressive industrial warfare against the world."[65] Other countries imposed a variety of trade restrictions in response to the Japanese export surge. It was during this period when the epithet "Japan, Inc." first appeared and when charges such as "social dumping" were first hurled at Japan.[66] Not everyone blamed Japan. As *Fortune* went on to say, "The Italian government, while its press screamed Yellow Peril and Social Dumping and Wake Up Europe, admitted that one reason why Japanese silks were selling in silk-making Italy might be that Japanese machinery and Japanese organization were better."[67] The *Fortune* article concluded that the Japanese export boom could not be explained solely by depreciation of the yen, government subsidies, or exploitation of workers and farmers. Rather, it could be attributed to "a conjunction of labor, exchange [rate], technical, and organizational advantages."[68]

Not all Japanese industries prospered during the 1930s. The silk industry struggled in the face of a severely depressed American market and competition from new materials such as nylon. By contrast, cotton textiles and rayon production thrived. The biggest growth occurred in heavy industries such as steel, shipbuilding, machine tools, machinery, and trucks. Prosperity in these industries came from greatly increased military spending (rising from 28 percent to 49 percent of the general national budget between 1930 and 1935) and from laws regulating specific industries.

Government Intervention: From Helping Hand to Iron Fist

In the early 1930s, the Japanese government began to intervene in industry more than it had in the past. After regaining tariff autonomy in 1911, the government used moderate tariffs to protect certain industries, particularly during the 1920s, but it did not make strong efforts to affect the overall industrial structure before 1930. One exception was a 1925 law mandating the formation of export cartels in certain industries. A much broader measure was the 1931 Major Industries Control Law which made cartel agreements enforceable on non-participants if two-thirds of a cartel's members so requested. As a result, the number of cartels operating in Japan increased dramatically, by one count rising from 12 in the 1927–29 period to 48 after 1930.[69] This policy of government-facilitated cartelization was based on German ideas about industrial rationalization, which had begun to percolate in Japan during the late 1920s.

Other rationalization measures soon followed. In 1934 the Japanese government combined the state-owned Yawata Iron Works and five private firms to create Nippon Steel. The government presided over a number of other large mergers, which spawned such firms as Oji Paper, Sanwa Bank, Mitsubishi Heavy Industries, and Sumitomo Metals. It also enacted specific laws governing militarily important industries. The first of these was the Oil Industry Law of 1934; it was followed by similar laws covering automobiles, artificial petroleum, steel, machine tools, aircraft manufacturing, and shipbuilding. These measures assisted domestic producers by limiting entry and competition, but also increased government control over the designated industries.

More extensive government intervention occurred in Manchukuo, which became a testing ground for Soviet-style economic plans. The military, which regarded the leading zaibatsu as corrupt and unpatriotic, tried to use centralized economic planning to develop this region. It relied upon the South Manchurian Railway Company to implement its five-year development plans. This approach failed because the South Manchurian Railway Company proved unable to manage heavy and chemical industries. The military then turned to a new breed of aggressive entrepreneurs, who presided over groups that came to be called "new zaibatsu." The new zaibatsu differed from the old in that they specialized in a narrower range of industries, exhibited less concentrated shareholding, and more enthusiastically supported the Japanese war effort. They also tended to focus on high-technology industries: Nissan in trucks, Riken in machinery, Nichitsu in chemicals, and Nakajima Aircraft. The "old" zaibatsu, which included many of the leading producers in heavy and chemical industries, were also active in the production of munitions and military supplies, but their relative position declined during this period.

After 1937, as the Japanese economy moved to a wartime footing, its industrial structure shifted markedly toward heavy industry and munitions production. Military spending rose dramatically, from 5 percent of GNP in 1936 to about 18 percent in 1942 and over 30 percent by 1943.[70] At the same time, government intervention became more pronounced and heavy-handed, especially after Japan entered World War II. Though business interests were able to defeat certain measures, the government eventually prevailed in exerting considerable authority over industry. The 1943 Munitions Company Law provided for shutting down firms considered non-essential to the war effort and for diverting their workers to other companies. It also authorized the stationing of government-appointed munitions supervisors at firms to make sure that they were doing their best to meet government-mandated production targets.

These measures had a tremendous impact on Japan's industrial structure. Light industry was devastated, as civilian businesses were shut down and their plant and equipment made into scrap metal for military production. By the end of World War II, only 33 percent of the capacity of Japan's mighty prewar textile industry remained.[71] Most of the destruction had come not from war damage but from government-ordered scrapping of equipment, leading a Japanese observer to conclude that the nation's " 'peace industries' were destroyed by their own government before a single American bomb had fallen."[72] By contrast, some heavy industries grew so rapidly during the war that even after extensive destruction, capacity remained higher than prewar levels. The annual capacity of steel, which had been 3 million tons in 1937, stood at 5.6 million tons in 1945. Over the same period, machine-tool production capacity rose from 22,000 to 54,000 units.[73] Even where heavy industries had been physically destroyed, the knowledge gained in operating the plants—the human capital—remained and could serve as the basis for the redevelopment of these industries after the war.

Government wartime controls had long-term effects not only on the composition of Japanese industry but also on the institutional superstructure.[74] One major development was the weakening of the power of large shareholders. Before the war, Japanese firms were highly dependent on large stockholders as a source of capital. Dividend rates were high and quite responsive to changes in profitability.[75] Complaints heard in the United States today about short-sighted, profit-hungry stockholders were then uttered in Japan.[76] Large-shareholder power had already been somewhat eroded by the growing presence and power of salaried managers following World War I. Developments during World War II accelerated the process. Wartime expansion demanded investments far greater than even the richest Japanese capitalists could afford. Bank borrowing and outside equity assumed a much larger role in Japanese corporate finance, thereby diluting zaibatsu ownership ties. Between 1928 and 1946, Mitsui family ownership of constituent firms fell from 91 percent to 67 percent. For Mitsubishi, the corresponding decrease was from 78 percent to 33 percent.[77]

Other key features of the postwar Japanese landscape appeared in embryonic form during World War II, often as unexpected byproducts of wartime measures. A 1942 law organized banks into loan consortia and stipulated that the lead banks of the consortia monitor borrowers. This system of delegated monitoring reemerged as the postwar "main bank" system.[78] During the war, the practice of subcontracting was promoted by the rapid expansion of heavy industry, as well as by the forced conversion of nonmilitary firms into munitions production. Elaborate subcontracting networks became a distinctive aspect of Japanese capitalism after the war. The government also promoted changes in labor relations, compelling firms to adopt seniority wage systems, pay fixed wages rather than piece rates, and give workers a more secure place in the firm.[79] In a limited way, these reforms anticipated the postwar development of the Japanese employment system. Some scholars attribute overall government policy toward industry during the postwar period to the knowledge gained by the elite bureaucrats who regulated the wartime economy.[80]

Whatever its long-term effects, wartime planning in Japan, as in Germany, failed miserably in the short run. There were frequent mismatches between supply and demand. Shortages of parts and raw materials led to hoarding, which was exacerbated by the strong rivalry between the Japanese navy and army. Japan's real GNP peaked in 1939, even before World War II began, and declined thereafter. Wartime controls had a severe impact on living standards, as Japanese officials reduced the resources devoted to consumption and diverted them to military production. A Japanese economic historian observed, "Compared even with Nazi Germany, which took care not to let production of consumer goods decline until about 1943, Japan's prioritizing of munitions production was extreme from the start and ignored the everyday needs of its own people and those in the territories it occupied."[81] When it finally surrendered in August 1945, Japan was an exhausted and devastated country.

The Japanese Economy in the Postwar Period

In the light of an analysis of its resources, the Japan of the next three decades appears likely to have one of two aspects if its population continues to grow to 100 million or more. (1) It may have a standard of living equivalent to that of 1930–34 if foreign financial assistance is continued indefinitely. (2) It may be "self-supporting," but with internal

political, economic and social distress and a standard of living gradually
approaching the bare subsistence level. Either of these alternatives seems
more likely than that of a Japan which will have made itself self-supporting at a 1930–34 standard through foreign trade and improved
resources utilization.

—Edward Ackerman, an American resources expert, in 1948 [82]

We have reached the crowning heights of Japan's rise as an economic
power. Her status as a commercial manufacturing and financial juggernaut is no longer a matter of debate or qualification. Japan's name is
now almost certain to be added to that very select list of nations—
Venice, Holland, England, Germany, and the United States—which have
successively stood at the cutting edge of economic change during the
past 500 years.

*—David Williams, professor of political science and editorial writer for the
Japan Times, 1994* [83]

THE ALLIED OCCUPATION (1945–1952): REFORM AND RECOVERY

From the Sino-Japanese War of 1894 until the early 1940s, Japan's economic expansion had been accompanied and influenced by its uninter-
rupted military success.[84] Now Japan had lost a bitter and brutally fought
war. It faced the formidable task of recovering from its vast losses. Some
3 million Japanese were killed during the war, and at least 25 percent of
the nation's capital stock was destroyed.[85] Its GNP stood at only 50
percent of the prewar level. Japan was stripped of its colonies, which
were important trading partners and which constituted a large portion
of the territory of the former Japanese empire. It confronted the problem
of finding employment for the 10 million men demobilized from the military or repatriated from colonies abroad. It also faced a severe and extended bout of inflation, which ran in the triple digits for three years after
the war. Key products were in short supply, including rice to feed the
Japanese people and coal to fuel the factories.

For the first time in its long history, Japan also faced the prospect of
prolonged occupation by a foreign power. Dominated by Americans, the
Allied Occupation was led by General Douglas MacArthur, the Supreme
Commander of the Allied Powers (SCAP). (Henceforth this acronym denotes not MacArthur but the entire Occupation bureaucracy.) SCAP initially aimed not to rebuild Japanese industry but merely to restore a basic
level of subsistence. A more important priority was to "defeudalize, de-
militarize, and democratize" Japan. Many of the young bureaucrats in
SCAP were New Dealers from the United States, who sought to refashion

Japan's institutions based on an idealized U.S. model.[86] They rewrote the Japanese constitution to include rights not guaranteed in America itself, such as equal rights for women. The new constitution also contained the famous "Renunciation of War" (Article 9), which stated that "the Japanese people forever renounce war" and the maintenance of "land, sea, and air forces." This idealism, while imbuing SCAP with a noble sense of purpose, doomed some of its naive reforms. SCAP's power was further limited by its indirect rule via the Japanese bureaucracy. And, in the words of a former Japanese prime minister, it was "hampered by its lack of knowledge of the people it had come to govern, and even more so, perhaps, by its generally happy ignorance of the amount of requisite knowledge that it lacked."[87]

The idealists in SCAP were also challenged by shifting priorities back in the United States. By 1948 the Cold War had begun in earnest, and consequently the United States no longer wished to keep Japan weak. The pressing need now was to make Japan a "bulwark against communism" in the Far East and to make its economy strong enough to survive without American aid. These new objectives led to a "reverse course," the term used to denote a partial undoing of SCAP's reforms. Many of the reform measures took the same circuitous path from 1945 to 1952: radical change, followed by some backsliding, and, in some cases, complete reversal. Some reforms were not well suited for Japanese soil, and failing to grow roots, withered and died. The most enduring policies were those which had indigenous support in Japan.

In this category is land reform, often regarded as the most successful of SCAP's initiatives. Before World War II, a significant percentage of farming was done by tenants, who were beholden to large and powerful landholders. During the war, the balance of power began to shift, as wartime price regulations and controls on rice worked against landowners.[88] This change, though important, paled in comparison to the measures taken after the war. SCAP regarded feudalistic landowner-tenant relations as one of the bases of Japanese militarism. It worked to break up large farms and eliminate absentee ownership. Landowners received a pittance for their land—at prevailing prices, the equivalent of 52 packets of cigarettes for one acre of land.[89] Although they complained bitterly, the policy was effective. Tenancy fell from 46 percent of the farming population to 10 percent between November 1946 and August 1950.[90] Land reform had the disadvantage of promoting smaller and less efficient farms, but this was more than offset by the advantage of a more stable and liberated rural populace.

Similar aims—to punish the "feudal" elements responsible for the war and to reduce Japan's future ability to wage war—motivated SCAP policies toward industry. Such measures included zaibatsu dissolution, other deconcentration measures, and the purge of prominent business leaders. SCAP blamed the zaibatsu for obstructing the development of a Japanese middle class which could have opposed the military. It set about destroying the key institution of the zaibatsu: the holding companies that served as their control centers. These holding companies were dissolved, and their shareholdings of other member firms were sold off at ridiculously low prices. Also imposed was a capital levy, which further reduced the economic power of the zaibatsu families. Overall, these large capitalists were dispossessed and their business groups dismantled.

SCAP targeted not only the zaibatsu families but also the top managers who actually exercised control of the corporations. It purged over 1,500 business leaders from their positions. These mass dismissals, also applied to Japanese leaders in politics and education, were highly unpopular in Japan. They were consequently reversed in 1950 and 1951, allowing some of the discharged managers to return to positions of national economic leadership.

The same sort of policy reversal occurred in SCAP's attempt to inhibit the concentration of economic power. In 1947, it forced the passage of the Elimination of Excess Concentration Law, under which MacArthur designated 325 Japanese companies to be reorganized or dissolved. After much lobbying by the companies and by U.S. conservatives, the law was emasculated, and only 19 companies were ultimately affected. Also enacted in 1947 was the Antimonopoly Law, the first of its kind in Japan and, as written, one of the most severe antitrust measures anywhere. Patterned after the U.S. Federal Trade Commission and Clayton Acts of 1914, this law went even further in some areas: holding companies and interlocking directorships were banned and exclusive licensing agreements with foreign companies were prohibited. This last provision was especially unpopular in a nation eager to reduce its technology gap with the West. It was deleted when the Antimonopoly Law was amended in 1949. The Antimonopoly Law was revised again in 1953, this time to loosen restrictions on cross-shareholding and to allow certain types of cartels. Though strengthened in a subsequent revision in 1977, the Antimonopoly Law remained much less restrictive than it was originally. Moreover, actual enforcement of antitrust law has been sporadic at best.

As for labor, SCAP pushed through legislation which guaranteed the right of workers to organize, bargain collectively, and strike. The freedom, indeed encouragement, to form unions sparked explosive growth of trade union membership, which rose from 496,000 workers in February 1946 to 6.6 million by July 1948.[91] The rebirth of labor unions fed radicalism, however, and SCAP was forced to crack down. In early 1947 it forbade a general strike that would have sent the convalescent Japanese economy back into a coma. This action, along with SCAP's ban of a possible strike by government workers the following year, reined in the radical fringe. Labor disputes declined sharply after 1948, before flaring up again in the early 1950s. This later burst of labor unrest would lead to a transformation of Japanese labor relations.

Many of SCAP's reforms proved important in the long run, but in the short run they failed to get the Japanese economy moving.[92] Growing conservatism in America and dissatisfaction with SCAP's economic policies led to the dispatch of a Detroit banker, Joseph Dodge, to Japan in 1949. Dodge reported directly to President Truman and thus had considerable authority. He was determined to tame Japan's raging inflation and to build up its economy so that it no longer needed extensive U.S. aid. In a three-month period, he laid down a series of tough policies that became known as the "Dodge Line." He forced the Japanese government to pass a balanced budget, slashed government subsidies, and prohibited the state-owned Reconstruction Finance Bank from issuing new bonds. Perhaps most important, Dodge ignored a long-standing and complicated debate about where to set the Japanese exchange rate and unilaterally decided on a rate of $1 = ¥360. This rate would remain unaltered for the next 22 years, even as the economic environment changed dramatically in Japan's favor. The Dodge Line halted the high inflation, and by making the yen convertible, it created the basic conditions necessary for Japanese trade to expand. Its immediate effect, however, was to plunge the economy into deeper recession.

Japanese Initiatives

Unlike the changes following the Meiji Restoration, many of which were internally generated, most of the post-World War II reform proposals came from Americans.[93] An important exception was the priority production system, which sought to focus Japan's economic resources on rebuilding a number of essential sectors: coal, electric power, steel, and shipping. A government-owned Reconstruction Finance Bank (RFB) was established, and its share of total loans received by certain industries was 71 percent for coal, 87 percent for electric power, and 65 percent for shipping.[94] Though Dodge prohibited the RFB from issuing any new credits, its function was later absorbed by the Japan Development Bank (created in 1951) and, to a lesser extent, the Export-Import Bank of Japan (1950). To supply long-term loans to capital-intensive industries, the Japanese government established two long-term credit banks, the Industrial Bank of Japan (reorganized in 1952) and the Long-Term Credit Bank of Japan (1952).

Priority production generated large increases in the output of coal and other designated goods, but recovery for the rest of the economy proceeded at a slow and unsteady rate. As the Allied Occupation of Japan came to a close in April 1952, Japan's per capita GNP was only $188, making it poorer than such countries as Brazil, Malaysia, and Chile.[95]

This miserable state proved a fertile ground for some Japanese entrepreneurs. In 1946 Akio Morita, Masaru Ibuka, and Tamon Maeda founded the company that would later become Sony. (Their first product was a rice cooker that failed to work.) That same year Soichiro Honda started a workshop to build bicycles with attached motors, leading eventually to the Honda Motor Company. In the long run, this sort of entrepreneurial effort led to the creation and growth of some of Japan's most celebrated companies. More important on an immediate basis, however, was the outbreak in 1950 of the Korean War, which sharply increased the demand for Japanese products. "Special procurement" expenditures by United Nations (mainly U.S.) forces accounted for 47 percent of the value of all Japanese exports between 1950 and 1953.[96] The Korean War lifted the Japanese economy out of its doldrums and paved the way for an era of unprecedented growth.

THE ERA OF HIGH-SPEED GROWTH (1953–1973)

By 1953 real per capita GNP had surpassed its prewar level, though the Economic Planning Agency waited until 1956 to announce that Japan's reconstruction was complete. Another notable event was the formation in 1955 of the Liberal Democratic Party (LDP), a business-oriented coalition supported by farmers. The LDP remained in power for the next

38 years, providing a climate of political stability in which the Japanese could focus almost single-mindedly on commerce and industry. Economic growth became priority number one, and the indefatigable Japanese "salaryman" became a fixture of urban life in Japan and a well-known image abroad.

In the late 1950s the nation entered the age of mass consumption. Buyers rushed to acquire consumer durables, first the "three sacred treasures"—refrigerator, washing machine, and black-and-white television—and later the "three C's": color television, car, and cooler (air conditioner). The rise of a mass-consumption society was supported and accompanied by a leveling of Japan's income distribution, which came to be among the world's most equal.[97]

Nothing encapsulated the atmosphere of this age better than the "Ten Year Income-Doubling Plan of 1961–70," announced by Prime Minister Hayato Ikeda, whom French President Charles de Gaulle had once derided as a "transistor salesman." Though some analysts dismissed it as an empty slogan or political posturing, the income-doubling plan was quite ambitious.[98] To be met, it required a decade of growth at the seemingly astronomical annual rate of 7.2 percent. Although the Japanese economy had experienced growth rates of this magnitude in the late 1950s, it was by no means certain that such a rate could be maintained for an entire decade. As it turned out, the goal of doubling income was more than fulfilled. Real output in 1970 was 2.8 times that of 1960, reflecting an average annual growth rate of over 9.3 percent. Japanese economic growth was so torrid that during a recession in 1965, the growth rate still exceeded 5 percent, a figure that would be considered stellar economic performance by any advanced industrial nation today. By 1973, Japan's income was an incredible 5.4 times its 1953 level (for per capita income the multiple was 4.1).[99] During this period, Japan overtook Canada in 1960, France and Britain in the mid-1960s, and West Germany in 1968 to become the second-largest economy in the noncommunist world.

The Development of the Japanese Firm

A key institution underlying the "miracle" was the Japanese firm, and during the 1953–73 period it evolved in several ways.[100] Permanent employment and seniority-based wages and promotion now spread to a much wider group of corporations, becoming in effect a norm to which all companies aspired, but which many small and medium-sized firms were unable to attain. Profit-sharing bonuses based not on individual merit but on the firm's overall performance were another prewar invention that became more prevalent at this time.

Enterprise unions, the third pillar of the Japanese employment system, emerged during the early postwar period. "Enterprise unions" are single-company unions encompassing both blue-collar and lower-tier white-collar workers. They are now the primary type of union in Japan, as opposed to the craft-wide and industry-wide unions which prevail in the United States and Europe. Even before World War II, Japanese workers tended to organize themselves by factory or workshop, not by craft or industry.[101] Modern enterprise unions arose during the 1950s, in a context of intense labor strife. Postwar liberalization had fostered left-wing unions more interested in class struggle than in rebuilding Japan. When these unions confronted Japanese management, the result was bitter, sometimes violent strikes, such as those which occurred at Nissan in 1953 and at the Miike Mining Company in 1959–60. Management tried to break up radically inclined unions by encouraging moderate workers to create more cooperative unions at the firm level. Ultimately this tactic proved successful. Japan is now regarded as a country in which organized labor is unusually quiescent, even though the rate of union membership is higher than in the United States (but lower than in Britain or Germany). Enterprise unions serve as a consultative organ for labor and management and, coupled with permanent employment, make Japanese workers generally more willing to accept the introduction of new technology than are workers in other industrial nations. Achieving labor peace was, however, not a simple or painless process.[102]

Some effects of the Japanese employment system are quite clear. Job tenure in Japan is on average much longer than it is in America and Europe, and the incremental gain in salary attributable to seniority is higher in Japan than in other industrial nations.[103] Other consequences are more subtle. Though the Japanese system appears rigid, it has several features that enhance its adaptability: variable compensation through bonuses, annual rather than multi-year contracts, and vague job assignments coupled with frequent rotation of employees. The sociologist Ronald Dore's notion of "flexible rigidities" aptly characterizes the Japanese employment system.[104]

Japanese companies differ from Western ones in ways other than their employment system. A major structural difference involves Japanese firms' management of information and personnel. U.S. companies tend to rely on a hierarchical chain of command in which decisions *about operations* are made at the top, based on information that flows upward. By contrast, decisions *about people* (hiring, promotion) are left to the discretion of local managers. Japanese firms have precisely the reverse orientation. They tend to have very centralized and powerful human resources departments but to give lower-level managers more leeway in making operational decisions. A prominent Japanese economist has suggested that this difference may help explain why Japanese companies appear to excel at industries where process innovation is important (such as steel and autos) and to be weak in sectors where product innovation is essential (aerospace and pharmaceuticals).[105]

The priorities and goals of the Japanese firm also appear to differ from those of its Western counterparts. Japanese managers tend to downplay the importance of shareholders as owners of the firm and to consider employees the true core of the firm. Surveys of corporate executives in the United States and Japan show that Japanese executives place far more weight on market share and new product development than do American managers, who are more concerned about return on investment and stock prices.[106] This finding has contributed to the widely held view that Japanese companies tend to pursue longer-term objectives than do their Western rivals.[107]

The inclination of Japanese corporations to pursue long-term objectives may derive less from the influence of culture than from their financial structure. Historically, Japanese firms were insulated from the pressures of the stock market in two ways. First, during the high-growth period they relied heavily on debt rather than retained earnings or new equity issues. Second, corporate equity came to be held primarily by other financial and nonfinancial corporations. It has been argued that this system of cross-shareholding insulated Japanese managers from the short-term, speculative nature of financiers and allowed for long-term investment plans.[108]

The Creation of New Interfirm Linkages

Widespread cross-shareholding is intimately related to another key development of this period, the creation of new interfirm linkages. Before World War II, both the old and new zaibatsu figured prominently in the

Japanese economy. In the postwar period, a wider variety of interfirm groups has appeared. Often referred to generically as *keiretsu*, there are four main types of groups.

One type is strongly reminiscent of the prewar zaibatsu: the conglomerate group, frequently referred to as "horizontal" keiretsu but more properly called *kigyo shudan* (enterprise group).[109] There are six main kigyo shudan, the so-called Big Six: the Mitsubishi, Mitsui, and Sumitomo groups, direct descendants of the prewar zaibatsu; plus the Fuyo, Sanwa, and Dai-ichi Kangyo groups. Fuyo has antecedents in the Yasuda zaibatsu, while the remaining two are postwar agglomerations organized around the Sanwa and Dai-ichi Kangyo banks.

Each of the Big Six kigyo shudan includes many firms and spans many different industries. Of these member firms, there is a core subgroup that meets periodically to discuss business matters concerning the group. This is the *shacho-kai* or president's club. Also at the heart of each group is a city bank (a large commercial bank) which serves as the "main bank" for member companies. The main bank is generally the largest source of loans for group firms, but it is not the exclusive lender. Companies typically borrow from a number of banks, including those outside the group. The main bank is usually an important shareholder of the client firm, thus serving a dual role as shareholder and lender. (In Japan, a bank can hold up to 5 percent of a firm's outstanding equity.) The main bank also frequently serves as the chief source of assistance when a client firm gets into trouble. In such cases, it may provide emergency loans, reduce interest charges, or even formulate a recovery plan and dispatch personnel to the client firm.[110]

Another major constituent of each group is the general trading company or *sogo shosha,* of which there are nine. The two largest prewar trading companies, Mitsui & Co. and Mitsubishi Corporation, were broken up by SCAP but later reconstituted themselves. The other sogo shosha had their origins in smaller prewar companies, with the exception of Sumitomo Corporation, which was a postwar creation. The sogo shosha deal in an enormous variety of goods, everything from noodles to subway cars. They handle an almost unbelievable volume of trade. In 1993, the six largest sogo shosha had sales of ¥86 trillion ($772 billion, or approximately the combined national output of China and Taiwan). In that same year, they handled 29 percent of Japanese exports and 43 percent of Japanese imports.[111] Given their size, the sogo shosha have a major impact on other countries. By one estimate, they handle 10 percent of U.S. overseas sales and 4 percent of world trade.[112] Within the group, the sogo shosha function as a key outlet to dispose of products and bring in raw materials. They are also a major source of financing for small companies.

Banks and trading companies lie at the heart of the kigyo shudan, but there are other links as well. Cross-shareholding, or reciprocal ownership of stock by member corporations, is pervasive within groups, with some 15 to 30 percent of a constituent firm's shares held by members of the same group, especially by financial institutions.[113] Group firms are also linked by personnel transfers, trade networks, collective industrial projects, and high-level executive councils which meet on a periodic basis. Western observers often regard the kigyo shudan as fixed and immutable, but both the number of member firms and the strength of their affiliations change over time.[114]

On the surface, the kigyo shudan appear quite similar to the zaibatsu, but there is one crucial difference: the zaibatsu were controlled by family-owned holding companies. The kigyo shudan lack holding companies and therefore have a much looser structure than their prewar counterparts. As Figure 12.2 (p. 453) shows, the ownership structures of the kigyo shudan are more complex and diffuse than those of the zaibatsu. As did the zaibatsu, kigyo shudan represent a large but not dominant portion of the Japanese economy. In 1992, nonfinancial companies belonging to the Big Six conglomerate groups made up only 0.1 percent of all incorporated firms, but they accounted for 15.2 percent of the paid-in capital, 13.8 percent of sales, and 10.6 percent of ordinary income.[115]

A second type of Japanese corporate group consists of production-oriented entities, known as "vertical" keiretsu. Some of Japan's premier manufacturing corporations, including the auto giants Toyota and Nissan and the electronic firms Matsushita, Hitachi, and Toshiba, stand at the top of these networks. Each group consists of a parent company, which acts largely as a design and assembly shop, plus tiers of subcontractors making parts for the main firm. As a result of this structure, the parent company is often much smaller than its American and European competitors. For instance, although Toyota's sales in 1987 were about half those of General Motors, its direct workforce was less than 8 percent of General Motors' 813,000 workers worldwide.[116]

A third type, also vertically oriented, is the "distribution" keiretsu.[117] They generally consist of small retailers forming the domestic distribution channel for a manufacturer. Matsushita Electric's extensive network of small outlets stocking its National brand (Panasonic is the brand abroad) helped it to become the largest producer of consumer electronics in Japan. The growth of specialty electronics outlets in recent years has eroded this advantage and pushed some of the more vulnerable Matsushita stores out of business. In automobiles, too, Japan's network of largely exclusive dealerships has been decried by foreign automakers trying to break into the Japanese market.

A fourth type of network consists of firms affiliated with large retailers or railway companies. These are often referred to as *guruhpu*, the Japanese pronunciation of the word "group."[118] Included in this category are Saison, Tobu, Daiei, and Ito-Yokado. Their existence, like that of the production keiretsu, may reflect the preference of Japanese firms to remain small and focused. Many of these groups have evolved as the parent company established new enterprises. When Ito-Yokado developed new businesses, for example, it periodically spun them off, so that subsidiaries such as Seven-Eleven Japan and Denny's Japan are now listed on the Tokyo Stock Exchange.

Though the keiretsu are frequently likened to cartels, they are not cartels in the usual definition of the word, that is, a group of firms in the same industry which collude to prevent price competition.[119] As will be discussed below, the Japanese government was very lenient toward and even promoted cartels in many industries, but these are quite distinct from keiretsu. If keiretsu were collusive, we would expect Japanese industries to be more concentrated than American ones, but this is not the case.[120] We would also expect keiretsu-affiliated firms to have higher profits than independent ones. Instead, members of kigyo shudan appear to be less profitable than independent firms.[121] Not only do firms in kigyo shudan perform worse than unaffiliated companies in the same industry, but industries in which members of kigyo shudan have a larger share tend to exhibit lower overall profitability.[122] This evidence suggests that competition *between members of different corporate groups* may account for the intense rivalry in many Japanese industries. The tendency of each kigyo shudan to have a representative firm in every major industry, the so-called one-set principle, may facilitate this severe competition.[123] Not all markets are so vigorously contested. Collusion is rampant in some highly visible sectors, such as construction. However, the fierce competitiveness of Japanese companies, along with their ability to cooperate with other firms when necessary, is both a surprise and puzzle to many Western observers.[124]

The "Developmental" State: The Role of the Japanese Government

Public policy in Japan has also played a role in its economic success, though how big a role is subject to much dispute. Clearly one of the most important tasks of economic policymaking is to get the macroeconomic fundamentals correct. The Japanese government certainly did this in the era of high-speed growth. It generated high saving, kept inflation under control, avoided accumulating large foreign and domestic debt, and restrained the growth of the government sector.

More controversial is Japanese government intervention at the microeconomic level, or what has come to be called "industrial policy." Two types of industrial policy should be distinguished. One was selective targeting. Some analysts argue that the Japanese government was not content to let perceived comparative advantage dictate what industries Japan would develop. Instead, it selectively intervened to alter the nation's industrial structure, first away from light industry to heavy and chemical industries, and then toward knowledge-intensive, high-technology ones. The main agency responsible for this targeting was the Ministry of International Trade and Industry (MITI), which used two primary criteria in selecting the industries: high elasticity of income demand (meaning that as incomes rose, consumers would buy proportionally more of these goods) and high value-added share (low cost of raw materials relative to a product's final price). The methods used to promote favored sectors were diverse. They included subsidized credit, preferential access to foreign exchange, government sponsorship of joint research projects, and tax incentives.

A second type of industrial policy was the use of cartels. The Japanese government not only promoted sunrise industries; it also acted to ease the adjustment burden of sunset industries and to keep cutthroat competition from breaking out in periods of slack demand. The term *kato kyoso,* or "excessive competition," is often used in Japan. The notion of excessive competition is perplexing to many Anglo-American economists, for whom "perfect competition" is the ideal.[125] By contrast, the Japanese, especially their economic bureaucrats, have been wary of allowing unfettered competition.[126] Fear of excessive competition is often cited as the basis for the sanction and sometimes deliberate creation of cartels in Japan. These cartels are called "recession cartels" in the case of temporarily affected industries and "rationalization cartels" if the industry is regarded as being in long-term decline. The widespread use of this technique can be seen by the sheer number of cartels that were authorized. By one count, in the mid-1960s there were over 1,000 cartels in operation, in roughly 20 percent of all manufacturing sectors, and 43 percent of all Japanese manufacturing output came from sectors involving some cartel activity.[127]

The means of government intervention was also unusual. In contrast to the formal, legalistic methods of regulation used in the United States, the Japanese government frequently resorted to informal, carrot-and-stick-type tactics, practices known collectively as administrative guidance. Administrative guidance is not authorized by any explicit law. Rather, its force comes from the ability of bureaucrats to punish or disadvantage those firms which disobey their "suggestions." Administrative guidance was practiced not just by MITI. The Ministry of Transportation used it in dealing with shipping and shipbuilding. The Ministry of Finance and the Bank of Japan used a form of it, called window guidance, to allocate credit.

Administrative guidance was facilitated by the common practice of placing retiring bureaucrats at high-ranking and lucrative jobs in the private sector, usually in an industry under the jurisdiction of their former ministry. Reflecting the considerable prestige attached to elite bureaucrats, who are generally top graduates of Japan's best universities, this practice is called *amakudari,* or "descent from heaven." Still, administrative guidance did not always work.[128] Over government opposition, Kawasaki Steel in 1953 built the world's most modern integrated steel complex, which became a huge financial success. MITI was also unable to consolidate the Japanese auto industry into two or three firms, as it had hoped.

Another type of intervention was the government's use of "visions" as guides to policy and signals to the private sector. Unlike the compulsory or even "indicative" plans used by more interventionist governments, the "visions" issued by MITI and the medium- or long-range "plans" issued by Japan's Economic Planning Agency consisted largely of predictions. These forecasts were often subsumed under a grand theme as to where the Japanese economy should be heading in the future.

The overall effectiveness of these policies is much debated, and the role of selective targeting is a particularly fierce controversy.[129] Some analysts assert that targeting was largely responsible for the superior performance and rapid structural change of the Japanese economy. The most prominent advocates of this view are political scientists and journalists. They tend to rely on case-study evidence, historical investigations of specific institutions, and the testimony and records of Japanese government officials. Chalmers Johnson's influential book *MITI and the Japanese Miracle* (1982) is the best-known example of this genre, but there are many others.[130]

By contrast, those arguing that industrial policy had little effect are largely economists, who focus less on the institutional environment than on statistical evidence. A study by two economists has shown that industries receiving the most government assistance did not record the greatest productivity growth, and that government assistance programs lacked consistency. Another study finds that government-authorized cartels had little impact on pricing behavior or margins of Japanese companies, and a third points to the small amount of resources allocated by MITI and other agencies as evidence that Japanese industrial policy was ineffective.[131]

Although the effectiveness of the Japanese government is debatable, the stellar performance of the Japanese economy during this period is not. Japan experienced both torrid growth and an enormous structural shift between 1955 and 1970. The agricultural population shrank dramatically, providing labor for factory employment (see Figure 12.1, p. 451). In distribution, another relatively backward industry, the rise of self-service supermarkets was heralded as a "distribution revolution." Most impressive was the growth of heavy and chemical industries, whose share of manufacturing output rose from 39 percent in 1955 to 60 percent in 1970.[132] Steel, automobiles, and consumer electronics were especially strong performers. Japan had begun this period as a maker of textiles and shoddy toys. In less than 20 years, it had become, in the words of a famous academic study, "Asia's new giant."[133]

CONFRONTING ECONOMIC MATURITY AND THE BUBBLE
ECONOMY (1974–1994)

As the 1970s began, there was widespread optimism about Japan's prospects, with some predictions that its economy would continue to grow at double-digit rates for the next decade.[134] This optimism prevailed in spite of worries about the environmental costs of rapid growth. A series of highly publicized pollution cases in the early 1970s led many Japanese for the first time since the war to question the wisdom of the nation's all-out pursuit of economic growth. When citizen concern had mounted to the point that normally staid newspapers angrily proclaimed, "To Hell with GNP," the Japanese government responded by passing some of the world's strictest environmental laws. In time, Japanese industry became not only more efficient in its use of energy, but also a leader in the production of pollution-control equipment.

Grappling with environmental problems was only the first of many adjustments Japan made during this period. As its economy matured, output growth fell to single-digit rates, and there was a shift from heavy and chemical industries toward cleaner, less energy-intensive, and more high-tech ones. The service sector also expanded. This restructuring was accelerated by two oil shocks and several episodes of yen appreciation.

In the midst of all these changes, Japan continued to outperform other advanced economies. By 1989, when the Showa emperor died and his son Akihito ascended to the throne, launching the Heisei (Achieving Peace) era, Japan had become an economic superpower. It was the world's largest net asset holder and the world's biggest aid donor. The Tokyo Stock Exchange even briefly had a larger capitalization than did the New York Stock Exchange. Measured at prevailing exchange rates, Japan's per capita income exceeded that of the United States. Much of this prosperity was genuine, the fruit of a 100-year struggle to "catch up and overtake" the West, but part of it reflected an abnormal and speculative environment of the late 1980s called the "bubble economy." When the bubble burst in the early 1990s, the Japanese economy experienced a prolonged downturn. Another shock came in 1993, when the Liberal Democratic Party was voted out of power for the first time since 1955. The collapse of the bubble and the apparent shakeup in Japan's political structure produced few immediate changes in Japanese capitalism. Probably more important in the long run than these temporary dislocations are demographic shifts, such as the rapid aging of Japan's population (by the early twenty-first century, likely the world's oldest) and the rise of a new generation of Japanese accustomed to affluence.

Overcoming Shocks to the System: The Japanese System Bends, But Holds Firm

All industrial economies were hurt by the sharp increase in oil prices in 1973, but resource-poor Japan was hit the hardest. Japan imports virtually all of its oil, which at the time comprised three-fourths of its total energy supply. Thus, the fourfold increase in the price of crude oil between September and December 1973 severely jolted Japanese industry. In 1974, for the first time in the postwar era, Japan's real output fell. At the same time, inflation soared to 24 percent. Unnerved by this stagflationary environment, the Japanese people coined the expression "oil shock."

The oil shock of 1973 seemed to threaten the foundations of the Japanese employment system, but managers fought valiantly to avoid layoffs. They found alternative ways to reduce redundant workers: voluntary retirement, natural attrition coupled with a stop in new hiring, transfers to other jobs within the company, or transfers to other firms. Companies began to reduce the scope of lifetime employment by relying more on part-time workers. Shareholders were also forced to bear much of the burden, as profit rates fell by more in Japan than in any other industrial country.

The first oil shock signaled the end of the high-growth period, not only for Japan but for all industrial nations. The second oil crisis of 1979 involved a greater absolute increase in the price of oil, but it was much less traumatic for Japan. Learning from the earlier, painful experience, its firms had reduced energy consumption and other production costs during the 1970s.

In addition to the two oil shocks, Japan faced a series of "yen shocks." Between 1949 and 1971, the yen's exchange rate was pegged at ¥360 to the dollar. As Japanese industry became more competitive, the yen became undervalued, further boosting Japanese exports. In 1971, however, the worldwide fixed exchange rate regime collapsed, and after 1973 the yen's value was determined by the market for foreign exchange. There followed three periods of *endaka,* or yen appreciation: the first from 1976 to 1978, the second between 1985 and 1988, and the third from

1990 to 1995, by which time the exchange rate had fallen to under ¥100 to the dollar (see Figure 12.3).

The oil and yen shocks not only affected overall growth but also forced structural changes. Some firms had little choice but to exit their industry. This was particularly true of small, labor-intensive firms in the textile industry and of companies in energy-intensive industries such as aluminum. Others moved upscale, exiting from the commodity part of the business, as some of the large Japanese textile, petrochemical, and shipbuilding producers did in developing specialty products. Another response was to diversify into other industries. This was a popular choice for some companies whose core businesses were in decline. One example is Kanebo, a textile company, which has ventured into cosmetics, food processing, pharmaceuticals, and housing construction.[135] Another option was to locate production abroad, and Japanese foreign direct investment will be discussed below. A final response was to slash production costs. Part of the cost cutting was accomplished by transferring tasks to low-wage subcontractors, who were urged to cut their own costs still further. Japanese firms also undertook massive investment in labor-saving technology. This phenomenon was particularly evident during the second and third bouts of endaka, when private capital investment as a percentage of GDP soared beyond its previous highs.[136]

Though Japan's industry structure and growth rate changed dramatically between 1974 and the mid-1990s, there was relatively little change in the institutions underlying Japanese business. The Japanese employ-

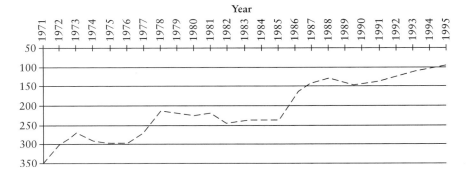

Figure 12.3   The Average Annual Yen-Dollar Exchange Rate

Source: International Financial Statistics Yearbook 1995 (Washington: International Monetary Fund, 1995), pp. 468–469; *International Financial Statistics,* May 1996, pp. 340–341.

ment system survived the oil and yen shocks largely intact. Participation of women in the Japanese labor force approached the U.S. level, but Japanese women remained largely excluded from the core of the corporate system.[137] Japanese firms became less dependent on bank finance, but the links between group firms remained solid. The sogo shosha remained gigantic, refuting many warnings of their imminent demise. There was a remarkable continuity in Japan's business institutions as the world economy moved from a time of high growth to one of low growth.

The role and effectiveness of government policy, however, changed somewhat in the 1970s and 1980s. For much of the high-growth period, Japan's economy had been heavily regulated and sheltered from international competition. Foreign pressure to open up its economy intensified as Japan became the world's second-largest industrial power. In response, Japan began slowly, often begrudgingly, to liberalize its economy. Deregulation sometimes involved major policy shifts, as with the 1979 revision of the Foreign Exchange Law, which made foreign exchange transactions permissible in principle rather than banned unless specifically approved. Usually, however, the process was a gradual series of incremental changes.

Deregulation measures generally came later in Japan than in other advanced industrial nations. Japan's privatization program, which included the sell-off of Japan National Railways, Japan Tobacco, and Nippon Telegraph and Telephone, followed earlier ones in the United Kingdom and the United States. Reform of the financial sector also came slowly. For example, the Ministry of Finance did not allow a futures market in Tokyo until 1989. In other sectors of the economy, there was little, if any, change. Agriculture, distribution, construction, and financial services remained highly regulated or protected in the mid-to-late-1990s.

Not just the speed, but the very concept of deregulation was different in Japan. In Japanese, the expression for deregulation, *kisei kanwa*, literally means "relaxation of regulations." Unlike "deregulation," which implies not just a change in the rules but the elimination of any need for regulators, the Japanese concept allows for continued bureaucratic supervision. As with the concept of kato kyoso (excessive competition) discussed earlier, this difference in terminology indicates a very different view of the market from that prevailing in Anglo-American countries.[138]

Even so, deregulation did reduce the policy instruments available to Japanese bureaucrats, who now found it more difficult to implement industrial policy. The growth of Japanese corporations made them less dependent on government beneficence, and thus less cooperative. At the same time, as Japan went from a technological laggard to a leader in many sectors, the choice of industries to target became less obvious. These changes did not lead the Japanese government to forsake long-term planning or to stop convening collaborative R&D projects. However, as one scholar put it, the Japanese government became less of a "planner" and more of a "referee" or an "arbiter."[139]

Japanese Trade and Investment: A Briar Patch of Conflict

Ironically, as Japan's government loosened controls on the domestic economy, its firms and products increasingly became targets of foreign government restrictions. Trade conflict was nothing new for Japan. Even before World War II, the dynamism of its textile industry had provoked the ire of other industrial countries. After the war, Japanese trade policies continued to be criticized. Textile conflict made a reappearance in the 1950s and 1970s, followed by bickering over steel and television receivers. In the early 1980s, the rise of the dollar made it difficult for American manufacturers of automobiles to compete, and they sought protection from the U.S. government. Ultimately, "voluntary" export restraints (VERs) were imposed by the United States on the Japanese steel and auto industries. Similar policies were imposed by European countries, so that by the mid-1980s some 30 to 40 percent of Japanese exports to America and the European Community were subject to a VER.[140] As the United States restricted Japanese access to its markets, it initiated a series of negotiations aimed at opening up the Japanese market. The first major initiative was the 1985 Market-oriented, Sector-specific (MOSS) talks. Next came the Structural Impediments Initiative (SII) of 1989–90, and then the aborted "framework" talks (ended on February 11, 1994). Over time the scope of these negotiations grew wider, and their outcomes less satisfactory to both sides.

With the rise of the yen and new barriers to their exports, many Japanese firms recognized the potential profitability of overseas production. They began to make acquisitions and build new plants in foreign countries. Although they invested all over the world, the United States was a particularly popular destination during the late 1980s. Many Americans viewed this investment with alarm.[141] However, careful analyses of Japanese foreign direct investment (FDI) in America have shown that it does not differ qualitatively from that of any other country, with the exception that U.S. subsidiaries of Japanese firms tend to import more components.[142] Japanese investments in the United States have not been very profitable, especially some of the speculative acquisitions of the late 1980s. In the 1990s, some of these purchases have been sold at a loss, and Japanese FDI has been increasingly directed at Asia.

Many people saw Japan's widening trade surpluses as evidence of a closed Japanese market, but the absolute magnitude of Japan's current account surplus (or the U.S. current account deficit) is determined primarily by macroeconomic forces, in particular the imbalance between national saving and national investment. In recent years, Japan has saved more than it has invested, and the United States has invested more than it has saved. Unless these macroeconomic imbalances are reduced, the overall current account positions of each country will not change. More problematic to many observers is the composition of Japanese trade. Compared to other industrial countries, Japan imports fewer manufactured goods and plays host to less investment from abroad. Japan engages in less intra-industry trade than do other industrial nations (that is, it does not tend to import goods that it exports, nor export goods that it imports).[143] Table 12.3 shows Japan's "unusual" trade pattern.

Whether these peculiarities reflect Japanese barriers is unclear. Japan has the lowest tariffs of any major industrial nation, so allegations that

Table 12.3 Japan's "Unusual" Trade Pattern

	Japan	U.S.	Germany	Britain
Intraindustry trade index (1990)[a]	0.58	0.83	0.73	0.79
Import share of manufactured goods consumption (1990)	6%	15%	15%	18%
Foreign firms' share of domestic sales (1986)	1%[b]	10%	18%	20%

a. The intraindustry trade index is a measure running from zero (if a country imports no goods that it exports, and vice-versa) to one (if it imports exactly the same amount as it exports in each sector). Intra-EC trade has been purged from its calculation, and from that of the import share figures.

b. This estimate is not based on very good data, and there are reasons to believe that it may be off by up to an order of magnitude. See David Weinstein, "Foreign Direct Investment and *Keiretsu*: Rethinking US and Japanese Policy," Harvard University, Sept. 11, 1995.

Source: C. Fred Bergsten and Marcus Noland, *Reconcilable Differences? United States–Japan Economic Conflict* (Washington: Institute for International Economics, 1993), table 3.3.

it is closed center on informal barriers. Some studies appear to support the frequent contention that keiretsu act as an obstacle to trade and foreign investment in Japan. Even if these groups limit foreign-firm participation, however, it is unclear whether they do so because they are very efficient and competitive, or whether barriers to entry keep more efficient foreign firms from entering certain sectors. Some observers are skeptical that business practices or government policy have greatly skewed Japan's pattern of trade. They point instead to Japan's unusual geographical, economic, and even cultural position.[144]

The "Bubble Economy"

The rise of the yen beginning in 1985 provoked fears of a serious recession in Japan. In response, and to accommodate its trading partners' demands for expansion of the Japanese economy, the government lowered interest rates. It thereby ignited rampant speculation. Asset prices skyrocketed, as investors used their growing liquidity to bid up the price of stocks and land. Some of this activity involved shady characters, but even normally conservative blue-chip Japanese firms engaged in what became known as *zaiteku,* or "financial engineering." Zaiteku was little more than a euphemism for gambling, as companies invested in property and stocks on the apparent assumption that their prices would continue to rise. Land and equity prices soared in the late 1980s, but eventually the speculative boom came to end. When it did, the ramifications spread throughout the corporate world. Japanese banks were especially afflicted by the fall in asset prices. In addition to being major holders of equity, they had made enormous loans using land as collateral. The collapse of stock prices shrank their capital base. At the same time, the downward spiral of land prices led to an explosion in bad debts.

The psychological shock of the bubble's collapse was as devastating as its economic impact. The Japan of the late 1980s had a buoyant, even arrogant attitude. Having caught up with and in some ways surpassed the West, Japanese people were enjoying their new affluence. The bursting of the bubble shattered some of this confidence. It also exposed a seamy underside of Japanese business, such as connections to organized crime and favoritism toward privileged insiders. Securities companies, for example, were shown to have compensated large clients for their short-term losses.

Some analysts believed that the bursting of the bubble would lead to dramatic changes in Japan, and several books presented "disaster" scenarios proclaiming the end of Japan as an economic superpower.[145] Others argued that, as with the oil shocks, the bursting of the bubble would cause temporary pain for Japanese industry but ultimately leave it stronger than before.[146]

Japanese Capitalism: A Paradigm to Emulate?

> Human capitalism is no more a "Japan" phenomenon than capitalism, born in eighteenth-century England, is an "English" phenomenon . . . Human capitalism has been the foundation of Japan's postwar economic rebirth. It took concrete shape in the course of the nation's accelerated economic growth . . . At the same time, its principles are rational and universal, and therefore transferable to other countries and cultures.
>
> —*Robert Ozaki, a Japanese-American economist, 1991* [147]

> It is America's model, not Japan's, to which rich societies, even in Asia, will tend to gravitate. America's founders were fired by universalist ideals, uncompromised by any national tradition. Japan's power as a role model is undermined by intense nationalism.
>
> —*Sebastian Mallaby in The Economist, July 9, 1994* [148]

Even before Japan became an economic power, it thought of itself (and was seen by others) as a model to emulate. A Western observer in 1902 described Japan's role "as that of the Schoolmaster of Asia," serving as "the chief influence to modernize China, to awaken Korea, to help Siam [Thailand]."[149] Unfortunately, Japan tried to fulfill this role through military conquest and colonization, first at the turn of the century and then more aggressively during the 1930s and early 1940s. Dispossessed of its colonial empire by defeat in World War II, Japan directed most of its national energies toward economic development. By the late 1960s, it had become a compelling economic model, especially for Asian nations. Some of them, including Malaysia and Singapore, explicitly adopted "Look East" policies, embracing Japan as a developmental model. South Korea and Taiwan, though as former colonies understandably less eager to acknowledge Japan as a teacher, in practice adhered even more faithfully to elements of the Japanese system.

The Japanese themselves have encouraged others to consider the "Japanese" or "Asian" model, even financing a recent World Bank study on the "East Asian Miracle."[150] But how well this paradigm applies to many developing countries is uncertain. An emerging controversy is the applicability of the Japanese system to the former communist nations of Eastern Europe. Some Western economists have suggested that these countries would be better off adopting the Japanese model than the American one. And some Japanese bureaucrats, academics, and corporate officials actively spread the gospel of Japanese capitalism in Eastern Europe.[151] Others warn that the Japanese model is inappropriate for this environment, just as it is in Africa or Latin America.[152]

The durability of the Japanese model is also debatable. For much of the postwar period, many observers—both Japanese and non-Japanese—maintained that the distinctive features of the Japanese economy represented faults or "distortions." As Japan developed, these distortions would disappear, and its economy would come to look more like those of rich Western nations, especially the United States. So far, many of these supposed defects have proven to be not only surprisingly resilient but also highly efficient. This is, of course, no guarantee that Japanese capitalism will not lose some of its singular characteristics over time. As this survey has shown, the past development of Japanese capitalism has not proceeded in a linear or otherwise predictable pattern. One clear lesson, however, is that modernization should not be confused with Westernization.

In the near future, Japan will assuredly remain an industrial and commercial superpower, although it is unlikely to be as dominant economically as Britain and the United States were at their peaks. Even so, Western observers have persistently underestimated Japan.[153] Going forward into the twenty-first century, those tempted to discount the strength of Japanese capitalism might heed the warning of a Russian medievalist: "History teaches nothing, but only punishes for not learning its lessons."[154]

PROLOGUE TO CHAPTER 13

In comparison with the earlier giants we have examined, such as Toyota, IBM, and the Deutsche Bank, the story of the humble 7-Eleven might seem an unusual chapter with which to end this book. But, as you'll discover, in business things aren't always what they seem.

As with the other companies we have discussed, the story of 7-Eleven began with specific ideas in the minds of individual entrepreneurs. In the United States, the key entrepreneur started to realize his vision in the 1920s. In Japan it didn't happen until the 1970s. There's a good deal of material in this chapter on convenience retailing in the United States, where the first 7-Eleven was born. But most of the text, and the real focus of the story, is on the Japanese side. There the chapter contains several surprises. One is that although the Japanese retail sector as a whole is less efficient than the American retail sector, 7-Eleven stores in Japan have performed much better than their American counterparts. The Japanese pupil not only surpassed its American teacher but also bailed it out and saved it from bankruptcy.

Another surprise, and the most important part of the chapter, is that the company operating 7-Eleven stores in Japan may constitute an authentic Third Industrial Revolution business. This company pioneered the innovative use of information technology, pushing it forward in ever more ingenious ways. As a matter of routine, it used on-line databases and point-of-sale computer terminals that recorded not only sales but also information about customers. It also developed novel ways to organize its suppliers, both manufacturers and wholesalers. The company had a very small workforce, and it carried so few tangible assets on its balance sheet that it might almost be regarded as a virtual corporation. Yet in market capitalization it ranked among the top 50 companies in the world.

How did such a striking situation evolve in convenience stores, of all places? How many kinds of companies will be able to exploit so thoroughly the forces of the Third Industrial Revolution? Is it possible that this is how business will be done in most industries during the twenty-first century?

In thinking about the experience of the Japanese 7-Eleven entrepreneur, Toshifumi Suzuki, you should ask yourself what forces and circumstances might have prevented the success he achieved. Why did he have such a hard time selling his ideas to his colleagues? When convenience stores finally did appear in Japan, why did they become so successful so fast?

In contrasting the differing experiences of 7-Eleven in America and Japan, would it be accurate to say that in the United States 7-Elevens remained stuck in business patterns characteristic of the Second Industrial Revolution, while their Japanese counterparts surged into the Third? This chapter suggests answers to that question.

❧13❧

7-ELEVEN IN AMERICA AND JAPAN

Jeffrey R. Bernstein

In March 1991, two Japanese firms paid $430 million to acquire a 70 percent share of the Southland Corporation. Southland was the operator of the 7-Eleven franchise chain of convenience stores in the United States and Canada and licenser of the 7-Eleven name to companies in 20 other countries. The cash infusion allowed Southland to emerge from bankruptcy. On the surface, this acquisition did not seem very different from other major Japanese takeovers of U.S. corporations during the late 1980s and early 1990s, such as Mitsubishi Real Estate's purchase of Rockefeller Center in 1989, Sony's acquisition of Columbia Pictures the same year, and Matsushita's takeover of MCA in 1990. However, the Southland acquisition was quite unusual in two major respects.

First, it occurred in retailing, an industry in which Japanese firms were not perceived as efficient.[1] The Japanese distribution system has been described as "premodern, archaic, Byzantine, outdated, anachronistic, or [a] maze."[2] Table 13.1 illustrates that relative to other industrialized nations Japan had many more retailers and wholesalers per capita, more layers of wholesalers, and smaller stores. Gigantic shopping malls and colossal individual stores such as Wal-Mart have a much smaller presence in Japan than in Europe and North America.

The second unusual aspect of the Southland acquisition was the identity of the buyers: Ito-Yokado (pronounced EE-toh YOH-kah-doh) and Seven-Eleven Japan. (The company uses the word "Seven" in its title instead of the digit "7" as in its logo.) Ito-Yokado was a Japanese retailing giant. Seventeen years earlier, it had licensed the 7-Eleven name from Southland and, as part of the deal, had received instruction in operating convenience stores. Ito-Yokado stood at the center of a retailing group that encompassed supermarkets, department stores, discount stores, spe-

Table 13.1 International Comparison of Distribution Systems, Mid-1980s

	U.K.	Germany (West)	U.S.	Japan
Retail Stores per 1000 residents	6.1	6.7	8.1	13.5
Wholesale Outlets per 1000 residents	n/a	2.1	1.6	3.4
Ratio of Wholesale Transactions to Retail Ones	n/a	1.8	1.9	4.2
Number of Workers per Retail Store	6.8	5.8	7.5	3.9
Market Share of Small Retailers (<10 workers)	23.3%	21.3%	13.7%	48.9%
Market Share of Large Retailers (>100 workers)	63.6%	44.9%	65.2%	15.0%

Sources: Service Sector Productivity (Washington: McKinsey Global Institute, 1992), exhibit 2D-13; and Motoshige Itoh, "The Japanese Distribution System and Access to the Japanese Market," in Paul Krugman, ed., *Trade with Japan: Has the Door Opened Wider?* (Chicago: University of Chicago Press, 1991), table 6.1.

cialty stores, and restaurants (including Denny's Japan). Another core member of this group—and the co-purchaser of Southland—was Seven-Eleven Japan, which Ito-Yokado had established to run its convenience-store operations. At the time of the Southland acquisition, Seven-Eleven Japan presided over 4,300 convenience stores in Japan and 58 in Hawaii.

The acquisition of Southland was one illustration of how far Seven-Eleven Japan had come in its short existence. At the same time, Southland's bankruptcy and subsequent bailout represented a fall from grace for the pioneer of the American convenience-store industry. But this tale of two convenience stores is more than just the story of two firms following different trajectories. It illustrates some of the differences between the retailing environments of Japan and the United States, and it illuminates aspects of the shift from the Second to the Third Industrial Revolution.[3]

In the Beginning: Southland's History to 1973

During the second half of the nineteenth century in the United States, the widespread application of mass-production techniques associated with the Second Industrial Revolution was accompanied by a retailing revolution.[4] In this period there arose chain stores such as the A&P, urban department stores such as Macy's and Filene's, and mail-order houses such as Sears, Roebuck and Montgomery Ward. By comparison with older kinds of stores, each of these three new types of retailers aimed for large sales volumes at low margins. Taking advantage of steep declines in transportation costs brought about by the railroads, the new retailers grew and prospered, helping to usher in a nationwide mass market. In the early twentieth century, rapidly expanding automobile ownership reduced the importance of catalog houses but promoted the growth of department stores and especially of chain stores. The decade of the 1920s has been called the "chain store age," because of the proliferation of drugstore, grocery, and apparel chains during those years.[5]

The convenience store dates from that same period. Southland, founded in 1927, claims to have been the world's first convenience-store chain.[6] It began as the Southland Ice Company, formed from a merger of four Dallas firms controlling 8 ice factories and 21 retail ice docks. A man named Claude Dawley brought about the merger as a means of expanding his family's ice business, and he convinced the wealthy Martin Insull of Middle West Utilities to provide financing. Also in 1927, an enterprising Southland dock employee named John Green, urged by his customers to provide some staple foods, began stocking bread, milk, and eggs in addition to ice. This venture proved to be quite popular and profitable, so it was expanded to the other ice docks. The name "Tote'm" (along with an Indian totem pole displayed out front) was adopted by these stores, each of which offered a small selection of groceries. Gasoline too was sold at some stores.

Tote'm Stores prospered even during the Great Depression. But Middle West Utilities went bankrupt, triggering a financial crisis that drove Southland itself into bankruptcy. At that point a 31-year-old member of Southland's board of directors named Joe Thompson was appointed receiver by the court, and he directed the company's reorganization. The repeal of Prohibition in 1933 was especially helpful to Southland. Its stores could now stock beer, plus more ice for keeping the beer cool. By 1939, it had recovered to the point that it operated 60 Tote'm Stores in the Dallas area.

During World War II, the ice industry boomed. Tote'm Stores flourished as well, with the beer business showing especially strong gains.

During the 1940s, Southland became the largest ice company in Dallas. Its most significant action during this decade was the decision in 1946 to adopt the "7-Eleven" name for its stores. This name, developed by a Dallas advertising agency, referred to the stores' operating hours: 7 A.M. to 11 P.M. By 1950, 80 7-Eleven stores were operating in the Dallas–Fort Worth area, and annual store revenues had increased to about $10 million.

In the early 1950s, the company expanded beyond Dallas–Fort Worth, opening new stores in Austin and Houston. In 1954, Southland moved outside Texas and opened five stores in Miami and Jacksonville. In the late 1950s, still more 7-Eleven stores were built in the Washington, D.C., area. Despite Southland executives' worries that convenience stores could not prosper in a colder climate, the new stores were immediately successful. Meanwhile, the company was also expanding locally, and it acquired its major competitor in Dallas in 1959. By 1960, Southland was operating a total of 490 convenience stores.

The 1960s were a time of even more rapid expansion, in part because of a change in leadership. Following the death of Joe Thompson in 1961, his son John became president. As John Thompson later recalled, "Dad wanted to expand, but he was just more cautious about it than we have been . . . He went through the Depression and saw the company go into bankruptcy. This would naturally make you very cautious."[7] Less apprehensive about the future than his father had been, John Thompson pushed hard to expand. In the period from 1960 to 1965, the number of Southland's convenience stores more than tripled, from 490 to 1,519, and by 1970 it climbed to 3,537.

Central to Southland's growth spurt was its acquisition in 1963 of Speedee Mart, a chain of 126 franchised convenience stores in California. As John Thompson acknowledged, "Speedee Mart gave us the know-how and expertise that we needed in franchising."[8] Southland now began franchising its stores for the first time. It would lease a fully equipped store to a franchisee who then paid Southland a percentage of the profits. Franchising enabled Southland to expand more quickly than it ever had before. The company continued to operate many stores of its own, however, and franchised stores never accounted for more than about half of 7-Eleven stores in the United States.

Southland also expanded geographically, so that by 1970 there were stores in 38 states, Washington, D.C., and three Canadian provinces.[9]

The number of shareholders grew from 317 in 1960 to almost 9,500 in 1972, the year Southland was listed on the New York Stock Exchange. By 1973, Southland had become a convenience-store empire, encompassing nearly 5,000 7-Eleven stores with revenues of $1.4 billion and net earnings of $23 million.[10]

REASONS FOR SOUTHLAND'S GROWTH

Southland's success had been facilitated by favorable market conditions. Large self-service supermarkets had arisen in the United States in the 1930s, but their growth had been constrained first by economic depression and then by wartime restrictions. Beginning in the 1950s, supermarkets rapidly began to drive neighborhood mom-and-pop stores out of business. This trend accelerated in the 1960s, thereby providing the convenience store with a niche: customers in a hurry, who wished to buy only a few items. Southland and other convenience chains exploited this niche by locating their stores near residential areas, more often in fast-growing suburbs than in urban centers. By lengthening their hours of operation, sometimes to 24 hours, convenience stores further differentiated themselves from supermarkets.[11]

Southland's superb performance did not come automatically, of course. The company displayed remarkable creativity and a willingness to experiment with new ideas, especially new product offerings. As noted earlier, Southland began even in the 1920s to sell gasoline at some of its ice docks. In 1935, it pioneered the use of paper milk cartons. Its best-known product innovation was the "Slurpee" frozen carbonated drink. This item was developed by a manufacturer of machines dispensing frozen beverages, but Southland created the Slurpee name and aggressively marketed the product in its stores. In 1965 it bought three dispensing machines on a trial basis. The following year, with machines in hundreds of its stores, it sold 150 million Slurpees. Naturally, not all product introductions were as successful as the Slurpee. A line of fast foods with microwave ovens, which Southland introduced in the late 1950s, proved to be ahead of its time.

Southland was also a leader in providing new services. By the mid-1950s, it sold money orders, television tube testers, and key-making machines. In the late 1960s, 7-Eleven stores rented out floor polishers, rug shampooers, and television sets. Some of these services soon became obsolete, but others are still offered today. After the U.S. Post Office, Southland remains the nation's second biggest seller of money orders, and it is the largest seller of state-sponsored lottery tickets. 7-Eleven became known as "the little store which has everything."[12]

In management, too, Southland exhibited some innovations. One was its early adoption of employee profit sharing, initiated in 1949. Another was its development in 1969 of a new distribution system. During that year Joe Hardin, the outgoing head of the Army and Air Force Exchange Service (the PX system), was hired to design the new system, the cornerstone of which was a network of regional Southland Distribution Centers. These centers used computerized methods of inventory control, merchandise handling, and delivery, in order to reduce in-store inventories and simplify small-lot delivery to stores. By 1973, three such centers were in operation, serving over half of all 7-Eleven stores. At that time, and even for a number of years afterward, this system was praised as state-of-the-art.[13]

The Coming of Convenience Stores to Japan

The convenience-store industry arose in Japan much later than it had in the United States. The reasons are rooted in the overall history of retailing in Japan.

The first large Japanese department stores emerged in the early 1900s, about 40 years after the appearance of their counterparts in the United States. Most of these Japanese stores had previously been retailers of kimonos or cotton apparel and had histories that stretched back several hundred years. For example, Mitsukoshi, which became Japan's first modern department store in 1904, had been established as a kimono dealer in 1673.[14] During the 1920s and 1930s, some different kinds of companies entered the department-store business. Many of these new entrants, such as Seibu and Tokyu, were railway enterprises. They situated their department stores within or adjacent to their busy terminals.

The rise of department stores in Japan, as in the United States and other countries, threatened the livelihood of many small shopkeepers. Like small retailers everywhere, they agitated for limits on aggressive price-cutting by the big stores, and tried to get public authorities to limit their expansion. To forestall government intervention, the Japan Department Store Association in the mid-1930s established voluntary restraints on the growth of department stores. These restraints proved unsatisfactory to small shopkeepers. In 1937 the Imperial Diet passed the landmark Department Store Law, placing the industry under strict regulation.

Conflict between small and large retailers, and between old retailing formats and newer ones, has been common across many countries. In the 1920s and 1930s, the United States was the scene of fierce battles between small and large retailers, over such matters as retail price maintenance, volume discounts, and the expansion of chain stores.[15] Small retailers in the United States won a few victories, such as the Robinson-Patman Act of 1936, which limited the extent to which big retailers could command volume discounts from wholesalers. In most cases, however, the big retailers prevailed, in large part because federal courts in the United States tended to rule unconstitutional any legislation discriminating against big retailers. In Japan, the outcome of the battle between small and large retailers more often went the other way. Consumers' interest in low prices was subordinated to the preservation of existing small stores.

After passage of the 1937 Department Store Law, and especially after the onset of World War II, friction between large and small retailers in Japan temporarily subsided. During the Allied Occupation of Japan, the Department Store Law was overturned, but the issue soon arose again, and in 1956 a similar provision was enacted. It too was known as the Department Store Law (DSL). The DSL required permission from Japan's Ministry of International Trade and Industry (MITI) for the opening or expansion of any retail store larger than 1,500 square meters, which is about the size of a small American supermarket. (For 10 major Japanese cities, the figure was set at 3,000 square meters.) In actual practice, MITI's permission was very difficult to obtain, and even for the successful applications, it often came only after four to seven years' delay.[16]

There was a loophole in the DSL, however, and a few shrewd businesspeople moved quickly to exploit it. The law applied to single businesses, so some entrepreneurs created stores with several floors, each less than 1,500 square meters and administered by a separate company. These multistoried general merchandise outlets, which carried groceries, clothing, and other household products at relatively low prices, became known as superstores. Some entrepreneurs even began to operate chains of superstores. Although such practices constituted a violation of the spirit of the DSL, regulatory authorities overlooked them in order to further the goal of modernizing the distribution sector.[17] Nor did small retailers complain much. There were not very many superstores, and in any case, Japan's economy during the 1960s grew at a real rate of more than 10 percent per year. Thus, the expansion of superstores did not prevent small stores from growing as well. The DSL did circumscribe the growth of established department stores, which were more conservative and more closely scrutinized by regulatory officials than the up-and-coming superstores. As a result, by the early 1970s some superstore chains had leapfrogged past the department stores to become the largest retailers in Japan (see Table 13.2).

THE BIRTH OF ITO-YOKADO

One of the most innovative of the new superstores was Ito-Yokado. By 1972, it was Japan's seventeenth largest retailer, with sales of ¥26 billion ($85 million).[18] By 1980, as Table 13.2 shows, Ito-Yokado was second in size only to Daiei (pronounced DIE-ay). Along with the Saison Group (which includes the superstore Seiyu and the department store Seibu), Daiei and Ito-Yokado have been the leaders of Japanese retailing and the two most direct competitors since the mid-1960s.[19] They have very different traditions.

Table 13.2   The Ten Largest Japanese Retailers, Ranked by Sales (¥ billion)

1960			1972			1980			1993		
Company		Sales	Company		Sales	Company		Sales	Company		Sales
Mitsukoshi	D	45	Daiei	S	305	Daiei	S	1,134	Daiei	S	2,073
Daimaru	D	45	Mitsukoshi	D	292	Ito-Yokado	S	688	Ito-Yokado	S	1,536
Takashimaya	D	39	Daimaru	D	213	Seiyu	S	599	Jusco	S	1,061
Matsuzakaya	D	37	Takashimaya	D	199	Jusco	S	554	Seiyu	S	1,050
Toyoko	D	30	Seiyu	S	167	Mitsukoshi	D	546	Nichii	S	822
Isetan	D	23	Seibu	D	155	Nichii	S	455	Mitsukoshi	D	801
Hankyu	D	21	Jusco	S	155	Daimaru	D	421	Takashimaya	D	724
Seibu	D	19	Matsuzakaya	D	149	Takashimaya	D	415	Seibu	D	681
Sogo	D	15	Nichii	S	144	Seibu	D	375	Uny	S	577
Matsuya	D	12	Uny	S	126	Uny	S	126	Daimaru	D	543

Note: D denotes department-store company, S superstore chain. Exchange rates were as follows: 1960: ¥360 = $1. 1972: ¥303 = $1. 1980: ¥227 = $1. 1993: ¥111 = $1.

Sources: For 1960–1980: Roy Larke, *Japanese Retailing* (London: Routledge, 1994), p. 109. For 1993: *Japan 1995: An International Comparison* (Tokyo: Keizai Koho Center, 1995), p. 28.

Daiei had roots in western Japan, specifically Osaka. Founded by Isao Nakauchi in 1957, it began as a discount pharmacy called The Housewives' Store Daiei. Nakauchi then diversified from drugs and cosmetics into groceries and a wide variety of household products. Building new stores and acquiring other superstore chains, he quickly expanded his business. By 1964, he presided over a chain of 20 superstores. Growth was paramount for Nakauchi. Later he would expand into domains unrelated to retailing, such as publishing, finance, and even professional baseball. Nakauchi placed a great premium on land ownership, as indicated by his stated belief that "in Japan business opportunities come only to those who own land and real estate."[20] In many ways, Daiei's expansion strategy was an extension of the personality of Isao Nakauchi, a brash leader throughout his storied career, unafraid of confrontation and often welcoming it.[21]

Ito-Yokado had its origins in Tokyo. Its founder, Masatoshi Ito, first worked at Mitsubishi Mining, but after World War II he resigned to help manage the family store. Following the death of his older brother in 1956, Masatoshi Ito took command of the family business, which at the time consisted of one medium-sized supermarket with 20 employees and annual sales of ¥100 million ($280,000). In 1961, Ito was invited by one of his suppliers, National Cash Register, to a group excursion to the United States. During this trip, the first of many visits to America by Ito, he was impressed by the prosperity of large chain stores he saw there. Ito became convinced that chain stores could thrive in Japan as well. In 1962 he incorporated the family business, using the name Yokado, and began opening superstores.[22] By 1964, he was presiding over a chain of eight superstores in the Tokyo area, and in 1965 he changed the company name to Ito-Yokado.

In its expansion, Ito-Yokado was more deliberate than Daiei and less reliant on acquisitions and diversification. In contrast to Daiei's push for growth, Ito-Yokado emphasized profitability. Whereas Daiei rushed to accumulate land and buildings for its stores, Ito-Yokado preferred to keep its asset base low and rent as many of its facilities as possible. This last difference had major implications for how the two superstore chains gained external financing. Daiei, with abundant real estate holdings that could be used as collateral, borrowed heavily from Japanese banks. Ito-Yokado, by contrast, had no such recourse and instead pioneered new ways to raise funds. These included innovative leaseback agreements and the sale of yen-denominated debentures to the Kuwaiti government, an almost unheard-of arrangement for a Japanese company.[23]

In spite of these differences, by the early 1970s both Daiei and Ito-Yokado, and indeed all superstores, confronted a common problem. Hurt by increasing competition from superstores and by slower Japanese economic growth, small retailers and wholesalers once again used their considerable political power to urge politicians to limit the expansion of superstore chains. Soon it became clear that superstore firms would no longer be able to build large stores as easily as they had in the past. To grow, they now would have to find other businesses in which expansion was less restricted. Though it was far from clear at the time, convenience stores were a solution to their dilemma.

THE RISE OF CONVENIENCE STORES

The convenience-store concept was already attracting interest in Japan, but mostly from hard-pressed small retailers and especially wholesalers, who began to organize "voluntary chains." Such chains were actually associations of small retailers. They were less tightly organized than franchised chains, and they demanded less standardization of store design and operating policy. They also offered less guidance and support to members.[24]

In 1969, a voluntary chain called My Shop became the first convenience store to open in Japan. Other voluntary chains soon followed, including Izumi Foods and K Mart. (The latter had no relation to the U.S. company. Japanese firms often used names derived from English to project a "modern" image.) On the whole, the voluntary-chain movement was embraced by government officials, who viewed it as a way of preserving small stores and increasing their productivity. In 1972, a bureau within MITI called the Small and Medium-Size Enterprise Agency published a "Convenience Store Manual" to help small retailers and wholesalers form voluntary chains.[25]

Other companies, mostly wholesalers and food manufacturers, also made tentative moves into convenience-store retailing. Then, in 1973, Seiyu became the first superstore chain to venture into convenience stores. It opened a pilot outlet under the name FamilyMart in a Tokyo suburb.[26]

Yet none of these initial efforts had the same galvanizing effect as the launch of Seven-Eleven Japan, which was the nation's first large-scale entry into the convenience-store sector. The decision to launch this enterprise was largely attributable to one man: Toshifumi Suzuki, a young executive who eventually became president of Ito-Yokado and chairman of Seven-Eleven Japan.[27]

Toshifumi Suzuki had begun his career at a publishing distributor. In 1963, when he was 31 years old, he met Masatoshi Ito and was so impressed that he quit his job in publishing and joined Ito's fledgling retail chain. By 1971, Suzuki had become a director of Ito-Yokado. In the spring of that same year, Suzuki made several trips to the United States to negotiate a licensing agreement with the Denny's restaurant chain. Through these trips, he came into contact with American convenience stores. He was particularly impressed by the number of 7-Eleven stores he encountered. In September 1971, he proposed starting a convenience-store franchise chain in Japan.[28]

Suzuki's proposal met with violent opposition at Ito-Yokado. Many managers inside the company believed that Ito-Yokado should continue building large stores to exploit economies of scale and scope. Other company officials, along with outside consultants, economists, and industry experts, maintained that the convenience-store concept offered nothing not already provided by the hundreds of thousands of traditional small shops in Japan. Suzuki, by contrast, argued that convenience stores could generate profits for Ito-Yokado while simultaneously easing friction between large and small stores. He saw the large number of small stores not as an obstacle but as an opportunity. Acutely aware of the low productivity of most small retailers in Japan, Suzuki envisioned a franchise system, under which Ito-Yokado would supply managerial techniques and support to small stores in return for a percentage of their profits. He looked to Southland, with its large network of 7-Eleven stores in the United States and Canada, as a source of knowledge about administering a franchise system. Suzuki eventually prevailed over the skeptics and convinced Masatoshi Ito at least to explore a deal with Southland.

Southland was not interested in the proposal at first, but again Suzuki persisted. Even after the initial resistance was overcome, negotiations bogged down on a number of sticking points. Southland demanded (1) a joint venture with Ito-Yokado; (2) a division of the Japanese market into two parts, with Ito-Yokado obtaining the rights to the 7-Eleven name for only eastern Japan; (3) a royalty equal to one percent of sales; and (4) the opening of at least 2,000 stores within eight years.

On the first two of these points, Ito-Yokado was emphatic: it would not take part in any joint venture, and it sought the rights for all of Japan.[29] It also pressed for a reduction in the royalty rate and in the minimum number of stores. Ultimately, Southland conceded the first two points and compromised on the last two. It lowered the royalty rate to 0.6 percent of sales and the minimum number of stores to 1,200.[30] On these terms, a licensing agreement was signed in November 1973.

The letter to shareholders in Southland's 1973 annual report declared, "We are extremely pleased that Southland will be participating in the modernization of Japan's retail food distribution system . . . We are extremely optimistic about the future of this venture."[31] Little did anyone know how prescient that assessment would prove to be.

The licensing agreement of 1973 resulted in the creation of Seven-Eleven Japan to operate the new Japanese convenience-store chain. At first, the new organization was called York Seven, "York" being an abbreviated form of "Yokado." It was set up as a wholly owned subsidiary of Ito-Yokado. Ito and Suzuki established a separate entity because they saw convenience stores as being fundamentally different from Ito-Yokado's core superstore business. For the same reason, almost all of York Seven's initial 15 employees had job experience from outside the retail sector. In the words of Seven-Eleven Japan's official corporate history, a "bunch of amateurs" had been entrusted with starting the new business.[32] Even so, Toshifumi Suzuki was York Seven's president, and Masatoshi Ito its chairman.

Before beginning operations, a subgroup of the "amateurs" was dispatched to America to receive training from Southland. Ito-Yokado already had a strong orientation toward profits, but the Japanese trainees were impressed with Southland's philosophy that convenience stores should not become embroiled in price competition with supermarkets.[33] They also realized the value of Southland's well-developed accounting system, which they perceived to be an important vehicle for building trust between the parent company and the franchisees.[34] But Suzuki and the other employees soon realized that the scope of potential borrowing from Southland was limited. To succeed in Japan, they would have to create a new system adapted specifically to the Japanese environment. Their many innovations will be discussed later in this chapter, but first it is worth looking at the results they achieved.

Seven-Eleven Japan and Its Performance

The corporate name York Seven was changed to Seven-Eleven Japan in 1978. Partially spun off by Ito-Yokado, it was listed on the Tokyo Stock Exchange in 1979. From the establishment of its first store in May 1974, Seven-Eleven Japan (including its years as York Seven) compiled a remarkable performance record. The number of stores rose steadily, hitting 1,000 in 1980, 2,000 in 1984, 3,000 in 1987, 4,000 in 1990, 5,000 in 1993, and 6,000 in 1995. Sales and profits also exhibited consistently strong growth (see Table 13.3).

Unlike superstores, whose initial expansion occurred during Japan's high-growth period, Seven-Eleven Japan managed to expand rapidly in an era of slower overall economic progress. The company also faced severe competition from new entrants into the convenience chain business. The most prominent rivals were Daiei's Lawson and the Saison Group's FamilyMart, but many smaller competitors emerged as well. (In

Table 13.3   The Growth of Seven-Eleven Japan

Year[a]	Store Sales (¥ million)	Revenue[b] (¥ million)	Net Income (¥ million)	Number of Stores	Number of Employees[c]	Inventory per Store (¥ 1000)	Gross Profit[d] (%)	Daily Sales[e] (¥ 1000)
1975	726	406	−158	15	45	n/a	n/a	n/a
1976	4,769	1,320	−41	69	91	n/a	n/a	n/a
1977	17,401	3,067	365	199	161	n/a	24.0	365
1980	109,775	16,619	1,815	801	489	7,739	25.0	436
1983	256,470	49,176	5,179	1,643	890	6,230	26.8	482
1986	453,616	83,757	11,628	2,651	1,189	5,471	27.4	506
1989	686,356	100,246	22,304	3,653	1,489	5,129	28.3	545
1992	1,081,871	162,820	40,674	4,687	1,814	5,165	29.0	670
1995	1,392,312	214,560	49,525	5,952	2,364	5,114	29.6	676

a. Refers to Seven-Eleven Japan's fiscal year, which ends on the last day of February of the calendar year.
b. Equals royalties from franchise stores, plus sales from company-owned stores, plus other revenues.
c. This figure does not include franchisees and their employees.
d. Average gross profit on merchandise sold in 7-Eleven stores in Japan.
e. Average daily sales per store.
Source: Compiled from sources obtained from Seven-Eleven Japan.

Table 13.4   The Five Leading Japanese Convenience Store Chains, 1995

	Store Name	Parent Company or Group	From Year	Store Sales (¥ bil.)	Number of Stores	Daily Sales[a] (¥ 1000)	Franchise Stores[b] (%)	Number of Prefectures Covered
1	Seven-Eleven	Ito-Yokado Group	1973	1,392	5,952	689	96	21
2	Lawson	Daiei Group	1975	821	5,139	450	80[d]	41
3	FamilyMart	Saison Group	1978[c]	471	3,454	513	97	31
4	Yamazaki Daily Store/Sun Every	Yamazaki Bread	1977	353	2,616	379	95	38
5	Circle K	Uny	1979	275	1,734	462	92	19

a. Average daily sales per store.
b. Area franchises are included as franchise stores in the calculation of these percentages.
c. A trial FamilyMart store was opened in 1973, but the full-scale launch of the business occurred in 1978.
d. Estimate from *Konbini* (Convenience Store), Fall-Winter 1995, p. 44.
Source: Compiled from *Konbini* (Convenience Store), Fall-Winter 1995 and Spring-Summer 1996.

1973, there were only 500 convenience stores in all of Japan, but by 1995, there were 46,834.)[35] Still, Seven-Eleven Japan quickly became the country's largest convenience chain and was still in this position in the mid-1990s (see Table 13.4).

Seven-Eleven Japan's accomplishments transcend the convenience-store sector. It is Japan's largest food retailer and, with parent Ito-Yokado, the most profitable Japanese retailer overall.[36] A 1995 study identified Seven-Eleven and Microsoft as the two firms that best synthesized the outstanding elements of Japanese and Western management practice.[37] In that same year, a survey conducted by Japan's leading business newspaper named Seven-Eleven Japan as the most exceptional Japanese company in any industry.[38]

Seven-Eleven Japan's enormous market value indicated how much investors appreciated its profitability and growth potential. By the mid-1990s, it had become the world's 46th-largest publicly traded noninsurance company, as measured by market capitalization. (Parent Ito-Yokado was ranked 70th.) Table 13.5 shows its size in relation to a number of well-known large companies.

Seven-Eleven Japan's achievements did not stop at the individual firm level. It also played an important role in the Ito-Yokado Group, through its ability to generate cash flow and through its influence on the operations of other companies in the group.[39] At a societal level, it served as an important conduit for introducing information technology into small stores

Table 13.5　World's Largest Public Noninsurance Corporations, Ranked by Market Value

Rank	Company (Country)	Market Value	Rank	Company (Country)	Market Value
4	Toyota Motor (Japan)	$78,788	55	Intel (U.S.)	$26,111
14	Wal-Mart Stores (U.S.)	57,469	64	Nippon Steel (Japan)	22,972
23	General Motors (U.S.)	36,990	69	Sony (Japan)	21,900
24	IBM (U.S.)	36,018	70	*Ito-Yokado (Japan)*	21,791
43	Microsoft (U.S.)	29,232	71	Deutsche Bank (Germany)	21,740
46	*Seven-Eleven Japan (Japan)*	28,344	86	McDonald's (U.S.)	19,161

Note: Market value as measured in $U.S. million, at prevailing exchange rates as of July 31, 1994.
Source: Wall Street Journal, September 30, 1994, p. R26.

and as a persistent force for rationalizing Japan's distribution channels. Similar to Wal-Mart in the United States, Seven-Eleven Japan exemplified the coming of the Third Industrial Revolution to retailing. Both it and its parent company Ito-Yokado have been likened to Wal-Mart, and Masatoshi Ito has been described as "the Sam Walton of Japan."[40]

GENERAL FACTORS BEHIND THE GROWTH OF SEVEN-ELEVEN JAPAN

At first glance, it may seem surprising that something as quintessentially American as the convenience store would prosper in Japan. Yet part of its appeal there may have sprung from its perception as foreign and therefore different from the typical Japanese small store. Perhaps to reinforce this impression, most of the major convenience chains in Japan adopted foreign-sounding names.[41] The perception of foreignness, rather than the reality, seemed to be the important thing. By one count, Seven-Eleven Japan directly imported only three items from the United States, and as of 1994, the share of all imported goods in Seven-Eleven Japan's sales was less than one percent.[42]

Seven-Eleven Japan was helped by some favorable market conditions, much as had been the case earlier with Southland in the United States. One factor, peculiar to Japan, was the changing regulatory environment. In 1974, the year the first 7-Eleven store opened in Japan, a new law limiting the spread of large stores went into effect. At first, this Large Store Law (LSL) was well received by nearly all retailers, for two reasons.[43] First, in contrast to the Department Store Law of 1956 (DSL), its stated purpose was to consider consumers' interests as well as to protect small retailers. In addition, the LSL adopted a notification and recommendation procedure that appeared less restrictive than that of the permit-based DSL.[44] In practice, however, the LSL was not implemented according to its statutory framework. Control of the process was ceded to regional associations of shopkeepers, who naturally opposed almost any opening of new stores. Over time, the LSL was made still more restrictive. In 1978 it was modified to cover even smaller stores of 500 square meters, and the approval process became still more decentralized and time-consuming.[45]

These regulatory shackles on large and medium-sized stores benefited convenience stores. Since chains such as Seven-Eleven Japan fulfilled both aspirations of the regulators—modernizing the distribution system while raising the productivity of small retailers—they were not required to limit their operating hours. The new stores were thus able to position themselves as being "time convenient," staying open longer than traditional small stores, sometimes even for 24 hours. This was extremely unusual in Japan, especially since the LSL limited the operating hours of large stores.[46] (In banking, too, the hours of operation for automatic teller machines were regulated for a long time, ostensibly to protect small banks.)[47] To emphasize this point, an early advertising campaign of Seven-Eleven Japan used the catch-line "Great, it's open!"

The LSL drove many superstores to follow Ito-Yokado and establish new convenience-store chains. Of the five largest such chains in Japan in the 1990s, four were affiliated with retailing groups organized around superstores: Seven-Eleven with Ito-Yokado, Lawson with Daiei, FamilyMart with Seiyu, and Circle K with Uny.[48] In general, convenience stores in Japan were not competitors of superstores but rather an alternate means of expansion by superstore companies. In America, by contrast, convenience stores usually arose as independent competitors to existing supermarkets.[49]

Corporate groups have been very important to the leading convenience chains in Japan. Many of the first products sold in 7-Eleven stores were selected by Ito-Yokado. Also, Seven-Eleven Japan was able to get wholesalers to accede to its requests even when it had only a few stores, largely because of Ito-Yokado's market power.[50] Lawson, a major competitor, needed the deep pockets of its parent Daiei to survive a disastrous start.[51]

The relationship between superstores and convenience stores in Japan suggests that the two types would not, as *sectors,* engage in fierce competition. Of course, individual superstores no doubt sought to steal business from their rivals' convenience stores. But price, the biggest weapon that large stores possessed relative to convenience stores, was traditionally not a key competitive variable in Japanese retailing. The lack of price competition in Japanese retailing, wrote one scholar of the industry, has resulted in "generally uniform prices for the same items across store types."[52]

With the prolonged recession in Japan during the 1990s, this situation began to change. The term "price destruction" *(kakaku hakai)* became a buzzword as some retailers sought to increase market share by drastically lowering prices. For instance, Daiei caused a stir by offering a private-label cola for ¥40 per can, one-third the price of branded products such as Coca-Cola. Still, the extent of "price destruction" should not be over-emphasized. Discount stores still occupied only a small part of the overall retail sector, and price competition remained tame by U.S. standards.[53]

Another reason convenience stores were relatively sheltered from competition from larger retailers was location. Because of high urban land prices, superstores tended to locate in the suburbs, but Japanese convenience stores were established in urban areas. Also, unlike their U.S. counterparts, Japanese convenience stores faced little competition from gas stations selling food and other items.[54] Nor was the competition from fast-food chains as severe as it was in the United States. Japanese convenience stores did compete with vending machines, which are ubiquitous in Japan. These machines offer everything from canned coffee to alcoholic beverages to magazines. By one estimate, there was one vending machine for every 30 people in Japan, as compared with one per 55 people in the United States.[55]

Even so, the main competition for convenience stores in Japan was the huge number of existing mom-and-pop stores. Food retailing, the bulk of convenience stores' business, was even more fragmented among thousands of tiny stores than was other retailing in Japan.[56] Traditional mom-and-pop stores usually could not match the convenience stores in the variety of goods or hours of operation. Nor did they provide the wide variety of services typically available at the new convenience stores, such as copying and facsimile machines, payment of utility bills, and even bicycle insurance. The broad array of services accounted for only a small fraction of sales, and by themselves were generally not profitable for the individual store.[57] But they certainly attracted customers. In addition, convenience stores had access to new managerial know-how and sophisticated guidance from large parent companies. Given all of these advantages, it was not surprising that they displaced large numbers of mom-and-pop stores.[58]

Contrary to many people's expectations, therefore, convenience stores fulfilled a need not being satisfied by traditional Japanese retailers. They offered what consumers regarded as the main advantages of traditional small stores, namely accessibility and customer service, while remedying their biggest disadvantage, an inadequate assortment of goods.[59]

Accessibility was important because of shopping patterns in Japan. Japanese homes were significantly less spacious than American ones and somewhat smaller than most European ones. The scarcity of storage space, in conjunction with a strong preference for freshness, led Japanese consumers to shop frequently. Because of the nation's relatively narrow and crowded roads, Japanese people tended to shop close by or use public transportation. All of these factors discouraged trips to the supermarket and made convenience stores relatively attractive. In addition, increased female participation in the workforce favored convenience stores, with their extended operating hours.

These elements help to account for the general growth of the convenience-store sector in Japan, but they cannot explain why some convenience chains outperformed others. Until the 1980s, nearly all participants in this industry prospered and grew. But after a deluge of new entries during the late 1970s and early 1980s, some convenience chains, especially small regional ones, encountered stagnant sales and declining profitability. Even between Seven-Eleven Japan and its large competitors, there were great disparities in performance, which suggest an important role for firm-specific factors.

FIRM-SPECIFIC REASONS FOR THE SUCCESS OF SEVEN-ELEVEN JAPAN

At least four strategies contributed to Seven-Eleven Japan's remarkable success: its franchise system and market-dominance strategy, its rationalization of distribution, its coordination of production of food products, and its investment in information technology. Each of these strategies merits a closer look.

The Franchise System and the Market-Dominance Strategy

Although Seven-Eleven Japan learned how to run a franchise system from Southland, it took a different approach. Southland's usual procedure was to buy or lease a plot of land, construct a store, and then arrange through a franchise contract to have someone else operate the store. Seven-Eleven Japan, in complete contrast, carefully selected existing mom-and-pop stores and persuaded their owners to convert their stores into 7-Elevens. This ingenious method did not encroach directly on the domain of small shopkeepers and thereby minimized potentially explosive political opposition. It also demanded little capital expenditure by Seven-Eleven Japan on property and development. (The company strictly avoided investing in real estate. Its head office, for instance, shared a modest, leased building with the other companies of the Ito-Yokado Group.)

From the beginning, Seven-Eleven Japan emphasized its commitment to small stores. Toshifumi Suzuki insisted that the very first 7-Eleven store in Japan be a franchise, rather than a company-managed pilot shop as Southland had recommended. Still, it was no easy task to get the franchise system off the ground. Convenience stores were an untried concept in Japan, and many store owners were reluctant to relinquish their independence and replace their store names with the 7-Eleven logo. The first franchisees were mainly young owners whose businesses were struggling and who were unsure about their future. In fact, the first 7-Eleven franchisee was a 23-year-old owner of a liquor store who saw little future growth in the liquor distribution business.[60] Only after he and other Seven-Eleven Japan franchisees began to show positive results did other types of store owners begin to take an interest.

Seven-Eleven Japan's service to its franchisees soon became famous in Japan, and for good reason. For example, should normal truck delivery routes be disrupted, the company proved willing to deliver goods by motorcycle, boat, or even helicopter.[61] Seven-Eleven Japan also reduced the risk for prospective franchisees by offering a guaranteed minimum level of profitability.[62] The company prepared detailed, comprehensive, yet easy-to-understand manuals for store operation and employee training.[63] A front-line employee, known as an Operation Field Counselor (OFC), became responsible for helping franchisees with decisions on ordering, merchandising, and display. Each OFC covered eight stores, which he (or, occasionally, she) visited twice a week, for at least two hours per visit.

This guidance was supplemented by considerable control from the top. Seven-Eleven Japan insisted on a strict contract with its franchisees. It stipulated that each store remain open every day of the year. The contract ran for 15 years, a very long period but one considered necessary to instill a sense of "business" into franchisees used to running a family proprietorship. In selecting prospective franchisees, Seven-Eleven Japan shrewdly targeted liquor-store owners, who possessed valuable and difficult-to-obtain liquor licenses and also tended to be in desirable high-traffic locations.

Seven-Eleven Japan also relied heavily on a "market-dominance" strategy. This term refers to a policy of expanding only into areas where new stores could be clustered. The faithfulness with which Seven-Eleven Japan has followed the market-dominance strategy can be seen by looking back at the last column of Table 13.4 (p. 505), which compares the geographic distribution of its stores with that of other chains. Despite having more stores than any of its rivals, in the mid-1990s Seven-Eleven Japan was active in only 21 of Japan's 47 prefectures. By so clustering its stores, the company served three goals: to block the entry of other convenience chains, to increase the efficiency of its distribution and franchise-support activities, and to increase its name recognition and improve the cost-effectiveness of its advertising expenditures within a given area.[64]

The market-dominance strategy was a double-edged sword, of course. Although it yielded many benefits, it also permitted competitors to gain a foothold in territories that might be difficult to break into later. Until the mid-1990s, for example, Seven-Eleven Japan stayed out of the lucrative Kansai region (Osaka, Kyoto, Nara, Kobe). As a result, in this area Daiei's Lawson chain became almost synonymous with convenience stores.[65] Overall, however, Seven-Eleven Japan's franchise approach seems to have worked well, and it has been replicated by other convenience chains in Japan.

Rationalization of Distribution

The second pillar of Seven-Eleven Japan's strategy was rationalization of distribution, which constituted a major departure from the traditional Japanese system. Under the traditional system, individual stores had access to manufacturers only through multiple layers of distribution. Each manufacturer would appoint a particular wholesaler to handle all of its products. The designated wholesaler, in turn, often relied on secondary and sometimes even tertiary wholesalers to distribute the goods to stores. This multi-tiered system of wholesalers was cumbersome and costly.

To attack this problem, Seven-Eleven in 1976 implemented a policy of vendor consolidation. Instead of allowing each manufacturer to pick its own wholesaler, Seven-Eleven Japan insisted that all manufacturers in an area deliver to a single wholesaler. That wholesaler became responsible for sorting and then delivering the products of multiple manufacturers to all 7-Eleven stores throughout the area. This reform greatly reduced the number of daily deliveries, as well as the complexity of delivery routes.

Also in 1976, Seven-Eleven Japan inaugurated what it called "combined distribution." Under this system, products were grouped by their delivery characteristics, most notably the temperature at which they were stored: frozen food ($-20°$ C), chilled food ($5°$ C), *bento,* or Japanese lunch boxes ($20°$ C), dry food and non-food (room temperature). Products in the same category were delivered to a Combined Distribution Center (CDC). There, the goods were sorted by store through an advanced digital picking system and then loaded into trucks for delivery. By 1996, Seven-Eleven Japan had 221 such CDCs (42 frozen, 42 chilled, 51 *bento* lunch box, 31 dry food, 41 non-food, and 14 liquor). They were located at 168 sites nationwide, and some sites had more than one CDC.

Significantly, Seven-Eleven Japan itself owned none of these CDCs. Nor did it own any of the trucks that shuttled goods between the CDCs and its stores. Rather, its suppliers and a few specialized distribution companies owned and operated the CDCs. Seven-Eleven Japan's own role was limited to coordinating, assisting, and supporting.[66] As Toshifumi Suzuki explained it, "Wholesalers had human resources, as well as sunk investments in land and buildings. Rather than make new investments ourselves, we aimed to lower costs and rationalize distribution by working together with existing wholesalers."[67]

Changing the existing distribution structure was not a simple or painless task, especially because the changes required that some existing relationships be severed. Yet Seven-Eleven Japan did not waver. As Suzuki went on to say, "I don't really pay much attention to how the industry has operated in the past. I think, 'If I do this, would it solve some problem?'"[68] In consolidating its distributors, Seven-Eleven Japan worked to minimize friction. It continued to pay a commission to the primary, manufacturer-designated wholesalers, even when they were no longer fulfilling any function in delivering products. (Seven-Eleven Japan did eliminate all secondary and tertiary wholesalers.) Although many wholesalers agreed to participate in the combined delivery system and found it to be quite lucrative, others, including one well-known wholesaler, balked at Seven-Eleven Japan's demands and refused to conduct further business with it.[69]

Seven-Eleven Japan's distribution reforms proved fruitful. Figure 13.1 shows that as the company progressively restructured its system, the number of trucks needed to service each store steadily decreased. Naturally, the capacity utilization of each truck increased. In the distribution of dry goods, for example, trucks serving Seven-Eleven Japan attained a capacity utilization of nearly 85 percent, while the average for other Japanese retailers remained in the 30 percent range.[70] In conjunction with the information technology investments (to be discussed below), Seven-Eleven Japan's distribution reforms dramatically lowered inventories and increased gross margins, even as store sales rose.

Another achievement was a much greater frequency of delivery for some products. For instance, starting in 1987, rice balls and boxed

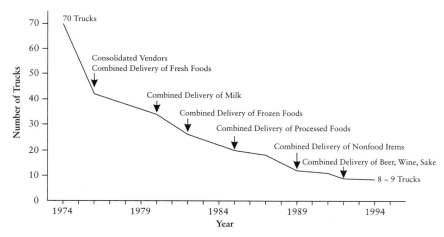

Figure 13.1 Number of Trucks Required to Serve Each Seven-Eleven Japan Store Daily

Source: Seven-Eleven Japan.

lunches were delivered to each store three times per day, and bread and dairy products twice a day. Fresh and fast food constituted an important share of Seven-Eleven Japan's sales, so its ability to provide fresher food products than the competition proved to be crucial. For goods where freshness is not as essential, delivery was less frequent. Processed foods, for example, were delivered only three times per week.

Coordinating the Preparation of Food Products

Seven-Eleven Japan had little success in selling the typical fast-food products sold in an American 7-Eleven store, such as Slurpees and hot dogs.[71] Instead, it chose to focus on traditional Japanese snack foods, such as rice balls and *bento* lunch boxes. However, it realized that to capture the latent demand for such products it would need to improve their quality. To do so, it intervened to organize the manufacturers of its fresh and fast-food products.

Firms making such products were often small. They usually lacked production and management expertise. To assist them, Seven-Eleven Japan established a cooperative association called Nihon Delica Foods. Beginning in 1979 with 10 makers of rice-based products, Nihon Delica Foods sought to raise quality and productivity by getting each participant to share its manufacturing knowledge with the others. Few members were willing to comply at first, but in due time the organization sponsored seminars on quality control and established a three-tiered quality ranking system (A, B, C). Firms receiving a C grade were expected to take decisive action to improve their performance. A company getting three Cs would be terminated as a supplier to Seven-Eleven Japan.[72]

By the mid-1990s, Nihon Delica Foods had expanded to some 100 companies, making not only rice-based items but also specialty bread products and side dishes. In addition to creating and administering quality standards, the organization undertook research on production methods and purchased raw materials in bulk. These efforts helped to improve the quality of fresh and fast-food products offered by Seven-Eleven Japan, as well as to standardize quality across all stores.

Just as some independent wholesalers were willing to build distribution centers dedicated to Seven-Eleven Japan, many manufacturers constructed plants that made products exclusively for sale in 7-Eleven stores. By 1995 there were 214 such plants.[73] Members of Nihon Delica Foods were especially dependent on the company as a buyer. Three-quarters of all plants belonging to the cooperative sold over 90 percent of their production to Seven-Eleven Japan.[74]

Use of Information Technology

Seven-Eleven Japan linked these dedicated manufacturers, its distributors, and its thousands of retail stores through a comprehensive computer network. Its rapid introduction of information technology and its efforts to upgrade the capabilities of this technology were a very important reason for Seven-Eleven Japan's continued success. The company spent substantial sums on upgrading, and its technological infrastructure has reportedly been changed over 80 times.[75]

The initial foray into information technology was aimed at simplifying the ordering process, which had previously been done by telephone.[76] The store owner had to call each vendor individually. In 1978, phone ordering was replaced by computer-processed order slips. The store owner would fill out these slips and send them to the district office, where they would be input into a computer system. In less than a year, the slips were replaced by a simple bar-code system for entering order data at a computer terminal in each store. Known as Terminal 7, this was Seven-Eleven Japan's first-generation system of information technology. Then in 1979 the company established an on-line network linking stores with suppliers and the head office. As a result, ordering became much easier and more accurate.

Simplifying the ordering process remained an important goal, but in time the emphasis shifted toward using Point-of-Sales (POS) data for ordering, merchandising, and developing new products. In 1982, the company introduced into every store POS cash registers as well as a new electronic order-booking system. This was the first large-scale use of POS data in Japan. Three years later, in 1985, the company replaced this system with one still more advanced. New POS registers, which allowed two-way transmission of data, were also added. (This enabled stores to monitor inventories of special seasonal gift items, which they could order for consumers but which they did not stock.)[77] A personal computer was installed in each store to allow owners and their employees to perform graphical analyses of POS data.

In 1990, Seven-Eleven introduced its fourth-generation information system, which had cost ¥23 billion ($158 million) to develop.[78] The new system consisted of three main items: a hand-held scanner terminal, which simplified the supervision of delivery; a notebook-sized graphic order terminal, which allowed employees to access selected POS data and place orders while walking around the store; and a new store computer with enhanced capabilities.

In 1991, all stores were linked to Seven-Eleven Japan's headquarters by an Integrated Services Digital Network that allowed for high-speed transmission of POS data. (The company claimed to have the largest such network in the world.)[79] Previously, only data related to rice-based lunch boxes and other fast foods had been sent via phone lines to the headquarters. Data for most products had been sent on floppy disks. This method caused delays of 7 to 10 days before stores could see the processed analysis. By contrast, with the digital network in place, POS data for one day was sent each evening to the host computer, where it was processed and the analysis made available by 7 A.M. the next morning. The high-speed links with manufacturers and the distribution centers also made quick-response delivery possible. For example, orders for sandwiches entered by store personnel by 10 A.M. were swiftly transmitted to manufacturers and distributors. The products were then delivered to stores by 6 P.M., in time for the dinner crowd.[80]

POS data were employed intensively in merchandising. When a sale was made, the store clerk entered into the register the customer's gender and approximate age, thereby providing information on who was buying what. Over time, control of this kind of information fundamentally altered the established balance of power in Japan among manufacturers, wholesalers, and retailers. Traditionally, Japanese retailers had tended to delegate product selection to wholesalers, who also helped to stock retailers' shelves and who allowed unsold merchandise to be returned for credit. In return for these services, wholesalers commanded premium prices. By contrast, Seven-Eleven Japan believed that its information capabilities told it directly which products sold and which did not. It was therefore able to forgo its right to return goods. By thus internalizing the risk of unsold items, it was able to demand lower prices. In addition, it could quickly drop poor-selling products. By the mid-1990s, Seven-Eleven Japan was annually replacing between one-half and two-thirds of the 6,000 products that it recommended to its stores.[81] This extremely rapid change in product selection was perhaps unmatched anywhere in the world.

The company also used its copious information on customer preferences and purchasing behavior to work with suppliers in developing new products, especially fresh and fast foods. Some examples included fresh-baked bread jointly developed with Ajinomoto and Itochu, beer with Suntory and Miller, ice cream with Morinaga, and ball-point pens with Gillette. These jointly developed products typically offered a higher profit margin than did national brands, and Seven-Eleven Japan intended to do even more of this "team merchandising" in the future. To increase its range of procurement sources and to enhance its product-development capabilities, it formed strategic alliances with Wal-Mart and with Germany's Metro Group.

Three other aspects of Seven-Eleven Japan's far-reaching investments in information technology are worth noting. First, as in distribution, much of the work in developing the information system was done in conjunction with other firms. Nomura Research Institute played a large role in developing the software and administering the network. In fact, Nomura owned the host computer. The hardware in 7-Eleven stores, too, was developed jointly with various manufacturers: Nippon Electric Company (NEC) created the store computer, Tokyo Electric Company built the register, and Nippondenso produced the scanner terminal. Seven-Eleven Japan usually insisted that any such products developed with its collaboration could not be sold to any competitors for two years.[82]

By relying on outside suppliers, Seven-Eleven Japan reduced the need for a large staff of computer experts. In the mid-1990s, only 50 of its employees worked in the systems development division, and only a small fraction of these had technical backgrounds in computers. The majority had experience in sales, and a few came from other areas such as accounting.[83] For Seven-Eleven Japan, the important competency was not technical know-how, which could be procured from specialists, but an understanding of what type of information was needed by its franchisees and by its staff at headquarters and in the field. This understanding enabled the company to offer useful suggestions for new product ideas to hardware and software vendors.

The company did, however, own the computer equipment in its franchised stores. It could use this technology as a means of "locking in" franchises. Its basic franchise fee was equal to 45 percent of its franchisees' gross profits, whereas those of its competitors Lawson and

FamilyMart were only in the 35 percent range. At least part of the difference was attributable to franchisees' desire to access Seven-Eleven Japan's superior information system.[84]

The company's main competitors eventually installed POS systems in their own stores, Lawson in 1988 and FamilyMart in 1989. So Seven-Eleven Japan no longer enjoyed a monopoly on the hardware. Still, it retained its first-mover position. In the mid-1990s, Seven-Eleven Japan remained a generation ahead of these two competitors in its information technology. Its franchisees also seemed to be well ahead of the competition in their ability to use the information.

This last point was especially important, because in making its investments in information technology, Seven-Eleven Japan sought to empower workers, rather than simply automate functions. This goal was evident in the company's approach to the reordering function. Seven-Eleven Japan could have installed a computerized replenishment system that automatically reordered items as they were sold. Instead it did something radically different. Its core idea here was called *tampin kanri,* which literally means "item-by-item control" but in fact carried much broader significance. Essential to tampin kanri was active participation in the ordering process by the store owner and other employees, including even part-timers. The person doing the ordering was taught to formulate a hypothesis, using data on previous sales and information relevant to purchasing behavior, such as the weather, day of the week, special events in the area, and so forth. Afterward, the clerk was taught to verify how well he or she had done, considering not only inventory losses on unsold items but also the opportunity cost of sales lost when the store ran out of certain items. Active participation of store owners, managers, and employees was seen as imperative. In this setting, the computer became a tool to support decisionmaking by individuals, not a replacement for their thinking.

In addition to giving franchisees latitude in the ordering decision, Seven-Eleven Japan maintained a relatively flat structure. This point was emphasized in its organizational chart, which was intentionally inverted: the franchised stores appeared at the top, the board of directors at the bottom. The aim here was to show the importance of those who actually did the selling of products.

For such a major company, Seven-Eleven Japan had in the mid-1990s a very small number of employees—fewer than 2,500, as compared to Wal-Mart's 675,000. (Of course, this figure did not include the approximately 120,000 people, mostly part-timers, employed by its franchisees.[85] Nor did it include suppliers.) Of Seven-Eleven Japan's employees, over one-third were the aforementioned Operation Field Counselors (OFC), who were in close contact with the stores. The OFCs were also integrated with headquarters. From all over Japan they gathered in Tokyo once a week for a meeting. Those at the next two levels, district and zone managers, also met in Tokyo once a week. The goal of these meetings was to provide Seven-Eleven Japan's home office with rapid, distortion-free feedback from franchisees and to make all OFCs aware of the tactics that seemed to be working in one group of stores. The OFCs could then disseminate this information rapidly throughout Seven-Eleven Japan's network of stores.

Seven-Eleven Japan delegated an immense range of responsibility to store personnel and to outside specialists. It believed that only a nimble organization would be equipped to respond to shifts in consumer demands and changes in the external environment.

Given this focus on ceaseless change, it is not surprising that Toshifumi Suzuki and his colleagues at Seven-Eleven Japan built their complex system through a process of continuous improvement. The history of Seven-Eleven Japan was not a story of one-shot innovations, followed by lulls before the next breakthrough innovation. Rather, it was a record of a careful overall strategy, implemented through endless small and medium-sized adjustments. Cumulatively these small changes helped to produce spectacularly successful results.

The Decline and Rebirth of Southland in the United States

During the 1970s and early 1980s, as Seven-Eleven Japan was expanding rapidly, Southland was also achieving strong growth. To do so, it overcame high inflation, intermittent government price controls, and a recession induced by the two oil shocks of the 1970s. Inflation was particularly difficult for Southland, as higher land prices increased its cost of developing new stores. Nonetheless, by 1976, it had attained $2 billion in sales and $40 million in net income.[86] Net income grew at a compound annual rate of 23 percent between 1980 and 1985, exceeding the 20 percent growth rate recorded for the 1960s. Southland reached its apogee in 1985. In that year it was the seventh-largest retailer in the United States, with 8,000 stores, $13 billion in total revenues, and $212 million in net earnings.[87]

During the 1980s, the American convenience-store sector became far more competitive. Competition had been increasing since the late 1960s, but the 1980s brought a rash of new entrants. During that single decade, the number of convenience stores doubled.[88] Several of the newcomers were major oil companies, which remodeled their gas stations to include mini-convenience stores—the so-called g-stores. To Southland and other convenience chains, the oil companies presented a formidable threat. They had deep pockets and large networks of prime corner locations for store sites. The extent of the g-stores' assault on the convenience store industry is illustrated in Table 13.6, which shows the largest chains in the United States and Canada over a 13-year period. In 1981, only one of the 10 largest chains belonged to an oil company. By 1993, 7 did.

A second threat to convenience stores came from supermarkets, which began to stay open for longer hours. In 1979, only one percent of independent supermarkets were open 24 hours a day, 7 days a week. By 1992, this figure had risen to 12 percent. In 1979, the median supermarket (including independents and chains) was open 82 hours per week. In 1992, the average independent supermarket was open 103 hours, and the average chain 129 hours.[89] Longer supermarket hours reduced the main advantage of convenience stores, their "time convenience," and thereby eroded the price premium they could command.

The boom in health and fitness also posed a threat to many American convenience stores. A substantial part of their sales had derived from beer, cigarettes, and fat-laden snack foods. Here the American pattern differed markedly from the Japanese. Table 13.7 shows the breakdown of products sold by Southland in the United States and Seven-Eleven in Japan.

Southland had two major responses to the product-market challenges of the 1980s. First, it created a two-tiered pricing scheme, charging low prices for beer and soda and higher, so-called insult prices for groceries and other goods. Second, it introduced new services, such as automated teller machines and video rentals. But neither of these responses represented the same degree of innovativeness that had characterized the com-

Table 13.6   The Ten Largest Convenience-Store Chains in the United States and Canada

1981			1987			1993		
Company		Stores	Company		Stores	Company		Stores
Southland	C	7,002	Southland	C	8,200	Southland	C	6,167
Circle K	C	1,194	Circle K	C	3,500	Circle K	C	2,575
Cumberland Farms	C	1,105	CT Food Mart	C	1,400	Amoco	G	1,892
Munford	C	1,080	Dairy Mart Convenience	C	1,207	Texaco	G	1,720
Convenient Food Mart	C	1,039	Cumberland Farms	C	1,205	Shell	G	1,625
UtoteM	C	936	Silcorp	C	1,042	Mobile	G	1,221
National Convenience Stores	C	832	National Convenience Stores	C	950	Chevron	G	1,180
Lawson	C	701	Texaco	G	900	BP Oil	G	1,105
Mac's Convenience Stores	C	701	Dillon Companies	C	853	Dairy Mart Convenience	C	1,079
Atlantic Richfield	G	685	Mobil	G	800	Marathon Oil	G	1,077

Note: C denotes convenience store, G denotes g-store (oil company).
Source: Convenience Store News Annual Report, 1981, 1987, and 1993.

Table 13.7   Composition of Sales at Southland and Seven-Eleven Japan, 1993

	Gasoline	Alcohol/ Tobacco	Soft Drinks	Confectionery Snacks	Deli, Dairy, Lunch Box, and Bakery	Magazines/ Newspapers	Processed Food and Other
Southland	22%	27%	10%	7%	23%	4%	7%
Seven-Eleven Japan	—	11%	10%	8%	49%	8%	14%

Source: Data from Seven-Eleven Japan.

pany earlier in its history. If anything, its pricing policy harkened back to the mass-retailing strategy of high volumes and low margins, a strategy from which Southland had hitherto abstained.

The company failed to differentiate itself from the new g-stores. In fact, tempted by the lure of easy money following the first oil shock, Southland itself became more dependent on gasoline sales. They rose from less than 3 percent of total sales in 1972 to over 25 percent in 1985.[90]

Meanwhile, Southland did not make the investments in information technology that might have improved its capabilities in merchandising and inventory management. Nor did it actively update its once-revolutionary distribution system. By the mid-1980s its nationwide system of five distribution and six food centers was outdated and overstretched. Management seemed content to keep opening new stores while making few adjustments to its operations. In the words of one former employee, "They had a hell of a bureaucracy. It was like congress; you couldn't get anything done. The mentality of existing management was build, build, build."[91]

Beginning in the late 1970s Southland engaged in a series of diversification ventures. It acquired companies in such industries as oil refining (Citgo), auto parts (Chief Auto Parts), snack foods (Pate Foods), and electronic safe controls (Tidel Systems). It also drifted into real estate speculation. In the early 1980s, it purchased Cityplace, a 160-acre parcel of land north of downtown Dallas. On this land it constructed an ostentatious new 42-story headquarters, and it laid out elaborate plans to develop the remainder of the property over the next 20 years.

In spite of increased product-market competition and a haphazard diversification scheme, Southland's performance did not appear to suffer, at least for a while. The company continued to enlarge its network of stores while generating real increases in same-store sales. In 1986, however, for the first time in 25 years, its revenues and net earnings fell. Even so, Southland appeared to be a healthy company, in no imminent danger of collapse.[92]

In addition to troubles within their own industry, however, American convenience stores in the 1980s were being challenged by a wave of takeovers, restructurings, and leveraged buyouts. Many of these financial maneuvers were based on the theory that companies tended to squander their free cash flow on unprofitable ventures, speculative acquisitions, and executive perquisites.[93] Thus, it might be worthwhile for an acquirer to buy up companies generating free cash flow, load them with debt, and then sell peripheral and underperforming lines of business, ultimately forcing free cash flow to be disgorged to shareholders. As this idea found acceptance, the retail sector in particular came to be perceived as replete with "cash cows" ripe for bust-up takeovers. During the 1980s, 5 of the 10 biggest leveraged buyouts in the United States were in retailing: Federated Department Stores, Safeway, Montgomery Ward, R. H. Macy, and Southland itself.[94]

The challenge to Southland came in 1987. Samuel Belzberg, a Canadian investor who owned 4.9 percent of Southland's common stock, informed the family members in control of the firm, John Thompson and his brothers Jere and Joe Jr., of his intent to acquire the company. Belzberg proposed a leveraged buyout at $65 per share, which was a 16 percent premium over market price. The Thompsons and other Southland executives were surprised by Belzberg's proposal. But in retrospect the takeover bid was not unpredictable, given the contemporary market mentality and the company's own actions in the early 1980s. In an era of bust-up takeovers, to diversify recklessly was to tempt fate.

Although the three Thompson brothers collectively owned less than 10 percent of the outstanding stock, they viewed Belzberg's proposal as an assault on their family business. In July 1987, they countered with a leveraged-buyout offer of their own: $77 per share, a 38 percent premium over market price and 20 times 1986 earnings.

The Thompsons' offer was successful in thwarting Belzberg, but almost immediately they had to cope with another shock—the stock market crash of October 1987. On a single day, the Dow Jones industrial average dropped by more than 500 points, one-fourth of its total value at the time. This stunning development sapped investors' confidence, particularly in the high-risk junk bonds with which the Thompsons had planned to finance their buyout. They therefore had to postpone their debt offering. When it was finally placed, the debt carried interest rates that were 1.5 to 4.0 percentage points greater than anticipated, resulting in about $30 million of additional annual after-tax interest expense.[95] The Thompsons were also forced to issue warrants entitling the bondholders to purchase up to 10 percent of the firm's common stock. Wall Street wags began referring to the Southland buyout as "the Texas chainstore massacre."[96]

To reduce its huge debt, Southland now embarked on an ambitious sell-off of assets. Its main divestitures included not only unrelated businesses, such as oil refining, auto parts, snack foods, and electronic safe controls, but also its core ice and dairy-products divisions and hundreds of its convenience stores.[97] It slashed capital expenditures from an annual average of $398 million between 1983 and 1986 to $111 million in 1988 and only $76 million in 1989. It sharply trimmed advertising as well, and stopped it altogether for most of 1988.[98]

These measures came at a time when Southland faced increasingly tough competition, and its performance suffered. Between 1988 and 1991, same-store sales declined at an annual real rate of over 2.5 percent. In 1988 Southland lost $216 million, in 1989 $1.3 billion, and in 1990

$277 million.[99] As if these difficulties were not enough, the property market in Dallas turned sour, and Southland could not find a buyer for its land at Cityplace or tenants for the vacant offices.

By early 1990, it was clear that Southland could not meet some of its debt covenants, not to mention interest and principal payments. It needed a restructuring, and especially the infusion of new equity. In March 1990, Southland officials approached Ito-Yokado as a potential savior.

JAPANESE ALLIES TO THE RESCUE

Ito-Yokado and Seven-Eleven Japan had already provided some assistance, though at arm's length. In 1988, the two companies had agreed to replace monthly royalty payments to Southland with an interest-free loan of ¥41 billion (about $300 million). The 7-Eleven brand name served as collateral for the loan.[100] In 1989, Seven-Eleven Japan purchased 58 7-Eleven stores in Hawaii, thereby providing Southland with still more cash. In 1990, Ito-Yokado and Seven-Eleven Japan again responded to Southland's calls for aid, this time offering to purchase a controlling interest in the company, conditional on a restructuring of its debt approved by 95 percent of its bondholders.

On the surface, the decision to rescue Southland seemed a bold step for Ito-Yokado. But officials at Ito-Yokado and Seven-Eleven Japan were concerned that Southland might go bankrupt or be acquired by another party. If either of those things happened, Seven-Eleven Japan's own image and brand equity might be damaged.[101] President Toshifumi Suzuki of Seven-Eleven Japan also believed that some money might be made by rebuilding Southland in the United States, using techniques he and his management team had pioneered in Japan.[102]

Working out a restructuring agreement acceptable to all parties required a complicated, messy series of negotiations. Talks began in March 1990 and lasted an entire year.[103] Meanwhile, Southland's financial condition steadily worsened. In October 1990, it filed for a "prepackaged" bankruptcy, and thereby earned the dubious distinction of becoming the first major company to use this procedure.[104] In March 1991, a restructuring agreement was finally concluded. For $430 million, Ito-Yokado and Seven-Eleven Japan jointly acquired 70 percent of Southland's equity.[105] Bondholders received new debt securities as well as 22 percent of the equity. Thompson family members retained 5 percent of the equity.

In 1992, Ito-Yokado increased its commitment to Southland by guaranteeing a $400 million line of credit.

Within the United States, the acquisition of Southland by Japanese purchasers generated little uproar. This was especially surprising because 7-Eleven constituted a piece of Americana and the early 1990s were a period when acquisitions by Japanese firms still made many Americans anxious. Perhaps there was little acrimony because Ito-Yokado and Seven-Eleven Japan had not initiated the takeover but had responded to Southland's pleas for assistance.

REBUILDING SOUTHLAND: SEVEN-ELEVEN JAPAN AS COACH

Seven-Eleven Japan already had some experience operating 7-Eleven stores in America. When they had taken over Southland's 58 Hawaiian stores in 1989, Seven-Eleven Japan officials were shocked at the high level of inventories, a level which had not changed in 18 years.[106] They were appalled by the small number of products offered—only about half the number in a typical 7-Eleven in Japan. They moved quickly to correct these perceived shortcomings by absorbing the Hawaiian stores into the Seven-Eleven Japan management system.

However, for Southland as a whole, with its thousands of franchised and company-operated stores in America, neither Toshifumi Suzuki nor Masatoshi Ito wanted the restructuring to be directed by a heavy hand from Japan. Given the widespread concern about Japanese takeovers of American companies in the late 1980s and early 1990s, a conspicuous Japanese shakeup might not make for good public relations. Even more important was Ito's and Suzuki's shared belief that retailing itself is fundamentally a domestic business. Suzuki likened Seven-Eleven Japan's role in Southland's rebuilding to that of a coach in a team sport. A coach sets the strategy and offers instruction to the players, but they themselves are responsible for playing the game.[107]

Under the influence of Seven-Eleven Japan, Southland drastically reduced the number of its stores.[108] It shed underperforming stores and tried to implement a type of market-dominance strategy. It began a massive store-remodeling program, which aimed to create a cleaner, more modern, shopper-friendly look that would be uniform across all 7-Eleven stores in the United States. Embracing a policy of "everyday fair pricing," the company lowered its exorbitant premiums over supermarket prices on most goods. At the same time, it stopped heavily discounting a few other products. It also urged franchisees to increase the number of products offered.

Southland sold off its distribution centers to the McLane Company, a subsidiary of Wal-Mart. It then outsourced much of its distribution to McLane, which took over the servicing of 7-Eleven stores through a nationwide network of 10 large distribution centers and 15 "rapid-response" centers. At the same time, it formed strategic alliances with other distribution companies, which built combined distribution centers to serve 7-Eleven stores. Many of these new centers specialized in fast delivery of fresh and fast-food products. To improve the quality of these products, Southland induced food manufacturers to establish factories and bakeries to make items exclusively for 7-Eleven stores. In the mid-1990s the company began delivering fresh foods daily instead of two or three times a week.[109]

To implement the Japanese notion of tampin kanri (employee input into the ordering process), Southland initiated a program called Accelerated Inventory Management (AIM). This program encouraged store clerks to take inventory frequently, even every few hours for fresh products, and to make merchandising decisions for themselves.[110] Unlike their Japanese counterparts, however, they could not rely at first on an electronic POS system. Instead they were expected to count items by hand. To offset the costs of this labor-intensive task, franchisees participating in AIM were offered a small reduction in franchise fees. Southland intended eventually to provide its stores with a new information system, similar to that in Japan but adapted to U.S. conditions.

Southland also moved to restructure its internal organization. The company centralized its merchandising, which had previously been done by each of five distribution centers. It also eliminated several layers of management and expanded the role of field counselors. They would no longer be merely a channel for delivering paperwork and information to the stores. Now they were charged with helping store personnel find solutions to problems. Southland also began to convene weekly video teleconferences of its staff in the field.

Ending several years of operating losses, Southland returned to the black in 1993 and remained profitable through the mid-1990s. Cost reductions from store closings explained part of this improvement. But same-store sales, which had fallen every year since 1988, also recovered.

In real terms they rose by 2 percent in 1994 and remained constant in 1995. Stores that implemented the AIM program and that underwent remodeling showed dramatic turnarounds. For 50 such company-owned stores located in Austin, Texas, the average same-store sales increase was 17 percent.[111]

Some of the changes instituted by Southland encountered resistance. More than a few franchisees balked at the AIM program, which they regarded as imposing unnecessary costs and infringing on their rights.[112] Attempts to replace direct-store deliveries (those made directly to the stores by manufacturers) also encountered resistance from suppliers and some franchisees. Opposition to these new programs and allegations of inadequate support prompted a number of dissatisfied franchisees to file suit against Southland.[113]

Meanwhile, the convenience-store business in the United States remained highly competitive. A trade publication described the challenge faced by Southland: "Competition is keen, the market is saturated, and while the game is the same, the rules have changed since 7-Eleven was synonymous with convenience."[114] Nor were these problems unique to Southland. Other large chains entering bankruptcy in the late 1980s included Circle K, National Convenience Stores, Cumberland Farms, and Sunshine-Jr. Stores.[115] Many retailing experts believed that the age of convenience stores in America had passed. They therefore doubted that the huge Japanese investment in Southland would yield a satisfactory return. The long-run effects of the changes at Southland under the coaching of Seven-Eleven Japan could not be forecast with much confidence.

As is always the case in business, the only sure thing was further change. The shifts that had already occurred in this industry in both Japan and the United States were quite extraordinary. Table 13.8 summarizes the differences in the historical evolution of convenience-store retailing in the two countries, and it provides a few comparative figures for Southland and Seven-Eleven Japan in the mid-1990s.

Of course, Table 13.8 does not address some important differences in the external environments of Japan and the United States, such as disparities in legal systems, educational levels of part-time employees, and crime rates. Crime, for example, was a major problem for convenience stores in the United States, but much less so in Japan. One survey found that 142 robberies of convenience stores were reported in Japan in 1994. A mere 8 of these incidents, or 6 percent, involved a gun.[116] For Japan

Table 13.8   7-Eleven in the United States and Japan

Historical Development	United States	Japan
Role of Convenience Stores:	Provide a more convenient alternative to supermarkets	Increase the productivity of mom-and-pop stores, while offering a higher level of convenience
Store Type:	Mix of directly managed and franchised stores; franchisees recruited to run newly built stores	Heavy emphasis on franchised stores, converted from existing small stores and managed by their owners
Store Location:	Residential areas	Urban areas, especially *shotengai* (traditional shopping districts)
Main Competition:	Gas stations, supermarkets	Mom-and-pop stores, vending machines
Supplier Relations:	Arm's-length, spot-market transactions	Long-term, but market-mediated
Information Technology:	Small investment, with no follow-up	Huge investment, frequent upgrading
Distribution Method:	Combined vertical integration (its distribution centers) with a reliance on manufacturers (direct-store deliveries)	Utilized existing wholesalers but reorganized their activities in order to promote efficiency

Current Characteristics	Southland	Seven-Eleven Japan
Store Sales ($ million)	$6,684	$15,337
Net Profit ($ million)	$92	$556
Number of Stores	5,630	5,952
Franchised Stores (%)	53	96
Floor Space Per Store (m²)	224	101
Employees	30,417	2,364

Source: Top half of the table is based on Nobuo Kawabe, *Sebun-Irebun no Keieishi* (Tokyo: Yuhikaku, 1994), table 15. Data in the bottom half come from the annual reports of Southland (fiscal year ending in December 1994) and Seven-Eleven Japan (fiscal year ending in February 1995).

as a whole, there were only 32 gun murders in 1995, as compared to over 15,000 in the United States in 1994.[117] This kind of cross-national divergence may not have mattered for some sectors of the economy, but it did for retailing.

Toward the Next Century: Retailing in a World of Ceaseless Change

Seven-Eleven Japan's long-term prospects in its home market seemed more secure than Southland's in the United States. However, one important development during the 1990s in Japan was a slow but steady loosening of regulations governing large stores. Inasmuch as a restrictive regulatory environment had helped convenience stores to thrive, this movement toward retail deregulation was hardly good news for Seven-Eleven Japan. In 1991, the Large Stores Law was amended. Size limits for new stores were doubled and permissible closing times for large stores were extended by an hour, from 6 P.M. to 7 P.M. More significantly, the maximum time allowed for MITI's approval or disapproval of new large stores was shortened to 18 months.[118]

In addition to these regulatory changes, the general economic malaise that gripped Japan in the years after 1991 dampened consumer optimism. Seven-Eleven Japan's performance held up well, but even it had some stumbles. Shop America, a mail-order initiative introduced by the company in 1991, failed to attract sufficient demand and was discontinued in 1994.[119] In 1992, increasing competition forced Seven-Eleven Japan to cut its prices on candy, processed food, and even rice-based lunch boxes.[120] This move was surprising given the company's long-standing antipathy toward discounting. Seven-Eleven Japan's market value, although still enormous, fell by about $1 billion (a 3 percent decline) from July 1994 to July 1995.[121] For the 1996 fiscal year, same-store sales declined for the first time in the company's history.[122]

Stagnant sales figures raised questions about market saturation. In many areas of Japan, the concentration of convenience stores had become intense. A poll undertaken by Lawson found that in Tokyo people encountered an average of 5.6 convenience stores on the way to work. In Osaka, the number was 4.4.[123] For Seven-Eleven Japan, the leading convenience store, the question of market saturation was particularly relevant. On a typical day, some 6 million customers—5 percent of Japan's population—visited a 7-Eleven store.[124] Seven-Eleven Japan was the biggest seller of fast food in Japan.[125] Annually it sold 800 million *bentos* and rice balls, 150 million sandwiches, 1 billion containers of soft drinks, and 400 million magazines.[126] How much larger could it grow?

In the mid-1990s, Toshifumi Suzuki was not terribly worried about the problem of market saturation. He insisted that there was still much room for Seven-Eleven Japan to expand geographically. After all, it was active in only half of Japan's prefectures. Nor was he worried much about competition from other convenience stores. As he put it, "The existence of competition is disagreeable from a shortsighted perspective; in the long run competition works as a positive force by promoting constant diligence."[127]

This view echoed what Joe Thompson Sr., Southland's pioneer and long-time president, had once told an associate who was worried about competition: "The other companies will hurt us to some extent, but on the other hand, they will help keep us on our toes." Thompson went on to say that "the company with the best organization is always the winner in the end."[128] Toshifumi Suzuki would undoubtedly agree on the importance of organizational capabilities. For him, however, there was no fixed destination in a world of ceaseless change. Asked about his biggest accomplishment, he replied, "I don't feel any sense of achievement. The world changes too much. A marathon has an end, but the world does not stop."[129]

He might have added, nor does capitalism.

❧ 14 ❧

RETROSPECT AND PROSPECT

Thomas K. McCraw

This has been a book about the creation of modern capitalism in four countries. The authors of the book have emphasized the roles played by entrepreneurs and innovative companies in the extraordinary economic success of those countries.

The approach has been comparative, in several ways. The authors have compared four national frameworks of capitalist growth. We have also compared business strategies across firms and across time. We have concerned ourselves with four different units of analysis—not only with countries and companies, but also with particular industries and individual entrepreneurs. And we have explored the interaction of each of the four units of analysis with the other three.

In this final chapter, it will be useful to restate what can be learned from this approach and to speculate about what remains to be learned. At the close of the twentieth century and the start of the twenty-first, historians and economists know much more about the anatomy of business and of economic growth than our counterparts did a century or two ago. But there is still a lot that we don't know.

What We Know

As mentioned in the Introduction, the capitalist era of the three industrial revolutions has been a profound discontinuity in the long course of human history. In Europe during the thousand years before 1700, per capita income rose at only about 0.11 percent per year, which would mean that it doubled about every 630 years. But between 1820 and 1990, from the First Industrial Revolution to the Third, it grew by a factor of 10 in Great Britain, 15 in Germany, 18 in the United States, and 25 in Japan.

How did such remarkable growth occur? The title of this book, "Creating Modern Capitalism," provides the beginnings of an answer, and the question itself is explicit in the book's subtitle: "How Entrepreneurs, Companies, and Countries Triumphed in Three Industrial Revolutions."

The United States was the productivity leader throughout this long period of high growth, except for the earliest years. It remained so at the end of the twentieth century, although its lead over other industrial countries had diminished. We can observe in Table 14.1 the type of convergence in productivity among countries that orthodox economic theory would predict, under assumptions of relatively free international flows of capital and technology.

Conventional theory would not predict, however, the lack of convergence and the radically different performances between the developed countries on the one hand and the developing countries on the other. Toward the close of the twentieth century, real per capita income in the advanced industrialized countries was *six times* the average for the rest of the world.[1] This is a far bigger spread than existed at the beginning of the First Industrial Revolution, when the difference was more on the order of 15 or 20 percent.[2]

For many countries, therefore, the direction of performance has not converged toward the high standards set by the leaders. Instead, it has gone the other way. The reasons for this are not very clear, and the whole question of why some countries became rich while others remained poor could hardly be more challenging or more important. As the Nobel Prize-winning economist Robert Lucas once put it, "The consequences for human welfare involved in questions like these are simply staggering: Once one starts to think about them, it is hard to think about anything else."[3]

This book has been concerned only with developed countries, and we might review here some of what economists and historians know about the mechanics of their performance. For one thing, we know that growth and development have been much stronger in capitalist economies than in noncapitalist ones. We also know, however, that not every capitalist country has been high-performing. So capitalism appears to be a necessary condition for strong growth, but not a sufficient one.

As set forth in the Introduction, for a country to be "capitalist" requires certain ingredients. It must have a market economy, and its legal system must protect private property and the sanctity of contracts. The

Table 14.1 Comparative Levels of Productivity, 1870–1987
(US GDP per man-hour = 100)

	1870	1913	1950	1973	1987
Germany	50	50	30	64	80
Japan	19	18	15	46	61
UK	104	78	57	67	80
USA	100	100	100	100	100

Source: Adapted from Angus Maddison, *Dynamic Forces in Capitalist Development: A Comparative View* (New York: Oxford University Press, 1991), p. 53.

"value" of a good or service must be determined not by some external notion such as a "just price," but instead by the simple test of what someone will pay for it. Property must be alienable. Wages must be paid in money. Entrepreneurial opportunity and technological advance must be encouraged. Capitalist systems depend heavily on investment credit, and the essence of capitalism itself is a psychological orientation toward the *future*—the pursuit of wealth and income as much for tomorrow as for today.

This orientation toward the future encourages continual innovation. So, above all else, capitalism is a perpetual motion machine. It never stands still. Individuals gain and lose fortunes. Companies prosper, falter, go bankrupt, and sometimes revive. Industries rise and decline. Whole national economies are in constant motion as well—moving forward most of the time, but occasionally backward when economic depressions and recessions occur. As Joseph Schumpeter wrote, "Stabilized capitalism is a contradiction in terms."

Of course, some of this constant motion is not unique to life in capitalist systems, but is inherent in the human condition. As the philosopher George Santayana once observed, human beings differ from other animals principally in their unquenchable aspirations. They are never satisfied. In capitalist countries during the last 300 years, their pursuits have most often focused on things economic. As Adam Smith put it in *The Wealth of Nations,* human beings seem to have a propensity "to truck, barter, and exchange one thing for another." Other animals show no such inclination. "Nobody ever saw a dog make a fair and deliberate exchange of one bone for another with another dog."[4]

Support for these remarks by Schumpeter, Santayana, and Smith appears on almost every page of this book. Evidence abounds particularly in the eight "company" chapters.

For Josiah Wedgwood, there was the continuous search for better techniques, recorded day by day in his Experiment Book. Wedgwood's creation of jasperware and other new forms of pottery, his systematic development of brand equity through selling to aristocrats, his organization of a factory workforce, and his installation of what amounted to a time clock—all of these activities bespoke an aspiration that knew no rest.

The same was true 150 years later in the case of Rolls-Royce. Henry Royce's restless quest for better designs of automotive and aero engines, Ernest Hives's search for a system in which he could subcontract production of the Merlin engine while still keeping control over its design and quality—these stories demonstrate the ceaseless adaptation and striving for improvement that are part of human nature, but are exaggerated by capitalist pressures.

They are exaggerated so powerfully because of the competitive nature of capitalism, as the case of August Thyssen and German steel shows. Like the other entrepreneurs discussed in this book, Thyssen seems to have been a driven personality. He was determined to serve the interests of himself, his family, his company, and the fatherland, all at the same time. To do this well, he had to compete with Krupp, Phoenix, and other elite German steel firms. And he had to do it within the peculiar constraints imposed by the cartel system. The result, as we have seen, was an obsession with detail on the part of Thyssen himself, and a corporate strategy that came to emphasize export markets, vertical integration, and a broad product line. Many other German firms followed similar strategies.

With the Deutsche Bank, we encountered another story remarkable for its dynamism. The early bank of Georg von Siemens first faltered, then prospered, then was faced with the stresses of war, followed by the fiscal lunacy of hyperinflation, and after that the unspeakable horrors of Nazi tyranny. Concurrently with the story of the Deutsche Bank's responses to these upheavals, we saw a vivid example of a company's structural evolution under capitalism: a commercial bank became a merchant bank, then also an investment bank, an investment trust, and finally a universal bank. That evolution came in response to new opportunities outside the firm and changing capabilities within it, rather than from some grand a priori plan.

In the first of our chapters on American companies, we witnessed the battle between Ford and General Motors for the top position in the most important industry of the twentieth century. We also encountered some colorful individuals. In the person of Henry Ford, we observed the original model for what has since become a familiar American character type: the multimillionaire as both genius and crackpot. Similarly, in Alfred Sloan we met the prototypical organization man: calculating but never callous, and supremely effective as a business manager.

In the chapter on IBM we again saw a compelling story of business overlain with deep personal drama. That drama was expressed in the title of Tom Watson Jr.'s autobiography: *Father, Son & Co.* The interaction we observed between the business story and the personal relationship suggests that Tom Jr. would not have embraced the "bet-the-company" gamble of System/360 had he not wanted to outdo his father.

Similarly with Kiichiro Toyoda, who took the funds generated by his father's licensing of looms to a British firm, and parlayed that stake into an enterprise that became the world's strongest car company. The Toyoda/Toyota story is an especially good example of the ways in which technology is transferred under capitalism: the technology of automatic looms from Britain to Japan and then back to Britain; the technology of cars from the United States to Japan, then back to the United States; and the spread of the Toyota Production System to many other industries and companies throughout the world. Thus it is with capitalism. Innovation spawns emulation, and first-mover advantages are never sufficient for a quiet life over the long run.

Toshifumi Suzuki made this point clear in his comment quoted at the end of the chapter on 7-Eleven in America and Japan. Suzuki himself transplanted the American-style convenience store to Japan, but he was forced to overcome adamant objections to the idea within his own company. Then, he and his colleagues proved to be so phenomenally successful that they were able to rescue their American partner from bankruptcy. Meanwhile, back in Japan, they built a model Third Industrial Revolution company: lean in assets, rich in knowledge and information technology, attuned to customer preferences, and able to change with dazzling speed.

As we have seen, the concept of the three industrial revolutions is problematical in some ways. The "revolutions" merge imperceptibly into one another, and they tend to arrive in different countries at different times. But there can be little question that the idea has enriched our understanding of national economic development. The four "country" chapters demonstrate that beyond much doubt.

Britain, the pioneer in the First Industrial Revolution, struggled more than the other three countries during the Second, in large measure because of its institutional legacy from the First. Similarly, the German economy, a preeminent performer in the key industries of the Second Industrial Revolution, encountered the Third with some apparent disadvantages that were the obverse of its virtues in the Second. At the close of the twentieth century, both Britain and Germany, like other European countries, struggled between the goals of strong economic performance and full social justice—between efficiency and equity, between lean staffing for individual companies and full employment for national economies. It is an old struggle. But it became more difficult as the demands of the Third Industrial Revolution intensified.

The United States, a top performer in all three Industrial Revolutions, confronted some especially challenging tradeoffs between economic success and social dislocation. All countries face these kinds of tradeoffs. But as the most entrepreneurially oriented, most "Schumpeterian" of all major economies, the United States was particularly conflicted. Its national ideology was not only individualistic but also egalitarian. More than the citizens of most countries, Americans have aspired to be both free and equal. But at the close of the twentieth century, it was not at all certain that the United States as a country could still have the best of both of those rather different worlds.

The case of Japan was in some respects the most interesting of all the country stories. Paradoxes abounded. Many Japanese people, having helped to accomplish an indisputable economic miracle during the decades after World War II, at century's end still regarded their own quality of life as unsatisfactory. For the average citizen, Japan was the safest of the four countries in which to live (far safer than the crime-ridden United States), but also the most congested. The Japanese government had the most capable and efficient civil servants, but also the most corruptible electoral system. Japan's economy was among the world's most productive, but was also the most heavily regulated of the four described in this book. Even in the apparently straightforward area of Gross National Product per capita, Japan's performance was anomalous. At the close of the twentieth century, the average person in Japan enjoyed an income about one-third greater than that of the average person in the United States, as measured by current exchange rates between the yen and the dollar. But goods and services were inordinately expensive in Japan. So, measured by purchasing power parity, the average Japanese person took in about 18 percent less than the average American. Spreads of such magnitude between ways of comparing incomes are not supposed to exist in a world of free mobility of the factors of economic production.[5]

Each of the four countries discussed in this book differs in some obvious ways from the other three, and from many others as well. The number of additional countries that appropriately could be analyzed in a history of capitalism is quite large—well over a hundred. We chose to write about Britain, Germany, the United States, and Japan because each of these nations has had a relatively long experience with capitalism, because each has been a star performer, and because each took a different path to capitalist success. There are numerous other champion performers: old ones such as France and the Netherlands, new ones such as Korea and Taiwan.

Most countries, of course, are not champions. Most have failed to develop their economies very effectively, and we could perhaps learn almost as much from the failures as from successes. But such a study would not be a book about effective innovation and the creation of modern capitalism.

As capitalism moves into the twenty-first century, some of the most interesting stories are likely to be found in what have come to be called "emerging markets": countries such as China, Brazil, Poland, and Thailand. Toward the end of the twentieth century, several of the companies we have discussed, headquartered in Britain, Germany, the United States, and Japan, set up large operations within those emerging markets. Economic analysts and planners in the emerging markets themselves carefully studied the records of the four nations depicted in this book, and learned a great deal about successful economic growth.

Nevertheless, there is still much that nobody understands very well about the process of growth. Additional knowledge awaits as economic history and business history continue to unfold.

What Is Still Unknown

History and economics are not experimental sciences. Human behavior does not lend itself to the predictability characteristic of physics and chemistry. No replicable experiments with any of our units of analysis (countries, industries, companies, entrepreneurs) are possible in the sense that scientists can experiment with matter, even living matter. No economist or historian has yet unlocked the equivalent of human DNA for economic life, nor is anyone likely to do so.

What *is* possible, using solid economic theory and rigorous empirical research, is to move forward gradually in our understanding of business behavior and economic growth. A great deal of splendid work has been done and is being done. We have tried to contribute to that stream of work, but we must acknowledge the impossibility of fully understanding either economics or history. The task of research has no end.

Chapter 3, "British Capitalism and the Three Industrial Revolutions," closed with a quotation from the German novelist Thomas Mann: "Very deep is the well of the past." Mann went on to say that because the well is so deep, "Should we not call it bottomless? For the deeper we sound, the further down into the lower world of the past we probe and press, the more do we find that the earliest foundations of humanity, its history and culture, reveal themselves unfathomable . . . the unresearchable plays a kind of mocking game with our researching ardours; it offers apparent holds and goals, behind which, when we have gained them, new reaches of the past still open out."[6]

So it is with the history of modern capitalism and of economic growth. As one studies these subjects, it becomes evident that the well of the past is bottomless. Precision and robust analysis become difficult. The field as a whole remains relatively disordered, because of the intractability of the issues and the almost infinite number of variables that must be taken into consideration.[7]

In historical comparisons of the sources of productivity growth, one fact stands out. In the nineteenth century, technological innovation was significantly embedded in the new use of capital-intensive machines for mass production. But in the twentieth century, and especially during the period after World War II, productivity growth became less a function of capital intensity than of knowledge intensity. Levels of education, the spread of information through the workforce, the mobility of technology, and the computer revolution became more important as sources of productivity growth than machine mass production per se.[8]

This much is clear, but the overall lesson remains how little economists or scholars from any other discipline really *know* about the sources of growth. They do not know how to measure the interactive effects of capital accumulation, technological progress, and labor productivity. They cannot figure out how to incorporate institutional and political factors into their analyses. So they have trouble saying anything conclusive about economic growth and the "residual" of productivity increases that can't be explained just by larger inputs of capital and labor.[9]

The subdiscipline of business history has something of crucial importance to contribute to the search for the sources of growth. The key here seems to lie within individual companies that are engaged in relentless competition with other companies: Thyssen versus Phoenix, Ford versus General Motors, Toyota versus Nissan. As the pioneering business historian Alfred D. Chandler Jr., has argued,

> At the core of this dynamic [growth of capitalism] were the organizational capabilities of the enterprise as a unified whole. These organizational capabilities were the collective physical facilities and human skills as they were organized within the enterprise . . . But only if these facilities and skills were carefully coordinated and integrated could the enterprise achieve the economies of scale and scope that were needed to compete in national and international markets and to continue to grow . . . Such organizational capabilities, of course, had to be created, and once established, they had to be maintained . . . [They] provided a dynamic for growth that helped to make the economies of the United States and Germany, in the three decades before World War I, the most productive and most competitive in the world . . . After World War II, such organizational capabilities became even more central to the competitiveness of enterprises, industries, and economies.[10]

In mainstream economics literature at the close of the twentieth century, the idea of "organizational capabilities," which is difficult to define and which inevitably contains an element of circular reasoning, has little currency. Nor does the group of ideas that go along with it: that the organization should be a focus of analysis and must be studied systematically; that developed capitalist economies can have very different organizational styles; and that the business enterprise is the best single place to look for an understanding of some of the mechanics of growth.[11]

Yet it seems very likely that a substantial portion of the elusive "residual" of total factor productivity growth can be located in the organizational capabilities of innovative firms such as those discussed in this book. Consider the surpassing importance of some of these firms (Toyota, IBM, the Deutsche Bank, Rolls-Royce) within their national economies. Consider the efficiency effects of the interactions of innovative companies with one another and with their competitors. Consider the effects of the "experience curve," multiplied across all the mass-produced items that have poured forth from the economies of star performers among nations. It is here that the empirical study of the firm should intersect with theoretical quests for the sources of economic growth.[12]

In the analyses of growth by Chandler and by the majority of economists as well, the role of public policy does not take a leading part. Most analysts do emphasize that the "basics" must be correct: a stable currency, the rule of law, protection of property rights, a good system of credit, and encouragement of competition. Beyond that, they don't usually go.[13]

In this book, however, we have seen that in all four of our successful national economies, activist public policies have been valuable and at times indispensable in promoting sustained growth. Often the most effective of these policies have been specific to a particular time and situation. They have not been general nostrums to be applied in all circumstances.

In the case of the United States, for example, it made a great deal of sense to have a protectionist trade policy for the nineteenth century. But it would make no sense at all to reinstitute one at the beginning of the twenty-first century. In Germany, the system of tariffs and cartels that prevailed from the 1880s to the 1910s obviously helped to thrust German business into the Second Industrial Revolution. But that system would be inappropriate if applied to the open global economy of the Third. In Japan, the thoroughgoing strategy of government intervention during and after the Meiji period of the late nineteenth century propelled the nation into the modern industrial era with a speed unmatched by any other country. Similarly for certain aspects of the "second" Japanese economic miracle, during the 1950s and 1960s. But the hand of affirmative regulation so effective during these periods proved less successful under other conditions, and during the 1990s pervasive interference with market forces seemed to slow the growth of the Japanese economy.

To improve our understanding of the process of growth, we obviously must analyze better the interaction between the business enterprise and its political and social environment. Because firms live in a world defined by national systems, in studying the one we automatically study the other. That is why in this book we chose to mix chapters on companies with chapters on countries. We are convinced that the systematic analysis of each is essential to further understanding of growth itself.

When we study the history of Rolls-Royce in Britain, we learn about the acute pressures of production for war. We observe the forced transition from small-batch production of luxury cars to very large-batch production of aero engines. We eventually encounter the company's need for government financial assistance to compete in the international market for large jet engines.

When we look at the history of Thyssen in Germany, we perforce learn about cartel policies and protective tariffs. We see that intensely competitive entrepreneurs such as August Thyssen will find ways to manage within the regulated environment, no matter how pervasive the regulation becomes.

When we examine the history of IBM in the United States, we begin to understand both the positive and negative effects of antitrust policy. In a broader sense, we see the evolution of a huge new market for data processing that arose within business during the Second Industrial Revolution. We then see that with the birth of the welfare state, exemplified by the Social Security Act of 1935, the market for IBM's punchcard systems multiplied enormously—only to grow by even bigger leaps during World War II. We see how national defense needs led the American government to develop a program of immense support for computer R&D, and promoted a three-way partnership among research universities, high-technology companies, and government agencies.

When we review the history of Toyota in Japan, we learn about the transition from making textile machinery to making trucks and automobiles, under pressure from a militarizing government in the 1930s. We see that the long-term success of Toyota required repeated governmental interventions in the early years, but that these interventions were by no means sufficient to ensure the firm's prosperity. It was the interfirm competition within the Japanese home market that provided the other big part of the environment for Toyota's success. Competition, especially with Nissan, spurred Toyota to its habit of relentless improvement and innovation, and to its record as the world leader in its industry.

These are the kinds of insights highlighted in this book. They are the fruits of comparative historical analysis: across time, as with the three industrial revolutions; across countries, as with our four star performers; across innovative firms, as in our eight company chapters; and across the individual managers and entrepreneurs whose lives so enrich these pages, and who collectively worked to create modern capitalism.

APPENDIX

STATISTICAL SUPPLEMENT *compiled by Jeffrey R. Bernstein*

TIMELINE *compiled by Rowena Olegario*

BASIC ECONOMIC DEFINITIONS *compiled by Jeffrey R. Bernstein*

Relative Sizes of U.S., Japan, United Kingdom, and Germany

Table A.1 Population by Country, 1700–1994 (in thousands)

Year	U.K.	Germany	U.S.	Japan
1700	8,400	15,000	251	30,000
1820	19,832	14,747	9,656	31,000
1870	29,312	23,055	40,061	34,437
1913	42,996	37,843	97,606	51,672
1950	50,363	49,983	152,271	83,563
1973	56,211	61,976	211,909	108,660
1994	58,202	66,802	261,558	125,188

Note: Except for 1700, figures are for midyear population adjusted to 1989 boundaries. Figures for Germany from 1820 onward thus refer to the population residing inside the former West Germany.

Sources: Angus Maddison, *Dynamic Forces in Capitalist Development* (New York: Oxford University Press, 1991), pp. 226–227; idem, *Monitoring the World Economy* (Paris: OECD, 1995), pp. 104–105.

Table A.2 Country Size and Population Density, 1992

	U.K.	Germany	U.S.	Japan
Area (1000 km²)	244	357	9,373	378
Population Density (people per km²)	238	225	27	328

Note: 1,000 km² = 386 mile², and 1 km² = 247 acres.

Source: Japan 1995: An International Comparison (Tokyo: Keizai Koho Center, 1994), p. 6.

Table A.3   Import Dependence for Fuels, 1991 (%)

	U.K.	Germany	U.S.	Japan
Coal	22.4	13.3	11.7	94.7
Oil	54.9	96.1	46.6	99.6
Natural Gas	9.5	77.3	11.4	96.0
Total Energy	39.1	50.3	22.8	82.6

Note: Import dependence is defined as (Net imports)/(Domestic production + Net imports) × 100. Total Energy is calculated using oil-equivalent data for coal, coke, oil, natural gas, hydroelectricity, and nuclear energy.
Source: Japan 1995: An International Comparison, p. 64.

Table A.4   Consumption of Energy, 1992

	U.K.	Germany	U.S.	Japan
Energy Consumption per Capita (kilograms of oil equivalent)	2,629	3,009	5,487	2,568
Energy Consumption per Unit of GDP (metric tons oil equivalent)	3.74	4.23	7.78	3.63

Source: Japan 1995: An International Comparison, pp. 59, 95.

Table A.5 Selected Socioeconomic Measures

	U.K.	Germany[a]	U.S.	Japan
Health Measures				
Life Expectancy in Years, 1900	51	47	47	44
Life Expectancy in Years, 1993	76	76	77	80
Infant Mortality (per 1000 births), 1993	7	6	9	4
Physicians (per 10,000 residents), c. 1990	16.4	25.6	21.4	17.0
Per Capita Caloric Intake, 1988	3,249	3,351	3,641	2,852
Marriage and Divorce Rates				
Marriages per 1000 people, 1970	14	12	17	14
Marriages per 1000 people, 1993	9	9	14	9
Divorces per 1000 married women, 1970	5[b]	5	15	4
Divorces per 1000 married women, 1993	13	7	21	6
Crime Statistics				
Homicides (per 100,000 inhabitants), 1988	7.4[b]	4.2	8.4	1.2
Robberies (per 100,000 inhabitants), 1988	62.6[b]	47.3	220.9	1.4
Homicide Arrests (per 100 offenses), 1988	81.5[b]	94.4	70.0	97.1
Robbery Arrests (per 100 offenses), 1988	23.3[b]	46.4	25.6	78.5
Average Years of Formal Education[c]				
For Working Population (ages 15–64), 1913	8.82	8.37	7.86	5.36
For Working Population (ages 15–64), 1950	10.60	10.40	11.27	9.11
For Working Population (ages 15–64), 1992	14.09	12.17	18.04	14.87
Communications and Media				
Telephone Lines (per 100 people), 1994	47	48	59	48
Cellular Phone Users (per 1000 people), 1992	26	10	43	13
Television Receivers (per 1000 people), 1993	435	559	816	618
Newspaper Circulation (per 1000 people), 1993	383	323	236	577
Transportation Infrastructure				
Length of Railway Lines in Use (000 km), 1870	21.5	18.9	85.2	0.0
Length of Railway Lines in Use (000 km), 1950	31.3	36.9	402.0	27.4
Stock of Passenger Cars in Use (million), 1950	2.3	0.5	40.3	0.05
Stock of Passenger Cars in use (million), 1996	20.3	39.9	146.0	40.8
Civil Aviation (billions of miles flown), 1996	58.8	12.6	480.0	69.3
Housing Conditions				
Floor Space Per Residence, c. 1990 (m²)	—	102	167	86
Sewerage Ratio, c. 1985 (% of houses)	95	91	73	44
Home Ownership Percentages, 1988	51.1	36.0	64.7	62.4

Continued on next page

Table A.5 (continued)

	U.K.	Germany[a]	U.S.	Japan
Consumer Prices (in 1991 $U.S.)	London	Hamburg	New York	Tokyo
Gasoline (1 liter)	0.89	0.89	0.60	1.05
Video Tape Recorder (1 unit)	970.00	1,213.48	397.75	587.78
Milk (1 liter)	0.91	0.79	1.19	1.65
Tissue Paper (5 boxes)	6.05	13.75	9.11	4.42

a. Information for Germany prior to 1991 refers to West Germany.

b. Figure for England and Wales.

c. Years of education as noted here is a weighted average, with years of primary education given a weight of 1, secondary 1.4, and higher education 2. This was done to accord with evidence on levels of earnings associated with different levels of education.

Sources: Health: Maddison, *Monitoring the World Economy,* p. 27; *Japan 1995: An International Comparison,* p. 87; *World Development Report, 1996* (New York: Oxford University Press, 1996), pp. 163, 215; George Thomas Kurian, *The New Book of World Ratings,* 3d ed. (New York: Facts on File, 1991), p. 235. Marriage and Divorce: *Statistical Abstract of the United States, 1996* (Washington: Census Bureau, 1996), p. 833. Crime: *Japan 1991: An International Comparison,* p. 92. Education: Maddison, *Monitoring the World Economy,* p. 37. Communications and Media: *Statistical Abstract of the United States, 1996,* p. 839. Transportation Infrastructure: Maddison, *Monitoring the World Economy,* pp. 64, 72; *World Almanac and Book of Facts, 1997* (New York: Press Publishing Co., 1997). Housing: *Japan 1995: An International Comparison,* pp. 85–86; Kurian, *New Book of World Ratings,* p. 221. Consumer Prices: *Japan Almanac, 1994* (Tokyo: Asahi Shimbun, 1994), p. 199.

Table A.6   Ownership of Publicly Listed Corporations by Sector, 1990–91 (%)

Owner	U.K.	Germany	U.S.	Japan
Financial Sector				
Banks	0.9	8.9	0.3	25.2
Insurance companies	18.4	10.6	5.2	17.3
Pension funds	30.4	—	24.8	0.9
Investment co. and other	11.1	—	9.5	3.6
Nonfinancial Sector				
Nonfinancial businesses	3.6	39.2	—	25.1
Households	21.3	16.8	53.5	23.1
Government	2.0	6.8	—	0.6
Foreign	12.3	17.7	6.7	4.2

Source: W. Carl Kester, "Industrial Groups as Systems of Contractual Governance," *Oxford Review of Economic Policy,* 8 (Autumn 1992): 24–44, table 4.

Table A.7   Number of Listed Companies, and Market Capitalization of Domestic Equity as a Percentage of GDP, 1990

	U.K.	Germany	U.S.	Japan
Number of Listed Domestic Companies	2,006	649	6,342	1,627
Market Capitalization of Listed Equity (% of GDP)	80.8	23.3	56.5	88.5

Source: Mitsuhiro Fukao, *Financial Integration, Corporate Governance, and the Performance of Multinational Companies* (Washington: Brookings, 1995), table 2-2, p. 21.

Table A.8   Gross Domestic Savings (% of GDP)

Year	U.K.	Germany	U.S.	Japan
Pre–World War II	12.3	20.0	18.7	11.7
1950–1959	16.2	26.8	18.4	30.2
1960–1984	18.1	23.7	18.0	32.5
1994	14	22	15	32

Sources: Figures for 1994: *World Development Report, 1996,* p. 213. Earlier data: C. Fred Bergsten and Marcus Noland, *Reconcilable Differences? United States–Japan Economic Conflict* (Washington: Institute for International Economics, 1993), p. 39.

Table A.9   Fixed Capital Formation as a Percentage of GDP, 1885–1995

Year	U.K.	Germany	U.S.	Japan
1885	7.4	10.7	21.2	—
1920	8.4	12.8	11.4	—
1950	13.2	19.1	16.8	25.5
1970	18.9	25.5	14.3	35.5
1995	15.1	21.7	14.2	28.4

Sources: Figures for 1885–1970: Thelma Liesner, *One Hundred Years of Economic Statistics* (London: Economist Publications, 1989), p. 8. Figures for 1995: calculated from data in International Monetary Fund, *International Financial Statistics,* Jan. 1997.

Table A.10   Unemployment Percentages

Year	U.K.	Germany	U.S.	Japan
1920	1.9%	1.7%	3.9%	5.3%[a]
1950–73	2.8	2.5	4.6	1.6
1974–83	7.0	4.1	7.4	2.1
1984–93	9.6	6.2	6.4	2.5

a. Japanese figure is for 1930 and comes from Liesner, *One Hundred Years of Economic Statistics.*

Sources: Maddison, *Dynamic Forces in Capitalist Development,* pp. 260–265; idem, *Monitoring the World Economy,* p. 84.

Table A.11   Strike Days (in thousands)

Year	U.K.	Germany	U.S.	Japan
1910	3,088[a]	17,848	—	—
1930	7,952[b]	4,029	26,200[b]	1,085
1950	1,389	380	38,800	5,468
1970	10,980	93	66,410	3,915
1990	1,093	364	5,926	140

a. U.K. figure from 1900.

b. U.K. figure from 1925, U.S. figure from 1927.

Source: Figures for 1910–1970: Liesner, *One Hundred Years of Economic Statistics.* Figures for 1990: *Japan 1995: An International Comparison,* p. 70.

Table A.12   Annual Hours Worked per Employed Person, 1870–1992

Year	U.K.	Germany	U.S.	Japan
1870	2,984	2,941	2,964	2,945
1913	2,624	2,584	2,605	2,588
1950	1,958	2,316	1,867	2,166
1973	1,688	1,804	1,717	2,042
1992	1,491	1,563	1,589	1,876

Source: Maddison, *Monitoring the World Economy,* p. 248.

Table A.13 Unionization Rates (union members as % of workers)

Year	U.K.	Germany	U.S.	Japan
1970	48.5	37.0	27.2	35.4
1980	52.6	39.4	22.6	30.8
1991	43.1	42.2	15.8[a]	24.2[b]

a. U.S. figure from 1992.
b. Japan figure from 1993.
Sources: Numbers for 1970 and 1980: Robert Price, "Trade Union Membership," in Ron Bean, ed., *International Labour Statistics: A Handbook, Guide, and Recent Trends* (London: Routledge, 1985), table 8.2. Others: *Japan 1995: An International Comparison,* p. 70.

Table A.14 Merchandise Exports as % of GDP

Year	U.K.	Germany	U.S.	Japan	World
1870	12.0	9.5	2.5	0.2	1.0
1913	17.7	15.6	3.7	2.4	5.0
1929	13.3	12.8	3.6	3.5	8.7
1950	11.4	6.2	3.0	2.3	9.0
1973	14.0	23.8	5.0	7.9	11.2
1992	21.4	32.6	8.2	12.4	13.5

Source: Maddison, *Monitoring the World Economy,* p. 38.

Table A.15 Total Government Expenditure (% of GDP at current prices), 1880–1992

Year	U.K.	Germany	U.S.	Japan
1880	9.9	10.0[a]	—	9.0[b]
1913	13.3	17.7	8.0	14.2
1938	28.8	42.4	19.8	30.3
1950	34.2	30.4	21.4	19.8
1973	41.5	42.0	31.1	22.9
1992	51.2	46.1[c]	38.5	33.5

a. Figure for 1881.
b. Figure for 1885.
c. Figure for 1990.
Source: Maddison, *Monitoring the World Economy,* p. 65.

Table A.16   Inflation, 1900–1993

Period	U.K.	Germany	U.S.	Japan
1900–1913	0.9	1.3	1.3	2.8
1920–1938	−2.6	−0.1[a]	−2.0	−0.3
1950–1973	4.6	2.7	2.7	5.2
1973–1983	13.5	4.9	8.2	7.6
1983–1993	5.2	2.3	3.8	1.7

a. Figure for 1924–1938, thus excluding the 1923 German hyperinflation.

Sources: Figures from 1900–1938: based on the compound annual growth rate of the GDP deflator; from Angus Maddison, *The World Economy in the 20th Century* (Paris: OECD, 1989), table 6.2, p. 70. Later figures: based on the average annual compound growth rate of the consumer price index, from Maddison, *Monitoring the World Economy*, p. 84.

Table A.17   Exchange Rates (Foreign Currency per $US), 1900–1995

Year	U.K. (£)	Germany (RM & DM)	U.S. ($)	Japan (¥)
1900	0.21	4.20	1.00	1.97
1913	0.21	4.20	1.00	1.97
1938	0.20	2.49	1.00	3.51
1950	0.40	4.20	1.00	360.00
1973	0.41	2.67	1.00	271.22
1995	0.63	1.43	1.00	94.06

Sources: Figures for 1900–1973: Maddison, *The World Economy in the 20th Century*, table D-9, p. 145. Figures for 1995: IMF, *International Financial Statistics*, Jan. 1997.

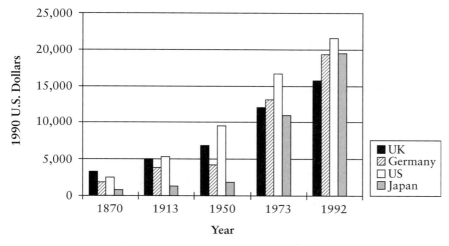

Figure A.1 Per Capita GDP, 1820–1992 (1990 $US)

Source: Angus Maddison, *Monitoring the World Economy, 1820–1992* (Paris: OECD, 1995), pp. 23–24.

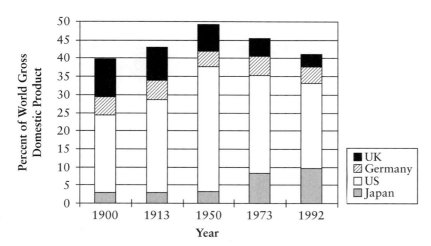

Figure A.2 Percentage Distribution of World Gross Domestic Product, 1900–1992

Source: Takashi Hikino and Alice Amsden, "Staying Behind, Stumbling Back, Sneaking Up, Soaring Ahead: Late Industrialization in Historical Perspective," in William J. Baumol, Richard R. Nelson, and Edward N. Wolff, eds., *Convergence of Productivity* (New York: Oxford University Press, 1994), p. 286.

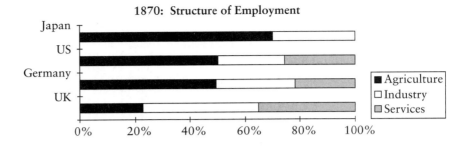

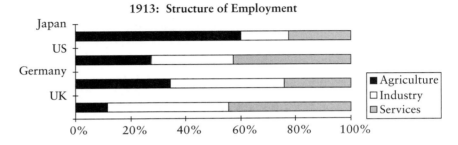

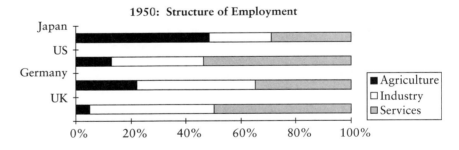

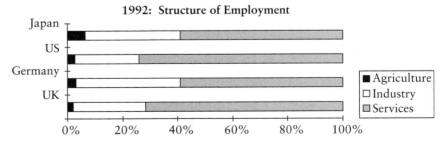

Figure A.3   Composition of Employment, 1870–1992

Note: For Japan in 1870, industry and services are combined.
Source: Maddison, *Monitoring the World Economy,* p. 39.

KEY DATES IN COUNTRY AND COMPANY CHAPTERS

Great Britain	Germany	United States	Japan
			Tokugawa period begins (1603)
			Country closed to foreign influence
1600			
		First permanent English-speaking settlement (1607)	
Glorious Revolution (1688)			
War against France (1688–97)			
Royal African Co. chartered (1672)			
Bank of England founded (1694)			
1700			
Union of England, Wales and Scotland (1707)	Prussia and Austria are largest German-speaking states, with several dozen others of various sizes included in the area making up present day Germany	Becomes independent of G. Britain (1776)	
First steam engine built (1712)		U.S. Constitution ratified (1789)	
South Sea Bubble episode (1720)		Alexander *Hamilton's Report on Manufactures* (1791)	
Josiah Wedgwood born (1730, d. 1795)		First Bank of the U.S. chartered (1791)	
Seven Years War against France (1756–63)			
Wedgwood opens first showrooms in London (1765)			
Watt dramatically improves steam engine (1765)			
Wedgwood invents jasperware (1774)			
Adam Smith publishes *Wealth of Nations* (1776)			
1800			

Great Britain	Germany	United States	Japan
		1800	
Defeats Napoleon at Waterloo (1815)	August Thyssen born (1842, d. 1926)	H. Clay's "American System" outlined (1824)	Perry forcibly opens Japan (1853)
Bank of England's monopoly ends (1826)	Thyssen opens hoop-iron mill (1867)	First protectionist tariff passed (1828)	Sakichi Toyoda born (1867, d. 1930)
First railway built (1830)	Deutsche Bank formed (1870)	Congress declines to recharter Second Bank of the U.S. (1836)	Meiji Restoration (1868)
Parliament widens franchise (1832)	Germany is unified (1871)	Civil War (1861–65)	Bank of Japan established (1882)
Corn Laws repealed (1846)	Thyssen & Co. founded (1871)	Henry Ford born (1863, d. 1948)	Imperial Constitution (1889)
Great Exhibition (1851)	Financial crisis (1873)	13th Amendment ends slavery (1865)	Commercial code introduced (1893)
Henry Royce born (1863, d. 1933)	Imperial Court upholds legality of cartels (1897)	Thomas Watson Sr. born (1874, d. 1956)	Kiichiro Toyoda born (1894, d. 1952)
Anti-union laws repealed (1869)		Alfred P. Sloan Jr. born (1875, d. 1966)	Sino-Japanese War (1894–95)
Charles Rolls born (1877, d. 1910)		Sherman Antitrust Law passed (1890)	
		4,227 U.S. companies merge into 257 combinations (1897–1904)	
		1900	

Great Britain	Germany	United States	Japan
		1900	Russo-Japanese War (1904–05)
			Toyoda Loom Works est'd. (1907)
			Taisho Period begins (1912)
			Showa Period begins (1926)
			Toyoda Automatic Loom Works est'd (1926)
			Toyoda signs licensing agreement with Platt Brothers (1929)
			Japan occupies Manchuria (1931)
			Toyoda establishes auto dept. (1933)
			Toyota Motor Co. spun off (1937)
			Allied occupation (1945–52)
		J.P. Morgan creates U.S. Steel: capitalized at $1.4 billion (1901)	
		Ford Motor Co. established (1903)	
		General Motors founded (1908)	
		Ford introduces Model T (1908)	
		Charles R. Flint establishes C-T-R (1911)	
		Federal Reserve System established (1913)	
		Tom Watson Jr. born (1914, d. 1993)	
		Sloan becomes president of GM (1923)	
		Ford produces 10 millionth car (1924)	
		Southland Ice Co. founded (1927)	
		Great stock market crash (1929)	
		Glass-Steagall Act separates commercial from investment banking (1933)	
		National Labor Relations and Social Security acts passed (1935)	
		Enters WWII (1941, ends 1945)	
		1950	
	Thyssen joins steel cartel (1904)		
	Thyssen cos. form "community of interest" (1915)		
	New German republic proclaimed (1918)		
	Versailles Treaty signed; Weimar Constitution adopted (1919)		
	Deutsche Bank workers strike (1919)		
	Period of hyperinflation (1922–23)		
	Thyssen joins VSt (1926)		
	Banking crisis (1931)		
	Hitler consolidates power (1933)		
	Krystallnacht (1938)		
	Nazis force Jews into ghettos (1941–42)		
	Occupation of Germany (1945–49)		
	Deutsche Bank broken up (1947–48)		
	New Deutsche Mark introduced (1948)		
	Soviets blockade W. Berlin (1948)		
	East and West Germany formally divided (1949)		
Labour Party formed (1900)			
Rolls-Royce founded (1906)			
Rolls-Royce produces Silver Cloud (1907)			
Enters World War I (1914, ends 1918)			
Rolls-Royce produces aircraft engines (1914)			
Universal suffrage enacted (1929)			
Goes off gold standard (1931)			
Enters World War II (1939, ends 1945)			
Adopts comprehensive welfare state (1945)			

1950

2000

Great Britain	Germany	United States	Japan
Wedgwood becomes public co. (1967)	Deutsche Bank recentralized (1952)	IBM begins producing computers (1950)	Formation of Liberal Dem. Party (1952)
Rolls-Royce files for bankruptcy (1971)	Deutsche Bundesbank created (1957)	War on Poverty (1964)	Department Store Law (1956)
Accepted into European Community (1973)	Berlin Wall built (1961)	IBM introduces System/360 (1964)	National Income Doubling Plan (1960)
Deregulation of securities industry (1986)	Berlin Wall falls; Germany reunited (1989)	Justice Dept. files suit against IBM (1969; dropped 1982)	Toyota launches Corolla (1966)
Wedgwood acquired by Waterford (1986)	Deutsche Bank's A. Herrhausen assassinated (1989)	Avg. real wages begin secular decline (1973)	Southland and Ito-Yokado sign licensing agreement (1973)
Rolls-Royce is privatized (1989)		IBM PC announced (1981)	First 7-Eleven store opens (1974)
		Southland files for prepackaged bankruptcy (1990)	Surpasses U.S. as leading producer of motor vehicles (1980)
			Collapse of bubble economy (1990)

Cartel. An agreement between firms in the same industry to fix prices, set production levels, or otherwise divide markets.

Consumption. In the context of GDP accounting, purchases of goods and services by households and individuals.

Economies of scale. A situation in which a proportionate increase in inputs (labor, capital) results in a greater than proportionate increase in output.

Economies of scope. A situation in which it is cheaper for a single firm to produce given quantities of mulitiple products than for multiple firms, each focusing on a single product, to produce the given quantities. (As Alfred Chandler has noted, economies of scope are often found in distribution rather than in the production process itself.)

Foreign direct investment (FDI). The purchase by domestic firms or individuals of (1) physical assets abroad or (2) a controlling share of a foreign firm's equity. The definition of "controlling share" is ambiguous; in the United States, it means 10 percent ownership.

Government spending. In the context of GDP accounting, government spending refers only to government purchases of goods and services (government consumption) and excludes transfer payments such as welfare payments and social security benefits.

Gross Domestic Product (GDP). The sum of the market values of all final goods and services produced within the borders of a country in a given period, usually one year. GDP thus represents a measure of national output. It can be analytically decomposed into consumption, investment, government spending, and net exports (see the separate definitions of these items).

In this book we use per capita GDP as our primary measure of economic performance, but GDP is a highly imperfect measure of economic well-being. GDP exaggerates national welfare by including as output such costs as pollution, resource depletion, and unproductive and undesirable expenditures such as crime-prevention devices. At the same time, GDP underestimates economic well-being by ignoring household and volunteer work and by not capturing improvements in productivity and quality.

Gross National Product (GNP). The sum of the market values of all final goods and services produced by a country's residents, regardless of their location in the world, in a given period. GNP = GDP plus residents' income from economic activity abroad minus nonresidents' income within the country. For most countries, there is little quantitative difference between GNP and GDP.

Inflation. The increase in the price level over a period of time.

Investment. In the context of GDP accounting, spending by firms on capital goods (such as production machinery, newly built structures, and office equipment) and on inventories. Investment also includes residential construction.

Labor productivity. A measure of output per labor input, such as output per worker or output per worker-hour.

Net exports. Exports minus imports. Exports are goods and services produced domestically but sold abroad; imports are goods and services produced abroad and consumed by domestic residents.

Nominal. Expressed in terms of the prices of the day (i.e., without adjustment for the effects of inflation).

Per capita. Per person

Purchasing power parity (PPP). A measure that converts incomes of different countries into dollars not on the basis of current exchange rates but according to their ability to purchase a standardized bundle of goods.

Real. Expressed in terms of constant prices (i.e., adjusted for the effects of inflation).

Total factor productivity (TFP). The increase in total output that is *not* attributable to increases in measured quantities of labor and capital inputs. It has been called the Solow residual (after Robert Solow, a Nobel Prize–winning economist). TFP is often said to represent a measure of "technological progress" or innovation, but its interpretation is far from clear. Still, TFP is considered important because it accounts for a large fraction of increases in output and labor productivity in developed countries, and because growth based only on accumulation of factor inputs is not expected to be sustainable (as the example of the former Soviet Union illustrates).

Value added. The difference between the price received by a firm when selling a given product and the cost of materials and services purchased from outside suppliers. The firm's own labor costs are not included in the latter figure. Thus, value added captures the firm's incremental addition to a product's selling price.

1. Introduction

1. I do not mean to suggest, of course, that there was no economic development or social change at all. Peter Mathias has reminded me that there was a good deal of change and development; that even though per capita growth rates were very low, there was population growth; and that asserting long-term economic stagnation might give the wrong impression about actual historical trends. I do want to emphasize that the best available aggregate numbers clearly show, in comparison with growth rates that came afterward, what can only be called stagnation.

2. William J. Baumol, Sue Anne Batey Blackman, and Edward N. Wolff, *Productivity and American Leadership: The Long View* (Cambridge, MA: MIT Press, 1989), p. 12. Reliable statistics on national income were not collected until the twentieth century, but the numbers quoted here represent the best available estimates. Scholars disagree over whether the "developed" world of today had a large lead over other countries in the years before industrialization. David S. Landes, in *The Unbound Prometheus: Technological Change and Industrial Development in Western Europe from 1750 to the Present* (Cambridge: Cambridge University Press, 1969), suggests that they did. For a strong argument that they did not, see Paul Bairoch, "Was There a Large Income Differential before Modern Development?" in Bairoch, *Economics and World History: Myths and Paradoxes* (Chicago: University of Chicago Press, 1993), pp. 101–110. All scholars seem to agree that the per capita income spread today between countries of the developed world and those of the less developed world is very much greater in both relative and absolute terms than it was on the eve of the First Industrial Revolution.

3. Karl Marx and Friedrich Engels, *The Manifesto of the Communist Party*, in Eugene Kamenka, ed., *The Portable Karl Marx* (New York: Viking, 1983), p. 209; Angus Maddison, *Dynamic Forces in Capitalist Development* (New York: Oxford University Press, 1991), pp. 6–7.

4. Joseph A. Schumpeter, *Capitalism, Socialism and Democracy* (New York: Harper, 1942, 3d ed. 1950), p. 79; idem, *Business Cycles: A Theoretical, Historical, and Statistical Analysis of the Capitalist Process*, 2 vols. (New York: McGraw-Hill, 1939), p. 1033.

5. I am referring here to thoroughgoing capitalist development in a country that became a major economic player. One could easily argue that capitalism in the Low Countries preceded that in Britain, or that important capitalist institutions developed in parts of pre-Renaissance Italy.

6. Of course, market forces could operate even within the framework of the just price, and they did. But their full play was severely constrained for those goods and services that came under such regimes.

7. On the issues covered in this paragraph and the next five, see Robert Heilbroner, *The Nature and Logic of Capitalism* (New York: Norton, 1985); idem, *The Making of Economic Society,* 8th ed. (Englewood Cliffs, N.J.: Prentice-Hall, 1989); Fernand Braudel, *Civilization and Capitalism,* 3 vols. (New York: Harper & Row, 1981–1984); Peter Laslett, *The World We Have Lost* (New York: Scribner, 1971); and Natalie Zemon Davis, *The Return of Martin Guerre* (Cambridge, MA: Harvard University Press, 1983).

8. Hobbes, *Leviathan,* ch. 13. Andrew Erdmann has reminded me that Hobbes was referring here to humankind in a state of nature, not to contemporary circumstances in a particular country. On the coming of time discipline, see E. P. Thompson, "Time, Work-Discipline, and Industrial Capitalism," *Past and Present,* 38 (Dec. 1967), pp. 56–97. It has been observed that in Algerian peasant society even in the twentieth century, "Haste is seen as a lack of decorum combined with diabolical ambition." Ibid., p. 59.

9. Arthur Young, *Political Essays concerning the Present State of the British Empire* (London, 1772), pp. 20–21.

10. The scholarly literature on the relationship between religion and capitalism has been accumulating for many decades, and has now reached immense proportions. The two classic texts are Max Weber, *The Protestant Ethic and the Spirit of Capitalism,* trans. by Talcott Parsons, intro. by Anthony Giddens (1904–05; New York: Charles Scribner's Sons, 1958); and R. H. Tawney, *Religion and the Rise of Capitalism: A Historical Study* (New York: Harcourt, Brace & World, 1926).

11. There is a huge literature on this subject. See, e.g., Michael Merrill, "Putting 'Capitalism' in Its Place: A Review of Recent Literature," *William and Mary Quarterly,* 3d ser., 52 (April 1995), pp. 315–326, esp. p. 322.

12. Scholars have long argued about what Blake meant by his reference to "dark Satanic mills." Some have even thought he was referring to universities. A recent biographer makes the case for the huge Albion flour mill in London. Peter Ackroyd, *Blake* (New York: Alfred A. Knopf, 1996), p. 130.

13. Joseph A. Schumpeter, *History of Economic Analysis,* ed. by Elizabeth Boody Schumpeter (New York: Oxford University Press, 1954), p. 541.

14. In the first few decades, the multiple was 14, the annual rate from 1870 to 1913 being 1.4 percent.

15. The term "industrial revolution" was popularized by the historian Arnold Toynbee, who used it in lectures delivered at Oxford University in the 1880–81 academic year. See Phyllis Deane, *The First Industrial Revolution,* 2d ed. (Cambridge: Cambridge University Press, 1984), p. 2, n. 1. Twentieth-century historians have conducted a long discourse over the appropriateness of the term. For a summary of the debate, see Charles P. Kindleberger, *World Economic Primacy: 1500 to 1990* (New York: Oxford University Press, 1996), pp. 129–132; and Mikuláš Teich and Roy Porter, eds., *The Industrial Revolution in National Context: Europe and the USA* (Cambridge: Cambridge University Press, 1996), pp. 1–12. For a survey of the ways in which the term has been used, see David Cannadine, "The Past and the Present in the English Industrial Revolution, 1880–1980," *Past & Present,* no. 103 (1984), pp. 130–172. My colleagues and I have been unable to pinpoint the origins of the terms "Second Industrial Revolution" and "Third Industrial Revolution." For a working definition of "Second Industrial Revolution," see Alfred D. Chandler Jr., *Scale and Scope: The Dynamics of Industrial Capitalism* (Cambridge, MA: Harvard University Press, 1990), pp. 62–63.

16. In 1970, two recent graduates of the Harvard Business School formed a company for the manufacture of something they called the "umbroller," an infant stroller that folded up like an umbrella. The product was a huge success.

2. Josiah Wedgwood and the First Industrial Revolution

All Wedgwood MSS references are to the Wedgwood collection deposited at Keele University or held at The Wedgwood Museum at Barlaston in Staffordshire. The author is grateful to The Trustees of The Wedgwood Museum for access to the collection. Quotations from its manuscripts are published by courtesy of The Trustees of The Wedgwood Museum, Barlaston, Stoke-on-Trent, Staffordshire, England, and copyright of this material remains vested in The Trustees of The Wedgwood Museum.

1. Statement c. 1759, quoted in Anthony Burton, *Josiah Wedgwood: A Biography* (New York: Stein and Day, 1976), p. 11.

2. John J. McCusker, *How Much Is That in Real Money? A Historical Price Index for Use as a Deflator of Money Values in the Economy of the United States* (Worcester, MA: American Antiquarian Society, 1992); *Economic Report of the President* (Washington: U.S. Government Printing Office, 1995), p. 272.

3. There is some historical dispute about the total number of pieces included in the set ordered by the Russian empress. The standard company histories place the number between 950 and 1,000.

4. Creamware was a durable, lead-glazed earthenware first made in England in the 1730s and named for its cream color. The description of the service is from

Mary Granville, Mrs. Delany, *Autobiography and Correspondence of Mrs. Delany* (London, 1862), vol. 1, p. 593.

5. Julia Wedgwood, *The Personal Life of Josiah Wedgwood* (London: Macmillan, 1915), p. 154.

6. Profit estimates vary from £200 to £500. See Wolf Mankowitz, *Wedgwood* (London: Dutton, 1953), p. 46; Robin Reilly, *Wedgwood* (London: Stockton, 1989), vol. 1, p. 72.

7. Josiah Wedgwood to Thomas Bentley, Sept. 1767, E. 18167–25, Wedgwood MSS, Keele University Library (original emphasis).

8. Nancy F. Koehn, *The Power of Commerce: Economy and Governance in the First British Empire* (Ithaca: Cornell University Press, 1994), pp. 26–50.

9. Henry Fielding, *An Enquiry into the Causes of the Late Increase of Robbers, with Some Proposals for Remedying this Growing Evil* (London, 1751), p. xi.

10. E. A. Wrigley and R. S. Schofield, *The Population History of England, 1541–1871: A Reconstruction* (Cambridge, MA: Harvard University Press, 1981), pp. 249–253; Lawrence Stone, *The Family, Sex and Marriage in England, 1500–1800* (London: Weidenfeld & Nicolson, 1977), p. 68; John Rule, *The Vital Century: England's Developing Economy, 1714–1815* (London: Longman, 1992), p. 9.

11. As Josiah wrote his partner in 1767, "I am in pursuit of so many objects, beside what my current run of business furnishes me with." Wedgwood to Bentley, 23 May 1767, E. 18147–25, Wedgwood MSS.

12. Quoted in G. W. and F. A. Rhead, *Staffordshire Pots and Potters* (London: Hutchinson, 1906), p. 223.

13. Wedgwood to Bentley, Nov. 8, 1766, E. 18132–35, Wedgwood MSS (original emphasis).

14. Lorna Weatherill, *The Pottery Trade and North Staffordshire, 1660–1760* (Manchester: Manchester University Press, 1971), p. 112. As Weatherill writes, "When a place acquired a population of between 1,000 and 2,000, it was well within the ranges of population of small market towns, as a few instances show . . . The second largest town in England [behind London with 675,000 inhabitants], Bristol, had a population of about 100,000 in the mid-eighteenth century, Birmingham 30,000, Manchester 45,000 and Norwich 50,000 . . . Other important towns had a much lower population, Canterbury, the largest town in [the county of] Kent, had 7,000 inhabitants in 1670, and in 1700 Nottingham also had a population of 7,000, which grew to nearly 14,000 by 1760" (p. 115).

15. Ibid., pp. 124–125.

16. Ibid., p. 126. Relative to numerous other contemporary shops, those in Burslem were advanced. Throughout the eighteenth century, many shop premises were informal. Sales across open windows of tradesmen's homes were common, so too were stalls in sheds or "bulks" set up against house or shop walls. "Some

were only big enough to provide a seat and roof; some were slept in at night by vagrants; some had a door and a bed on the floor and their tenants had no other home. One cold night in 1768, for instance, a [London] cobbler was found frozen to death in his pavement stall." Dorothy Davis, *A History of Shopping* (London: Routledge & Kegan Paul, 1966), p. 191. Even within larger commercial quarters, many merchants did not devote significant money or effort to displaying goods. Before 1750, a minority of stores had cupboards and shelves. Goods were often heaped in back rooms and attics, then brought out for interested customers. Such premises soon became a "splendid muddle . . . Even as late as the [1770s], in a progressive shop like [the London haberdashery and drapery] Flint and Palmer's it took numerous assistants hours every night to tidy away the goods tumbled during the day." Ibid., p. 193.

17. Eliza Meteyard, *The Life of Josiah Wedgwood* (London: Hurst and Blackett, 1865–1866), vol. 1, p. 182.

18. Burslem's roads were comparable to others in Britain before 1750. As Daniel Defoe wrote in 1720, "I saw an ancient lady [near Brighton in southeast England], and a lady of very good quality, I assure you, drawn to church in her coach with six oxen; nor was it done in frolic or humour, but mere necessity, the way being so stiff and deep [with mud], that no horses could go in it." *A Tour through the Whole Island of Great Britain* (London: P. Davies, 1927), vol. 1, p. 129.

19. Robin Reilly, *Wedgwood: The New Illustrated Dictionary* (Woodbridge, Suffolk: Antique Collectors' Club, 1995), pp. 143, 336.

20. Weatherill, *Pottery Trade,* p. 79.

21. Ibid., pp. 32–34. Before 1971 when Great Britain moved to decimalization—a coinage system based on 100 pence to the pound—the pound consisted of 20 shillings; each shilling consisted of 12 pence; a pound was thus worth 240 pence.

22. Ibid., p. 44. By way of comparison, a baker in Burslem in 1724 had equipment and inventories valued at £12, while the capital and stock of the Coalbrookdale ironworks were worth £3,000 in 1718. Ibid., p. 48.

23. In 1740, a farm laborer earned between £12 and £17 annually, an unskilled nonfarm worker £20, and a collier less than £22 ($3,200 in today's dollars). A bushel of wheat in 1740 cost 4 shillings and a pound of beef 1 or 2 pence. A calf could be purchased for between 6 and 9 shillings. See Robin Reilly, *Josiah Wedgwood* (London: Macmillan, 1992), p. 2. Wage data are from Peter H. Lindert and Jeffrey G. Williamson, "English Workers' Living Standards during the Industrial Revolution: A New Look," *Economic History Review,* 2nd ser., 36 (1983), p. 4, and Thomas Malthus, *Principles of Political Economy* (London: Reeves and Turner, 1836), pp. 241–251, quoted in Peter H. Lindert, "English Population, Wages, and Prices: 1541–1913," in Robert I. Rotberg and Theodore K. Rabb, eds., *Population and History: From the Traditional to the Modern World* (Cambridge: Cambridge University Press, 1986), p. 52. As several eco-

nomic historians have pointed out, wage data, like other numbers for the early eighteenth century, are limited and subject to large margins of error.

24. As early as 1700, pottery manufacture bore more resemblance to medium- and larger-scale production than to domestic or cottage industries, such as lacemaking or straw plaiting. The term "cottage industry" or "putting-out system" refers to a variety of handicraft production processes undertaken for the market by rural households as a means of supplementing agricultural incomes during slack seasons. Maxine Berg, *Age of Manufactures, 1700–1820* (New York: Oxford University Press, 1986), p. 79.

25. Ibid., p. 26.

26. N. F. R. Crafts, "The Industrial Revolution," in Roderick Floud and Donald McCloskey, eds., *The Economic History of Britain since 1700* (Cambridge: Cambridge University Press, 1994), vol. 1, p. 49.

27. Peter H. Lindert, "English Occupations, 1670–1811," *Journal of Economic History,* 40 (1980), pp. 685–712. As Lindert notes, eighteenth-century occupational labels were often imprecise. "We know from literary evidence that persons with one label often had many occupations, both in a single year and (especially) over their adult lives. Weavers farmed and farmers wove, in unknown proportions" (p. 693). See also Crafts, "Industrial Revolution," p. 45, and *British Economic Growth during the Industrial Revolution* (Oxford: Oxford University Press, 1985), pp. 12–14; and Peter Mathias, "The Social Structure in the Eighteenth Century: A Calculation by Joseph Massie," *Economic History Review,* 2nd ser., 10 (1957), pp. 30–45.

28. Koehn, *Power of Commerce,* p. 32. Agricultural output figure is from Crafts, "Industrial Revolution," p. 47.

29. Crafts, "Industrial Revolution," pp. 47–48.

30. On the historiographical debates surrounding the timing of the Industrial Revolution, see David Cannadine, "The Past and the Present in the English Industrial Revolution, 1880–1980," *Past & Present,* no. 103 (1984), pp. 131–172, and Julian Hoppitt, "Understanding the Industrial Revolution," *Historical Journal,* 30 (1987), pp. 211–224.

31. No other eighteenth-century European economy has received so much attention. See John Brewer, *Sinews of Power: War, Money, and the English State, 1688–1783* (New York: Knopf, 1989), p. 179.

32. According to recent research, farm output grew at an average rate of 0.1 or 0.2 percent per annum from 1760 to 1780. Crafts, "Industrial Revolution," p. 47.

33. Crafts, *British Economic Growth,* p. 23.

34. Lindert, "English Occupations," p. 709.

35. Simon Kuznets, *Modern Economic Growth* (New Haven: Yale University Press, 1966), pp. 88–89. There is scholarly controversy about the magnitude of Britain's industrialization. Crafts estimates industry's contribution to British output at about 20 percent in 1800. But he does not include commerce, services, or

mining. Crafts, "Industrial Revolution," p. 45, and *British Economic Growth,* pp. 62–63. According to the economic historian W. A. Cole, industry accounted for half of real output in 1800. "Factors in Demand, 1700–1800," in Roderick Floud and Donald McCloskey, eds., *The Economic History of Britain since 1700* (Cambridge: Cambridge University Press, 1981), vol. 1, pp. 40, 64.

36. In 1800, about 80 percent of the U.S. labor force was engaged in agricultural activities. See Richard K. Vedder, *The American Economy in Historical Perspective* (Belmont, CA: Wadsworth, 1976), p. 227. In France, approximately 40 percent of the nation's output was nonagricultural. See Myron P. Guttman, *Toward the Modern Economy: Early Industry in Europe, 1500–1800* (Philadelphia: Temple University Press, 1988), p. 117.

37. In the 1750s and 1760s, an extensive division of labor developed in many of the larger metalware workshops and factories. Here is how the British statesman Shelburne described the organization of work he observed on a 1766 tour of a Birmingham manufactory: "Instead of employing the same hand to finish a button or any other thing, they subdivide it into as many different hands as possible, finding beyond doubt that the human faculties by being confined to a repetition of the same thing become more expeditious and more to be depended on than when obliged or suffered to pass from one to another. Thus a button passes through fifty hands, and each hand perhaps passes a thousand in a day; likewise, by this means, the work becomes so simple that, five times in six, children of six or eight years old do it as well as men, and earn from ten pence to eight shillings a week." Lord Shelburne to Lady Shelburne, 19 May 1766, quoted in Lord Fitzmaurice, ed., *Life of William Earl of Shelburne* (London: Macmillan, 1912), vol. 1, pp. 276–277.

38. Supplies of west country clay were limited and relatively expensive until the Weaver River canal opened in 1733. Reilly, *Wedgwood,* vol. 1, p. 21.

39. Josiah C. Wedgwood, *Staffordshire Pottery and Its History* (New York: McBride, Nast, 1913), pp. 46–47.

40. Meteyard, *Life of Wedgwood,* vol. 1, p. 142; Wedgwood, *Staffordshire Pottery,* p. 61; A. H. Church, *Josiah Wedgwood: Master-Potter* (New York: Dutton, 1908), p. 21.

41. Weatherill, *Pottery Trade,* p. 35.

42. Enoch Booth, a master potter in Tunstall, Staffordshire, is generally credited with pioneering these techniques.

43. Meteyard, *Life of Wedgwood,* vol. 1, p. 203.

44. Reilly, *Wedgwood,* vol. 1, pp. 25–26. See also Julia Wedgwood, *Personal Life of Wedgwood,* pp. 8–9; Alison Kelly, *The Story of Wedgwood* (London: Faber & Faber, 1975), p. 11; Meteyard, *Life of Wedgwood,* vol. 1, pp. 199–200; and Llewellyn Jewitt, *Life of Josiah Wedgwood* (London: Virtue Brothers, 1865), p. 89.

45. In the eighteenth century, "manufacturer" designated a workman or master, as

well as an industrialist. P. Mantoux, *The Industrial Revolution in the Eighteenth Century: An Outline of the Beginnings of the Modern Factory System* (London: J. Cape, 1928), p. 375.

46. Burton, *Josiah Wedgwood*, p. 19.

47. Ibid.

48. There is no documentary evidence regarding Josiah's employment between 1739 and 1744. Reilly, *Wedgwood*, vol. 1, p. 26.

49. "Smallpox, unlike a disease such as influenza, did not sweep across the country as a national epidemic. Rather it seems to have been endemic at a regional level, returning to individual communities when there was a sufficient number of young children who had not previously been exposed to it." Wrigley and Schofield, *Population History of England*, p. 669. Before 1800, about one in seven people infected with the disease died. Fernand Braudel, *The Structures of Everyday Life: The Limits of the Possible* (New York: Harper & Row, 1979), p. 79.

50. Reilly, *Wedgwood*, vol. 1, p. 27; Meteyard, *Life of Wedgwood*, vol. 1, pp. 228–230; Burton, *Josiah Wedgwood*, p. 21; Jewitt, *Life of Wedgwood*, pp. 102–103; and Julia Wedgwood, *Personal Life of Wedgwood*, p. 16. In 1779, Wedgwood drew up a list of books he wished to own. "Besides county and other histories," the list included "travel [logs], and books on mathematics and science, especially chemistry . . . a large number of works of general literature: Bacon's works, [Laurence] Sterne's Letters, Churchill's [the Duke of Marlborough] Works, Hesiod, Horace, Cicero, Caesar . . . Bolingbroke on History, [James] Beattie [a Scottish poet] on Truth" and others. Julia Wedgwood, *Personal Life of Wedgwood*, p. 18.

51. "As [Wedgwood] was later to prove," Robin Reilly writes, "there were few tasks performed by craftsmen in his factories which he was unable to perform himself, often rather better than those he employed." *Wedgwood*, vol. 1, p. 27.

52. Quoted in Meteyard, *Life of Wedgwood*, vol. 1, p. 222.

53. A journeyman is a person who has served an apprenticeship at a trade and is certified to work at it assisting or under another person.

54. Reilly, *Wedgwood*, vol. 1, p. 29. When Whieldon retired in 1780, his fortune was estimated at £10,000 or ($1.3 million today). Mankowitz, *Wedgwood*, p. 27.

55. Weatherill, *Pottery Trade*, p. 51.

56. According to estimates later drawn up by Josiah Wedgwood, annual sales at his father's pottery in 1715 were £185. *Staffordshire Pottery*, p. 49.

57. Most of the ornamental goods Josiah sold in Birmingham and Sheffield were agateware, pottery made of various local clays, blended to imitate marble and other natural stones.

58. E. Anthony Wrigley, "Urban Growth and Agricultural Change: England and the Continent in the Early Modern Period," in Rotberg and Rabb, eds., *Population and History*, pp. 126, 133.

59. Ibid., p. 126.

60. On the expansion of consumer goods in the eighteenth century, see Eric L. Jones, "The Fashion Manipulators: Consumer Tastes and British Industries, 1660–1800," in Louis P. Cain and Paul J. Uselding, eds., *Business Enterprise and Economic Change: Essays in Honor of Harold F. Williamson* (Kent, OH: Kent State University Press, 1973), pp. 201–207; Lorna Weatherill, *Consumer Behaviour and Material Culture in Britain, 1660–1760* (London: Routledge, 1988), pp. 25–42; Neil McKendrick, "Home Demand and Economic Growth: A New View of the Role of Women and Children in the Industrial Revolution," in Neil McKendrick, ed., *Historical Perspectives: Studies in English Thought and Society* (London: Europa, 1974), pp. 152–210; idem, "The Consumer Revolution of Eighteenth-Century England," in Neil McKendrick, John Brewer, and J. H. Plumb, eds., *The Birth of a Consumer Society: The Commercialization of Eighteenth-Century England* (Bloomington: Indiana University Press, 1982), pp. 9–99; D. E. C. Eversley, "The Home Market and Economic Growth in England, 1750–80," in E. L. Jones and G. E. Mingay, eds., *Land, Labour and Population in the Industrial Revolution* (London: Edward Arnold, 1967), pp. 206–259.

61. Lord Shelburne to Lady Shelburne, 19 May 1766, quoted in Fitzmaurice, *Life of Shelburne,* vol. 1, p. 276.

62. Josiah Wedgwood's Experiment Book, E. 19121–29, Wedgwood MSS.

63. The numerical code constituted a form of shorthand. It also had the advantage, as Josiah noted, "of not being intelligible without the key." Quoted in Burton, *Josiah Wedgwood,* p. 25.

64. John Wedgwood's Account Book, City Museum and Art Gallery, Stoke-on-Trent, cited in Reilly, *Wedgwood,* vol. 1, p. 42. Burton puts the annual rent at £10. *Josiah Wedgwood,* p. 27.

65. Eversley, "Home Market and Economic Growth," p. 257.

66. Weatherill, *Consumer Behaviour,* pp. 24–42.

67. McKendrick, "Consumer Revolution," p. 10.

68. Meteyard, *Life of Wedgwood,* vol. 1, p. 215; Jones, "Fashion Manipulators," p. 206. Annual sugar consumption also rose rapidly during this period, from about 12 pounds per person annually in 1730 to 24 pounds in 1790. Carole Shammas, "Changes in English and Anglo-American Consumption 1550 to 1800," in John Brewer and Roy Porter, eds., *Consumption and the World of Goods* (London: Routledge, 1993), p. 182.

69. Quoted in McKendrick, "Consumer Revolution," p. 10.

70. In 1768, Josiah commented on the importance of a single shade: "With respect to the colour of my ware, I endeavour to make it as pale as possible to continue it *cream-colour,* and find my customers in general . . . think the alteration I have made in that respect a great improvement. But it is impossible that any one colour, even though it were to come down from heaven, should please every

taste, and I cannot *regularly* make two cream colours . . . without having two works for that purpose." Quoted in Mankowitz, *Wedgwood,* p. 44.

71. Quoted in *The Selected Letters of Josiah Wedgwood,* ed. Ann Finer and George Savage (London: Cory, Adams & Mackay, 1965), p. 7.

72. Landscapes, commemorative scenes, foliage, flowers, and birds were all popular subjects in the later eighteenth century. Wedgwood used Sadler & Green, a Liverpool firm, for his escalating printing needs. As soon as possible, he insisted on exclusive designs for his creamware, and consistently provided Sadler & Green engravers with new subjects for individual pieces and whole services. Mankowitz, *Wedgwood,* p. 53. The quantities of creamware sent to Liverpool for transfer-printing rose from £30 a month in 1763 to more than £600 a month in 1771. Reilly, *Wedgwood,* vol. 1, p. 48.

73. Consignments intended for export were probably fired in Liverpool.

74. In addition to the growing number of molds he commissioned, Wedgwood also ordered large quantities of biscuit (unglazed) earthenware from other local potters for use with his own glazes.

75. Meteyard, *Life of Wedgwood,* vol. 1, p. 329–331.

76. According to Wedgwood's 1762 records, daily wages for these hands varied from 2½ pence to 1 shilling, 2 pence. Burton, *Josiah Wedgwood,* p. 41.

77. As Wedgwood grew older and his success escalated, he became increasingly prone to psychosomatic ailments. His symptoms—rapid weight loss, blurred vision, shortness of breath—were real and consistently correlated with moments of frustration and anxiety, usually surrounding his business. See, for example, Wedgwood to Bentley, 12 Oct. 1772, quoted in Reilly, *Wedgwood,* vol. 1, p. 100.

78. In the 1760s, his fitness regime involved "riding on Horsback from 10 to 20 miles a day . . . [and eating] Whey and yolks of eggs in abundance, with a mixture of Rhubarb and soap just to keep my body open." Wedgwood to Bentley, 26 July 1767, E. 18160–25, Wedgwood MSS.

79. Meteyard, *Life of Wedgwood,* vol. 1, p. 299.

80. Reilly, *Wedgwood,* vol. 1, p. 46.

81. As Neil McKendrick has noted, Bentley "provided many of the mercantile ideas, the commercial contacts, entrepreneurial gambits, social introductions, and knowledge of the market that were to prove so valuable to [Wedgwood & Bentley's] business." See Neil McKendrick, "Josiah Wedgwood and Thomas Bentley: An Inventor-Entrepreneurship Partnership in the Industrial Revolution," *Transactions of the Royal Historical Society,* 14 (1964), p. 6.

82. See Reilly, *Josiah Wedgwood,* pp. 98–99, 240–242.

83. Robert E. Schofield, *The Lunar Society of Birmingham: A Social History of Provincial Science and Industry in Eighteenth-Century England* (Oxford: Clarendon Press, 1963), p. 44.

84. Burton, *Josiah Wedgwood,* pp. 36–37.

85. John Money analyzes the eighteenth-century political experience of the Mid-

lands in *Experience and Identity: Birmingham and the West Midlands, 1760–1800* (Manchester: Manchester University Press, 1977). On the larger role of manufacturers and merchants in transportation initiatives, see Koehn, *Power of Commerce,* pp. 42–43. On the financing of eighteenth-century turnpikes and canals, see G. R. Hawke and J. P. P. Higgins, "Transport and Social Overhead Capital," in Floud and McCloskey, eds., *Economic History of Britain since 1700* (1981), vol. 1, pp. 227–252.

86. Josiah Wedgwood to John Wedgwood, 1 Feb. 1765, E. 18059–25, Wedgwood MSS.

87. Thomas Bentley, *A View of the Advantages of Inland Navigation with a Plan of a Navigable Canal* (London, 1766), p. 42. The canal was completed in 1771 at a total cost of £300,000. It reduced transport costs for raw materials and finished goods from 10 pence per ton-mile to 1½ pence. Reilly, *Wedgwood,* vol. 1, p. 57.

88. Wedgwood also served as treasurer for the canal's newly formed investment company, the Proprietors of the Navigation from the Trent to the Mersey. Before he assumed his (unpaid) post, he was required to post a £10,000 bond. Burton, *Josiah Wedgwood,* p. 59.

89. Documentation of Josiah and Sarah's marriage settlement and other monetary arrangements between them have not survived. But there can be little doubt, as Reilly notes, that Josiah's marriage "was of great financial importance to him." In 1764, for example, Sarah's brother lent Josiah £500 for improvements to one of his workshops. When Sarah's father died in 1782, she inherited £20,000 or about $2.5 million today. Reilly, *Josiah Wedgwood,* p. 36.

90. Reilly, *Wedgwood,* vol. 1, p. 55.

91. George Stubbs's 1780 painting of the Wedgwood family captures a comfortable intimacy between Josiah and Sarah that is curiously at odds with the formal, genteel setting of the group portrait.

92. As Josiah wrote his brother, "I have just begun a Course of experiments for a white body & glaze which promiseth well hitherto. Sally is my chief helpmate in this as well as other things, & that she may not be hurried by having too many *Irons in the fire* as the phrase is I have ordered the spinning wheel [brought] into the Lumber room. She hath learned my [code] characters, at least to write them, but can scarcely read them at present." Josiah Wedgwood to John Wedgwood, 6 March 1765, E. 18070–25, Wedgwood MSS (original emphasis).

93. Wedgwood to Bentley, Jan. 1768, E. 25–18183, quoted in Reilly, *Wedgwood,* vol. 1, p. 55.

94. This estimate is based on Wedgwood's 4 Feb. 1770 letter to Bentley, E. 18288–25, Wedgwood MSS, and inventory figures from Wedgwood's accounts, W/M 1713, Wedgwood MSS.

95. The construction costs for the factory and surrounding buildings amounted to almost £10,000. Accounts, 28632–43, Wedgwood MSS.

96. In the 1760s it was a generally accepted, though mistaken, notion that much of the pottery unearthed in Italy was Etruscan.

97. Reilly, *Wedgwood,* vol. 1, p. 57.

98. Wedgwood to Bentley, 31 May 1767, E. 18149–25, Wedgwood MSS (original emphasis).

99. By the early 1770s, Wedgwood was worried about collection and sales costs, his sales representatives' initiative, and the general condition of his various showrooms. Wedgwood to Bentley, 1 Sept. 1772, E. 18397–25, Wedgwood MSS.

100. Wedgwood to Bentley, 14–18 June 1768, E. 18199–25, Wedgwood MSS.

101. Burton, *Josiah Wedgwood,* p. 82.

102. To commemorate the opening of the factory, six blackware vases were made in the classical style. Each bore the inscription: "One of the first Day's productions at Etruria in Staffordshire by Wedgwood and Bentley." On the reverse was inscribed "Artes Etruriae Renascuntur" ("The art of Etruria is reborn"). In November 1769, Wedgwood and his family moved into their new mansion. They celebrated by hosting a dinner in the Burslem town hall for 120 of Wedgwood's workmen. Kelly, *The Story of Wedgwood,* p. 28.

103. Neil McKendrick, "Josiah Wedgwood and Factory Discipline," *Historical Journal,* 1 (1961), p. 31.

104. Wedgwood was certain that the "same hands cannot make fine & coarse—expensive & cheap articles so as to turn to any good account to the Master." Wedgwood to Bentley, 19 Sept. 1772, quoted in McKendrick, "Factory Discipline," p. 32.

105. Robin Reilly, "A Lifetime of Achievement," in Hilary Young, ed., *Genius of Wedgwood* (London: Victoria and Albert Museum, 1995), p. 48.

106. Josiah claimed to have introduced the engine-turning process to the pottery industry. Commonplace Book, 28408–39, Wedgwood MSS. See also Reilly, *Wedgwood,* vol. 1, pp. 691–693.

107. Reilly, *Wedgwood,* vol. 1, p. 691.

108. Weatherill, *Pottery Trade,* p. 82.

109. In 1765, Josiah noted to a member of Parliament that the "principal of [our export] markets are the [American] Continent & [the West Indian] islands." Wedgwood to William Meredith, 2 March 1765, E. 18067–25, Wedgwood MSS. As Reilly points out, Wedgwood meant America not Europe, when he referred to the "Continent." Reilly, *Wedgwood,* vol. 1, p. 95. Creamware, cauliflower ware, agate, and tortoiseshell were in great demand in colonial America during the 1760s. Josiah Wedgwood and Thomas H. Ormsbee, *Staffordshire Pottery* (London: R. M. McBride, 1947), pp. 49–50. See also T. H. Breen, "An Empire of Goods: The Anglicization of Colonial America, 1690–1776," *Journal of British Studies,* 25 (1986), pp. 467–499.

110. R. P. Thomas and D. N. McCloskey, "Overseas Trade and Empire, 1700–

1860," in Floud and McCloskey, eds., *The Economic History of Britain since 1700* (1981), vol. 1, p. 87.

111. Cole, "Factors in Demand," p. 39.

112. Ibid.

113. Thomas and McCloskey, "Overseas Trade and Empire," p. 91.

114. Wedgwood to Thomas Bentley, 13 Sept. 1769, E. 18252–25, Wedgwood MSS (original emphasis).

115. Wedgwood to Bentley, 11 Feb. 1771, in *The Letters of Josiah Wedgwood*, ed. Lady Farrar (Manchester: E. J. Morten, 1973), vol. 2, p. 7 (original emphasis).

116. Wedgwood to Bentley, 5 Aug. 1772, E. 18384–25, Wedgwood MSS (original emphasis).

117. McKendrick, "Josiah Wedgwood and the Commercialization of the Potteries," in McKendrick, Brewer, and Plumb, eds., *Birth of a Consumer Society*, pp. 127–132. See also Reilly, *Josiah Wedgwood*, pp. 219–220. It is not precisely clear how Wedgwood and Bentley financed this initiative. They were helped by a relatively swift and largely positive response on the part of their targeted customers. As Wedgwood wrote to Bentley: "If a few more should turn up with letters as these promises of farther *commissions* we may in the end have no great reason to repent what we have done." Wedgwood to Bentley, 29 July 1772, E. 18383–15, Wedgwood MSS quoted in Reilly, *Josiah Wedgwood*, p. 220.

118. Quoted in Reilly, *Josiah Wedgwood*, p. 220.

119. Less than two years after the parcels were sent from Britain, all but three of the customers who had purchased the pottery had paid in full. McKendrick, "Wedgwood and the Commercialization of the Potteries," p. 130.

120. Wedgwood to Bentley, 7 June 1773, E. 18489–25, Wedgwood MSS.

121. Reilly, *Josiah Wedgwood*, p. 213. See also Mankowitz, *Wedgwood*, pp. 149–150.

122. According to one eighteenth-century traveler to Britain, the extravagance of the lower and middling classes had "risen to such a pitch as never before seen in the world!" G. C. Lichtenberg, *Lichtenberg's Visits to England*, ed. Margaret L. Mare and W. H. Quarrel (Oxford: Oxford University Press, 1938), p. 122.

123. Nathaniel Forster, *An Enquiry into the Causes of the Present High Price of Provisions* (London, 1767), p. 41.

124. C. Knick Harley, "Reassessing the Industrial Revolution: A Macro View," in Joel Mokyr, ed., *The British Industrial Revolution: An Economic Perspective* (Boulder, CO: Westview, 1993), p. 194.

125. Peter H. Lindert and Jeffrey G. Williamson, "Reinterpreting Britain's Social Tables, 1688–1913," *Explorations in Economic History*, 20 (1983), p. 102.

126. Wedgwood to Bentley, 2 Aug. 1770, E. 18314–25, Wedgwood MSS.

127. Josiah Wedgwood, *Catalogue of Cameos, Intaglios, Medals, Bas-Reliefs, Busts and Small Statues* (1787, 6th ed.), p. 1, Wedgwood Museum, Barlaston.

128. Neil McKendrick, "Josiah Wedgwood: An Eighteenth-Century Entrepreneur in Salesmanship and Marketing Techniques," *Economic History Review,* 2nd ser., 12 (1960), pp. 353–379.

129. Ibid., p. 358.

130. Wedgwood to Bentley, 23 Aug. 1772, E. 18392–25, Wedgwood MSS (original emphasis).

131. The 1790 Travellers' Book instructed salesmen to "arrive [at a given dealer or residence] very early in the morning or at 6 in the evening." Travellers' Book, 1790, E. 23571–12, Wedgwood MSS, p. 2. The book also contained information on the creditworthiness of customers.

132. Wedgwood to Bentley, 14 Nov. 1773, E. 18498–25, Wedgwood MSS.

133. It had always been his aim, Wedgwood wrote in 1787, "to improve the quality of the articles of my manufacture, rather than to lower their price." Wedgwood to Charles Twigg, 18 June 1787, E. 8636–10, Wedgwood MSS. See also Memorandum, 19 Sept. 1772, E. 18407–25, Wedgwood MSS.

134. In 1773, Wedgwood noted that his tableware prices were two to three times as high as the industry average and considered cutting prices. Wedgwood to Bentley, 14 April 1773, E. 18451–25, Wedgwood MSS.

135. 1770 Price List, 9484–52, Wedgwood MSS. Wedgwood offered retailers quantity discounts as well as a 5 percent price reduction for paying in cash.

136. Wedgwood to Bentley, 14 April 1773, E. 18457–25, Wedgwood MSS.

137. In 1770, Wedgwood and 25 other master potters agreed to maintain specified minimum prices for a range of table and other useful ware products. This is one of the earliest recorded examples of industrial price collusion in the eighteenth century. E. 9484–52, Wedgwood MSS.

138. Wedgwood to Bentley, 21 and 22 April 1771, quoted in Finer and Savage, eds., *Selected Letters,* p. 106; McKendrick, "Eighteenth-Century Entrepreneur," pp. 354–355.

139. McKendrick, "Wedgwood and the Commercialization of the Potteries," p. 126. See also Ralph M. Hower, "The Wedgwoods—Ten Generations of Potters," *Journal of Economic and Business History,* 4 (1932), p. 305.

140. The Chinese market presented significant challenges to Wedgwood. He was particularly concerned about porcelain manufacturers there copying his patterns and products and selling these new designs in Europe. Wedgwood to Bentley, 23 Jan. 1771, W/M 1441, Moseley Collection, Wedgwood MSS.

141. Arthur Young, *A Farmer's Tour through the East of England* (London, 1771), vol. 4, pp. 360–362. For Wedgwood's list of export destinations in 1786, see Wedgwood Ledger 10, p. 200, Wedgwood MSS.

142. McKendrick, "Wedgwood and the Commercialization of the Potteries," p. 135. See also Reilly, *Josiah Wedgwood,* p. 217.

143. On the organization of work in British and American potteries, see Frank Bur-

chill and Richard Ross, *A History of the Potters' Union* (Hanley: Ceramic and Allied Trades Union, 1977), pp. 28, 33; Marc Jeffrey Stern, *The Pottery Industry of Trenton: A Skilled Trade in Transition, 1850–1929* (New Brunswick: Rutgers University Press, 1994); John Thomas, *The Rise of the Staffordshire Potteries* (Bath: Adams & Dart, 1971); and Richard Whipp, *Patterns of Labour: War and Social Change in the Pottery Industry* (London: Routledge, 1990).

144. E. P. Thompson, "Time, Work-Discipline and Industrial Capitalism," *Past & Present*, no. 38 (1967), pp. 71, 73.

145. Commonplace Book, E. 28408–39, Wedgwood MSS.

146. E. 19114–26, p. 2, Wedgwood MSS.

147. E. 28408–39, Wedgwood MSS, quoted in McKendrick, "Factory Discipline," p. 41.

148. Marc Stern has pointed out to me that the punch-clock was not universally adopted by other eighteenth-century potters. As late as the 1920s, many U.S. potteries lacked time clocks.

149. Wedgwood to Bentley, 7 Oct. 1769, E. 18265–25, Wedgwood MSS.

150. McKendrick, "Factory Discipline," p. 38.

151. "Some Regulations and Rules made for this Manufactory more than Thirty Years Back," 1810, 4045–5, Wedgwood MSS.

152. The fine for most offenses was 2 shillings, 6 pence, which amounted to about 12 percent of an apprentice's weekly pay and about a quarter of a less-skilled worker's paycheck. Commonplace Book, 28409–39, Wedgwood MSS. On Wedgwood's efforts to discipline his workforce in the context of modern organizational theory, see Steven Postrel and Richard Rumelt, "Incentives, Routines, and Self-Command," *Industrial and Corporate Change*, 1 (1992), pp. 397–425.

153. Wedgwood to Bentley, 9 April 1773, E. 18455–25, Wedgwood MSS, quoted in McKendrick, "Factory Discipline," p. 34.

154. Wedgwood to Bentley, 19 May 1770, E. 18301–25, Wedgwood MSS (original emphasis).

155. Wedgwood began training female apprentices in the 1770s. Commonplace Book, 28409–39, Wedgwood MSS.

156. Wedgwood to Bentley, 23 Aug. 1772, E. 18392–25, Wedgwood MSS.

157. Hamilton was honored to have his collection emulated and sent Wedgwood drawings and models of various vases. "It is with infinite satisfaction," he wrote the potter in 1786, "that I reflect on having been in some measure instrumental in introducing a purer taste of forms & Ornaments by having placed my Collection of Antiquities in the British Museum, but a Wedgewood and a Bentley were necessary to diffuse that taste so universally, and it is to their liberal way of thinking & . . . acting that so good a taste prevails at present in Great

Britain." Quoted in Reilly, "A Lifetime of Achievement," p. 59. See E. 22495–30, Wedgwood MSS.

158. Wedgewood to Bentley, 1 May 1769, E. 18240–25, Wedgwood MSS (original emphasis).

159. Wedgwood to Bentley, 2 Aug. 1770, E. 18314–25, Wedgwood MSS (original emphasis).

160. Wedgwood to Bentley, 14 Feb. 1769, quoted in Reilly, *Wedgwood,* vol. 1, p. 349.

161. Wedgwood to Bentley, 1 Oct. 1769, E. 18264–25, Wedgwood MSS (original emphasis).

162. Reilly, *Wedgwood,* vol. 1, p. 350.

163. Wedgwood to Bentley, 19 Nov. 1769, E. 18269–25, Wedgwood MSS.

164. Wedgwood to Bentley, 4 Feb. 1770, E. 18288–25, Wedgwood MSS, quoted in Reilly, *Wedgwood,* vol. 1, p. 351.

165. Price Book of Workmanship, E. 30023–54, Wedgwood MSS.

166. Wedgwood to Bentley, 23 Aug. 1772, E. 18392–25, Wedgwood MSS (original emphasis).

167. Wedgwood to Bentley, 19 Nov. 1769, E18269–25, Wedgwood MSS.

168. Josiah Wedgwood, *An Address to the Young Inhabitants of the Pottery* (Etruria, 1783), p. 21.

169. In 1782, a riot broke out at Etruria. This was chiefly a result of a disastrous harvest that had resulted in escalating food prices and shortages. The uprising occurred when a barge loaded with cheese and flour and bound for the Staffordshire potteries was redirected to Manchester. Rioters seized the vessel and sold its contents at reduced prices. The protesters were finally dispersed by the local militia. Reilly, *Josiah Wedgwood,* pp. 142–143.

170. Wedgwood to Bentley, 25 Oct. 1777, E. 18788–25, Wedgwood MSS, quoted in Reilly, *Josiah Wedgwood,* p. 135.

171. McKendrick, "Eighteenth-Century Entrepreneur," p. 353.

172. Waterford Wedgwood paid an interim dividend in 1994.

3. British Capitalism and the Three Industrial Revolutions

1. Attendance figures from Eric de Maré, *London 1851: The Year of the Great Exhibition* (London: Folio Press, 1973), p. 74.

2. Charlotte Brontë to Patrick Brontë, 7 June 1851, quoted in Juliet Barker, *The Brontës* (London: Weidenfeld and Nicolson, 1994), pp. 676–677.

3. N. F. R. Crafts, "The Eighteenth Century: A Survey," in Roderick Floud and Donald McCloskey, eds., *The Economic History of Britain since 1700* (Cambridge: Cambridge University Press, 1981), vol. 1, p. 18.

4. In 1690, the great landowners and gentry owned about 75 percent of Britain's land. In the eighteenth century, the historian Richard Brown has written, "power, economic and political, lay in the possession and exploitation of land . . . In England there were major changes in landownership between the fifteenth and eighteenth centuries which consolidated the position of the great landowners and the gentry and made them into the dominant economic, political and social force in the country." Brown, *Society and Economy in Modern Britain, 1700–1850* (London: Routledge, 1991), pp. 266–267.

5. Charles Davenant, *Discourses on the Publick Revenues, and on the Trade of England* (London, 1698), pt. 1, p. 38.

6. See John Brewer, *Sinews of Power: War, Money and the English State 1688–1783* (New York: Knopf, 1989); the 75 percent figure is mentioned on p. 40.

7. These conflicts were the Nine Years War, also known as King William's War or the War of English Succession (1689–97), the War of Spanish Succession (1702–13), the Wars of Jenkins's Ear and Austrian Succession (1739–48), the Seven Years War (1756–63), the American War of Independence (1775–83), and the Great War with France, also known as the Napoleonic Wars (1793–1802, 1803–15).

8. Nancy F. Koehn, *The Power of Commerce: Economy and Governance in the First British Empire* (Ithaca: Cornell University Press, 1994), pp. 4–5.

9. Ibid., p. 4.

10. Brewer, *Sinews of Power*, pp. 88–114.

11. Ibid., p. 114.

12. The Bank's legal monopoly lasted until 1826. The institution became an official government agency only after World War II.

13. On debt financing, see P. G. M. Dickson, *The Financial Revolution in England: A Study in the Development of Public Credit, 1688–1756* (New York: Macmillan, 1967).

14. Larry Neal, "The Finance of Business during the Industrial Revolution," in Roderick Floud and Donald McCloskey, eds., *Economic History of Britain since 1700* (Cambridge: Cambridge University Press, 1994), vol. 1, p. 172.

15. Peter Mathias, "Capital, Credit, and Enterprise in the Industrial Revolution," in *The Transformation of England: Essays in the Economic and Social History of England in the Eighteenth Century* (New York: Columbia University Press, 1979), p. 94. Short-term credit needs included buying raw materials, providing customer credit, and inventories. Mathias notes that the "relative slowness of the distribution system in the eighteenth century meant that a very high level of stocks had to be financed relative to turnover" (p. 94).

16. Ibid.

17. Neal, "Finance of Business," p. 151.

18. Julian Hoppit, "The Use and Abuse of Credit in Eighteenth Century England," in Neil McKendrick, ed., *Business Life and Public Policy* (Cambridge: Cambridge University Press, 1986), p. 66.

19. S. D. Chapman, *The Rise of Merchant Banking* (London: George Allen & Unwin, 1984), pp. 1–15.

20. In 1750, London had 675,000 inhabitants. By 1801, more than 950,000 people lived in the nation's capital. E. Anthony Wrigley, "Urban Growth and Agricultural Change: England and the Continent in the Early Modern Period," in Robert I. Rotberg and Theodore K. Rabb, eds., *Population and History: From the Traditional to the Modern World* (Cambridge: Cambridge University Press, 1986), p. 126.

21. E. A. Wrigley, *People, Cities and Wealth* (Oxford: Basil Blackwell, 1987), pp. 142–156.

22. On the relationship between international authority and economic strategy, see Paul Kennedy, *The Rise and Fall of the Great Powers: Economic Change and Military Conflict from 1500 to 2000* (London: Unwin Hyman, 1988), and Koehn, *Power of Commerce,* pp. 1–23.

23. Josiah Child, *A New Discourse of Trade,* 3d ed. (London, 1718), p. 152.

24. Koehn, *Power of Commerce,* pp. x–xii, 61–104.

25. R. P. Thomas and D. N. McCloskey, "Overseas Trade and Empire, 1700–1860," in Floud and McCloskey, eds., *Economic History of Britain,* (1981), vol. 1, p. 91.

26. Phyllis Deane, *The First Industrial Revolution,* 2d ed. (Cambridge: Cambridge University Press, 1979), pp. 57–59.

27. Economic historians continue to debate the role of colonial trade in eighteenth-century industrialization. W. A. Cole and other scholars have argued that Britain's exports to colonial markets accounted for as much as 40 percent of the increase in industrial output over the century. See Cole, "Factors in Demand, 1700–80," in Floud and McCloskey, eds., *Economic History of Britain,* (1981), vol. 1, p. 41. Ralph Davis, R. P. Thomas, D. N. McCloskey, and others deny that imperial commerce significantly influenced industrial development. See Ralph Davis, *The Industrial Revolution and British Overseas Trade* (Leicester: Leicester University Press, 1979), pp. 62–64; Thomas and McCloskey, "Overseas Trade and Empire," pp. 100–102.

28. John Rule, *The Vital Century. England's Developing Economy, 1714–1815* (London: Longman, 1992), p. 268.

29. Lucy S. Sutherland, *The East India Company in Eighteenth Century Politics* (Oxford: Clarendon Press, 1952). See also John Keay, *The Honourable Company: A History of the English East India Company* (New York: Macmillan, 1991); K. N. Chaudhuri, *The Trading World of Asia and English*

East India Company, 1660–1760, (Cambridge: Cambridge University Press, 1978).

30. Deane, *First Industrial Revolution,* p. 56.
31. Ibid.
32. S. D. Chapman, *Merchant Enterprise in Britain* (Cambridge: Cambridge University Press, 1992), pp. 68–69.
33. J. R. Ward, *The Finance of Canal Building in Eighteenth Century England* (Oxford: Oxford University Press, 1974).
34. William Albert, *The Turnpike Road System in England, 1663–1840* (Cambridge: Cambridge University Press, 1972).
35. G. R. Hawke and J. P. P. Higgins, "Transport and Social Overhead Capital," in Floud and McCloskey, eds., *Economic History of Britain,* (1981), vol. 1, p. 233.
36. W. T. Jackman, *The Development of Transportation in Modern England* (London: F. Cass, 1962), cited in Hawke and Higgins, "Transport and Social Overhead Capital," p. 234.
37. See G. N. von Tunzelmann, *Steam Power and British Industrialization to 1860* (Oxford: Clarendon Press, 1978). Von Tunzelmann argues that the steam engine had only a limited effect until the mid-nineteenth century.
38. Michael Flinn, *The History of the British Coal Industry* (Oxford: Clarendon Press, 1984), vol. 2.
39. See G. R. Hawke, *Railways and Economic Growth in England and Wales, 1840–1870* (Oxford: Clarendon Press, 1970).
40. D. A. Farnie, *English Cotton Industry and the World Market, 1815–1896* (Oxford: Clarendon Press, 1979), pp. 24, 57–63.
41. Leslie Hannah, *The Rise of the Corporate Economy,* 2d ed. (London: Methuen, 1983), p. 10.
42. N. F. R. Crafts, *British Economic Growth during the Industrial Revolution* (Oxford: Oxford University Press, 1985), p. 23.
43. Ibid., p. 143.
44. Anthony Howe, *The Cotton Masters, 1830–1860* (Oxford: Clarendon Press, 1984), p. 2.
45. On the importance of regional development, see Sidney Pollard, *Peaceful Conquest: The Industrialization of Europe, 1760–1970* (Oxford: Oxford University Press, 1981).
46. See Hannah, *Rise of the Corporate Economy.*
47. David J. Jeremy, *Transatlantic Industrial Revolution: The Diffusion of Textile Technologies between Britain and America 1790–1830s* (Cambridge, MA: MIT Press, 1981), p. 255.
48. Ibid., pp. 40–42.
49. Farnie, *English Cotton Industry,* p. 215. See also Howe, *Cotton Masters,* p. 5.

50. On the social status of British cotton mill owners, see Howe, *Cotton Masters*. On the international nature of the cotton textile industry, see Farnie, *English Cotton Industry*.

51. See Sidney Pollard, *The Genesis of Modern Management* (Cambridge, MA: Harvard University Press, 1965), pp. 90–91.

52. Peter Mathias, "Financing the Industrial Revolution," in Peter Mathias and John Davis, eds., *The First Industrial Revolutions* (Oxford: Basil Blackwell, 1989), p. 82.

53. P. L. Cottrell, *Industrial Finance, 1830–1914* (London: Methuen, 1980), p. 179.

54. Neal, "Finance of Business," p. 169. See also Peter Mathias, *The First Industrial Nation: An Economic History of Britain*, 2d ed. (London: Methuen, 1983), pp. 154–155.

55. Mathias, "Financing the Industrial Revolution," p. 83.

56. David Cannadine, *The Decline and Fall of the British Aristocracy* (New Haven: Yale University Press, 1990).

57. Brown, *Society and Economy in Modern Britain*, p. 267; Cannadine, *Decline and Fall of the British Aristocracy*, pp. 8–15.

58. S. D. Chapman, *Merchant Enterprise in Britain*, p. 289.

59. See Ann Prior and Maurice Kirby, "The Society of Friends and the Family Firm, 1700–1830," in Geoffrey Jones and Mary Rose, eds., *Family Capitalism* (London: F. Cass, 1993), pp. 66–85; François Crouzet, *The First Industrialists: The Problem of Origins* (Cambridge: Cambridge University Press, 1985); Katrina Honeyman, *Origins of Enterprise: Business Leadership in the Industrial Revolution* (Manchester: Manchester University Press, 1982).

60. See Walter L. Arnstein, *The Bradlaugh Case* (Oxford: Clarendon Press, 1965; rpt. Columbia: University of Missouri Press, 1983).

61. Koehn, *Power of Commerce*, pp. 28–30, 105–147, 185–200. For a dissenting view, see P. J. Cain and A. G. Hopkins, "Gentlemanly Capitalism and British Expansion Overseas: The Old Colonial System, 1688–1850," *Economic History Review*, 39 (1986), pp. 501–525. On the role of manufacturing interests in late eighteenth-century politics, see Vivian Dietz, "Before the Age of Capital: Manufacturing Interests and the Pittite State" (Ph.D. diss., Princeton University, 1991).

62. These fears were unfounded; Wedgwood and other manufacturers were either mistaken about the intentions of the proposed treaty or misinformed by Opposition politicians interested in defeating the government's policies. See Robin Reilly, *Josiah Wedgwood, 1730–1795* (London: Macmillan, 1992), p. 265.

63. Josiah Wedgwood to Matthew Boulton, 21 February 1785, E. 19098–26, Wedgwood MSS, Keele University, quoted in ibid., p. 263.

64. Ibid.
65. Robin Reilly, *Wedgwood* (London: Stockton, 1989), vol. 1, p. 116.
66. Edmund Burke, *Reflections on the Revolution in France* (1790), ed. Thomas Mahoney (New York: Bobbs-Merrill, 1955), pp. 57–59.
67. G. R. Searle, *Entrepreneurial Politics in Mid-Victorian England* (Oxford: Oxford University Press, 1993).
68. Samuel Smiles, *Self-Help* (1859; London: John Murray, 1958), pp. 360–362.
69. Adapted from B. R. Mitchell and Phyllis Deane, *Abstract of British Historical Statistics* (Cambridge University Press, 1962), p. 98.
70. Mathias, *First Industrial Nation,* p. 229.
71. R. C. O. Matthews, C. H. Feinstein, and J. C. Odling-Smee, *British Economic Growth, 1856–1973* (Stanford: Stanford University Press, 1982), p. 432.
72. On the collapse of free trade in 1931, see R. W. D. Boyce, *British Capitalism at the Crossroads, 1919–1932* (Cambridge: Cambridge University Press, 1987).
73. Alfred Maizels, *Industrial Growth and World Trade* (Cambridge: Cambridge University Press, 1963), p. 220.
74. Matthews, Feinstein, and Odling-Smee, *British Economic Growth, 1856–1973,* p. 435.
75. Youssef Cassis, "British Finance: Success and Controversy," in J. J. Van Helten and Y. Cassis, eds., *Capitalism in a Mature Economy: Financial Institutions, Capital Exports and the British Economy, 1870–1939* (Aldershot: Edward Elgar, 1990), p. 1.
76. Sidney Pollard, "Capital Exports, 1870–1914: Harmful or Beneficial?" *Economic History Review,* 38 (1985), p. 500. Numbers are from Frederick Lavington, *The English Capital Market* (London: Methuen, 1921).
77. Lance Davis and Robert Huttenback, *Mammon and the Pursuit of Empire: The Political Economy of British Imperialism, 1860–1912* (Cambridge: Cambridge University Press, 1986), pp. 303–304.
78. Ibid., pp. 42–43.
79. See D. K. Fieldhouse, *Economics and Empire, 1830–1914* (London: Weidenfeld and Nicolson, 1973).
80. Robert I. Rotberg, *The Founder: Cecil Rhodes and the Pursuit of Power* (New York: Oxford University Press, 1988).
81. John Dunning and Howard Archer, "The Eclectic Paradigm and the Growth of UK Multinational Enterprise, 1870–1983," *Business and Economic History,* 16 (1987), pp. 19–21; Geoffrey Jones, *The Evolution of International Business* (London: Routledge, 1996), pp. 29–31.
82. Henry Dyer, *Dai Nippon: The Britain of the East* (London: Blackie & Son, 1904), pp. 427–428.

83. E. E. Williams, "Economic Decay of Great Britain," *Contemporary Review,* 79 (1901), p. 631.

84. Mitchell and Deane, *Abstract of British Historical Statistics,* p. 334. Adapted from A. H. Imlah, *Economic Elements in the Pax Britannica* (Cambridge: Harvard University Press, 1958).

85. On British investment in the United States, see Mira Wilkins, *The History of Foreign Investment in the United States to 1914* (Cambridge, MA: Harvard University Press, 1989), pp. 155–167.

86. Mathias, *First Industrial Nation,* p. 293.

87. For some of the reasons for this, see Steven Tolliday, *Business, Banking, and Politics: The Case of British Steel, 1918–1939* (Cambridge, MA: Harvard University Press, 1987).

88. Hannah, *Rise of the Corporate Economy,* p. 22.

89. See Clive Trebilcock, *The Vickers Brothers* (London: Europa, 1977); R. P. T. Davenport-Hines, "Vickers as a Multinational before 1945," in Geoffrey Jones, ed., *British Multinationals* (Aldershot: Gower, 1986), pp. 43–74.

90. Hudson Maxim, "High Explosives and Smokeless Powders," *Mechanical Engineer,* 3, no. 58 (1899), p. 129. Hudson Maxim, inventor of smokeless cannon powder and high explosives, was the brother of Sir Hiram Maxim, inventor of the Maxim Automatic [Machine] Gun and head of the Maxim Gun Company, which later became part of Vickers, Son & Maxim, Ltd.

91. World War I was the first total war, or all-out war of attrition. It was the first in which civilian populations were actively mobilized for war service, with the result that they too sometimes became military targets along with the troops.

92. A century earlier, in 1805, the British Admiral Horatio Nelson had ended a similar threat by defeating Napoleon's navy in the Battle of Trafalgar, and had become one of the most honored heroes in the nation's history.

93. D. A. Farnie, "The Structure of the British Cotton Industry, 1846–1914," in Akio Okochi and Shin-ichi Yonekawa, eds., *The Textile Industry and Its Business Climate* (Tokyo: University of Tokyo Press, 1982), p. 69.

94. See A. J. Robertson, "Lancashire and the Rise of Japan, 1910–1937," in Mary Rose, ed., *International Competition and Strategic Response in the Textile Industries since 1870* (London: Frank Cass, 1991), pp. 87–105.

95. J. H. Porter, "Cotton and Wool Textiles," in Neil Buxton and Derek Aldcroft, eds., *British Industry between the Wars* (London: Scolar Press, 1979), pp. 25–30.

96. See John Singleton, "Showing the White Flag: The Lancashire Cotton Industry, 1945–1965," in Rose, ed., *International Competition and Strategic Response,* pp. 129–149.

97. See William Lazonick, "Industrial Organization and Technological Change: The Decline of the British Cotton Industry," *Business History Review,* 57

(summer 1983), pp. 195–236; Bernard Elbaum and William Lazonick, *The Decline of the British Economy* (Oxford: Clarendon Press, 1986); William Mass and William Lazonick, "The British Cotton Industry and International Competitive Advantage: The State of the Debates," *Business History*, 32 (Oct. 1990), pp. 9–65.

98. Hannah, *Rise of the Corporate Economy*, p. 24.

99. See W. J. Reader, *Imperial Chemical Industries: A History* (Oxford: Oxford University Press, 1970); Charles Wilson, *The History of Unilever* (London: Cassell, 1954), vol. 1.

100. See Alfred D. Chandler Jr., *Scale and Scope: The Dynamics of Industrial Capitalism* (Cambridge, MA: Harvard University Press, 1990).

101. Mathias and Davis, eds., *First Industrial Revolutions*, p. 370.

102. See Leslie Hannah and J. A. Kay, *Concentration in Modern Industry* (London: Macmillan, 1977), pp. 64–82.

103. See T. R. Gourvish, "British Business and the Transition to a Corporate Economy: Entrepreneurship and Management Structure," in R. P. T. Davenport-Hines and Geoffrey Jones, eds., *Enterprise, Management and Innovation in British Business, 1914–1980* (London: Frank Cass, 1988).

104. George Orwell, *The Road to Wigan Pier* (1937; New York: Harcourt, Brace, Jovanovich, 1958); pp. 18–19.

105. See Michael Turner, *Enclosures in Britain, 1750–1830* (London: Macmillan, 1984); J. M. Neeson, *Commoners: Common Right, Enclosure and Social Change in England, 1700–1820* (Cambridge: Cambridge University Press, 1993); Robert C. Allen, *Enclosure and the Yeoman* (Oxford: Clarendon Press, 1992).

106. See E. P. Thompson, "The Moral Economy of the English Crowd in the Eighteenth Century," *Past & Present*, no. 50 (Feb. 1971); rpt. in E. P. Thompson, *Customs in Common* (New York: New Press, 1991).

107. Historically, Europe's population had gone through periods of dramatic growth, only to be decimated by disease, famine, and war. The so-called Black Death (bubonic plague) of the 1300s had wiped out as much as a third to a half of all Europeans.

108. See Neil McKendrick, John Brewer, and J. H. Plumb, *The Birth of a Consumer Society: The Commercialization of Eighteenth Century England* (Bloomington: Indiana University Press, 1982).

109. Quoted by James Boswell, *Life of Johnson*, ed. R. W. Chapman (Oxford: Oxford University Press, 1983), pp. 658–659.

110. Charlotte Brontë, *Shirley* (London: Penguin, 1985), p. 62.

111. Friedrich Engels, *The Condition of the Working Class in England*, ed. and trans. W. O. Henderson and W. H. Chaloner (Oxford: Basil Blackwell, 1958), p. 43.

112. Sidney Pollard, "Labour in Great Britain," in Peter Mathias and M. M.

Postan, eds., *Cambridge Economic History of Europe* (Cambridge: Cambridge University Press, 1978), vol. 7.

113. M. A. Bienefeld, *Working Hours in British Industry: An Economic History* (London: Weidenfeld and Nicolson, 1972), pp. 47, 106–118, 143.

114. Charles Dickens, *Hard Times* (London: Methuen, 1987), pp. 33–34.

115. Sidney Pollard, "Management and Labor in Britain during the Period of Industrialization," in Keiichiro Nakagawa, ed., *Labor and Management* (Tokyo: University of Tokyo Press, 1979), pp. 60–61.

116. Quotation from Douglas A. Reid, "The Decline of Saint Monday, 1766–1876," *Past & Present*, no. 71 (May 1976), p. 90.

117. Quotation from Ivy Pinchbeck, *Women Workers and the Industrial Revolution, 1750–1850* (1930; London: Frank Cass, 1969), p. 280.

118. Crafts, *British Economic Growth*, p. 156.

119. H. A. Clegg, Alan Fox, and A. F. Thompson, *A History of British Trade Unions since 1889* (Oxford: Oxford University Press, 1964), vol. 1, p. 313. On resistance, see John Saville, "Trade Unions and Free Labour: The Background to the Taff Vale Decision," in Asa Briggs and John Saville, eds., *Essays in Labour History* (London: Macmillan, 1967), pp. 317–350.

120. Andrew Kilpatrick and Tony Lawson, "On the Nature of Industrial Decline in the UK," *Cambridge Journal of Economics*, 4 (March 1980), p. 86.

121. See Elbaum and Lazonick, eds., *Decline of the British Economy*.

122. Derek Aldcroft, "Investment in and Utilization of Manpower: Great Britain and Her Rivals, 1870–1914," in Barrie Ratcliffe, ed., *Great Britain and Her World, 1750–1914* (Manchester: Manchester University Press, 1975), p. 304.

123. Clegg, Fox, and Thompson, *History of British Trade Unions*, vol. 1, pp. 423–465.

124. Eric Hobsbawm, *Labouring Men* (New York: Basic Books, 1964), p. 361; also 344–370.

125. On the impact of World War II on British business, see Peter Howlett, "British Business and the State during the Second World War," in Jun Sakudo and Takao Shiba, eds., *World War II and the Transformation of Business Systems* (Tokyo: University of Tokyo Press, 1994).

126. It is often asked how Winston Churchill could have won the war and yet lost the 1945 election. In fact, Churchill's wartime cabinet had been a multiparty coalition, in which he himself was a Conservative but in which Labour Party members were responsible for much of the government's domestic policy.

127. See Wayne Lewchuk, "The Motor Vehicle Industry," in Elbaum and Lazonick, eds., *Decline of the British Economy*, pp. 135–161. See also Roy Church, *The Rise and Decline of The British Motor Industry* (London: Macmillan, 1994).

128. N. F. R. Crafts and N. W. C. Woodward, eds., *The British Economy Since 1945* (Oxford: Clarendon Press, 1991), p. 12.

129. Hamish McRae and Frances Cairncross, *Capital City* (London: Methuen, 1991), p. 136.

130. Maximilian Hall, *The City Revolution* (New York: St. Martin's, 1987), p. 34.

131. See Stephen George, *An Awkward Partner: Britain in the European Community* (Oxford: Oxford University Press, 1994).

132. Crafts, *British Economic Growth*, p. 73.

133. Graham Turner, *Business in Britain* (London: Eyre and Spottiswoode, 1969), p. 431, quoted in John F. Wilson, *British Business History, 1720–1994* (Manchester: Manchester University Press, 1995), p. 181.

134. I am indebted to Professor Geoffrey Jones for suggesting the points made in this sentence and the preceding two. See esp. Jones, *The Evolution of International Business* (London: Routledge, 1996), pp. 225–229.

135. See R. P. T. Davenport-Hines, *Glaxo: A History to 1962* (Cambridge: Cambridge University Press, 1992).

136. On British companies in international markets, see Geoffrey Jones, ed., *British Multinationals: Origins, Management and Performance* (Aldershot: Gower, 1986), and R. P. T. Davenport-Hines and Geoffrey Jones, eds., *British Business in Asia since 1860* (Cambridge: Cambridge University Press, 1989). On the influence of the British oil industry on foreign countries, see Geoffrey Jones, *The State and the Emergence of the British Oil Industry* (London: Macmillan, 1981).

137. Thomas Mann, *Joseph and His Brothers*, trans. H. T. Lowe-Porter (1934; New York: Alfred A. Knopf, 1978); p. 3.

4. Rolls-Royce and the Rise of High-Technology Industry

1. See M. H. Evans, *In the Beginning: The Manchester Origins of Rolls-Royce* (Derby: Rolls-Royce Heritage Trust, 1984). General references include Roy Church, *The Rise and Decline of the British Motor Industry* (Cambridge: Cambridge University Press, 1994); Wayne Lewchuk, *American Technology and the British Vehicle Industry* (Cambridge: Cambridge University Press, 1987); and James Foreman-Peck, Sue Bowden, and Alan McKinley, *The British Motor Industry* (Manchester: Manchester University Press, 1995).

2. Donald Bastow, *Henry Royce—Mechanic,* Historical Series no. 12 (Derby: Rolls-Royce Heritage Trust, 1989), pp. 9–10.

3. Ibid., p. 17.

4. Quoted by Ian Lloyd, *Rolls-Royce: The Growth of a Firm* (London: Macmillan, 1978), p. 19.

5. Ibid., p. 18.

6. A wholly owned subsidiary of Vickers Limited—see below.

7. Ronald Harker, *The Engines Were Rolls-Royce* (New York: Macmillan, 1979), p. 13.

8. Beginning in the late 1930s, Rolls-Royce gradually took over the job of making the bodies for its cars. It acquired two major coachmaking firms, Park, Ward in 1938 and H. J. Mulliner in 1958, after which Rolls-Royce and Bentley bodies were standardized and custom bodies became a rarity.

9. Rolls-Royce Archives (subsequently RRA).

10. Wilton Oldham, *The Hyphen in Rolls-Royce* (London: G. T. Foulis, 1967), pp. 90–91.

11. S. B. Saul, "The Motor Industry in Britain to 1914," *Business History*, 5 (1962), table 1, cited by Church, *Rise and Decline*, pp. 1–2.

12. Quoted by Lloyd, *Growth*, p. 34.

13. Ibid., p. 37.

14. The separate design facility away from Derby got Royce away from the shop floor, where he was sometimes a burden. See Lewchuk, *American Technology*, p. 145.

15. Quoted by Lloyd, *Growth*, p. 47.

16. Ibid., p. 45–48.

17. Ibid., p. 55.

18. Ibid., p. 58.

19. Harker, *The Engines Were Rolls-Royce*, p. 9, and RRA.

20. In some respects Rolls-Royce was not prepared for the harsh new reality of aerial warfare. In early 1916, the Derby works was bombed by a German zeppelin. The damage was not serious, but nerves were strained nonetheless. Claude Johnson responded by sending the following telegram to all Rolls-Royce employees: "I am sure all the men will stick to their jobs, and will not let the enemy have the satisfaction of knowing that they have frightened any Rolls-Royce man so much that he has refused to assist in making the Rolls-Royce Aero Engines, which are destined to drop bombs on thousands of Germans and blow them into smithereens." Source: RRA.

21. *Aeroplane*, 2 Jan. 1918, pp. 33–34.

22. Ibid.

23. Lloyd, *Growth*, pp. 83–84.

24. Quoted by Ian Lloyd, *Rolls-Royce: The Years of Endeavour* (London: Macmillan, 1978), p. 4.

25. Ibid., pp. 4–5.

26. Ibid., pp. 116–117.

27. Henry Royce to Arthur Sidgreaves, 9 March 1931, RRA. In all quotations from Royce, the emphases are his.

28. Quoted by Lloyd, *Years of Endeavour*, p. 144.

29. Royce to Sidgreaves, 6 March 1931, RRA.

30. Ibid.
31. Royce to Ernest Hives, 28 Dec. 1926, RRA.
32. Royce to Basil Johnson (copy to Ernest Hives), 25 Nov. 1926, RRA.
33. Royce to Works, 11 June 1930, RRA.
34. RRA.
35. Royce to Sidgreaves, 6 March 1931, RRA.
36. Royce memo, 2 June 1931, RRA.
37. Quoted by Harker, *Engines Were Rolls-Royce,* p. 125.
38. As General Manager, Hives was officially second in charge behind the company's Managing Director, Sir Arthur Sidgreaves. This arrangement lasted until Sidgreaves's retirement at the end of World War II.
39. Quoted by Alec Harvey-Bailey, *Rolls-Royce—Hives: The Quiet Tiger,* Rolls-Royce Historical Series no. 7 (Paulerspury, UK: Sir Henry Royce Memorial Foundation, 1985), p. 22.
40. Managing a company of skilled craftsmen required not only a firm hand, but also diplomacy. For instance, during World War II, Rolls-Royce was asked to contribute to a propaganda campaign on "British Craftsmanship," in which a single Rolls-Royce employee would be honored in the press. The idea did not play well in Derby. Arthur Sidgreaves replied to the Air Ministry that singling out one employee "would, so far as we are concerned, do more harm than good. As a matter of fact we could pick out probably a dozen, but even then we should cause quite a lot of jealousy and ill feeling amongst others who would think they ought to have been included." Sidgreaves to E. L. Baddley, 24 July 1944, Hives Files (henceforth HF), RRA.
41. Quoted by Lloyd, *Years of Endeavour,* p. 189.
42. RRA. Figure 4.1 is adapted from a larger document. The original was undated, but the names suggest it was prepared sometime between 1946 and 1949.
43. W. A. Robotham, *Silver Ghosts and Silver Dawn* (London: Constable, 1970), p. 275.
44. Alec Harvey-Bailey, *The Merlin in Perspective,* Historical Series no. 2 (Derby: Rolls-Royce Heritage Trust, 1981), p. 14.
45. C. F. Andrews and E. B. Morgan, *Supermarine Aircraft* (London: Putnam, 1981), pp. 209–227.
46. 20 Sept. 1940. RRA.
47. RRA "The Expansion of Rolls-Royce by the Use of Sub-Contractors," Aug. 1949, p. 1. The quotation by Hives is from the late 1930s and was reproduced here.
48. Hives to Beaverbrook, 23 June 1940, HF.
49. Hives memo, 2 Nov. 1937, HF.
50. Hives to Charles Craven, 14 Sept. 1941, HF. Hives to Beaverbrook, 10 Feb. 1941, HF.

51. RRA.
52. RRA.
53. Hives to T. C. L. Westbrook, 15 Nov. 1941, HF.
54. Hives to Beaverbrook, 10 Oct. 1940, HF.
55. Sir Stanley Hooker, *Not Much of an Engineer* (Shrewsbury, UK: Airlife, 1984), pp. 58–59.
56. Hives to E. N. Plowden, 4 June 1945, HF.
57. Hives to MAP, 28 Sept. 1943, HF.
58. See M. M. Postan, *British War Production* (London: HMSO and Longmans, 1952), p. 411.
59. Hives to Beaverbrook, 17 Nov. 1940, HF.
60. Hives report to MAP, 24 June 1941, HF.
61. Hives report to MAP, 16 Oct. 1940, HF.
62. Hives report to MAP, 3 March 1942, HF.
63. Harvey-Bailey, *The Merlin in Perspective*, pp. 13–16.
64. Ibid., p. 18.
65. In fact the demand for tank engines was so great that the supply of rejected aero-engine parts proved insufficient and so parts had to be manufactured from scratch.
66. Beaverbrook to Rolls-Royce, 12 Sept. 1941, HF.
67. Hives memo, 3 March 1942, HF.
68. Sidgreaves to Sir Archibald Sinclair, 15 Aug. 1942, HF.
69. Hives to Sir Henry Tizard, 2 June 1941, HF.
70. Hooker, *Not Much of an Engineer*, p. 73.
71. Harker, *Engines Were Rolls-Royce*, p. 105.
72. R. A. MacCrindle and P. Godfrey, *Rolls-Royce Limited: Investigation under Section 165 (a) (i) of the Companies Act 1948* (London: HMSO, 1973), p. 4.
73. St. John Elstub, *Productivity of the National Aircraft Effort: Report of a Committee appointed by the Minister of Technology and the President of the Society of British Aerospace Companies, 1967*, ch. 7, para. 63.
74. MacCrindle and Godfrey, *Rolls-Royce Limited*, p. 100.
75. Lord Plowden, *Report of the Committee of Inquiry into the Aircraft Industry* (London: HMSO, 1965), p. 15.
76. Ibid., p. 11.
77. In the race to build this new generation of jets, General Electric and Pratt & Whitney benefited greatly from a US government contract in the mid-1960s, which gave both companies full funding to design a large jet engine for the massive C-5A military transport plane. GE's entry won the contest, but both companies were able to develop successful civil versions of their C-5A engines. The GE CF-6 became the launch engine for the Mc-

Donnell-Douglas DC-10, while the Pratt & Whitney JT-9D was the launch engine for the Boeing 747.

78. Quoted by Keith Hayward, *Government and British Civil Aerospace* (Manchester: Manchester University Press, 1983), p. 104.

79. *Economist*, 14 Nov. 1970, p. 67.

80. Hayward, *Government and British Civil Aerospace,* pp. 107–108.

81. *Air Transport World,* Nov. 1992.

82. There were calls in Parliament and elsewhere for the RB211 to be dropped as a condition for the government's rescue of Rolls-Royce. However, it was reported in the press that a majority of the board of directors were convinced that Rolls-Royce could not continue without the RB211 contract. The board's resolve to finish the RB211 may have influenced the government's decision to save the project along with the rest of the company. *Aviation Week and Space Technology,* 8 Feb. 1971, p. 27.

83. *Economist,* 13 March 1971, p. 64.

84. Hayward, *Government and British Civil Aerospace, p. 120.*

85. *Aviation Week and Space Technology,* 22 Feb. 1971, p. 25.

86. In early 1995, the Rolls-Royce Trent 800 became the first civil aero engine ever certified at 90,000-lb. thrust—this engine powers the Boeing 777. In November 1995, Singapore Airlines ordered 157 Trent 800s for its new 777 fleet. This was reported to be the single largest order in Rolls-Royce's history. *Financial Times,* 15 Nov. 1995, p. 1.

87. The consortium included Pratt & Whitney (U.S.), FiatAvio (Italy), MTU (Germany), and the Japanese Aero Engine Corporation. The engine powers several planes, including the Airbus A320 and the McDonnell-Douglas MD-90.

88. In the mid-1990s, a Delta Airlines RB211 held a record for flying 27,500 consecutive hours without overhaul. Source: Mr. David Blencoe, Rolls-Royce plc.

5. German Capitalism

1. The following works offer overviews of the various "economic orders," their policies, and their economic histories: Richard H. Tilly, ed., *Geschichte der Wirtschaftspolitik: Vom Merkantilismus zur Sozialen Marktwirtschaft* (Munich: R. Oldenbourg Verlag, 1993); Hans Jaeger, *Geschichte der Wirtschaftsordnung in Deutschland* (Frankfurt (Main): Suhrkamp, 1988); Knut Borchardt, *Grundriß der deutschen Wirtschaftsgeschichte* (Göttingen: Vandenhoeck & Ruprecht, 1985); Friedrich-Wilhelm Henning, *Die Industrialisierung in Deutschland 1800 bis 1914* (Paderborn: Schoningh, 1989); idem,

Das Industrialisierte Deutschland 1914 bis 1990 (Paderborn: Schoningh, 1991); Hans-Joachim Braun, *The German Economy in the Twentieth Century* (London: Routledge, 1990); Gerold Ambrosius, *Staat und Wirtschaft im 20. Jahrhundert* (Munich: R. Oldenbourg Verlag, 1990); Karl Hardach, *The Political Economy of Germany in the Twentieth Century* (Berkeley: University of California Press, 1980). On *Wirtschaftsordnung*, see Alan Peacock and Hans Willgerodt, *German Neo-Liberals and the Social Market Economy* (New York: St. Martin's, 1989); idem, *Germany's Social Market Economy: Origins and Evolution* (New York: St. Martin's, 1989).

2. Introductory surveys of early modern Germany include Michael Hughes, *Early Modern Germany, 1477–1806* (Philadelphia: University of Pennsylvania Press, 1992); John Gagliardo, *Germany under the Old Regime, 1600–1790* (London: Longman, 1991); Mary Fulbrook, *A Concise History of Germany* (Cambridge: Cambridge University Press, 1990). On the "German problem," see Gordon A. Craig, *The Germans* (New York: Putnam, 1982).

3. Thomas Nipperdey, *Deutsche Geschichte 1800–1866: Bürgerwelt und starker Staat* (Munich: C. H. Beck, 1983), p. 11.

4. James J. Sheehan, *German History, 1770–1866* (Oxford: Clarendon Press, 1989), p. 40.

5. Ibid., pp. 235–274, 291–310, esp. 371–388; Hans-Ulrich Wehler, *Deutsche Gesellschaftsgeschichte*, vol. 1: *Vom Feudalismus des Alten Reiches bis zur Defensiven Modernisierung der Reformära 1700–1815* (Munich: C. H. Beck, 1987); T. C. W. Blanning, *The French Revolution in Germany: Occupation and Resistance in the Rhineland, 1792–1802* (Oxford: Oxford University Press, 1983); Reinhart Koselleck: *Preußen zwischen Reform und Revolution: Allgemeines Landrecht, Verwaltung und soziale Bewegung von 1791 bis 1848* (1967; Stuttgart: Ernst Klett Verlag, 1975).

6. Sheehan, *German History*, pp. 391–410.

7. Ibid., pp. 899–911; Gordon A. Craig, *Germany, 1866–1945* (New York: Oxford University Press, 1978); Jonathan Sperber, "Master Narratives of Nineteenth-Century German History," *Central European History*, 24, no. 1 (1991), pp. 69–91.

8. On Imperial Germany, see Volker R. Berghahn, *Imperial Germany 1871–1914: Economy, Society, Culture and Politics* (Oxford: Berghahn Books, 1994); John Lowe, *The Great Powers, Imperialism, and the German Problem, 1865–1925* (London: Routledge, 1994); Klaus Hildebrand, *Das Vergangene Reich, Deutsche Außenpolitik von Bismarck bis Hitler,* (Stuttgart: Deutsche Verlags-Anstalt, 1995); Thomas Nipperdey, *Deutsche Geschichte 1866–1918*, vols. 1–2 (Munich: C. H. Beck, 1990/91); Hans-Ulrich Wehler, *The German Empire, 1871–1918* (Leamington Spa: Berg 1985); David Blackbourn and Geoff Eley, The *Peculiarities of German History: Bourgeois Society and Politics in Nineteenth-Century Germany* (Oxford: Oxford Uni-

versity Press, 1984); Richard J. Evans, *Rethinking German History: Nineteenth-Century Germany and the Origins of the Third Reich* (London: Allen and Unwin, 1987); James J. Sheehan, ed., *Imperial Germany* (New York: New Viewpoints, 1976); Ralf Dahrendorf, *Society and Democracy in Germany* (New York: Norton, 1967); Fritz Fischer, *Germany's Aims in the First World War* (London: Chatto & Windus, 1967); idem, *From Kaiserreich to Third Reich* (London: Allen & Unwin, 1986).

9. D. E. Schremmer, "Taxation and Public Finance: Britain, France, and Germany," *Cambridge Economic History of Europe,* vol. 8, ed., Peter Mathias and Sidney Pollard (Cambridge, 1989), p. 457; Peter-Christian Witt, *Wealth and Taxation in Central Europe: The History and Sociology of Public Finance* (Leamington Spa: Berg, 1987).

10. See Eric Owen Smith, *The German Economy* (London: Routledge, 1994), esp. pp. 60–78; Berghahn, *Imperial Germany,* pp. 196–201, 243–244.

11. See R. H. Dumke, "Tariffs and Market Structure: The German *Zollverein* as a Model for Economic Integration," in *German Industry and German Industrialisation: Essays in German Economic and Business History in the Nineteenth and Twentieth Centuries,* ed. W. R. Lee (London, 1991), pp. 77–115; Richard H. Tilly, *Vom Zollverein zum Industriestaat: Die Wirtschaftlich-Soziale Entwicklung Deutschlands 1834 bis 1914* (Munich: Deutscher Taschenbuch Verlag, 1990), pp. 39–49; Jaeger, *Geschichte der Wirtschaftsordnung,* pp. 56–61; Wehler, *Deutsche Gesellschaftsgeschichte,* vol. 2, pp. 125–139, 556–558.

12. Rainer Fremdling, "Germany," in *Railways and the Economic Development of Western Europe, 1830–1914,* ed. Patrick O'Brien (New York, 1983), pp. 121–147; idem, "Railroads and German Economic Growth: A Leading Sector Analysis with a Comparison to the United States and Great Britain," *Journal of Economic History,* 38 (1977), pp. 586–587. On state promotion of railroads, see Eric Dorn Brose, *The Politics of Technological Change in Prussia: Out of the Shadow of Antiquity, 1809–1848* (Princeton: Princeton University Press, 1993), esp. pp. 3–25, 209–240; Colleen A. Dunlavy, *Politics and Industrialization: Early Railroads in the United States and Prussia* (Princeton: Princeton University Press, 1994); W. R. Lee, "Economic Development and the State in Nineteenth-Century Germany," *Economic History Review,* 41, no. 3 (1988), pp. 346–367.

13. Manfred Pohl, "Die Entwicklung des deutschen Bankwesens zwischen 1848–1870" and "Festigung und Ausdehnung des deutschen Bankwesens zwischen 1870 und 1914," in *Deutsche Bankengeschichte,* vol. 2 (Frankfurt (Main): Fritz Knapp Verlag, 1982); James Brophy, "The Political Calculus of Capital: Banking and the Business Class in Prussia, 1848–1856," *Central European History,* 25, no. 2 (1992), pp. 149–176.

14. Rainer Fremdling, "Foreign Competition and Technological Change: British

Exports and the Modernisation of the German Iron Industry from the 1820s to the 1860s," in *German Industry and German Industrialization*, pp. 53–55.

15. Hubert Kiesewetter, *Industrielle Revolution in Deutschland 1815–1914* (Frankfurt (Main): Suhrkamp, 1989); Richard H. Tilly, "Germany," in *Patterns of European Industrialization: The Nineteenth Century*, ed. Richard Sylla and Gianni Toniolo (London: Routledge, 1991), pp. 175–196. On the mechanical engineering industry, Gary Herrigel, *Industrial Constructions: The Sources of German Industrial Power* (Cambridge: Cambridge University Press, 1996), pp. 100–106. On the early steel industry, Ulrich Wegenroth, *Enterprise and Technology, The German and British Steel Industries, 1865–1895* (Cambridge: Cambridge University Press, 1994). On technological culture, see Joachim Radkau, *Technik in Deutschland vom 18. Jahrhundert bis zur Gegenwart* (Frankfurt: Suhrkamp, 1989), pp. 133–148.

16. J. J. Lee, "Labour in German Industrialisation," *Cambridge Economic History of Europe*, vol. 7: *The Industrial Economies: Capital, Labor and Enterprise*, ed. Peter Mathias and M. M. Postan (Cambridge: Cambridge University Press, 1978), pp. 442–491; Jürgen Kocka, *Lohnarbeit und Klassenbildung: Arbeiter und Arbeiterbewegung in Deutschland 1800–1875* (Berlin: J. H. W. Dietz, 1983); idem, *Arbeitsverhältnisse und Arbeiterexistenzen: Grundlagen der Klassenbildung im 19. Jahrhundert* (Bonn: J. H. W. Dietz, 1990); Michael J. Neufeld, *The Skilled Metalworkers of Nuremberg: Craft and Class in the Industrial Revolution* (New Brunswick: Rutgers University Press, 1989); Richard J. Evans, *Proletarians and Politics: Socialism, Protest and the Working Class in Germany before the First World War* (New York: St. Martin's, 1990), esp. pp. 48–71.

17. Quoted in Clive Trebilcock, *The Industrialization of the Continental Powers, 1780–1914* (London, 1981), pp. 62–64; Jaeger, *Geschichte der Wirtschaftsordnung*, pp. 80–81; Otto Keck, "The National System for Technical Innovation in Germany," in *National Innovation Systems: A Comparative Analysis*, ed. Richard R. Nelson (New York, 1993), pp. 115–157; Radkau, *Technik in Deutschland*, pp. 155–171.

18. Wolfram Fischer, *Unternehmerschaft, Selbstverwaltung und Staat: Die Handelskammern in der deutschen Wirtschafts und Staatsverfassung des 19. Jahrhunderts* (Berlin: Duncker & Humblot, 1964); *Zur Politik und Wirksamkeit des Deutschen Industrie und Handelstages und der Industrie- und Handelskammern 1861 bis 1949*, ed. Hans Pohl (*Zeitschrift für Unternehmensgeschichte*, supplement 53) (Stuttgart: Franz Steiner Verlag, 1987); Herrigel, *Industrial Constructions*, pp. 51–58.

19. This has usually been called "organized capitalism." See Heinrich A. Winkler, ed., *Organisierter Kapitalismus: Voraussetzungen und Anfänge* (Göttin-

gen: Vandenhoeck & Ruprecht, 1974); J. J. Puhle, "Historische Konzept des entwickelten Industriekapitalismus: 'Organisierter Kapitalismus' und 'Korporatismus,'" *Geschichte und Gesellschaft*, 2 (1984), pp. 165–184.

20. P. L. Payne, "Iron and Steel Manufactures," in Derek H. Aldcroft, ed., *Development of British Industry and Foreign Competition, 1875–1914* (London, 1968), pp. 71–99.

21. Keck, "National System for Technical Innovation," pp. 125–130; Gottfried Plumpe, "Konzentrationsbewegung und Wiedereingliederung der deutschen Wirtschaft in ihre weltwirtschaftlichen Beziehungen nach dem ersten Weltkrieg" in *Kartelle und Kartellgesetzgebung in Praxis und Rechtsprechung vom 19. Jahrhundert bis zur Gegenwart,* ed. Hans Pohl (Stuttgart, 1985), p. 129.

22. See Steven B. Webb, "Tariffs, Cartels, Technology and Growth in the German Steel Industry 1879–1914," *Journal of Economic History,* 40, no. 2 (1980), pp. 302–329; idem, "Tariff Protection for the Iron Industry: Cotton, Textiles and Agriculture in Germany, 1879–1914," *Jahrbücher für Nationalökonomie und Statistik,* vol. 192 (1977/78), pp. 336–357; Hans Pohl, ed., *Die Auswirkungen von Zöllen und anderen Handelshemmnissen auf Wirtschaft und Gesellschaft vom Mittelalter bis zur Gegenwart* (Stuttgart: Franz Steiner Wiesbaden, 1987), esp. the contribution by Karl Hardach.

23. Norbert Horn, Hein Kötz, Hans G. Leser, *German Private and Commercial Law: An Introduction* (Oxford: Clarendon Press, 1982). Norbert Horn, "Aktienrechtliche Unternehmensorganisation in der Hochindustrialisierung (1860–1920): Deutschland, England, Frankreich und die USA im Vergleich," in *Recht und Entwicklung der Großunternehmen im 19. und frühen 20. Jahrhundert: Wirtschafts-, sozial- und rechtshistorische Untersuchungen zur Industrialisierung in Deutschland, Frankreich, England und den USA,* ed. Norbert Horn and Jürgen Kocka (Göttingen: Vandenhoeck & Ruprecht, 1979), pp. 123–189.

24. Carl-Ludwig Holtfrerich, "Relations between Monetary Authorities and Governmental Institutions: The Case of Germany from the 19th Century to the Present," in Gianni Toniolo, ed., *Central Banks' Independence in Historical Perspective* (Berlin: Walter de Gruyter, 1988), pp. 105–159.

25. The discussion is based largely on Richard Tilly, "On the Development of German Big Banks as Universal Banks in the 19th and 20th Centuries: Engine of Growth or Power Block?" *German Yearbook on Business History 1993,* ed. German Society for Business History (Munich: K. G. Saur, 1994), pp. 110–130; idem, "Banking Institutions in Historical and Comparative Perspective: Germany, Great Britain and the United States in the Nineteenth and Early Twentieth Century," *Journal of Institutional and Theoretical Economics,* 145 (1989), pp. 189–209; idem, "German Banking, 1850–1914:

Development Assistance to the Strong," *Journal of Economic History,* 15, (1986), pp. 113–152; Volker Wellhöner, *Großbanken und Großindustrie* (Göttingen: Vandenhoeck & Ruprecht, 1989).

26. Wilfried Feldenkirchen, "Banking and Economic Growth: Banks and Industry in Germany in the Nineteenth Century and Their Changing Relationship during Industrialisation," in *German Industry and German Industrialisation,* ed. Lee, pp. 116–147.

27. Manfred Pohl, *Emil Rathenau and die AEG* (Berlin: AEG Aktiengesellschaft, 1988), pp. 65–77.

28. Alfred D. Chandler Jr., *Scale and Scope: The Dynamics of Industrial Capitalism* (Cambridge, MA: Harvard University Press, 1990); Wilfried Feldenkirchen, "Concentration in German Industry, 1870–1939," in *The Concentration Process in the Entrepreneurial Economy since the Late 19th Century* (*Zeitschrift für Unternehmensgeschichte,* supplement 55), ed. Hans Pohl Wiesbaden: Franz Steiner Verlag, 1988), pp. 113–146. Table 1 is adapted from the appendix.

29. Bernard P. Bellon, *Mercedes in Peace and War: German Automobile Workers, 1903–1945* (New York: Columbia University Press, 1990), pp. 13–19.

30. Jürgen Kocka, "Entrepreneurs and Managers in German Industrialization," in *Cambridge Economic History of Europe,* vol. 7, pp. 492–589; idem, "The Rise of Modern Industrial Enterprise in Germany," in *Managerial Hierarchies: Comparative Perspectives on the Rise of the Modern Industrial Enterprise,* ed. Alfred D. Chandler and Herman Daems (Cambridge, MA: Harvard University Press, 1980), pp. 77–116; Bernd Dornseifer, "Zur Bürokratisierung deutscher Unternehmen im späten 19. und frühen 20. Jahrhundert," *Jahrbuch für Wirtschaftsgeschichte* (1993), pp. 69–91; Jeffrey R. Fear, "Thyssen & Co., Mülheim (Ruhr) 1871–1934: The Institutionalization of the Corporation" (diss., Stanford University, 1993).

31. The chemical industry dominated by BASF, Bayer and Hoechst epitomized this type of science-based innovation. See David Landes, *The Unbound Prometheus: Technological Change and Industrial Development in Western Europe from 1750 to the Present* (Cambridge: Cambridge University Press, 1969), esp. p. 274; Chandler, *Scale and Scope,* pp. 474–486.

32. Keck, "National System for Technical Innovation," pp. 130–133; Jeffrey Allan Johnson, *The Kaiser's Chemists: Science and Modernization in Imperial Germany* (Chapel Hill: University of North Carolina Press, 1990); Rudolf Vierhaus and Bernhard vom Brocke, eds., *Forschung im Spannungsfeld von Politik und Gesellschaft, Geschichte und Struktur der Kaiser-Wilhelm/Max-Planck-Gesellschaft* (Stuttgart: Deutsche Verlags-Anstalt, 1990).

33. Peter Hayes, "Industrial Factionalism in Modern German History," *Central European History*, 24, no. 2 (1991), pp. 122–131.

34. Klaus Megerle, *Württemberg im Industrialisierungsprozeß Deutschlands: Ein Beitrag zur regionalen Differenzierung der Industrialisierung* (Stuttgart: Klett-Cotta, 1982), pp. 177–180.

35. Herrigel, *Industrial Constructions*, pp. 33–71.

36. Megerle, *Württemberg*, p. 134, rpt. in Herrigel, *Industrial Constructions*, p. 17.

37. Robert Gellately, *The Politics of Economic Despair: Shopkeepers and German Politics, 1890–1914* (London: Sage, 1974); David Blackbourn, "The Mittelstand in German Society and Politics, 1871–1914," *Social History* (Jan. 1977), pp. 409–433.

38. See Erich Maschke, "Outline of the History of German Cartels from 1873–1914," in *Essays in European Economic History, 1789–1914*, ed. F. Crouzet, W. H. Chaloner, and W. M. Stern (London: Edward Arnold, 1969); Robert Liefmann, *Cartels, Concerns and Trusts* (New York: Arno, 1977); Gerald Feldman, *Iron and Steel in the German Inflation, 1916–1923* (Princeton: Princeton University Press, 1977), esp. pp. 3–49; Lon LeRoy Peters, "Cooperative Competition in German Coal and Steel," *1893–1914* (diss., Yale University, 1981); Martin F. Parnell, *The German Tradition of Organized Capitalism: Self-Government in the Coal Industry* (Oxford: Clarendon Press, 1994); Fritz Blaich, *Kartell- und Monopolpolitik im kaiserlichen Deutschland: Das Problem der Marktmacht im deutschen Reichstag zwischen 1879 und 1914* (Düsseldorf: Droste Verlag, 1973); Hans Pohl, ed., *Kartell- und Monopolpolitik in Praxis und Rechtsprechung vom 19. Jahrhundert bis zur Gegenwart* (Stuttgart: Klett Verlag, 1985).

39. Feldenkirchen, "Concentration in German Industry."

40. *Entscheidung des Reichsgerichts in Civilsachen*, vol. 38, 4 Feb. 1897 (Leipzig, 1897), pp. 155–162.

41. Tony Freyer, *Regulating Big Business: Antitrust in Great Britain and America, 1880–1990* (Cambridge: Cambridge University Press, 1992).

42. Robert Liefmann, *Kartelle und Trusts und die Weiterbildung der volkswirtschaftlichen Organisation* (Stuttgart, 1910), pp. 109–142.

43. Feldenkirchen, "Concentration in German Industry."

44. Gustav Schmoller, *Grundriß der Allgemeinen Volkswirtschaftslehre*, pt. 1 (Leipzig, 1900), pp. 450–454. Similar skepticism about competitive capitalism could be found all around continental Europe; see Harm Schröter, "Small European States and Cooperative Capitalism, 1920–1960," in *Big Business and the Wealth of Nations*, ed. Alfred D. Chandler Jr., Takashi Hikino, and Franco Amatori (Cambridge: Cambridge University Press, 1997).

45. Dick Geary, "Socialism and the German Labour Movement before 1914,"

in *Labour and Socialist Movements in Europe before 1914,* ed. Dick Geary (Oxford: Berg, 1989), pp. 101–136. The comprehensive work in German is Gerhard A. Ritter and Klaus Tenfelde, *Arbeiter im Deutschen Kaiserreich 1871 bis 1914* (Bonn: J. H. W Dietz Nachf., 1992).

46. On factory paternalism and local industrial relations, see S. H. F. Hickey, *Workers in Imperial Germany: The Miners of the Ruhr* (Oxford: Clarendon Press, 1985); Elaine Glovka Spencer, *Management and Labor in Imperial Germany: Ruhr Industrialists as Employers, 1896–1914* (New Brunswick, NJ: Rutgers University Press, 1984).

47. See Gerhard A. Ritter, *Social Welfare in Germany and Britain: Origins and Development* (Leamington Spa: Berg, 1986); Volker Hentschel, "German Economic and Social Policy, 1815–1939," in *Cambridge Economic History of Europe,* vol. 8: *The Industrial Economies: The Development of Economic and Social Policies,* ed. Peter Mathias and Sidney Pollard (Cambridge: Cambridge University Press, 1989), esp. pp. 793–801.

48. Werner Milert and Rudolf Tschirbs, *Von den Arbeiterausschüssen zum Betriebsverfassungsgesetz: Geschichte der betrieblichen Interessenvertretung* (Cologne: Bund-Verlag, 1991); Hans-Jürgen Teuteberg, *Geschichte der industriellen Mitbestimmung in Deutschland: Ursprung und Entwicklung ihrer Vorläufer im Denken und in der Wirklichkeit des 19. Jahrhunderts* (Tübingen: J. C. B. Mohr, 1961).

49. Berghahn, *Imperial Germany,* Tables 79–81.

50. Gerald D. Feldman, *Army, Industry and Labor in Germany 1914–1918* (Princeton: Princeton University Press, 1966); Richard Bessel, *Germany after the First World War* (Oxford: Clarendon Press, 1993), pp. 1–48; Gerald D. Feldman, *The Great Disorder: Politics, Economics, and Society in the German Inflation, 1914–1924* (New York: Oxford University Press, 1993).

51. Feldman, *Great Disorder,* pp. 56, 89.

52. Feldman, *Great Disorder,* pp. 41, 57, 66–96. See also Bernard Bellon, *Mercedes in Peace and War,* pp. 83–135.

53. Ute Daniel, "Women's Work in Industry and Family: Germany, 1914–1918," in *The Upheaval of War: Family, Work and Welfare in Europe, 1914–1918,* ed. Richard Wall and Jay Winter (Cambridge: Cambridge University Press, 1988), pp. 268–278; Ulrich Herbert, *A History of Foreign Labor in Germany 1880–1980: Seasonal Workers/Forced Laborers/Guest Workers* (Ann Arbor: University of Michigan Press, 1990), pp. 87–119.

54. Feldman, *Great Disorder,* pp. 56–66, 192–195.

55. Jürgen Reulecke, "Der Erste Weltkrieg und die Arbeiterbewegung im rheinisch-westfälischen Industriegebiet," in *Arbeiterbewegung an Rhein und Ruhr: Beiträge zur Geschichte der Arbeiterbewegung in Rheinland-Westfalen,* ed. Jürgen Reulecke (Wuppertal: Hammer, 1974), pp. 228–234. Reinhard Rürup, "Einleitung," in *Arbeiter- und Soldatenräte im rheinisch-west-*

fälischen Industriegebiet: Studien zur Geschichte der Revolution 1918/19, ed. Reinhard Rürup (Wuppertal: Hammer, 1975), pp. 7–38.

56. See the appropriate pages on Rudolf Wissel and Wichard von Moellendorf in Feldman, *Great Disorder.*

57. Eberhard Kolb, *The Weimar Republic* (London: Unwin Hyman, 1988); Detlev Peukert, The *Weimar Republic: The Crisis of Classical Modernity* (New York: Hill and Wang, 1989); Hans Mommsen, *The Rise and Fall of Weimar Democracy* (Chapel Hill: University of North Carolina Press, 1996); Bessel, *Germany after the First World War.*

58. Gerald D. Feldman, "German Business between War and Revolution: The Origins of the Stinnes-Legien Agreement," in *Entstehung und Wandel der Modernen Gesellschaft,* ed. Gerhard A. Ritter (Berlin: De Gruyter, 1970), pp. 312–341; Gerald D. Feldman and Irmgard Steinisch, *Industrie und Gewerkschaften 1918–1924: Die überforderte Zentralarbeitsgemeinschaft* (Stuttgart: Deutsche Verlags-Anstalt, 1985).

59. Gustav Stolper, Karl Häuser, and Knut Borchardt, *The German Economy, 1870 to the Present* (New York, 1967), p. 80.

60. On factory councils, see Werner Plumpe, "Die Betriebsräte in der Weimarer Republik: Eine Skizze zu ihrer Verbreitung, Zusammensetzung und Akzeptanz," in *Unternehmen zwischen Markt und Macht: Aspekte deutscher Unternehmens- und Industriegeschichte im 20. Jahrhundert,* ed. Werner Plumpe und Christian Kleinschmidt (Essen: Klartext, 1992), pp. 42–60.

61. Feldman, *Great Disorder,* p. 849.

62. Bernd Weisbrod, *Schwerindustrie in der Weimarer Republik: Interessenpolitik zwischen Stabilisierung und Krise* (Wuppertal, 1978), pp. 36–51; Feldman, *Iron and Steel in the German Inflation,* pp. 11–15; Stolper, Häuser, and Borchardt, *German Economy,* pp. 74–78.

63. Feldman, *Great Disorder,* pp. 309–384; John Maynard Keynes, *The Economic Consequences of the Peace* (London: Macmillan, 1919).

64. Feldman, *Great Disorder;* Steven B. Webb, *Hyperinflation and Stabilization in Weimar Germany* (New York: Oxford University Press, 1989); Michael L. Hughes, *Paying for German Inflation* (Chapel Hill: University of North Carolina Press, 1988).

65. Feldman, *Great Disorder,* pp. 708–725 for various preliminary plans.

66. Ibid.; William C. McNeil, *American Money and the Weimar Republic: Economics and Politics on the Eve of the Great Depression* (New York: Columbia University Press, 1986).

67. Feldman, *Iron and Steel,* pp. 210–279.

68. Pohl, *Entstehung und Entwicklung des Universalbankensystems,* pp. 67–69.

69. Feldman, *Great Disorder,* pp. 837–858; Theo Balderston, *The Origins and Course of the German Economic Crisis: November 1923 to May 1932* (Ber-

lin: Haude & Spener, 1993), pp. 406–407; Knut Borchardt, "Germany's Experience of Inflation" and "Constraints and Room for Manoeuvre in the Great Depression of the Early Thirties: Towards a Revision of the Received Historical Picture," in *Perspectives on Modern German Economic History and Policy,* trans. Peter Lambert (Cambridge: Cambridge University Press, 1991), pp. 132–160.

70. Mary Nolan, *Visions of Modernity: American Business and the Modernization of Germany* (New York: Oxford University Press, 1994); Mauro F. Guillén, *Models of Management: Work, Authority, and Organization in a Comparative Perspective* (Chicago: University of Chicago Press, 1994), pp. 91–121; Robert Brady, *The Rationalization Movement in German Industry* (Berkeley: University of California, 1933).

71. Heidrun Homburg, *Rationalisierung und Industriearbeit: Arbeitsmarkt— Management—Arbeiterschaft im Siemens-Konzern Berlin 1900–1939* (Berlin: Haude & Spener, 1991), pp. 264–268.

72. Chandler, *Scale and Scope,* pp. 506–592; Feldenkirchen, "Concentration Process," pp. 131–139; idem, *Siemens 1918–1945* (Munich: Piper, 1995); Gottfried Plumpe, *Die I.G. Farbenindustrie AG: Wirtschaft, Technik und Politik 1904–1945* (Berlin: Duncker & Homblot, 1990), pp. 96–199. Peter Hayes, *Industry and Ideology: IG Farben in the Nazi Era* (Cambridge: Cambridge University Press, 1987), pp. 1–68; Gerald D. Feldman, "Die Deutsche Bank vom Ersten Weltkrieg bis zur Weltwirtschaftskrise 1914–1933," in *Die Deutsche Bank 1870–1995* (München: C. H. Beck, 1995), pp. 239– 246; Bernard Bellon, *Mercedes in Peace and War,* pp. 209–210; Wilfried Feldenkirchen, "Big Business in Interwar Germany: Organizational Innovation at Vereinigte Stahlwerke, IG Farben, and Siemens," *Business History Review,* 61 (autumn 1987), pp. 417–451.

73. See *International Cartels in Business History,* ed. Akira Kudo and Terushi Hara (Tokyo: University of Tokyo Press, 1992); Gillingham, *Coal, Steel, and the Rebirth of Europe,* pp. 19–28.

74. Nolan, *Visions of Modernity,* esp. pp. 30–82, 179–205; John Gillingham, "The Deproletarianization of German Society: Vocational Training in the Third Reich," *Journal of Social History,* 9, no. 3 (1986), pp. 423–432.

75. See Knut Borchardt, "Constraints and Room for Manoeuvre" and "Economic Causes of the Collapse of the *Weimar Republic*," in *Perspectives on Modern German Economic History and Policy,* pp. 143–183; Harold James, *The German Slump: Politics and Economics, 1924–1936,* (Oxford: Clarendon Press, 1986), esp. pp. 190–245; Balderston, *German Economic Crisis,* esp. pp. 49–81; Nolan, *Visions of Modernity,* pp. 154–172.

76. Director Hermann Dahl, 18 Jan. 1924 quoted in Feldman, *Great Disorder,* p. 811.

77. Weisbrod, *Schwerindustrie,* pp. 415–456; Johannes Bähr, *Staatliche Schli-*

chtung in der Weimarer Republik: Tarifpolitik, Korporatismus und industrieller Konflikt zwischen Inflation und Deflation 1919–1932 (Berlin: Colloquium, 1989), esp. pp. 250–274.

78. Balderston, *German Economic Crisis,* pp. 400–435. Barry Eichengreen, *Golden Fetters: The Gold Standard and the Great Depression, 1919–1939* (New York: Oxford University Press, 1992).

79. Ian Kershaw, ed., *Weimar: Why Did German Democracy Fail?* (New York: St. Martin's, 1990); Jürgen Baron von Kruedener, ed., *Economic Crisis and Political Collapse: The Wrimar Republic, 1924–1933* (New York: Berg, 1990). Peter D. Stachura, ed., *The Nazi Machtergreifung* (London: Allen & Unwin, 1983); Larry Eugene Jones, *German Liberalism and the Dissolution of the Weimar Party System, 1918–1933* (Chapel Hill: University of North Carolina Press, 1988).

80. Martin Broszat, *Hitler and the Collapse of Weimar Germany* (Leamington Spa: Berg, 1989); Klaus P. Fischer, *Nazi Germany: A New History* (New York: Continuum, 1995), pp. 74–263; Thomas Childers, "The Middle Classes and National Socialism," in *The German Bourgeoisie,* ed. David Blackbourn and Richard J. Evans (London: Routledge, 1991), pp. 318–337.

81. Henry Ashby Turner, Jr., *Big Business and the Rise of Hitler* (New York: Oxford University Press, 1985), pp. 204–219; Thomas Childers, "Big Business, Weimar Democracy, and Nazism: Henry Turner's German Big Business and the Rise of Hitler," *Business History Review,* 62 (Spring 1988), pp. 128–133.

82. Avraham Barkai, *Nazi Economics: Ideology, Theory, and Practice* (New Haven: Yale University Press, 1990).

83. Ian Kershaw, *The Nazi Dictatorship: Problems and Perspectives in Interpretation* (London: E. Arnold, 1993); idem, *The "Hitler Myth": Image and Reality in the Third Reich* (Oxford: Oxford University Press, 1987); Detlev Peukert, *Inside Nazi Germany: Conformity, Opposition, and Racism in Everyday Life* (New Haven: Yale University Press, 1987); David F. Crew, ed., *Nazism and German Society, 1933–1945* (London: Routledge, 1994).

84. James, *The German Slump,* pp. 343–419; Peter Hayes, "Polycracy and Policy in the Third Reich: The Case of the Economy," in *Reevaluating the Third Reich,* ed. Thomas Childers and Jane Caplan (New York: Holmes & Meier), pp. 190–210.

85. Jeffrey Herf, *Reactionary Modernism: Technology, Culture, and Politics in Weimar and the Third Reich* (Cambridge: Cambridge University Press, 1984); Michael Prinz and Rainer Zitelmann, eds., *Nationalsozialismus und Modernisierung* (Darmstadt: Wissenschaftliche Buchgesellschaft, 1991).

86. Steven Tolliday, "Enterprise and State in the West German Wirtschaftswunder: Volkswagen and the Automobile Industry, 1939–1962," *Business History Review,* 69 (autumn 1995), pp. 273–350; Simon Reich, *Fruits of Fascism: Postwar Prosperity in Historical Perspective* (Ithaca: Cornell Uni-

versity Press, 1990); R. J. Overy, "Cars, Roads, and Economic Recovery in Germany, 1932–1938," in *War and Economy in the Third Reich* (Oxford: Clarendon Press, 1994), pp. 68–89.

87. R. J. Overy, "Introduction" and "Unemployment in the Third Reich," in *War and Economy in the Third Reich*, pp. 1–67.

88. On rearmament, see R. J. Overy, "Hitler's War Plans and the German Economy, 1933–1939," in *War and Economy in the Third Reich*, pp. 177–204, esp. pp. 185–192; Hayes, *Industry and Ideology*, pp. 163–188.

89. Hayes, *Industry and Ideology*, pp. 133–139, 144–161, 172–86.

90. Quoted in Harold James, "Economic Recovery in the 1930s," in *Reevaluating the Third Reich*, p. 130. Richard Overy, "Heavy Industry in the Third Reich: The Reichswerke Crisis," in *War and Economy in the Third Reich*, pp. 93–118. See also Volker R. Berghahn, "Big Business in the Third Reich," *European History Quarterly*, 21 (1991), pp. 97–108.

91. Bernard P. Bellon, *Mercedes in Peace and War*, pp. 218–238.

92. Tim Mason, *Social Policy in the Third Reich: The Working Class and the National Community* (Providence, RI: Berg, 1993); Matthias Frese, *Betriebspolitik im "Dritten Reich": Deutsche Arbeitsfront, Unternehmer und Staatsbürokratie in der westdeutschen Großindustrie 1933–1939* (Paderborn: Ferdinand Schöningh, 1991). Tilla Siegel, *Leistung und Lohn in der nationalsozialistischen "Ordnung der Arbeit"* (Opladen: Westdeutscher Verlag, 1989). Marie-Luise Recker, *Nationalsozialistische Sozialpolitik im Zweiten Weltkrieg* (Munich: R. Oldenbourg, 1985); Ronald Smelser, *Robert Ley: Hitler's Labor Front Leader* (New York: Berg, 1988).

93. Raul Hilberg, *The Destruction of the European Jews* (New York: Holmes & Meier, 1985); Hannah Arendt, *Eichmann in Jerusalem: The Banality of Evil* (1964; rpt. New York: Penguin, 1977); Eberhard Jäckel, *Hitler's World View: A Blueprint for Power* (Cambridge, MA: Harvard University Press, 1981); Christopher R. Browning, *The Path to Genocide: Essays on Launching the Final Solution* (Cambridge: Cambridge University Press, 1992); idem, *Ordinary Men: Reserve Police Battalion 101 and the Final Solution in Poland* (New York: HarperCollins, 1992); Daniel Goldhagen, *Hitler's Willing Executioners: Ordinary Germans and the Holocaust* (New York: Knopf, 1996).

94. Hayes, *Industry and Ideology*, pp. 90–94, 126–127, 196–199; Ron Chernow, *The Warburgs: The Twentieth-Century Odyssey of a Remarkable Jewish Family* (New York: Vintage, 1993).

95. Ian Kershaw, *Popular Opinion and Political Dissent in the Third Reich: Bavaria 1933–1945* (Oxford: Clarendon Press, 1983), pp. 224–277.

96. R. J. Overy, "Hitler's War and the German Economy: A Reinterpretation," in *War and Economy in the Third Reich*, pp. 233–314.

97. I am paraphrasing Peter Hayes, "Polycracy and Policy," p. 200. R. J. Overy, "Rationalization and the 'Production Miracle' in Germany during the Second World War," in *War and Economy in the Third Reich*, pp. 343–375; Albert Speer, *Inside the Third Reich* (New York: Avon, 1970); Matthias Schmidt, *Albert Speer: The End of a Myth* (New York: St. Martin's, 1984); Gitta Sereny, *Albert Speer: His Battle with Truth* (New York: Knopf, 1995).

98. Overy, "Rationalization and the 'Production Miracle,'" pp. 366–374; Alan Kramer, *The West German Economy, 1945–1955* (New York: Berg, 1991), pp. 17–24.

99. Geyer, *Deutsche Rüstungspolitik*, pp. 165–167; Jeffrey Fear, "Die Rüstungsindustrie im Gau Schwaben 1939–1945," *Vierteljahrshefte für Zeitgeschichte*, pt. 2 (1987), pp. 193–216. Michael Geyer, "Die Wehrmacht in der Kostenfalle: Finanzierung und Struktur der NS-Rüstungswirtschaft," *Journal für Geschichte*, 3 (1982), pp. 11–18.

100. Ulrich Herbert, *A History of Foreign Labor;* idem, "Labor as Spoils of Conquest, 1933–1945," *Nazism and German Society 1933–1945*, ed. David F. Crew (London: Routledge, 1994), pp. 219–273; John Gillingham, *Industry and Politics in the Third Reich* (New York: Columbia University Press, 1985), pp. 112–138.

101. Quoted in Herbert, *History of Foreign Labor*, p. 174.

102. Quoted in Overy, "Heavy Industry," p. 106.

103. Primo Levi, *Survival in Auschwitz and the Reawakening: Two Memoirs* (1960, 1965; rpt. New York: Summit, 1986).

104. Hayes, *Industry and Ideology*, pp. 343–361.

105. Charles S. Maier, *The Unmasterable Past: History, Holocaust and German National Identity* (Cambridge, MA: Harvard University Press, 1988); Richard J. Evans, *In Hitler's Shadow: West German Historians and the Attempt to Escape from the Nazi Past* (London: I. B. Taurus, 1989); Peter Baldwin, ed., *Reworking the Past: Hitler, the Holocaust, and the Historians' Debate* (Boston: Beacon, 1990).

106. Mary Fulbrook, *The Divided Nation: A History of Germany, 1918–1990* (Oxford: Oxford University Press, 1992), pp. 129–167.

107. Charles S. Maier, ed., *The Cold War in Europe* (New York: M. Wiener, 1991); Michael J. Hogan, *The Marshall Plan: America, Britain, and the Reconstruction of Western Europe, 1947–1952* (Cambridge: Cambridge University Press, 1987); David Reynolds, ed., *The Origins of the Cold War in Europe: International Perspectives* (New Haven: Yale University Press, 1994); Wilfried Loth, *The Division of the World, 1941–1955* (New York: St. Martin's, 1988).

108. Christoph Buchheim, "The Currency Reform in West Germany in 1948,"

German Yearbook on Business History 1989–92, ed. German Society for Business History (Munich: K. G. Saur, 1993), pp. 85–120; Kramer, *West German Economy,* pp. 134–176.

109. Mary Fulbrook, *The Two Germanies, 1945–1990* (London, 1992); A. James McAdams, *Germany Divided: From the Wall to Reunification* (Princeton University Press, 1993); Henry A. Turner, *Germany from Partition to Reunification* (New Haven: Yale University Press, 1992).

110. Eric Owen Smith, *The German Economy* (London: Routledge, 1994), pp. 60–78; Dennis L. Bark and David R. Gress, *A History of West Germany,* vol. 1: *From Shadow to Substance, 1945–1963* (Oxford: Blackwell, 1993), pp. 231–302.

111. Ian Derbyshire, *Politics in Germany: From Division to Unification* (Edinburgh: Chambers, 1991); William E. Paterson and David Southern, *Governing Germany* (Oxford: Blackwell, 1991); Andrei S. Markovits, *The German Left: Red, Green and Beyond* (New York: Oxford University Press, 1993).

112. A. J. Nicholls, *Freedom with Responsibility: The Social Market Economy in Germany, 1918–1963* (Oxford: Clarendon Press, 1994); Alan Peacock and Hans Willgerodt, *German Neo-Liberals and the Social Market Economy;* idem, *Germany's Social Market Economy.*

113. Smith, *The German Economy,* p. 11; Keck, "National System for Technical Innovation," pp. 133–137, table 4.4; Haruhiro Fukui, Peter H. Merkl, Hubertus Müller-Groeling, and Akio Watanabe, *The Politics of Economic Change in Postwar Japan and West Germany* (New York: St. Martin's, 1993).

114. Kramer, *West German Economy, 1945–1955,* pp. 117–121.

115. Gerold Ambrosius, "Das Wirtschaftssystem," *Die Geschichte der Bundesrepublik Deutschland,* vol. 2: *Wirtschaft,* ed. Wolfgang Benz (Frankfurt (Main): Fischer Taschenbuch, 1989), pp. 23–27, table 6.

116. Barry Eichengreen, ed., *Europe's Post-War Recovery* (Cambridge, 1995); H. Giersch, K.-H. Paqué, and H. Schmieding, *The Fading Miracle: Four Decades of Market Economy in Germany* (Cambridge, 1992), pp. 95–101; Charles S. Maier, ed., *The Marshall Plan and Germany: West German Development within the Framework of the European Recovery Program* (New York: Berg, 1991); Alan S. Milward, *The Reconstruction of Western Europe, 1945–1951* (Berkeley: University of California Press, 1984).

117. Derek W. Urwin, *The Community of Europe: A History of European Integration since 1945* (London: Longman, 1995); Allan M. Williams, *The European Community: The Contradictions of Integration* (Oxford: Blackwell, 1991).

118. Giersch, Paqué, and Schmieding, *The Fading Miracle;* Smith, *German*

Economy; W. R. Smyser, *The German Economy: Colossus at the Cross-roads* (New York: St. Martin's, 1993), pp. 47–52.

119. Smith, *German Economy,* pp. 139–167; Smyser, *German Economy,* pp. 47–52; David Marsh, *The Most Powerful Bank: Inside Germany's Bundesbank* (New York: Random House, 1992), pp. 3–19; Ellen Kennedy, *The Bundesbank: Germany's Central Bank in the International Monetary System* (London: Royal Institute of International Affairs, 1991); Hans-Hermann Francke and Michael Hudson, *Banking and Finance in West Germany* (New York: St. Martin's, 1984), pp. 22–43.

120. Smith, *German Economy,* pp. 319–415; Jeremy Edwards and Klaus Fischer, *Banks, Finance and Investment in Germany* (Cambridge, 1994); Francke and Hudson, *Banking and Finance in West Germany.*

121. Parnell, *The German Tradition of Organized Capitalism,* esp. pp. 151–173, 225–240; Herrigel, *Industrial Constructions,* pp. 166–170; Smith, *German Economy,* pp. 37–91.

122. Peter J. Katzenstein, ed., *Industry and Politics in West Germany: Toward the Third Republic* (Ithaca: Cornell University Press, 1989).

123. Volker R. Berghahn, *The Americanisation of West German Industry 1945–1973* (Leamington Spa: Berg, 1986); idem, "West German Reconstruction and American Industrial Culture, 1945–1960," in *The American Impact on Postwar Germany,* ed. Reiner Pommerin (Providence: Berghahn, 1995), pp. 65–81.

124. On cartel policy, see Smith, *German Economy,* pp. 434–447.

125. Ibid., pp. 273–311; Andrei S. Markovits, *The Politics of the West German Trade Unions: Strategies of Class and Interest Representation in Growth and Crisis* (Cambridge: Cambridge University Press, 1986); Siegfried Mielke and Fritz Vilmar, "Die Gewerkschaften," *Die Geschichte der Bundesrepublik Deutschland,* vol. 2, pp. 82–139.

126. J. Shearman, "Corporate Governance: An Overview of the German Aufsichtsrat," *Journal of Business Law* (Sept. 1995), pp. 517–531; Stephen Overell, "UK Firms Jump the EWC Gun," *People Management,* 1, no. 25 (Dec. 21, 1995), p. 9; "European Works Councils: Social Partners Anticipate a Directive," *International Labor Review,* 134, no. 1 (1995), pp. 91–103; "European Works Councils and the UK," *IRS Employment Review,* 581 (April 1995), pp. 13–16.

127. P. J. Katzenstein, "Industry in a Changing West Germany," in Katzenstein, ed., *Industry and Politics in West Germany,* p. 7; Ambrosius, "Das Wirtschaftssytem," pp. 52–57; W. Abelshauser, *Wirtschaftsgeschichte der Bundesrepublik Deutschland, 1945–1980* (Frankfurt [Main]: Suhrkamp, 1983), pp. 103–111.

128. Mielke and Vilmar, "Die Gewerkschaften," pp. 82–139, table 8.

129. Bark and Gress, *History of West Germany,* vol. 1, pp. 441–448; Susanne Miller and Heinrich Potthoff, *A History of the SPD: From 1848 to the Present* (Leamington Spa: Berg, 1986).

130. Smith, *German Economy,* pp. 118–125; Giersch, Paqué, and Schmieding, *Fading Miracle,* pp. 139–154; Smyser, *German Economy,* pp. 16–23.

131. Smith, *German Economy,* pp. 60–75; J. Alber, "Germany," in *Growth to Limits: The Western European Welfare States since World War II,* vol. 2, ed. Peter Flora, (Berlin: de Gruyter, 1986), pp. 4–149.

132. Giersch, Paqué, and Schmieding, *Fading Miracle,* pp. 151–154, 176–184; Abelshauser, *Wirtschaftsgeschichte,* pp. 111–118; Chris Flockton, "Federal Republic of Germany," in *The National Economies of Europe,* ed. David Dyker (London: Longman, 1992), pp. 32–68.

133. Irwin L. Collier Jr., "Rebuilding the German Welfare State," in *Germany's New Politics,* ed. David P. Conradt, Gerald R. Kleinfeld, George K. Romoser, and Christian Soe (Tempe, AZ: German Studies Review, 1995), pp. 235–252. On Kohl's election, see Bark and Gress, *History Of West Germany,* vol. 2: *Democracy and Its Discontents, 1963–1991,* pp. 376–399.

134. Josef Esser and Wolfgang Fach, "Crisis Management 'Made in Germany': The Steel Industry," in Katzenstein, ed., *Industry and Politics in West Germany,* pp. 221–248; Herrigel, *Industrial Constructions,* pp. 143–254; Kirsten S. Wever and Christopher S. Allen, "Is Germany a Model for Managers?" *Harvard Business Review* (Sept./Oct. 1992), pp. 36–42; Christopher S. Allen, "From Social Market to Mesocorporatism to European Integration: The Politics of German Economic Policy," in *From Bundesrepublik to Deutschland: German Politics after Unification,* ed. Michael G. Huelshoff, Andrei S. Markovits, and Simon Reich (Ann Arbor: University of Michigan Press, 1993), pp. 61–76; Philip Glouchevitch, *Juggernaut: The German Way of Business: Why It Is Transforming Europe— and the World* (New York: Simon & Schuster, 1992), pp. 121–133.

135. Lothar Späth, *Facing the Future: Germany Breaking New Ground* (Berlin: Springer-Verlag, 1985).

136. Even in the nineteenth century the Germans were held to be a "slow-moving" people. One English observer noted in 1906: "The Germans are slow, directed, careful, methodical, and thorough in their work . . . They are not an entrepreneurial and adventurous people . . . they need time to think and act; they need their regularity, their usual surroundings, their mapped out way. But they have the unequalled capacity to find the right way and follow it without wavering." Quoted in Radkau, *Technik in Deutschland,* p. 173.

137. Peter Lawrence, *Managers and Management in West Germany* (New York: St. Martin's, 1980); Ulrich Wengenroth, "Germany," in *Big Business and the Wealth of Nations,* ed. Alfred D. Chandler Jr., Takashi Hikino, and

Franco Amatori (Cambridge: Cambridge University Press, 1997); Stanley Hutton and Peter Lawrence, *German Engineers: The Anatomy of a Profession* (Oxford: Clarendon Press, 1981).

138. Herrigel, *Industrial Constructions;* Smith, *German Economy,* pp. 419–421; Glouchevitch, *Juggernaut,* pp. 54–71; Hermann Simon, "Lessons from Germany's Midsize Giants," *Harvard Business Review* (March/April 1992), pp. 115–123; idem, *Hidden Champions: Lessons from 500 of the World's Best Unknown Companies* (Boston, MA: Harvard Business School Press, 1996); Günter Rommel, Jürgen Kluge, Rolf-Dieter Kempis, Raimund Diederichs, and Felix Brüch, *Simplicity Wins: How Germany's Mid-Sized Industrial Companies Succeed* (Boston: Harvard Business School Press, 1995).

139. "Who Is First in the Market, Sells," *Forbes,* 148 (Sept. 16, 1991), pp. 64–65.

140. Konrad H. Jarausch, *The Rush to German Unity* (New York: Oxford University Press, 1994); Conradt, Kleinfeld, Romoser, and Soe, eds., *Germany's New Politics;* Huelshoff, Markovits, and Reich, eds., *From Bundesrepublik to Deutschland;* Gerlinde Sinn and Hans-Werner Sinn, *Jumpstart: The Economic Unification of Germany* (Cambridge, MA: MIT Press, 1992).

6. *August Thyssen and German Steel*

1. For overviews, see Paul Arnst, *August Thyssen und Sein Werk* (Leipzig: G. A. Gloeckner, 1925); Walter Däbritz, "August Thyssen" ms, c. 1944, in the Mannesmann-Archiv (MA), Dusseldorf, and Thyssen-Archiv (TA), Duisburg; Wilhelm Treue, *Die Feuer Verlöschen Nie: August Thyssen-Hütte 1890–1926* (Düsseldorf/Vienna: Econ-Verlag, 1966); Wilhelm Treue und Helmut Uebbing, *Die Feuer Verlöschen Nie: August Thyssen-Hütte 1926–1966* (Düsseldorf/Vienna: Econ-Verlag, 1969); Horst A. Wessel, ed., *Thyssen & Co. Mülheim a.d. Ruhr: Die Geschichte einer Familie und ihrer Unternehmung* (Stuttgart: Franz Steiner, 1991); Helmut Uebbing, *Wege und Wegmarken: 100 Jahre Thyssen 1891–1991,* ed. Thyssen AG, Duisburg (Berlin: Siedler, 1991); Carl-Friedrich Baumann, *Schloß Landsberg und Thyssen,* ed. Thyssen Aktiengesellschaft and August Thyssen-Stiftung Schloß Landsberg (Duisburg/Mülheim [Ruhr], 1993); and Jeffrey R. Fear, "Thyssen & Co., Mülheim (Ruhr), 1871–1934: The Institutionalization of the Corporation" (Ph.D. diss., Stanford University, 1993).

2. *New York Times* (5 April 1926), clippings in MA: R 2 30 00.

3. On Thyssen's personal life, see Stephan Wegener, "Die Familie Thyssen Aachen-Eschweiler-Mülheim a.d. Ruhr," pp. 13–52; Carl-Friedrich Baumann, "August Thyssen: Ein Bürger Mülheims," in *Thyssen & Co.,* ed. Wessel,

pp. 179–198; Baumann, *Schloß Landsberg und Thyssen;* Dolores L. Augustine, *Patricians and Parvenus: Wealth and High Society in Wilhelmine Germany* (Oxford/Providence: Berg, 1994).

4. The closest thing to an autobiography available is an article sent by Thyssen to the *Mülheimer Zeitung* in March 1922, rpt. in *Tradition: Zeitschrift für Firmengeschichte und Unternehmerbiographie* (now the *Zeitschrift für Unternehmensgeschichte* or *ZUG*), 3, no. 3 (Aug. 1958), pp. 140–150.

5. TA: A/1727, interview with Klara Scholten-Bagel, 2 Nov. 1938; Baumann, *Schloß Landsberg und Thyssen,* p. 53.

6. Baumann, *Schloß Landsberg und Thyssen,* p. 53.

7. Däbritz, *August Thyssen,* p. 23; Lutz Hatzfeld, "Thyssen & Co., Mülheim—Werks- und Firmengeschichte" in *Thyssen & Co.,* ed. Wessel, pp. 64–77.

8. MA: R 2 30 09, 22 May 1882, fol. 22–25. The contractor in question was a predecessor firm of DEMAG, which is still one of the leading mechanical engineering firms in Germany.

9. The following discussion is based on Fear, "Thyssen & Co.," chs. 2–3.

10. H. Thomas Johnson and Robert S. Kaplan, *Relevance Lost: The Rise and Fall of Management Accounting* (Boston: Harvard Business School Press, 1991); Richard P. Brief, "Nineteenth Century Accounting Error," *Journal of Accounting Research* (Spring 1965), pp. 12–31.

11. TA: A/1801, interview with Heinrich Dinkelbach, Dec. 1942.

12. Thyssen to the *Mülheimer Zeitung, ZUG,* pp. 143–144.

13. TA: A/1771, A/1774 Däbritz correspondence with Franz Dahl. See also Däbritz, *Thyssen;* W. Treue, *Feuer Verlöschen Nie.* On Dahl, see TA: PA Press Biographies; Carl-Friedrich Baumann, "Franz Dahl: Reorganisator und Planer der Hüttenwerke von August Thyssen," *Niederrheinische Unternehmer* (Feb. 1987), p. 104; "Franz Dahl," *Stahl und Eisen,* 70 (1950), p. 632. On the growth of the German steel industry, see Wilfried Feldenkirchen, *Die Eisen- und Stahlindustrie des Ruhrgebiets 1879–1914: Wachstum, Finanzierung und Struktur ihrer Großunternehmen* (Wiesbaden: Franz Steiner, 1982). For a summary in English, see Rainer Fremdling, "The German Iron and Steel Industry in the 19th Century," in *Changing Patterns of International Rivalry: Some Lessons from the Steel Industry* (International Conference on Business History, Proceedings of the Fuji Conference), ed. Etsuo Abe and Yoshitaka Suzuki (Tokyo: University of Tokyo Press, 1991), pp. 118–130.

14. Däbritz, *Thyssen,* pp. 101–104; Treue, *Feuer Verlöschen Nie,* 55–56; MA: R 2 30 09, fol. 410–412, 418–420; TA: A/1727, Däbritz interview with Kalle, 25 July 1939. On Kalle, see Gertrud Milkereit, "Julius Kalle," *Neue Deutsche Biographie,* vol. 11, 1977; Carl-Friedrich Baumann, "Julius Kalle:

Ein Leben für Bandeisen," *Niederrheinische Unternehmer* (Feb. 1991), p. 112.

15. Feldenkirchen, *Eisen- und Stahlindustrie,* has extensive financial information on the GDK and other German steel firms; Volker Wellhöner, *Großbanken und Großindustrie im Kaiserreich* (Göttingen: Vandenhoeck & Ruprecht, 1989). See also Gertrud Milkereit, "Einige Überlegungen zum Verhältnis zwischen Industrie und Banken," in *Wirtschaftskräfte und Wirtschaftswege, III. Auf dem Weg zur Industrialisierung,* ed. Jürgen Schneider et al. (Stuttgart: Klett-Cotta, 1978), pp. 521–528; Maximilian Müller-Jabusch, *Oscar Schlitter* (Berlin: R. Scherpe, 1955), pp. 52–54.

16. TA: A/1727, interview with Klara Scholten-Bagel, 2 Nov. 1938.

17. Charles Medalen, "State Monopoly Capitalism in Germany: The Hibernia Affair," *Past and Present,* no. 78 (Feb. 1978), pp. 82–112.

18. Treue, *Feuer Verlöschen Nie,* 144. For quotas, see Feldenkirchen, *Eisen- und Stahlindustrie,* Tab.: 28–29.

19. TA: A/9569, Thyssen to Carl Klönne, 16 July 1902. The discussion is also based on Däbritz, *August Thyssen,* 246–253; Treue, *Feuer Verlöschen Nie,* pp. 114–119. Franz Dahl gave a detailed technical description of the steel works in "Die Anlagen des Stahlwerks Thyssen A.G. in Hagendingen (Lothr.)," *Stahl und Eisen,* 21, no. 13 (1921), pp. 430–443.

20. TA: A/786 Gewerkensammlung, 30 Dec. 1905.

21. Quoted from Thyssen/Klönne correspondence, 18 Dec. 1902, in Treue, *Feuer Verlöschen Nie,* p. 140.

22. This is the main thesis of Arnst, *August Thyssen und Sein Werk.*

23. On Thyssen's relationship to the cartels see Wolfgang Pieper, *Theodor Wuppermann und die Vereinigung Rheinisch-Westfälischer Bandeisenwalzwerke* (Köln: Rheinisch-Westfälisches Wirtschaftsarchiv zu Köln, 1963). Franz Dahl felt Thyssen was "cartel-friendly" because he was often short of cash; see TA: A/1771, interview with Dahl, 28 Jan. 1939; TA: A/1767, interview with Julius Lamarche, 19 Oct. 1940; TA: A/1727, interview with Jakob Hasslacher, 7 Nov. 1939.

24. Wellhöner, *Großbanken und Großindustrie,* pp. 80–87.

25. Quoted in ibid., p. 86.

26. TA: A/1727, interview with Jakob Hasslacher, 7 Nov. 1939

27. Maximilian Müller-Jabusch, *Oscar Schlitter,* pp. 52–54. Schlitter was Klönne's successor.

28. Arnst, *August Thyssen und Sein Werk,* p. 66.

29. Hidemasa Morikawa, *Zaibatsu: The Rise and Fall of Family Enterprise Groups in Japan* (Tokyo: University of Tokyo Press, 1992).

30. See "Denkschrift der Konzerne" and "Stellungnahme der Treuhandverwaltung. . .," in *Die Neuordnung der Eisen- und Stahlindustrie im Gebiet*

der Bundesrepublik Deutschland: Ein Bericht der Stahltreuhändervereinigung (Munich/Berlin: C. H. Beck, 1954), esp. pp. 567–576.

31. Christian Kleinschmidt, *Rationalisierung als Unternehmensstrategie: Die Eisen- und Stahlindustrie des Ruhrgebiets zwischen Jahrhundertwende und Weltwirtschaftskrise* (Essen: Klartext, 1993).

32. TA: A/1783, 22 March 1913.

33. TA: A/681/1, 11 April 1913.

34. Fear, "Thyssen & Co.," pp. 203–204. TA: A/1784.

35. Jürgen Kocka, "Family and Bureaucracy in German Industrial Management 1850–1914: Siemens in Comparative Perspective," *Business History Review*, 45 (summer 1971), pp. 133–156.

36. Fear, "Thyssen & Co.," pp. 216–223, 238–243, ch. 9. The rationale for reorganizing the VSt into a Konzern, advocated by a former Thyssen manager, Heinrich Dinkelbach, should also be consulted. TA: A/1801 Interview with Heinrich Dinkelbach, Dec. 1942, regarding the founding of the VSt; TA: A/3482, A/9415 Niederscrift, "Abschliessende Darstellung der Umorganisation der Vereinigte Stahlwerke A.G., Düsseldorf," 25 April 1934; MA: R 1 40 35.1, "Außerordentliche Generalversammlung der Vereinigte Stahlwerke A.-G."; MA: R 1 50 03 (1) "Die Gliederung der Vereinigte Stahlwerke A.G. nach dem jetzigen Stande und nach der beabsichtigten Neuordnung," 4 Aug. 1933; TA: VSt/950, "Die Gliederung der Vereinigte Stahlwerke A.G. nach dem jetzigen Stande und nach der beabsichtigten Neuordnung" ["Letzte Fassung"], 7 Oct. 1933.

37. Fear, "Thyssen & Co.," pp. 142–149, 272–285. See esp. TA: A/643 [Denkschrift], "Die Thyssen'schen Handelsniederlassungen, ihr Entstehen, ihr Wesen und ihre Aufgabe," 26 Jan. 1918.

38. Fear, "Thyssen & Co.," pp. 204–216.

39. Ibid., p. 225. See esp. TA: A/760/5.

40. TA: A/1773, interview with Wilhelm Späing, 3 Jan. 1941.

41. Fear, "Thyssen & Co.," pp. 322–326. See esp. TA: A/639/2 [Gutachten], 20 May 1921, Späing; TA: A/847/7, "Niederschrift," 3 Feb. 1921.

42. Fear, "Thyssen & Co.," p. 218; Däbritz, *Thyssen*, pp. 169–171, 174–179.

43. Fear, "Thyssen & Co.," pp. 144–173, 228–232. See esp. the statutes of the CAO in MA: R 1 31 05, 1 Dec. 1906. Thyssen composed these statutes personally and the head of the auditing department of the VSt 25 years later requested them for guidance. See TA: A/1345, Dr. Berthold Gr[aff] to Heinrich Kindt, 1 Dec. 1932. For the CAO's activities, see TA: A/701/2; TA: A/681/2; MA: R 1 35 83.

44. Fear, "Thyssen & Co.," pp. 254–256. See TA: A/813/2.

45. Kocka, "Family and Bureaucracy"; Morikawa, *Zaibatsu*, pp. 182–188.

Mitsui had a similar debate about a centralized or decentralized structure at the same time as Thyssen. For the American examples, see Alfred D. Chandler Jr., *Strategy and Structure: Chapters in the History of the American Industrial Enterprise* (Cambridge, MA: MIT Press, 1962).

46. Baumann, "Ein Bürger Mülheims," p. 186; Augustine, *Patricians and Parvenus.*

47. TA: A/1771, interview with Kern und Wallmann, 8 Nov. 1940, and memories of Anton Mittler, Thyssen's butler.

48. Hjalmar Schacht, *Confessions of "The Old Wizard": The Autobiography of Hjalmar Horace Greeley Schacht* (Westport, Conn.: Greenwood Press, 1955), pp. 133–35.

49. TA: A/1771.

50. MA: R 2 30 09, 20 April 1891, pp. 100–101.

51. Baumann, "Ein Bürger Mülheims," p. 191; Augustine, *Patricians and Parvenus,* pp. 130–133.

52. Gisbert Knopp, *Schloß Landsberg* (Duisburg/Mülheim [Ruhr], 1993).

53. TA: A/1771, interview with Carl Wallmann, 4 Nov. 1940.

54. Schacht, "Confessions of the Old Wizard," pp. 133–35; Baumann, "Ein Bürger Mülheims," pp. 185–190; MA: R 2 30 09, 15 Feb. 1894, pp. 307–308, 309–310; 18 Dec. 1894, pp. 349–350.

55. Baumann, "Ein Bürger Mülheims," p. 186. See Lutz Hatzfeld, "Anekdoten um August Thyssen," in *Thyssen & Co.,* ed. Wessel, pp. 199–211.

56. MA: R 2 30 10, 3 May 1903, p. 409.

57. TA: A/1727, interview with Jakob Hasslacher, 7 Nov. 1939; Baumann, "Ein Bürger Mülheims"; Baumann, *Schloß Landsberg und Thyssen.*

58. Quoted in Baumann, "Ein Bürger Mülheims," 183, from TA: A/9578, 10 Dec. 1905.

59. TA: A/847/7, "Niederschrift," 3 Feb. 1921.

60. Fritz Thyssen, *I Paid Hitler* (New York: Farrar & Rinehart, 1941), pp. 120–127.

61. TA: A/1801, interview with Dinkelbach, Dec. 1942; TA: A/1727, interview with Rabes, Schleifhaken, Murrmann, Späing, Rekate, Kuepper, 5 Dec. 1938; TA: A/1773, Späing to Walther Däbritz, 13 Feb. 1941; Conrad Matschoss, "August Thyssen und Sein Werk: Zur Erinnerung an die Begründung des ersten Werkes am 1. April 1871," *Zeitschrift des Vereines deutscher Ingenieure,* no. 14 (2 April 1921), p. 38.

62. Fear, "Thyssen & Co.," pp. 289–290; MA: R 1 35 70 (1), "Niederschrift," 11 Oct. 1920; TA: A/1727, interview with Rabes, Schleifhaken, Murrmann, Späing, Rekate, Kuepper, 5 Dec. 1938.

63. TA: A/1771, interview with Dahl, 28 Jan. 1939, and interview with Wallman, 4 Nov. 1940.

64. Fear, "Thyssen & Co.," pp. 487–489; TA: A/1801, interview with Dinkelbach, Dec. 1942. Thyssen valued "leadership personalities."

65. TA: A/1727, interview with Jakob Hasslacher, 7 Nov. 1939.

66. MA: R 1 30 10, Commercial Register.

67. Augustine, *Patricians and Parvenus,* pp. 130–133. Wegener, "Die Familie Thyssen," pp. 28–39.

68. Wegener, "Die Familie Thyssen," pp. 28–39.

69. Quoted in ibid., p. 50, n. 20, from TA: A/195 70, correspondence Carl Klönne/Thyssen. TA: A/1801, Däbritz interview with Albert Vögler, 11 Jan. 1943, and Dinkelbach, Dec. 1942, 2 March 1943. TA: A/3271, Däbritz interview with Scheifhacken and Dinkelbach, 1 Jan. 1940.

70. Quoted in Treue, *Feuer Verlöschen Nie,* p. 164.

71. Wegener, "Die Familie Thyssen," 35–39. Augustine, *Patricians and Parvenus,* pp. 130–133. Also TA: A/1806; MA: R 5 35 10 (1), letters, 6 June 1918, 1 Oct. 1918, 10 Oct. 1918; and R 5 35 15.

72. TA: A/681/1, 24 Nov. 1915; TA: A/635/12, 15 Dec. 1915, Späing; TA: A/747/1, "Interessengemeinschaftsvertrag," 20 Dec. 1915.

73. Baumann, *Schloß Landsberg und Thyssen,* p. 15. Thyssen once wrote that the war "first intervened" in his company affairs "between 1918 and 1925."

74. Irmgard Steinisch, "Linksradikalismus und Rätebewegung im westlichen Ruhrgebiet: Die revolutionären Auseinandersetzungen in Mülheim an der Ruhr," in *Arbeiter- und Soldatenräte im rheinisch-westfälischen Industriegebiet,* ed. Reinhard Rürup (Wuppertal: Hammer, 1975), pp. 155–237, is the best account of the radicalization of workers in Mülheim.

75. MA: M 30.141, *Das Mülheimer Werk der Siemens-Schuckertwerke AG,* ed. Siemens-Schuckertwerke A.G. (Berlin: VDI-Verlag, 1937); Hatzfeld, "Werks- und Firmengeschichte," pp. 166–167.

76. Harald Wixforth, *Banken und Schwerindustrie in der Weimarer Republik* (Diss: Bielefeld, 1990), p. 206.

77. TA: A/6377, F. Bartscherer, 18 March 1927.

78. MA: R 1 35 32 (5), "H. A. Brassert, Inc. Reporting-Consulting-Operating Iron and Steel Industries," 1 Jan. 1925.

79. MA: R 1 35 32 (6), "Dortmunder Denkschrift über einen Zusammenschluss in der Stahlindustrie," Albert Vögler.

80. TA: A/1801, "Konzentrationspläne in der deutschen Eisenindustrie: Grubenvorstandssitzung der Gewerkschaft August Thyssen-Hütte," 14 July 1919.

81. See Fear, "Thyssen & Co.," pp. 346–360. See also Gert von Klass, *Albert Vögler: Einer der Grossen des Ruhrreviers* (Tübingen: Rainer Wunderlich

Verlag, 1957), p. 143. Thyssen wrote Vögler personally. The letter, which has since been lost, had been in the possession of Dinkelbach and Späing; Vögler, Dinkelbach, and Späing all independently confirm its existence. TA: A/3271, Däbritz interview with Scheifhacken and Dinkelbach, 19 Feb. 1960; TA: A/1801, Däbritz interview with Dinkelbach, Dec. 1942.

82. Quoted in Baumann, *Schloß Landsberg und Thyssen*, p. 70.

83. Quoted in Stephan Wegener, "Die Familie Thyssen: Aachen—Eschweiler—Mülheim a.d. Ruhr," in *Thyssen & Co.*, ed. Wessel, p. 46, from a letter from Heinrich to Fritz, Julius, and Hans Thyssen, 24 Sept. 1925.

84. TA: A/1807.

85. *Das Spezial-Archiv der deutschen Wirtschaft, Vereinigte Stahlwerke Aktiengesellschaft, Düsseldorf 1927: Aufbau Werke, Zechen u. Rohstoffbetriebe Konzern- u. Gründer-Gesellschaften, Statistik & Finanzen* (Berlin: R. & H. Hoppenstedt, 1927); *Allgemeiner Führer*, ed. Vereinigte Stahlwerke AG (Ausgabe, 1930); *Coal, Iron and Steel: A Review of the Vereinigte Stahlwerke Aktiengesellschaft*, ed. Vereinigte Stahlwerke AG, Presseabteilung (Düsseldorf, 1937); Paul Ufermann, *Der deutsche Stahltrust* (Berlin: Verlagsgesellschaft des Allgemeinen deutschen Gewerkschaftbundes, 1927). H. Apfelstedt, *Konzerne der deutschen Eisen- und Stahl-Industrie, Interessengebiete und Verflechtungen*, ed. Spezial-Archiv der Deutschen Wirtschaft (Berlin: R. & H. Hoppenstedt, 1933); *Die Vereinigte Stahlwerke AG: Ihr Aufbau und Ihre Bedeutung für Deutschland und die Weltwirtschaft*, ed. Schwarz, Goldschmidt, & Co. (Berlin, 1926); Robert Brady, *The Rationalization Movement in German Industry: A Study in the Evolution of Economic Planning* (Berkeley: University of California Press, 1933). Brady argues that the VSt exemplified the rationalization movement in the 1920s. Gerhard Mollin, *Montankonzerne und "Drittes Reich": Der Gegensatz zwischen Monopolindustrie und Befehlswirtschaft in der deutschen Rüstung und Expansion, 1936–1944* (Göttingen: Vandenhoeck & Ruprecht, 1988); Gustav-Hermann Seebold, *Ein Stahlkonzern im Dritten Reich: Der Bochumer Verein 1927–1945* (Wuppertal: Hammer, 1981); Wilfried Feldenkirchen, "Big Business in Interwar Germany: Organizational Innovation at Vereinigte Stahlwerke, IG Farben, and Siemens," *Business History Review*, 61 (autumn 1987), pp. 417–451; Fear, "Thyssen & Co.," esp. pp. 366–382.

86. TA: VSt/1388, AVI-Abkommen; Ulrich Nocken, "Inter-Industrial Conflicts and Alliances as Exemplified by the AVI-Agreement," in *Industrielles System und politische Entwicklung in der Weimarer Republik*, ed. Hans Mommsen, Dietmar Petzina, and Bernd Weisbrod (Düsseldorf: Droste Verlag, 1974), pp. 693–704; Ulrich Nocken, "Corporatism and Pluralism in Modern Ger-

man History," *Industrielle Gesellschaft und politisches System: Beiträge zur politischen Sozialgeschichte,* ed. Dirk Stegmann et al. (Bonn: Verlag Neue Gesellschaft, 1978), pp. 37–56; Bernd Weisbrod, *Schwerindustrie in der Weimarer Republik: Interessenpolitik zwischen Stabilisierung und Krise* (Wuppertal: Hammer, 1978), pp. 114–119.

87. Feldenkirchen, "Big Business in Interwar Germany." For a contentious example of internal decisionmaking see Fear, "Thyssen & Co.," pp. 407–418.

88. Feldenkirchen, "Big Business in Interwar Germany"; Fear, "Thyssen & Co.," pp. 425–472; TA: VSt/1567–1595; esp. VSt 1575, "Vorschlag für eine Vereinfachung der kaufmännischen Organisation," 23 June 1931.

89. Walther Rohland, *Bewegte Zeiten: Erinnerungen eines Eisenhüttenmannes* (Stuttgart: Seewald, 1978). Mollin, *Montankonzerne und "Drittes Reich"*; Volker R. Berghahn, *The Americanisation of West German Industry, 1945–1973* (Cambridge: Cambridge University Press, 1986), pp. 51–71.

90. Uebbing, *Wege und Wegmarken,* pp. 42–47.

91. Klass, *Albert Vögler.*

92. Fritz Thyssen, *I Paid Hitler*; Baumann, *Schloß Landsberg und Thyssen,* pp. 24–31, 55–74; Wegener, "Die Familie Thyssen," pp. 46–49.

93. Fear, "Thyssen & Co.," pp. 472–480; K. H. Herchenröder und J. Schäfer, *Die Nachfolger der Ruhrkonzerne* (Düsseldorf: Econ-Verlag, 1953). Berghahn, *Americanisation,* pp. 213–230; *Die Neuordnung der Eisen- und Stahlindustrie im Gebiet der Bundesrepublik Deutschland: Ein Bericht der Stahltreuhändervereinigung* (München/Berlin: C. H. Beck, 1954), pp. 523–620; Dietmar Petzina, "Wirtschaft und Arbeit im Ruhrgebiet 1945 bis 1985," in *Das Ruhrgebiet im Industriezeitalter: Geschichte und Entwicklung,* Band I (Düsseldorf: Schwann, 1990), pp. 500–505; Gabriele Müller-List, *Neubeginn bei Eisen und Stahl im Ruhrgebiet: Die Beziehungen zwischen Arbeitgebern und Arbeitnehmern in der nordrhein-westfälischen Eisen- und Stahlindustrie 1945–1948* (Düsseldorf: Droste, 1990), esp. pp. 93–119.

94. Uebbing, *Wege und Wegmarken,* pp. 48–67.

95. Ibid., p. 70.

96. Baumann, *Schloß Landsberg und Thyssen,* p. 31.

97. Uebbing, *Wege und Wegmarken,* pp. 82–84; Horst A. Wessel, *Kontinuität und Wandel: 100 Jahre Mannesmann, 1890–1990* (Düsseldorf: Mannesmann AG, 1990), pp. 401–412.

98. Jeffrey R. Fear, Thomas Wesson, and John B. Goodman, *Thyssen AG—1994,* HBS Case, N1–795–009 (17 Oct. 1994).

99. "Family Sells Last of Stake in Thyssen," *New York Times* (5 Sept. 1995), p. D1.

7. The Deutsche Bank

1. Quoted in Lothar Gall, "The Deutsche Bank from its Founding to the Great War, 1870–1914," in Gall et al., *The Deutsche Bank, 1870–1995* (London: Weidenfeld & Nicolson, 1995), p. 106.

2. "The World's 1000 Largest Banks," *Institutional Investor,* Aug. 1995, p. 94.

3. The figures on equity holdings and voting blocks are for 1986. See Jürgen Böhm, *Der Einfluß der Banken auf Großunternehmen* (Hamburg: Steuer- und Wirtschaftsverlag, 1992), pp. 225–226; Arno Gottschalk, "Der Stimmrechtseinfluß der Banken in den Aktionärsversammlungen von Großunternehmen," *WSI Mitteilungen,* 1988, pp. 295–296. The data on supervisory board seats are for 1994 and were provided by the Deutsche Bank press office.

4. See Hans E. Büschgen, "Deutsche Bank from 1957 to the Present: The Emergence of an International Financial Conglomerate," in Gall et al., *The Deutsche Bank,* pp. 785–796.

5. Gall, "Deutsche Bank from Its Founding to the Great War," pp. 2–5, 7.

6. Jakob Riesser, *The German Great Banks and their Concentration* (Washington: Government Printing Office, 1911), 3d ed., p. 421.

7. "Deutsche Bank," in Manfred Pohl, ed., *Handbook on the History of European Banks* (Brookfield, VT: Edward Elgar, 1994), p. 384; Gall, "Deutsche Bank from Its Founding to the Great War," pp. 2–3, 10; Manfred Pohl, "Selected Documents on the History of the Deutsche Bank," in *Studies on Economic and Monetary Problems and on Banking History* (Mainz: Hase & Koelher, 1988), p. 769.

8. Gall, "The Deutsche Bank," pp. 13–14.

9. Ibid., p. 14. See also Karl Helfferich, *Georg von Siemens: Ein Lebensbild aus Deutschlands großer Zeit* (Krefeld: Richard Scherpe, 1956), pp. 11–15.

10. "Glimpses of Deutsche Bank's Early Days—through the Papers of Hermann Wallich," in *Studies on Economic and Monetary Problems,* p. 395; Manfred Pohl, "Deutsche Bank's East Asia Business (1870–1875): A Contribution to the Economic History of China and Japan," ibid., p. 426.

11. "Glimpses of Deutsche Bank's Early Days," p. 389. These paragraphs were reconstructed by Fritz Seidenzahl from a variety of collections of Wallich's papers.

12. Pohl, "Deutsche Bank's East Asia Business," pp. 426–427; Gall, "The Deutsche Bank," pp. 17–18; Riesser, *The German Great Banks,* pp. 422–424.

13. Riesser, *The German Great Banks,* pp. 424.

14. Pohl, "Deutsche Bank's East Asia Business," esp. pp. 448–450.

15. Quoted in Riesser, *The German Great Banks,* p. 424.

16. Before 1870, German firms and individuals were served by a wide variety of banking institutions. The short-term credit needs of firms were handled

by private merchant banks and joint-stock banks. Private bankers were also involved with long-term financing. But as investment projects grew in size, especially with the advent of the railroads, long-term finance increasingly became the domain of bank syndicates and joint-stock banks. Transfers of funds between firms were sometimes coordinated by private note-issue banks, but more typically such payments were handled through the thick branch networks of government banks (especially the Prussian Bank established in 1846). Land purchases were generally financed by specialized mortgage banks. And while it was unusual for individual Germans to hold bank deposits in the mid-nineteenth century, those who did often carried accounts at public savings banks. See Holger L. Engberg, *Mixed Banking and Economic Growth in Germany, 1850–1931* (New York: Arno Press, 1981), pp. 20–28; Richard H. Tilly, "Banking Institutions in Historical and Comparative Perspective: Germany, Great Britain and the United States in the Nineteenth and Early Twentieth Century," *Journal of Institutional and Theoretical Economics,* 145 (1989), pp. 191–193; idem, "A Short History of the German Banking System," in *Handbook on the History of European Banks,* pp. 301–304.

17. Engberg, *Mixed Banking,* p. 101.

18. Manfred Pohl, "The Deutsche Bank during the 'Company Promotion' Crisis (1873–1876)," in *Studies on Economic and Monetary Problems,* pp. 277–278; Riesser, *The German Great Banks,* pp. 115–116.

19. "Glimpses of the Deutsche Bank's Early Days," pp. 387–388.

20. Ibid., p. 389; Gall, "The Deutsche Bank," p. 20.

21. Gall, "The Deutsche Bank," p. 19; Riesser, *German Great Banks,* p. 473.

22. Gall, "The Deutsche Bank," p. 19; Erich Achterberg, "Georg von Siemens—Banker," in *Studies on Economic and Monetary Problems,* pp. 314–316. Short-term loans were often referred to as discounts because banks would buy commercial paper from firms "at a discount." In discounting commercial paper, a bank would purchase a firm's promise to pay an amount of money at some specified future time. For example, a bank might buy a firm's promise to pay 100 marks one month later. If the bank bought the firm's promise for 99 marks, then the discount would be one mark and the discount rate (or interest rate) would be approximately one percent per month. Performing this discount is equivalent to the bank lending the firm 100 marks for one month at an interest rate of about one percent per month. If the bank sold the commercial paper to the Reichsbank for 98 marks, then the bank would have "rediscounted" the paper at the Reichsbank.

23. Annual Reports of the Deutsche Bank for 1880, 1890, 1900, 1910, and 1913. See esp. the respective balance sheets.

24. Gall, "The Deutsche Bank," pp. 29–30.

25. Sometimes the bank rolled over short-term current-account loans on an ongoing basis, thus effectively transforming them into long-term loans. Although historians are not sure just how common this practice was, it is likely that it was normally done only in anticipation of an upcoming security issue. See Engberg, *Mixed Banking,* pp. 100–101; also Hugh Neuburger and Houston H. Stokes, "German Banks and German Growth, 1883–1913: an Empirical View," *Journal of Economic History,* vol. 34, no. 3 (1974), esp. p. 715; and Rainer Fremdling and Richard Tilly, "German Banks, German Growth, and Econometric History," *Journal of Economic History,* 36, no. 2 (1976), esp. pp. 418–420. On the limited role of current accounts in long-term industrial financing, see also Volker Wellhöner and Harald Wixforth, "Unternehmensfinanzierung durch Banken—Ein Hebel zur Etablierung der Bankenherrschaft? Ein Beitrag zum Verhältnis von Banken und Schwerindustrie in Deutschland während des Kaiserreichs und der Weimarer Republik," in Dietmar Petzina, ed., *Zur Geschichte der Unternehmensfinanzierung* [*Schriften des Vereins für Socialpolitik,* new series, vol. 196] (Berlin: Duncker & Humblot, 1990), pp. 11–33, esp. 17.

26. Gall, "The Deutsche Bank," pp. 30–31.

27. Ibid., pp. 30–45.

28. Ibid., pp. 31, 34; Engberg, *Mixed Banking,* pp. 143–145.

29. Gall, "The Deutsche Bank," pp. 38–39.

30. Volker Wellhöner, *Großbanken und Großindustrie im Kaiserreich* (Göttingen: Vandenhoeck u. Ruprecht, 1989), p. 217; Georg Siemens, *History of the House of Siemens,* vol. 1, trans. A. F. Rodger (Freiburg: Karl Alber, 1957), pp. 152–159; Gall, "The Deutsche Bank," pp. 36–37; Wilfried Feldenkirchen, *Siemens, 1918–1945* (Munich: Piper, 1995), pp. 35, 660; Hans Otto Eglau, *Wie Gott in Frankfurt* (Düsseldorf: Econ Verlag, 1989), pp. 22–23.

31. The Gross National Product for Germany in 1913 has been estimated at 52.4 billion marks; see esp. Walther G. Hoffmann, *Das Wachstum der Deutschen Wirtschaft Seit der Mitte des 19. Jahrhunderts* (Berlin: Springer-Verlag, 1965), table 248, p. 826. Although it is inappropriate to compare assets with income, the Gross National Product number (which is equivalent to total national income) offers some sense of the magnitudes involved. In 1913, 52.4 billion marks was worth $12.5 billion, or about $187 billion in 1995 dollars.

32. *Untersuchung des Bankwesens 1933,* II. Teil: Statistics (Berlin: Carl Heymanns Verlag, 1934), pp. 138, 114, 122; Annual Report of the Deutsche Bank, 1913. According to Theo Balderston, who relies on an additional

source with a broader definition of the banking system, total system assets equaled 68 billion marks in 1913; "German Banking between the Wars: The Crisis of the Credit Banks," *Business History Review,* 65 (autumn 1991), p. 556. Based on this definition, Deutsche Bank assets amounted to 3.2 percent of total system assets.

33. Gall, "The Deutsche Bank," pp. 22, 89. Although the bank was involved in a wide variety of ventures, not all of them were successful. The international ones, in particular, entailed great risks. At the insistence of Georg Siemens, for example, the Deutsche Bank became heavily involved beginning in the 1880s in financing the Northern Pacific Railroad in the United States. When the Northern Pacific nearly collapsed in the early 1890s, Siemens used his own personal funds to buy back shares from some clients who had invested on his recommendation. Ultimately, the Deutsche Bank, together with the American banking house of J. P. Morgan, worked to reorganize the railroad and succeeded in bringing share values back to their original levels. But the whole experience was a trying one. A historian has observed that "Northern Pacific's insolvency was perhaps the hardest test that Siemens had to face." It is some measure of the Deutsche Bank's extraordinary success in its early years that Siemens' "hardest test" involved a venture that ultimately broke even and may have yielded a profit for its investors. See Achterberg, "Georg von Siemens," p. 318; Gall, "The Deutsche Bank," pp. 62–64.

34. Gerald D. Feldman, "The Deutsche Bank from World War to World Economic Crisis, 1914–1933," in *The Deutsche Bank, 1870–1995,* pp. 135, 130. See also Annual Reports of the Deutsche Bank, 1914–1918.

35. Annual Report of the Deutsche Bank, 1918 (English version), p. 3.

36. Quoted in Feldman, "The Deutsche Bank," p. 160.

37. Ibid., pp. 163–164.

38. A. J. P. Taylor, *The Course of German History* (1945; London: Methuen, 1982), pp. 222–223; Karl Erich Born, "Deutsche Bank during Germany's Great Inflation after the First World War," in *Studies on Economic and Monetary Problems,* p. 496.

39. Annual Report of the Deutsche Bank, 1919 (English version), p. 11.

40. Gall, "The Deutsche Bank," pp. 67–77; Feldman, "The Deutsche Bank," pp. 141–145. The Bank's involvement with the Baghdad Railway during the war provided the bank's directors with their first exposure to policies of genocide. Managing director Arthur Gwinner received reports in 1915 from Franz Günther, vice president of the Anatolian Railway Company, that the Turks were sending trainloads of Armenians off into the desert and that the cars were coming back empty. "One has to go far back into the history of humanity," Günther observed, "to find something comparable in its bestial horribleness as the extermination of the Armenians in today's Turkey. The

pogroms against the Jews in Russia, which I know, are child's play and one has to go back to the expulsion of the Moors from Spain and the persecution of the Christians by Rome to find an analogy to what is taking place here." Günther concluded, "It appears that the government wants to eradicate the entire tribe, root and branch, for this is the only thing that can result from their behavior, and if things go on this way, they may only too well succeed." The Deutsche Bank contributed money to help the Armenians, but did no more since the Ottoman Empire was a wartime ally of Germany. Günther quoted in Feldman, "The Deutsche Bank," p. 142. The story is also based on the author's interview with Martin Müller, assistant archivist at the Deutsche Bank, 11 Oct. 1995.

41. See esp. Born, "Deutsche Bank during Germany's Great Inflation," pp. 499–500, 511. When the management released their annual report for 1919, it is not surprising that their mood was somber rather than joyful. "Having regard to the sad conditions which have come upon our country as a consequence of the disastrous conclusion of the war," the report announced, "we are abstaining from celebrating [our fiftieth anniversary]." See Annual Report of the Deutsche Bank, 1919 (English version), p. 9.

42. Gerald D. Feldman, *Iron and Steel in the German Inflation, 1916–1923* (Princeton: Princeton University Press, 1977), app. 1, p. 472; Don Paarlberg, *An Analysis and History of Inflation* (Westport, CT: Praeger, 1993), pp. 53–66.

43. Konrad Heiden, *Der Fuehrer: Hitler's Rise to Power,* trans. Ralph Manheim (Boston: Houghton Mifflin, 1944), pp. 125–127.

44. Annual Report of the Deutsche Bank, 1922 (English version), p. 8.

45. Feldman, "The Deutsche Bank," pp. 193–196.

46. See Annual Report of the Deutsche Bank, 1922 (English version), p. 10; Manfred Pohl and Angelika Raab-Rebentisch, *Deutsche Bank: Dates, Facts, and Figures, 1870–1993* (Mainz: Hase & Koehler, 1994), pp. 35, 78; Born, "Deutsche Bank during Germany's Great Inflation," pp. 498–499.

47. Born, "Deutsche Bank during Germany's Great Inflation," pp. 509–511; Feldman, "The Deutsche Bank," p. 200.

48. Born, "Deutsche Bank during Germany's Great Inflation," pp. 506–509; Feldman, "The Deutsche Bank," p. 205.

49. Theo Balderston, "German Banking between the Wars: The Crisis of the Credit Banks," *Business History Review,* 65 (autumn 1991), pp. 564–576.

50. See Wilfried Feldenkirchen, "Big Business in Interwar Germany: Organizational Innovation at Vereinigte Stahlwerke, IG Farben, and Siemens," *Business History Review,* 61, no. 3 (autumn 1987), pp. 417–451.

51. Quoted in Feldman, "The Deutsche Bank," pp. 202–203.

52. Ibid., p. 220–221.

53. Ibid., pp. 232–233. On concentration in the banking industry, see esp. Manfred Pohl, *Konzentration im deutschen Bankwesen, 1848–1980* (Frankfurt: Fritz Knapp Verlag, 1982), pp. 285–357.

54. Feldman, "The Deutsche Bank," pp. 230–236.

55. Balderston, "German Banking between the Wars," pp. 574–576; Feldman, "The Deutsche Bank," pp. 234, 237–238.

56. *Untersuchung des Bankwesens 1933*, I. Teil, I. Band, p. 512; Balderston, "German Banking between the Wars," pp. 564, 568–569, 581–584.

57. Angus Maddison, *Dynamic Forces in Capitalist Development: A Long-Run Comparative View* (New York: Oxford University Press, 1991), tables A.7, pp. 212–213, and F.3, pp. 316–317.

58. Prices were falling as well, but at a much slower rate. In real terms, the value of deposits in 1931 stood at 72 percent of their 1929 level.

59. Annual Report of the Deutsche Bank, 1937 (English version), balance-sheet historical summary.

60. Feldman, "The Deutsche Bank," pp. 258–268. See also Fritz Seidenzahl, "The Deutsche Bank's Help for the Danatbank at the Height of the Crisis in July 1931," in *Studies on Economic and Monetary Problems*, pp. 135–145.

61. Balderston, "German Banking between the Wars," pp. 596–598.

62. Hans E. Büschgen, "Banking in Germany, Britain and the United States—A Comparative Appraisal," in *Studies on Economic and Monetary Problems*, esp. pp. 269–270; Feldman, "The Deutsche Bank," pp. 268, 270, 271.

63. *Untersuchung des Bankwesens 1933*, I. Teil, I. Band, p. 512.

64. Annual Report of the Deutsche Bank und Disconto-Gesellschaft, 1933 (English version), p. 5.

65. Harold James, "The Deutsche Bank and the Dictatorship, 1933–1945," in *The Deutsche Bank, 1870–1995*, pp. 294–295.

66. Ibid.; Ernst Wilhelm Schmidt, *Männer der Deutschen Bank und der Disconto-Gesellschaft* (Düsseldorf, 1957), pp. 118, 72.

67. Quoted in James, "The Deutsche Bank and the Dictatorship," p. 296.

68. Ibid., p. 297; Schmidt, *Männer der Deutschen Bank,* p. 62. On the role of four prominent Jewish bankers (Max Warburg, Oscar Wassermann, Jakob Goldschmidt, and Georg Solmssen) during the Weimar period and the rise of Nazism, see Gerald D. Feldman, "Jewish Bankers and the Crises of the Weimar Republic," *Leo Baeck Memorial Lecture* 39 (New York: Leo Baeck Institute, 1995).

69. James, "The Deutsche Bank and the Dictatorship," pp. 298, 300–301, 342–344; Feldman, "The Deutsche Bank," pp. 249, 254–256, 273.

70. Annual Reports of the Deutsche Bank, 1929, 1937, 1944; Balderston, "German Banking between the Wars," pp. 602–603.

71. Kristallnacht (the night of broken glass) describes an explosion of violence

against Jews and Jewish property all across Germany on the night of 9 November 1938. Almost 100 Jews lost their lives that night, many synagogues were burned down or otherwise vandalized, and over 7,000 Jewish businesses were destroyed. The Deutsche Bank felt the impact in a variety of ways. The very next day, for example, the Gestapo began looking for Hermann Wallich's son Paul. Hermann Wallich had served with Georg Siemens as one of the first managing directors of the Deutsche Bank back in 1870. Hermann had died in 1928. Although Paul had been baptized as a baby, had vigorously renounced Judaism as an adult, and had probably even helped to arrange a loan from the United States for Adolf Hitler, he ended up on the Gestapo's list of Jews to arrest. In order to escape prosecution, he jumped off a bridge and killed himself on 11 November. He wrote in a suicide note to his wife (who was safe because she was a Christian): "I wanted to do it tomorrow, but now I've decided to do it today as I don't want to run into any danger . . . I am so tired and know that I'll be doing you and the children no good if I act any differently . . . You needn't resist placing the Nazi flag outside the old house at the Glienicke Bridge. The power that I've succumbed to is a world power. Do not be ashamed of my end, but do acknowledge the victor, as I myself am doing. I shall be thinking of you, my most beloved, in the last moment. All the best to you and the children." One of Paul's children, Henry C. Wallich, was then in the United States and would later become a governor of the Federal Reserve Board. After the war, Henry served with the American occupation force and helped to reconstruct the devastated German economy; and he remained a lifelong friend of the Deutsche Bank. See Katie Hafner, *The House at the Bridge: A Story of Modern Germany* (New York: Scribner, 1995), pp. 25–26, 45–48. See also Werner E. Mosse, "Problems and Limits of Assimilation: Hermann and Paul Wallich, 1833–1938," *Leo Baeck Institute Yearbook,* 33 (1988), pp. 43–65.

72. See Herbert Wolf, "Zur Kontrolle und Enteignung jüdischen Vermögens in der NS-Zeit—Das Schicksal des Rohtabakhändlers Arthur Spanier," *Bankhistorisches Archiv Zeitschrift zur Bankengeschichte,* June 1990, pp. 55–62. See also Jewish-account files from the Deutsche Bank's Mannheim branch, Historisches Archiv der Deutschen Bank.

73. Oswald Rösler, Aktennotiz, 20 July 1943, Bundesarchiv Potsdam, R 8119 F, P 6855, fol. 179–179a. The first third of this quotation is cited and translated in James, "The Deutsche Bank and the Dictatorship," pp. 328–329. On bank involvement in the "Aryanization" of Jewish property, see ibid., pp. 305–308; and esp. Christopher Kopper, *Zwischen Marktwirtschaft und Dirigismus: Bankenpolitik im "Dritten Reich," 1933–1939* (Bonn: Bouvier Verlag, 1995), esp. pp. 220–291.

74. James, "The Deutsche Bank and the Dictatorship," pp. 332–335.

75. Ibid., pp. 341–342, 349–350.

76. Ibid., pp. 355–356.

77. Carl Ludwig Holtfrerich, "The Deutsche Bank, 1945–1957: War, Military Rule and Reconstruction," in Gall et al., *The Deutsche Bank*, p. 367. According to Holtfrerich, the various members of the Deutsche Bank's managing board "had been arrested, suspended, or fired" within a short time of Germany's defeat. The Financial Division operated under the authority of the U.S. Treasury Department. "Since 1940/41, the Treasury Department under the leadership of Henry Morgenthau had attracted the most ardent opponents of National Socialism: Jews who had emigrated from Germany, intellectuals from the left, and devotees of Roosevelt's New Deal . . . They took their task particularly seriously, which had been officially stated as dismantling the financial apparatus of Nazi expansion to ensure that Germany would never again threaten world peace." Karl Heinz Roth, "Nachwort," in Finance Division—Financial Investigation Section, Office of Military Government for Germany, United States, *Ermittlungen gegen die Deutsche Bank, 1946/1947* (Nördlingen: Franz Greno, 1985), pp. 531–532.

78. Holtfrerich, "The Deutsche Bank, 1945–1957," pp. 417–418. For the Financial Division's report, see Finance Division—Financial Investigation Section, *Ermittlungen gegen die Deutsche Bank*.

79. Holtfrerich, "The Deutsche Bank, 1945–1957," pp. 373–377, 433–434.

80. See Manfred Pohl, "The Dismemberment and Reconstruction of Germany's Big Banks, 1945–1957," in *Studies on Economic and Monetary Problems*, esp. pp. 343–347; "Germany's Capital Needs; Has Credit Policy Been Too Restrictive?" *The Banker*, 91, no. 282 (July 1949), pp. 17–21.

81. Quoted in Holtfrerich, "The Deutsche Bank, 1945–1957," p. 409.

82. See Büschgen, "Banking in Germany, Britain and the United States," pp. 263–275. On the British position, see esp. Holtfrerich, "The Deutsche Bank, 1945–1957," pp. 410–411, 422.

83. "Die Dezentralisation der Grossbanken," 2 Nov. 1949, Historisches Archiv der Deutschen Bank, Rheinisch-Westfälische Bank, 6.

84. Ibid.

85. Report to the Occupation Authorities (from Clemens Plassmann), 31 Dec. 1945, Historisches Archiv der Deutschen Bank, Rheinisch-Westfälische Bank, 411.

86. Quoted in Holtfrerich, "The Deutsche Bank, 1945–1957," p. 430.

87. "The Future Structure of German Joint Stock Banks," (Memorandum, English version), 12 Feb. 1950, Historisches Archiv der Deutschen Bank, Rheinisch-Westfälische Bank, 64, pp. 16–17.

88. Ibid., pp. 5, 6.

89. Holtfrerich, "The Deutsche Bank, 1945–1957," pp. 468, 469–485.

90. Annual Report of the Deutsche Bank, 1994 (English version), p. 5.

91. Hans E. Büschgen, "Deutsche Bank from 1957 to the Present: The Emergence of an International Financial Conglomerate," in Gall et al., *The Deutsche Bank,* pp. 700, 715, 703–705, 698; interview with Herbert Wolf, Commerzbank AG, 13 Oct. 1995.

92. Büschgen, "Deutsche Bank from 1957 to the Present," p. 541. Already in 1958, an internal bank report about the punch-card system was (in Büschgen's words) "almost euphoric about the rationalization achieved."

93. Ibid., pp. 542–544.

94. Ibid., pp. 657, 625, 681.

95. Ibid., pp. 748–783.

96. *Deutsche Bank: Dates, Facts and Figures,* p. 79.

97. See esp. Annual Reports of the Deutsche Bank, 1913, 1957, 1994.

98. Büschgen, "Deutsche Bank from 1957 to the Present," pp. 530, 741–743.

99. Ibid., pp. 593–594, 771–772; John Garper, "Deutsche Bank Details Merger of Global Operations: Investment Banking Arms United with Those of Morgan Grenfell," *Financial Times,* 6 July 1995, p. 27.

8. Henry Ford, Alfred Sloan, and the Three Phases of Marketing

1. *Statistical Abstract of the United States* (Washington: Government Printing Office, 1994); *World Almanac, 1994* (New York: Press Pub. Co., 1994); *Information Please Almanac, 1994* (New York: McGraw-Hill, 1994).

2. Angus Maddison, *Phases of Capitalist Development: A Long-Run Comparative View* (Oxford: Oxford University Press, 1991), p. 7: in 1985 dollars, U.S. GDP per capita was $1,048 in 1820, $2,247 in 1870, $4,854 in 1913, $8,611 in 1950, $14,103 in 1973, and $18,317 in 1989. The average of Maddison's sample of 16 rich countries, including the United States, in 1989 was $14,486, still significantly below the American level.

3. James J. Flink, "Automobile," in Glenn Porter, ed., *Encyclopedia of American Economic History* (New York: Scribner's, 1980), p. 1168.

4. James J. Flink, *The Car Culture* (Cambridge, MA: MIT Press, 1975), p. 70.

5. *Business Week,* 28 Feb. 1994, p. 52.

6. Flink, "Automobile," p. 1169 and passim.

7. The Three Phases model of marketing originated in Richard S. Tedlow, *New and Improved: The Story of Mass Marketing in America* (1990; Boston: Harvard Business School Press, 1996). See also Richard S. Tedlow and Geoffrey Jones, eds., *The Rise and Fall of Mass Marketing* (London: Routledge, 1993).

8. Steven Klepper and Kenneth Simons, "Innovations and Industry Shakeouts," *Industrial and Corporate Change,* forthcoming.

9. Ford, like most modern auto companies, dealt primarily through franchised dealers. But prior to 1916, Ford operated a few company-owned and operated outlets, understandably against the wishes of its regular dealers. In 1916, the firm decided "to discontinue the further sale and delivery of cars at retail by us or through our branch houses." See "Discontinuance of Retail Selling and Shop Service," general letter no. 210, 17 Nov. 1916, Accession 78, Box 1, General Letters Numbered, Ford Archives, Henry Ford Museum and Greenfield Village, Dearborn, Michigan (subsequently FA).

10. This paragraph and the next four are based on Richard S. Tedlow, "The Great Cola Wars: Coke vs. Pepsi," in *New and Improved,* pp. 22–111.

11. The literature on Henry Ford and his company is immense. The standard account remains the three-volume work by Allan Nevins, with the collaboration of Frank Ernest Hill: *Ford: The Times, the Man, the Company* (New York: Scribner's, 1954); *Ford: Expansion and Challenge 1915–1933* (New York: Scribner's, 1957); and *Ford: Decline and Rebirth 1933–1962* (New York: Scribner's, 1963). See also Reynold M. Wik, *Henry Ford and Grass Roots America* (Ann Arbor: University of Michigan Press, 1972).

12. Nevins and Hill, *Ford: The Times, the Man, the Company,* pp. 574–582.

13. David A. Hounshell, *From the American System to Mass Production: The Development of Manufacturing Technology in the United States* (Baltimore: Johns Hopkins University Press, 1984), pp. 218, 223; David L. Lewis, *The Public Image of Henry Ford: An American Folk Hero and His Company* (Detroit: Wayne State University Press, 1976), p. 367.

14. From *The Automobile,* 14 (11 Jan. 1906), 107–19, rpt. in John B. Rae, ed., *Henry Ford* (Englewood Cliffs, NJ: Prentice Hall, 1969), p. 18.

15. John B. Rae, *The American Automobile* (Chicago: University of Chicago Press, 1965), pp. 58–60; Lewis, *Public Image,* p. 43.

16. Samuel S. Marquis, *Henry Ford: An Interpretation* (Boston: Little, Brown, 1923), quoted in Rae, ed., *Henry Ford,* p. 78; Henry Ford with Samuel Crowther, *Moving Forward* (Garden City, NY: Doubleday, 1931), pp. 28–29.

17. Federal Trade Commission, *Report on the Motor Vehicle Industry* (Washington: Government Printing Office, 1939), quoted in Rae, ed., *Henry Ford,* p. 91. The price declines are all the more noteworthy because the numbers are in current dollars and the period was one of moderate but sustained inflation.

18. James Dalton, "What Will Ford Do Next?" *Motor* (May 1926), rpt. in Alfred D. Chandler Jr., ed. and comp., *Giant Enterprise: Ford, General Motors, and the Automobile Industry: Sources and Readings* (New York: Harcourt, Brace & World, 1964), p. 106.

19. Tedlow, *New and Improved,* p. 127; Charles E. Sorensen, with Samuel T. Williamson, *My Forty Years with Ford* (New York: Norton, 1956), rpt. in

Rae, ed., *Henry Ford,* pp. 127–130. For a thorough discussion of the evolution of the assembly line at Ford see Hounshell, *From the American System to Mass Production,* pp. 237–256.

20. H. L. Arnold and F. L. Faurote, *Ford Methods and the Ford Shops* (New York: Engineering Magazine Company, 1915), pp. 1–3, 16–18, 31–33, 112, 135–136, 137–39, rpt. in Rae, *Henry Ford,* pp. 63–69.

21. See Nevins and Hill, *Ford: The Times, The Man, The Company,* pp. 512–541; Stephen Meyer III, *The Five Dollar Day: Labor Management and Social Control in the Ford Motor Company, 1908–1921* (Albany: State University of New York Press, 1981); Daniel M. G. Raff, "Wage Determination Theory and the Five-Dollar Day at Ford" (Ph.D. diss., MIT, 1987).

22. Lewis, *Public Image,* p. 481. See also Keith Sward, *The Legend of Henry Ford* (New York: Holt, Rinehart and Winston, 1948).

23. Lewis, *Public Image,* p. 212.

24. Bruckberger, *Image of America* (New York: Viking 1959), rpt. in Rae, ed., *Henry Ford,* pp. 159–161.

25. Lewis, *Public Image,* pp. 218–229.

26. Marquis, *Henry Ford: An Interpretation,* quoted in Rae, *Henry Ford,* p. 78.

27. Lewis, *Public Image,* p. 43.

28. Quoted in Rae, ed., *Henry Ford,* p. 27. Records at the Ford Archives show some of the mixed results of this policy of price-cutting. Unit sales for the fiscal year August 1916 through July 1917 were just over 730,000, an increase of about one-half over the previous year. Profits were down 40 percent because of the steep price cut, but the company still earned more than $30 million. See "Statistical Statement Showing Percent of Profit to Cost per Car by Year," Fair Lane Papers, Accession 7, Box 123, FA, and *Standard Catalogue of American Cars,* Collection 629.2, Box 49, FA, pp. 530–531.

29. Quoted in Rae, ed., *Henry Ford,* pp. 23–24.

30. Lewis, *Public Image,* p. 102.

31. "Alfred P. Sloan Jr.: Chairman," *Fortune,* April 1938, pp. 73 ff., is the source of much of this paragraph and the next three. See also Sloan in collaboration with Boyden Sparkes, *Adventures of a White Collar Man* (New York: Doubleday, 1941); and Sloan, *My Years with General Motors* (New York: Doubleday, 1963).

32. Sloan, *White-Collar Man,* pp. 3, 12, 20–22, and passim.

33. "Alfred P. Sloan Jr.: Chairman," p. 110.

34. Sloan, *My Years with General Motors,* p. 15.

35. Ibid., pp. 4, 9.

36. Ibid., p. 13.

37. Sloan, *White Collar Man,* pp. 96–99.

38. Ibid., p. 133.

39. "Alfred P. Sloan Jr.: Chairman," pp. 111–114.

40. Ibid., pp. 73–74.

41. Peter F. Drucker, "Why *My Years with General Motors* is Must Reading," intro. to Sloan, *My Years with General* Motors, p. viii; Tedlow, *New and Improved,* p. 153.

42. Professor David L. Lewis has reminded the authors that during the 1920–21 crisis, Henry Ford did close his plants from 25 Dec. 1920 to 5 Feb. 1921.

43. Tedlow, *New and Improved,* p. 162. In *My Years with General Motors* (p. 305), Sloan reports that "From 1919 to 1963 GMAC financed for distributors and dealers, as distinguished from consumers, over 43 million new cars, in addition to other products of the corporation. In the same period GMAC financed a total of over 46 million cars for consumers, 21 million new and 25 million used." Ford Motor Company, of course, did eventually develop a similar service, but throughout the 1920s Henry Ford resisted most forms of installment selling.

44. Chandler, ed. and comp., *Giant Enterprise,* pp. 1–2.

45. Roland Marchand, "The Corporation Nobody Knew: Bruce Barton, Alfred Sloan, and the Founding of the General Motors 'Family,'" *Business History Review,* 65 (winter 1991), pp. 825–875; Daniel M. G. Raff, "Making Cars and Making Money in the Interwar Automobile Industry: Economies of Scale and Scope and the Manufacturing behind the Marketing," ibid., pp. 721–753.

46. On the Model A, see Hounshell, *From the American System to Mass Production,* pp. 279–296.

47. For a thorough and systematic analysis of the Ford-GM contest see Arthur J. Kuhn, *GM Passes Ford, 1918–1938: Designing the General Motors Performance-Control System* (University Park: Pennsylvania State University Press, 1986).

48. In this paragraph and the next six, we rely on the work of Alfred D. Chandler Jr., esp. *Giant Enterprise,* plus *Strategy and Structure: Chapters in the History of the American Industrial Enterprise* (Cambridge, MA: MIT Press, 1962), and *The Visible Hand: The Managerial Revolution in American Business* (Cambridge, MA: Harvard University Press, 1977).

49. As Chandler makes clear in *Strategy and Structure,* Sloan was not the only inventor of the multidivisional structure. It was more or less simultaneously developed in other American firms as well, such as DuPont. It also had antecedents in nineteenth-century railroads, and, in some respects, in European companies as well, as Chapter 6 of this book suggests.

50. John A. Byrne, *The Whiz Kids: Ten Founding Fathers of American Business—and the Legacy They Left Us* (New York: Doubleday, 1993); Richard S. Tedlow, "From the Edsel to the Taurus: New Ways to Bring Product to Market at the Ford Motor Company" (MS, 1996).

51. Henry R. Luce, "The American Century," *Life,* 17 Feb. 1941, pp. 61–65.

52. Peter G. Peterson, *The United States in the Changing World Economy*, vol. 2: *Background Material* (Washington: Government Printing Office, 1971), p. 5 and chart 9.

53. Lawrence J. White, *The Automobile Industry since 1945* (Cambridge, MA: Harvard University Press, 1971), pp. 290–291.

54. Ibid.

55. Ibid., pp. 292–293.

56. Ibid., pp. 305–306.

57. Sloan's own enthusiastic description of this process appears in *My Years with General Motors*, pp. 264–278.

58. White, *The Automobile Industry since 1945*, p. 304.

59. Cited in Michael A. Cusumano, *The Japanese Automobile Industry: Technology and Management at Nissan and Toyota* (Cambridge, MA: Harvard University Press, 1985), p. 193.

60. James J. Flink, *The Automobile Age* (Cambridge: MIT Press, 1988), p. 286.

61. Ibid., pp. 286–287.

62. Ibid., p. 289.

63. Ibid., pp. 287–293.

64. Ibid., pp. 281–293.

65. Ibid. Flink cautions the reader that the Eldorado was not a typical Detroit product. It did offer front disc brakes as an option and also featured other characteristics making it more advanced than its American contemporaries. For the American response to radial tires, see Richard S. Rosenbloom, Don Sull, and Richard S. Tedlow, "Technological Discontinuity and the U.S. Tire Industry: The Radial Age" *Industrial and Corporate Change*, forthcoming.

66. Cusumano, *The Japanese Automobile Industry*, pp. 103–130; Tedlow, "From the Edsel to the Taurus."

67. Flink calls 1968 the year of the "big breakthrough" for foreign cars in the American market. *The Automobile Age*, p. 339.

68. These data can be traced through *Ward's Automotive Yearbook* (Detroit: Ward's Communications) for the applicable years.

69. Ibid.

70. Department of Commerce, *Trade Highlights of the United States* (Washington: Government Printing Office, various years).

71. From 1980, when Japan surpassed the United States, to 1994 inclusive, 179.1 million were manufactured in Japan and 150.6 million in the United States, including transplants. These data can be traced through *Ward's Automotive Yearbook* for the applicable years.

72. Henry Ford with Samuel Crowther, *My Life and Work* (Garden City, NY: Doubleday, 1923), p. 30.

73. Ibid., pp. 103, 105–106.

74. Ibid., pp. 91–92.

75. Ford, *Moving Forward,* p. 8.
76. Ibid., p. 29.
77. Rpt. in Rae, ed., *Henry Ford,* pp. 54–56.

9. American Capitalism

1. Carl N. Degler, *Out of Our Past: The Forces That Shaped Modern America* (New York: Harper, 1959), p. 1. The topic of American capitalism is so very broad that no list of citations short of a separate book detailing its exceptionally rich historiography could do justice to the trove of relevant scholarship. But in the notes for this chapter, I have added to the source citations some references to the abundant literature on the subject. I am very deeply indebted to scores of scholars in many fields, only some of whose works can be mentioned here. The interested reader is invited to pursue particular aspects of American capitalism further in two reference works that contain extensive bibliographies: Glenn Porter, ed., *Encyclopedia of American Economic History* (New York: Scribner's, 1980); and Stanley I. Kutler, ed., *Encyclopedia of the United States in the Twentieth Century* (New York: Scribner's, 1996) vol. 3. A useful textbook with ample bibliographies is Mansel G. Blackford and K. Austin Kerr, *Business Enterprise in American History,* 3d ed. (Boston: Houghton Mifflin, 1994).
2. Paul W. Gates, *History of Public Land Law Development* (Washington: Public Land Law Review Commissions, 1968); Malcolm Rohrbough, *The Land Office Business: The Settlement and Administration of American Public Lands* (New York: Oxford University Press, 1968); Merrill Jensen, *The New Nation: A History of the United States during the Confederation* (New York: Knopf, 1950).
3. Bernard Bailyn, *The New England Merchants in the Seventeenth Century* (Cambridge, MA: Harvard University Press, 1955); Edmund S. Morgan, *Visible Saints: The History of a Puritan Idea* (New York: New York University Press, 1963).
4. Frederic B. Tolles, *Meeting House and Counting House: The Quaker Merchants of Colonial Philadelphia, 1682–1763* (Chapel Hill: University of North Carolina Press for the Institute of Early American History and Culture, 1948); Thomas M. Doerflinger, *A Vigorous Spirit of Enterprise: Merchants and Economic Development in Revolutionary Philadelphia* (Chapel Hill: University of North Carolina Press for the Institute of Early American History and Culture, 1986).
5. Philip D. Curtin, *The Atlantic Slave Trade: A Census* (Madison: University of Wisconsin Press, 1969), esp. pp. 215, 232; Robert W. Fogel and Stanley

L. Engerman, *Time on the Cross: The Economics of American Negro Slavery* (Boston: Little, Brown, 1974), p. 18.

6. Abbot Emerson Smith, *Colonists in Bondage: White Servitude and Convict Labor in America, 1607–1776* (Chapel Hill: University of North Carolina Press, 1947); Bernard Bailyn, *The Peopling of British North America* (New York: Knopf, 1990); David Hackett Fischer, *Albion's Seed: Four British Folkways in America* (New York: Oxford University Press, 1989); David W. Galenson, *White Servitude in Colonial America: An Economic Analysis* (New York: Cambridge University Press, 1981); idem, "The Rise and Fall of Indentured Servitude in the Americas: An Economic Analysis," *Journal of Economic History,* 44 (March 1984), esp. pp. 1–14, 24–26. German immigrants usually came as "redemptioners" who had to redeem the loans for their passage from ship captains, either in cash or through the indentured labor of a family member. Social aspects of indentured servitude are emphasized in Sharon V. Salinger, *"To Serve Well and Faithfully": Labor and Indentured Servants in Pennsylvania, 1682–1800* (New York: Cambridge University Press, 1987).

7. Gavin Wright, "The Origins of American Industrial Success, 1879–1940," *American Economic Review,* 80 (Sept. 1990), pp. 651–688.

8. Winifred Barr Rothenberg, *From Market-Places to a Market Economy: The Transformation of Rural Massachusetts, 1750–1850* (Chicago: University of Chicago Press, 1992); Allan Kulikoff, *The Agrarian Origins of American Capitalism* (Charlottesville: University Press of Virginia, 1992); Christopher Clark, *The Roots of Rural Capitalism: Western Massachusetts, 1780–1860* (Ithaca: Cornell University Press, 1990). See also Gordon S. Wood, "Inventing American Capitalism," *New York Review of Books,* 9 June 1994, pp. 44–48.

9. "Immigration," *Concise Dictionary of American History,* ed. Wayne Andrews (New York: Scribner's, 1961), pp. 442–448; Richard N. Current et al., *American History: A Survey,* 7th ed. (New York: Knopf, 1987), p. 526. This latter source gives the percentages quoted as immigrants, but the authors undoubtedly meant first- or second-generation immigrants.

10. Maldwyn A. Jones, *American Immigration* (Chicago: University of Chicago Press, 1960); idem, "Immigration," in Porter, ed., *Encyclopedia of American Economic History,* pp. 1068–1086; Thomas Kessner, *The Golden Door: Italian and Jewish Immigrant Mobility* (New York: Oxford University Press, 1977); John Bodnar, *The Transplanted: A History of Immigrants in Urban America* (Bloomington: Indiana University Press, 1985). "Immigration," *Concise Dictionary of American History,* pp. 442–448. In the late nineteenth century, Congress passed a series of laws designed to limit Asian immigration.

11. See, e.g., John Higham, *Strangers in the Land: Patterns of American Nativism* (New Brunswick: Rutgers University Press, 1955).

12. Jefferson, *Notes on the State of Virginia*, ed. William Peden (Chapel Hill: University of North Carolina Press, 1955), pp. 164–165.

13. Hamilton, *Report on Manufactures*, 5 Dec. 1791, in Harold Syrett et al., eds., *The Papers of Alexander Hamilton* (New York and London: Columbia University Press, 1961–78), vol. 10, p. 252.

14. It is arguable that today's leading agricultural nation is not the United States but China, with its huge farm population. The United States remains the most efficient producer and the top exporter, however.

15. On Hamilton, Jefferson, and the nature of American capitalism after the Revolution, see esp. Drew R. McCoy, *The Elusive Republic: Political Economy in Jeffersonian America* (Chapel Hill: University of North Carolina Press for the Institute of Early American History and Culture, 1980); Stanley Elkins and Eric McKitrick, *The Age of Federalism: The Early American Republic* (New York: Oxford University Press, 1993); E. A. J. Johnson, *The Foundations of American Economic Freedom: Government and Enterprise in the Age of Washington* (Minneapolis: University of Minnesota Press, 1973); Joyce Appleby, *Capitalism and a New Social Order: The Republican Vision of the 1790s* (New York: New York University Press, 1984); Gordon S. Wood, *The Radicalism of the American Revolution* (New York: Knopf, 1991); and James Willard Hurst, "Alexander Hamilton, Law Maker," *Columbia Law Review*, 78 (April 1978), pp. 483–547.

16. Ronald E. Shaw, *Erie Water West: A History of the Erie Canal, 1792–1854* (Lexington: University of Kentucky Press, 1966); Carter Goodrich, "Internal Improvements Reconsidered," *Journal of Economic History*, 30 (June 1970), pp. 289–311.

17. Harry N. Scheiber, *Ohio Canal Era: A Case Study of Government and the Economy, 1820–1861* (Athens: Ohio University Press, 1969); Carter Goodrich, *Government Promotion of American Canals and Railroads, 1800–1890* (New York: Columbia University Press, 1960).

18. On the regional diversity of the American economy, see Diane Lindstrom, "Domestic Trade and Regional Specialization," in Porter, ed., *Encyclopedia of American Economic History*, pp. 264–280. Charles G. Sellers, in *The Market Revolution: Jacksonian America, 1815–1846* (New York: Oxford University Press, 1991), argues that many Americans were ambivalent about exposing themselves to market forces, and moved upland or westward in order to escape the pressures of developing markets. A rejoinder to this interpretation is William Gienapp, "The Myth of Class in Jacksonian America," *Public Policy History*, 6 (1994), pp. 232–259.

19. These quotations and others like them may be found in Frank W. Taussig, ed., *State Papers and Speeches on the Tariff* (Cambridge, MA: Harvard

University Press, 1892); and George B. Curtiss, *The Industrial Development of Nations and a History of the Tariff Policies of the United States, and of Great Britain, Germany, France, Russia and Other European Countries*, vols. 2 and 3 (Binghamton, NY: Curtiss, 1912).

20. Quoted in Taussig, ed., *State Papers and Speeches on the Tariff*, pp. 258, 265. See also Robert V. Remini, *Henry Clay, Statesman for the Union* (New York: Norton, 1991), ch. 13.

21. The Second Inaugural Address is in Roy P. Basler, ed., *The Collected Works of Abraham Lincoln* (New Brunswick: Rutgers University Press, 1953), pp. 332–333.

22. For a summary of the literature on the economic effects of the Civil War and other American wars, see Claudia D. Goldin, "War," in Porter, ed., *Encyclopedia of American Economic History*, pp. 935–957.

23. See J. J. Pincus, "Tariffs," in ibid., esp. p. 440; Frank W. Taussig, *The Tariff History of the United States*, 8th ed. (New York: Putnam's, 1930); Sidney Ratner, *The Tariff in American History* (New York: Van Nostrand, 1972).

24. See, e.g., G. R. Hawke, "The United States Tariff and Industrial Protection in the Late Nineteenth Century," *Economic History Review*, 2d ser., 28 (Feb. 1975), pp. 84–99; Bennett D. Baack and John Ray, "Tariff Policy and Comparative Advantage in the Iron and Steel Industry," *Explorations in Economic History*, 11 (fall 1973), pp. 3–23; and Keith Head, "Infant Industry Protection in the Steel Rail Industry," *Journal of International Economics*, 37 (Nov. 1994), pp. 141–165. Lance Davis et al., *American Economic History: The Development of a National Economy* (Homewood, IL.: Irwin, 1969), table 16–2, shows that American manufacturers benefited far more than any other segment of the economy from tariff protection.

25. For this paragraph and the next three, see James Willard Hurst, *Law and the Conditions of Freedom in the Nineteenth Century United States* (Madison: University of Wisconsin Press, 1956); idem, *The Legitimacy of the Business Corporation in the Law of the United States, 1780–1970* (Charlottesville: University Press of Virginia, 1970); Morton Keller, *Affairs of State: Public Life in Late Nineteenth Century America* (Cambridge, MA: Harvard University Press, 1977), chs. 10–11; Morton Horwitz, *The Transformation of American Law, 1780–1860* (Cambridge, MA: Harvard University Press, 1977); *The Transformation of American Law, 1870–1960: The Crisis of Legal Orthodoxy* (New York: Oxford University Press, 1992); Lawrence Friedman, *A History of American Law* (New York: Simon and Schuster, 1973); and Stanley I. Kutler, *Privilege and Creative Destruction* (Philadelphia: Lippincott, 1971).

26. Robert A. Lively, "The American System: A Review Article," *Business History Review*, 29 (March 1955), p. 82.

27. On this subject see the works cited in note 25, plus those surveyed in the

article cited in note 26. In addition, see Ellis W. Hawley, *The New Deal and the Problem of Monopoly: A Study in Economic Ambivalence* (Princeton: Princeton University Press, 1966); Morton Keller, *Regulating a New Economy: Public Policy and Economic Change in America, 1900–1933* (Cambridge, MA: Harvard University Press, 1990); and Louis Galambos and Joseph Pratt, *The Rise of the Corporate Commonwealth: U.S. Business and Public Policy in the Twentieth Century* (New York: Basic Books, 1988).

28. On the war experience and its relation to American ideology see Robert D. Cuff, *The War Industries Board: Business-Government Relations during World War I* (Baltimore: Johns Hopkins University Press, 1973); Barry D. Karl, *The Uneasy State* (Chicago: University of Chicago Press, 1983); Donald Nelson, *Arsenal of Democracy* (New York: Harcourt, Brace, 1946); Alan Brinkley, *The End of Reform: New Deal Liberalism in Recession and War* (New York: Knopf, 1995); Otis L. Graham Jr., *Toward a Planned Society: From Roosevelt to Nixon* (New York: Oxford University Press, 1976); Paul A. C. Koistenen, *The Military-Industrial Complex: A Historical Perspective* (New York: Praeger, 1981).

29. Harris Corporation, "Founding Dates of the 1994 *Fortune 500* U.S. Companies," *Business History Review,* 70 (spring 1996), pp. 69–90.

30. George Rogers Taylor, *The Transportation Revolution, 1815–1860* (New York: Holt, Rinehart, 1951); John F. Stover, *American Railroads* (Chicago: University of Chicago Press, 1961).

31. See Charles Francis Adams Jr., *Railroads: Their Origin and Problems* (New York: Putnam's Sons, 1878); Alfred D. Chandler Jr., ed. and comp., *The Railroads: The Nation's First Big Business* (New York: Harcourt, Brace and World, 1965); and Frank Dobbin, *Forging Industrial Policy: The United States, Britain, and France in the Railway Age* (Cambridge: Cambridge University Press, 1994).

32. Charles Francis Adams Jr., *Notes on Railroad Accidents* (New York: Putnam's Sons, 1879); U.S. Bureau of the Census, *Historical Statistics of the United States: Colonial Times to 1970* (Washington: Government Printing Office, 1975), II, p. 740.

33. Chandler, ed. and comp., *The Railroads,* pp. 3–18.

34. Colleen Dunlavy, *Politics and Industrialization: Early Railroads in the United States and Prussia* (Princeton: Princeton University Press, 1994), pp. 56–63; Alfred D. Chandler Jr., *The Visible Hand: The Managerial Revolution in American Business* (Cambridge, MA: Harvard University Press, 1977), p. 95; Henry Adams, *The Education of Henry Adams* (Boston: Houghton Mifflin, 1918), p. 240.

35. *Historical Statistics,* II, p. 731.

36. Export figures: ibid., pp. 898–899.

37. Paul Uselding, "Manufacturing," in Porter, ed., *Encyclopedia of American*

Economic History, pp. 409–411; John Kendrick, "Productivity," ibid., pp. 157–166; *Historical Statistics*, I, pp. 200–201, 224. The figures for total capital invested are in current dollars, which understates the rise from 1879 to 1899 and slightly overstates the rise from 1899 to 1914. The numbers for capital invested per worker are in constant dollars. On the engineering and technical side of American manufacturing see David A. Hounshell, *From the American System to Mass Production, 1800–1932: The Development of Manufacturing Technology in the United States* (Baltimore: Johns Hopkins University Press, 1984).

38. John Moody, *The Truth about the Trusts* (New York: Moody, 1904); Glenn Porter, *The Rise of Big Business, 1860–1920*, 2d ed. (Arlington Heights, IL: Harlan Davidson, 1992); Chandler, *Visible Hand*, pts. 1–4; *Historical Statistics*, I, p. 224.

39. The average during 1880–1930 was five new companies per year that were still part of the *Fortune* 500 at the end of the twentieth century. For all other years of American national history, the average is only 1.5. See Harris Corporation, "Founding Dates of the 1994 *Fortune* 500 U.S. Companies."

40. See Chandler, *Visible Hand*, and Richard S. Tedlow, *New and Improved: The Story of Mass Marketing in America* (1990; Boston: Harvard Business School Press, 1996).

41. As in the previous list, the numbers of companies enumerated for each decade is in approximate proportion to the rate of their founding. That is, four companies are listed for each decade from 1930 to 1990, whereas seven to nine were listed for each decade from 1880 to 1930, because the rate of founding of present-day *Fortune* 500 companies was proportionally higher during those earlier decades.

42. See Mansel G. Blackford, "Small Business in America: A Historiographic Survey," *Business History Review*, 65 (spring 1991), pp. 1–26.

43. See Chandler, *Visible Hand*, esp. pp. 315–344; Thomas K. McCraw, *Prophets of Regulation* (Cambridge, MA: Harvard University Press, 1984), pp. 65–142; and Jeremy Atack, "Firm Size and Industrial Structure in the United States during the Nineteenth Century," *Journal of Economic History*, 46 (June 1986), pp. 463–475.

44. Alfred D. Chandler Jr., *Scale and Scope: The Dynamics of Industrial Capitalism* (Cambridge, MA: Harvard University Press, 1990), table 5, p. 19.

45. See the chapter on the Soviet Union by Andrei Yudanov in Alfred D. Chandler Jr., Takashi Hikino, and Franco Amatori, eds., *Big Business and the Wealth of Nations* (Cambridge: Cambridge University Press, 1997).

46. Harold F. Williamson and Arnold R. Daum, *The American Petroleum Industry: The Age of Illumination, 1859–1899* (Evanston, IL: Northwestern University Press, 1959), pp. 474–475, 483–484.

47. U.S. Bureau of Corporations, *Report of the Commissioner of Corporations*

on the Tobacco Industry, pt. 3 (Washington: Government Printing Office, 1915), pp. 158–160.

48. U.S. Federal Trade Commission, *Report on the Motor Vehicle Industry* (Washington: Government Printing Office, 1939), quoted in John B. Rae, ed., *Henry Ford* (Englewood Cliffs, NJ, 1969), p. 91. The price declines for the Model T are all the more remarkable because the period 1908–24 was one of moderate but sustained inflation.

49. This is a central thesis of Chandler, *Visible Hand.* See also Glenn Porter and Harold C. Livesay, *Merchants and Manufacturers: Studies in the Structure of Nineteenth-Century Marketing* (Baltimore: Johns Hopkins University Press, 1971); and Alexander J. Field, "Modern Business Enterprise as a Capital-Saving Innovation," *Journal of Economic History,* 47 (June 1987), pp. 473–485. Theoretical aspects of the rise of big business during the Second Industrial Revolution, including the integration of manufacturing and marketing, are explored in Oliver E. Williamson, *Markets and Hierarchies: Analysis and Antitrust Implications* (New York: Free Press, 1975); idem, *The Economic Institutions of Capitalism: Firms, Markets, Relational Contracting* (New York: Free Press, 1985); and William Lazonick, *Business Organization and the Myth of the Market Economy* (Cambridge: Cambridge University Press, 1991).

50. On manufacturing sectors not characterized by big business see Philip Scranton, "Diversity in Diversity: Flexible Production and American Industrialization, 1880–1930," *Business History Review,* 65 (spring 1991), pp. 27–90. On nineteenth-century social and economic history, and esp. their interaction, see Walter Licht, *Industrializing America: The Nineteenth Century* (Baltimore: Johns Hopkins University Press, 1995).

51. Jesse Markham, "Survey of the Evidence and Findings on Mergers," in *Business Concentration and Price Policy* (Princeton: Princeton University Press, 1955), p. 157. See also Ralph Nelson, *Merger Movements in American Industry, 1895–1956* (Princeton: Princeton University Press, 1959); William Z. Ripley, *Trusts, Pools, and Corporations* (Cambridge, MA: Harvard University Press, 1905); and Naomi R. Lamoreaux, *The Great Merger Movement in American Business, 1895–1904* (Cambridge: Cambridge University Press, 1985). For a vivid example of the merger process see Alfred S. Eichner, *The Emergence of Oligopoly: Sugar Refining as a Case Study* (Baltimore: Johns Hopkins University Press, 1969).

52. Alfred D. Chandler Jr., "Government versus Business: An American Phenomenon," in John T. Dunlop, ed., *Business and Public Policy* (Boston: Harvard University Graduate School of Business Administration, 1980), pp. 1–11; Thomas K. McCraw, "Business and Government: The Origins of the Adversary Relationship," *California Management Review,* 26 (winter 1984), pp. 33–52.

53. A notable example of this kind of prediction, though in this particular case made more in optimism than in fear, was Edward Bellamy's bestselling futuristic novel *Looking Backward, 2000–1887,* published in 1888.

54. See McCraw, *Prophets of Regulation,* ch. 3, esp. pp. 138–141.

55. Again the literature on this subject is vast. On views expressed in contemporary periodicals, see Louis P. Galambos, *The Public Image of Big Business in America, 1880–1940: A Quantitative Study in Social Change* (Baltimore: Johns Hopkins University Press, 1975). On the interrelations between economics and politics growing out of the trust question, see Martin J. Sklar, *The Corporate Reconstruction of American Capitalism, 1890–1916: The Market, the Law, and Politics* (Cambridge: Cambridge University Press, 1988).

56. The standard source on Rockefeller is Allan Nevins's sympathetic biography, *John D. Rockefeller: The Heroic Age of American Enterprise,* 2 vols. (New York: Scribner's, 1940); the classic muckraking analysis is Ida M. Tarbell, *The History of the Standard Oil Company* (New York: Macmillan, 1904). Less biased than either of these books is Ralph W. and Muriel E. Hidy, *Pioneering in Big Business, 1882–1911: History of Standard Oil (New Jersey)* (New York: Harper, 1955).

57. The Sherman Act of 1890 is 26 Stat. 209, *U.S. Statutes at Large.* The early criminal cases under the Sherman Act were notably unsuccessful.

58. The Federal Trade Commission Act of 1914 is 38 Stat. 719, *U.S. Statutes at Large.*

59. Richard Hofstadter, "What Happened to the Antitrust Movement? Notes on the Evolution of an American Creed," in Earl F. Cheit, ed., *The Business Establishment* (New York: Wiley, 1964), pp. 113–151; Suzanne Weaver, *Decision to Prosecute: Organization and Public Policy in the Antitrust Division* (Cambridge, MA: MIT Press, 1977); Robert H. Bork, *The Antitrust Paradox: A Policy at War with Itself* (New York: Basic Books, 1978).

60. Richard A. Posner, "A Statistical Study of Antitrust Enforcement," *Journal of Law and Economics,* 13 (Oct. 1970), pp. 306, 411; Walton Hamilton and Irene Till, *Antitrust in Action,* Temporary National Economic Committee Monograph no. 16 (Washington: Government Printing Office, 1940), pp. 135–141; and the "Bluebook" of antitrust, *The Federal Antitrust Laws, with Summary of Cases Instituted by the United States* (Chicago: Commerce Clearing House, 1951 and subsequent years).

61. On the beneficial consequences of forced divestiture, see William S. Comanor and F. M. Scherer, "Rewriting History: The Early Sherman Act Monopolization Cases," *International Journal of the Economics of Business,* 2, no. 2 (1995), pp. 263–289, which focuses on the differing fates of Standard Oil and U.S. Steel but speculates about IBM and AT&T as well. See also George David Smith, *From Monopoly to Competition: The Transforma-*

tions of Alcoa, 1888–1986 (New York: Cambridge University Press, 1988). A dissenting view is Peter Temin with Louis Galambos, *The Fall of the Bell System: A Study in Prices and Politics* (Cambridge: Cambridge University Press, 1987).

62. On competition policies see Norbert Horn and Jürgen Kocka, eds., *Law and the Formation of the Big Enterprises in the 19th and early 20th Centuries* (Göttingen: Vandenhoeck & Ruprecht, 1979); Tony Freyer, *Regulating Big Business: Antitrust in Great Britain and America, 1880–1990* (Cambridge: Cambridge University Press, 1992); and F. M. Scherer, *Competition Policies for an Integrated World Economy* (Washington: Brookings, 1994).

63. See John J. McCusker and Russell R. Menard, *The Economy of British America, 1607–1789* (Chapel Hill: University of North Carolina Press for the Institute of Early American History and Culture, 1985); E. James Ferguson, *The Power of the Purse: A History of American Public Finance* (Chapel Hill: University of North Carolina Press for the Institute of Early American History and Culture, 1961); Curtis P. Nettels, *The Emergence of a National Economy, 1775–1815* (New York: Holt, Rinehart and Winston, 1962); Douglass C. North, *American Economic Growth, 1790–1860* (Englewood Cliffs, NJ: Prentice-Hall, 1960); and Edwin J. Perkins, *American Public Finance and Financial Services, 1700–1815* (Columbus: Ohio State University Press, 1993).

64. Allen G. Bogue, "Land Policies and Sales," in Porter, ed., *Encyclopedia of American Economic History* pp. 588–589.

65. On Hamilton and banking, see esp. Broadus Mitchell, *Alexander Hamilton: The National Adventure, 1788–1804* (New York: Macmillan, 1962), and Forrest McDonald, *Alexander Hamilton: A Biography* (New York: Norton, 1979).

66. See Bray Hammond, *Banks and Politics in America from the Revolution to the Civil War* (Princeton: Princeton University Press, 1957); and Walter B. Smith, *Economic Aspects of the Second Bank of the United States* (Cambridge, MA: Harvard University Press, 1958).

67. Jackson's veto message is in James D. Richardson, ed., *A Compilation of Messages and Papers of the Presidents, 1789–1897* (Washington: Government Printing Office, 1896), II, pp. 576–591.

68. John James, *Money and Capital Markets in Postbellum America* (Princeton: Princeton University Press, 1978); Irwin Unger, *The Greenback Era: A Social and Political History of American Finance, 1865–1879* (Princeton: Princeton University Press, 1964); Milton Friedman and Anna J. Schwartz, *A Monetary History of the United States, 1867–1960* (Princeton: Princeton University Press, 1963); and Richard Sylla, "Federal Policy, Banking Market Structure, and Capital Mobilization in the United States, 1863–1913," *Journal of Economic History*, 29 (Dec. 1969), pp. 657–686.

69. Richard H. Timberlake, *Money, Banking, and Central Banking* (New York: Harper & Row, 1965); Robert Craig West, *Banking Reform and the Federal Reserve, 1863–1913* (Ithaca: Cornell University Press, 1977); Friedman and Schwartz, *Monetary History of the United States.*

70. *Historical Statistics,* II, p. 1019.

71. See Richard H. K. Vietor, *Contrived Competition: Regulation and Deregulation in America* (Cambridge, MA: Harvard University Press, 1994), chs. 5 and 6.

72. Chandler, ed. and comp., *The Railroads,* pp. 43–70.

73. Peter Wyckoff, *Wall Street and the Stock Markets: A Chronology, 1644–1971* (Philadelphia: Chilton, 1972); Thomas R. Navin and Marian V. Sears, "The Rise of a Market for Industrial Securities, 1887–1902," *Business History Review,* 24 (June 1955), pp. 105–138.

74. Jonathan Lurie, *The Chicago Board of Trade, 1859–1905: The Dynamics of Self-Regulation* (Urbana: University of Illinois Press, 1979); Vincent P. Carosso, *Investment Banking in America: A History* (Cambridge, MA: Harvard University Press, 1970); Richard Sylla and George David Smith, "Capital Markets," in Kutler, ed., *Encyclopedia of the United States,* III, pp. 1209–1241; Wyckoff, *Wall Street,* pp. 150–151.

75. Wyckoff, *Wall Street,* pp. 150–151.

76. Ibid., p. 179; *Historical Statistics,* II, p. 1007.

77. New York Stock Exchange, *Fact Book, 1991* (New York: NYSE, 1991).

78. Richard Sylla, Jack W. Wilson, and Charles P. Jones, "U.S. Financial Markets and Long-Term Economic Growth, 1790–1989," in Thomas Weiss and Donald Schaefer, eds., *American Economic Development in Historical Perspective* (Stanford: Stanford University Press, 1994), p. 46. During the late nineteenth century real returns were somewhat higher for all types of securities than they were in the twentieth.

79. See Olivier Zunz, *Making America Corporate, 1870–1920* (Chicago: University of Chicago Press, 1990).

80. See Vincent P. Carosso, *Investment Banking in America* (Cambridge, MA: Harvard University Press, 1970); idem, *The Morgans: Private International Bankers, 1854–1913* (Cambridge, MA: Harvard University Press, 1987), esp. chs. 12 and 13.

81. The issue of separation of ownership from control was remarked by Adam Smith and other commentators almost as soon as corporations became familiar in Britain in the eighteenth century. The question was often discussed in the United States in the late nineteenth century, and it was first explicated at length by Adolf A. Berle and Gardiner C. Means in their landmark book *The Modern Corporation and Private Property* (New York: Macmillan, 1932). For arguments that the separation is a positive force for economic growth, see Chandler, *Scale and Scope,* and Bernard Elbaum and William

Lazonick, eds., *The Decline of the British Economy* (New York: Oxford University Press, 1986).

82. See e.g., Michael C. Jensen, "Eclipse of the Public Corporation," *Harvard Business Review,* 89 (Sept./Oct. 1989), pp. 61–74. The issue at stake here, which revolves around agency theory, remains one of the most controversial questions confronting modern business practice as well as economic scholarship. A relatively early exchange of arguments may be found in the special issue of the *Journal of Law and Economics,* 26 (June 1983), devoted to a 50-year retrospective on Berle and Means's *The Modern Corporation and Private Property.* See also Thomas K. McCraw, "In Retrospect: Berle and Means," *Reviews in American History,* 18 (Dec. 1990), pp. 578–596.

83. Chester Barnard, *The Functions of the Executive* (Cambridge, MA: Harvard University Press, 1938), p. 289.

84. JoAnne Yates, *Control through Communication: The Rise of System in American Management* (Baltimore: Johns Hopkins University Press, 1989).

85. See Albert Fink, "Classification of Operating Expenses," in *Annual Report of the Louisville & Nashville Railroad Company for the year ending 30 June 1874* (Louisville, 1874), pp. 37–47, 63–64, reprinted in Alfred D. Chandler Jr., Thomas K. McCraw, and Richard S. Tedlow, *Management Past and Present: A Casebook on the History of American Business* (Cincinnati: South-Western, 1996), pp. 2-25–2-32.

86. Frederick W. Taylor, *The Principles of Scientific Management* (New York: Harper's, 1911). See also Daniel Nelson, *Frederick W. Taylor and the Rise of Scientific Management* (Madison: University of Wisconsin Press, 1980). On the efficiency movement as an American fad, see Samuel Haber, *Efficiency and Uplift: Scientific Management in the Progressive Era, 1890–1920* (Chicago: University of Chicago Press, 1962).

87. See the sections on Du Pont and General Motors in Alfred D. Chandler Jr., *Strategy and Structure: Chapters in the History of the Industrial Enterprise* (Cambridge, MA: MIT Press, 1962).

88. Kenneth Flamm, *Creating the Computer: Government, Industry, and High Technology* (Washington: Brookings Institution, 1988); Thomas J. Watson Jr. and Peter Petre, *Father, Son & Co.: My Life at IBM and Beyond* (New York: Bantam, 1990); Emerson W. Pugh, *Building IBM: Shaping an Industry and Its Technology* (Cambridge, MA: MIT Press, 1995).

89. Alfred P. Sloan Jr., *My Years with General Motors* (New York: Doubleday, 1963), p. 54 and passim. See also Sloan, in collaboration with Boyden Sparkes, *Adventures of a White Collar Man* (New York: Doubleday, 1941).

90. Barnard, *Functions of the Executive,* p. 194. In the original, this entire statement is printed in italics.

91. For a survey of information systems from the nineteenth century onward, see James Beniger, *The Control Revolution* (Cambridge, MA: Harvard Uni-

versity Press, 1986); for an analysis of computer-mediated work, see Shoshana Zuboff, *In the Age of the Smart Machine: The Future of Work and Power* (New York: Basic Books, 1988).

92. Mira Wilkins, *The Emergence of Multinational Enterprise: American Business Abroad from the Colonial Era to 1914* (Cambridge, MA: Harvard University Press, 1970); Fred V. Carstensen, *American Enterprise in Foreign Markets: Studies of Singer and International Harvester in Imperial Russia* (Chapel Hill: University of North Carolina Press, 1984).

93. Mira Wilkins, *The Maturing of Multinational Enterprise: American Business Abroad From 1914 to 1970* (Cambridge, MA: Harvard University Press, 1974); Raymond Vernon, *Sovereignty at Bay: The Multinational Spread of U.S. Enterprises* (New York: Basic Books, 1971).

94. The classic statement of this view is Louis Hartz, *The Liberal Tradition in America* (New York: Harcourt, Brace, 1955).

95. Quoted in Henry Steele Commager, ed., *America in Perspective: The United States through Foreign Eyes* (New York: Random House, 1947; Mentor paperback, 1948), pp. 232–238.

96. Chicago: University of Chicago Press.

97. Boston: Houghton Mifflin.

98. See Richard H. K. Vietor, "Economic Performance," in Kutler, ed., *Encyclopedia of the United States,* III, pp. 1155–1182; and Frank Levy, *Dollars and Dreams: The Changing American Income Distribution* (New York: Russell Sage Foundation, 1987).

99. See James T. Patterson, "Wealth and Poverty," in Kutler, ed., *Encyclopedia of the United States,* III, pp. 1067–1090.

100. Ibid.

101. Michael M. Weinstein, "Why They Deserve It," *New York Times Magazine,* 19 Nov. 1995, p. 103, citing a study by Graef Crystal.

102. See Edward Wolff, "Trends in Household Wealth in the United States, 1962–83 and 1983–89," *Review of Income and Wealth,* 40, no. 2 (1994), and "How the Pie Is Sliced," *American Prospect,* Summer 1995, both cited in Steven Sass, "Passing the Buck: The Intergenerational Transfer of Wealth," Federal Reserve Bank of Boston *Regional Review* (Summer 1995), pp. 12–17; and Lee Soltow, "Distribution of Income and Wealth," in Porter, ed., *Encyclopedia of American Economic History,* pp. 1087–1119.

103. *Historical Statistics,* I, p. 178. The percentages are higher, of course, for nonagricultural employment. Whereas in 1945 the unionized portion of the workforce as a whole was 21.9 percent, it was 35.5 percent of the nonagricultural workforce. This difference abated as the years passed and fewer people worked in agricultural employment.

104. For a survey of the literature on American labor organization, see Melvyn

Dubofsky, *Industrialism and the American Worker, 1865–1920,* 2d ed. (Arlington Heights, IL, 1985), which contains an extensive annotated bibliography. A comprehensive analysis is David Montgomery, *The Fall of the House of Labor: The Workplace, the State, and American Labor Activism, 1865–1925* (Cambridge: Cambridge University Press, 1987). For the shift in government policy during the 1930s and the strike at General Motors on 1936–37, see Sidney Fine, *Sit-Down* (Ann Arbor: University of Michigan Press, 1968). See also Robert H. Zieger, *The CIO: 1935–1955* (Chapel Hill: University of North Carolina Press, 1995). Biographies of labor leaders include Harold C. Livesay, *Samuel Gompers and Organized Labor in America* (Boston: Little, Brown, 1978); Melvyn Dubofsky and Warren Van Tine, *John L. Lewis: A Biography* (New York: Quadrangle/New York Times Books, 1977); Irving Howe and B. J. Widdick, *The UAW and Walter Reuther* (New York: Random House, 1959); and Steven Fraser, *Labor Will Rule: Sidney Hillman and the Rise of American Labor* (New York: Free Press, 1992). On the changing nature of employment, see Robert B. Reich, *The Work of Nations* (New York: Knopf, 1991).

105. Elliot Brownlee, "Taxation," in Kutler, ed., *Encyclopedia of the United States,* III, pp. 1309–1330.

106. *Historical Statistics,* I, p. 8; II, pp. 1102–1103; *Statistical Abstract of the United States* (Washington: Government Printing Office, 1982), pp. 6, 264, 266–267. See Ballard C. Campbell, *The Growth of American Government: Governance from the Cleveland Era to the Present* (Bloomington: Indiana University Press, 1995).

107. Harold Syrett et al., eds., *The Papers of Alexander Hamilton* (New York and London: Columbia University Press, 1961–78), vol. 18, pp. 101–103. Capitalization and spelling are as in the original.

108. On recent American performance and future prospects see Nicolas Spulber, *The American Economy: The Struggle for Supremacy in the 21st Century* (Cambridge: Cambridge University Press, 1995), which contains cross-national comparative data.

109. "Back on Top? A Survey of American Business," *Economist,* 16–22 Sept. 1995, pp. 13–14.

110. For a summary of the literature of optimism, together with a pessimistic verdict, see Robert H. Hayes, "U.S. Competitiveness: 'Resurgence' versus Reality," *Challenge,* March-April 1996, pp. 36–44.

111. See Alfred D. Chandler Jr., "The Competitive Performance of U.S. Industrial Enterprises since the Second World War," *Business History Review,* 68 (spring 1994), pp. 1–72.

112. Joseph A. Schumpeter, *Capitalism, Socialism and Democracy,* 3d ed. (1942; New York: Harper, 1950), p. 79.

113. Ibid., pp. 81, 83–84.
114. "Back on Top?" p. 18.

10. IBM and the Two Thomas J. Watsons

1. S&P *Industry Surveys,* "The Computer Industry," 24 Nov. 1994, p. 76. "Information technology" is the "merging of computing and high-speed communications links carrying data, sound, and video." *Webster's New World Dictionary of Computer Terms,* 4th ed., comp. Donald Spencer (New York: Prentice Hall, 1992), p. 206.

2. James W. Cortada, *Historical Dictionary of Data Processing Organizations* (New York: Greenwood Press, 1987), pp. 2, 9. See also James W. Cortada, *Before the Computer: IBM, NCR, Burroughs, and Remington Rand and the Industry They Created, 1865–1956* (Princeton: Princeton University Press, 1993); and James R. Beniger, *The Control Revolution: Technical and Economic Origins of the Information Society* (Cambridge, MA: Harvard University Press, 1986).

3. Kenneth Flamm, *Targeting the Computer: Government Support and International Competition* (Washington: Brookings Institution, 1987), p. 7; idem, *Creating the Computer: Government, Industry, and High Technology* (Washington: Brookings Institution, 1988), p. 16.

4. Flamm, *Creating the Computer,* ch. 3. For a history of semiconductors, see Ernest Braun and Stuart Macdonald, *Revolution in Miniature: The History and Impact of Semiconductor Electronics* (New York: Cambridge University Press, 1978).

5. Flamm, *Targeting the Computer,* pp. 6–8.

6. IBM annual report, 1990.

7. On the British industry, see John Hendry, *Innovating for Failure: Government Policy and the Early British Computer Industry* (Cambridge, MA.: MIT Press, 1990); Martin Campbell-Kelly, *ICL: A Business and Technical History* (New York: Oxford University Press, 1989); Tim Kelly, *The British Computer Industry: Crisis and Development* (London: Croom Helm, 1987); and Simon Lavington, *Early British Computers* (Bedford, MA.: Digital Press, 1980).

8. Flamm, *Creating the Computer,* p. 135; see also chs. 5 and 6. On Europe and Japan, see Flamm, *Targeting the Computer,* ch. 5. On Japan, see Marie Anchordoguy, *Computers Inc.: Japan's Challenge to IBM* (Cambridge, MA: Harvard University Press for the Council on East Asian Studies, 1989); and Martin Fransman, *Japan's Computer and Communications Industry: The Evolution of Industrial Giants and Global Competitiveness* (New York: Oxford University Press, 1995).

9. David B. Yoffie, *Strategic Management in Information Technology* (Englewood Cliffs, NJ: Prentice Hall, 1994), p. 32.

10. Alfred D. Chandler Jr., "The Computer Industry—The First Fifty Years" (MS, 15 Nov. 1995), p. 10; *Statistical Abstract of the United States* (Washington: Government Printing Office, 1994), p. 761.

11. *Webster's New World Dictionary of Computer Terms,* pp. 250–251.

12. Chandler, "The First Fifty Years," p. 10.

13. Ibid.

14. "The Computer Industry: The Third Age," *Economist,* 17 Sept. 1994, p. 4.

15. A transistor is a "device used for controlling the flow of current between two terminals." Bell Laboratories developed the first transistors in 1947. *Webster's New World Dictionary of Computer Terms,* p. 430.

16. "The Computer Industry: The Third Age," p. 4.

17. An "open architecture" is a nonproprietary design that allows other makers to design components for a machine. In contrast to IBM, Apple Computer decided not to license its proprietary operating system until 1994. Until then, the company lacked a clone market for its Macintosh chips, software, operating system, and peripherals. Throughout the 1980s and early 1990s, Apple struggled against the "Wintel" (Microsoft Windows and Intel chips) juggernaut. According to one industry observer, Apple's decision not to go with an open architecture in the early 1980s may have been "one of the most serious fumbles in the history of corporate America." Apple's share of the microcomputer market, as measured by revenue, was 17 percent in 1993, placing it third behind IBM and Compaq. S&P *Industry Surveys,* p. 84; "PC Makers Adapt to Slim Margins," *Datamation,* 15 June 1994, p. 55.

18. Thomas J. Watson Jr. and Peter Petre, *Father, Son & Co.: My Life at IBM and Beyond* (New York: Bantam, 1990), ch. 2. See also William Rodgers, *THINK: A Biography of the Watsons and IBM* (New York: Stein and Day, 1969).

19. Watson and Petre, *Father, Son & Co.,* ch. 2; on Patterson, see Samuel Crowther, *John H. Patterson, Pioneer in Industrial Welfare* (Garden City, NY: Garden City Pub. Co., 1926); Judith Selander, *Grand Plans: Business Progressivism and Social Change in Ohio's Miami Valley, 1890–1929* (Lexington: University Press of Kentucky, 1988).

20. Emerson W. Pugh, *Building IBM: Shaping an Industry and Its Technology* (Cambridge, MA: MIT Press, 1995), p. 248.

21. Watson and Petre, *Father, Son, & Co.,* p. ix.

22. Ibid., p. 82.

23. Quoted in Pugh, *Building IBM,* p. 46.

24. See Geoffrey D. Austrian, *Herman Hollerith: Forgotten Giant of Information Processing* (New York: Columbia University Press, 1982).

25. Lou Mobley and Kate McKeown, *Beyond IBM: Leadership, Marketing and Finance for the 1990s* (Washington: Enter Publishing, 1989), p. 5.
26. Cortada, *Before the Computer*, p. 153.
27. Watson and Petre, *Father, Son & Co.*, p. 33.
28. Ibid., pp. 113, 134.
29. Steven W. Usselman, "IBM and Its Imitators: Organizational Capabilities and the Emergence of the International Computer Industry," *Business and Economic History*, 22, no. 2 (winter 1993), pp. 1–35; quotation pp. 9–10.
30. Watson and Petre, *Father, Son & Co.*, pp. 173–179.
31. Mobley and McKeown, *Beyond IBM*, pp. 15–16.
32. Ibid.
33. Watson and Petre, *Father, Son & Co.*, p. 218.
34. Emerson Pugh, who worked at IBM for many years, disputes Tom Jr.'s account of T.J.'s resistance to computer technology. "By not emphasizing his own early role," writes Pugh, "Watson, Sr., provided his son with ownership of the company's thrust into electronics. The master salesman had made one of the more important sales of his life. His son had chosen to be responsible for the company's activities in electronics. The senior Watson could now concentrate on traditional . . . products and a planned expansion of the electric typewriter business." *Building IBM*, p. 149.
35. Watson and Petre, *Father, Son & Co.*, p. ix. The next five paragraphs are based primarily on the account in this book, which is Tom Jr.'s autobiography.
36. Ibid., p. 201.
37. See Nancy Stern, *From ENIAC to UNIVAC: An Appraisal of the Eckert-Mauchly Computers* (Bedford, MA: Digital Press, 1981).
38. See Charles J. Bashe, Lyle R. Johnson, John H. Palmer, and Emerson W. Pugh, *IBM's Early Computers* (Cambridge, Mass: MIT Press, 1986).
39. Flamm, *Creating the Computer*, pp. 87–88. See also Kent C. Redmond and Thomas M. Smith, *Project Whirlwind: The History of a Pioneer Computer* (Bedford, MA: Digital Press, 1980). Magnetic core memory, or magnetic core storage, is a system that "retains stored data in the event of a power loss." A circuit board is "the thin insulating board used to mount and connect various electronic components and microchips in a pattern of conductive lines. This circuit pattern is etched into the board's surface." *Webster's New World Dictionary of Computer Terms*, pp. 248, 54.
40. Pugh, *Building IBM*, p. 237.
41. Watson and Petre, *Father, Son & Co.*, p. 242.
42. Usselman, "IBM and Its Imitators," pp. 11–12.
43. Watson and Petre, *Father, Son & Co.*, p. 227.
44. Ibid., p. 228. Steven Usselman has pointed out that the parallel development of the 701 and 702 did not turn out exactly as IBM had expected. Company

executives thought that the developments in connection with the 701, for which it had 18–20 orders, would spill over to the 702, the commercial version. But 702 sales lagged (about 5 were built). Overall, however, the rapidly falling cost of memory eroded the distinction between the scientific and the commercial markets by opening up opportunities for programming.

45. Flamm, *Creating the Computer,* p. 83.

46. Franklin M. Fisher, James W. McKie, and Richard B. Mancke, *IBM and the U.S. Data Processing Industry: An Economic History* (New York: Praeger, 1983), pp. 56–57.

47. Steven Usselman questions the interpretation that "IBM behaved in a highly unusual (and remarkably enlightened) fashion in making this transition" from electromechanical accounting equipment to electronic computers. Instead, he believes that the transition was logical and natural, given the organizational capabilities IBM had developed. He also argues that "IBM was a market-oriented company, and scientific computing represented an obvious opportunity, one that did not threaten its established base at all." "IBM and Its Imitators," pp. 8–9.

48. David Mercer, *The Global IBM: Leadership in Multinational Management* (New York: Dodd, Mead, 1988), p. 49 and ch. 8; Yoffie, *Strategic Management,* p. 35.

49. Fisher et al., *IBM and the U.S. Data Processing Industry,* p. 65. Twelve major U.S. companies manufactured digital computers in 1956. In 1965, only six of these continued as significant producers, and by 1986 only IBM, NCR, and UNISYS (a merger of Sperry Rand and Burroughs) remained of the original twelve. In 1991, NCR was acquired by AT&T. Flamm, *Creating the Computer,* p. 81; Yoffie, *Strategic Management,* p. 49.

50. Watson and Petre, *Father, Son, & Co.,* pp. 347–348.

51. Flamm, *Creating the Computer,* pp. 90–91.

52. Ibid., p. 98.

53. Watson and Petre, *Father, Son & Co.,* pp. 346–347. See also Emerson W. Pugh, *Memories That Shaped an Industry: Decisions Leading to IBM System/360* (Cambridge, MA: MIT Press, 1984); Emerson Pugh, Lyle R. Johnson, and John H. Palmer, *IBM's 360 and Early 370 Systems* (Cambridge, MA: MIT Press, 1991).

54. IBM introduced the 1401 in 1959. At the time, the 1401 was the least expensive entry-level computer available and could perform seven times as many instructions as the 650.

55. Charles H. Ferguson and Charles R. Morris, *Computer Wars: How the West Can Win in a Post-IBM World* (New York: Times Books, 1993), p. 7.

56. Flamm, *Creating the Computer,* pp. 99–101; William O. Ingle, under the supervision of Professor Joseph L. Bower, "The IBM 360: Giant as Entre-

preneur," Harvard Business School Case no. 9-389-003. The powerful effects of IBM's backward integration have been underscored by Steven Usselman.

57. Flamm, *Targeting the Computer,* pp. 127–131.

58. James Cortada, *Historical Dictionary of Data Processing Biographies* (New York: Greenwood Press, 1987), p. 277.

59. Alfred D. Chandler Jr. "Computers and Semiconductors," (MS, August 1994), pp. 19–22.

60. Ibid.

61. Watson and Petre, *Father, Son & Co.,* p. 293; Paul Carroll, *Big Blues: The Unmaking of IBM* (New York: Crown, 1993), p. 64.

62. Yoffie, *Strategic Management,* p. 32.

63. Watson and Petre, *Father, Son & Co.,* p. 147.

64. Quoted in Cortada, *Before the Computer,* p. 121. The song has additional verses.

65. Mobley and McKeown, *Beyond IBM,* p. 8.

66. Pugh, *Building IBM,* pp. 55–57.

67. Ibid., p. 57.

68. Watson and Petre, *Father, Son, & Co.,* pp. 46, 66.

69. Mobley and McKeown, *Beyond IBM,* pp. 8–9, 14.

70. Watson and Petre, *Father, Son, & Co.,* p. 254.

71. Ibid., p. 253.

72. Ibid., pp. 285–290.

73. Mobley and McKeown, *Beyond IBM,* p. 23.

74. Flamm, *Creating the Computer,* pp. 83–84.

75. Watson and Petre, *Father, Son & Co.,* p. 285–286.

76. Ibid., p. 303.

77. Ibid., pp. 291–292.

78. Ibid., p. 308.

79. Ibid., pp. 301.

80. Ibid., p. 142.

81. The author is indebted to Steven Usselman for calling attention to this point.

82. Ibid., p. 216.

83. Ibid., pp. 217–219.

84. "Old, Onerous, and Still on the Books," *Business Week,* 7 Nov. 1994. See also Nancy S. Dorfman, *Innovation and Market Structure: Lessons from the Computer and Semiconductor Industries* (Cambridge, MA: Ballinger, 1987). Dorfman believes that government policy has been less important than other factors in the evolution of these industries.

85. Watson and Petre, *Father, Son & Co.,* p. 270. IBM has since attempted to have the consent decree overturned. The antitrust story in computing is

traced in Steven W. Usselman, "Fostering a Capacity for Compromises: Business, Government, and the Stages of Innovation in American Computing," *IEEE Annals of the History of Computing,* 18, no. 2 (1996), pp. 30–39.

86. The following account of *U.S. v. IBM* and *Control Data v. IBM* is based on Watson and Petre, *Father, Son, & Co.,* ch. 29.

87. Ibid., p. 380.

88. Again the author is indebted to Steven Usselman for highlighting this point.

89. Ibid., p. 386.

90. Even as late as 1989, IBM derived half of its revenues and an even higher proportion of its profits from products based on the System/360 architecture and its extensions. By then, IBM's high exposure to the upper end of the computer market had become a serious problem, as the industry shifted to lower-priced, consumer-oriented personal computers, which did not use the System/360 architecture. Pugh, *Building IBM,* p. 311. A workstation is "a configuration of computer equipment designed for use by one person at a time." *Webster's New World Dictionary of Computer Terms,* p. 454.

91. See e.g., Robert X. Cringely, *Accidental Empires: How the Boys of Silicon Valley Make Their Millions, Battle Foreign Competition, and Still Can't Get a Date* (Reading, MA: Addision-Wesley, 1992); AnnaLee Saxenian, *Regional Advantage: Culture and Competition in Silicon Valley and Route 128* (Cambridge, MA: Harvard University Press, 1994); Michael Malone, *The Big Score: The Billion-Dollar Story of Silicon Valley* (Garden City, NY: Doubleday, 1985); Everett Rogers and Judith K. Larsen, *Silicon Valley Fever: Growth of High-Technology Culture* (New York: Basic Books, 1984). The author is grateful to Stuart W. Leslie for calling attention to these works.

92. Yoffie, *Strategic Management,* pp. 36, 38, 277. Japanese companies were not immune to the cutthroat competition that increasingly characterized the industry. In the mid-1990s Hitachi, Fujitsu, and NEC were faced with ailing mainframe and minicomputer businesses.

93. Ibid., pp. 277–278.

94. IBM's entry into PCs may well have saved the U.S. semiconductor industry. Intel became the world's largest microprocessors producer and helped maintain U.S. supremacy over Japanese rivals. Chandler, "The First Fifty Years," pp. 64–65.

95. The disk operating system is "a collection of software stored on disk that controls the operation of the computer system . . . Typically, it keeps track of files, saves and retrieves files, allocates storage space, and manages other control functions associated with disk storage." The microprocessor is "the complex chip that is the central processing unit (CPU) of the computer." *Webster's New World Dictionary of Computer Terms,* pp. 123, 262.

96. See James Chposky and Ted Leonsis, *Blue Magic: The People, Power and*

Politics behind the IBM Personal Computer (New York: Facts on File, 1988).

97. The RISC technology enhances the speed of the microprocessor by reducing the number of operations. In this technology, the software takes over many of the functions formerly handled by the microprocessor.

98. "The Computer Industry: The Third Age," p. 8.

99. See Richard N. Langlois, "External Economies and Economic Progress: The Case of the Microcomputer Industry," *Business History Review* 66 (spring 1992), pp. 1–50.

100. Carroll, *Big Blues,* p. 4; "The New World of Work," *Business Week,* 17 Oct. 1994; "Is He Too Cautious for IBM?" *Fortune,* 3 Oct. 1994; "The Computer Industry: The Third Age," p. 8.

101. Thomas M. Liptak, *U.S. v. IBM* (transcript), pp. 84, 620–684, 621. Research for this appendix was done at the Charles Babbage Institute, University of Minnesota, which holds a copy of the transcript.

102. Frank Cary, *U.S. v. IBM* (transcript), pp. 101,612–101,613.

103. Cary, p. 101,613.

104. Cary, p. 101,612.

105. Cary, p. 101,718.

106. John Opel, *U.S. v. IBM* (transcript), p. 1,437.

107. Opel, pp. 1,456–1,457.

108. Cary, p. 101,776.

109. Thomas J. Watson Jr., *U.S. v. IBM* (transcript), p. 29,045.

110. Cary, p. 101,711.

111. Cary, p. 101,784.

112. See Pugh, *Memories That Shaped an Industry,* p. 197. On System/360, see Pugh, Johnson, and Palmer, *IBM's 360 and Early 370 Systems.*

113. Bob O. Evans, *U.S. v. IBM* (transcript), p. 101,050.

114. Evans, p. 101,052.

115. Evans, p. 101,054.

116. Evans, p. 101,061.

117. Evans, p. 101,064.

118. Evans, pp. 101,065–101,066.

119. Evans, p. 101,100.

120. Evans, p. 101,105.

121. Evans, p. 101,067.

122. Evans, p. 101,127.

123. Evans, p. 101,128.

124. Evans, p. 101,073.

125. Evans, p. 101,198. Steven Usselman has pointed out that Evans's statement was perhaps not strictly accurate, because IBM had drastically re-

defined the machines since 1961 and had added new members of the line. The decision to announce all of the machines at once came very late.

126. Evans, pp. 101,125–101,126.
127. Evans, p. 101,174.
128. Evans, pp. 101,118–101,119.
129. Evans, pp. 101,118–101,119.
130. T. Vincent Learson, *U.S. v. IBM* (transcript), pp. 26,938–26,948.

11. *Toyoda Automatic Looms and Toyota Automobiles*

1. Penelope Francks writes of the Japanese textile industry's "almost total reliance on one machine supplier, Platt Brothers." Platt Brothers accounted for 87 percent of the spindles used in Japanese thread spinning in 1909, and even as Japanese imports of spinning machinery declined in the 1920s, it maintained a 70 percent share of the import market. Francks, *Japanese Economic Development: Theory and Practice* (London: Routledge, 1992), p. 185; D. A. Farnie, "The Textile Machine-making Industry and the World Market," *Business History* 32 (Oct. 1990), p. 153; and William Mass and Hideaki Miyajima, "Technology Transfer and the First Japanese Economic Miracle," paper presented at the Harvard Business History Seminar, 14 Dec. 1992, p. 23.

   In this chapter and the following two, Japanese personal names are written using Western order: given name first and family name second. Also, macrons are omitted in the romanization of Japanese words.

2. See, e.g., William Mass and Hideaki Miyajima, "The Organization of the Developmental State: Fostering Private Capabilities and the Roots of the Japanese 'Miracle,'" *Business and Economic History* 22, no. 1 (1993), pp. 151–168.

3. Much of this section is based on Toyota's official company history, *Toyota: A History of the First 50 Years* (Toyota City: Toyota Motor Corporation, 1988), pp. 23–38; Yukiyasu Togo and William Wartman, *Against All Odds: The Story of the Toyota Motor Corporation and the Family That Created It* (New York: St. Martin's Press, 1993), pp. 1–39; and Mass and Miyajima, "Technology Transfer," pp. 36–63.

4. *Toyota: A History,* p. 26.

5. Sakichi initially left Kiichiro in the care of his parents while he went to Nagoya. Only after he remarried did Kiichiro come to live with him. See Togo and Wartman, *Against All Odds,* pp. 19, 26.

6. *Toyota: A History,* p. 27.

7. Ibid., p. 28. Mitsui & Company is the English name that was later adopted for Mitsui Bussan. In Chapters 11–13, I generally use current (mid-1990s) names for Japanese corporations.

8. In Japanese, the company's name had been changed from Toyoda Shoten to Toyoda Shokai, but in English both "shoten" and "shokai" can be translated as "company."

9. *Toyota: A History,* p. 30.

10. Sakichi retained a 30 percent share of Toyoda Loom Works' profits until 1912, when he exchanged this right for a lump-sum payment of ¥80,000. This move turned out to be a major error on his part, as he would have earned ¥3 million in royalties between 1914 and 1919 alone had he retained his claim. In the early 1920s, Sakichi also became embroiled in a patent disagreement with Toyoda Loom Works. See Mass and Miyajima, "Technology Transfer," pp. 42–43, 46–47.

11. Indeed, Mass and Miyajima conclude, "It is likely that Kiichiro was principally responsible for the company's inventions after 1921." Ibid., p. 55.

12. Farnie, "Textile Machine-making Industry," p. 155.

13. W. Mark Fruin, *The Japanese Enterprise System* (New York: Oxford University Press, 1994), pp. 336–341.

14. Mary B. Rose, "International Competition and Strategic Response in the Textile Industries since 1870," *Business History* 32 (1990), table 1, p. 3. On the Japanese displacement of the British, see William Mass and William Lazonick, "The British Cotton Industry and International Competitive Advantage: The State of the Debates," *Business History* 32 (1990), pp. 9–65.

15. On British reactions to the Japanese challenge, see Alex J. Robertson, "Lancashire and the Rise of Japan," *Business History* 32 (1990), pp. 87–103.

16. In the 1880s, the largest British cotton-spinning firm, as measured by the number of spindles, was over seven times the size of its Japanese counterpart. By 1938, the largest British firm, actually a loose amalgamation of 45 different spinning firms, had just over twice the number of spindles and less than one-fifteenth the number of looms of its largest Japanese rival. See Shin-ichi Yonekawa, "The Growth of Cotton Spinning Firms: A Comparative Study," in Akio Okochi and Shin-ichi Yonekawa, eds., *The Textile Industry and Its Business Climate,* International Conference on Business History 8 (Tokyo: University of Tokyo Press, 1982), pp. 1–38.

17. See Mass and Lazonick, "British Cotton Industry," pp. 39, 42–43.

18. In 1913, ring spindles made up 19 percent of all spindles in Britain, 87 percent in the United States, and 98 percent in Japan. Naosuke Takamura, "Japanese Cotton Spinning Industry during the Pre-World War I Period," in Okochi and Yonekawa, eds., *Textile Industry,* pp. 277–285, Table 1.

19. Females comprised 81 percent of the workers in cotton textiles in Japan in 1930, as opposed to only 39 percent in the southern United States. See Gary Saxonhouse and Gavin Wright, "Two Forms of Cheap Labor in Textile History," in *Technique, Spirit, and Form in the Making of Modern Economies,* Supplement 3 of *Research in Economic History* (1984), p. 6.

20. Mass and Lazonick, "British Cotton Industry," p. 23. The percentage of automatic looms in Lancashire remained less than 12 percent as late as 1955.

21. Alice Amsden's study of South Korean development illustrates that Korean textile firms, at one time the largest Korean firms, were unable to make the transition into more advanced industries. Instead, firms in heavy industry, such as Hyundai in cement and Lucky-Goldstar in plastics, formed the basis of modern industry in Korea. *Asia's Next Giant* (New York: Oxford University Press, 1989).

22. Farnie, "Textile Machine-making Industry," pp. 156, 168n.

23. Ibid., p. 167. This figure is based upon the value of textile machinery exports, but the figure for volume is similar.

24. Ibid., p. 160.

25. On competition in this industry, see Mass and Miyajima, "Technology Transfer," pp. 49–51.

26. Togo and Wartman, *Against All Odds,* p. 34; *Toyota: A History,* p. 23; Eiji Toyoda, *Toyota: Fifty Years in Motion* (Tokyo: Kodansha International, 1987), p. 23.

27. Fruin, *Japanese Enterprise System,* p. 260.

28. *Toyota: A History,* p. 41; Michael Cusumano, *The Japanese Automobile Industry* (Cambridge, MA: Harvard University Press, 1985), app. A.

29. *Toyota: A History,* p. 42. Mass and Miyajima ("Technology Transfer," pp. 61–62) make the important point that Kiichiro undertook this expensive technological upgrading at a time when Toyoda Automatic Loom Works was unable to fill all the outstanding orders for its machines. Thus, instead of expanding capacity to meet demand for looms—the conservative strategy—Kiichiro opted to channel resources into a new and very risky activity.

30. Cusumano, *Japanese Automobile Industry,* p. 59.

31. Ibid., p. 65.

32. *Toyota: A History,* p. 65.

33. The Japanese government later named Diesel Jidosha Kogyo, the predecessor of Isuzu Motors, as an authorized producer. Koichi Shimokawa, *The Japanese Automobile Industry* (London: Athlone, 1994), p. 6.

34. Cusumano, *Japanese Automobile Industry,* pp. 385–386.

35. *Toyota: A History,* p. 60.

36. Ibid., p. 65.

37. Togo and Wartman, *Against All Odds,* p. 76.

38. Cusumano, *Japanese Automobile Industry,* pp. 61, 46.

39. Ibid., pp. 63–64; *Toyota: A History,* pp. 76–77.

40. Eiji Toyoda recalls, "There were nuns and geishas, and even convicted criminals." *Fifty Years in Motion,* p. 64.

41. Ibid., pp. 71–72.

42. Ibid., p. 80. Toyota did become a producer of prefabricated houses.
43. Fruin, *Japanese Enterprise System,* pp. 265–266.
44. Cusumano, *Japanese Automobile Industry,* p. 147.
45. Ibid., pp. 160–162.
46. *Toyota: A History,* pp. 111–112.
47. Naoto Ichimata, quoted in Yoshiro Miwa, "Subcontracting Relationships: The Automobile Industry," in Ken-ichi Imai and Ryutaro Komiya, eds., Ronald Dore and Hugh Whittaker, trans., *Business Enterprise in Japan* (Cambridge, MA: MIT Press, 1994), p. 142, n. 3.
48. Cusumano, *Japanese Automobile Industry,* p. 19.
49. Ibid., p. 387.
50. Ibid., p. xix. The Japanese government employed a number of other measures, not protectionist in orientation, that also stimulated the industry. For instance, beginning in 1951, the Ministry of Transportation implemented an auto inspection system (*shaken*). Under this system, expensive inspections were required every two years after the purchase of a new car. (In 1983 the first inspection only was changed to three years after purchase.) Many Japanese, rather than pay for the costly second inspection, opted to buy a new car.
51. David Halberstam, *The Reckoning* (New York: Avon, 1986), pp. 263–268; Cusumano, *Japanese Automobile Industry,* pp. 33–45.
52. Toyoda, *Fifty Years in Motion,* p. 109. Other accounts give a different impression of Eiji's reaction. According to Toyota's official 30-year history, Eiji sent a communiqué from Ford to headquarters stating that "he thought there were some possibilities to improve the [Toyota] production system." And in 1982, Eiji told Ford's president, Philip Caldwell: "There is no secret to how we learned to do what we do, Mr. Caldwell. We learned it at the Rouge." See James P. Womack, Daniel T. Jones, and Daniel Roos, *The Machine That Changed the World: The Story of Lean Production* (New York: HarperCollins, 1990), p. 49, and Halberstam, *Reckoning,* p. 81.
53. *Toyota: A History,* p. 114, and p. 4 of Koichi Shimokawa, "Interview with Eiji Toyoda: A New Leap Forward," *The Wheel Extended,* 3, no. 4 (1987), pp. 3–9. For more on the Toyota suggestion system, see Yuzo Yasuda, *40 Years, 20 Million Ideas: The Toyota Suggestion System* (Cambridge, MA: Productivity Press, 1991).
54. Toyoda, *Fifty Years in Motion,* p. 115.
55. *Toyota: A History,* pp. 130–131.
56. Data for 1950–84 from Cusumano, *Japanese Automobile Industry,* pp. 98–99. For the remaining years, I relied upon *The Automobile Industry: Toyota and Japan* (Toyota City: Toyota Motor Corporation, 1995) and several issues of *Japanese Motor Business.*
57. Cusumano, *Japanese Automobile Industry,* p. 98. Of course, Toyota expe-

rienced a major strike that year, so its production was unusually low. However, Nissan was the larger and more experienced automobile firm at the time.

58. Ibid., p. 74 and p. 78.
59. Ibid., p. 220.
60. Ibid., p. 182.
61. Ibid., p. 307.
62. For more on Kamiya's role, see his autobiography, *My Life with Toyota* (Toyota City: Toyota Motor Sales, 1976).
63. Ibid., p. 37. Even so, Kamiya did not complain, because his salary was set at a level equal to that of the directors of Toyoda Automatic Loom.
64. Organizing a larger dealer network was not Kamiya's only contribution. Under his leadership Toyota Motor Sales pioneered many innovations in Japanese automobile marketing and distribution, a few of which are described in the Appendix to this chapter. However, the brief description there does not adequately convey the important contributions of Toyota Motor Sales or the creative vision of Kamiya. See ibid., esp. Ch. 4; Togo and Wartman, *Against All Odds,* pp. 134–136; and Shimokawa, *Japanese Automobile Industry,* pp. 83–85.
65. Numbers from a 1977 study by MITI's Small and Medium-Sized Enterprise Agency reported in Fruin, *Japanese Enterprise System,* fig. 7.1. On Toyota's subcontracting, see Kazuo Wada, "The Development of Tiered Inter-firm Relationships in the Automobile Industry: A Case Study of Toyota Motor Corporation," *Japanese Yearbook on Business History* 8 (1991), pp. 451–475, and Cusumano, *Japanese Automobile Industry,* pp. 241–261.
66. Cusumano argues that the auto companies' reluctance to invest is illustrated by their extremely high rates of capacity utilization. *Japanese Automobile Industry,* p. 238.
67. Toyoda, *Fifty Years in Motion,* p. 165 and p. 127.
68. Toyoda, *Fifty Years in Motion,* p. 135. Many of the names Nissan gave its cars, such as Cedric, Bluebonnet, and Fair Lady, sprang from the Anglophilism of Nissan's long-time president, Katsuji Kawamata. See Halberstam, *Reckoning,* pp. 441–442.
69. *Toyota: A History,* p. 174.
70. Ibid., p. 197.
71. Toyoda, *Fifty Years in Motion,* p. 122; Togo and Wartman, *Against All Odds,* p. 237.
72. *Toyota: A History,* p. 69.
73. Ibid., pp. 69–73.
74. See Taiichi Ohno, *Toyota Production System: Beyond Large-Scale Production* (Cambridge, MA: Productivity Press, 1988); Cusumano, *Japanese Au-*

tomobile Industry, pp. 267–307; Togo and Wartman, *Against All Odds,* pp. 114–119, 130–131; *Toyota: A History,* pp. 141–145; Kazuo Wada, "The 'Flow Production' Method in Japan," in Haruhito Shiomi and Kazuo Wada, eds., *Fordism Transformed: The Development of Production Methods in the Automobile Industry* (New York: Oxford University Press, 1995), pp. 12–27; Koichi Shimokawa, "From the Ford System to the Just in Time Production System," *Japanese Yearbook on Business History,* 10 (1993); and Kazuhiro Mishina, "The Logic of the Toyota Production System," Harvard Business School Working Paper 94–065, April 1994.

75. Cusumano, *Japanese Automobile Industry,* p. 285.

76. On Ohno and the 1950 strike, see ibid., p. 306, and Wada, " 'Flow Production' Method," p. 23. The Toyota system certainly demanded much exertion from workers. Its factories consistently ran beyond full capacity, requiring substantial amounts of overtime. Satoshi Kamata, who worked at Toyota for six months, criticized its treatment of workers and suppliers in a 1973 book, *Jidosha Zetsubo Kojo (The Automobile Factory of Despair),* which was translated into English as *Japan in the Passing Lane* (New York: Pantheon, 1982). More recently, some observers have denounced lean production as "management by stress." See, e.g., Mike Parker and Jane Slaughter, "Unions and Management by Stress," in Steve Babson, ed., *Lean Work: Empowerment and Exploitation in the Global Auto Industry* (Detroit: Wayne State University Press, 1995), pp. 41–53.

77. Togo and Wartman, *Against All Odds,* pp. 131, 198.

78. Cusumano, *Japanese Automobile Industry,* p. 319.

79. Ibid., p. 6.

80. See Womack et al., *Machine That Changed the World,* pp. 43–45, esp. figs. 2.2 and 2.3.

81. Ibid., p. 46.

82. GM had little incentive to develop anything path-breaking, because anything truly revolutionary might have bankrupted Chrysler and decimated Ford's market share. Such an outcome would surely have provoked antitrust action and possibly the dissolution of GM.

83. Cusumano, *Japanese Automobile Industry,* p. 129.

84. Hal Sperlich, a top product man at both Ford and Chrysler, quoted in Halberstam, *Reckoning,* p. 46.

85. Some U.S. executives displayed unbridled contempt for small cars. Henry Ford II, the grandson of the legendary auto magnate, called compact cars "little shitboxes." K. T. Keller, Chrysler's top executive, bellowed to a designer who showed him a small car, "Chrysler builds cars to sit in, not to piss over." Quoted in ibid., pp. 468, 41.

86. *Toyota: A History,* p. 211.

87. Halberstam, *Reckoning,* p. 34.
88. Cusumano, *Japanese Automobile Industry,* p. 391. For passenger cars, Japan's share was even higher, as Figure 11.2 illustrates.
89. *Toyota: A History,* p. 317. Toyota measures market share exclusive of the minicar segment of the Japanese market, since it does not produce minicars.
90. Paul J. Ingrassia and Joseph B. White, *Comeback: The Fall and Rise of the American Automobile Industry* (New York: Simon and Schuster, 1994), p. 340.
91. Ibid., p. 194; Womack et al., *Machine That Changed the World,* pp. 131–132.
92. Michael C. Jensen, "The Modern Industrial Revolution, Exit, and the Failure of Internal Control Systems," *Journal of Finance,* July 1993, p. 858; "When GM's Robots Ran Amok," *Economist,* 10 Aug. 1991, pp. 64–65.
93. Ingrassia and White, *Comeback,* p. 278. GM was not alone in these non-automotive ventures. Between 1985 and October 1989, Ford spent $8.5 billion on acquisitions, including Jaguar, a California savings and loan, and two consumer finance companies. Chrysler also got into the diversification game, buying Gulfstream Aerospace, FinanceAmerica, and Lamborghini. Most of these ventures, including those of GM, were financial disasters.
94. The VER applied to Japanese cars. Japanese trucks faced a steep 25 percent tariff and thus posed less of a threat to U.S. automakers.
95. Whether Tatsuro Toyoda deserves the credit for these results is not clear. One automobile industry analyst, Maryann Keller, has argued that "NUMMI wasn't the result of Tatsuro's efforts, since other executives effectively laid the groundwork." She quotes an insider as saying, "At Toyota, regardless of how high the rank might be, everyone bowed to Shoichiro. But at Toyota Motor Sales, Tatsuro bowed to others." Keller, *Collision: GM, Toyota, Volkswagen and the Race to Own the 21st Century* (New York: Doubleday, 1993), pp. 67, 64.
96. On the plant's operations, see Kazuhiro Mishina, "Toyota Motor Manufacturing, U.S.A., Inc.," Harvard Business School Case #693-019, 1992.
97. Womack et al., *Machine That Changed the World,* p. 241.
98. The Japanese auto companies did not increase prices in proportion to the yen's appreciation. Instead, they passed on only part of the increase in yen-denominated costs to U.S. customers. Also, as Japanese firms amassed brand loyalty, some consumers steadfastly purchased Japanese cars, even though they became more expensive than their U.S. competitors.
99. C. Fred Bergsten and Marcus Noland, *Reconcilable Differences? United States–Japan Economic Conflict* (Washington: Institute for International Economics, 1993), p. 114. The authors also point out (p. 123) that "although the Japanese market has been historically closed, this does not ex-

plain why Germany and Great Britain export more cars to Japan than the Big Three, and France and Sweden nearly as many."

100. Ingrassia and White, *Comeback,* pp. 136–137; Womack et al., *Machine That Changed the World,* p. 86.

101. Ingrassia and White, *Comeback,* p. 433. On this agreement see Neil Weinberg, "Toyota Loves GM," *Forbes,* 18 Dec. 1995, pp. 262–266.

102. Ingrassia and White, *Comeback,* p. 460.

103. "U.S. Big Three Trail Japan in Productivity," *New York Times,* 15 May 1995, p. D5.

104. As of the early 1990s, all three of Eiji's sons were working at companies in the Toyota Group. Shoichiro's son, who was working for Toyota's Corolla division, has been mentioned as a possible future leader of Toyota Motor. Keller, *Collision,* pp. 63, 74.

105. Womack et al., *Machine That Changed the World,* p. 118.

106. On quality control, see Cusumano, *Japanese Automobile Industry,* pp. 320–373, and Izumi Nonaka, "The Development of Company-Wide Quality Control and Quality Circles at Toyota Motor Corporation and Nissan Motor Co., Ltd.," in Shiomi and Wada, eds., *Fordism Transformed,* pp. 139–159.

107. William K. Tabb, *The Postwar Japanese System* (New York: Oxford University Press, 1995), p. 90.

108. Togo and Wartman, *Against All Odds,* p. 164.

12. Japanese Capitalism

1. Quoted in Endymion Wilkinson, *Japan versus the West: Image and Reality* (London: Penguin, 1991), p. 101.

2. Quoted in Robert Whiting, *You Gotta Have Wa* (New York: Vintage, 1989), p. 5.

3. Many Japanese also believe firmly in their own uniqueness. There is a vast literature on what is called *nihonjinron* ("theorizing on the Japanese"). Some of these works go so far as to argue that Japanese people differ not only in culture but in physiology. Among their nonsensical assertions: the Japanese brain operates differently from those of other people and Japanese intestines are longer than those of other races. See Karel van Wolferen, *The Enigma of Japanese Power* (London: Macmillan, 1989), pp. 346–357, and Peter Dale, *The Myth of Japanese Uniqueness* (London: Routledge, 1986).

4. Alan Blinder, "There Are Capitalists, Then There Are Japanese," *Business Week,* 8 Oct. 1990, p. 21. See also Blinder, "More Like Them," *American Prospect,* winter 1992, pp. 51–61.

5. Robert Ozaki, *Human Capitalism: The Japanese Enterprise System as World Model* (New York: Penguin, 1991), pp. 7, 158; Eisuke Sakakibara, *Beyond Capitalism: The Japanese Model of Market Economics* (Washington: Economic Strategy Institute, 1993), p. 1. See also Hiroyuki Itami, "The 'Human-Capital-ism' of the Japanese Firm as an Integrated System," in Kenichi Imai and Ryutaro Komiya, eds., Ronald Dore and Hugh Whittaker, trans., *Business Enterprise in Japan: Views of Leading Japanese Economists* (Cambridge, MA: MIT Press, 1994), pp. 73–88; Ronald Dore, "What Makes the Japanese Different?" in C. Crouch and D. Marquand, eds., *Ethics and Markets: Cooperation and Competition within Capitalist Economies* (Oxford: Blackwell, 1993), pp. 66–79; and Koji Matsumoto, *The Rise of the Corporate System* (London: Kegan Paul, 1991).

6. The best-known revisionists are Chalmers Johnson, James Fallows, Clyde Prestowitz, Karen van Wolferen, Pat Choate, and Eamonn Fingleton. Four of these summarized their position in "Beyond Japan-bashing: The 'Gang of Four' Defends the Revisionist Line," *U.S. News and World Report,* 7 May 1990.

7. Although he differentiates Anglo-American and Japanese modes of capitalism, one Japanese economist has written that "the principle of the Invisible Hand is just as applicable to the Japanese economy (and possibly more so) as it is to the Western economies." Hiroyuki Odagiri, *Growth through Competition, Competition through Growth* (Oxford: Oxford University Press, 1992), p. 19. Some observers even assert that Japan more closely approaches "pure" capitalism than do Western economies. See, e.g., Katsuhito Iwai, "Nihon Koso Ga Junsui na Shihonshugi (It's Japan That Is Pure Capitalism)," in Nihon Keizai Shimbun, ed., *Watakushi no Shihonshugi* (My Capitalism) (Tokyo: Nihon Keizai Shimbun, 1993), pp. 132–137.

8. Quoted in Wilkinson, *Japan versus the West,* p. 105.

9. G. C. Allen, *A Short Economic History of Modern Japan,* 4th ed. (London: George Allen & Unwin, 1981), p. 15.

10. See Thomas C. Smith, "'Merit' as Ideology in the Tokugawa Period," in Ronald Dore, ed., *Aspects of Social Change in Modern Japan* (Princeton: Princeton University Press, 1967), rpt. in Thomas C. Smith, *Native Sources of Japanese Industrialization* (Berkeley: University of California Press, 1988), pp. 156–172.

11. Camoens, *The Lusiads,* 1572, Canto X, line 131, quoted in Wilkinson, *Japan versus the West,* p. 105.

12. Much of the information in this paragraph comes from Noel Perrin, *Giving Up the Gun: Japan's Reversion to the Sword, 1543–1879* (Boston: David R. Godine, 1979), summarized in David Weinstein, "Structural Impediments to Investment in Japan: What Have We Learned over the Last 450 Years?"

in Masaru Yoshitomi and Edward M. Graham, eds., *Foreign Direct Investment in Japan* (Brookfield, VT: Edward Elgar, 1996), pp. 136–172.

13. The characterization of Japan as a "closed country" for 200 years is somewhat misleading. In fact, Japan continued to engage in trade with the Chinese and the Dutch throughout this period, thereby maintaining a channel for the inflow of information on developments in the outside world. See Robert L. Innes, "The Door Ajar: Japan's Foreign Trade in the Seventeenth Century" (Ph.D. diss., University of Michigan, 1980); Kazui Tashiro, "Foreign Relations during the Edo Period: *Sakoku* Reexamined," *Journal of Japanese Studies,* 8, no. 2 (summer 1982), pp. 283–306; Ronald P. Toby, *State and Diplomacy in Early Modern Japan: Asia in the Development of the Tokugawa Bakufu* (Princeton: Princeton University Press, 1984); and Christopher Howe, *The Origins of Japanese Trade Supremacy: Development and Technology in Asia from 1540 to the Pacific War* (Chicago: University of Chicago Press, 1996), pp. 22–41.

14. My concise description of Tokugawa society does not show the full extent of the advances in commercial capitalism during this period. For further detail see Conrad Totman, *Early Modern Japan* (Berkeley: University of California Press, 1993); Chie Nakane and Shinzaburo Oishi, *Tokugawa Japan: The Social and Economic Antecedents of Modern Japan* (Tokyo: University of Tokyo Press, 1990); Tessa Morris-Suzuki, *The Technological Transformation of Japan: From the Seventeenth to the Twenty-First Century* (Cambridge: Cambridge University Press, 1994), pp. 13–54; and Ronald P. Toby, "Both a Borrower and a Lender Be: From Village Money Lender to Rural Banker in the Tempo Era," *Monumenta Nipponica,* 46 (winter 1991), pp. 483–512.

15. Takatoshi Ito, *The Japanese Economy* (Cambridge, MA: MIT Press, 1992), p. 30. As in contemporary futures markets, trading of futures exceeded that of the underlying asset; in 1749, a total of 110,000 bales of rice were traded in coupons in Osaka, while only 30,000 bales actually existed. See Johannes Hirschmeier and Tsunehiko Yui, *The Development of Japanese Business, 1600–1980,* 2d ed. (London: George Allen & Unwin, 1982), p. 31.

16. E. Sydney Crawcour, "The Tokugawa Heritage," in William Lockwood, ed., *The State and Economic Enterprise in Japan* (Princeton: Princeton University Press, 1965), pp. 17–44; Thomas C. Smith, "Farm Family By-Employments in Japan," *Journal of Economic History,* 29, no. 4 (Dec. 1969), rpt. in Smith, *Native Sources,* pp. 71–102.

17. Ito, *Japanese Economy,* p. 18.

18. Ryoshin Minami, *The Economic Development of Japan: A Quantitative Study,* 2d ed. (New York: St. Martin's, 1994), p. 17.

19. See Thomas P. Rohlen, "Learning: The Mobilization of Knowledge in the

Japanese Political Economy," in Shumpei Kumon and Henry Rosovsky, eds., *The Political Economy of Japan*, vol. 3: *Cultural and Social Dynamics* (Stanford: Stanford University Press, 1992), pp. 321–363, and Merry White, *The Japanese Educational Challenge: A Commitment to Children* (New York: Free Press, 1987).

20. Minami, *Economic Development of Japan*, p. 29; Akira Hayami, "Population Changes," in Marius Jensen and Gilbert Rozman, eds., *Japan in Transition: From Tokugawa to Mejii* (Princeton: Princeton University Press, 1986), pp. 280–317.

21. Joel Kotkin, *Tribes: How Race, Religion and Identity Determine Success in the New Global Economy* (New York: Random House, 1992), p. 26. Japanese education was initially not very oriented toward science or engineering, at least compared to that in continental Europe. See David Landes, "Japan and Europe: Contrasts in Industrialization," in William Lockwood, ed., *The State and Economic Enterprise in Japan* (Princeton: Princeton University Press, 1965), pp. 109–110.

22. D. Eleanor Westney, *Imitation and Innovation* (Cambridge, MA: Harvard University Press, 1987), p. 19; Weinstein, "Structural Impediments," p. 140; Hazel Jones, *Live Machines: Hired Foreigners in Meiji Japan* (Vancouver: University of British Columbia Press, 1980).

23. Each student sent abroad cost about 1,000 yen per year, while the annual cost of primary school for one student was 1.2 yen. Hirschmeier and Yui, *Development of Japanese Business*, p. 78.

24. Kazushi Ohkawa and Henry Rosovsky, *Japanese Economic Growth* (Stanford: Stanford University Press, 1973), p. 17.

25. See Ichiro Inukai and A. R. Tussing, "*Kogyo Iken*: Japan's Ten Year Plan, 1884," *Economic Development and Cultural Change* 16, no. 1 (1967); Morris-Suzuki, *Technological Transformation*, pp. 99–103.

26. For a fascinating portrait of Matsukata, see Haru Matsukata Reischauer, *Samurai and Silk: A Japanese and American Heritage* (Cambridge, MA: Harvard University Press, 1986).

27. Minami, *Economic Development of Japan*, pp. 74, 77.

28. Quoted in Wilkinson, *Japan versus the West*, p. 121.

29. "Men, Yen, and Machines," *Fortune*, Sept. 1936, pp. 67–68.

30. I am paraphrasing the definition of Hidemasa Morikawa, *Zaibatsu: The Rise and Fall of Family Enterprise Groups in Japan* (Tokyo: Tokyo University Press, 1992), p. xvii.

31. Takafusa Nakamura, *Lectures on Modern Japanese Economic History, 1926–1994* (Tokyo: Long-Term Credit Bank of Japan, 1994), p. 6. The companies owned by these American families generally dominated one industry. Their Japanese counterparts, by contrast, had stakes in many different industries but were usually not nearly as dominant in any one of them.

32. Hirschmeier and Yui, *Development of Japanese Business*, pp. 137, 140; Masaaki Kobayashi, "Japan's Early Industrialization and the Transfer of Government Enterprises: Government and Business," *Japanese Yearbook in Business History*, 2 (1985), pp. 54–80.

33. Keiichiro Nakagawa, "Business Management in Japan—A Comparative Historical Study," *Industrial and Corporate Change*, 2, no. 1 (1993), pp. 38–39.

34. Tsunehiko Yui, "Development, Organization, and International Competitiveness of Industrial Enterprises in Japan, 1880–1915," *Business and Economic History*, 2d ser., 17 (1988), p. 41.

35. This assertion is the main theme of W. Mark Fruin's *The Japanese Enterprise System* (New York: Oxford University Press, 1992). He argues that contemporary Japanese firms are smaller, less diversified, and less vertically integrated than their U.S. counterparts, and that, relative to American corporations, they tend to have smaller head offices and a larger concentration of personnel at the factory level. He attributes these qualitative features of Japanese corporations to Japan's experience as a late-developing country.

36. On these sectors, see William D. Wray, *Mitsubishi and the N.Y.K., 1870–1914: Business Strategy in the Japanese Shipping Industry* (Cambridge, MA: Harvard University Press, 1984); Shinya Sugiyama, *Japan's Industrialization in the World Economy, 1859–1899: Export Trade and Overseas Competition* (London: Athlone Press, 1988); Howe, *Origins of Japanese Trade Supremacy*.

37. Allen, *Short Economic History*, pp. 94–95, 98; Hirschmeier and Yui, *Development of Japanese Business*, p. 191.

38. Fruin, *Japanese Enterprise System*, pp. 103–109.

39. Minami, *Economic Development of Japan*, pp. 100, 175.

40. Analysts making this argument include Allen, *Short Economic History*, p. 75; Ito, *Japanese Economy*, p. 28; and Henry Rosovsky, "What Are the 'Lessons' of Japanese Economic History?" in A. Youngson, ed., *Economic Development in the Long Run* (London: Allen and Unwin, 1972), p. 232.

41. Fruin, *Japanese Enterprise System* , p. 116.

42. Industrial histories include Barbara Molony, *Technology and Investment: The Prewar Japanese Chemical Industry* (Cambridge, MA: Harvard University Press, 1990); Yukiko Fukasaku, *Technology and Industrial Development in Pre-war Japan: Mitsubishi and Nagasaki Shipyard, 1884–1934* (London: Routledge, 1992); Seiichiro Yonekura, *The Japanese Iron and Steel Industry, 1850–1990: Continuity and Discontinuity* (New York: St. Martin's, 1994); and Steven J. Ericson, *The Sound of the Whistle: Railroads and the State in Meiji Japan* (Cambridge, MA: Harvard University Press, 1996).

43. Yonekura, *Japanese Iron and Steel Industry*, pp. 47–48, 54.

44. Allen, *Short Economic History,* p. 85.
45. Hirschmeier and Yui, *Development of Japanese Business,* p. 149.
46. I have used the modern English forms of Japanese company names (e.g., Mitsubishi Corporation, rather than Mitsubishi Shoji, and Mitsui & Company, rather than Mitsui Bussan) in the interest of simplicity.
47. Allen, *Short Economic History,* p. 101.
48. These figures and the above material on banking come from Nakamura, *Lectures,* p. 29.
49. Allen, *Short Economic History,* p. 110.
50. Fruin, *Japanese Enterprise System,* p. 62.
51. Hirschmeier and Yui, *Development of Japanese Business,* p. 153.
52. Ibid., pp. 156–157.
53. Ibid., pp. 157, 160.
54. "The organization of Japanese and Western industry was probably more similar in 1910 than in 1970," writes Rodney Clark in *The Japanese Company* (New Haven: Yale University Press, 1979), p. 258. Andrew Gordon concurs: "Ironically enough, the social relations of industrial production most resembled those in the West at the outset [before the 20th century]." Gordon, *Evolution of Labor Relations in Japan* (Cambridge, MA: Harvard University Press, 1985), p. 413.
55. Fruin, *Japanese Enterprise System,* p. 77; Nakagawa, "Business Management in Japan," p. 33; Hirschmeier and Yui, *Development of Japanese Business,* p. 120; Penelope Francks, *Japanese Economic Development: Theory and Practice* (London: Routledge, 1992), pp. 207–208.
56. Hirschmeier and Yui, *Development of Japanese Business,* p. 207.
57. See Gordon, *Evolution of Labor Relations;* Francks, *Japanese Economic Development,* pp. 208–209; and Thomas C. Smith, "The Right to Benevolence: Dignity and Japanese Workers, 1890–1920," *Comparative Studies in Society and History,* 26, no. 4 (1984), rpt. in Smith, *Native Sources,* pp. 235–270.
58. By contrast, white-collar workers at large firms often did receive such benefits in the 1920s. See Eisuke Daito, "Recruitment and Training of Middle Managers in Japan, 1900–1930," in Kesaji Kobayashi and Hidemasa Morikawa, eds., *Development of Managerial Enterprise,* International Conference on Business History, vol. 12 (Tokyo: University of Tokyo Press, 1986), pp. 151–184. Still, one indication of the much greater applicability of these practices in postwar Japan is that the stability of employment was far less in prewar than in postwar Japan. See Tetsuji Okazaki, "The Japanese Firm under the Wartime Planned Economy," in Masahiko Aoki and Ronald Dore, *The Japanese Firm* (New York: Oxford University Press, 1994), p. 357.
59. Richard Caves and Masu Uekusa, "Industrial Organization," in Hugh Pat-

rick and Henry Rosovsky, eds., *Asia's New Giant* (Washington: Brookings, 1976), p. 465.

60. Nakamura, *Lectures*, pp. 41–42.

61. "The Farm 'Depression' in Japan," *Fortune*, Sept. 1936, p. 28.

62. Chalmers Johnson, *MITI and the Japanese Miracle* (Stanford: Stanford University Press, 1982), p. 111. By contrast, Hidemasa Morikawa argues that dollar buying was a "normal contingency measure" and that Mitsui Bank, far from reaping windfall profits, recorded losses during the second half of 1931. *Zaibatsu*, pp. 224–225.

63. Japan's imperialist expansionism was, of course, another important motivation for this attack. Japanese leaders at the time spoke of liberating Asia from European domination and creating a Greater East Asian Co-Prosperity Sphere. For other Asian nations, though, the "prosperity" of Japanese rule proved elusive. Japanese colonialism was even more oppressive and brutal than that of the Europeans.

Because my focus is Japanese business history and not Japanese history in general, I do not attempt to explain the complex causes of Japan's colonialism. On the period of Japan's outward economic and political expansion see Howe, *Origins of Japanese Trade Supremacy*, pp. 335–425; Peter Duus, Ramon H. Myers, and Mark Peattie, eds., *The Japanese Informal Colonial Empire, 1895–1937* (Princeton: Princeton University Press, 1989); idem, *The Japanese Colonial Empire, 1895–1945* (Princeton: Princeton University Press, 1984).

Nor do I mention Japan's wartime atrocities, except to say that Japanese soldiers did commit some monstrous crimes, including the massacre and rape of tens or hundreds of thousands of Chinese civilians after the fall of Nanking; the deportation of Korean and Chinese civilians to Japan to work as slave laborers in Japanese factories; the use of prisoners of war in medical experiments; and the establishment of brothels where Korean, Chinese, and some Japanese women were forced to serve as prostitutes for Japanese soldiers. Most of these crimes are customarily not reported in the history textbooks used in Japanese schools. For a comparison of the ways in which Germans and Japanese have addressed their wartime conduct, see Ian Buruma, *The Wages of Guilt: Memories of War in Germany and Japan* (New York: Penguin, 1994).

64. Johnson, *MITI and the Japanese Miracle*, p. 121.

65. "The Proof of the Pudding," *Fortune*, Sept. 1936, p. 176.

66. Although it is widely believed that the term "Japan, Incorporated" was invented in the late 1960s or early 1970s, the term appears in ibid., p. 77. The term "social dumping" appears in the same issue of *Fortune*, in "The Rising Sun of Japan," p. 53.

67. "The Rising Sun of Japan," p. 52.

68. "The Proof of the Pudding," p. 174.

69. Nakamura, *Lectures,* p. 74.

70. Ibid., p. 99.

71. Ibid., p. 125.

72. Johnson, *MITI and the Japanese Miracle,* p. 165.

73. Nakamura, *Lectures,* p. 125.

74. See Jun Sakudo and Takao Shiba, eds., *World War II and the Transformation of Business Systems,* International Conference on Business History, vol. 20 (Tokyo: University of Tokyo Press, 1993), and Jerome B. Cohen, *Japan's Economy in War and Reconstruction* (Minneapolis: University of Minnesota Press, 1949).

75. Okazaki, "The Japanese Firm under the Wartime Planned Economy," pp. 357–358.

76. One manager lamented, "In Japan, there are capitalists who buy up stock for speculative reasons, control the future course of the company, make imprudent plans to increase stock, attempt to raise the market value of the stock, and then sell their shares of stock to make big profits. [Others] not only try to cut operating expenses but even discontinue welfare facilities for employees. Such avaricious capitalists keep the employees in a miserable state and endanger the basis of existence of the company." Quoted in Hidemasa Morikawa, "The Increasing Power of Salaried Managers in Japan's Large Companies," in William Wray, *Managing Industrial Enterprise: Cases from Japan's Prewar Experience* (Cambridge, MA: Harvard University Press, 1989), p. 42.

77. Nakamura, *Lectures,* p. 127. Shares owned by the zaibatsu holding companies, as well as shares owned directly by the Mitsui and Mitsubishi families, are included in these figures.

78. Okazaki, "The Japanese Firm under the Wartime Planned Economy," p. 369; Nakamura, *Lectures,* p. 126.

79. Gordon, *Evolution of Labor Relations,* chs. 7 and 8.

80. See, e.g., Johnson, *MITI and the Japanese Miracle,* p. 115.

81. Nakamura, *Lectures,* p. 120.

82. Quoted in Shigeto Tsuru, *Japan's Capitalism: Creative Defeat and Beyond* (New York: Cambridge University Press, 1993), p. 12.

83. David Williams, *Japan: Beyond the End of History* (New York: Routledge, 1994), p. 4.

84. See Kozo Yamamura, "Success Illgotten? The Role of Meiji Militarism in Japan's Technological Progress," *Journal of Economic History,* 37 (March 1977), pp. 113–135; Richard J. Samuels, *Rich Nation, Strong Army: National Security and the Technological Transformation of Japan* (Ithaca: Cornell University Press, 1994).

85. This figure is the one most often cited, but other estimates exist. For example, a figure of 40 percent is given in Hugh Patrick and Henry Rosovsky, "Japan's Economic Performance: An Overview," in Patrick and Rosovsky, eds., *Asia's New Giant,* p. 9.

86. Theodore Cohen, a former SCAP official, wrote a book entitled *Remaking Japan: The American Occupation as New Deal* (New York: Free Press, 1987). Perry Miller, a Harvard professor visiting Japan in the early 1950s, described the goal of Occupation policy as "to make of Japan, a new Middle West—not of course, the Middle West as it is, or in fact ever was, but as it perpetually dreams of being." Quoted in David Halberstam, *The Reckoning* (New York: Avon, 1986), pp. 276–277. The notion of "remaking Japan" ran so strong that there was even a proposal to substitute Roman characters for the Chinese symbols used in Japanese writing. See Tsuru, *Japan's Capitalism,* p. 35; Frank Gibney, *Japan: The Fragile Superpower* (New York: Norton, 1975), p. 155.

87. Shigeru Yoshida, twice prime minister of Japan (1946–47 and 1948–54), quoted in Johnson, *MITI and the Japanese Miracle,* p. 174. Of course, as Andrew Gordon pointed out to me, sometimes ignorance can be bliss. Had SCAP officials been more apprised of political realities in Japan, they might have hesitated to push their slate of reforms, many of which were ultimately beneficial.

88. Nakamura, *Lectures,* p. 128.

89. Tsuru, *Japan's Capitalism,* p. 21.

90. Nakamura, *Lectures,* p. 141.

91. Tsuru, *Japan's Capitalism,* p. 24.

92. On the reforms, see Juro Teranishi and Yutaka Kosai, eds., *The Japanese Experience of Economic Reforms* (New York: St. Martin's, 1993).

93. This is not to dismiss the importance of Japanese officials in devising and implementing reforms during this period. In June 1945—even before the war ended—a committee of Japanese government officials began meeting to discuss plans for the postwar reconstruction. Their report, published in September 1946, gives a frank and careful assessment of the problems Japan was likely to face, as well as some suggested policy responses. It has been published in English as Saburo Okita, ed., Special Survey Committee, Ministry of Foreign Affairs, *Postwar Reconstruction of the Japanese Economy* (Tokyo: University of Tokyo Press, 1992).

94. Nakamura, *Lectures,* p. 162.

95. Patrick and Rosovsky, "Japan's Economic Performance," p. 11.

96. Figures based on Nakamura, *Lectures,* table 4.6. They include not only special procurement orders placed directly by the military, but also dollars spent by troops and their families in Japan.

97. This was *not* the case in the prewar period, when the gap between the rich

and the poor was much wider in Japan. See Minami, *Economic Development of Japan*, pp. 300–302. Nor could prewar Japan be described as a mass-consumption society. In September 1936, *Fortune* (pp. 67, 116) described the Japanese domestic market as "a little insulated universe of goods entirely different from the goods she manufactures and sells to her foreign clientele," and the Japanese people as being able to "*still get along without more things than any other industrial people*" (original italics).

98. Indeed, it has been compared to Kennedy's pledge to land an American on the moon by the end of the decade. Williams, *Beyond the End of History*, p. 137.

99. Figures from Edward Denison and William Chung, "Economic Growth and Its Sources," in Patrick and Rosovsky, eds., *Asia's New Giant*, pp. 67–151.

100. One of the earliest books on the Japanese firm is James Abegglen's *Japanese Factory* (Glencoe, IL: Free Press, 1958). By praising various distinctive Japanese institutions, this book shocked many Japanese observers, who were used to thinking of these features as "distortions" or flaws relative to more advanced Western economies. More recent literature includes Clark, *The Japanese Company*; James Abegglen and George Stalk, *Kaisha, the Japanese Corporation* (New York: Basic Books, 1986); Masahiko Aoki, ed., *The Economic Analysis of the Japanese Firm* (New York: Elsevier, 1984); Masahiko Aoki, "Toward an Economic Model of the Japanese Firm," *Journal of Economic Literature*, 28 (March 1990), pp. 1–27; Aoki and Dore, eds., *The Japanese Firm*; Ken-ichi Imai and Ryutaro Komiya, eds., Ronald Dore and Hugh Whittaker, trans., *Business Enterprise in Japan: Views of Leading Japanese Economists* (Cambridge, MA: MIT Press, 1994); and Masahiko Aoki, "The Japanese Firm in Transition," in Kozo Yamamura and Yasukichi Yasuba, eds., *The Political Economy of Japan*, vol. 1: *The Domestic Transformation* (Stanford: Stanford University Press, 1987), pp. 263–288.

101. "Prewar unions, weak or strong, were organized by factory or by enterprise and, most important, they all *acted* at the factory level." Gordon, *Evolution of Labor Relations in Japan*, p. 341.

102. "It is astonishing how easily foreign admirers of the tranquility of Japanese society during the 1970s forget the strikes, riots, demonstrations, and sabotage that marked the period 1949–61." Johnson, *MITI and the Japanese Miracle*, p. 197. Even today, the quiescence of Japanese enterprise unions should not be interpreted as weakness. If threatened, workers may protest vigorously, even over issues that would be seen as conventional in the United States. See Nicholas D. Kristof, "AT&T Cutbacks in Japan Rattle Old Sensibilities," *New York Times*, 22 March 1995, p. D8; Andrew Gor-

don, "Contests for the Workplace," in Andrew Gordon, ed., *Postwar Japan as History* (Berkeley: University of California Press, 1993).

103. Masanori Hashimoto and John Raisian, "Employment Tenure and Earnings Profiles in Japan and the United States," *American Economic Review,* 75, no. 4 (1985), pp. 721–735.

104. Ronald Dore, *Flexible Rigidities* (Stanford: Stanford University Press, 1986).

105. Aoki, "Toward an Economic Model." See also Ozaki, *Human Capitalism,* p. 102.

106. See Abegglen and Stalk, *Kaisha,* table 7-8, p. 177; Mitsuhiro Fukao, *Financial Integration, Corporate Governance, and the Performance of Multinational Companies* (Washington: Brookings, 1995), table 3-1, p. 40. As Abegglen and Stalk point out, despite the low priority that Japanese managers supposedly place on shareholder welfare, returns to shareholders of Japanese companies have historically been quite high.

107. See Paul Sheard, "Long-termism and the Japanese Firm," in Mitsuaki Okabe, ed., *The Structure of the Japanese Economy* (New York: St. Martin's, 1995), pp. 25–52.

108. Many economists take exception to this view. They argue that rational shareholders would not be short-sighted, as stock prices presumably reflect the present discounted value of all future cash flows. If anyone is likely to behave myopically, it is managers, whose limited tenure at the firm might lead them to make decisions that are good in the short run (while they are employed at the firm) but detrimental in the long run (by which time they will have retired). Indeed, some have argued that insulation from capital markets via corporate cross-shareholding has hurt Japanese shareholders. See, e.g., Frank Lichtenberg and George Pushner, "Ownership Structure and Corporate Performance in Japan," NBER Working Paper no. 4092, 1992.

109. The terminology surrounding these groups is muddled. The horizontal keiretsu are not horizontal in the sense that they involve firms in the same industry (the conventional usage of "horizontal" in economics). They are essentially conglomerate groups.

110. Perhaps the best-known case of intervention was the rescue of Toyo Kogyo (Mazda) after the first oil shock. For a list of cases in which a main bank helped a client firm in financial distress, see Paul Sheard, "The Main Bank System and Corporate Monitoring and Control in Japan," *Journal of Economic Behavior and Organization,* 11, no. 3 (1989), pp. 399–422, table A.1.

111. Calculated using data from *Japan 1995: An International Comparison* (Tokyo: Keizai Koho Center, 1994).

112. Michael Yoshino and Thomas Lifson, *The Invisible Link: Japan's Sogo*

Shosha and the Organization of Trade (Cambridge, MA: MIT Press, 1986), p. 2.

113. Michael Gerlach, "Business Alliances and the Strategy of the Japanese Firm," *California Management Review,* Fall 1987, p. 132; idem, *Alliance Capitalism: The Social Organization of Japanese Business* (Berkeley: University of California Press, 1992).

114. There are also tricky classification problems. One has to be careful not to include companies affiliated with a group's main bank but not with the group itself. Though Sony has traditionally had close ties with Mitsui (now Sakura) Bank, it would be misleading to classify Sony as part of the Mitsui Group. Depending on the membership criteria or source used, the boundaries of these groups vary widely. Some of the prominent listings of keiretsu affiliation exhibit surprisingly little correlation; see David Weinstein and Yishay Yafeh, "Japan's Corporate Groups: Collusive or Competitive? An Empirical Investigation of *Keiretsu* Behavior," *Journal of Industrial Economics,* 43 (Dec. 1995), pp. 359–376.

115. This estimate comes from the Fair Trade Commission of Japan, *Nihon no Dairoku Kigyo Shudan no Jittai* (The Essence of Japan's Six Large Enterprise Groups) (Tokyo: Toyo Keizai Shimposha, 1994), p. 113. The fact that membership is defined as participation in a group's shacho-kai leads to a downward bias in these figures. The importance of these groups is also understated by these figures because they do not include financial companies, where the kigyo shudan are especially strong, or the subcontracting and distribution chains cascading downward from member firms which preside over their own vertical keiretsu. All of these caveats about the precision of this estimate do not negate the basic point that the kigyo shudan are large but not dominant.

116. Fruin, *Japanese Enterprise System,* table 1.4, pp. 52–53.

117. On the distribution keiretsu, see Hideto Ishida, "Anticompetitive Practices in the Distribution of Goods and Services in Japan," *Journal of Japanese Studies,* 9 (summer 1983), pp. 317–334.

118. In practice, expressions such as *keiretsu* and *guruhpu* are not always used in ways consistent with my categorization. For instance, the word guruhpu is frequently used to denote kigyo shudan (as in the Mitsubishi guruhpu) or production keiretsu (as in the Toyota guruhpu). Nevertheless, my usage here has the benefit of drawing clear analytical distinctions between the different types of interfirm linkages in Japan.

119. For an example of this analytic confusion, see Robert Cutts, "Capitalism in Japan: Cartels and Keiretsu," *Harvard Business Review,* July-Aug. 1982, pp. 48–55.

120. See Caves and Uekusa, "Industrial Organization"; Tomio Iguchi, "Aggregate Concentration, Turnover, and Mobility among the Largest Manu-

facturing Firms in Japan," *Antitrust Bulletin,* 32, no. 4 (1987), pp. 939–965.

121. This finding, dating back at least to Caves and Uekusa's 1976 chapter, "Industrial Organization," has been replicated by many other researchers, including Iwao Nakatani, "The Economic Role of Financial Corporate Grouping," in Aoki, ed., *Economic Analysis of the Japanese Firm;* W. Carl Kester, "Capital and Ownership Structure: A Comparison of U.S. and Japanese Manufacturing Corporations," *Financial Management,* spring 1986, pp. 5–16; Hesna Genay, "Japan's Corporate Groups," *Economic Perspectives,* 15, no. 1 (1991), pp. 20–30; Jeffrey Bernstein, "The Financing Arrangements of Japanese Corporations: A Competitive Advantage?" (thesis, Amherst College, 1991); and Lichtenberg and Pushner, "Ownership Structure and Corporate Performance."

122. Weinstein and Yafeh, "Japan's Corporate Groups."

123. The term comes from Yoshikazu Miyazaki, "Rapid Economic Growth in Post-war Japan—With Special Reference to 'Excessive Competition' and the Formation of 'Keiretsu,'" *Developing Economies,* 5 (1967), pp. 329–350. There are many exceptions to this rule. A group may have no member firm in a particular industry, and in other industries it may have multiple representatives.

124. For instance, in a study of 10 nations, Michael Porter writes that Japan "is characterized by some of the fiercest domestic rivalry of any nation juxtaposed with large areas of little or no rivalry." Porter, *The Competitive Advantage of Nations* (New York: Free Press, 1991), p. 416.

125. "To an economist raised, like myself, in an orthodox tradition, the visceral reaction to *kato kyoso* talk is 'Impossible!' and the subsequent intellectual reaction is extreme suspicion," writes Martin Brofenbrenner in "'Excessive Competition' in Japanese Business," *Monumenta Nipponica,* 21 (1966), pp. 114–124. Many Japanese economists trained in the neoclassical tradition are also wary of the concept of excessive competition. See, e.g., Ryutaro Komiya, "Introduction," in Ryutaro Komiya, Masahiro Okuno, and Kotaro Suzumura, eds., *Industrial Policy in Japan* (San Diego: Academic Press, 1988), pp. 1–22.

126. A MITI official, Yoshihiko Morozumi, stated in 1962, "Free competition provides neither the most suitable scale nor a guarantee of proper prices. Free competition means excessive equipment and low profits." See Daniel Okimoto and Thomas Rohlen, eds., *Inside the Japanese System* (Palo Alto: Stanford University Press, 1988), p. 80. The economist Kotaro Suzumura has characterized Japanese thinking on the role of competition as "competition is bad, cooperation is good" in his "Kyoso, Kisei, Jiyu" (Competition, Regulation, and Freedom), in Hiroyuki Itami, Tadao Kagono, and Motoshige Itoh, eds., *Nihon no Kigyo Shisutemu: Kigyo to Shijo* (Japan's

Corporate System: The Firm and The Market) (Tokyo: Yuhikaku, 1993), p. 124.

127. David Weinstein, "Administrative Guidance and Cartels in Japan (1957–1988)," *Journal of the Japanese and International Economies,* 9 (1995), pp. 200–223.

128. For a rich case study of administrative guidance by MITI, see Frank Upham, "The Man Who Would Import: A Cautionary Tale about Bucking the System in Japan," *Journal of Japanese Studies,* 17 (summer 1991), pp. 323–343.

129. "Nothing in the Western concern with modern Japan engages the intellectual passions quite like the issue of industrial policy." Williams, *Beyond the End of History,* p. 75. Though Williams is certainly correct about the passion involved, the debate often seems less an intellectual exercise than an ideological dispute.

130. Williams, *Beyond the End of History;* Clyde Prestowitz, *Trading Places* (New York: Basic Books, 1988); James Fallows, *Looking at the Sun* (New York: Pantheon, 1994); Thomas Huber, *Japan's Strategic Economy* (Boulder, CO: Westview, 1994). Also see Motoshige Itoh, Kazuhiro Kiyono, Masahiro Okuno-Fujiwara, and Kotaro Suzumura, *The Economic Analysis of Industrial Policy* (San Diego: Academic Press, 1991).

131. See Richard Beason and David Weinstein, "Growth, Economies of Scale, and Targeting in Japan (1955–1990)," *Review of Economics and Statistics,* 78 (May 1996), pp. 286–295; Weinstein, "Administrative Guidance and Cartels"; Philip Trezise, "Industrial Policy Is Not the Major Reason for Japan's Success," *Brookings Review* (spring 1983), pp. 13–18. See also Komiya, "Introduction," in Komiya, Okuno, and Suzumura, eds., *Industrial Policy,* pp. 1–22; David Friedman, *The Misunderstood Miracle: Industrial Development and Political Change in Japan* (Ithaca: Cornell University Press, 1988); Kent Calder, *Strategic Capitalism: Private Business and Public Purpose in Japanese Industrial Finance* (Princeton: Princeton University Press, 1993); Scott Callon, *Divided Sun: MITI and the Breakdown of Japanese High-Tech Industrial Policy, 1975–1993* (Stanford: Stanford University Press, 1995).

132. Minami, *Economic Development of Japan,* p. 100.

133. Patrick and Rosovsky, eds., *Asia's New Giant.*

134. See Tsuru, *Japan's Capitalism,* p. 120; Hugh Patrick and Henry Rosovsky, "Prospects for the Future," in Patrick and Rosovsky, eds., *Asia's New Giant,* p. 908.

135. Hirschmeier and Yui, *Development of Japanese Business,* p. 313.

136. Williams, *Beyond the End of History,* pp. 55–56.

137. In 1988, the rate of female labor force participation was 49 percent in Japan and 57 percent in the United States. Ito, *Japanese Economy,* table

8.1, p. 210. Still, the so-called glass ceiling was even tougher to penetrate in Japan than in Western countries. It is no accident that the *Japan Almanac*, a book of facts and figures published by the Asahi Newspaper, contains on the same page data on "the female and foreign labor force," since both are essentially outsiders to the Japanese corporate system.

138. See Glen S. Fukushima, "'*Kisei Kanwa*' Is Not 'Deregulation,'" *Tokyo Business Today*, June 1995, p. 48.

139. Ronald Dore, "Kyodotai ga Kojin ni Yusen suru Nihon" (Japan: Giving Preference to the Collective over the Individual), in Yusuke Fukuda and Ronald Dore, eds., *Nihongata Shihonshugi Nakushite Nan no Nihon ka* (If Japanese Capitalism Disappears, What Happens to Japan? (Tokyo: Kobunsha, 1993), p. 147.

140. Wilkinson, *Japan versus the West*, p. 193.

141. See, e.g., Michael Crichton, *Rising Sun* (New York: Knopf, 1992); Berry James, *Trojan Horse: The Ultimate Japanese Challenge to Western Industry* (London: Mercury, 1989); Kozo Yamamura, ed., *Japanese Direct Investment in the United States: Should We Be Concerned?* (Seattle: Society of Japanese Studies, 1989); Robert Kearns, *Zaibatsu America: How Japanese Firms Are Colonizing Vital U.S. Industries* (New York: Free Press, 1992); Martin Tolchin and Susan Tolchin, *Selling Our Security* (New York: Penguin, 1992); Daniel Burstein, *Yen: Japan's New Financial Empire and Its Threat to America* (New York: Fawcett Columbine, 1988).

142. Figures for value-added and R&D per worker are similar in American subsidiaries of Japanese firms, American affiliates of other foreign firms, and American-owned firms. See Edward Graham and Paul Krugman, *Foreign Direct Investment in the United States,* 3d ed. (Washington: Institute for International Economics, 1995); Richard Caves, "Japanese Investment in the United States: Lessons for the Economic Analysis of Foreign Investment," *World Economy,* Dec. 1992; Bill Emmott, *Japanophobia: The Myth of the Invincible Japanese* (New York: Times Books, 1993).

143. See Edward J. Lincoln, *Japan's Unequal Trade* (Washington: Brookings, 1990).

144. A symposium in the *Journal of Economic Perspectives,* 7, no. 3 (summer 1993), provides an overview of this controversy.

145. A surprising number of such books were written by people with a connection to *The Economist,* including Bill Emmott, *The Sun Also Sets* (New York: Simon and Schuster, 1989); Brian Reading, *Japan: The Coming Collapse* (London: Weidenfeld & Nicholson, 1992); and Christopher Wood, *The Bubble Economy* (Boston: Atlantic Monthly Press, 1992) and *The End of Japan, Inc.* (New York: Simon & Schuster, 1994).

146. See, for example, John Curran, "Why Japan Will Emerge Stronger," *Fortune,* 18 May 1992; Eamonn Fingleton, *Blindside: Why Japan Is Still on*

Track to Overtake the U.S. by the Year 2000 (New York: Buttonwood Press, 1995); Fallows, *Looking at the Sun;* Williams, *Beyond the End of History;* Chalmers Johnson, *Who Governs?* (New York: Norton, 1995).

147. Ozaki, *Human Capitalism,* p. 2.

148. Sebastian Mallaby, "Oriental Renaissance: A Survey of Japan," *Economist,* 9 July 1994, p. 18.

149. J. Barrett, "New Japan, Schoolmaster of Asia," *Review of Reviews,* Dec. 1902, cited in Wilkinson, *Japan versus the West,* p. 129.

150. World Bank, *The East Asian Miracle: Economic Growth and Public Policy* (New York: Oxford University Press, 1993).

151. See Alan Blinder, "Should the Former Socialist Economies Look East or West for a Model?" paper presented to the Tenth World Congress of the International Economic Association in Moscow, 28 Aug. 1992; Williams, *Beyond the End of History,* pp. 157–164; Ozaki, *Human Capitalism,* p. 59; Fukao, *Financial Integration,* p. 85; Robert Neff, "Japanese Fusion: Business Thrives under the State's Protective Wing," *Business Week,* special issue on 21st-century capitalism, 24 Jan. 1995.

152. See, e.g., Jeffrey Sachs, "Reforms in Eastern Europe and the Former Soviet Union in Light of the East Asian Experience," *Journal of the Japanese and International Economies,* 9 (Dec. 1995), pp. 454–485. Colin Mayer also suggests caution in assuming that Japanese (or even German) corporate governance systems will be easily transferable to Eastern European countries. See his comments in Fukao, *Financial Integration,* p. 91.

153. A number of authors decry this phenomenon, including James Abegglen, *Sea Change* (New York: Free Press, 1994), p. 58; Wilkinson, *Japan versus the West,* pp. 97–98, 106, 151–152; Fallows, *Looking at the Sun,* p. 13; Williams, *Beyond the End of History,* p. 193; and Fingleton, *Blindside,* p. 1.

154. Vassily Kliuchesky, quoted in Robert Heilbroner, *21st Century Capitalism* (New York: Norton, 1993), p. 13.

13. 7-Eleven in America and Japan

1. The efficiency of the Japanese distribution system is much debated. By some measures, the performance of the Japanese retail sector looks quite poor; e.g., the McKinsey Global Institute estimates that the labor productivity of Japanese general merchandise retailers was only 44 percent of that of their U.S. counterparts in 1987. *Service Sector Productivity* (Washington: McKinsey Global Institute, 1992), Exhibit 2D-3. Other purported signs of inefficiency include the large number of small retailers and wholesalers and the tight regulations in this sector. See, e.g., Thomas K. McCraw and Patricia

O'Brien, "Production and Distribution: Competition Policy and Industry Structure," in Thomas K. McCraw, ed., *America versus Japan* (Boston: Harvard Business School Press, 1986), pp. 77–116. Others argue that the Japanese system is not necessarily inefficient. Takatoshi Ito notes that retail gross profit margins in Japan do not differ from those in other developed nations. See his *Japanese Economy* (Cambridge, MA: MIT Press, 1991), pp. 400–403. David Flath has argued that many of the distinctive characteristics of Japanese retailing, such as the large number of small stores, largely reflect indigenous factors that make small stores relatively more efficient in Japan. See his "Why Are There So Many Retail Stores in Japan?" *Japan and the World Economy*, 2 (1990), pp. 365–386.

2. Arieh Goldman, "Evaluating the Performance of the Japanese Distribution System," *Journal of Retailing*, 68 (1992), pp. 11–39; quotation p. 12.

3. This last point is a major theme of Nobuo Kawabe, *Sebun-Irebun no Keieishi* (A Business History of Seven-Eleven) (Tokyo: Yuhikaku, 1994).

4. This section follows ibid., pp. 27–36, and McCraw and O'Brien, "Production and Distribution," pp. 106–107.

5. For data on the growth of the leading U.S. chain stores during this period, see table 2 (p. 199) in Thomas K. McCraw, "Competition and 'Fair Trade': History and Theory," *Research in Economic History*, 16 (1996), pp. 185–239.

6. The material on Southland's early history is drawn largely from Allen Liles, *Oh Thank Heaven! The Story of the Southland Corporation* (Dallas: Southland Corporation, 1977).

7. Ibid., p. 253.

8. Ibid., p. 163.

9. Ibid., p. 188.

10. Ibid., p. 226.

11. In the summer of 1963, several 7-Eleven stores in Las Vegas began to stay open for 24 hours each day. At about the same time, a store in Austin, Texas, began experimenting with 24-hour operation to capitalize on crowds following football games at the University of Texas. The trend toward 24-hour operation increased markedly during the 1960s. Ibid., pp. 192–194.

12. Ibid., p. 107.

13. The 1978 *Convenience Store News Annual Report* (pp. 46–47) describes Southland's distribution centers as embodying "the most advanced computer technology and merchandising handling methods."

14. Mitsukoshi does not even have the longest history of existing Japanese department stores. This honor belongs to Matsuzakaya, which was established as a kimono dealer in Nagoya in 1611. See Roy Larke, *Japanese Retailing* (London: Routledge, 1994), p. 172.

15. The classic reference is Joseph Cornwall Palamountain Jr., *The Politics of Distribution* (Cambridge, MA: Harvard University Press, 1955). See also McCraw and O'Brien, "Production and Distribution," pp. 104–106.

16. McCraw and O'Brien, "Production and Distribution," p. 108.

17. Interview with Professor Yoshihiro Tajima of Gakushuin University, who served on an advisory panel to MITI during this period, conducted by Jeffrey Rayport in March 1991 (hereafter cited as Tajima interview, 1991). See also McCraw and O'Brien, "Production and Distribution," p. 108, and Jeffrey Rayport, "Japanese Retailing System: Tokugawa Period to the Present," industry note prepared for Thomas K. McCraw, April 1991, p. 39.

18. *Sebun-Irebun Japan: Owarinaki Inobeshon 1973–1991* (Seven-Eleven Japan: Ceaseless Innovation 1973–1991) (Tokyo: Seven-Eleven Japan, 1991), p. 5.

19. On the Saison Group, see Thomas Havens, *Architects of Affluence: The Tsutsumi Family and the Seibu-Saison Enterprises in Twentieth-Century Japan* (Cambridge, MA: Harvard University Press, 1994), and Leslie Downer, *The Brothers: The Hidden World of Japan's Richest Family* (New York: Random House, 1994).

20. Quoted in Yoshihiro Sakaguchi, *Daiei—Nakauchi Isao vs. Yokado—Masatoshi Ito* (Tokyo: Paru Shuppan, 1990), p. 19.

21. In his memoirs, Nakauchi wrote, "The history of Daiei is a history of fighting. We challenged ourselves and trained ourselves through fights against manufacturers and distributors." Quoted in Mariko Tatsuki, "The Rise of the Mass Market and Modern Retailers in Japan," in Etsuo Abe and Robert Fitzgerald, *The Origins of Japanese Industrial Power* (London: Frank Cass, 1995), pp. 70–88; quotation p. 83.

22. Yokado was the name of the Ito family store, which had been founded by Masatoshi Ito's uncle in 1920. At that time, there was a popular clothing store called Nikkado. Ito's uncle chose a very similar name for his shop, substituting "Yo" for the first of the three Chinese characters in Nikkado. The character "yo" meant sheep and referred to the year of the Chinese zodiac in which Ito's uncle had been born. As for the other two Chinese characters, the second one, "ka," connoted brilliance or gorgeousness, and the third, "do," indicated a room, hall, or shop.

23. M. Colyer Crum and David M. Meerschwam, "From Relationship to Price Banking: The Loss of Regulatory Control," in McCraw, ed., *America versus Japan*, pp. 261–297, esp. 291–292.

24. Larke, *Japanese Retailing*, p. 148. See also Michael Y. Yoshino, *The Japanese Marketing System: Adaptations and Innovations* (Cambridge, MA: MIT Press, 1971), pp. 194–197.

25. *Konbiniensu Sutoa Manyuaru* (Convenience Store Manual) (Tokyo: Small and Medium-Sized Enterprise Agency, 1972). This study was written by the

Distribution Economics Institute of Japan. See *Sebun-Irebun Japan 1973–1991*, p. 3.

26. *Konbini Meijin* (Convenience Store Expert) (Tokyo: Mainichi Shimbunsha, 1996), p. 10; Havens, *Architects of Affluence*, p. 160; and Toshiyuki Yahagi, *Konbiniensu Sutoa Shisutemu no Kakushinsei* (The Innovativeness of Convenience Store Systems) (Tokyo: Nihon Keizai Shimbun, 1994), p. 39.

27. That Suzuki was the major force in creating Seven-Eleven Japan is undisputed. Suzuki is also usually credited as the initial source of the idea to start a convenience store chain. See, e.g., Sakaguchi, *Daiei vs. Yokado*, p. 108; Kawabe, *Sebun-Irebun no Keieishi*, p. 173; Akio Iwabuchi, *Sebun-Irebun: Akinai no Shinjigen e* (Seven-Eleven: Toward a New Dimension in Commerce) (Tokyo: O.S. Publishing), p. 68; and Norihiko Morishita, *Sebun-Irebun Suzuki Toshifumi: Kyoi no Keiei Tetsugaku* (Seven-Eleven's Toshifumi Suzuki: An Astonishing Management Philosophy) (Tokyo: Paru Publishing, 1991). However, Professor Yoshihiro Tajima, a long-time associate of Masatoshi Ito, claimed to have suggested a licensing agreement with Southland to Ito around 1967. Tajima interview, 1991. See also p. 70 of Leigh Sparks, "Reciprocal Retail Internationalisation: The Southland Corporation, Ito-Yokado and the 7-Eleven Convenience Stores," in Gary Akehurst and Nicholas Alexander, eds., *The Internationalisation of Retailing* (London: Frank Cass, 1996), pp. 57–96.

28. Iwabuchi, *Sebun-Irebun: Akinai no Shinjigen e*, p. 68.

29. Southland has often been criticized for "cashing out" by not entering into a joint venture with Ito-Yokado. Typical is the following statement by James C. Morgan and J. Jeffrey Morgan: "Southland Corporation's licensing of 7-Eleven chain stores to Ito-Yokado in Japan is one of the classic examples of how Americans are, for easy-money and short-term gains, losing out on major opportunities for global expansion." *Cracking the Japanese Market: Strategies for Success in the New Global Economy* (New York: Free Press, 1991), p. 168. Such criticism is overly harsh and perhaps even misleading.

30. A few sources, such as Iwabuchi, *Sebun-Irebun: Akinai no Shinjigen e*, p. 72, and Takeshi Yamashita, *Sebun-Irebun vs. Rohson* (Seven-Eleven vs. Lawson) (Tokyo: Paru Publishing, 1995), p. 68, place the royalty rate at 0.5 percent. However, the 0.6 percent figure comes from Seven-Eleven Japan's corporate history. According to that same source, the royalty payment to Southland was lowered to 0.3 percent in 1982. See *Sebun-Irebun Japan 1973–1991*, p. 12.

31. Southland Corporation's 1973 annual report, reprinted in Liles, *Oh Thank Heaven*, p. 221.

32. The term "bunch of amateurs" comes from *Sebun-Irebun Japan 1973–1991*, p. 23.

33. Ibid., p. 25. In my interview with Suzuki, he mentioned only the importance

of Southland's accounting system. Interview with Toshifumi Suzuki, Chairman of Seven-Eleven Japan, 27 March 1996, hereafter cited as Suzuki interview, 1996.

34. Of course, as Richard Tedlow has emphasized to me, it is extremely difficult to build trust between the franchiser and its franchisees. Even if, as in Southland's accounting system, the rules for administering the division of profits seem quite fair, there will nonetheless be conflict about the share of profits that each party will receive.

35. *Konbini* (Convenience Store), spring-summer 1996, p. 28.

36. *Tokyo Business Today,* Sept. 1993, p. 26.

37. Ikujiro Nonaka and Hirotaka Takeuchi, *The Knowledge-Creating Company* (New York: Oxford University Press, 1995), pp. 245–246.

38. "Shui ni Sebun-Irebun (Seven-Eleven at the Top)," *Nihon Keizai Shimbun,* 27 Feb. 1995, p. 1.

39. An important example of this was Ito-Yokado's Reform Program, launched following its first-ever drop in profits in 1982. Spearheaded by Toshifumi Suzuki, the Reform Program introduced many elements of Seven-Eleven Japan's system (e.g., POS terminals, risk merchandising, and its store manager conference) into Ito-Yokado. See David Wylie and Walter Salmon, "Ito-Yokado," Harvard Business School Case no. 9-589-116, rev. 1992; "Ito-Yokado Rolls a Seven-Eleven," *Chain Store Age Executive,* Jan. 1991, p. 38; and Ryoichi Higurashi, "Ito-Yokado Co.: High-Tech Merchant Management Back to Basics," *Tokyo Business Today,* April 1989, pp. 46–47.

40. See, for example, Gale Eisenstodt, "Information Power," *Forbes,* 21 June 1993, p. 44, and "Ito-Yokado Rolls a Seven-Eleven," pp. 34–48.

41. In 1991, Seven-Eleven Japan even launched a "Shop America, World Import Catalog." However, many of the items in the Shop America catalog were made in Japan, and relatively few were made in America. The catalog sales operation did not catch on, and in 1994 Seven-Eleven Japan discontinued it. See Yamashita, *Sebun-Irebun vs. Rohson,* pp. 198–200.

42. The estimate of three items comes from Michael R. Czinkota and Jon Woronoff, *Unlocking Japan's Markets: Seizing Marketing and Distribution Opportunities in Today's Japan* (Chicago: Probus, 1991), p. 124. The one percent figure comes from Yamashita, *Sebun-Irebun vs. Rohson,* p. 227.

43. A better translation would be "the Large-Scale Retail Stores Law." Following Larke, *Japanese Retailing,* p. 104, I have adopted the simplified "Large Stores Law."

44. Yoshimasa Tsuruta and Toshiyuki Yahagi, "Daitenho Shisutemu to Sono Keigaika (The System of the Large-Scale Retail Stores Law and Its Skeletonization)," in Yoshiro Miwa and Kiyohiko Nishimura, eds., *Nihon no Ryutsu* (Japanese Distribution) (Tokyo: Tokyo University Press, 1990), pp. 283–324.

45. The average length of time required to open a store for the 6 largest superstores between 1972 and 1986 was 51 months, and the average reduction in size (from initial proposal to final outcome) was 33.6 percent. In some cases, the approval process required much more time, as demonstrated by an Ito-Yokado store that had to wait 10 years (and reduce floor space by 80 percent) before it could open a branch in Shizuoka prefecture. Tsuruta and Yahagi, "Daitenho Shisutemu," table 10-3, p. 300, and table 10-4, p. 302. Moreover, the number of applications for new stores fell dramatically while the LSL was in effect. Ibid., table 10-1, p. 290; McCraw and O'Brien, "Production and Distribution," pp. 110–111; Frank Upham, "The SII and the Japanese Retail Industry," in Suzanne Berger and Ronald Dore, eds., *National Diversity and Global Capitalism* (Ithaca: Cornell University Press, 1996), pp. 263–297, esp. p. 278.

46. 1991 statistics show that of all food retailers in Japan—including convenience stores—a mere 2 percent were open 24 hours. Yahagi, *Konbiniensu Sutoa Shisutemu,* p. 50.

47. Restrictions on the operating hours of automatic teller machines appear to have been loosened in the early 1990s, with at least one bank (Citibank) offering 24-hour access.

48. I refer to Daiei's convenience-store subsidiary and its stores as "Lawson" for simplicity, because the names changed several times. For example, the name was changed to Lawson, Inc., in June 1996. For the seven preceding years, from 1989, the company name had been Daiei Convenience Systems. Also, until 1992 Daiei used two names for its stores: Lawson and Sun Chain. Then the latter name was dropped. I am grateful to Professor Nobuo Kawabe of Waseda University for his help in clarifying this convoluted history.

49. A few American supermarkets have participated in the convenience-store business. Safeway entered the business but quickly withdrew when it realized that it was not equipped to operate in this industry. White Hen Pantry, a convenience-store chain, was owned by the supermarket Jewel. None of the largest convenience-store chains, however, is affiliated with a supermarket. See Kawabe, *Sebun-Irebun no Keieishi,* p. 125.

50. Interview with Mitsuaki Muneoka of the Nomura School of Advanced Management, by Jeffrey Rayport, 15 March 1991, hereafter cited as Muneoka interview, 1991. The flow of information and assistance was not unidirectional. This was the case initially, with deep-pocketed superstores providing human and physical capital for their convenience-store subsidiaries, but subsequently it was the convenience-store chains which taught the superstores how to use information technology, as illustrated by Seven-Eleven Japan's key role in Ito-Yokado's Reform Program.

51. Lawson's initial campaign, which promoted party goods for holidays not observed in Japan, flopped badly, and Daiei was forced to relaunch its con-

venience-store business. Yoshihiro Sakaguchi, *Daiei: Kyoi no Kakudai Sen-ryaku no Zenbo* (Daiei: All Aspects of an Astonishing Strategy of Business Expansion) (Tokyo: Seinen Shokan, 1990).

52. Goldman, "Evaluating the Performance," p. 33. Others have noted the lack of a price differential between convenience stores and supermarkets in Japan. See, e.g., Motoshige Itoh and Shigeru Matsushima, "Nihon no Ryutsu—Mittsu no Henka (Japanese Retailing—Three Changes)," in Motoshige Itoh, ed., *Ryutsu ga Nihon wo Kaeru* (Retailing Will Change Japan) (Tokyo: Nihon Hyoronsha, 1990), p. 55.

53. For a skeptical view about "price destruction," see Shin'ya Arai, "'Price Busting' Is a Fad," *Keizai Koho Center Forum*, Jan. 1995, pp. 7–8.

54. Again, this situation began to change in the 1990s. By the end of 1995, one Japanese convenience-store chain owned by a Japanese oil company called am/pm was operating 33 combined gas stations/convenience stores. See *Konbini Meijin*, p. 94. Also, the loosening of restrictions on oil marketing in Japan stimulated superstores, especially Daiei and Jusco, to consider installing gasoline pumps at some of their stores.

55. This estimate is derived using 1991 population figures for Japan, 1989 population figures for the United States, and figures on the number of vending machines from Matt Durbin, "The Vending Machine Phenomenon," *Mangajin*, no. 28, Aug. 1993, p. 8.

56. Arieh Goldman presents data on the food and non-food retail sectors in Japan and the United States, which he uses to argue that "the structure of [Japan's] nonfood sector is quite similar to that of the US and that the structural differences are largely confined to the retail food sector." Goldman, "Japan's Distribution System: Institutional Structure, Internal Political Economy, and Modernization," *Journal of Retailing*, 67 (1991), pp. 154–183; quotation p. 156.

57. Larke, *Japanese Retailing*, p. 153, reports that services accounted for less than 3 percent of sales in 1990. Yohei Sato, *Do Shite mo Sebun-Irebun ni Katenai Konbini Kakusha no Kenkyu* (A Study of Several Convenience Stores That, Try as They Might, Cannot Beat Seven-Eleven) (Tokyo: Yell Publishing, 1993), p. 70, discusses the low profitability of these services.

58. See George Fields, "The Japanese Distribution System: Myths and Realities," *Tokyo Business Today*, July 1989, p. 58. Some retailing analysts have predicted that convenience stores will force more than half the mom-and-pop stores out of business within 10 years. Carla Rapoport, "Ready, Set, Sell—Japan is Buying," *Fortune*, 11 Sept. 1989, p. 164.

59. These priorities are drawn from a survey of consumer behavior undertaken by MITI, as detailed in Small and Medium-Size Enterprise Agency, *Small Business in Japan, 1989* (Tokyo: MITI), pp. 126–127.

60. *Sebun-Irebun Japan 1973–1991*, p. 30.

61. In 1996, while guiding me around a distribution center located in a summer resort town, Mr. Moriya Unozawa, a managing director of Seven-Eleven Japan, indicated that on some very busy weekends the company has had to use such unorthodox and costly delivery methods. See also Kawabe, *Sebun-Irebun no Keieishi,* p. 218, and Yamashita, *Sebun-Irebun vs. Rohson,* p. 128.

62. *Sebun-Irebun Japan 1973–1991,* p. 52. See also J. Travis Millman, "Politics, Policy, and the Rise of 7-Eleven Japan" (undergraduate thesis, Harvard College, March 1990), p. 59.

63. Nonaka and Takeuchi, *The Knowledge-Creating Company,* p. 245.

64. The list of potential benefits of the market-dominance strategy comes from a Seven-Eleven handout, but it is reproduced in several books, including Ryuichi Kunitomo, *Sebun-Irebun no Joho Kakumei* (Seven-Eleven's Information Revolution) (Tokyo: Paru Publishing, 1993), p. 228, and Kawabe, *Sebun-Irebun no Keieishi,* p. 183.

65. Sakaguchi, *Daiei: Kyoi no Kakudai Senryaku no Zenbo,* p. 21.

66. Its main competitors took a more active role in the distribution of goods for their stores. Lawson sought to produce and deliver daily foods itself. Half of its convenience delivery centers were owned by Daiei. Sato, *Do Shite mo,* p. 58. FamilyMart fell between Seven-Eleven Japan and Lawson, delivering about 25 percent of its products itself and relying on vendors to distribute the remainder. Yamashita, *Sebun-Irebun vs. Rohson,* p. 146.

67. Suzuki interview, 1996.

68. Ibid.

69. The most prominent example is Meiji-ya, a well-known wholesaler of dry goods. In 1989, it either quit or was terminated as a supplier to Seven-Eleven Japan, allegedly for not agreeing to build a distribution center dedicated to Seven-Eleven Japan. See Millman, "Politics, Policy, and the Rise of 7-Eleven," pp. 90–91. The Meiji-ya case is also referred to in the Muneoka interview, 1991.

70. The 85 percent figure comes from documents obtained from Seven-Eleven Japan. The same documents also give 30 to 35 percent as the average capacity utilization for trucks serving the typical Japanese store. The latter figure is consistent with a 30 percent estimate given by Motoshige Itoh, *Chosen Suru Ryutsu* (Challenging Distribution) (Tokyo: Kodansha, 1994), p. 155.

71. *Sebun-Irebun Japan 1973–1991,* pp. 111–112.

72. Yamashita, *Sebun-Irebun vs. Rohson,* p. 160, and Yahagi, *Konbiniensu Sutoa Shisutemu,* ch. 9.

73. Seven-Eleven Japan, Co., 1995 Annual Report, p. 7. As in the case of the distribution centers, Seven-Eleven Japan's enormous buying power gave it a powerful weapon to use in convincing manufacturers to construct dedi-

cated plants. If Seven-Eleven requests that such a factory be built, said an executive at Ajinomoto, "we have no choice but to comply." Quoted in Millman, "Politics, Policy, and the Rise of 7-Eleven," p. 89.

74. Yahagi, *Konbiniensu Sutoa Shisutemu,* p. 131.

75. "Sebun-Irebun Japan," *Chain Store Age,* 1 Jan. 1992, p. 112. Makoto Usui, the general manager of Seven-Eleven Japan's Information Systems Development Department, emphasized that most of these changes have involved software upgrades rather than new hardware.

76. This paragraph and the next rely on Millman, "Politics, Policy, and the Rise of 7-Eleven," pp. 69–72, and *Sebun-Irebun Japan 1973–1991,* pp. 185–205.

77. In Japan, there are two main periods for gift-giving, December (*oseibo* and Christmas) and July *(ochugen).* The year-end oseibo season and the mid-year ochugen season are times when individuals and corporations give gifts to those for whom they feel a particular obligation (e.g., bosses or customers). By one estimate, this semi-obligatory gift-giving accounts for nearly one-fourth of total Japanese spending on personal and company gifts. See Larke, *Japanese Retailing,* p. 51.

78. This figure comes from Yohei Sato, *Do Shite mo,* p. 95, and includes expenditures by Nomura Research Institute and Nippon Telegraph and Telephone.

79. *Sebun-Irebun 1973–1991,* p. 209.

80. This is based on materials I received from Seven-Eleven Japan on the Atsugi Combined Distribution Center. A slightly different example was Warabeya, a maker of rice-based products. It received orders by 11 A.M., and its products appeared in stores by 6:30 P.M. See Yahagi, *Konbiniensu Sutoa Shisutemu,* pp. 142–147.

81. Sparks, "Reciprocal Retail Internationalisation," p. 76; Kawabe, *Sebun-Irebun no Keieishi,* p. 216.

82. Interview with Makoto Usui, General Manager, Information Systems Development Department, 28 March 1996, hereafter cited as Usui interview, 1996.

83. Ibid., 1996.

84. Iwabuchi, *Sebun-Irebun: Akinai no Shinjigen e,* p. 37. Of course, these higher fees are associated with better performance of Seven-Eleven Japan stores. In 1991, the average daily sales of a 7-Eleven store was ¥630,000. For Lawson and Family Mart, the comparable figures were ¥490,000 and ¥550,000 respectively. Sato, *Do Shite mo,* p. 19.

85. Ryuichi Kunimoto estimates that there are 20 workers per 7-Eleven store. See his *Sebun-Irebun: Tencho no "Hitozukuri" no Manyuaru* (Seven-Eleven: A Manual for Employee Development) (Tokyo: Paru Publishing, 1993), p. 4.

The 120,000 figure comes from multiplying 20 workers per store by 6,000 stores.

86. Liles, *Oh Thank Heaven,* p. 257.

87. Data for Southland in the early 1980s drawn from Southland's 1985 annual report. The growth rate for Southland's earnings in the 1960s comes from Liles, *Oh Thank Heaven,* p. 185.

88. Hideki Nakahara, "Suzuki Toshifumi no 'Stop!' no Dosei de Hajimatta 'Darasu no Atsui Ichinichi'" ("One Hot Dallas Day" That Began With Toshifumi Suzuki Roaring "Stop!"), *Keiei Juku,* 31 Dec. 1991, p. 96.

89. *Progressive Grocer,* "Annual Report of the Grocery Industry," 1980 and 1993.

90. Kawabe, *Sebun-Irebun no Keieishi,* p. 250.

91. Quotation from Jim Hood, "The New Southland: Will the Empire Strike Back?" *Convenience Store People,* 4 (Feb. 1993), reprint obtained from Southland. However, another former employee faulted Southland for too hastily implementing a restructuring plan recommended in the mid-1980s by the consulting firm McKinsey & Company. See Allen Liles, "Road to Long-Term Ruin: Is That Where Restructuring Mania Is Taking U.S.?" *Barron's,* 27 Jan. 1992, p. 15.

92. For example, Southland's interest coverage ratio (the ratio of earnings before interest and taxes to interest expense) was a comfortable 5.15 in 1986 and had been relatively constant for the past six years.

93. Free cash flow is cash flow in excess of that required to fund all projects with positive net present values when discounted at appropriate discount rates. See Michael Jensen, "Agency Costs of Free Cash Flow, Corporate Finance, and Takeovers," *American Economic Review,* 76 (May 1986), pp. 323–329, and idem, "Eclipse of the Public Corporation," *Harvard Business Review,* Sept.-Oct. 1989, pp. 61–74.

94. *Hoover's Handbook of American Business, 1991* (Austin: Reference Press, 1991), p. 51.

95. Estimates of how much interest rates on the debt were increased to satisfy reluctant investors ranged from 1.5 to 4.0 percentage points. This back-of-the-envelope calculation was arrived at as follows. Suppose interest rates were 2 percentage points higher as a consequence of Black Monday, as the crash of 1987 came to be called. The Thompsons raised $2.2 billion in public debt, so interest expense was $44 million greater than planned. Since interest payments are tax deductible, the relevant cost is the after-tax interest expense. Assuming a corporate tax rate of 34 percent, this amounts to $29 million.

96. John Taylor, "The Texas Chain Store Massacre," *Forbes,* 6 Feb. 1989, pp. 54–62.

97. For a list of Southland's divestitures between 1988 and early 1990 see Richard Ruback, "Southland Corporation (B)," Harvard Business School, Case no. 9-291-039, 1991, Exhibit 1. According to its 1994 annual report, Southland sold its last non-convenience-store business, the Citijet fixed-base operation at the Dallas airport, in 1993.

98. Ruback, "Southland Corporation (B)," p. 5.

99. The 1989 losses were so large because they included a $947 million write-off of goodwill (resulting from the sale of various assets) and a $56 million charge incurred in a debt exchange.

100. The deal was structured so as to minimize the tax liabilities of Southland. Had Southland simply sold its license to Seven-Eleven Japan, it would have had to pay 38 percent tax on the proceeds. See *Sebun-Irebun 1973–1991*, pp. 245–246.

101. This concern is not uncommon among Japanese firms. W. Carl Kester writes that Japanese companies' "bidding activity abroad has been more *defensive* of an established relationship than an offensive or proactive deployment of cash to take advantage of what they view as undervalued dollar assets." And he cites Ito-Yokado's offer to purchase 75 percent of Southland as a response to "impending financial distress on the part of a foreign strategic ally." Kester, *Japanese Takeovers: The Global Contest for Corporate Control* (Boston: HBS Press, 1991), pp. 270, 135.

102. Toshifumi Suzuki wrote, "If we [the Ito-Yokado group] had not stepped in, Seven-Eleven of the United States might very well have either fallen into outside hands or gone bankrupt." Suzuki, "The Quest to Rebuild Seven-Eleven Founder Southland," *Tokyo Business Today,* Sept. 1991, p. 44. However, in an interview he emphasized that this fear was not the only reason for purchasing Southland. Disagreeing with those who think the age of convenience stores has passed in America, Suzuki emphasized that he believes that there are still profits to be made in convenience-store retailing in the United States. Suzuki interview, 1996.

103. This process is documented in great detail in Richard Ruback, "Southland Corporation (B)" and "Southland Corporation (C)," Case no. 9-292-004, Harvard Business School, 1991.

104. A prepackaged bankruptcy involves the submission of a reorganization plan and solicitation of approval for that plan prior to filing for bankruptcy. The process reduces the "uncertainty and disruption associated with bankruptcy." Ruback, "Southland Corporation (B)," p. 6.

105. Subsequently their stake was reduced to 64 percent.

106. Suzuki, "The Quest to Rebuild Seven-Eleven," p. 45.

107. Suzuki interview, 1996. The influence of the Japanese parent companies, though less obtrusive than one might expect, should not be underestimated. As one retailing scholar put it, "There is an undoubted 'Japaniza-

tion' of The Southland Corporation underway, but one typically that is not based on occupying offices or direct edicts but rather on underlying processes and influences." Sparks, "Reciprocal Retail Internationalisation," p. 90.

108. Except where noted, information below on the changes at Southland comes from Southland's 1995 Annual Report and 1995 10-K Form. For more detail on these changes, see Masaaki Kotabe, "The Return of 7-Eleven . . . from Japan: The Vanguard Program," *Columbia Journal of World Business,* 30 (winter 1995), pp. 70–81.

109. Kawabe, *Sebun-Irebun no Keieishi,* p. 280.

110. Kotabe, "The Return of 7-Eleven," p. 74. As Kotabe emphasizes, under the new system Southland has sought to instill a stronger feeling of "ownership" in its front-line employees, including even part-time clerks. Each clerk is assigned a section of shelf space and is responsible for ordering and managing inventories of the selected products. In addition, Southland instituted a graduated profit-sharing plan for 7-Eleven store clerks. Each employee's share increased with the length of employment.

111. Kawabe, *Sebun-Irebun no Keieishi,* p. 285. Kotabe, "The Return of 7-Eleven," gives additional information on the improvement of Southland's financial performance. See also Karen Lowry Miller, "Listening to Shoppers' Voices," *Business Week,* Reinventing America Special Issue 1992, p. 9.

112. Dissenters included the chairman of the National Coalition of 7-Eleven Franchises, which represented two-thirds of Southland franchises. "The Changemakers," *Convenience Store Decisions,* Sept. 1993, reprint from Southland.

113. Jeffrey Tannenbaum, "Franchisee Lawsuit Seeks $1 Billion from Southland," *Wall Street Journal,* 8 April 1994, p. B2. As of the mid-1990s, several of these lawsuits were still ongoing. See Southland's 1995 10-K Form, pp. 26–28.

114. Hood, "The New Southland."

115. "Down But Not Out," *Forbes,* 18 Jan. 1993, p. 19.

116. "Konbini Goto Bosai Taisaku (Countermeasures for Convenience-Store Robberies)," *Konbini,* Fall-Winter 1995, pp. 130–134.

117. Nicholas D. Kristof, "In Japan, Nothing to Fear but Fear Itself," *New York Times,* 19 May 1996, p. E4.

118. On the deregulation of retailing, see Upham, "The SII and the Japanese Retail Industry," and Larke, *Japanese Retailing,* pp. 117–125.

119. Part of the reason for Shop America's demise appears to have been diminished consumer demand for foreign branded products as a result of the recession. Seven-Eleven Japan also ran into government restrictions concerning the import of certain foreign products, such as cosmetics. See Ya-

mashita, *Sebun-Irebun vs. Rohson*, pp. 198–200. Earlier, Seven-Eleven Japan had feuded with the American who had originally been its partner in the Shop America venture. See Sara Kahlili, "Shop America Feud: Mail-Order Bust," *North American International Business* 4, no. 5, pp. 46–49.

120. Yamashita, *Sebun-Irebun vs. Rohson*, pp. 202–203.

121. In dollar terms, Seven-Eleven Japan's market value fell from $28.3 billion to $27.5 billion over this period. *Wall Street Journal,* 30 Sept. 1994, p. R26; 2 Oct. 1995, p. R31. Since the yen was appreciating, the fall in yen terms was even greater. Seven-Eleven Japan reports that its market value fell from ¥2.8 trillion in March 1994 to ¥2.4 trillion in September 1995, a 15 percent decline.

122. Same-store sales decreased by 0.3 percent in the year ending 29 Feb. 1996. "Corporate Outline: An Introduction to Seven-Eleven Japan Co., Ltd. for Investors," Seven-Eleven Japan, 1996, p. 23.

123. "Odoriba Dassuru Arata na Taido: Mittsu no Kiken na Choko no Ura de (A New Movement to Move beyond a Turning Point: Behind Three Symptoms of Danger)," *Nikkei Business,* 9 Oct. 1995, p. 23.

124. By comparison, a 1996 newspaper article estimated that 7 percent of Americans visited a McDonald's restaurant each day. Stephen Drucker, "Who Is the Best Restaurateur in America?" *New York Times Magazine,* 10 March 1996, p. 45.

125. Kawabe, *Sebun-Irebun no Keieishi,* pp. 205–206; Itoh, *Chosen Suru Ryutsu,* pp. 5, 86.

126. Itoh, *Chosen Suru Ryutsu,* p. 85.

127. Quote from Takeshi Sugano and Tetsuya Taniguchi, "Konbini ni Tsuzuke: Ugokidashita 'Sei Hai Han' Kakumei (Follow Convenience Stores: A Revolution Achieved in Production, Distribution, and Sales)," *Nikkei Business,* 9 Oct. 1995, p. 21.

128. Liles, *Oh Thank Heaven,* p. 104.

129. Suzuki interview, 1996.

14. *Retrospect and Prospect*

1. Angus Maddison, *Dynamic Forces in Capitalist Development: A Long-Run Comparative View* (Oxford: Oxford University Press, 1991), p. 1.

2. Paul Bairoch, *Economics and World History: Myths and Paradoxes* (Chicago: University of Chicago Press, 1993), pp. 108–110.

3. Robert Lucas, "On the Mechanics of Economic Development," *Journal of Monetary Economics,* 22 (July 1988), pp. 2–42.

4. Adam Smith, *An Inquiry into the Nature and Causes of the Wealth of Nations,* ed. with an intro. by Edwin Cannan (1776; Chicago: University of Chicago Press, 1976), p. 17.

5. See Kenneth Rogoff, "The Purchasing Power Parity Puzzle," *Journal of Economic Literature,* 34 (June 1996), pp. 647–668. At current exchange rates, Japan had a GNP per capita of $34,630 in 1994, as compared to $25,880 in the United States. For the same year, the index for purchasing power parity was 81.7 for Japan, 100.0 for the United States. See *World Development Report, 1996* (New York: Oxford University Press for the World Bank, 1996), p. 189.

6. Thomas Mann, *Joseph and His Brothers,* trans. H. T. Lowe-Porter (1934; New York: Knopf, 1978), p. 3.

7. For an overview of the literature, see H. W. Arndt, *The Rise and Fall of Economic Growth: A Study in Contemporary Thought* (Chicago: University of Chicago Press, 1978, 1984). As an index of the state of the art of understanding this subject as it stood a generation ago, in the 1970s, consider the following comments by the economists Robert Solow and Peter Temin. This passage is from their introduction to the *Cambridge Economic History of Europe,* a standard reference work: "It is easy to provide definitions of the three traditional factors of production—land, labour, and capital—but hard to translate these definitions into workable rules for use . . . Even after the best possible adjustment is made for quality changes in inputs and output, a positive residual is likely to remain as a reflection of a genuine increase in the productivity of the economic system." Robert M. Solow and Peter Temin, "Introduction: The Inputs for Growth," *Cambridge Economic History of Europe,* vol. 7, ed. Peter Mathias and M. M. Postan (Cambridge: Cambridge University Press, 1978), pp. 1, 7, 9, 24, 26. The term "residual" was coined by the development economist Evsey Domar.

A later article by the economic historian Moses Abramowitz reinforced this impression of incomplete understanding. What, he wondered, "was this Residual, this total factor productivity growth" which accounted for most economic growth but could not be attributed to increases in capital, labor, and other inputs? Most economists interpreted the residual as deriving from technological progress, but Abramowitz disagreed. As he pointed out, the standard techniques of growth accounting do not directly measure the *interactions* of the factors of growth. The assumption seems to be that they function independently of one another, and therefore can simply be added up. The trouble is that they don't add up to anything like the total growth that has actually occurred. The fallacy, according to Abramowitz, was first pointed out in 1964 by Richard Nelson, and the "lesson of interdependence has emerged in other ways as well, notably in Kenneth Arrow's hypothesis about learning by doing and in Nathan Rosenberg's learning by using. The lesson of interaction, indeed, emerges in numerous historical and empirical studies . . ." Abramovitz, "The Search for the Sources of Growth: Areas of Ignorance, Old and New," *Journal of Economic History,* 53 (June 1993), pp. 221–222. See also Maurice FG. Scott, "Explaining Economic Growth," *American Economic Review,* 83 (May 1993), pp. 421–425.

8. Abramovitz, "The Search for the Sources of Growth," pp. 222–237.

9. This has changed somewhat under the "new growth economics" pioneered by Paul Romer, Robert Barro, Robert Lucas, and others, which attaches more importance to education and intellectual capital. But still the question remains open, resistant to analysis by conventional econometric methods.

10. Alfred D. Chandler Jr., *Scale and Scope: The Dynamics of Industrial Capitalism* (Cambridge, MA: Harvard University Press, 1990), pp. 594–596. The powerful implications of this book and of Chandler's *The Visible Hand: The Managerial Revolution in American Business* (Cambridge, MA: Harvard University Press, 1977), for the study of productivity have not been fully appreciated by economists.

11. Chandler's rough categorization here is that the United States represents "competitive capitalism," the United Kingdom "family capitalism," and Germany "cooperative capitalism." The economic historian William Lazonick also attaches great importance to organizational capabilities in shaping national competitiveness and different styles of capitalism. See esp. Lazonick, *Business Organization and the Myth of the Market Economy* (Cambridge: Cambridge University Press, 1991).

12. The obvious difficulty in demonstrating the connection says nothing about the likelihood of there being such a connection, or of its importance. The work of Paul Romer, Robert Lucas, Robert Barro, and other neoclassical economists is fully consistent with this hypothesis because of its emphasis on knowledge, technology, and learning.

On the whole, historians and management scholars are readier to acknowledge the relevance of organizational capabilities to total factor productivity than are mainstream academic economists. The management scholar Michael Porter, in *The Competitive Advantage of Nations* (New York: Free Press, 1990), has made a noteworthy attempt to untangle the reasons for differential performances across countries. He emphasizes the importance of locational clusters of firms in the same industry or related industries. In his view, the international competitive sucess of such industries as Italian ceramic tiles, Swedish mining equipment, Japanese consumer electronics, and American medical equipment derives in part from their physical clustering within small geographic areas of their home countries. This clustering not only facilitates the ready exchange of information, but also promotes intensified competitive pressures. For Porter, this constant spur of competition is the key to industrial success on international markets. The development of organizational capabilities is driven by the constant pressure of interfirm competition. Porter's overall approach, as he puts it, is "more Schumpeterian than neoclassical" (p. 778, n. 46). Like Schumpeter and

Chandler, he sees capitalism as a relentless process of change. In his view, national competitive advantage derives directly from the performance of individual companies. It requires that those companies, if they are to endure and prevail, be subjected to continual competition, reinforced by discriminating home-country consumers. Because Porter's analytical emphasis falls overwhelmingly on the power of interfirm competition, he acknowledges but does not highlight the role of government.

13. For some exceptions, which include surveys bearing on particular aspects of the subject, see Helen Shapiro and Lance Taylor, "The State and Industrial Strategy," *World Development,* 18 (1990), pp. 861–878; Abramovitz, "The Search for the Sources of Growth," pp. 217–243; Pranab Bardhan, "Economics of Development and the Development of Economics," *Journal of Economic Perspectives,* 7 (spring 1993), pp. 129–142; and Martin Bell and Keith Pavitt, "Technological Accumulation and Industrial Growth: Contrasts between Developed and Developing Countries," *Industrial and Corporate Change,* 2 (1993), pp. 157–211.

Thomas K. McCraw (Ph.D., University of Wisconsin) is the Isidor Straus Professor of Business History at the Harvard Business School and editor of the *Business History Review*. His many books include *Prophets of Regulation* (1984; Pulitzer Prize, Newcomen Book Award), *Management Past and Present* (1996, with Alfred D. Chandler Jr. and Richard S. Tedlow), and the edited volumes *America versus Japan* (1986) and *The Essential Alfred Chandler* (1988). His current research is on American business since 1920, the history of economic thought, and the development and effects of public policies toward competition.

Jeffrey R. Bernstein is a Ph.D. candidate in business economics at Harvard University. He has an A.M. from Harvard and an A.B. in economics from Amherst College. He has a longstanding interest in Japanese business, and he spent a year at Kyushu University as a Fulbright Scholar. His current research spans the fields of international trade, industrial organization, and corporate finance.

Peter Botticelli is a professional business analyst with a Ph.D. in modern European history from the University of Illinois. In 1966–97, he worked for the Competition and Strategy Group at the Harvard Business School, for whom he wrote teaching cases on the history of strategic management and on Intel Corporation. Mr. Botticelli's research specialties include the management consulting industry and the commercial development of high technologies in aerospace and computing.

Jeffrey R. Fear (Ph.D., Stanford) is Assistant Professor of History at the University of Pennsylvania and a former Harvard-Newcomen Postdoctoral Fellow in Business History. He is the author of a number of articles on German business history and a contributor to the volume edited by Alfred D. Chandler Jr. et al., *Big Business and the Wealth of Nations* (1997). His current research concerns the history of German management and business history in a comparative perspective.

Nancy F. Koehn (Ph.D., Harvard) is Associate Professor of Business Administration at the Harvard Business School. She is the author of *The Power of Commerce: Economy and Governance in The British Empire* (1994), as well as a contributor to Michael G. Rukstad, ed., *Macroeconomic Decision Making* *in the* World Economy (1986) and *Management Past and Present* (1996). Her current research focuses on consumer behavior and business strategy in the three industrial revolutions.

David A. Moss (Ph.D., Yale) is Assistant Professor of Business Administration at the Harvard Business School. His book *Socializing Security: Progressive-Era Economists and the Origins of American Social Policy* (1996) examines the intellectual and institutional origins of the American welfare state. His current research includes an historical investigation of public policy responses to risk in the United States and a comparative study of a contemporary employment policies in Europe and North America.

Rowena Olegario is a doctoral candidate in American history at Harvard University. She is writing her dissertation on credit and its role in the creation of the American business culture in the nineteenth century. Prior to entering Harvard, she was a Senior Associate with Coopers & Lybrand's market analysis group in New York, where she specialized in the retail industry. She received a B.A. in history from Yale University.

Richard S. Tedlow (Ph.D., Columbia) is Class of 1957 Professor of Business Administration at the Harvard Business School. His work as a business historian has centered on the history of marketing. He is the author of *New and Improved: The Story of Mass Marketing in America* (1990), which is available in Japanese and French translations as well as in English. He is the coauthor (with Alfred D. Chandler Jr. and Thomas K. McCraw) of *Management Past and Present* (1996) as well as numerous other books and articles. His current research concerns the changing role of the Chief Executive Officer of the large American business corporation during the twentieth century.

ACKNOWLEDGMENTS

Modern capitalism is a subject of extraordinary breadth and complexity, and some of the scholars who have written about it are giants. We build on their work with respect and appreciation. The endnotes provide detailed evidence of our indebtedness, and the list here of the people who helped us directly—many of whom are among the world's leading scholars of business, business history, and economic history—amplifies the long roster of authors cited in the notes. To all of these people, we are grateful for inspiration and example.

Our book is the product of a three-year collaboration involving more than 50 scholars and about 265 students. The eight authors know each other well, and we criticized, condensed, and marked up one another's drafts. It was a fundamentally interactive process, and almost every author worked on almost every chapter. So a lot of reciprocal obligations are embedded in the book. In addition, the editor wishes to note that all authors were remarkably patient with and responsive to his own relentless stream of requests for still more changes.

After writing their drafts, the authors vetted each chapter at least once, and sometimes twice, in formal presentations to Harvard's Business History Seminar. The members of this seminar, about 35 students and professors from half a dozen universities and several academic disciplines, went over every chapter with great care. At each meeting, a pair of faculty commentators, whose names are included in the list below, analyzed a chapter before its discussion by the whole seminar. Also, each of the seminar's Ph.D. students, also listed below, wrote a critique of the chapter, and these documents proved very helpful.

After the authors revised each chapter in response to critiques from the seminar, we taught the material to the entire class of MBA students who entered the Harvard Business School in January 1996. In numerous discussions, and in response to a series of detailed questionnaires, these students provided us with some useful new perspectives; and we revised our chapters still again.

Each chapter was then submitted to several outside experts—historians, economists, and other scholars—based in North America, Europe, and Japan. Their names are included in the list below, and their evaluations proved to be extraordinarily helpful in saving us from errors of fact and distorted interpretation. We are grateful indeed for the help of these specialists.

Aside from scholarly assistance, we benefitted from the services of two uncommonly careful editors: Mr. Max Hall, who used his matchless tact to persuade us to abandon faulty constructions and flights of fancy in favor of clear English; and Ms. Camille Smith of Harvard University Press, whose acute eye caught a number of awkward sentences, mixed images, and other flaws.

For reading the original manuscript for the Press, and for providing invaluable suggestions, we thank Professors Mansel G. Blackford of The Ohio State University, Robert D. Cuff of York University, and Leslie Hannah of the London School of Economics and Political Science.

For critiques of the introductory chapter, which was originally published as Harvard Business School Case 796-100, the author thanks Professors David Collis of the Harvard Business School, Robert D. Cuff of York University, and Peter Mathias of Downing College, Cambridge University, all of whom also commented on the chapter entitled "British Capitalism and the Three Industrial Revolutions"; Professor Gerald Feldman of the University of California, Berkeley, who also provided detailed comments on "German Capitalism" and "The Deutsche Bank"; Professors Morton Keller of Brandeis University and K. Austin Kerr of The Ohio State University, both of whom also commented on "American Capitalism"; Professor Steven Usselman of the Georgia Institute of Technology, who also gave a valuable critique of "IBM and the Two Thomas J. Watsons" based on his own work in progress; and Ms. Susan McCraw of the Boston Bar, who also commented on "American Capitalism" and provided crucial organizational advice about "British Capitalism and the Three Industrial Revolutions."

For critiques of "Josiah Wedgwood and the First Industrial Revolution" (originally HBS 796-079), the author is grateful to Professors John Brewer of the European University Institute (Florence); Marc Stern of Bentley College; Cynthia A. Montgomery and Alvin J. Silk of the Harvard Business School, both of whom also commented on "Rolls-Royce and the Rise of High-Technology Industry"; and Sven Beckert of Harvard

University, who also commented on "American Capitalism" and helped on all three of the chapters on Germany. Geoffrey Verter, a Research Associate at the Harvard Business School, provided indispensable archival assistance, as did Gaye Blake-Roberts, Curator of The Wedgwood Museum, and Martin Phillips, Archivist at Keele University.

For critiques of "British Capitalism and the Three Industrial Revolutions" (originally HBS 796-182), the author thanks, in addition to those already mentioned, Professor Walter Arnstein of the University of Illinois; and Professor Geoffrey Jones of the University of Reading and Dr. Mary B. Rose of the Management School of Lancaster University, both of whom also commented on "Rolls-Royce and Rise of High-Technology Industry."

For critiques of "Rolls-Royce and the Rise of High-Technology Industry" (originally HBS 796-171), in addition to those already mentioned, the author is indebted to Professor Roy Church of the University of East Anglia, Professor Wayne Lewchuk of McMaster University, and Mr. M. H. Evans, Mr. S. L. Shepherd, and their colleagues at Rolls-Royce plc.

For critiques of "German Capitalism" (originally HBS 797-020), the author thanks, in addition to those already mentioned, Professor F. M. Scherer, Kennedy School of Government, Harvard University, who also commented on "American Capitalism"; Mr. Uwe Lembke, who also commented on "The Deutsche Bank"; Professors Wilfried Feldenkirchen of Friedrich-Alexander Universität, Karen Wruck of the Harvard Business School, and Andrei S. Markovits of the University of California, Santa Cruz, all of whom also commented on the chapter entitled "August Thyssen and German Steel." Professor Markovits commented on "The Deutsche Bank" as well.

For the chapter entitled "August Thyssen and German Steel" (originally HBS 796-005), in addition to those already cited, the author is grateful to the archivists of Thyssen and of Mannesmann, particularly Mr. Carl-Friedrich Baumann, Mr. Horst A. Wessel, and Dr. Manfred Rasch. Dr. Rasch, Thyssen AG Archivist, supplied Thyssen photographs and granted permission to use them, as did Franz Steiner Verlag Wiesbaden GmbH, of Stuttgart.

For critiques of "The Deutsche Bank" (originally HBS 796-106), the author thanks, in addition to those listed above, Professor Jay O. Light of the Harvard Business School and Herr Professor Dr. Manfred Pohl of

Deutschebank AG. Dr. Ronaldo Schmitz of the Deutsche Bank Managing Board was exceedingly generous with his time and influential assistance in the preparation of the chapter. Mr. Martin Müller, Assistant Archivist, Deutsche Bank, was very helpful in the primary research, and Dr. Herbert Wolf assisted in interpreting Nazi documents. Mr. Nicolaj Siggelkow, a Harvard Ph.D. student and Research Associate, was indispensable to the research, both in Harvard's Baker Library and at the bank's historical archives in Frankfurt.

For "Henry Ford, Alfred Sloan, and the Three Phases of Marketing" (originally HBS 796-169), the authors are grateful to Professors David Lewis of the University of Michigan Business School and David Hounshell of Carnegie-Mellon University. For helping to locate photographs, the authors thank Mr. Albert F. Bartovics of Baker Library's Historical Collections, Harvard Business School; for supplying photographs and permission to use them, the Ford Motor Company; for photographs, trade cards, and permission to use them, General Motors Media Archives.

For critiques of "American Capitalism" (originally HBS 796-101), the author thanks, in addition to those already listed, Professors George C. Lodge and Richard H. K. Vietor of the Harvard Business School.

For critiques of "IBM and the Two Thomas J. Watsons" (originally HBS 797-021), in addition to those mentioned above, the author is indebted to Professor Stuart Leslie of Johns Hopkins University; and Professors Debora L. Spar and Richard S. Rosenbloom of the Harvard Business School, both of whom also commented on "Toyoda Automatic Looms and Toyota Automobiles." Mr. Kevin D. Corbitt of the Charles Babbage Institute, University of Minnesota, facilitated the research for the appendix to the IBM chapter. Mr. Robert Godfrey, IBM Archivist, supplied IBM photographs and granted permission to use them.

For critiques of "Toyoda Automatic Looms and Toyota Automobiles" (originally HBS 796-083), the author thanks, in addition to those already mentioned, Professors Michael Cusumano of the Sloan School of Management, MIT, and Koichi Shimokawa, Hosei University, Faculty of Business Administration. Professor William Mass of the University of Massachusetts, Lowell, kindly granted permission to cite his unpublished work. Toyota Motor Corporate Services of North America, New York office, granted permission to use photographs, which were supplied by Toyota.

For critiques of "Japanese Capitalism" (originally HBS 796-084), the author is indebted to Professors Andrew Gordon and Henry Rosovsky of Harvard; W. Carl Kester of the Harvard Business School; William Wray of the University of British Columbia; and David Weinstein, University of Michigan Business School, who also provided the diagrams of *zaibatsu* and *keiretsu* organizational structures reproduced in the chapter. Ms. Myral Bernstein made helpful editorial suggestions, as did Mr. Takuo Imagawa of Harvard and Mr. Kenji Nishimura of the Harvard Business School.

For critiques of "7-Eleven in America and Japan" (originally HBS 797-030), the author is grateful to Professors Nobuo Kawabe of Waseda University; Masaaki Kotabe, University of Hawaii at Manoa, College of Business Administration; and John Deighton and Walter J. Salmon of the Harvard Business School. Mr. Mitsuru Yamada of Ito-Yokado was exceptionally helpful in coordinating the author's visit to Seven-Eleven Japan and in handling requests for information. Mr. Masatoshi Ito, the founder of Ito-Yokado, took time to talk with the author, and Mr. Toshifumi Suzuki, the guiding entrepreneur behind Seven-Eleven Japan, granted a very helpful interview. Other managers of Seven-Eleven Japan were also a great assistance: Mr. Joriya Unozawa explained the distribution system and guided the author on a tour of a manufacturing facility and distribution center; Mr. Makoto Usui explained and gave demonstrations of information technology systems, assisted by Mr. Haruo Uchida. Seven-Eleven Japan gave permission to use photographs. Mr. Hirotsugu Sakai of Mitsubishi Research Institute collected articles on Seven-Eleven Japan and also transcribed interviews. Ms. Hiroko Nagai, Harvard University, helped in summarizing and translating other materials, and Mr. Susumu Ogawa, Kobe University, provided useful comments on the Japanese convenience-store sector.

For assistance with the maps of the United States and Japan, we thank the staff of the Harvard Map Room. The maps of Germany were also developed there, using the "Centennia" historical atlas software, a product of Clockwork Software, Inc., Chicago, IL, http://www.clockwk.com. For the maps of the United Kingdom and Ireland, we thank Mr. Peter Amirault of Type A, Somerville, MA; and, for help in facilitating our use of these maps, Ms. Eleanor Jaynes and Ms. Aimee Hamel of the Harvard Business School.

All eight authors, and particularly the editor, owe a special debt to

Professor Emeritus Alfred D. Chandler Jr. of the Harvard Business School. His distinguished body of work helped to inspire our approach, and in the Business History Seminar he himself read and commented on all the chapters.

The editor is also very grateful to the Department of History at the University of Wisconsin–Madison for the honor of its invitation to deliver the 1995 Merle Curti Lectures. Some of the key ideas for this book were developed during the preparation of those lectures, and the editor particularly thanks Professors Stanley I. Kutler and Colleen Dunlavy of the University of Wisconsin for their kindness and their help.

We deeply appreciate the generous financial assistance of the Division of Research of the Harvard Business School throughout the three years of this book's preparation. Deans John H. McArthur and Kim B. Clark were enthusiastic supporters of the project, as were Senior Associate Deans for Research F. Warren McFarlan and Dwight B. Crane. The faculty Research Directors most closely involved were Professors Richard S. Tedlow, Richard H. K. Vietor, and Cynthia A. Montgomery, all of whom helped immensely. We are also grateful to former Senior Associate Dean Leonard Schlesinger, who originally proposed that we undertake the work that led to the book.

The Ph.D. students who wrote critiques of our chapters in the Business History Seminar were Mr. Nicholas Barberis, Mr. Terrence Burnham, Mr. George Chacko, Mr. Thomas Eisenmann, Mr. Raymond Fisman, Mr. Roger Hallowell, Ms. Leslie Jeng, Mr. Shahir Kassam-Adams, Mr. Vassil Konstantinov, Mr. Partha Mohanram, Mr. Jan Rivkin, Mr. Mark Seasholes, Mr. Nicolaj Siggelkow, Mr. Jürgen Weiss, and Mr. Jeffrey Wurgler. We are very grateful for their insights.

Ms. Margaret C. Murphy of the Harvard Business School oversaw the entire production of the book, from its genesis as draft chapters through hundreds of changes as it was presented successively in whole or in part to various audiences. She skillfully shepherded its text, tables, charts, and endnotes through their many iterations. Without her unremitting work and her dexterity with multiple software packages, the final version could not have been submitted to the publisher on time. Ms. Murphy took up just where her predecessor, Ms. Pamela Sawyer, had left off. Ms. Sawyer had done equally outstanding work in the early stages of the book, prior to her departure to become Editorial Coordinator of the *Business History Review*.

Ms. Laura Bureš, a Research Associate at the Harvard Business School, carried out two important phases of the project with grace and aplomb. She coordinated the mailings to all of the outside experts, and she kept careful track of permissions to reproduce photographs, maps, and other materials.

To all of these collaborators, and to the librarians and archivists of Baker, Widener, Lamont, and other repositories at Harvard and elsewhere whose treasures were yielded up for this book, we give our fervent thanks. For any errors that remain, we alone are responsible.